MODERN LAW OF CONTRACTS

Breach and Remedies

HOWARD O. HUNTER
Professor of Law
Emory University School of Law

WG&L
WARREN, GORHAM & LAMONT
Boston • New York

WARREN, GORHAM & LAMONT, INC.
210 SOUTH STREET
BOSTON, MASSACHUSETTS 02111

ISBN 0-88712-506-9

Library of Congress Catalog Card No. 86-50054

PRINTED IN THE UNITED STATES OF AMERICA

In memory of Owen

Preface

Modern Law of Contracts: Breach and Remedies is the first book in a two-volume treatise that combines a treatment of the traditional common law of contracts with a consideration of the current commercial law of sales. This volume focuses on the identification of a breach and the results that flow from a breach. When does one occur? What are the respective rights and duties of the parties to a contract after a breach? What are the claims available to the non-breaching party? What are excuses that justify a breach? These are the kinds of questions that lawyers face every day, and the rules of damage recovery are among the most dynamic in commercial law. The practicing lawyer needs to be as informed as possible about current trends because there have been, and are likely to be, significant changes in the treatment of damages.

Volume II, which will be published in the near future, will consider problems of formation, competency, consideration, and closely related issues. It will address questions such as: Who is competent to make a contract? What constitutes an offer? When and how is an offer accepted? What is sufficient to create an implied contract? What is consideration and why is it important? When is a contract imposed by law on a person without his consent and what does this mean for the development of the law of contracts?

This treatise is designed to provide straightforward, practical analysis of common issues in commercial law and to place this analysis in a historical context. It is difficult, for instance, to apply the damage rules of Article 2 of the UCC without an understanding of their antecedents and the reasons for their development. At the same time, it is important to be aware of the continuing relationship between common-law developments and the statutory law of sales. A proper grounding in each assists in the application of the other. Indeed, the two should not be separated. One of the goals of this treatise is to make clear that the UCC does not exist in a vacuum; it is an outgrowth of the general law of contracts and the two are complementary. That is one of the major justifications for another treatise on contract law — too many either focus almost entirely on traditional common-law issues or on the specific application of provisions of the UCC.

Another goal of this treatise is to highlight some of the areas of contract law that are in greatest flux. In this volume, for example, Chapter 11 is devoted to a consideration of a variety of damage awards — attorney's fees, punitive damages, mental distress damages — that have not been part of the usual recovery in a contract action but that have become more common in recent years. In Chapter 12 there is a lengthy consideration of the commercial impracticability defense under Section 2-615 of the UCC, a defense that is being asserted more and more as economic conditions become more volatile and as contracts deal with difficult technological problems.

Acknowledgments

The publication of any book is an enormous task and every author receives support from many people. Certainly that has been true in my case, but there have been several who have been especially important and I would be remiss if I did not acknowledge my appreciation publicly.

The staff of the Emory University Law Library have answered my every request cheerfully, promptly, and accurately. Special thanks go to Deborah Mann, the Reference Librarian, for tracking down numerous hard-to-find citations, to Mark Butler for keeping my office full of books, and to Robin Mills, our Librarian, for her commitment to service and to excellence.

Tom Morgan, who was Dean of the Law School during most of the time that I worked on this volume, was unfailingly supportive. He provided research support and encouraged this effort in every way. Now that Tom has returned to the ranks of faculty, he no doubt has an even better understanding of the importance of administrative support and encouragement for the research and publishing work of the faculty.

Theresa L. Kitay of the Class of 1987 was a diligent and productive research assistant. Proofreading and checking footnotes is not the most exciting work, but she did it with a smile and she did it well. She probably has a better knowledge of the "blue book" than any other student at Emory.

Of course I have had the support of my family who have been patient with my mounds of books and reams of paper, and I thank both Emily and Susan for their patience. In addition to moral encouragement, Susan gave me a tangible item of great importance in the preparation of this volume — a word processor and printer that brought me out of the era of foolscap and pencils and into the world of computer technology. Writing a book on a word processor may not be as romantic as writing one by hand, but it certainly is a great deal easier. It also improves author-editor relationships because editorial changes are so much simpler.

The American Law Institute graciously gave permission to reprint certain portions of the following:

Restatement of Contracts, Copyright (1932) by the American Law Institute; reprinted with the permission of the American Law Institute.

Restatement (Second) of Contracts, Copyright (1981) by the American Law Institute; reprinted with the permission of the American Law Institute.

Uniform Commercial Code and Official Commentary, Copyright (1978) by the American Law Institute; reprinted with the permission of the American Law Institute.

HOWARD O. HUNTER

Atlanta, Georgia
April 1986

Summary of Contents

Table of Contents

CHAPTER 1
Contract Theory and Remedial Choices

CHAPTER 2
Present Breaches and the Rights and Obligations of the Nonbreaching Party

CHAPTER 3
Anticipatory Breaches

CHAPTER 4
Warranties

CHAPTER 5
Conditions

CHAPTER ***6***
Equitable Remedies

CHAPTER 7
General Rules of Damages for Breach of Contract

CHAPTER 8
Damages and Other Remedies for Breach of Contract in Specific Situations

CHAPTER 9
Quasi-Contracts and Restitutionary Remedies

CHAPTER 10
Agreed Remedies for Breach

CHAPTER 11
Extracontractual Damages

CHAPTER 12
Excuses for Nonperformance

CHAPTER 1

Contract Theory and Remedial Choices

¶ 1.01 INFLUENCE AND BASIS OF CONTRACT LAW

The law of contracts affects everyone. Virtually every human relationship in western, industrialized societies involves some aspect of the law of contracts, from the most personal to the most common, standardized commercial transaction. This is not surprising, because the law of contracts is all about the way people organize their lives within a community. The division of labor, whether customary or by explicit agreement, is an example of the fundamentals of contract law at work. Contracts provide a means to assure stability and predictability in both personal and commercial relationships. They attempt to regularize the future and, in that sense, represent one of man's most important intellectual powers — the ability to contemplate the future.[1] Contract law, at least as it is understood in western societies, is also a means for the vindication of individual interests. Unlike customs passed down from generation to generation by which people live in certain accepted patterns with little individual modification, the regime of contract law

[1] See generally MacNeil, "The Many Futures of Contract," 47 S. Cal. L. Rev. 691 (1974).

is based upon the principle of free, independent actors who make their own decisions and their own deals.

Nevertheless, contract law can be confusing and inconsistent. This is, in part, the result of its basis in individual action. There are as many contracts as there are contracting parties. In this country, the confusion and inconsistency of contract law also result from the development of legal rules in the Anglo-American system through the common law.[2] Case law, by its very nature, develops from idiosyncratic disputes. The UCC is the only comprehensive American effort to systematize a body of contract law by statute.[3] It has been a successful effort, but the UCC itself draws upon the common law for much of its substance, and it is filled with a suffi-

---

[2] Contract law is important even in socialist nations with centrally controlled economies and in countries such as France with civil law systems. But nowhere does contract play quite the role in the law as it does in nations such as England with a strong common-law background where the law of contracts has developed piecemeal from several hundred years of human existence and multitudes of individual transactions.

[3] Many statutes, such as bankruptcy laws, insurance regulations, antitrust laws, consumer protection statutes, and credit disclosure laws, affect the making and enforcement of contracts. The Uniform Sales Act (1906), the predecessor to Article 2 of the UCC, attempted to bring statutory order to the law of contracts, but it never received the same widespread approval as the UCC. Unlike other laws, the UCC is the only statute that expressly addresses a wide range of contract issues, rather than a discrete problem or area of the law that has ramifications in the area of contracts. In addition, it has been adopted, at least in part, by all fifty states and the District of Columbia.

In 1893, the English Parliament adopted the British Sale of Goods Act, which had its roots in the Law Merchant. In the United States, the National Conference of Commissioners on Uniform State Laws decided to propose a similar model law to the state legislatures. Professor Samuel Williston served as a principal draftsman, and the Uniform Sales Act was published in 1906. Several states adopted the model law, sometimes with modifications, but it failed to satisfy the demand for a systematic approach to commercial transactions because it only covered a small aspect of contract law. In the late 1940s, the Commission on Uniform State Laws and the American Law Institute jointly undertook the task of drafting a new model law. The principal draftsman was Professor Karl Llewellyn. The result was the UCC, which was published in 1952. It has since gone through several modifications and the most current Official Text dates from 1978. For an interesting debate about some of the merits and drawbacks of the UCC, see Williston, "The Law of Sales in the Proposed Uniform Commercial Code," 63 Harv. L. Rev. 561 (1950) and Corbin, "The Uniform Commercial Code — Sales: Should It Be Enacted?" 59 Yale LJ 821 (1950).

cient number of ambiguities to provide a continuing source of case law.[4]

Two interrelated and perennial issues in contract law are the extent to which there are public aspects of private transactions and, therefore, the extent to which there is a justification for state intrusion. The first, and perhaps most important, question of state intrusion is whether there is a justification for the public enforcement of a private agreement. If a husband and wife agree on a division of household responsibilities (for example, he will collect the children from school on Monday, Wednesday, and Friday; she will do so on Tuesday and Thursday), there is little reason for the rest of the world, through the agency of the state, to be concerned about whether each performs adequately.[5] Indeed, the older English law courts were somewhat reluctant to become involved in matters of private agreement. They left many such matters to local, commercial, and ecclesiastical courts.[6] The origins of assumpsit in the common-law courts were in cases sounding at least partly in notions of trespass.[7]

Many of the ambiguities that plague the law of contracts — but which give it a peculiarly human and humane flavor — are reflected in the remedies that are available when there is some promissory failure or default. If there is a remedy at all, this amounts to a recognition that there is something important about the transaction. If there were not, there would be little reason to bring to bear the government's enforcement authority on the offending party. All kinds of remedies are available for a broken promise, however, and it is the *choice* of remedies made by the law

---

[4] This book considers the operation of various sections of the UCC from Article 2, which governs sales transactions. Other parts of the UCC, such as Article 3 on commercial paper or Article 9 on secured transactions, are important aspects of contract law, but they are beyond the general scope of this book.

[5] Of course, the community does have an interest in the stability of marriages and the care of children, and public-law responsibilities are placed upon parents. In addition, a growing body of law is devoted to marital contracts and their enforceability.

[6] See generally 1 Page, *The Law of Contracts* 11 (1920); Kessler & Gilmore, *Contracts* 20 (2d ed. 1970) (hereinafter cited as Kessler & Gilmore).

[7] See, e.g., Horse Doctor's Case, YB Hil. 19 Henry VI, f. 5, pl. 49 (1441), reprinted in Kessler & Gilmore 24.

that defines as much as anything the public-law aspects of private consensual transactions. This book is devoted to the questions of what constitutes a breach of a promissory undertaking, what kinds of remedies are available for such a breach, and what excuses can be invoked as justifications by the defaulting party. Through an analysis of these issues, it is possible to identify the major themes of contract theory in the Anglo-American legal system.

¶ 1.02 CONTRACT AS A MORAL DUTY

One school of thought examines contract law through the discipline of moral philosophy, albeit with strong ecclesiastical influences.[8] Everyone is familiar with the common saying that a man's word is his bond, and young children learn from their parents that it is wrong to break a promise. Honesty and truth-telling are highly prized virtues in the western tradition. A promise carries with it a notion of solemnity. If someone expresses aspirations, hopes, or expectations, others may be disappointed if he does not fulfill them, but their level of expectation is different when the same person makes a promise. Then they trust the promise-maker to follow through and bring the promise to fruition or, at the very least, to try his best to do so. The question is whether the same kinds of expectations should carry over into the public law of contracts.

To be sure, most of ordinary contracting, whether between businessmen or private parties, depends on a strong element of trust in the words of each party; each expects the other honestly to fulfill the promises made. But should courts make them do so? Should the courts do what Shylock asked of the Duke of Venice and enforce a man's bond regardless of the consequences?[9] The strength of the ecclesiastical tradition is most readily apparent in the courts of equity, where the preferred remedy is specific performance. That remedy holds a promisor exactly to his promise re-

---

[8] Perhaps the best known of the modern texts in this area is Fried, *Contract as Promise* (1981).

[9] No modern court will enforce a contract that puts someone's life at risk, although holding a person to his promises may sometimes put his career or business at risk.

gardless of events that occur in the meantime, unless specific performance is objectively impossible.

The moral standard that requires individuals to keep their promises certainly has had an important effect on the development of contract law. The common-law courts, however, have never been willing to hold people expressly to their promises. The preferred remedy at law always has been substitutional, partly as a result of the early reluctance of the law courts to become involved in matters of private agreement and partly as a result of other policies (e.g., reluctance to force a person to perform a personal service against his will, difficulties of enforcement). Under the common law, the disappointed party does not necessarily get the performance that he wanted; rather, he gets the value of the performance, or an approximation of it, in money. Specific performance has remained the preferred remedy in cases involving the transfer of real property, but in virtually all other contracts the preference is for some other kind of remedy. Thus, whatever may be said about the moral duty to keep promises, the fact remains that the law courts have never held promisors strictly to their undertakings. This reflects the commonsense understanding of the law courts that circumstances change and people are sometimes wrong in their predictions and expectations. The law recognizes some flexibility for changing facts and changing minds. A blind adherence to the principle of promissory obligation would lack that flexibility.

Another approach to the justification of promissory enforcement through remedies that are both specific and substitutional is experiential.[10] This is the genesis of the doctrine of reliance. For example, if John makes a promise to Peter, then Peter, relying on John to keep his word, may expend efforts or money in preparation for the performance of John's promise. If John reneges, Peter's disappointment can be measured by the cost of his reliance. This cost may not accurately measure Peter's disappointment in not having the full benefit of John's performance, but it does provide a means to put Peter back where he was before John made a promise to him. This sketchy outline of the theory of reliance illustrates another approach to promissory liability that focuses on the prom-

---

[10] This is the general thesis of Atiyah, *The Rise and Fall of Freedom of Contract* (1979).

isee and his actions rather than on the promisor and his moral obligations.[11]

¶ 1.03 CONTRACT AS A MARKET MECHANISM

The view of contract most in favor among modern commentators is that of a set of rules designed to enhance efficiency: Those rules or customs of the common law that seem to work against efficient outcomes in some cases are the subject of criticism, while others that reward an efficient choice are heaped with praise.[12] There is much truth in the view of contract law as a means to promote economic efficiency, but such a view only tells part of the story.

Oliver Wendell Holmes said that there was nothing wrong with breaching a contract if the performing party found it difficult or uneconomic to perform, although the breaching party might have to pay damages.[13] The rules of common-law remedies generally sustain his view. The breaching party rarely has to perform according to his undertaking but must answer only in damages. The calculation of damages is an inexact science, but there are rules that make it possible to predict the scope of damage liability within a reasonably close range.[14] Damages should not be more than the value of the bargain to the other party, although some-

---

[11] See ¶¶ 3.01[2], 3.01[3], 3.02[3].

[12] See, e.g., Barton, "The Economic Basis of Damages for Breach of Contract," 1 J. Legal Stud. 277 (1972); Farber, "Reassessing the Economic Efficiency of Compensatory Damages for Breach of Contract," 66 Va. L. Rev. 1443 (1980); Goetz & Scott, "Liquidated Damages, Penalties and the Just Compensation Principle: Some Notes on an Enforcement Model and a Theory of Efficient Breach," 77 Colum. L. Rev. 554 (1977); Goetz & Scott, "Enforcing Promises: An Examination of the Basis of Contract," 89 Yale LJ 1261 (1980); Goetz & Scott, "The Mitigation Principle: Toward a General Theory of Contractual Obligation," 69 Va. L. Rev. 967 (1983); Jackson, " 'Anticipatory Repudiation' and the Temporal Element of Contract Law: An Economic Inquiry Into Contract Damages in Cases of Prospective Nonperformance," 31 Stan. L. Rev. 69 (1978); Ulen, "The Efficiency of Specific Performance: Toward a Unified Theory of Contract Remedies," 83 Mich. L. Rev. 341 (1984).

[13] Holmes, *The Common Law* 235, 236 (Howe ed. 1963); see also Globe Ref. Co. v. Landa Cotton Oil Co., 190 US 540 (1903).

[14] See ¶ 7.02. The nonbreaching party has the correlative duty to try to minimize damages. See ¶ 7.03.

times there may be consequential damages.[15] More recently, a few courts have begun to suggest the availability of punitive damages for the purposeful breach of a contract.[16] Nevertheless, it remains true that a party to a contract usually can predict the approximate cost of completing his obligation and can compare it with the potential gain or savings from a breach. It may make sense to go into default rather than to continue with what seems to be a losing deal. The general approach of contract law is to allow an "efficient" breach and not to punish the breaching party who makes a decision that is economically wise.

Of course, there may be any number of subjective issues involved in deciding whether to continue with performance. It may be more important for a businessman's credibility in the marketplace to continue with a losing deal and to keep promises rather than to try to save money on a bad transaction, or there may be sentimental reasons for going ahead that can never be translated objectively into a monetary equivalent. In addition, the law does recognize (from the traditions of the equity courts) that some contracts are so important that they should be enforced specifically. The performing party cannot be assured that he will be able to answer in money damages only. The most common of these are contracts for the transfer of real property. It may seem anomalous in an age of tract houses and virtually identical condominiums that the law treats each parcel of real estate as unique, but that is the prevailing rule and neither the seller nor the buyer can avoid the demands of specific enforcement.[17] The same rules hold for contracts involving the transfer of "unique" chattels. Although the rule for chattels developed in connection with things such as family heirlooms or art objects, it has been extended to include goods that are not unique but that are in particularly short supply.[18] If the

[15] See ¶¶ 7.03[4], 8.02[2][f], 8.02[3][d].

[16] See ¶ 11.03.

[17] See ¶ 6.02. The nondefaulting party may choose the damage remedy as an alternative, but the breaching party cannot be assured of that choice in advance unless there is an election of remedies clause in the agreement. Such a clause is itself subject to review for fairness and consistency with the overall rules of remedies. See ¶ 10.03.

[18] See ¶ 6.03.

party in default does not obey an order for specific performance, he may find himself in contempt and fined or even jailed.[19]

The Holmes approach to contract remedies is the norm in the common-law courts. It is possible to cut losses on a bad deal and to be no worse off than by going ahead with performance; often one may be in a better position because an opportunity is gained to enter another transaction. With the application of the rule requiring the nonbreaching party to mitigate, the ultimate damage liability may be considerably less than the cost of full performance. This provides an incentive to terminate losing transactions and to move on to other and better agreements. Nevertheless, there is still the possibility of being held to specific performance of certain kinds of obligations. The law has not gone as far as the commentators in recognizing the virtues of an efficient breach. On the contrary, remnants of the principle that promises are made to be kept — not broken according to the convenience of the parties — continue to exist.[20]

¶ 1.04 STATE INTRUSION AND PRIVATE LAW

In the background of all the rules of contract law is the lingering question first raised by the law courts several centuries ago. To what extent is state intrusion into this quintessentially private area of the law justified? The decision to favor, in general, the legal remedy of money damages as a substitute for performance reflects the hesitance of the courts to become too closely involved in the private law of contracts. At the same time, the development of the rules for excusing performance, such as the doctrines of impossibility, frustration of purpose, and, especially, the doctrine of unconscionability, has involved courts directly in the interpretation and application of the most detailed aspects of individual contracts. Indeed, courts have rewritten any number of agreements to comply with some external objective sense of justice or fairness

---

[19] See ¶ 6.01.

[20] The principle that promises are made to be kept remains even in the UCC. Section 2-716, for instance, provides that "specific performance may be decreed where the goods are unique or in other proper circumstances." That section also provides the buyer with a right to replevy goods identified to the contract.

despite the law of the contract that the parties have created as between themselves.[21]

In the twentieth century there has been an interesting movement toward greater public involvement in even the most intimate private agreements. This is apparent in cases concerning the relationships between cohabitants, in those concerning both antenuptial and postnuptial contracts,[22] and in others concerning the personal decision about the choice of a contracting partner.[23] At the same time there has been an explosion of standardized agreements that have depersonalized most ordinary consumer transactions, although courts have reviewed many of these kinds of agreements for substantive fairness.[24]

What is apparent is that the basic issues of contract law have remained largely unchanged for several hundred years. The specific rules of proof, damages, other remedies, and excuses may have changed over time, but the questions asked as courts have tried to fashion these rules have not changed greatly. Should the state be involved at all in a transaction? Does its toleration or recognition mean that the state should lend its weight to the enforcement of an obligation? Should a promisor be held to his promise or should he be allowed to break it? If he does break a promise

---

[21] Rewriting agreements is obviously what courts have done for a long time with contracts for some purpose that is illicit or against a significant public policy, as, for example, a contract to fix prices. But courts often become involved in second-guessing intent and deciding the merits of relative bargaining power in transactions that are neither illegal nor against public policy on their face. In so doing, courts place considerations of public-law interests in justice above private-law interests in making and enforcing purely private agreements.

[22] See generally Hunter, "An Essay on Contract and Status: Race, Marriage and the Meretricious Spouse," 64 Va. L. Rev. 1039 (1978); Weitzman, "Legal Regulation of Marriage: Tradition and Changes," 62 Calif. L. Rev. 1169 (1974).

[23] See, e.g., Runyon v. McCrary, 427 US 160 (1976). Racial discrimination in the choice of a contracting partner may lead to liability for damages in a private action brought pursuant to 42 USC § 1981. The law provides that all citizens shall have the same right to make contracts as white citizens; it was one of the post-Civil War civil rights statutes and was enacted in 1870. Act of May 31, 1870, c. 114, § 16, 16 Stat. 144.

[24] The importance of standardized agreements and their possible use in increasing fairness in consumer transactions has been the subject of critical commentary for most of this century. See, e.g., Isaacs, "The Standardizing of Contracts," 27 Yale LJ 34 (1917); Rehbinder, "Status, Contract and the Welfare State," 23 Stan. L. Rev. 941 (1971).

and is not required to perform, what remedies are available to the other party — the value of the performance in money, transactional costs, the value of lost opportunities, punitive damages, attorneys' fees? How is the value of a performance determined? Should the focus be on the value to the disappointed party or on an objective market standard? What are the obligations, if any, of the nondefaulting party?

This book attempts to answer these questions in the context of the law of contracts as it now stands. When there is no precise answer, only a series of guidelines can be given. The questions remain constant, however, and probably will as long as the prevailing structure of the law remains essentially the same.

CHAPTER 2

Present Breaches and the Rights and Obligations of the Nonbreaching Party

¶ 2.01 DEFINITION OF "BREACH"

A "breach" is any failure in performance or payment. In the great majority of cases it is simple enough to decide whether there has been a breach. More difficult questions usually involve one of the following issues: (1) whether the breach is substantial enough to justify suspension of performance by the other party; (2) what remedies are available to the nonbreaching party; and (3) how to calculate damages. Moreover, the contract may involve subtle questions of "satisfaction" that make it difficult to determine if there has been a breach or if one party correctly has exercised a right to terminate all or part of his performance.

This chapter focuses on some of the questions that are directly connected with the relationships of the parties one to the other where there is a present failure of performance or payment. The central problem is whether courts will require parties to adhere strictly to the letter of a contract and, if so, whether a failure by one party, however slight, will justify repudiation or termination by the other party. Almost invariably the nonbreaching party will have a claim for damages arising from any breach, although the damages may be nominal. The question raised is not whether there is a claim for damages but whether there is an excuse from further performance by the nonbreaching party. Can the buyer refuse to pay? Can the seller refuse to make any more deliveries? Can the builder walk off the job? This usually involves a decision about the materiality of the breach and brings into play the competing policies of the perfect tender rule and the substantial performance rule.

¶ 2.02 SUBSTANTIAL PERFORMANCE AND THE PERFECT TENDER RULE

[1] Historical Background

The common-law courts have long stated the principle that performance in accordance with the terms of the contract is a prerequisite to recovery on the contract. If the performing party fails to perform as the contract stipulates, the standard rule is that he is left without a remedy. The corollary is that full performance acts as a discharge; anything less does not.[1] The other party can keep the nonconforming goods or accept the improperly constructed building without having to pay the price. As the New York Court of Appeals said about a performing party in *Smith v. Brady*,[2]

[1] Farnsworth, *Contracts* § 8.8, at 575 (1982) (hereinafter cited as Farnsworth).

[2] Smith v. Brady, 17 NY 173 (1858).

a famous case from the middle of the nineteenth century: "If he fails to perform when the requirement is plain, and where he can perform if he will, he has no right to call upon the courts to make a new contract for him; nor ought he to complain if the law leaves him without remedy."[3] There is more than a little method in this strict rule. In the earliest contract cases, courts considered covenants to be independent. If one party did not perform, this did not excuse the other from performing, although the latter might have an action for breach.[4] Obviously, this approach could put the nonbreaching party at a disadvantage. He might have little interest in paying the contract price to someone who had already breached one promise in the hope that a court would eventually find in his favor and give him a judgment for the return of his money, which long since might have been spent. By making performance a condition to performance by the other side, the nonbreaching party was not faced with the problem of paying and then suing to get his money back.[5]

If there is to be a single, straightforward performance, the rule makes sense and is applied. The buyer who orders a carload of apples does not have to accept a carload of tomatoes. Indeed, not only is the buyer freed from the obligation to pay, he also has a claim for damages against the seller for breach of contract.[6] But few contracts are so simple. Courts soon recognized that there were many instances in which it was not fair to say that the performing party could get nothing. What if the performing party made eleven of twelve perfect installments in an installment contract and the twelfth was modestly nonconforming? Should the nonperforming party be allowed to retain the whole performance, most of which was satisfactory, without having to pay anything? What if a builder completed a house that varied somewhat from the specifications or the architect's drawings? Should the owner be

---

[3] Id. at 190.

[4] See ¶ 6.01[3].

[5] See generally Farnsworth § 8.9, at 576–582.

[6] The buyer should be able to collect the profit he would have made on the resale of the apples less his mitigation, or the difference between the contract price and the market price of the apples at the time and place of delivery, or the difference between the contract price and the cost of a cover contract. See ¶¶ 7.03[4], 7.05, 8.02[3].

allowed to accept the house and pay nothing for it because there were variations? What if there are variations in performance but the performing party proffers evidence that the nonperforming party has accepted similar variations in the past or that variations of this sort are common in the trade? What if the contract specifications are ambiguous or involve a question of personal satisfaction that is not susceptible to objective definition?

Judges have been ingenious in responding to these questions, for they have managed to maintain the principle that the performing party is under a duty to adhere strictly to the terms of the agreement while they have fashioned ways to ensure fairness. The party who receives a nonconforming tender may have to pay its value[7] although he retains an action for breach. If the variance is slight or within the scope of acceptable trade practice, a court may decide, in effect, that there has been no breach. In the background of these decisions are two strong policies: the avoidance of forfeiture and the avoidance of economic waste.

The enunciation of the rule of strict performance and perfect tender and the development of ways around the harsh results that could accompany the application of the rule were at the heart of a series of cases decided by the New York Court of Appeals over a period of about seventy years beginning in the 1850s.[8] *Smith v. Brady,*[9] the case quoted in the preceding paragraphs, involved a construction contract. The contract called for the builder to construct several cottages, in which the joists were to be twelve inches apart and the beams in the third floors were to be sixteen inches apart. The contractor built them sixteen and twenty-four inches apart, respectively. Apparently this did not make the cottages structurally unsound, although they were not as solidly built as the owner had desired. The contractor, however, saved the cost of about 200 joists as well as the labor and time of installing them. There was little difficulty in finding that the contractor was in breach, and the court clearly enunciated a standard of strict adher-

---

[7] Payment is made in this instance using the principles represented by the terms "quantum meruit" or "quantum valebant."

[8] There are excerpts from the major cases and an excellent discussion of them in Kessler & Gilmore, *Contracts* 878–901 (2d ed. 1970).

[9] Smith v. Brady, 17 NY 173 (1858).

ence as a prerequisite to recovery on the contract by the performing party.[10]

The most important facts in *Smith v. Brady* were not emphasized in the court's written opinion. The suit was for the final payment. The owner had made installment payments as the construction went along, and he was not seeking to have them returned. He simply did not want to make the final payment. Thus, the contractor received at least some of the payment due under the agreement for a performance that was nonconforming, and he saved the expense of buying and installing a large number of joists. The owner received cottages that were nonconforming, but at a price lower than contract. Whether the court would have followed through on its rule of strict performance and have required the contractor to refund the installment payments had the owner sought that relief is questionable. The court may have invoked the doctrines of waiver or of repose to avoid undoing what were closed aspects of the transaction.[11]

The doctrine of waiver became important in the next major case decided by the New York Court of Appeals, *Avery v. Wilson*.[12] The contract was for a single delivery of 699 boxes of glass. At the buyer's request, the seller made an initial partial delivery of 365 boxes. The parties then fell into a dispute. When the seller later offered to complete delivery, the buyer refused to accept any more deliveries and refused to pay for the glass that had been delivered. In an action by the seller for the price of 365 boxes, the buyer defended by arguing that there had been an imperfect tender. The court had little trouble finding for the seller by reasoning that when the buyer elected to receive a partial delivery, accepted the delivery, and appropriated the goods to his uses, he waived the condition of full performance and became liable for the

---

[10] Even so, the court left an opening for the development of a substantial performance rule by saying: "It is true that such contracts [for the construction of a building] embrace a variety of particulars, and that slight omissions and inadvertences may sometimes very innocently occur. These should be indulgently regarded, and they will be so regarded by courts and juries." Id. at 190.

[11] Of course, if courts truly wanted to enforce a doctrine of perfect tender, they would require specific performance, but the common-law courts have never been so inclined except in cases involving the transfer of title to land. See generally Chapter 6.

[12] Avery v. Wilson, 81 NY 341 (1880).

price of what was delivered. By using the doctrine of waiver, the court was able to retain the stated rule of *Smith v. Brady* that perfect tender is a condition of the obligation to pay and to avoid the harsh result demanded by the buyer. The court could have reached the same result by treating the actions of the parties as a modification of the original agreement. It could have used a theory of unjust enrichment to find that the buyer was obligated to pay something for the glass received and used even if the contract itself was not enforceable.[13]

By 1900, the rule in *Smith v. Brady* had become even weaker, as noted by the New York Court of Appeals in the case of *Spence v. Ham*:[14]

> But there has been a relaxation of that rule, and now on such a contract there may be a recovery without a literal or exact performance of it. It is now the rule that where a builder has in good faith intended to comply with the contract, and has substantially complied with it, although there may be slight defects caused by inadvertence or unintentional omissions, he may recover the contract price, less the damages on account of such defects.[15]

The most significant decision, not only in New York but in general, came in 1921 when Judge Cardozo wrote the opinion in *Jacob & Youngs, Inc. v. Kent*.[16] The contract was to construct a country residence for a total consideration of $77,000. After installment payments were made, a balance was due of slightly less than $3,500. The owner refused to pay because he discovered that the builder had used a different brand of pipe from that specified in the contract for some of the plumbing in the house.[17] The owner

---

[13] For more on waiver in similar cases, see Clark v. West, 193 NY 349, 86 NE 1 (1908).

[14] Spence v. Ham, 163 NY 220, 57 NE 412 (1900).

[15] Id. at 225, 57 NE at 413. The burden of proving substantial performance was on the performing party. In this particular case the performing party failed to carry that burden because there were material and substantial deviations. Again, this was a suit for the balance due on a construction contract after there had been installment payments made.

[16] Jacob & Youngs, Inc. v. Kent, 230 NY 239, 129 NE 889 (1921).

[17] The architect had not issued his final certificate either, but the court never made much of that fact.

wanted the plumbing just as specified, but much of the offending pipe was buried in walls and floors. To take it out and to repair the resulting damage would have been costly and time-consuming. The builder saw no point in doing so and was able to show that the pipe he substituted was of equal quality and size. The only difference was in the name stamped on the pipe. Judge Cardozo sided with the builder and stated:

> The courts never say that one who makes a contract fills the measure of his duty by less than full performance. They do say, however, that an omission, both trivial and innocent, will sometimes be atoned for by allowance of the resulting damage, and will not always be the breach of a condition to be followed by a forfeiture.[18]

In Judge Cardozo's view, a contract might contain covenants of three different types. First, some are independent: A party is bound to perform regardless of the performance of the other party. Second, others are clearly dependent and are essentially the same as conditions.[19] The performance of one party is necessary to the obligation of the other party to perform the reciprocal covenant. Third, some are mixed. They may be dependent in form, but if the variation in performance is not substantial they may be treated as if they were independent. In *Jacob & Youngs* there was no question that there had been a breach. It was also true that the contract as written and the general rule still prevailing in New York made performance in accordance with the contract a condition to the obligation of payment (or at least payment of the final balance). But the court treated the covenants as independent because the deviation was insignificant and did not impair the value of the perfor-

---

[18] Jacob & Youngs, Inc. v. Kent, 230 NY 239, 241, 129 NE 889, 890 (1921). Judge Cardozo spoke of an omission that was "trivial" or " innocent." Despite the general rule that willfulness is not a factor in determining contract damages as it might be in a tort case (see ¶ 11.03), a willful defaulter does have more difficulty in relying on the substantial performance rule, although he may be able to recover in quantum meruit. See Kauranen v. Mattaliano, 347 Mass. 583, 199 NE2d 214 (1964); Andre v. McGuire, 305 Mass. 515, 26 NE2d 347 (1940); Lee, "The Plaintiff in Default," 19 Vand. L. Rev. 1023 (1966); Restatement (Second) of Contracts § 241 (1981).

[19] See ¶ 5.01[3].

mance. Furthermore, replacement of the pipe would have been wasteful.[20]

The importance of the opinion in *Jacob & Youngs* cannot be overstated. It continues to be the standard both for the analysis of the respective rights of parties when there is a breach and for the determination of whether there has been substantial compliance with the contract so that the paying party is obligated for the price with perhaps a claim for nominal damages for the breach. Although the Cardozo opinion did not do away with the basic principle that strict adherence to the contract is the norm, it made straightforward what courts had been doing through the use of collateral doctrines such as waiver. Some breaches are less important than others, and some are so insignificant as not to matter.[21] There is a tendency to find substantial performance when the variance is one for which the nonbreaching party can be adequately compensated in damages.[22]

The influence of the Cardozo opinion was apparent in the discussion of material breach in the first Restatement of Contracts,

---

[20] According to Judge Cardozo, one determines whether there has been a significant departure from the contract by reference to considerations of justice and the presumable intentions of the parties. Did the owner really want pipe of a certain brand in the walls of his house, or did he want a satisfactory country house with plumbing of good quality? Is making a builder tear up perfectly good walls and floors just an action to satisfy a whim about the brandname of pipes? Obviously, the Cardozo approach can involve courts in subjective second-guessing, but to those critics who were concerned about the loss of objectivity and the certainty of the perfect tender approach, Judge Cardozo said:

> "Those who think more of symmetry and logic in the development of legal rules than of practical adaptation to the attainment of a just result will be troubled by a classification where the lines of division are so wavering and blurred. Something, doubtless, may be said on the score of consistency and certainty in favor of a stricter standard. The courts have balanced such considerations against those of equity and fairness, and found the latter to be weightier."

Jacob & Youngs, Inc. v. Kent, 230 NY 239, 242, 243, 129 NE 889, 891 (1921).

[21] Massachusetts, which is usually the guardian of traditions in contract law, adopted a substantial performance rule long before New York. See, e.g., Bowen v. Kimball, 203 Mass. 364, 89 NE 542 (1909); Hayward v.Leonard, 24 Mass. 181 (1828). In the former case the court said that a builder who proceeds in good faith can recover the contract price upon substantial performance with a deduction for the value of imperfections or omissions.

[22] Farnsworth § 8.12, at 592, 593 (1982).

which suggested a variety of factors to be taken into account in deciding whether a breach was "material" and, therefore, whether the nonbreaching party could repudiate.[23] These factors were applied, for example, by the Michigan Supreme Court in a 1957 decision on a contract for the lease, installation, and maintenance of a neon sign.[24] The agreement ran for a term of thirty-six months. There was no problem with the installation, but the lessee became dissatisfied with the lessor's maintenance: Someone threw a tomato at the sign, there was a little rust on it, some children scribbled on part of it, and there were cobwebs. The lessee called these problems to the attention of the lessor and became irritated when the lessor did not respond quickly and the sign's appearance continued to be marred.[25] The lessee suspended payments, and the lessor sued for breach. The lessee responded by arguing that the lessor's failure to respond promptly to demands for maintenance was a breach of the agreement that justified his suspension of payments. The court disagreed. The lessor might have been in breach, but it was not a material breach. The lessee was still bound to make the lease payments, and any claim he had was for damages arising from the lessor's partial and immaterial breach.[26]

A significant issue in *Jacob & Youngs* was the measurement of any damages. There was essentially no difference in the value of the house as built and the value the house would have had if the

---

[23] Section 275 of the first Restatement of Contracts (1932) suggested six factors to be taken into account in deciding whether a breach was "material" and therefore justified a repudiation by the other party: (1) the extent to which the injured party will receive substantially what he anticipated; (2) the extent to which the injury can be compensated in damages; (3) the extent to which the party in breach has performed or made preparations for performance; (4) the degree of hardship to be imposed on the breaching party by a repudiation as opposed to the hardship suffered by the nonbreaching party; (5) whether the breaching party acted willfully, negligently, or innocently; and (6) the likelihood that the party in breach will perform the remainder of the agreement.

[24] Walker & Co. v. Harrison, 347 Mich. 630, 81 NW2d 352 (1957). An edited version of this case together with a discussion of its principles appears in McGovern, *Cases, Statutes and Readings on the Law of Contracts* 191, 192 (1980).

[25] It was the tomato stain that really seemed to have the lessee upset. He said that he became angry every time he looked at it.

[26] Even though the lessee lost the lawsuit, he did manage to get the lessor's attention. Within a week of the suspension of payments the sign was cleaned.

contractor had used the specified pipe. Judge Cardozo noted this, and there is little doubt that the absence of any difference in value influenced his view of the problem. On the other hand, the repair cost would have been substantial. Suppose that a court says there is a breach for which the injured party may seek damages, but that the breach is not significant enough to justify forfeiture or repudiation of the obligation to pay. If the injured party sues for breach, is he entitled to the cost of repair or replacement, or is he only entitled to the difference in value? There is no clear answer. Courts tend to say that the general rule is that the injured party is entitled to repair or replacement cost, but the difference-in-value approach is used when it would be unfair to apply the general rule.[27] "Unfairness" often seems to turn on the question of waste. The approach of the first Restatement,[28] for instance, was to allow the recovery of the repair or replacement cost unless that would result in economic waste, which would have been the case had the owner in *Jacob & Youngs* prevailed.[29]

If there is a material breach and the nonbreaching party may suspend or terminate performance with justification, he must still proceed with care. For instance, if there are several contracts between the buyer and the seller, the buyer may suspend payments or set off damages against the payments due only on the contract in breach, not on any other contracts between the parties.[30]

---

[27] See, e.g., Ficara v. Belleau, 331 Mass. 80, 117 NE2d 287 (1954); Bellizi v. Huntley Estates, Inc., 3 NY2d 112, 143 NE2d 802 (1957).

[28] Restatement (First) of Contracts § 346 (1932).

[29] As a corollary, the injured party should not get more than he bargained for whichever measure may be used. In Ficara v. Belleau, 331 Mass. 80, 117 NE2d 287 (1954), the plaintiff and the defendant had a contract to install a heating and cooling system for $6,200. The parties had a falling out and the seller/installer walked off the job after having been paid a total of $4,200. The plaintiff was able to get the job completed for another $2,361. He sued for that amount, but the court sensibly limited his recovery to $361, the difference between the original contract price and the cost to complete. This clarified a rather open-ended approach to damages suggested by the same court in the earlier case of Glaser v. Schwartz, 276 Mass. 54, 176 NE 613 (1931).

[30] See, e.g., Travenol Laboratories, Inc. v. Zotal, Ltd., 394 Mass. 95, 474 NE2d 1070 (1985).

[2] Perfect Tender and the UCC

The UCC carries forward the perfect tender rule in language as strict as that used by the New York Court of Appeals in the pre-Civil War *Smith v. Brady* case.[31] Section 2-601 reads:

> Subject to the provisions of this Article on breach in installment contracts (Section 2-612) and unless otherwise agreed under the sections on contractual limitations of remedy (Sections 2-718 and 2-719), if the goods or the tender of delivery fail in any respect to conform to the contract, the buyer may
> (a) reject the whole; or
> (b) accept the whole; or
> (c) accept any commercial unit or units and reject the rest.

According to a 1984 decision from Texas,[32] there is no room for a substantial performance argument under Section 2-601. It demands complete performance and nothing else.[33] Even so, the court admitted that there were some limitations on the requirements of Section 2-601. A defendant may introduce evidence of trade usage to explain or to supplement the contract if there is some ambiguity.[34] In the same manner, a buyer is subject to the general duty of good faith imposed by Section 2-103, and the court will entertain evidence that is presented for the purpose of proving that the buyer's motivation in rejecting the tender was avoidance of the bargain and not dissatisfaction with a tender of impaired value.[35]

---

[31] For a general discussion and criticism, see Priest, "Breach and Remedy for the Tender of Nonconforming Goods Under the Uniform Commercial Code: An Economic Approach," 91 Harv. L. Rev. 960 (1978).

[32] Printing Center of Texas, Inc. v. Supermind Publishing Co., 669 SW2d 779 (Tex. Civ. App. 1984).

[33] The court cited Mitsubishi Goshi Kaisha v. J. Aron & Co., 16 F2d 185 (2d Cir. 1926), for the proposition that commercial law demands strict conformity to the contract, and it rejected the suggestion in Del Monte Corp. v. Martin, 574 SW2d 597 (Tex. Civ. App. 1978), that the question of substantial compliance was appropriate for the jury. A recent New Jersey decision says essentially the same thing. Ramirez v. Auto-Sport, 88 NJ 277, 440 A2d 1345 (1982).

[34] Printing Center of Texas, Inc. v. Supermind Publishing Co., 669 SW2d 779, 784 (Tex. Civ. App. 1984).

[35] Id. The seller does have the burden of proving bad-faith rejection by the buyer. Rejection for a minor defect in a falling market makes the buyer's rejection appear suspicious. Neumiller Farms, Inc. v. Cornett, 368 So. 2d 272 (Ala. 1979).

Section 2-601, however, is like all other sections of the UCC in that it cannot be read alone; it must be considered together with a number of other related sections. The duty of good faith stated in Section 2-103 must be considered along with Section 2-508, which gives a seller the right to cure a nonconforming tender.[36] Section 2-602 details the manner in which a buyer is to make a rejection, and Section 2-605 provides that a buyer may be found to have waived nonconformities by not stating them to the seller in a timely or clear manner. Regardless of nonconformity, a buyer may find that he has accepted the goods under Section 2-606 if he "does any act inconsistent with the seller's ownership" or if he accepts part of a commercial unit.[37] Even after acceptance, however, a buyer may be able to revoke his acceptance under Section 2-608 if the nonconformity of the tender "substantially impairs its value to him." Section 2-612 establishes special rules for installment contracts, and these contracts are excluded from the coverage of Section 2-601 to the extent that Section 2-612 applies. Finally, Section 2-614 provides several justifications for substituted performance by a seller where, through no fault of the parties, the planned form of carriage or delivery becomes unavailable but there is a reasonable substitute. Section 2-614 also protects the parties when the contract method of payment becomes impossible by reason of intervening government action. Of course, the contract itself may allow for less than perfect tender or specify the remedies in the event that performance is at variance with the agreement. In considering these sections and their relationship to one another, a careful lawyer also must bear in mind the various remedial sections (e.g., Sections 2-703 through 2-719) and their interrelationships.[38]

The interplay among various sections of the UCC was particularly apparent in the case of *Lanners v. Whitney*,[39] a decision of the Oregon Supreme Court. The buyer took delivery of a secondhand

---

[36] If the buyer fails to allow the seller an opportunity to cure under Section 2-508, he may find himself in breach. See ¶ 5.04[9]. Furthermore, Section 2-508(2) gives the seller a reasonable time to substitute a conforming tender for a rejected "nonconforming tender which the seller had reasonable grounds to believe would be acceptable." This language suggests that sometimes less-than-perfect tender would be acceptable as full performance.

[37] Even so, he may still have an action for breach. See UCC § 2-607.

[38] See ¶ 8.02 and generally Chapter 10.

[39] Lanners v. Whitney, 247 Ore. 223, 428 P2d 398 (1967).

airplane that the seller represented to be airworthy and certified by the Federal Aviation Administration. It was neither, but the buyer only became aware of these shortcomings some time later, after incurring expenses for various repairs. The dissatisfied buyer then brought suit for a rescission (i.e., an unmaking of the contract), but the trial court rejected the buyer's demand. Rescission is an extraordinary remedy and the trial court reasoned that the buyer had a satisfactory remedy for money damages. On appeal, the buyer was successful and the trial court was reversed. The appellate court recognized that the buyer's action arose under the UCC and that there was no need to resort to the use of extraordinary remedies. As one commentator analyzed the case:

> The buyer wanted to return the plane to the seller. That was possible since he could simply "reject" the plane as nonconforming (2-601), if he had not yet "accepted" it (2-606). Even if he had "accepted," he could still "revoke" his acceptance under the facts of this case and then return the plane (2-608). In either event, he had a right to a return of the money he had paid (2-711). Added to this, he could recover his out-of-pocket expenses for repairs and storage (2-715), and damages, if he so desired, for the seller's failure to meet his contract in the first place (2-713). What's more, he could retain the plane by way of security to assure the repayment of at least some of the money that was now due (2-711(3)).[40]

[a] What Constitutes Nonconformity

Technically, any failure, however small, is a nonconformity that justifies rejection under Section 2-601. In fact, courts applying this section tend to bring into play considerations relating to the substantiality of the nonconformity and to decide cases based on their context. For instance, delivery of a car without a spare tire was a substantial nonconformity that justified rejection under Section 2-601. The buyer's job required him to travel extensively, particularly in the early morning hours. He had ordered special high-quality tires on the car, and a spare was important to him for safety reasons. He did not want to be stranded with a flat tire on a

---

[40] Quinn, *Uniform Commercial Code Commentary and Law Digest* ¶ 2-601[A][9][b] (1978).

highway late at night.[41] By comparison, delivery of an expensive agricultural fertilizer applicator without the calibration chart was not a nonconforming tender. The calibration chart was essential to the proper operation of the machinery, but the information was available to the buyer by telephone on a toll-free number. The seller had requested a chart from the manufacturer, and it was expected shortly.[42]

Other examples of nonconformity justifying rejection include the following: a Chevrolet Camaro that was delivered without requested undercoating and polymer finish,[43] soybeans with a germination rate of 67 percent instead of the 80 percent rate represented by the seller,[44] persistent overheating of a truck engine,[45] and an excess of the quantity delivered over the quantity ordered.[46] There is authority for the proposition that the question of conformity is one for a jury,[47] but at least one court has suggested that it is a matter of legal interpretation for the courts.[48]

[b] Timeliness and Form of the Notice of Nonconformity and Rejection

A buyer who is dissatisfied with goods that are delivered must give the seller timely notice[49] of his dissatisfaction and a reasonably clear statement of what he considers to be the nonconform-

---

[41] Colonial Dodge, Inc. v. Miller, 121 Mich. App. 466, 328 NW2d 678, 40 UCC Rep. 1 (1984).

[42] Evco Distrib., Inc. v. Commercial Credit Equip. Co., 6 Kan. App. 2d 205, 627 P2d 374 (1981).

[43] Jakowski v. Carole Chevrolet, Inc., 180 NJ Super. 122, 433 A2d 841 (1981).

[44] Jacob Hartz Seed Co. v. Coleman, 271 Ark. 756, 612 SW2d 91 (1981).

[45] Capitol Dodge Sales, Inc. v. Northern Concrete Pipe, Inc., 131 Mich. App. 149, 346 NW2d 535, 38 UCC Rep. 114 (1983).

[46] Van Dorn Co. v. Future Chem. & Oil Corp., 753 F2d 565, 40 UCC Rep. 119 (7th Cir. 1985). In this case the buyer was found to have accepted the excess goods even though it rightfully could have rejected the excess.

[47] See, e.g., O'Neal Ford, Inc. v. Earley, 13 Ark. App. 189, 681 SW2d 414 (1985); Frontier Mobile Home Sales v. Trigleth, 256 Ark. 101, 505 SW2d 516 (1974); Dopieralla v. Arkansas La. Gas Co., 255 Ark. 150, 499 SW2d 610 (1973).

[48] Printing Center of Texas, Inc. v. Supermind Publishing Co., 669 SW2d 779 (Tex. Civ. App. 1984).

[49] UCC § 2-602.

ity.[50] If the buyer were not required to give notice and to specify the reasons for rejection, the seller would not have a reasonable opportunity to cure. Furthermore, the notice protects the buyer from an inadvertent acceptance of the goods.[51]

The notice of nonconformity must be timely,[52] but the requirements of timeliness vary greatly with the particulars of different agreements. A transfer of title and physical acceptance of goods, for instance, do not necessarily mean that a subsequent notice of nonconformity is untimely. In Michigan, for example, a buyer was interested in purchasing a secondhand truck but was concerned when it overheated during a test drive. After the seller assured him that the problem was minor, the buyer agreed to purchase the truck if the problem could be fixed. He took possession and title, but the overheating problem continued, despite the seller's attempts to cure. The buyer's subsequent rejection and tender of the truck back to the seller was timely.[53] The buyer's patience in allowing the seller an opportunity to repair while continuing discussions does not make a notice of rejection untimely when the seller's efforts appear to be unavailing.[54]

Some buyers do not buy for their own use but for immediate resale to third parties. Sometimes the goods pass through the buyer's warehouse, but in other cases they may travel directly to the buyer's vendees. The buyer may make spot inspections of the goods, but if the seller is reputable it is just as likely that the goods will pass through unopened and uninspected. This happened in a Pennsylvania case where the buyer did not open tool sets ordered from the seller because they came sealed in vinyl pouches that were packed in shipping cartons. The cartons were sent on to the buyer's vendees, but the buyer began to receive complaints from

---

[50] UCC § 2-605.

[51] Even if there is an acceptance, all is not lost. The buyer may still have remedies for breach of warranty. See, e.g., Tonka Tours, Inc. v. Chadima, 354 NW2d 519, 39 UCC Rep. 122 (Minn. Ct. App. 1984).

[52] See, e.g., UCC § 2-602(1); Seasons Coal Co. v. City of Cleveland, 10 Ohio St. 3d 77, 461 NE2d 1273 (1984).

[53] Capitol Dodge Sales, Inc. v. Northern Concrete Pipe, Inc., 131 Mich. App. 149, 346 NW2d 535, 38 UCC Rep. 114 (1983).

[54] Lafayette Stabilizer Repair, Inc. v. Machinery Wholesaler Corp., 750 F2d 1290 (5th Cir. 1985).

his vendees about the tool kits. The court found that his notice to the seller was timely because of the time and expense required to inspect each carton of goods.[55]

A court will look askance, however, at a buyer who belatedly asserts a nonconformity defense in a suit to collect the balance due on a delivery. This was the case where a mail-order distribution company asserted that it was justified in refusing to pay for a shipment from a publisher because the publisher had been more than two months late in making delivery. The court might have been more sympathetic to the defense to the publisher's suit for the price, but the buyer had made no objection to the late delivery for two years and only asserted it as a justification after the seller brought suit.[56]

Courts have held that the requirements for particularity in stating the reasons for a rejection are different for merchants and consumers, although this difference is not apparent on the face of Section 2-605, the governing provision of the UCC.[57] The Official Commentary suggests somewhat more stringent standards for merchants than for consumers,[58] but it is not clear that the drafters intended that there be any hard and fast rule that the notice re-

---

[55] In re HP Tool Mfg. Corp., 38 UCC Rep. 110 (Bankr. ED Pa. 1984).

[56] Simon & Schuster, Inc. v. Howe Plastics & Chems. Co., 105 AD2d 604, 481 NYS2d 82, 39 UCC Rep. 1266 (Sup. Ct. 1984).

[57] Section 2-605 reads:

"(1) The buyer's failure to state in connection with rejection a particular defect which is ascertainable by reasonable inspection precludes him from relying on the unstated defect to justify rejection or to establish breach

"(a) where the seller could have cured if it stated seasonably; or

"(b) between merchants when the seller has after rejection made a request in writing for a full and final written statement of all defects on which the buyer proposes to rely.

"(2) Payment against documents made without reservation of rights precludes recovery of the payment for defects apparent on the face of the documents."

[58] For instance, Section 2-605, Official Comment 2, states that a rejection without stating reasons would be "commercial bad faith" and probably evidence that a buyer is "seeking to get out of a deal which has become unprofitable." Official Comment 3 mentions "a formal demand" in the case of "a merchant buyer," but at the same time Official Comment 1 says that "the present section rests upon a policy of permitting the buyer to give a quick and informal notice of defects in a tender without penalizing him for omissions in his statement."

quirements for merchants be substantially different from those for consumers. The prevailing rule, however, holds merchants to a stricter standard. In the words of one court:

> What constitutes adequate notice from an inexperienced consumer may not be sufficient in a transaction between professionals. We agree with the rationale of the above-cited cases which require more than minimal notice, and higher standards of commercial good faith, where both parties are merchants engaged in ongoing transactions.[59]

Oral notice suffices if it is clear.[60] Whether the notice is seasonable or sufficient is usually a jury question.[61]

[c] Buyer's Acceptance of Nonconforming Tender

A buyer always has the option to accept nonconforming goods, thereby either waiving the condition of perfect tender or making a de facto modification of the contract.[62] Problems arise when the buyer does not explicitly accept nonconforming goods, but by his action or inaction finds that the law has presumed acceptance. Failure to make an effective rejection,[63] acting in a way that is inconsistent with the seller's ownership,[64] or accepting part of a commercial unit[65] results in an acceptance, even if the goods are nonconforming and the buyer intended to reject. The buyer, therefore, must be careful if he has reason to doubt that the goods are conforming, or he may discover that he has lost his right of rejection.

---

[59] Industrial Fiberglass v. Jandt, 361 NW2d 595, 598, 40 UCC Rep. 133, 137 (ND 1985). To the same effect, see K&M Joint Venture v. Smith Int'l, Inc., 669 F2d 1106 (6th Cir. 1982); Standard Alliance Indus. v. Black Clawson Co., 587 F2d 813 (6th Cir. 1978), cert. denied, 441 US 923 (1979); Eastern Airlines, Inc. v. McDonnell Douglas Corp., 532 F2d 957 (5th Cir. 1976).

[60] Delano Growers' Coop. Winery v. Supreme Wine Co., 393 Mass. 666, 473 NE2d 1066 (1985).

[61] Rowe Int'l, Inc. v. J-B Enters., Inc., 647 F2d 830 (8th Cir. 1981); Wilson v. Marquette Elecs., Inc., 630 F2d 575 (8th Cir. 1980).

[62] UCC §§ 2-601(b), 2-606(1)(a).

[63] UCC § 2-606(1)(b).

[64] UCC § 2-606(1)(c).

[65] UCC § 2-606(2).

In general, a buyer has the opportunity to inspect before he loses the right to reject. Some contracts require payment on the presentation of documents before the delivery of goods and before any inspection. Payment in accordance with such a contract is not an acceptance of the goods that precludes rejection after inspection.[66] This only makes sense. It would be anomalous to say that a buyer accepted nonconforming goods (unless the nonconformity appears in the documents) before he has had a chance to look at them. Furthermore, the seller's right to payment is conditional on delivery of conforming goods.[67] Proper delivery after payment is akin to a condition subsequent, and if it fails, the seller has no right to retain payment.[68] The opportunity to inspect before losing the right of rejection can be important even if payment is not due on the presentation of documents because delivery often takes place somewhere other than the buyer's place of business (e.g., FOB seller's dock or FOB common carrier).[69]

Carelessness is the main culprit in most cases involving the loss of the right of rejection. For example, in *CMI Corp. v. Leemar Steel Co.*,[70] the buyer received the goods on March 23, inspected them five days later, and wrote up a rejection report because they were nonconforming. The buyer never mailed the rejection report, however. Instead, an employee of the buyer telephoned the seller on April 13 to say that there was a problem with the goods. On April 24, other employees approved and paid the seller's invoice, again without any specific notice of nonconformity. Meanwhile, the seller tried to work with the buyer to straighten out the prob-

---

[66] Tonka Tours, Inc. v. Chadima, 354 NW2d 519, 39 UCC Rep. 122 (Minn. Ct. App. 1984). In this case, however, the buyer proceeded to act in a way that was inconsistent with the seller's ownership after inspection and, for that reason, lost the right to reject.

[67] In re Gold Coast Seed Co., 751 F2d 1118, 40 UCC Rep. 479 (9th Cir. 1985).

[68] For a discussion of conditions, see generally Chapter 5.

[69] See, e.g., Warrior Tombigee Transp. Co. v. 5,775,674 Net Tons of Coal, 570 F. Supp. 1405 (SD Ala. 1983) (sale FOB barge meant that seller completed performance and was entitled to payment when coal was loaded on barge); see also United Cal. Bank v. Eastern Mountain Sports, Inc., 546 F. Supp. 945 (D. Mass. 1982), aff'd mem., 705 F2d 439 (1st Cir. 1983); Travenol Laboratories, Inc. v. Zotal, Ltd., 394 Mass. 95, 474 NE2d 1070 (1985).

[70] CMI Corp. v. Leemar Steel Co., 733 F2d 1410, 38 UCC Rep. 798 (10th Cir. 1984).

lem. By July the buyer had become frustrated and tried to reject, but the court said that it was too late. The buyer's actions and the failure to send notice of rejection until July after delivery in March, inspection the same month, and payment in April constituted an acceptance. In a somewhat similar case, a buyer "accepted" nonconforming goods when they were held in the buyer's possession for three months, stamped with the buyer's identifying marks, and manufactured into parts.[71] Another buyer tried unsuccessfully to reject after holding possession of goods for two years and even reselling some of them.[72]

[d] Revocation of Buyer's Acceptance of Nonconforming Tender

Even if a buyer has accepted goods, either expressly or by implication, he may still be able to revoke the acceptance pursuant to Section 2-608 and to reject the goods. There are several hurdles to an effective revocation under Section 2-608. The buyer must show that the goods are nonconforming and then must demonstrate that the nonconformity "substantially impairs" the value of the goods "to him."[73] The buyer also must show either (1) that he accepted the goods "on the reasonable assumption" that the seller would be able to cure the nonconformity and that the seller has not done so "seasonably,"[74] (2) that he was induced to accept the goods by the seller's assurances, or (3) that he accepted nonconforming goods because of the difficulty that would be involved in discovering their defects.[75] The revocation of acceptance must occur within a "reasonable time" after discovery of the defects and "before any substantial change in condition of the goods which is

---

[71] Intervale Steel Corp. v. Borg & Beck Div., Borg-Warner Corp., 578 F. Supp. 1081 (ED Mich. 1984). The most important factor was the buyer's use of the goods to manufacture certain parts, although the time element was also critical. Stamping the goods with the buyer's marks was evidence of acts inconsistent with the seller's ownership but, standing alone, would not have been determinative.

[72] Eaton Corp. v. Magnavox Corp., 581 F. Supp. 1514 (ED Mich. 1984).

[73] UCC § 2-608(1).

[74] UCC § 2-608(1)(a).

[75] UCC § 2-608(1)(b).

not caused by their own defects."[76] The choice of a revocation does not preclude the buyer from seeking damages for the breach as well.[77] Thus, the buyer is not faced with the dilemma of electing remedies while trying to decide what to do with goods that are unsatisfactory but happen to be in his possession.

Often, the most difficult problem is to determine what is a "substantial impairment" of value to the buyer. The focus is on the buyer's needs, not on any external market determinations of value.[78] The Official Commentary to Section 2-608 states:

> For this purpose the test is not what the seller had reason to know at the time of contracting; the question is whether the nonconformity is such as will in fact cause a substantial impairment of value to the buyer though the seller had no advance knowledge as to the buyer's particular circumstances.

Not surprisingly, a number of the cases arising under Section 2-608 have involved automobile sales. Even though a buyer has a number of advantages under Sections 2-601 and 2-608, he still has to provide the seller with a reasonable opportunity to make good on the transaction. This duty sometimes catches a consumer who becomes especially irritated by delivery of an automobile that turns out to be a "lemon." A Rhode Island buyer took delivery of a new car but returned it and stopped payment on his check because the car was missing a window sticker, floor mats, and bumper guards, and also had a dented hood. He contended that his revocation was timely and correct because the value of the automobile to him was substantially impaired. The court said that it would not even consider the question of substantial impairment because the buyer did not give proper notice and an opportunity to cure. The buyer was without a remedy, and to his chagrin the court ruled that the seller had a claim for damages for nonacceptance under Section 2-703,

---

[76] UCC § 2-608(2). The revocation is not effective until the buyer informs the seller of it. Id. A revoking buyer has the same responsibilities, as well as the same rights, as one who rejects prior to acceptance. UCC § 2-608(3). This means, among other things, that the buyer is bound by the provisions of Sections 2-603 and 2-604 on the handling and salvage of rejected goods.

[77] UCC § 2-608, Official Comment 1.

[78] Not every court is in agreement with this. See, e.g., Hays Merchandise, Inc. v. Dewey, 78 Wash. 2d 343, 474 P2d 270 (1970).

plus other damages (including storage fees) under Sections 2-708 and 2-710.[79]

In comparison, the buyer of another car was almost too patient. Her new automobile was in the repair shop four out of the first six months of ownership. Despite repairs, it still was difficult to start and stalled in traffic. The buyer even introduced evidence that her employer was dissatisfied because she had missed work as a result of problems with the car. The seller had had ample opportunities to cure and had failed to do so. The buyer's revocation of acceptance was good.[80]

In yet another automobile case, the buyer purchased a used car with a "limited" warranty that provided for certain "exclusive" remedies. Revocation and rejection were not among the remedies. Within three days of the purchase, the car developed severe problems that needed extensive and expensive repairs. The buyer informed the seller of these problems and demanded revocation. The court said that she had a right to revocation because the defects substantially impaired the value of the car to her and the limited warranty with exclusive remedies did not defeat her right to revoke and to reject.[81]

Sometimes a buyer can use the nonconforming goods and still revoke the acceptance if the alternatives to temporary use would be inconsistent with the policies in favor of minimizing damages and avoiding waste. A group of radiologists on Long Island entered into an agreement for the purchase of a CAT scanner after consid-

---

[79] Palmisciano v. Tarbox Motors, Inc., 39 UCC Rep. 146 (RI Super. Ct. 1984).

[80] Jackson v. Rocky Mountain Datsun, Inc., 693 P2d 391, 39 UCC Rep. 885 (Colo. Ct. App. 1984). For a similar case involving a buyer who was plagued with defects in a new DeLorean, see Freeman v. Hubco Leasing, Inc., 253 Ga. 698, 324 SE2d 462 (1985). In fact, the buyer's first DeLorean broke down on the way home from the dealership. The dealer immediately replaced it with another, which also developed a series of problems. The dealer gave up on repairs after several months because the manufacturer was not compensating him for warranty expenses.

[81] O'Neal Ford, Inc. v. Earley, 13 Ark. App. 189, 681 SW2d 414 (1985). For the proposition that signing an agreement with a limited warranty does not affect the right to revoke an acceptance, see also Ford Motor Credit Co. v. Harper, 671 F2d 1117 (8th Cir. 1982); Blankenship v. Northtown Ford, Inc., 420 NE2d 167 (Ill. App. Ct. 1981).

ering the products of several vendors and after fairly lengthy discussions with the seller. The scanner that was delivered was not the one the radiologists had ordered, and they made their dissatisfaction known to the seller immediately. The seller represented that a cure would be possible, but despite ongoing negotiations the seller was never able to come up with a satisfactory tender. In the meantime the radiologists used the nonconforming scanner. The court ruled that this did not affect their ability to revoke, because the market was so competitive that they had to have a scanner, regardless of its capabilities, and another suitable for their use would not be available from any vendor for some time. Using the nonconforming scanner was a reasonable way to mitigate damages and did not constitute a waiver of the right to revoke and reject.[82]

[e] Installment Agreements and Section 2-612

Many commercial sales agreements contemplate a series of performances rather than a single performance. Section 2-612(1) defines an "installment contract" as one that "requires or authorizes the delivery of goods in separate lots to be separately accepted, even though the contract contains a clause 'each delivery is a separate contract' or its equivalent." Somewhat different rules apply to determining the rights of a buyer upon a breach of either a part or the whole of an installment contract.

A buyer may reject a nonconforming installment, but only if the nonconformity "substantially impairs the value of that installment and cannot be cured" or if the problem is a defect in the contract documents.[83] This is significantly different from the perfect tender standard of Section 2-601. Indeed, it is more a substantial performance than a perfect tender rule, because the onus is on the buyer to show that the nonconformity "substantially impairs" the value of the installment. Interestingly, this section does not define value by reference to the buyer's uses, as does Section 2-608 on revocation of acceptance. The "substantial impairment" requirement of Section 2-612(2) is apparently an objective rather than a subjective standard. Unless the defect in an installment is so

[82] Computerized Radiological Servs. v. Syntex Corp., 595 F. Supp. 1495 (EDNY 1984).

[83] UCC § 2-612(2).

great as to constitute a default on the entire agreement as defined in Section 2-612(3), the buyer must accept a nonconforming installment when the seller gives "adequate assurance of its cure." This explicitly limits the buyer's right of rejection by the seller's right to cure under Section 2-508.

The contract may specify what amounts to a substantial impairment. In the absence of language in the agreement,[84] the Official Commentary suggests the following:

> Substantial impairment of the value of an installment can turn not only on the quality of the goods but also on such factors as time, quantity, assortment, and the like. It must be judged in terms of the normal or specifically known purposes of the contract. The defect in required documents refers to such matters as the absence of insurance documents under a CIF contract, falsity of a bill of lading, or one failing to show shipment within the contract period or to the contract destination. Even in such cases, however, the provisions on cure of tender apply if appropriate documents are readily procurable.[85]

If a buyer is concerned about the quality of an installment (or a seller is worried about a buyer's ability to pay) and about possible problems with future installments but is uncertain that he can prove substantial impairment of value, he may be able to demand adequate assurances of performance under Section 2-609.[86] This puts the seller on notice that the buyer has concerns and protects the buyer from an inadvertent waiver of the nonconformity.

Some defects in the delivery of an installment may be so serious that the buyer considers the entire agreement to be in default. Section 2-612(3) takes this problem into account:

---

[84] Even so, the Official Comment says that a strict compliance clause "must . . . have some basis in reason, must avoid imposing hardship by surprise and is subject to waiver or to displacement by practical construction." UCC § 2-612, Official Comment 4.

[85] Id.

[86] Section 2-609 provides, in part, that "when reasonable grounds for insecurity arise with respect to the performance of either party the other may in writing demand adequate assurance of due performance and until he receives such assurance may if commercially reasonable suspend any performance for which he has not already received the agreed return."

> Whenever nonconformity or default with respect to one or more installments substantially impairs the value of the whole contract there is a breach of the whole. But the aggrieved party reinstates the contract if he accepts a nonconforming installment without seasonably notifying of cancellation or if he brings an action with respect only to past installments or demands performance as to future installments.

A buyer must be careful, however, because the courts generally require that the defects in one installment be very substantial before the buyer is entitled to reject the entire agreement.[87] The same applies to a seller who becomes upset because a buyer misses an installment payment.[88]

[f] Substituted Performance and Section 2-614

Sometimes, through no fault of either party, it is not possible to send the goods by the designated carrier or to the location specified in the contract. If that occurs, the parties are not excused. Section 2-614 provides that as long as there is a "commercially reasonable substitute" available, the seller must use that substitute and the buyer must accept it. This provision limits the perfect tender rule of Section 2-601 and modifies the general rules on impossibility and frustration of purpose.[89]

Section 2-614 makes good sense. There is no reason that a contract should fail because the carrier that the parties expected to use is on strike when another carrier of comparable quality is able to deliver the goods. As exemplified in one case, it was no excuse that rail cars were unavailable to transport goods when no attempt was made either to use trucks or to show that an alternative carrier would be unreasonably expensive.[90] Essentially the same rule applies to payments when an intervening government regulation affects the manner of payment contemplated by the agreement.[91]

---

[87] See, e.g., Kirkwood Agri-Trade v. Frosty Land Foods Int'l, Inc., 650 F2d 602 (5th Cir. 1981).

[88] See, e.g., Laredo Hides Co. v. H&H Meat Prods. Co., 513 SW2d 210 (Tex. Civ. App. 1974).

[89] See generally Chapter 12. Compare, e.g., UCC §§ 2-613 (casualty to identified goods) and 2-615 (excuse by failure of presupposed conditions).

¶ 2.03 PERFORMANCE TO THE "SATISFACTION" OF THE OTHER PARTY AND THE DUTY OF GOOD FAITH

"Satisfaction" clauses and the problems that arise from them are common in publishing contracts. A recent case involving the actor Tony Curtis and the Doubleday publishing house provides a good example.[92] Curtis wrote a novel in the mid-1970s that Doubleday published with some success for both publisher and author. It was a first effort by Curtis and apparently his editor at Doubleday worked with him so closely that he was almost a coauthor. Curtis came up with an idea and an outline for another book and signed a contract with Doubleday that provided for an advance of $100,000, one half on signing and the other half on submission of a manuscript in a form acceptable to Doubleday, plus royalties on sales of the book. The contract specifically provided that if the manuscript was not "acceptable" to Doubleday, the agreement would be void. The manuscript was due October 1, 1978, but Curtis had difficulty meeting the due date, and through various negotiations the contractual deadline was eventually moved to late 1981.[93] The editor who worked on Curtis' first book did not work on the second one, and although the new editor spent a good deal of time on the chapters Curtis submitted, he did not undertake to rewrite them as extensively as the first editor had done. After lengthy internal dis-

---

[90] Nora Springs Coop. Co. v. Brandau, 247 NW2d 744 (Iowa 1976).

[91] Section 2-614(2) states:

"If the agreed means or manner of payment fails because of domestic or foreign governmental regulation, the seller may withhold or stop delivery unless the buyer provides a means or manner of payment which is commercially a substantial equivalent. If delivery has already been taken, payment by the means or in the manner provided by the regulation discharges the buyer's obligation unless the regulation is discriminatory, oppressive or predatory."

[92] Doubleday & Co. v. Curtis, 763 F2d 495 (2d Cir. 1985).

[93] Many such contracts have a "time-is-of-the-essence" clause. In an interesting footnote, the court stated that waiver of such a time clause will convert the contract into one to be completed within a "reasonable" time. Doubleday & Co. v. Curtis, 763 F2d 495 (2d Cir. 1985), citing Schenectady Steel v. Bruno Trimpoli Gen. Constr. Co., 43 AD2d 234, 350 NYS2d 920, aff'd, 34 NY2d 939, 316 NE2d 875, 359 NYS2d 560 (1974).

cussions[94] and editorial conferences, Doubleday decided that the Curtis manuscript was not publishable. The publisher rejected the manuscript and sued Curtis for the return of the advance on the grounds that he had breached the agreement (and thereby the condition for performance by Doubleday had failed to occur) by not submitting a satisfactory manuscript. Curtis countered by arguing that Doubleday's refusal to accept the completed manuscript was a breach and that it had not acted in good faith because it had not provided him with sufficient editorial counsel.

The court found for Doubleday and Curtis had to return the $50,000. The court said: "[W]e hold that a publisher may, in its discretion, terminate a standard publishing contract, provided that the termination is made in good faith, and that the failure of an author to submit a satisfactory manuscript was not caused by the publisher's bad faith."[95]

The key to this decision is that a publisher must reject a manuscript in good faith and must not lead the author on by acting as if the submissions are satisfactory when, in fact, the publisher has decided to drop the project. In the publishing industry, bad faith can be inferred from evidence showing that a publisher refused or failed to give editorial assistance to an author.[96] But good faith does not mean that the publisher must be skillful. There is no obligation to operate at high quality; there is only an obligation to make an honest appraisal of a manuscript and an honest attempt at editorial guidance.[97] Courts use a similar approach when considering whether a publisher has promoted a book satisfactorily. The publisher must make an initial good-faith effort, but there is no need to throw good money after bad or to spend large sums promoting a book that is not likely to have large sales.[98]

Although the publishing industry has its own trade practices, courts treat contracts from other professions in much the same

---

[94] Doubleday had a lucrative "can't lose" paperback contract with New American Library and thus a strong incentive to go ahead with the project.

[95] Doubleday & Co. v. Curtis, 763 F2d 495 (2d Cir. 1985).

[96] Dell Publishing Co. v. Whedon, 577 F. Supp. 1454 (SDNY 1984); Harcourt Brace Jovanovich v. Goldwater, 532 F. Supp. 619 (SDNY 1982).

[97] Doubleday & Co. v. Curtis, 763 F2d 495 (2d Cir. 1985).

[98] See, e.g., Zilg v. Prentice Hall, Inc., 717 F2d 671 (2d Cir. 1983).

way. The case of *Baker v. Chock Full O' Nuts Corp.*[99] involved a contract to develop and mount an advertising campaign. The client had to pay only upon completion of the promotion to its "satisfaction." The court implied a requirement that the client could refuse to pay only upon "honest dissatisfaction." It is not clear from the opinion exactly how one is to decide what is honest dissatisfaction, but apparently a court can review the decision of the terminating party to determine whether it meets some objective standard of fairness.

Publishing contract cases provide good examples of the problem of second-guessing what is essentially a subjective decision by one of the parties about the quality of the performance. The problem, at heart, is one of deciding who has acted in good faith and who has not. At least since the early part of this century when Judge Cardozo, in the famous case of *Wood v. Lucy, Lady Duff-Gordon,*[100] said that a contract may be "instinct with an obligation, imperfectly expressed," courts have sought to hold contracting partners to a duty of good faith one to the other.[101] The UCC explicitly imposes the duty of good faith on all parties to contracts that it governs.[102] Thus, even an agreement that by its terms leaves the question of satisfaction or acceptability entirely to the discre-

---

[99] Baker v. Chock Full O' Nuts Corp., 30 AD2d 329, 292 NYS2d 58 (1968).

[100] Wood v. Lucy, Lady Duff-Gordon, 222 NY 88, 118 NE 214 (1917). Lucy, Lady Duff-Gordon was a predecessor to modern designers whose names appear on a wide range of personal apparel and other objects. She agreed to give Wood the "exclusive" right to place her indorsement on the designs of others (e.g., for clothes, fabrics, parasols) for a period of one year and from year to year thereafter until terminated. They were to share the profits from the sale of these "designer" items. To Wood's chagrin, he found that Lady Duff-Gordon was allowing her name to be used on other products without his knowledge and without sharing the profits with him. She defended against his claim of breach by arguing that there was no consideration flowing from him; the contract did not require him to do anything. In support of Wood's position, Judge Cardozo found that there was an implied duty in the agreement for Wood to use reasonable efforts to promote the goods with Lucy's name attached and that this implied obligation was sufficient consideration to make the contract enforceable.

[101] See, e.g., Parev Prods. Co. v. I. Rokeach & Sons, Inc., 124 F2d 147 (2d Cir. 1941); Kirke La Shelle Co. v. Paul Armstrong Co., 262 NY 79, 188 NE 163 (1933).

[102] Section 1-203 states that "every contract or duty within this Act imposes an obligation of good faith in its performance or enforcement."

tion of one party can be interpreted to include an element of good faith as a limit on the exercise of unfettered discretion.[103]

¶ 2.04 SHIFTING THE RISK OF NONPERFORMANCE: THE QUESTION OF TITLE

A party to a contract should always ask who has the risk of loss at a given time in the transaction. This can be important in deciding what action (if any) to take in response to a breach by the other party. If the subject matter of the agreement is property rather than services, the nonbreaching party does not want to run the risk of jeopardizing the property if he bears the risk of loss, regardless of his rights against the breaching party. After all, the property has some value, and it is in the interest of both parties to preserve that value. It may have more substance than a claim against the breaching party that may not be reduced to judgment for one, two, or more years, by which time there may not be any assets to satisfy the judgment. Determination of title and risk of loss is also important in deciding insurance coverage. An insured party must have an "insurable interest" in the property that is the subject of an insurance policy, and, in general, this means that the insured party must have some risk of loss in the property.

Although risk of loss usually follows title, it may precede actual legal transfer of title, especially when formal transfer of title lags behind the exchange of consideration and physical possession. This is certainly the approach of most courts in cases involving sales of cars, trucks, and similar chattels for which there is a state title law. Actual title and the risk of loss transfer from seller to buyer when the parties sign the sales agreement, the buyer executes a promissory note and chattel mortgage (or delivers full payment), and the seller hands over the keys. It might be several weeks before a certificate of title is issued by the state, but that

---

[103] This is wholly aside from the separate issue of whether the agreement, or its interpretation by one of the parties, is unconscionable. See discussion at ¶ 12.06.

does not govern.[104] A similar rule applies for auctions. Title and risk of loss pass when the gavel comes down, subject only to any conditions stated in advance.[105]

In cases governed by the UCC, the determination of title and risk of loss follows the guidelines of Section 2-509. In the absence of a contrary agreement, the manner and place of delivery govern. If the contract requires the seller to deliver at a certain location, risk passes upon delivery at that location.[106] If the contract does not specify a particular location for delivery, title usually passes upon delivery by the seller to the carrier.[107] If a case does not fall within either of these general alternatives, the rule is that the risk of loss passes to the buyer upon receipt when the seller is a merchant and upon tender of delivery when the seller is not a merchant.[108] The old common-law rule was that tender occurred when

---

[104] Motors Ins. Corp. v. Safecon Ins. Co., 412 SW2d 584 (Ky. Ct. App. 1967); Galemore v. Midwest Nat'l Fire & Casualty Ins. Co., 443 SW2d 194 (Mo. Ct. App. 1969); Safeco Ins. Co. v. Lapp, 695 P2d 1310 (Mont. 1985); Dairylea Coop., Inc. v. Rossal, 64 NY2d 1, 473 NE2d 251, 483 NYS2d 101, 39 UCC Rep. 1666 (1984); Nationwide Mut. Ins. Co. v. Hayes, 276 NC 620, 174 SE2d 511 (1970). Contra Firemen's Fund Ins. Cos. v. Blais, 14 Mass. App. Ct. 254, 438 NE2d 360, cert. denied, 440 NE2d 1177 (1982).

[105] Taylor & Martin, Inc. v. Hiland Dairy, Inc., 676 SW2d 859 (Mo. Ct. App. 1984). This may vary with the facts. In an odd case involving the auction sale of a house that was to be moved from the property to another location, the seller retained an insurable interest and risk of loss in the house when he remained in possession and residence subsequent to the auction while waiting for the buyer to make his arrangements. St. Paul Fire and Marine Ins. Co. v. Toman, 351 NW2d 146 (SD 1984). The court said that the contract was subject to the UCC because the house was to be moved from its location. It was not sold as an improvement to the real estate but as a separate chattel.

[106] See, e.g., In re Coast Trading Co., 744 F2d 686 (9th Cir. 1984); Warrior Tombigee Transp. Co. v. 5,775,674 Net Tons of Coal, 570 F. Supp. 1405 (SD Ala. 1983); Murray v. Conrad, 346 NW2d 814 (Iowa 1984).

[107] UCC § 2-509(1)(a).

[108] UCC § 2-509(3). Official Comment 3 states:

> "The underlying theory of this rule is that a merchant who is to make physical delivery at his own place continues meanwhile to control the goods and can be expected to insure his interest in them. The buyer, on the other hand, has no control of the goods and it is extremely unlikely that he will carry insurance on goods not yet in his possession."

For a general discussion of Section 2-509, see Silver v. Wycombe, Meyer & Co., 124 Misc. 2d 717, 477 NYS2d 288 (Civ. Ct. 1984).

the seller actually held out what was to be delivered. The modern approach is that tender is made when there is an "offer of performance . . . accompanied with a manifested present ability to make it good."[109]

One of the more interesting and audacious arguments on passage of title occurred in a New York shoplifting case. The defendant entered a delicatessen where the cashier noticed that she placed a 40-cent package of gum in her purse. She then selected a 25-cent package of chips and tendered a dollar to the cashier, who returned 35 cents in change after adding in the price of the gum. The defendant protested that she had been shortchanged. Her protest escalated into an argument with the owner's son. She attacked him with a knife before she could be subdued and the police arrived. She was charged with first-degree robbery for taking the gum and using a dangerous weapon in the process. Her lawyer tried to have the robbery charge dropped on the grounds that title to the gum passed when the cashier returned only 35 cents in change. The court rejected the argument, because there was no agreement. According to the court, the UCC requires some meeting of minds, and the defendant, by protesting the shortchange and fighting about it, clearly did not intend to enter a contract for the purchase of the chewing gum.[110]

A lawsuit involving a shipload of rotten tomatoes presented questions about the risk of loss in a context that was more usual. The contract was CIF (cost, insurance, and freight) Bridgetown, Barbados, but the buyer would not accept the tomatoes when they arrived because they were spoiled. He shipped them back to the seller without paying, and the seller then sued the carrier for the price. The carrier tried to dismiss the suit because a contract CIF normally means that the buyer is to pay on the delivery of documents, not on the delivery of goods. The documents, which were in order, were presented to the buyer, but the buyer failed to pay and then rejected the goods upon their arrival. The carrier argued that the buyer's obligation for the price ripened when the documents were presented, and, therefore, the buyer was in default. (Of

---

[109] Restatement (Second) of Contracts § 263 comment b (1981); Farnsworth § 8.10, at 583.

[110] People v. Walden, 124 Misc. 2d 615, 478 NYS2d 501 (1984).

course, if the buyer were liable for the price, he also had an action for damages for the spoiled tomatoes and, having paid in advance, possibly could have revoked under Section 2-608.) However, the evidence showed that the buyer and seller had an understanding extrinsic to the written agreement that the buyer could inspect before paying. Thus, the trade practices of the parties governed, despite the explicit language of the contract. Neither title nor risk of loss ever passed to the buyer, and the seller could seek recompense for the loss of value of the contract, assuming, of course, that the carrier breached the contract of carriage so as to cause the tomatoes to spoil.[111]

---

[111] William D. Branson, Ltd. v. Tropical Shipping & Constr. Co., 598 F. Supp. 680 (SD Fla. 1984). The court dismissed the action because the seller had received compensation from his insurance carrier. The court reasoned that the claimant, if any, was the seller's insurer by way of subrogation. This decision was contrary to the collateral source rule by which courts do not take into account whether the plaintiff has insurance or not. That is a matter of a business decision made by the insured party wholly separate from the transaction giving rise to the claim against the defendant. See Dobbs, *Remedies* § 8.10 (1973).

CHAPTER **3**

Anticipatory Breaches

¶ 3.01 ORIGINS OF THE DOCTRINE OF ANTICIPATORY BREACH

[1] Nature of Anticipatory Breach and Effect on Nonrepudiating Party

Contract law, in general, deals with the future. The parties to an agreement make mutual promises about future actions or payments and, based on their expectations of performance, are able to make subsequent plans for their business or personal lives. This chapter considers the problems that arise upon repudiation, when one party to the contract informs the other party that he does not intend to perform his contractual obligations. Although he is not technically in breach (because it is not yet time for him to do anything and he could always change his mind and perform satisfactorily when the time comes), the party who announces that he does not plan to perform defeats the purposes of assuring predictability and encouraging stability in business relationships.

The basic problems involve the nonrepudiating party. When informed of the other party's potential nonperformance, is he free from his own contractual obligations? Can he seek another partner? Must he seek another agreement in order to minimize the possible consequences if the repudiating party indeed carries out his announced plans? May he bring suit against the repudiating party for breach even though the time for performance has not yet arrived? How does he calculate damages?

This chapter provides some answers to these questions. The general rule is that an unequivocal repudiation in advance of the time for performance is equivalent to a complete present breach. The nonrepudiating party is freed from his responsibility to perform and may sue immediately for breach of contract. There are, however, some variations on this general rule. One difficulty that arises in many instances is determining whether there has in fact been a repudiation. A party to a contract may say or do any number of things that make the other party uneasy but that do not amount to a repudiation. The uneasy party who decides that there has been a repudiation may do so at his own risk and may himself be in danger of breaching the agreement. The UCC provides an approach to this problem that has been used with a good deal of success and that is also useful by way of analogy to other contracts not subject to the UCC. This approach allows the concerned party to demand assurances of performance. If the assurances are not forthcoming or are inadequate, he may then assume that there has been a breach and proceed accordingly.

[2] A Landmark Decision: *Hochster v. De La Tour*

Until the middle of the nineteenth century, common-law courts would not allow an action for breach of contract until the time for performance had arrived and the performing party had failed to perform. Even if the obligor had announced an unequivocal repudiation and performance had become impossible, the reasoning was that there could be no damage to the promisee until the time for performance was due.[1] This approach changed with the decision in the famous case of *Hochster v. De La Tour,*[2] which was decided in 1853. The plaintiff in that case had agreed to be a traveling companion for the defendant on a tour of Europe from June 1 to September 1 for a fixed fee. On May 11 the defendant repudiated the agreement, and the plaintiff then brought suit for breach of contract on May 22. The main point of contention was whether the plaintiff's suit was premature. The defendant was under no obligation of performance until June 1, and he still had more than a week in which he could have changed his mind and have reinstated the original agreement. In fact, the case was not heard until early July, by which time the plaintiff had managed to secure alternative employment. The defendant's counsel argued that his client's repudiation on May 11 was not a breach but an offer to rescind, which could be accepted or rejected. If the plaintiff had wanted to preserve his rights under the contract and reject the offer to rescind, the defendant argued, he should have remained willing and able to perform his obligations throughout the term of the contract; that is, until September 1. By accepting other employment, the plaintiff had accepted the offer of rescission and could not complain about a breach of contract.

The court rejected this line of argument and held for the plaintiff while making two important points. First, the defendant's unequivocal repudiation of May 11 relieved the plaintiff from his obligations of performance and freed him to seek other employment, which also made sense because it minimized the damages that might otherwise accrue. Second, the plaintiff could file suit prior to the time for performance because there had been a repudiation and he could seek damages as upon a breach of the entire

[1] See, e.g., Phillpotts v. Evans, 151 Eng. Rep. 200 (Ex. 1839).

[2] Hochster v. De La Tour, 118 Eng. Rep. 922 (QB 1853).

contract.[3] In other words, an unequivocal repudiation in advance of the time for performance was the same as a present breach of the entire contract.[4]

[3] Further Amplifications of the *Hochster* Rule

The holding in *Hochster* has become the generally accepted rule in both England and the United States. The Supreme Judicial Court of Massachusetts expressly rejected the *Hochster* rule in *Daniels v. Newton,*[5] decided in 1874, but twenty-six years later the United States Supreme Court followed *Hochster* in *Roehm v. Horst,*[6] and every other American jurisdiction that has considered the issue has followed the lead of the Supreme Court. Even though Massachusetts has not overruled the *Daniels* decision,[7] its legislature has adopted the UCC, which includes a section on anticipatory breach that codifies the principles of the *Hochster* decision.[8]

---

[3] In truth, *Hochster* may not have been the first case to decide that an anticipatory repudiation would support a present action for breach. One commentator has suggested that the honor should go to an earlier case from New York, Masterton v. Mayor of Brooklyn, 7 Hill 61 (NY 1845). Jackson, " 'Anticipatory Repudiation' and the Temporal Element of Contract Law: An Economic Inquiry Into Contract Damages in Cases of Prospective Nonperformance," 31 Stan. L. Rev. 69, 74 n.17 (1978) (hereinafter cited as Jackson). There is no doubt, however, that *Hochster* is the more famous decision.

[4] Current law is little changed. See Restatement (Second) of Contracts §§ 253, 255 (1981).

[5] Daniels v. Newton, 114 Mass. 530 (1874). In that decision the court stated the classic objections to allowing a suit to proceed before the time that performance was due:

> "Until the plaintiff has either suffered loss or wrong in respect of that which has already vested in him in right, or has been deprived of or prevented from acquiring that which he is entitled to have or demand, he has no ground on which to seek a remedy by way of reparation. The conduct of the defendant is no wrong to the plaintiff until it actually invades some right of his. Actual injury and not anticipated injury is the ground of legal recovery. The plaintiff's rights are invaded by repudiation of the contract only when it produces the effect of nonperformance, or prevents him from entering upon or completing performance on his part, at a time when and in the manner in which he is entitled to perform it or have it performed."

Id. at 539.

[6] Roehm v. Horst, 178 US 1 (1900).

[7] See, e.g., Johnson v. Starr, 321 Mass. 566, 74 NE2d 137 (1947).

[8] UCC § 2-610; see also UCC § 2-609; infra ¶ 3.02[9].

The drafters of both the first and second Restatements of Contracts recognized the principles of *Hochster* as the prevailing rules to govern anticipatory repudiations in American common-law cases.[9]

Despite its approval in the law courts, the *Hochster* decision has not met with unanimous approval among the commentators.[10] The most severe critic was Professor Williston. In his view, a court that entertained an action for breach before the contracted time for performance imposed an obligation on the promisor that the promisor had not been willing to assume — an obligation not to state any negative intentions before the time for performance. Williston said that a promisor could agree not to repudiate, but that there was no good reason for a court to impose such a promise on him. Furthermore, he could not see that the promisee suffered any injury until the date when performance was due and not forthcoming. The promisee had no right to anything before then.[11] The courts did not pay much attention to Williston's criticisms, however, and other commentators tended to support the development of the *Hochster* rule.[12] One of the most influential statements was made by Judge Learned Hand:

> A promise to perform in the future by implication includes an engagement not deliberately to compromise the probability of

---

[9] Restatement (First) of Contracts § 318 (1932); Restatement (Second) of Contracts § 253 (1981).

[10] Most critics are quick to point out that the *Hochster* case could have been decided more simply. It would have been consistent with the law prevailing then for Hochster to have been excused from further performance and allowed to seek other employment, and it would not have worked much of a hardship if he had waited until June 1 to commence his lawsuit. The change came in allowing him to sue on a complete breach immediately.

[11] See generally Williston, "Repudiation of Contracts (Pts. 1 and 2)," 14 Harv. L. Rev. 317, 421 (1901); Williston, *A Treatise on the Law of Contracts* §§ 1300, 1302, 1319, 1320, 1326, 1330 (W. Jaeger 3d ed. 1968) (hereinafter cited as Williston).

[12] This was certainly true of the other great treatise writer, Professor Corbin. See 4 Corbin, *Contracts* § 959 (1963). Other important early writings on the doctrine of anticipatory repudiation include: Ballantine, "Anticipatory Breach and the Enforcement of Contractual Duties," 22 Mich. L. Rev. 329 (1924); Beale, "Damages Upon Repudiation of a Contract," 17 Yale LJ 443 (1908); Limburg, "Anticipatory Repudiation of Contracts," 10 Cornell LQ 135 (1925); Vold, "The Tort Aspect of Anticipatory Repudiation of Contracts," 41 Harv. L. Rev. 340 (1928).

> performance. . . . Such intermediate uncertainties as arise from the vicissitudes of the promisor's affairs are, of course, a part of the risk, but it is hard to see how, except by mere verbalism, it can be supposed that the promisor may within the terms of his undertaking gratuitously add to those uncertainties by announcing his purpose to default.[13]

Today there is little question that the weight of the cases and of the critical commentary is in favor of the general principles enunciated in *Hochster*.[14]

Supporting the general rules of *Hochster* as a matter of principle is one thing, but applying the rules to a variety of situations involves a number of problems. Straightforward, unequivocal repudiation is less the norm than it is the exception. Often the first difficulty is to determine whether there has even been a repudiation. If a repudiation can be determined, the promisee then has to decide his best course of action. Sometimes the repudiating party changes his mind; then the question becomes what power, if any, he has to restore the contract. Finally, there is almost always a problem in calculating damages. Although damage issues are discussed in later chapters,[15] it is important to be aware of some of the questions raised by a premature breach in calculating the injury suffered by the promisee.

¶ 3.02 THE PROMISEE'S REACTIONS TO ANTICIPATORY BREACH

[1] Acts or Statements That Constitute Anticipatory Breach

The performing party is always free to breach the agreement by failing to perform if he is willing to bear the costs of a breach.

---

[13] Equitable Trust Co. v. Western Pac. Ry., 244 F 485, 502 (SDNY 1917), aff'd, 250 F 327 (2d Cir.), cert. denied, 246 US 672 (1918), cited with approval in Farnsworth, *Contracts* § 8.20, at 628, 629 (1982) (hereinafter cited as Farnsworth).

[14] See, e.g., Farnsworth 628, 629; Jackson 74 n.17; Rosett, "Partial, Qualified, and Equivocal Repudiation of Contract," 81 Colum. L. Rev. 93 (1981) (hereinafter cited as Rosett, "Repudiation of Contract"); Rosett, "Eight Cases and Section 251," 67 Cornell L. Rev. 841 (1982) (hereinafter cited as Rosett, "Eight Cases").

[15] See generally Chapters 7 and 8.

Unless the contract is subject to specific enforcement,[16] the performing party usually can estimate the cost of breaching and compare that with the cost of performing. Sometimes it may be wiser to cut losses on what has turned out to be a bad bargain and to break a promise than to adhere doggedly to the contract at a mounting risk of loss.[17] If the performing party thinks that it may be preferable to fail to perform than to go ahead with the deal, an early announcement of the intention not to perform is wise. This gives the other party a chance to make alternative arrangements and improves the chances for a reasonable cover contract that minimizes the exposure of the breaching party to a claim for damages.

In the simplest case, therefore, the performing party clearly announces an intention not to perform.[18] Such an unequivocal statement is as much a breach as a failure to perform.[19] Examples include the death of the performing party,[20] a farmer's statement before planting time that he would not plant a corn crop because the season had been too wet,[21] the termination of timber cutting and the filing of a petition for reorganization under the bankruptcy laws by a logging company,[22] the return of a purchase order by a buyer stamped "cancel" together with a statement that the buyer would refuse any deliveries,[23] and a buyer's stop-payment order on his check.[24]

In the majority of cases, however, the promisor is less certain about his repudiation. Perhaps from a fear of being branded as one who does not keep his word, a party who questions the wisdom of

---

[16] See generally Chapter 6.

[17] See ¶¶ 7.02, 7.03 for discussions of the concept of efficient breach.

[18] See, e.g., Government of Republic of China v. Compass Communications Corp., 473 F. Supp. 1306 (DDC 1979).

[19] Wolgin v. Atlas United Fin. Corp., 397 F. Supp. 1003 (ED Pa. 1975); Abrams v. Brent, 362 SW2d 155 (Tex. Civ. App. 1962).

[20] Bonebrake v. Cox, 499 F2d 951 (8th Cir. 1974). Death might be an excuse for a breach. See ¶ 12.03[3][a].

[21] Oloffson v. Coomer, 11 Ill. App. 3d 918, 296 NE2d 871 (1973). Whether the breach would be excused because of poor weather is another question that would arise in connection with the assertion of an impossibility defense.

[22] In re Humboldt Fir, Inc., 426 F. Supp. 292 (ND Cal. 1977).

[23] Whewell v. Dobson, 227 NW2d 115 (Iowa 1976).

[24] Goldstein v. Stainless Processing Co., 465 F2d 392 (7th Cir. 1972).

performing may couch his repudiation in terms that are not meant to look like a repudiation. He may state that for one reason or another the contract is no longer binding. If the other party has a good reason to doubt the argument that the contract has lost its binding effect, such a statement may be interpreted as a repudiation.[25] What is reasonable to construe as a repudiation depends on the history of the relationship between the parties as much as anything else.[26]

Often, a party states that he will continue to perform only if the other party agrees to certain additional conditions (although he may argue that these conditions are not really additional but within the spirit of the agreement).[27] In one case, a lessor of 144 television sets asked the lessee to execute UCC-1 financing statements on the sets. The lessee refused to take delivery and to sign the forms because this additional condition was not a requirement of the original lease agreement.[28] In another case — a classic "add-on" — a seller refused to deliver a yacht unless the buyer paid an additional $550 for a rescue boat, even though the rescue boat was included within the terms of the original agreement.[29] Whether a demand is for an additional performance or a condition that goes beyond the contract is often a fact issue for a jury.[30]

---

[25] See, e.g., Rapid Transit Lines, Inc. v. Transit Ads, Inc., 401 SW2d 276 (Tex. Civ. App. 1966).

[26] See, e.g., American Bronze Corp. v. Streamway Prod., 8 Ohio App. 3d 223, 456 NE2d 1295 (1982).

[27] See, e.g., Kromer v. Photo-Scan Corp., 305 F. Supp. 461 (ND Tex. 1969); Humphrey v. Placid Oil Co., 142 F. Supp. 246 (ED Tex. 1956), aff'd, 244 F2d 184 (5th Cir. 1957); Jon-To Farms, Inc. v. Goodpasture, Inc., 554 SW2d 743 (Tex. Civ. App. 1977); Laredo Hides Co. v. H&H Meat Prods. Co., 513 SW2d 210 (Tex. Civ. App. 1974).

[28] Tenavision, Inc. v. Neuman, 45 NY2d 145, 379 NE2d 1166, 408 NYS2d 36 (1978). The lessee may have been correct in principle, but it turned out that this was not an anticipatory breach because the lessor was willing to deliver the sets anyway and not to require execution. By refusing delivery even after the lessor communicated a willingness to deliver and to forgo the UCC-1 statements, the lessee wound up in breach.

[29] Puget Sound Marina, Inc. v. Jorgensen, 3 Wash. App. 476, 475 P2d 919 (1970).

[30] See, e.g., Created Gemstones, Inc. v. Union Carbide Corp., 47 NY2d 250, 391 NE2d 987, 417 NYS2d 905 (1979); Comment, "Anticipatory Repudiation Under the Uniform Commercial Code: Interpretation, Analysis and Problems," 30 Sw. LJ 601 (1976).

[2] Four Variables That Determine Repudiation

One commentator has suggested that there are four important variables to keep in mind in trying to decide whether there has been a repudiation. These are: (1) the type of contract involved, (2) the character of the communication from the party suspected of repudiation, (3) the reasons for insecurity and the possible contract failure, and (4) the actual ability of the parties to perform.[31]

The type of contract obviously affects issues of repudiation. In a volatile commodities market, even the hint of a party's intention not to perform may suffice as a repudiation that justifies the other party in seeking a cover contract. If the nonrepudiating party waits too long, the market may rise or fall dramatically, and delay will work against the principle of mitigation.[32] More patience may be in order if the contract is for a custom service.

The character of the communication also must be examined. A communication directly from the performing party should receive more weight than information from a third party. In context, however, even a bit of gossip may justify the nonrepudiating party in taking some self-help measures, such as temporarily suspending payments.[33]

What are the reasons for failure to perform? If one party learns that deliveries will be delayed because the other has mechanical troubles with its delivery vehicles, the news may be cause for concern but not necessarily a justification for treating the expected delays as a form of repudiation. Trucks and other vehicles can be repaired and deliveries can be rescheduled. Learning that the performing party has filed for bankruptcy, however, is another matter.

---

[31] Rosett, "Repudiation of Contract" 104.

[32] The case of Pillsbury Co. v. Ward, 250 NW2d 35 (Iowa 1977), is a good example. A buyer of soybeans requested that the seller delay delivery of an order. The seller was faced with the problem of a rapidly rising market. Because the seller's crop was only 2,000 bushels and the contract called for 3,000, the seller would have to purchase 1,000 bushels on the market to satisfy the contract. This arrangement was satisfactory to the seller as long as delivery was timely, but delays in delivery meant that he would have to buy in a rising market and would probably lose money. He did not have the storage facilities or capital necessary to buy 1,000 bushels and hold them for the buyer's convenience.

[33] See, e.g., Clem Perrin Marine Towing, Inc. v. Panama Canal Co., 730 F2d 186, 38 UCC Rep. 490 (5th Cir. 1984).

Finally, what can realistically be expected of the repudiating party? For example, if one party learns that a contracting partner has died or is otherwise incapacitated from performance, that may be a legitimate basis for acting as if there has been a repudiation, unless the contract can be performed equally well by someone else closely associated with the incapacitated party. For instance, if a client has an agreement with a partner in a law firm for representation in a lawsuit, the death of that partner may not incapacitate the firm. Unless it is a small firm and each lawyer has a specialized practice, other lawyers may be able to carry on the representation.

[3] Reaction of the Nonrepudiating Party

If one party repudiates the contract, what should the other party do? Traditionally, the nonrepudiating party has had three options. First, he can treat the repudiation as an offer to rescind, accept it as such, and then act as if the contract were extinguished. Second, he can treat the repudiation as a breach, suspend performance, and bring suit upon it promptly. Third, he can do nothing and await the time for performance, allowing the repudiating party the opportunity to retract and to reinstate the contract.[34]

These three options only tell part of the story. If there has indeed been a repudiation, the nonrepudiating party may run afoul of the good-faith duty to minimize damages if he does nothing.[35] That is, he may find it difficult to collect the full measure of damages if he waits an unreasonably long time after a clear repudiation before he does anything to protect his own interests. On the other hand, there is no good reason to hold that the nonrepudiating party waives a right to claim damages because he elects to treat the repudiation as a form of rescission. Of course, he is free to do so, and the requirements of good business relations may dictate that he simply accept the termination of the agreement and not make any additional claims on the other party. If the repudiation is complete, however, the nonrepudiating party is free from his contractual obligations, free to enter another agreement, and has the right to claim

---

[34] See, e.g., Simpson v. Scott, 189 Va. 392, 53 SE2d 21 (1949).

[35] See ¶ 7.07.

damages for the breach, limited by his own efforts to minimize damages.

[4] Rescission and Repudiation

A party who repudiates a contract refuses to perform the contractual duty or obligation he owes to the other party to the contract. Rescission necessarily involves a repudiation of the contract, but goes a step further in undoing the contract entirely, restoring both parties to the positions they would have had if no contract ever was made. A recent case involving a dispute over a custom-built truck illustrates the interplay between rescission and repudiation. In *Palmer v. Idaho Peterbilt, Inc.*,[36] the buyer and seller were somewhat unhappy with each other. The buyer was concerned about delays in getting the truck, and the seller was worried about the buyer's ability to pay for the truck. After some discussions, the seller returned the buyer's $500 deposit and cancelled the deal. The buyer deposited the check, but instead of accepting the seller's offer of a rescission, treated the seller's actions as a repudiation and sued for breach of contract based on the seller's anticipatory repudiation. The court held for the buyer.[37]

The aggrieved party runs into the most problems when he acts as if there has been a repudiation but the facts do not support him. That happened in *Tenavision, Inc. v. Neuman*,[38] where the lessee of television sets balked at executing UCC-1 financing statements as requested by the lessor because nothing in the lease agreement required him to do so. Although the lessor backed off on the demand for the financing statements and tendered the sets, the lessee refused delivery. The court found the lessee to be in breach, even though he may have been right in the first instance in refusing to sign the UCC-1 forms.[39]

---

[36] Palmer v. Idaho Peterbilt, Inc., 102 Idaho App. 800, 641 P2d 346 (1982).

[37] If the seller had reason to believe he would not be paid, he should have demanded assurances under Section 2-609 before returning the check to the buyer and terminating the agreement. See infra ¶ 3.02[9].

[38] Tenavision, Inc. v. Neuman, 45 NY2d 145, 379 NE2d 1166, 408 NYS2d 36 (1978). See supra ¶ 3.02[1].

[39] Id.

In another case, a seller apparently was concerned about the buyer's payments and suspended deliveries on ten separate installment contracts until the buyer had made more substantial payments on four earlier contracts under which there had been partial deliveries. The buyer's payments on the first partial deliveries were not made in accordance with the contract, but the deviations were insufficient to justify the seller's suspension of performance. The seller claimed that the buyer was in breach by reason of an anticipatory repudiation, but the court disagreed and found the opposite to be true: The seller was the breaching party for suspending performance on the ten upcoming contracts.[40] As this case demonstrates, the party claiming breach may find himself to be in breach and liable for damages. This can be somewhat tricky because the failure to note an apparent repudiation or breach may result in a waiver or a de facto modification of the contract.[41]

[5] Partial Repudiation

It is not uncommon for a party to perform a portion of the contractual agreement, but to repudiate or fail to perform some other portion. The obligee may have some freedom of action if there is a partial repudiation, but not as much as if the repudiation was total. In general, the obligee must pay for the value of the completed performance. A partial repudiation, therefore, rarely justifies a complete suspension of the obligee's performance. The first Restatement distinguished repudiations that amounted to total breaches and supported an immediate claim for damages from those that discharged the obligee's future obligations and justified suspension of performance (some repudiations do both).[42] This approach meant that the obligee often proceeded at risk if there was some question about whether the repudiation was truly

[40] National Farmers Org. v. Bartlett & Co., 560 F2d 1350 (8th Cir. 1977); see also Neal-Cooper Grain Co. v. Texas Gulf Sulphur Co., 508 F2d 283 (7th Cir. 1974); Pittsburgh-Des Moines Steel Co. v. Brookhaven Manor Water Co., 532 F2d 572 (7th Cir. 1976).

[41] See ¶ 12.05. An occasional acceptance of late performance or partially nonconforming performance, without additional circumstances, does not constitute a waiver. Commercial Credit Corp. v. Taylor, 448 SW2d 190 (Tex. Civ. App. 1969).

[42] Restatement (First) of Contracts § 318 comments d, g, h, i (1932).

unequivocal. The UCC and more recent cases[43] give the obligee more flexibility. If the obligee is concerned about the actions or statements of the obligor, he can request assurances of performance.[44] This removes some of the risk, although there is always the danger that even a partial suspension of performance will be treated as a breach rather than as a justified response to a repudiation.

Distinguishing a total repudiation from a partial one is essentially a matter of common sense. A debtor who is a few days late on an installment payment may be in breach, but perhaps the breach is not a reason to accelerate the entire debt, especially in a typical consumer credit context. In a commercial context, late payment of a major debt obligation, where both parties clearly understand that time is of the essence, is a different matter.[45] The importance of context cannot be overstated. As one commentator has said, "Sellers in rapidly rising markets who carp about small matters deserve . . . skepticism." [46] Of course, the obligee can always retain a right to seek damages for breach, in whole or in part, as long as there is no waiver. The obligee does not need to suspend performance or to bring suit in order to prevent a waiver. In general, it is sufficient to note that the other party has failed to perform in accordance with the agreement and that the obligee does not intend to waive his right to seek an appropriate remedy for that failure.

---

[43] Restatement (Second) of Contracts § 256 (1981).

[44] See infra ¶ 3.02[6] for a discussion of demand for assurance.

[45] See, e.g., Gateway Aviation, Inc. v. Cessna Aircraft Co., 577 SW2d 860 (Mo. Ct. App. 1978) (installment payment contract for purchase of aircraft with chattel mortgage; buyer was late in making payments, failed to maintain, license, or insure aircraft, and moved aircraft from location specified in contract).

[46] Rosett, "Eight Cases" 852, citing and discussing Teeman v. Jurek, 312 Minn. 292, 251 NW2d 698 (1977) (seller was trying to get out of grain contracts because of rapidly rising market and tried to make an excuse out of a host of minor discrepancies in weights and grading requirements of the buyer; although seller demanded assurances and received them, he still acted as if there had been a repudiation, but to no avail). But compare Westinghouse Elec. Corp. v. CX Processing Laboratories, Inc., 523 F2d 668 (9th Cir. 1975) (buyer refused to make payment citing a breach by seller; buyer's refusal was an anticipatory repudiation because suspension of performance was not justified by reason of the seller's breach, but the court said that buyer's repudiation was not actionable by reason of the seller's own breach).

[6] Nonrepudiating Party's Demand for Assurances — Interplay of Common Law and the UCC

For self-protection, the nonrepudiating party may request assurances of performance in accordance with the terms of the contractual agreement. This avoids the risk of acting as if there has been a repudiation only to find out that a court later disagrees and holds the nonrepudiating party liable for breach. It also clarifies the situation and stabilizes the relationships of the parties. If a reasonable demand for assurances is made and none is forthcoming, that itself is evidence of a repudiation. The nonrepudiating party is then in a good position to suspend performance and to seek appropriate damages. This is the approach taken both in Section 2-609 [47] of the UCC and Section 251 of the second Restatement.[48]

There are some technical differences between Section 2-609 of the UCC and its counterpart in the second Restatement. First, the UCC requires that the request for assurances be made in writing, although this requirement has been interpreted rather loosely.[49] No such requirement is made in the Restatement. Second, Section 2-609(4) of the UCC defines a "reasonable time" for response to a demand for assurances as thirty days, whereas the second Restate-

---

[47] Section 2-609(1) reads:

"A contract for sale imposes an obligation on each party that the other's expectation of receiving due performance will not be impaired. When reasonable grounds for insecurity arise with respect to the performance of either party the other may in writing demand adequate assurance of due performance and until he receives such assurance may if commercially reasonable suspend any performance for which he has not already received the agreed return."

[48] Section 251 of the second Restatement reads:

"(1) Where reasonable grounds arise to believe that the obligor will commit a breach by nonperformance that would of itself give the obligee a claim for damages for total breach under section 243, the obligee may demand adequate assurance of due performance and may, if reasonable, suspend any performance for which he has not already received the agreed exchange until he receives such assurance.

"(2) The obligee may treat as a repudiation the obligor's failure to provide within a reasonable time such assurance of due performance as is adequate in the circumstances of the particular case."

[49] See, e.g., ARB v. E-Sys., Inc., 663 F2d 189 (DDC 1980) (oral demands coupled with written internal memoranda of the company to whom the demands were addressed satisfied the writing requirement).

ment does not suggest a specific time. Although the Official Commentary to Section 2-609 states that the thirty-day time "is laid down to free the question of reasonable time from uncertainty in later litigation," [50] there is little doubt that courts can be somewhat flexible in their interpretation of the thirty-day limit. The whole thrust of Section 2-609 is toward a standard of commercial reasonableness based on the facts particular to the case. Nonetheless, the thirty-day standard provides a useful guideline that common-law courts use by way of analogy. Finally, Section 2-609 says that "reasonable grounds for insecurity" justify a demand for assurances, but the second Restatement requires an apprehension of a complete breach. This suggests that the common law may require a more substantial or material threat than the UCC as a predicate to the demand for assurances.[51] This is merely speculation; no court has so held. These technical differences are minor, and for the most part Section 2-609 of the UCC and Section 251 of the second Restatement are substantively identical.[52]

Section 2-609 protects both parties to an agreement. It provides the concerned party with an opportunity to determine whether there is any real basis for concern and to protect his own interests without running the risk of breaching the contract himself. On the other hand, it allows the performing party an opportunity opportunity informally to explain his actions or to assure the obligee of his good intentions. Both parties can negotiate amicably and perhaps satisfy each other before there is any intervention by lawyers and judges. If Section 2-609 is to work, however, the obli-

[50] UCC § 2-609, Official Comment 5.

[51] Section 251 of the second Restatement should not be read in a vacuum; it should be considered together with Sections 241 (defining materiality), 243 (providing for an action immediately for a total breach), and 237 (stating that the obligation to perform is conditional on there being no uncured material breaches by the other party).

[52] This is the thesis of Rosett, "Eight Cases." Professor Rosett's view is that Section 2-609 has never developed into a "lawyer's tool." Lawyers do not write "Section 2-609 letters" on behalf of their clients demanding assurances. Instead, the section has been employed by judges as a way to sort out laymen's negotiations during the course of a contract performance. The parties do what seems sensible and in their best interests (e.g., suspending performance, making concerned telephone calls, or stopping payments), and a judge later decides that what they did fell within the scope of Section 2-609. For a collection of a number of leading cases decided under Section 2-609, see id. at 842, 843 n.5.

gee must make use of it. For that reason, some obligees have found themselves in trouble because they did not make use of their rights under the section to demand assurances when they could have done so. Courts have reasoned that the failure to request assurances under Section 2-609 takes away the corresponding right of the obligor to cure or to give assurances.[53] The same reasoning should apply to cases that are not within the coverage of the UCC.

[7] Reasonable Insecurity

Reasonable insecurity is one party's reasonable basis for believing that the other party might fail to uphold his part of the bargain. It may not be good for business for a suspicious party to demand assurances and thereby to insult the other party who has no thought of reneging. At the same time, however, there is a danger in waiting too long. The issue of reasonable insecurity involves the state of mind of the party who is concerned. The question is not whether the obligor actually intends to default, but whether the obligee has a good-faith reason to believe that he might. It is essentially a question of fact.[54] The case of *Clem Perrin Marine Towing, Inc. v. Panama Canal Co.*[55] is a good example. The charterer of a tug had an option to buy the boat. A third party mentioned in a telephone conversation with the charterer that the owner of the tug had failed to make some of the payments on the first mortgage. In addition, the third party continued, the owner had encumbered the tug with a third mortgage, even though two mortgages already were outstanding when the charter/purchase option agreement was made. This was a sufficient basis for the charterer to demand assurances and to suspend his performance until they were forthcoming. It turned out that the owner's financial condition was not nearly as bleak as was feared, but the charterer

---

[53] See, e.g., Continental Grain Co. v. McFarland, 628 F2d 1348 (4th Cir. 1980); National Farmers Org. v. Bartlett & Co., 560 F2d 1350 (8th Cir. 1977); Harlow & Jones, Inc. v. Advance Steel Co., 424 F. Supp. 770 (ED Mich. 1976).

[54] See, e.g., AMF, Inc. v. McDonald's Corp., 536 F2d 1167 (7th Cir. 1976); Cherwell-Ralli, Inc. v. Rytman Grain Co., 180 Conn. 714, 433 A2d 984 (1980); Financial Bldg. Consultants, Inc. v. St. Charles Mfg. Co., 145 Ga. App. 768, 244 SE2d 877 (1978).

[55] Clem Perrin Marine Towing, Inc. v. Panama Canal Co., 730 F2d 186, 38 UCC Rep. 490 (5th Cir. 1984).

was justified in acting as he did because the third party was a reliable source known to both parties who had helped to put the deal together in the first place.

If the party asked to give assurances of due performance does not do so or does so inadequately, his actions may constitute an explicit repudiation.[56] The case of *Creusot-Loire International, Inc. v. Coppus Engineering Corp*.[57] illustrates this point. The suit involved a contract for the sale and installation of burners in an ammonia plant under construction in Yugoslavia. The buyer became concerned because of information that similar burners installed by the seller in a plant in Sri Lanka were inadequate and did not meet specifications. The buyer asked for assurances, and the seller did not respond at all from February until the following September. Then all the seller said was that the burners would work adequately. The court agreed with the buyer that both the timing and the content of the assurances were inadequate and that the buyer was justified in suspending performance.

On the other hand, the party who receives assurances cannot simply dismiss them for personal or idiosyncratic reasons. The standard of acceptability for assurances is objective and based on commercial reasonability. The Official Commentary to Section 2-609 states the following:

> The adequacy of the assurance given is not measured as in the type of "satisfaction" situation affected with intangibles, such as in personal service cases, cases involving a third party's judgment as final, or cases in which the whole contract is dependent on one party's satisfaction, as in a sale on approval. Here, the seller must exercise good faith and observe commercial standards.[58]

Giving assurances is not enough. The party who makes them must also live up to them. Even if the performing party makes a

---

[56] See, e.g., International Therapeutics, Inc. v. McGraw-Edison Co., 721 F2d 488 (5th Cir. 1983) (buyer refused to give assurances); see also AMF, Inc. v. McDonald's Corp., 536 F2d 1167 (7th Cir. 1976).

[57] Creusot-Loire Int'l, Inc. v. Coppus Eng'g Corp., 585 F. Supp. 45 (SDNY 1983).

[58] UCC § 2-609, Official Comment 4, citing James B. Berry's Sons Co. of Ill. v. Monark Gasoline & Oil Co., 32 F2d 74 (8th Cir. 1929).

good-faith effort and runs into technical problems, that does not suffice as an excuse.[59] The concerned party is entitled both to assurances and to performance in accordance with them. Of course, there may be some other excuse for nonperformance, such as impossibility or commercial impracticability, but the question under Section 2-609 is whether or not there is a breach.[60]

[8] Exception to the Doctrine of Anticipatory Breach for Unilateral Agreements

There is one large exception to the doctrine of anticipatory breach: It does not apply in connection with the repudiation of a unilateral agreement or after there has been performance in a typical bilateral agreement. The reasoning behind the exception is simple. In a typical unilateral contract (a promise for an act), there is in theory no contract until there has been performance. The acceptance is in the performance. If the performing party announces that he will not perform, he does not breach the agreement; rather, he rejects the offer, and the contract never comes into existence. Similarly, if the party promising to pay repudiates the promise before the performance of the other party, he has withdrawn the offer rather than breached the contract because the contract has not yet come into being. The argument continues that when there has been full performance under a bilateral agreement, there cannot be an anticipatory repudiation because there is no performance due — there is no failure of performance to anticipate. If there is a breach, it is one in the ordinary course.

This exception to the doctrine of anticipatory breach has been criticized,[61] and exceptions to the exception have weakened its effect. In addition, the "simple" reasoning of the exception overlooks a host of problems. The concept of unilateral contracts is not as straightforward as it was fifty years ago. Greater use of the concepts of reliance and promissory estoppel has resulted in fewer

---

[59] See, e.g., ARB, Inc. v. E-Sys., 663 F2d 189 (DDC 1980); Erwin Weller Co. v. Talon, Inc., 295 NW2d 172 (SD 1980).

[60] An acceptable excuse for the breach that relieves the breaching party of liability raises other issues, which are discussed in Chapter 12.

[61] See, e.g., Farnsworth § 8.20, at 630, 631, noting that Texas has refused to recognize the exception. Pitts v. Wetzel, 498 SW2d 27 (Tex. Civ. App. 1973).

typical unilateral contract situations. The substantial performance rule embedded in Section 45 of the first Restatement further expanded the concept of bilateral agreements. It is not necessary for the performing party to complete performance in order to accept the promisor's offer of payment; it is enough if the performing party makes a substantial effort to do so. That suffices as an acceptance, and the contract is treated as an ordinary bilateral contract. If the performing party stops prior to completion of his contractual obligation, he is in breach. Similarly, if the paying party repudiates while the other party is in the midst of performance, he is in breach.[62] In general, many contracts that are unilateral in their original form become bilateral in operation and, therefore, do not fall within the exception to the anticipatory breach rule.[63]

Contracts to pay money and option contracts are common examples of those that fall within the exception to the anticipatory breach doctrine. The exception states that the payee (1) is not entitled to receive anything until the time for the payment arrives and (2) can suffer no damage until then as long as there is not a normal market for cover. If it ever had any credence, however, this argument has none in the modern financial world. The payee has an expectation of a payment at a date certain in the future. It is an easy matter to calculate the present value of that expectation, which, if dashed, is as much a present injury as the loss of an expectation of some other kind of performance. In addition, al-

---

[62] A typical casebook example involves a landowner who offers a farm worker a set fee for plowing a field. Under strict unilateral contract theory, the worker could collect nothing unless he finished the job, and the owner would be free to repudiate anytime before the plowing is completed. (The worker could also walk off the job with impunity.) But under Section 45 of the first Restatement, the worker would "accept" the offer and both parties would be bound to a bilateral agreement (as if they had exchanged mutual promises about work and payment) when the worker made a substantial effort. What constitutes a substantial effort is a question of fact, but it is no doubt less than plowing two-thirds of the field and no doubt more than just buying fuel for the tractor. Even if there were not substantial progress sufficient to constitute an acceptance prior to the owner's revocation, the owner could still be held for good-faith reliance expenses or the fair market value of work done by the worker on his behalf. See discussion at ¶¶ 7.01, 9.02.

[63] Insurance contracts (especially disability policies) constitute one of the principal categories of contracts still covered by the exception, but to some extent that is because the law of insurance is something of a category unto itself. See generally Farnsworth § 8.20, at 632, 633.

though an old adage of the law posits that it is never impossible to pay money (thus precluding the impossibility defense for an insolvent debtor [64]), any creditor knows that it is quite possible to be unable to collect on a debt and to know that the debt is bad long before it comes due. Many contracts involving a promise to pay money are forms of investments, and there is an active market in which the payee could make an alternative investment of the present value of a debt due in the future that might diminish his damages substantially.

The exception makes the most sense in a typical option agreement for land or some other commodity. The holder of the option pays a consideration for the option, which therefore is an executed agreement. He may or may not exercise the option. If he announces a decision not to exercise the option, he is not in breach. The following scenario may be a problem, however. The option holder indicates that he probably will not exercise the option, which is interpreted by the other party as a clear rejection. After the other party sells the property to a third party, the option holder changes his mind. Despite the possible difficulties, such a situation can be handled by ordinary rules of breach, and the doctrine of anticipatory breach need not apply. A sale of the property subject to option during the option period to a third party is a *present* breach of the option contract.

This exception is a holdover from the earlier criticism of the whole doctrine of anticipatory breach.[65] There is no good reason for the continued existence of the exception other than in those cases in which there really is no need for a doctrine of anticipatory breach because a repudiation can be handled as a form of present breach. It is an anachronism that many courts avoid by construing contracts to be bilateral or by finding that there is still some performance due. Unfortunately, the exception continues in the second Restatement and is set out in rather broad, general terms.[66]

---

[64] See, e.g., Levy Plumbing Co. v. Standard Sanitary Mfg. Co., 68 SW2d 273 (Tex. Civ. App. 1933). Of course, an insolvent debtor may resort to use of the bankruptcy laws.

[65] See, e.g., Williston §§ 1302, 1326–1330.

[66] See Restatement (Second) of Contracts §§ 243, 253 (1981); UCC § 2-611. For a criticism of the retention of the exception, see Rosett, "Repudiation of Contract" 100, 101.

[9] Retraction of the Repudiation

If the repudiating party has a change of heart, he can retract his repudiation and restore the contract as if nothing had happened as long as the other party has not changed his position materially in the meantime.[67] The nonrepudiating party can always accept the offer to reinstate the agreement, but he does not have to do so if he has relied on the repudiation to make a material change in his own position in the interim. If a partial breach accompanies the repudiation, the nonrepudiating party retains a claim for damages for the partial breach even if a retraction reinstates the agreement.[68] What constitutes a "material" change in position on the part of the nonrepudiating party is largely a question of fact. A "cancellation" that amounts to an "acceptance" of the repudiation may be enough.[69] Certainly, entering into a cover contract would be a material change. The retraction must occur prior to the time for performance.[70] There is no set manner for making a retraction, but it must be communicated clearly to the aggrieved party as a retraction.[71]

¶ 3.03 ANTICIPATORY REPUDIATION AND CALCULATION OF DAMAGES

[1] Problems of Calculating Damages in Anticipatory Repudiation Cases

The various remedies available in actions for the breach of contracts and the means for calculating damages are subjects of

[67] Restatement (Second) of Contracts § 256 (1981). After the nonrepudiating party has changed his position, he can ignore the retraction if the change is material. See, e.g., Roehm v. Horst, 178 US 1 (1900); Fowler v. A&A Co., 262 A2d 344 (DC 1970).

[68] In this sense, Section 256 of the second Restatement operates very much the same as Section 2-508 of the UCC. For a discussion of Section 2-508, see ¶ 5.04[9]; see also Restatement (Second) of Contracts § 256 comment a; Rosett, "Repudiation of Contract" 97; White & Summers, *Handbook of the Law Under the Uniform Commercial Code* 319 n.74 (2d ed. 1980).

[69] See, e.g., Sumner v. Fel-Air, Inc., 680 P2d 1109, 1118, 38 UCC Rep. 91, 106 n.26 (Alaska 1984), citing and applying UCC § 2-609.

[70] UCC § 2-611(1).

[71] UCC § 2-611(2); Pittsburgh-Des Moines Steel Co. v. Brookhaven Manor Water Co., 532 F2d 572 (1976).

later chapters in this book.[72] This section highlights some of the problems inherent in the calculation of damages where there has been an anticipatory repudiation because there are a few special difficulties that are not present in ordinary contract cases. Indeed, one of the criticisms of the anticipatory repudiation doctrine has been that it is difficult to calculate damages with any degree of accuracy. Invariably there must be some projection into the future because the breach occurs before the time for performance. This objection is overstated, however. As a practical matter, many cases do not come up for trial until after the time for performance.[73] In this event, there is no need to speculate about the market because direct evidence of the market's own actions is available.[74] Furthermore, many ordinary contract cases require some projections into the future in deciding damages. The valuation of a business or an investment opportunity, the estimation of lost profits, and the calculation of lost wages or other earnings may all require some guesswork based upon the most reasonable projections that can be made. An educated approximation of future losses is certainly not unique to anticipatory breach cases.

The United States Supreme Court stated the standard common-law rule for the measurement of damages in an anticipatory breach case in *Roehm v. Horst*.[75]

> [The] plaintiff is entitled to compensation based, as far as possible, on the ascertainment of what he would have suffered by the continued breach of the other party down to the time of complete performance, less any abatement by reason of circumstances of which he ought reasonably to have availed himself. If a vendor is to manufacture goods, and during the process of manufacture the contract is repudiated, he is not bound to complete the manufacture, but the measure of damage is the

---

[72] See especially Chapters 6, 7, and 8.

[73] That was true even of the famous *Hochster* case.

[74] There may be some cases in which it is necessary to ignore the market. If the breach occurs at t1 and performance at t2 was to have been based upon fair market value at t2, but the trial occurs at t3, the court may have to ignore market changes between t2 and t3.

[75] Roehm v. Horst, 178 US 1 (1900).

> difference between the contract price and the cost of performance.[76]

This approach recognizes that the time for performance is the critical time for the calculation of damages, which is generally consistent with the common-law rules in ordinary cases and with the goal of providing the nonbreaching party with his benefit of the bargain or a close approximation. It also recognizes the duty to mitigate.

The method for determining damages set out in the *Roehm* opinion works reasonably well in cases such as *Hochster* where there is an established contract consideration and time is not of the essence. There was no question about Mr. Hochster's salary for the summer that he was to be a traveling companion. All the court needed to do was take that gross figure and use it as a basis for calculating the actual benefit to Hochster as mitigated by his subsequent alternative employment. In principle, many cases are as simple, and there is certainly no difficulty in calculating present values of future streams of income. The more difficult cases involve rapidly rising or falling markets, in which timing is critical. Are damages to be measured when the repudiation occurs, when the nonrepudiating party "covers," or when the performance is due? The differences can be enormous.[77]

[2] Options for the Aggrieved Party Provided by the UCC

Section 2-610 provides the aggrieved party with options. He may:

> (a) for a commercially reasonable time await performance by the repudiating party; or
>
> (b) resort to any remedy for breach (Section 2-703 or Section 2-711), even though he has notified the repudiating party that he would await the latter's performance and has urged retraction; and
>
> (c) in either case suspend his own performance or proceed in

---

[76] Id. at 20, 21.

[77] To a greater or lesser extent this is a problem in every case that involves a contract-market calculation. See ¶ 7.05.

accordance with the provisions of this Article on the seller's right to identify goods to the contract notwithstanding breach or to salvage unfinished goods (Section 2-704).

Although Section 2-610 provides the aggrieved party with a good deal of flexibility, it does not fix the time for measuring damages. Indeed, it leaves that question as ambiguous as ever, and perhaps even more so. The references in Section 2-610(b) to Sections 2-703 and 2-711 are to the general outlines of the remedies available to sellers and buyers upon a breach. A buyer, for instance, may choose to cover and then seek damages for the contract-cover differential under Section 2-712. The measurement time is then determined by referring to the cover contract. A buyer also may choose to recover the contract-market differential by seeking damages for nondelivery under Section 2-713. In this remedy, the time for measurement is "when the buyer learned of the breach," not the time when performance was due. An aggrieved seller may recover the difference between the contract price and a commercially reasonable resale (the seller's "cover") under Section 2-706 or he may seek the difference between the contract price and the market price "at the time and place for tender" under Section 2-708(1). In some instances, the seller may sue for the price under Section 2-709.

The remedy sections of the UCC thus suggest at least three different times at which damages can be measured: (1) when the buyer learns of a breach by the seller; (2) when either the buyer or the seller covers; or (3) when performance is due. Section 2-610 adds another wrinkle by allowing the aggrieved party to await performance "for a commercially reasonable time" after learning of the repudiation.[78]

[3] Establishing "Commercially Reasonable Time"

In *Cosden Oil & Chemical Co. v. Karl O. Helm Aktiengesellschaft,*[79] the Court of Appeals for the Fifth Circuit recently consid-

---

[78] See, e.g., First Nat'l Bank of Chicago v. Jefferson Mortgage Co., 576 F2d 479 (3d Cir. 1978); Cargill, Inc. v. Stafford, 553 F2d 1222 (10th Cir. 1977).

[79] Cosden Oil & Chem. Co. v. Karl O. Helm Aktiengesellschaft, 736 F2d 1064, 38 UCC Rep. 1645 (5th Cir. 1984).

ered this problem of timing. Helm used large quantities of polystyrene, a petrochemical, in its manufacturing processes. In anticipation of petrochemical shortages that were likely to occur as a result of the Iranian revolution and the general turmoil in the Middle East, Helm decided to purchase a substantial quantity of polystyrene. It entered into two contracts in January 1979 with Cosden, one for 1,250 metric tons of high-impact polystyrene at $0.2825/lb. and another for 250 metric tons of general quality polystyrene at $0.2650/lb. The contracts called for delivery, at Helm's direction, in one or more lots during January and February 1979. In addition, Helm had options on two more purchase orders to be exercised by January 31. Helm exercised both options. Cosden almost immediately ran into problems. There was a harsh winter and barges carrying the raw materials to Cosden's processing plants were stuck in the frozen Illinois and Mississippi Rivers. New equipment in a Cosden plant failed to operate properly, and there were substantial production delays. Meanwhile, the price of polystyrene was rising. Cosden notified Helm that it would be late in filling the first purchase order and that it was cancelling the other three contracts because it had insufficient production capacity. Cosden relied on the force majeure clause in the contracts as an excuse.

After receiving the notice from Cosden, Helm decided to encourage Cosden to proceed to fill the first order, but Helm planned to retain amounts due in payment of the first order sufficient to offset what it expected damages to be on the other three. Helm did not tell Cosden of its plan to retain a setoff until delivery. When that happened, Cosden sued Helm for nonpayment, and Helm counterclaimed for breach of the other three purchase orders.

In essence, both parties were in the wrong and the crux of the case dealt with sorting out the damages. Cosden's force majeure defense did not carry the day, and there was no question about its repudiation of the other three purchase orders. That repudiation, however, did not justify Helm's partial suspension of performance if the first agreement was truly a separate one. (If this were an integrated, unitary transaction, partial suspension might have been acceptable.) Neither party made proper use of Section 2-609.[80] For the purposes of this discussion, the most important part of the court's opinion was its consideration of the issue of time in the calculation of damages in a Section 2-610 suit. After noting the varying possibilities, the court stated: "In the anticipatory repudiation context, the buyer's specific right to wait for a commercially reasonable time for choosing his remedy must be read together with the general damages provision of Section 2-713 to extend the time for measurement beyond when buyer learns of the breach."[81]

The court reasoned that the purpose of the commercially reasonable waiting period in Section 2-610 was to balance the incentives of buyers and sellers in a rising market. If damages are fixed at the time of repudiation, a seller will prefer to repudiate early in order to minimize damages and to increase his flexibility in playing the market as it goes up. On the other hand, setting damages as of the date of performance — the traditional common-law approach — defeats a buyer's incentive to cover and to mitigate.[82]

There is still the open question of what is a commercially reasonable time. In *Cosden,* the court suggested that it was some time after the discovery of the repudiation, but in *Oloffson v. Coomer,*[83] the court used the day on which the seller notified the buyer of his repudiation. That was the same day that would have been appropriate under Section 2-713 without any additional waiting period, as Section 2-610 seems to contemplate. In *Oloffson,* the buyer could have covered immediately in a rising market. He did

---

[80] The court made clear its opinion that an aggrieved party must request assurances under Section 2-609 and not get them before the suspension of performance or the termination of payments. Id. at 1074, 38 UCC Rep. at 1659, citing Tennell v. Estene Cotton Co., 546 SW2d 346 (Tex. Civ. App. 1976).

[81] Cosden Oil & Chem. Co. v. Karl O. Helm Aktiengesellschaft, 736 F2d 1064, 38 UCC Rep. 1645, 1655 (5th Cir. 1984), citing Calamari & Perillo, *The Law of Contracts* § 14.20 (2d ed. 1977); Peters, "Remedies for Breach of Contracts Relating to the Sale of Goods Under the Uniform Commercial Code: A Roadmap for Article Two," 73 Yale LJ 199, 263–268 (1963); Sebert, "Remedies Under Article Two of the Uniform Commercial Code; An Agenda for Review," 130 U. Pa. L. Rev. 360, 372–380 (1981); Wallach, "Anticipatory Repudiation and the UCC," 13 UCC LJ 48 (1980).

[82] Cosden Oil & Chem. Co. v. Karl O. Helm Aktiengesellschaft, 736 F2d 1064, 1072, 38 UCC Rep. 1645, 1655, 1656 (5th Cir. 1984).

[83] Oloffson v. Coomer, 11 Ill. App. 3d 918, 296 NE2d 871 (1973).

not do so, but kept imploring the seller to change his mind and waited several months before covering. The buyer had a third-party vendee during the whole period and knew that he would eventually have to cover or be in breach as the seller on his other contract. The court seemed to have little sympathy with his failure to seek an early cover, although it would certainly have been consistent with Section 2-610 for the court to have allowed him some time to try to change the seller's mind.[84]

---

[84] The seller had contracted to sell his crop of corn, and he informed the buyer on June 3 that he did not intend to plant corn because the season had been too wet. There was then very little time for the seller to change his mind and retract because of the lateness of the year. No doubt that influenced the court's reasoning as well.

CHAPTER 4

Warranties

¶ 4.01 ESTABLISHING THE IDENTITY OF WARRANTIES IN CONTRACT LAW

The use of the word "warranty" in contract law can be confusing. It is sometimes used in the sense of a promise or a covenant to accomplish a task or to produce goods. At other times, it is used to convey the sense of a guarantee of truthfulness, especially when it is used together with the word "representation." Contracts commonly include lists of representations that are warranted to be true by a party to the contract. The word "warrant" seems to add a degree of seriousness to statements made in the contract, such as those about a business' financial soundness or a seller's title to various assets. In its most common application, the word "warranty" is used to describe the quality or quantity of goods delivered in a typical chattel sale. This means that although a warranty is collateral to the main subject of the transaction (e.g., a transfer of title from seller to buyer for a consideration of an automobile), it may be critical in determining whether the transaction's main purpose has been accomplished.[1]

Sometimes the words "warranty" and "condition"[2] are used interchangeably,[3] typically in insurance transactions. Insurance applications often require the applicant to warrant responses to a variety of questions. If one of these responses is false and the question is material to the risk assumed by the insurer, the insurance policy may be void. The representation of the applicant, called a warranty, thus becomes a condition to the insurer's obligation to perform. It becomes important to establish whether a warranty is considered to be a promise or a condition in deciding available remedies if breach of contract occurs. If there is a breach of the contract or of one promise within the contract, the breaching party may have to pay damages or be subject to another remedy on

[1] This is perhaps why one commentator has said, "The word is also much used in the law of the sales of goods to refer to a representation that has also become a promise, or a condition, or both, in the contract of sale." Murray, *Grismore on Contracts* § 120, at 172 (rev. ed. 1965) (hereinafter cited as Murray/Grismore).

[2] For a discussion of the theory of conditions, see generally Chapter 5.

[3] Some commentators include the law of warranties within their consideration of the law of conditions. See, e.g., Calamari & Perillo, *The Law of Contracts* § 11-24 (2d ed. 1977); Murray/Grismore § 120; Murray, *Murray on Contracts* § 136 (1974) (hereinafter cited as Murray, *Contracts*).

the contract.[4] If there is a failure of a condition, however, the entire agreement may be void, returning the parties to the status quo before the contract was made.[5]

In this chapter, the word "warranty" has its most common meaning of an affirmation of quality, quantity, and title in connection with a sale. An express warranty is explicitly made by the words or actions of the seller.[6] A warranty also may be implied in law from the circumstances of the sale, even if the seller is silent. With some exceptions, the parties may exclude warranties if the seller is explicit and the buyer knows of the exclusion.

The identity of warranties, their scope, and the question of effective exclusion have given rise to an enormous amount of litigation since the end of World War II. There is no way to treat the subject of warranties exhaustively in this book, and it is particularly impossible to consider all the consumer protection legislation that creates warranties as a matter of law and that provides a wide range of remedies for unhappy buyers.[7] At least a passing acquaint-

---

[4] See generally Chapters 6, 7, and 8. If the breach is of a promise central to the transaction and is material, it may excuse the nonbreaching party from further performance. See generally Chapter 2.

[5] Of course, it may not be possible to get the parties back to the precise status quo ante. For a general consideration of the remedial problems, see Chapter 5.

[6] A standard definition of "express warranty" is contained in the Supreme Court's opinion in the case of Shippen v. Bowen, 122 US 575, 581 (1887), cited in 8 Williston, *A Treatise on the Law of Contracts* § 970, at 483, 484 (3d ed. 1964) (hereinafter cited as Williston):

> "Any affirmation of the quality or condition of the thing sold (not uttered as a matter of opinion or belief) made by the seller at the time of sale, for the purpose of assuring the buyer of the truth of the fact affirmed, and inducing him to make the purchase; if so received and relied on by the purchaser, is an express warranty. And in cases of oral contracts, on the existence of these necessary ingredients to such a warranty, it is the province of the jury to decide, upon considering all the circumstances attending the transaction."

See also Distillers Distrib. Corp. v. Sherwood Distilling Co., 180 F2d 800 (4th Cir. 1950). This is essentially the same definition used in the Uniform Sales Act § 12. It has been expanded somewhat by Section 2-313 of the UCC. See infra ¶ 4.04[2].

[7] Perhaps the most prominent legislation in the area of warranties is the Magnuson-Moss Warranty Act, 15 USC §§ 2301–2312 (1982). In addition, some state laws such as New York's "lemon law" supersede the UCC in sales of used cars and imply a nonexcludable warranty of serviceability in the sale of every used car. Rice v. RM Burritt Motors, Inc., 124 Misc. 2d 712, 477 NYS2d 278 (1984).

ance with the law of warranties is nevertheless important because warranty issues frequently arise in contract cases. This chapter therefore focuses on the common-law origins of express and implied warranties, the modern understanding of these terms, and the influence of the UCC on the common law of warranties.[8]

¶ 4.02 COMMON-LAW ORIGINS OF WARRANTY

[1] Ecclesiastical Background: Ethical Duties of Buyers and Sellers

The English law of warranties grew from medieval ecclesiastical concepts of trust and Christian ethics that antedate the common-law development of the law of assumpsit. According to the Christian tradition, all human endeavors, being nothing more than preparation for entrance into the kingdom of God, were governed by the teachings of the Church. In exchanges of goods and services this meant that both the seller and buyer were held to standards of fair dealing, honesty, and full disclosure. The ethical requirements of trade are outlined in *Summa Theologica,* the famous treatise of Thomas Aquinas, who was a respected lawyer as well as a noted theologian.[9] No formality was necessary to create a warranty. As Aquinas wrote, "between a simple word and an oath God draws no distinction."[10] The buyer was under similar ethical duties. If after his purchase he found he owned something worth more than the price he had paid for it, he was morally bound to give additional consideration to the seller. There is no doubt, however, that the standards bore most heavily on sellers. As one commentator

---

[8] A fuller consideration of warranty issues and their statutory bases is offered in Clark & Smith, *The Law of Product Warranties* (1984) and Wallach, *The Law of Sales Under the Uniform Commercial Code* (1981).

[9] The lawyer in Aquinas sometimes shone through the churchman. He thought that there was no question that the seller should disclose any latent defects in his wares, but he equivocated on the requirements for disclosing patent defects. After all, the buyer could inspect and could make use of his powers of observation. If he failed to inspect or if he overlooked a patent defect, nothing had been kept from him and he bought at his own risk. Aquinas did admit that perhaps the truly moral man would disclose everything, patent as well as latent, and thus protect the buyer from his own shortcomings as well as from any deceit or sharp dealing by the seller.

[10] Quoted in 2 Pollock & Maitland, *History of the English Law* 195 (2d ed. 1903).

has noted, "In ecclesiastical polity there was no place for the notion that the seller was not responsible for the goodness of his wares."[11]

[2] Secular Responses to Warranty

The explosion of commerce that accompanied the voyages of exploration and the growth of a merchant class became too much to be handled by ecclesiastical guidance alone. Changes in European society also were reflected in the Reformation, which weakened the central authority of the Church. In England especially, the Church became closely identified with secular authority. Even before the Reformation, other means to assure certain warranties and to enforce them against sellers began to develop. Towns, other political subdivisions, and trade guilds adopted extensive regulations of weights and measures, quality of goods, and freshness of foodstuffs that were applied to bakers, barbers, chandlers, weavers, and a host of other craftsmen. Instead of relying on the fear of God (or of the clergy) or on a disappointed buyer's ability to pursue an action for judicial redress, the towns and guilds imposed regulatory standards on sellers and manufacturers and enforced them with physical punishments.[12] Regulatory authorities did not forget that moral duty applied to all God's subjects and often provided for postsale amendments of the price term to reflect the greater or lesser quality of the goods sold. "The object of the law was to insure to every good offered for sale a fair price, full measure, and good workmanship."[13]

The theft that was fairly common during the medieval period often caused buyers to doubt title to the goods they purchased. A

---

[11] Hamilton, "The Ancient Maxim Caveat Emptor," 40 Yale LJ 1133, 1141 (1931) (hereinafter cited as Hamilton). Much of this discussion borrows from Professor Hamilton's classic article. He relies, inter alia, on Wilson, *A Discourse on Usury* (1572); Bunyan, *The Life and Death of Mr. Badman* (1680); Baxter, *A Christian Directory: Or a Summ of Practical Theologie and Cases of Conscience* (1678).

[12] Hamilton 1146–1150. For instance, "night work was forbidden to spurriers, founders, armorers, and other workers in metal, because it gave opportunity to introduce false iron for tin and to gild false copper." Id. at 1149.

[13] Id. at 1150, citing a statute of Berwick from 1249 and a similar one from the Grimsby Charter of 1259.

modern free-market advocate might argue that the market price naturally includes a discount for the possibility of a cloud on title. Nonetheless, perhaps from a concern for the honest seller who might be unfairly tainted by an unscrupulous fence, English towns developed a useful mechanism that is the basis for the implied warranty of title accompanying chattel sales. Every town had a designated market day (in London it was every day except the Sabbath), and it became the rule that a chattel sold at the "market overt" was sold with clear title. The reasoning was that if the goods were stolen, the rightful owner would see them in the market and make claim, a rationale that had much more substance in the small villages of fifteenth- and sixteenth-century England than it does in a more mobile society.[14]

Warranties also played a part in the development of the Law Merchant. Unless there was express agreement to the contrary, the Law Merchant made three basic assumptions: (1) the buyer relied on the seller's word as to the quality of the goods; (2) if sale was by sample, the bulk of merchandise would conform to the sample; and (3) failure of a warranty would justify confiscation of the goods and damages to the wronged party.[15]

[3] The Rule of Caveat Emptor and Development of Modern Concepts of Warranty

During the Middle Ages and the Renaissance, English common law developed separately without any real form of action satisfactory for the redress of warranty breaches except in actions for deceit or fraud.[16] This reflected the ecclesiastical origins of the concept of warranty — a failed warranty violated a public duty of fair dealing rather than breached a promise privately made. Actions sounding in assumpsit (that is, for the recovery of damages for the nonperformance of a contract) were not available for warranty breaches until the late seventeenth century, and then the concept of warranty as conceived by Aquinas and the medieval Church fathers ran into the more recently articulated rule of caveat

[14] Id. at 1146, 1147.

[15] Id. at 1161.

[16] See generally Williston § 970, at 487.

emptor. This rule basically states that a buyer is responsible for examining, judging, and testing the goods he purchases. A 1603 opinion[17] first stated the rule of caveat emptor, but it was at least two centuries before the doctrine assumed its full force and limited the availability of remedies for the breach of warranties.[18]

By the middle of the nineteenth century, the common law of warranties in England and in the United States was largely an exception to the standard of caveat emptor, at least in sales of personalty. In a treatise published in 1844, William Story wrote:

> The general rule of law, applicable to all sales, is that the buyer buys at his own risk; *caveat emptor;* unless the vendor give an express warranty; or unless the law imply a warranty, from the nature of the thing sold, and the circumstances of the sale; or unless the vendor have been guilty of a fraudulent representation, or concealment in regard to the things sold.[19]

In summary, Story wrote: (1) the affirmation that is said to be a warranty must relate to the goods sold; (2) the seller must have intended that the warranty be an affirmation with respect to those goods; (3) the warranty must be contemporaneous with the sale; and (4) the warranty requires no specific language. The warranty may be limited by the seller. Statements of "puffing" or the opinions of the seller are not warranties, although what constitutes puffing and what constitutes a clear affirmation are questions of

---

[17] Chandelor v. Lopus, 79 Eng. Rep. 3 (Ex. 1603). This case involved the sale of what turned out to be a worthless bezoar stone, an item reputed to have certain magical qualities.

[18] Professor Hamilton sharply criticized the means by which the rule of caveat emptor was developed and suggested that it was inconsistent with prior English law:

> "The raw materials of a judicial doctrine of caveat emptor were scant enough. An excerpt or two from Fitzherbert or whoever wrote his books, a neat distinction between the civil and the common law pried from its context in Coke, a persuasive but doctored line of Latin lifted from a venerable document, the prescribed tests for the validity of a declaration in deceit, the dubious support of a handful of none too relevant cases — and that was all. But the words were there, ready to bear the ideas of a later age; and with interpretation, the great creator, was to prove equal to the occasion."

Hamilton 1169.

[19] Story, *A Treatise on the Law of Contracts Not Under Seal* § 528 (1844) (hereinafter cited as Story).

fact that depend on the circumstances. The language of a warranty is to be interpreted in accordance with common usage and understanding in the trade; if a technical term is used, it is understood in accordance with its appropriate technical definition. A warranty made after a sale is void for want of consideration. A general warranty of quality does not cover patent defects observable by the buyer unless the buyer is unable to make an examination of the goods.[20]

The rules of express warranties set out by Story more than 140 years ago could easily be listed in a contemporary book as a general outline of the law of express warranties. The most significant change in the development of warranties from medieval times has been in presumptions. Medieval and Renaissance ecclesiastics presumed that transactions were to be made on the basis of fairness and full disclosure. By the middle of the nineteenth century, the presumption was that the buyer had to look out for himself and that the law would only intervene under limited circumstances. This reflects a change in the understanding of the role of public authority in making and enforcing private agreements and also evinces the change from the use of trespass to the use of assumpsit as the basis of judicial remedies. In an assumpsit, or contract, action, the focus is necessarily on the promises and undertakings of the parties one to the other. In a trespass, or tort, action, however, the focus is on the duty owed, as a matter of public law, from one party to the other regardless of the undertakings of each.

Story also described a series of implied warranties that were actionable in assumpsit, but that had developed from the tort actions for fraudulent misrepresentation and concealment:

> This new form of action [assumpsit] led to many changes and modifications in the law, and accounts for many discrepancies and contradictions in the older cases. By the old rule of the common law, the doctrine of *caveat emptor* applied to all sales, where there was not an express warranty. But in the Roman law, the rule is *caveat venditor,* in all cases. And ever since the form of *assumpsit* was introduced, as the form of pleading upon cases of implied warranty, there has been a tendency in the common law to approximate to the rule of the

[20] Id. at §§ 529–532.

Roman law, which implies a warranty, that the goods sold are merchantable, and fit for the purpose for which they are known to be bought.[21]

When Story wrote his treatise in 1844, he found that the law recognized five implied warranties: (1) title; (2) merchantability (the quality demanded and expected by the buyer); (3) fitness for a particular purpose (goods manufactured for a specific purpose made known to the manufacturer by the buyer); (4) absence of latent defects (seller knows that buyer relies on his judgment, or seller is the manufacturer and thus can provide against defects); and (5) conformity of the bulk to a sample.[22] In Story's day the seller could avoid the implied warranty of title by stating that he had less than clear title and was quitclaiming nothing more than his interest in the goods subject to the claims of others.[23] The implied warranty of merchantability applied only when the buyer's inspection of goods was impracticable.[24] The warranty of fitness for a particular purpose was not a warranty for any use to which the buyer might put the goods, but only of the goods' general suitability.[25] The reasoning behind the implied warranty against latent defects reflected early ecclesiastical influences: "The ground of this warranty is the implied trust and confidence reposed in the seller by the buyer, with the buyer's tacit consent; and, therefore, whenever this reason fails, the warranty fails."[26]

Forty years later, the rule of *caveat emptor* was even stronger. Parsons' *Law of Contracts,* a treatise that became well-known after its publication in 1883, states, "If there be no express warranty, the common law, in general, implies none. Its rule is, unquestionably, both in England and in this country, *caveat emp-*

---

[21] Id. at § 534.

[22] Id. at §§ 533–540.

[23] Id. at § 535.

[24] Id. at § 536.

[25] Id. at § 538.

[26] Id. at § 539. Story also pointed out that the uses of warranty are limited. The law of warranties does not apply where the thing delivered is fundamentally different from the thing bargained for. In such a case the proper remedy is in mistake or fraud, not in warranty. Id. at § 541.

tor."[27] Although the rule of caveat emptor did not excuse fraud, that was about all it did not excuse.[28] There was one significant exception for instances in which the seller had information about the goods that was not available to anyone else, including the buyer. The rule of caveat emptor did not apply in such a situation.[29]

Despite the general requirement that the buyer look out for himself, the law did continue to recognize a few implied warranties, such as title, fitness for a particular purpose,[30] and conformity of the bulk to the sample. If goods were sold on examination, however, a buyer could not rely on the sample and bought at risk unless he examined the whole. A buyer could not rely on advertising circulars as warranties; they were regarded merely as sales puffery. What was a mere opinion rather than an affirmation equivalent to a warranty was a question of law, although whether the seller intended a warranty and whether the buyer relied on it were questions of fact.[31] The seller could avoid all express and implied warranties by refusing to warrant and by selling "as is" or "with all faults."[32]

In the past few decades, the pendulum has begun to swing back against the strict application of the rule of caveat emptor and toward a more expansive application of both express and implied warranties. Although twenty years ago the rule still stood that the buyer was expected to look out for himself, the law began to be somewhat more protective of the buyer and less solicitous of the seller. For instance, the question of warranty or opinion became more often than not a question of fact for the jury.[33] That circum-

---

[27] 1 Parsons, *The Law of Contracts* 618 (7th ed. 1883) (hereinafter cited as Parsons).

[28] Active fraud was actionable, but silence did not constitute fraud: "the seller may let the buyer cheat himself *ad libitum,* but must not actively assist him in cheating himself." Id. at 620.

[29] Id. at 625, 626.

[30] As something of a corollary, there developed an implied warranty of wholesomeness for foodstuffs purchased for immediate use. Id. at 632. However, there was no implied warranty for defects in goods that were observable with an ordinarily careful inspection. Hoffman v. Oates, 77 Ga. 701 (1886).

[31] Parsons 622–631.

[32] Id. at 633, 634. This avoidance did not exclude liability for fraud. A warranty in writing could not be enlarged by parol.

[33] Williston § 970, at 490.

stance did not necessarily favor the buyer, but it was likely that jurors might be more sympathetic to a good-faith buyer who suffered a bad deal than to a seller who profited from sharpness, even if not from deceit. Some cases dropped the requirement of showing an intent to warrant by reasoning that positive statements of quality should be taken as affirmations of fact, and thus as warranties.[34] This was carried farther by cases that held that buyers could rely on mass advertising claims as warranties, not merely as puffing.[35] The buyer did not have to prove reliance on an express warranty, which was assumed from his agreement to purchase, and the buyer was no longer under a duty to inspect on an express warranty. He could rely on the seller's word instead.[36]

From the mid-nineteenth to mid-twentieth centuries, there was no great change in the articulation of the common law of warranties. There was a subtle shift in emphasis, however. In the 1844 Story treatise, caveat emptor is clearly the rule and warranties, express or implied, are exceptions, but there is an undercurrent of the doctrines expressed much earlier by Aquinas in the emphasis given to implied warranties, such as the warranty for merchantability. Later in the century, Parsons propounded a much more strongly held view of the caveat emptor maxim. In his 1883 treatise, caveat emptor is indeed the law, and warranties are a minor exception. The buyer must operate at risk or be sure that he takes precautions. By the mid-twentieth century and the time of the third revision of Williston's treatise, the rule of caveat emptor still applies, and quite strongly, but there is a trend in Williston to treat the law of warranties as a subject unto itself and not just as a

---

[34] Id. § 971, at 491, 492.

[35] Id. § 971A, at 495.

[36] Id. §§ 972, 973, at 497–500. Williston noted that buyers typically rely on both the seller's warranties and their own inspection, and he could see no reason to exculpate the seller because the buyer's inspection did not uncover the problem. He used as an example the well-known case of Turner v. Central Hardware Co., 353 Mo. 1182, 186 SW2d 603 (1945). The buyer went to a hardware store to purchase a ladder for use in his work. He had seen the model advertised and it was represented to be capable of supporting far more than his weight. He looked it over in the store, the clerk maintained that it was a good product for his use, and Turner bought it. When he first used the ladder, a rung broke, and Turner fell and injured himself as a result. Despite the buyer's inspection in the store, the court held the seller to his warranty.

minor exception to the general rule that the buyer should beware.[37] For instance, Williston describes statements made during negotiations that induce the sale as the basis of warranties and therefore relevant to the determination of their scope in a particular case.[38] He goes on to say that "In early times, intentions not expressed by words were disregarded; today, they are frequently given effect by the recognition of implied meanings."[39] Williston's approach to the common-law cases and the decisions of common-law judges was no doubt influenced by the passage of numerous consumer protection statutes that had the effect of expanding the availability of warranties for the protection of unwary buyers.

This short excursion into the history of the law of warranties is an attempt to provide an understanding of some of the problems that have arisen in warranty litigation in the late twentieth century. If nothing else, it demonstrates that concern with warranties has been cyclical. For the past fifty years, courts and legislatures have been increasingly concerned with buyers and the overall fairness of an exchange. This development is a shift from the strict application of the doctrine of caveat emptor that characterized late nineteenth-century cases and reflects some of the earlier principles derived from the ecclesiastical law. Even in times of greatest deference to sellers, however, courts have consistently implied some warranties (e.g., title warranties) and have been willing to hold sellers to the letter of their express warranties.

---

[37] This trend is also evident in case law. For instance, in a 1948 decision, the Court of Appeals for the Fifth Circuit, applying Mississippi law, noted that caveat emptor overcame neither express warranties or fraud (which was not surprising) nor a laundry list of implied warranties (which indicated some weakening of the doctrine). McElroy v. Long, 170 F2d 345 (5th Cir. 1948).

[38] Williston § 974, at 506, 507.

[39] Id. § 975, at 508. Although the longstanding rule from the days of the market overt held that a seller in possession impliedly warranted good title, most earlier cases held that a seller not in possession did not warrant title. Williston noted that fewer and fewer modern courts drew a distinction between sellers in possession and those not in possession. Most courts implied a warranty of title as an incident of sale regardless of possession. If the seller had doubts about the title, he could protect himself by limiting his representations of title and by simply quitclaiming. Id. § 976, at 508, 509. It has always been the rule that there is no implied warranty of title by one who does not profess any claim to title in his own right (e.g., a sheriff at an execution sale or a trustee in bankruptcy).

¶ 4.03 CHARACTER AND NATURE OF WARRANTIES

[1] Express and Implied Warranties

A party who makes an express or implied warranty assures against defects in the quantity or quality of the goods being sold.[40] Certain warranties are incidental to any sale of chattels and are part of the consideration unless excluded or limited by the parties to the sale.[41] However, a problem may arise in deciding what is and what is not an express warranty.

There is nothing complicated about the definition of an "express warranty." It is the seller's affirmation of fact to the buyer of the quality or quantity of goods, title, or restrictive covenants to real property as an inducement to a sale.[42] It must be made before or at the time of the sale; postsale statements are gratuitous, without consideration, and unenforceable in common-law cases.[43] Nevertheless, it later may be questioned whether the seller's statements to the buyer were affirmations of fact, mere opinions, or puffing upon which the buyer should not have relied. Depending on the vintage of the case or the treatise, classic examples involve either the sale of a horse or an automobile. The seller's statement that a horse is sound is an express warranty of its soundness.[44] The statement that the seller *believes* the horse to be sound is simply an

---

[40] See, e.g., Saranac Automatic Mach. Corp. v. Duke, 67 F2d 436 (5th Cir. 1933).

[41] See, e.g., Wilson v. Taylor, 106 Ga. App. 720, 128 SE2d 83 (1962); AE Speer, Inc. v. McCorvey, 77 Ga. App. 715, 49 SE2d 677 (1948).

[42] It is sometimes said that it must be shown that the buyer relied on the seller's statements as warranties and that the seller intended them as such, knowing that the buyer was relying on them. Bel v. Adler, 63 Ga. App. 473, 11 SE2d 495 (1940). The more common approach, however, presumes reliance from the fact of the buyer's purchase and treats affirmations of fact as inducements intended to cause reliance. See generally Williston § 972.

[43] See, e.g., Brooks v. Matthews, 78 Ga. 739, 3 SE 627 (1887); Baldwin v. Daniel, 69 Ga. 782 (1883); Widincamp v. Patterson, 33 Ga. App. 483, 127 SE 158 (1925). The UCC varies this rule somewhat. See UCC § 2-313; infra ¶ 4.04[2].

[44] There may be varieties of soundness. A horse may be sound for breeding but not for racing. Another may be sound for simple pleasure riding but not for foxhunting. The scope of the warranty depends on the purchaser's intended uses as much as anything, and reason dictates that the seller should not be held to a complete warranty of soundness for all purposes if the buyer has indicated that he intends to purchase only for breeding or for light pleasure use.

opinion in which the seller does not warrant soundness; he only warrants his belief. The buyer thus purchases the horse at risk. If the seller knows the horse is unsound and lies, the buyer may have an action for deceit, but not for breach of warranty. The seller's statement that the horse is suitable for the buyer may not be a warranty of soundness for all purposes, but can reasonably be construed as a warranty of soundness for the buyer's purposes. Similar shades of meaning apply with respect to a seller's comments about a car or any other piece of equipment he is selling. Whether the seller's statements are warranties or opinions is usually a question of fact, but the tendency of courts has been to hold positive statements of quality to be warranties.[45]

Implied warranties come from two sources. They are either imposed by operation of law to serve a publicly identified goal (e.g., an implied warranty of title), or they develop from a common trade practice. For example, samples have long been used as a means to induce sales in bulk because it is time-consuming, inefficient, and often impossible for a buyer to examine an entire order before it is delivered. By relying on the quality of the sample, the buyer saves time and energy, and by implying a warranty of conformity to the whole, the law imposes a duty that protects against unscrupulous sellers. If a buyer does inspect the goods he purchases, he may waive the implied warranty and rely instead on his own inspection. An implied warranty also may be based on the particular circumstances of a transaction and the expressed interests of the buyer.

The implied warranties of merchantability and fitness for a particular purpose reflect ordinary trade practices and common understandings of the parties' relative knowledge and expectations of trust. The warranty of merchantability assumes that the seller intends that the product for sale will perform ordinarily well for products of its type. It is not a warranty of quality under any circumstances, but simply an understood affirmation that the product is indeed what it seems to be. The warranty of fitness for a particular purpose is more specific. The buyer has in some way let the seller know that he intends to use the product in a specific

---

[45] See generally Williston §§ 970, 971.

application. If the product is sold for the buyer's specific purpose, the seller makes an implied warranty that it is good for that purpose. Whether the product is merchantable for ordinary use is irrelevant if the product fails for the buyer's expressed particular purpose.

A common-law seller can avoid all warranty problems by excluding warranties altogether.[46] A sale "as is," "with all faults," or "with no warranties express or implied" means that the buyer takes the goods at risk. If the product fails, the buyer's only remedy is in tort if he can prove that the seller acted fraudulently or deceitfully. There are also statutory limitations on the seller's common-law right to exclude warranties.[47]

[2] The Rule of Privity

The concept of privity has led to a series of interesting cases at the intersection of the law of contracts and the law of torts. A warranty action is "on" the contract and is separate and distinct from any action for fraud or other tort that may arise from the same transaction.[48] The rule of privity holds that breach of warranty is a breach of a private, voluntary undertaking rather than a breach of a public duty.[49] It creates a right of action only between the parties to the agreement, even though the failure of the warranted goods may have caused injury to third persons.[50]

---

[46] Some courts have held that express warranties exclude implied warranties. Moultrie Repair Co. v. Hill, 120 Ga. 730, 48 SE 143 (1904); Malsby v. Young, 104 Ga. 205, 30 SE 854 (1898).

[47] See, e.g., Rice v. RM Burritt Motors, Inc., 124 Misc. 2d 712, 477 NYS2d 278 (1984).

[48] For traditional statements of the principle, see, e.g., Burge v. Stroberg, 42 Ga. 88 (1871); Barfield v. Farkas, 40 Ga. App. 559, 150 SE 600 (1929).

[49] For a criticism of this argument, see Seavey, 45 Harv. L. Rev. 209 (1931) (book review). Seavey argued that tort liability is premised on an act by the tortfeasor that is voluntary in the same way that the decision to enter into a contract is voluntary. Both involve decisions to engage in relationships with other people with the knowledge that certain obligations will accompany the decision to act.

[50] For a classic application of the privity rule, see Winterbottom v. Wright, 10 M&W 109, 152 Eng. Rep. 402 (Ex. 1842).

The privity rule can create problems for a consumer who purchases defective goods from middlemen instead of from the manufacturer, who might be held responsible for the defect. In this mass-consumption society, there is little real privity between manufacturers and the ultimate users of their products. The courts have tried to take care of this problem by expanding the concept of product liability in tort[51] and by holding that manufacturers may warrant goods to their ultimate consumers through advertising or mass warranties, such as those that accompany automobile sales.[52]

Although some statutes have removed the privity requirement or limited its application,[53] the privity rule has prevented plaintiffs from recovering damages in several warranty actions. For example, a cotton mill employee who injured his hand on a machine at the mill could not maintain an action against the machine's manufacturer for breach of warranty because he was not in privity with the manufacturer. He was merely an employee of the machine's buyer.[54] Similarly, in one of the many recent asbestos cases, plaintiffs who were suffering from asbestosis could not maintain a warranty action against the manufacturer of the asbestos materials

---

[51] This has resulted in the creation of a subfield of torts that has become almost a separate area of the law and in the blurring of the lines of distinction between tort and contract liability. See generally Restatement (Second) of Torts § 402A (1977); Calabresi, "Some Thoughts on Risk Distribution and the Law of Torts," 70 Yale LJ 499 (1961); Kessler, "Products Liability," 76 Yale LJ 887 (1967); Prosser, "The Assault Upon the Citadel (Strict Liability to the Consumer)," 69 Yale LJ 1099 (1960); Prosser, "The Fall of the Citadel (Strict Liability to the Consumer)," 50 Minn. L. Rev. 791 (1966). Two of the most important cases in the area are Henningsen v. Bloomfield Motors, Inc., 32 NJ 358, 161 A2d 69 (1960) and MacPherson v. Buick Motor Co., 217 NY 382, 111 NE 1050 (1916).

[52] The consideration for the warranty is payment of the purchase price by the consumer. Studebaker Corp. v. Nail, 82 Ga. App. 779, 62 SE2d 198 (1950). This does not necessarily apply to endorsers of goods (e.g., the Good Housekeeping Seal of Approval) because courts tend to insulate them from contract liability by reason of the privity doctrine. The endorser may be liable in tort on a theory of negligent misrepresentation or product liability. See e.g., Hanberry v. Hearst Corp., 276 Cal. App. 2d 680, 81 Cal. Rptr. 519 (1969); Annot., 39 ALR3d 181 (1971).

[53] See, e.g., UCC § 2-318; infra ¶ 4.04[7].

[54] Watkins v. Barber-Colman Co., 625 F2d 714 (5th Cir. 1980).

because they were employees of the purchasers, not the purchasers themselves.[55] Although there has been substantial weakening of the privity rule, it can still be a trap for the unwary.

[3] Warranty of Title

Title to chattels or to real property is one of the oldest of implied warranties. Many sellers expressly warrant title. A standard real estate warranty deed includes a clear guarantee of title, but even in the absence of a warranty deed the law implies a warranty of clear title by the seller. In a quitclaim deed, a seller specifically excludes any warranty of title and only purports to transfer his claim to the property, whatever it may be. Similarly, in an executor's deed of assent or bill of sale, the executor transfers the title held by his decedent but he makes no independent warranties. The same holds for other fiduciaries, such as trustees,[56] conservators, guardians, trustees in bankruptcy, receivers, and public officials who sell pursuant to judicial direction.

For several centuries the rule of implied warranty of title also has applied to chattel sales. As discussed previously, this rule has its origins in the open markets of English towns, where it was developed as a title-laundering device to deal with the chronic problem of stolen goods.[57] The rule has changed little over the centuries, and, unless a seller explicitly excludes a warranty of title, the law implies that he sells with good title free and clear of all clouds.[58]

---

[55] Starling v. Seaboard Coast Line Ry. Co., 533 F. Supp. 183 (SD Ga. 1982); see also Best Canvas Prods. & Supplies, Inc. v. Ploof Truck Lines, Inc., 713 F2d 618 (11th Cir. 1983); Spiller v. Tennessee Trailers, Inc., 97 FRD 347 (ND Ga. 1982).

[56] Of course, there are instances in which a trustee invests in land or other property in the management of the trust corpus. The trust then may be an owner and subject to the implied warranty of title upon a subsequent transfer. This rule of limited liability applies to properties held in legal name by fiduciaries for others. The trustee has no greater title to real estate than the title held by the settlor at the time the property was put into trust.

[57] See supra ¶ 4.02[2].

[58] See, e.g., Bond & Maxwell v. Perrin, 145 Ga. 200, 88 SE 954 (1916); Wilson v. Eargle, 98 Ga. App. 241, 105 SE2d 474 (1958). The UCC codifies this rule in Section 2-312. See infra ¶ 4.03[1].

[4] UCC Applicability to Contract Transactions and the Common Law of Warranties

Because most chattel sales occur within the coverage of the UCC, the modern common law of warranties is of somewhat limited application. However, there are specific instances of important warranty law applications outside the UCC. Cases that do not fall under UCC coverage (notably insurance cases) are subject to other regulation. It is not quite correct to refer to these as common-law cases, but the term is useful shorthand for non-UCC decisions.

In many contracts cases, especially those that involve the transfer of goods and the provision of services, one of the first questions often is whether the UCC applies. Is the agreement primarily for the sale of chattels and therefore under UCC coverage, or is it primarily a contract for services to which the transfer of chattels is merely incidental? Article 2 of the UCC applies only to the sale of "goods," which are defined as "all things (including specially manufactured goods) which are movable at the time of identification to the contract for sale other than the money in which the price is to be paid, investment securities . . . and things in action."[59] The general test for UCC coverage is to determine whether the primary purpose and main thrust of the contract is the sale of goods or services. This almost always requires a factual inquiry into the particulars of the transaction and the intentions of the parties.[60]

Construction and equipment installation contracts often raise questions of UCC applicability because they invariably involve both services and the transfer of chattels. The Kansas Supreme Court, for instance, decided that the UCC did not apply to a con-

---

[59] UCC § 2-105(1). "Goods" also includes the "unborn young of animals and growing crops and other identified things attached to realty." For further guidance on the coverage of Article 2, see UCC §§ 2-102–2-107.

[60] See, e.g., Bonebrake v. Cox, 499 F2d 951 (8th Cir. 1974). The contract at issue in that case was for the sale and installation of bowling equipment. Although the agreement contemplated construction work to install the equipment, the court found that the UCC applied because the main purpose was the sale and purchase of bowling equipment to replace items that had been destroyed in a fire. See also Northwestern Equip., Inc. v. Cudmore, 312 NW2d 347 (ND 1981); Allied Indus. Serv. Corp. v. Kasle Iron & Metals, Inc., 62 Ohio App. 2d 144, 405 NE2d 307 (1977).

tract for the design and construction of a display booth.[61] Although one party sold a substantial amount of goods to another, the main purpose of their agreement was the design and construction of the booth. The transfer of title to the lumber, nails, and other materials needed to construct the booth was held to be incidental to the service aspects of the agreement.

On the other hand, a New Jersey court applied the UCC to a contract for the installation of overhead garage doors because the installer's main purpose was to sell a set of doors. The installation was a service to the consumer that was incidental to the sales transaction.[62] The courts have split just about evenly in deciding whether contracts for the sale and installation of heating, air conditioning, electrical, and plumbing equipment are covered by the UCC.[63]

An interesting recent case is *Skelton v. Druid City Hospital Board,*[64] a 1984 decision of the Alabama Supreme Court. The plaintiff was a patient who underwent an operation for the repair of a hernia. During the operation, a suture needle broke off and lodged in the patient's body. He subsequently brought suit for breach of warranty against the hospital as the seller of the needle and as a merchant that trades in such items.[65] The hospital argued that it was neither a seller nor a merchant of the needle because its primary purpose was to provide services. Although it charged pa-

---

[61] Care Display, Inc. v. Didde-Glaser, Inc., 225 Kan. 232, 589 P2d 599 (1979).

[62] Meyers v. Henderson Constr. Co., 147 NJ Super. 77, 370 A2d 547 (1977).

[63] Holding that the UCC applies, see, e.g., Baker v. Compton, 455 NE2d 382 (Ind. Ct. App. 1983); Alden Wells Veterinarian Clinics, Inc. v. Wood, 324 NW2d 181 (Minn. 1982); Mayflower Farms v. Tech-Mark, Inc., 64 Ore. App. 121, 666 P2d 1384 (1983). Holding that the UCC does not apply, see, e.g., Althoff Indus., Inc. v. Elgin Medical Center, Inc., 95 Ill. App. 3d 517, 51 Ill. Dec. 386, 420 NE2d 800 (1981); Semler v. Knowling, 325 NW2d 395 (Iowa 1982); Geelan Mechanical Corp. v. Dember Constr. Corp., 97 AD2d 810, 468 NYS2d 680 (1983). In comparison, courts have consistently applied UCC Article 2 to the sale and installation of carpeting. See, e.g., Colorado Carpet Installation, Inc. v. Palermo, 647 P2d 686 (Colo. Ct. App. 1982), aff'd, 668 P2d 1384 (Colo. 1983); Lipson v. Hawthorne Indus., Inc., 148 Ga. App. 751, 252 SE2d 639 (1979).

[64] Skelton v. Druid City Hosp. Bd., 459 So. 2d 818 (Ala. 1984).

[65] A "seller" is any person "who sells or contracts to sell goods." UCC § 2-103(1)(d). A "merchant" is one "who deals in goods of the kind or otherwise by his occupation holds himself out as having knowledge or skill peculiar to the practices or goods involved in the transaction." UCC § 2-104(1).

tients for items used during surgery, those items were incidental to the hospital's main purpose, which was to provide the services necessary for proper medical and surgical care. The court disagreed and found that the hospital was both a seller and a merchant of the needle and similar items used during surgery. The court noted that the hospital did indeed charge for such items; perhaps most important, the court also noted that the patient had to rely on the hospital's expertise in selecting and using goods of satisfactory quality. No consumer choice was available once the patient and his doctor selected the hospital. This decision subjected the hospital to an implied warranty of fitness for the particular purpose intended imposed by Section 2-315 of the UCC.[66]

Whether the UCC applies is certainly not a final decision of substantive liability, but it can be quite important in determining the relative likelihood of the plaintiff's success. The UCC sets forth relatively clear, general standards of liability for both express and implied warranties, and a significant body of case law expounds upon the ambiguities of the statute. If a product fails and damages result, the parties have a reasonable framework in which to gauge the degree of the seller's liability. Outside the UCC, there is substantially less certainty. The UCC also eliminates the privity requirement for warranty actions that cause personal injury to certain identified groups of people.[67] To the extent that express or implied warranties apply to a service contract, it may be that they apply only to performance taken as a whole, not to the quality of every item involved in the contract. The failure of a single suturing needle may not amount to a breach of a warranty of ordinary surgical care.[68] If a medical treatment is unsuccessful, the patient may have an action for medical malpractice or negligence, but in a warranty action liability is easier to prove.[69]

---

[66] For further discussion of UCC § 2-315, see infra ¶ 4.04[4].

[67] In general, this is limited to members of the buyer's family. See UCC § 2-318; infra ¶ 4.04[7].

[68] It is unlikely (although possible) that a doctor would warrant the absolute success of an operation. See, e.g., Hawkins v. McGee, 84 NH 114, 146 A 641 (1929) (doctor said that operation on boy's crabbed hand would make it "a 100 percent good hand," but skin graft to palm of hand from boy's chest subsequently grew hair; held, evidence supported finding of express warranty).

[69] On the other hand, tort damages may be more desirable to the plaintiff because they are not as limited as contract damages.

¶ 4.04 WARRANTIES UNDER THE UCC

[1] Affirmation of Title: Section 2-312

The majority of warranty cases today arise under the UCC. Sections 2-312 through 2-318 deal directly with express and implied warranties, although other sections come into play in determining the scope of the applicability of the specific warranty sections.

Section 2-312 codifies and expands upon the implied warranty of title. It creates the presumption that a seller has good title and the right to transfer it [70] and that a buyer takes the goods free from any security interest, lien, or encumbrance, other than those he already knows of at the time of contracting.[71] A seller may exclude or limit the warranty of title either by specific language or by showing that the buyer knew of any clouds on the title and purchased subject to them.[72] Although merchants and sellers both warrant sales free from third-party claims (except as disclosed), a sale made in accordance with a buyer's specifications requires the buyer to hold the seller harmless from third parties for complying with the specifications.[73] This requirement protects the seller from claims for infringement of trademark, copyright, patent, or similar rights and puts the burden of these claims on the party that furnishes the specifications.[74]

The implied warranty of title under Section 2-312 arises whether or not the seller possesses the goods at the time of contracting.[75] The slightest disturbance of title violates the seller's implied warranty. The buyer need not lose possession or control of the property; it is enough that he has to respond to an adverse claim, even if it is finally determined to be without merit. The seller's good faith is no defense.[76] The question is not whether the

---

[70] UCC § 2-312(1)(a).

[71] UCC § 2-312(1)(b). The buyer is at risk only for liens he knew about at the time of contracting, not for any that arose between the time of contracting and closing, unless the buyer also knew of them and agreed to take at risk.

[72] UCC § 2-312(2).

[73] UCC § 2-312(3).

[74] UCC § 2-312, Official Comment 3.

[75] UCC § 2-312, Official Comment 1.

[76] UCC § 2-312, Official Comments 4, 5.

buyer will prevail against other claimants, but whether he must contend with a substantial shadow on title.[77]

Two recent cases illustrate the reach of Section 2-312. *Jefferson v. Jones* involved the purchase of a motorcycle. Everything about the sale was aboveboard; however, the seller made a clerical error in filling out the application for the certificate of title and inscribed an incorrect vehicle identification number. Two years later, the buyer was stopped by a policeman for a minor traffic offense, and when the policeman noted the discrepancy between the number on the title and the number on the motorcycle, he impounded the motorcycle. It took some time and considerable legal expense for the buyer to prove the validity of his title and to get his motorcycle back. The seller was liable for breach of the implied warranty of title and had to pay all the buyer's expenses.[78]

The California case of *De LaHoya v. Slim's Gun Shop* involved the sale of a pistol. The buyer paid $140 to Slim's for the firearm, and both parties completed the papers necessary for the transfer of title. The seller, a licensed gun dealer, assumed that his title to the pistol was good and that he was acting in good faith. When the buyer later took the pistol to a shooting range, another shooter, who happened to be an off-duty policeman, asked to look it over. The policeman checked the identification number of the pistol and determined that it was stolen property. The buyer was arrested, and expensive legal maneuvering was needed to prove his innocence. The seller had to return the purchase price and pay the buyer's legal expenses.[79]

[2] Express Warranties: Section 2-313

Section 2-313 identifies three ways in which a seller can create an express warranty. The first is largely a restatement of the common-law definition of express warranty; that is, an affirmation of fact about the goods being sold that becomes a part of the basis of

---

[77] Wright v. Vickaryous, 611 P2d 20 (Alaska 1980).

[78] Jefferson v. Jones, 286 Md. 544, 408 A2d 1036 (1979).

[79] De LaHoya v. Slim's Gun Shop, 80 Cal. App. 3d, supp. 6, 146 Cal. Rptr. 68 (1978).

the bargain.[80] The second way to warrant quality is to describe the goods. If the description becomes a part of the basis of the bargain, it creates an express warranty of conformity to the description.[81] Third, if the seller uses a sample or model in making a sale, he may expressly warrant conformity of the bulk to the sample or model.[82]

The seller is not required to use any specific language or specifically intend to warrant the quality of the goods,[83] nor must the buyer show reliance on the seller's claims, as long as the seller's affirmations are part of the basis of the bargain.[84] However, the seller's opinion is merely that; even an opinion about the value of goods[85] is not a warranty.[86] The drafters of the UCC recognized that sellers often make statements of value or commendation that neither the seller nor the buyer reasonably understands to be affirmations of fact; rather, these statements are understood to be part of the seller's attempt to persuade the buyer to make the purchase.[87] In short, there is a difference between puffing and a warranty.[88] There also is no specific time limitation on a warranty,

---

[80] UCC § 2-313(1)(a) states: "Any affirmation of fact or promise made by the seller to the buyer which relates to the goods and becomes part of the basis of the bargain creates an express warranty that the goods shall conform to the affirmation or promise."

[81] UCC § 2-313(1)(b) states: "Any description of the goods which is made part of the basis of the bargain creates an express warranty that the goods shall conform to the description."

[82] UCC § 2-313(1)(c) states: "Any sample or model which is made part of the basis of the bargain creates an express warranty that the whole of the goods shall conform to the sample or model."

[83] UCC § 2-313(2).

[84] See UCC § 2-313, Official Comment 3; Campus Sweater and Sportswear Co. v. MB Kahn Constr. Co., 515 F. Supp. 64 (DSC 1979), aff'd, 644 F2d 877 (4th Cir. 1981).

[85] See, e.g., Hall v. TL Kemp Jewelry, Inc., 71 NC App. 101, 322 SE2d 7 (1984) (buyer paid $1,900 for bracelet that seller appraised at $2,650 for insurance, but two other appraisers put its value at $900 and $595, respectively; seller's statement about value was not a warranty of value).

[86] Id.

[87] See UCC § 2-313, Official Comment 8. For a consideration of what is opinion and what is an affirmation of fact in a complex transaction, see, e.g., Royal Business Machs., Inc. v. Lorraine Corp., 633 F2d 34 (7th Cir. 1980).

[88] See, e.g., Chase Resorts, Inc. v. Johns-Manville Corp., 476 F. Supp. 633 (ED Mo. 1979), aff'd, 620 F2d 203 (8th Cir. 1980).

which may be made before, at the time of, or after the sale. This is a departure from the common-law rule that postsale warranties are mere nullities and without consideration. Under Section 2-313, a postsale affirmation may be a warranty if it is intended to induce the buyer's future purchases.[89] The Official Commentary to Section 2-313 deals with the question of consideration by stating the following: "If language is used after the closing of the deal (as when the buyer when taking delivery asks and receives an additional assurance), the warranty becomes a modification, and need not be supported by consideration if it is otherwise reasonable and in order."[90]

A New York decision involving the sale and purchase of a CAT scan x-ray system, *Computerized Radiological Services, Inc. v. Syntex Corp.*,[91] illustrates the operation of Section 2-313 in most of its particulars. A group of radiologists on Long Island decided to purchase a CAT scan system in order to have the most advanced diagnostic equipment. The evidence showed that the doctors needed fast, efficient, accurate equipment because almost all radiological work comes from referrals from physicians who want fast, accurate diagnoses. The plaintiffs were in competition with other radiologists, and they wanted to be the first to offer CAT scans. When they decided to purchase a system, they had a choice of one well-established brand (the pioneer in the field) or two or three other more recent systems, including the product sold by the defendant. The defendant offered two basic systems: One was used only to scan heads, the other was used on the whole body. The basic technology of both systems used what was called a wet pack, an awkward procedure that was soon due to be superseded by new technology. The plaintiffs examined the sales literature of competing companies and talked to sales representatives. They

---

[89] See, e.g., Downie v. Abex Corp., 741 F2d 1235 (10th Cir. 1984) (seller sent brochures to buyer for distribution to buyer's customers with obvious hope that this would lead to increased business for the buyer and more purchases from the seller). For purposes of the statute of limitations, an express warranty of future performance arises at the time of the transaction, not at the time of manufacture. See UCC § 2-725(2); Ferguson v. Sturm, Ruger & Co., 524 F. Supp. 1042 (D. Conn. 1981).

[90] UCC § 2-313, Official Comment 7.

[91] Computerized Radiological Servs. v. Syntex Corp., 595 F. Supp. 1495 (EDNY 1984).

attended a session at which the defendant set up a whole-body, advanced dry model. The salesperson told the radiologists that a head-only model could be simply and inexpensively upgraded to a whole-body model by adding a simple kit. The defendant's price for the system was lower than the principal competitor's price, and, more important, the defendant offered the radiologists a much smaller down payment and a less onerous payment schedule. The plaintiffs purchased the defendant's system. However, instead of getting a head-only, dry system that could be easily upgraded, they received a head-only, wet-pack system that could not be upgraded simply. Soon thereafter, the defendant went out of the CAT scan business.

The documents of sale did not purport to warrant that the machine delivered was anything other than what it was. However, the court said that the seller's promotional sales literature, the oral representations of its sales personnel, and the model machine shown to the plaintiffs amounted to express warranties that the defendant would provide a machine with the latest technological capabilities that could perform whole-body scans when minor modifications were made. The plaintiffs clearly expressed what they wanted, and the court had little difficulty in deciding that the defendant's representations (statements of sales representatives, brochures, sales documents, and model machine) affirmed the quality of its equipment. These representations thus formed part of the inducement and were part of the basis of the bargain. This case demonstrates that in applying Section 2-313, courts are willing to look beyond the written agreement and to take into account evidence extrinsic to the documents in determining the extent of the seller's warranties.[92]

In *Interco, Inc. v. Randustrial Corp.*,[93] a seller was surprised to find that an express warranty was implied by language in its catalog that described the characteristics of a product. The buyer

---

[92] When the head-only, wet-pack scanner arrived in the plaintiffs' offices, they might have been able to rescind the deal on the basis of a fundamental mistake as to subject matter (see Chapter 8). They also could have rejected the goods as nonconforming tender under Section 2-601 (see Chapter 5). For another case holding a seller to oral representations made during the course of negotiations, see Werner v. Montana, 117 NH 721, 378 A2d 1130 (1977).

[93] Interco, Inc. v. Randustrial Corp., 533 SW2d 257 (Mo. Ct. App. 1976).

bought and used the product, a floor-refinishing agent, with good results.[94] When the buyer used it again on the basis of prior use and the refinisher's description in the manufacturer's catalog, the results were unsatisfactory. The floors were worse than they had been before the refinisher was applied, although even the seller admitted that the buyer used the product correctly.[95] The court found that the seller's catalog description amounted to an express warranty and that the failure of the product, as alleged by the plaintiff, made out a prima facie case of breach of warranty.[96] However, whether in fact there was a breach and the extent of the warranty were decisions for the jury.[97]

A statement that is not a warranty may become one because of the way the seller uses it. For example, a veterinarian offered his opinion to the owner of a racehorse that the animal's "funny"

---

[94] The product was described as follows: "Sylox is a hard yet malleable material which bonds firm to wood floors for smooth and easy hand-trucking. Sylox will absorb considerable flex without cracking and is not softened by spillage of oil, grease or solvents." Id. at 260. The plaintiff had used it to smooth out the ground floor of an older warehouse and had been pleased with the result.

[95] When the buyer used the product a second time, there apparently was too much give-and-take in the floor.

[96] The court said:

> "An important factor is whether the seller assumes to assert a fact of which the buyer is ignorant or whether the seller merely expresses an opinion on which the buyer may be expected to have an opinion and be able to express his own judgment. Weiss v. Rockwell Mfg. Co., 9 Ill. App. 3d 906, 293 NE2d 375 (1973); General Supply and Equip. Co. v. Phillips, 490 SW2d 913 (Tex. Civ. App. 1972); Carpenter v. Alberto Culver Co., 28 Mich. App. 399, 184 NW2d 547 (1970). . . . It is manifest that the words so used were meant to induce purchases through the assurance that considerable flex would be absorbed and were not mere opinion."

Interco, Inc. v. Randustrial Corp., 533 SW2d 257, 263 (Mo. Ct. App. 1976). For another case suggesting that a catalog description is an express warranty, see Peterson v. North Am. Plant Breeders, 218 Neb. 258, 354 NW2d 625 (1984). In Gladden v. Cadillac Motor Car Div., Gen. Motors Corp., 83 NJ 320, 416 A2d 394 (1980), a seller was held to statements in a brochure about the quality of automobile tires.

[97] Interco, Inc. v. Randustrial Corp., 533 SW2d 257, 263, 264 (Mo. Ct. App. (1976), citing Hawkeye-Sec. Ins. Co. v. Thomas-Grain Fumigant Co., 407 SW2d 622 (Mo. Ct. App. 1966). On the jury question, see also Judd Constr. Co. v. Bob Post, Inc., 516 P2d 449 (Colo. Ct. App. 1973); Jansse v. Hook, 1 Ill. App. 3d 318, 272 NE2d 385 (1971); Ertl Co. v. Lange Plastics Co., 158 NW2d 93 (Iowa 1968); Barb v. Wallace, 45 Md. App. 271, 412 A2d 1314 (1980); Opera v. Hym, Inc., 86 AD2d 373, 450 NYS2d 615 (1982).

breathing noises were not of any significance in terms of its soundness. That opinion was not a warranty; it was simply a statement of the veterinarian's expert opinion of the animal's health. However, when the owner had the substance of the veterinarian's opinion read over a loudspeaker at an auction, it became his warranty to the bidders that the funny noises were not evidence of the horse's unsoundness. It turned out that the veterinarian was wrong, and the owner faced a breach of warranty action brought by the disappointed purchaser.[98] Similarly, sellers have been found to have made express warranties by describing their goods as "safe" and "practically foolproof,"[99] "in good shape and good working order,"[100] "designed to safely carry working loads up to 20,000 pounds per panel,"[101] "failsafe,"[102] "mechanically A-1,"[103] "fully guaranteed,"[104] "runs good,"[105] and "built to operate safely and efficiently."[106] Most warranty cases involve problems with the quality of goods sold, but there also may be an express warranty of quantity. For example, a petroleum company became involved in a warranty case when it promised supplies of natural gas that exceeded available sources.[107]

---

[98] Slyman v. Pickwick Farms, 15 Ohio App. 3d 25, 472 NE2d 380 (1984).

[99] McCormack V. Hankscraft Co., 278 Minn. 322, 154 NW2d 488 (1967).

[100] Acme Equip. Corp. v. Montgomery Coop. Creamery Ass'n, 29 Wis. 2d 355, 138 NW2d 729 (1966).

[101] Hawkins Constr. Co. v. Matthews Co., 190 Neb. 546, 209 NW2d 643 (1973).

[102] Downie v. Abex Corp., 741 F2d 1235 (10th Cir. 1984).

[103] Jones v. Kellner, 5 Ohio App. 3d 242, 451 NE2d 548 (1982). This statement appeared in a newspaper ad for the car. It broke down as the buyer was driving home.

[104] Jones v. Cranman's Sporting Goods, 142 Ga. App. 838, 237 SE2d 402 (1977). This statement accompanied a rifle delivered to retailer and was held to be an express warranty of quality that passed to the ultimate consumer.

[105] Ekizian v. Capurro, 111 Misc. 2d 372, 444 NYS2d 361 (1981). This statement was construed to be an express warranty that the cylinder head on a car was not cracked.

[106] Falcon Tankers, Inc. v. Litton Sys., Inc., 380 A2d 569 (Del. 1977). This statement was an express warranty in connection with the sale of oil tankers that was breached when cargo pumps and expansion joints failed.

[107] Gulf Oil Corp. v. Federal Power Comm'n, 563 F2d 588 (3d Cir. 1977), cert. denied, 434 US 1062, reh'g denied, 435 US 981, cert. dismissed, 435 US 911 (1978).

Although an as-is sale excludes all warranties,[108] courts sometimes overlook as-is clauses in the documents if the seller or his agent has made substantial oral representations as part of the inducement to the purchaser.[109] If written clauses suggest a warranty, they may be read to override an as-is clause. A contract in one case stated that all property was sold "as is," but another contract clause described the "rolling stock" as being in "operating condition." This phrase created a warranty of the rolling stock.[110]

[3] Implied Warranties of Merchantability: Section 2-314

[a] Requirement That Seller Be Merchant of Goods or Services

Section 2-314 codifies and expands the common-law warranty of merchantability. It has produced substantial litigation as buyers and sellers have wrestled with the concept of merchantability within a wide range of circumstances. The warranty arises only in transactions that involve a merchant, rather than a casual seller or a seller who is not a merchant of the goods sold. "Obviously this qualification restricts the implied warranty to a much smaller group than everyone who is engaged in business and requires a professional status as to particular kinds of goods."[111] Section 2-104(1) defines a "merchant" as

> [A] person who deals in goods of the kind or otherwise by his occupation holds himself out as having knowledge or skill peculiar to the practices or goods involved in the transaction or to whom such knowledge or skill may be attributed by his employment of an agent or broker or other intermediary who

---

[108] Tenwick v. Byrd, 9 Ark. App. 340, 659 SW2d 950 (1983).

[109] See, e.g., Knipp v. Weinbaum, 351 So. 2d 1081 (Fla. Dist. Ct. App. 1977), cert. denied, 357 So. 2d 188 (Fla. 1978).

[110] Sires v. Luke, 544 F. Supp. 1155 (SD Ga. 1982). To the same effect, see Woods v. Secord, 122 NH 323, 444 A2d 539 (1982).

[111] UCC § 2-104, Official Comment 2, discussing applicability to UCC § 2-314.

by his occupation holds himself out as having such knowledge or skill.[112]

For instance, a supermarket is unquestionably a merchant for many purposes, but it is not a merchant of shopping carts provided for customers to use in carrying their selections. Both the supermarket and the customer are users of the carts, and only the manufacturer or the wholesale distributor is a merchant of the shopping carts.[113]

A retailer, however, is generally a merchant of the goods in his store within the meaning of Section 2-314 even if merchandise arrives from manufacturers in sealed containers and the retailer only displays or makes it available to customers.[114] Although the manufacturer or producer remains liable to the ultimate purchaser for sealed goods that he places in the chain of distribution,[115] it may be more convenient for a dissatisfied buyer to sue the retailer than to bring a distant manufacturer to court.

---

[112] In fact, the intended meaning of "merchant" in Section 2-314 may be even narrower than this; Section 2-314 speaks of a seller who is "a merchant with respect to goods of that kind." Vince v. Broome, 443 So. 2d 23 (Miss. 1983).

[113] See, e.g., Keen v. Dominick's Finer Foods, Inc., 49 Ill. App. 3d 480, 364 NE2d 502 (1977); Grimm v. Scoa Indus., 9 Pa. D. & C. 3d 742 (1979). Several other questions arose in these cases. Because neither shopper in *Keen* or *Grimm* bought the supermarket cart, the first issue was whether Article 2 applied in the absence of a sale. There is support for treating an equipment lease as a sale within the coverage of the UCC. See, e.g., Barco Auto Leasing Corp. v. PSI Cosmetics, Inc., 125 Misc. 2d 68, 478 NYS2d 505 (1984). But neither court thought that the use of a shopping cart could be construed as a lease of equipment. The argument that use of the cart was a necessary incident of the sale of goods was also rejected. Of course, an injured shopper may have other actions against the store (e.g., negligence) or the manufacturer (e.g., product liability or a warranty action).

[114] This has long been the rule with automobiles, partly because an automobile is a complicated machine that can be quite dangerous and because the cars that arrive at an auto dealership are inspected by expert mechanics using sophisticated equipment. Few consumers have such capabilities. When one car dealer buys from another, however, he may not be able to rely on the implied warranty of merchantability if he has had an opportunity to inspect. See, e.g., Hummel v. Skyline Dodge, Inc., 41 Colo. App. 572, 589 P2d 73 (1978). For an example of a case holding the retailer liable for breach of warranty on the sale of prepackaged and unopened goods, see Pierce v. Liberty Furniture Co., 141 Ga. App. 175, 233 SE2d 33 (1977).

[115] See, e.g., Peterson v. North Am. Plant Breeders, 218 Neb. 258, 354 NW2d 625 (1984). This case also said that the defendant's catalog description of seed corn might be an express warranty.

A person who primarily provides services also may be a merchant of the goods used in connection with his services. A Wisconsin plumber was held to be a merchant of pumps he installed even though he relied on the manufacturer's warranty that he passed along to his customers.[116] On the other hand, a milliner was held not to be the merchant of a pressing machine used to manufacture headwear because the milliner's business was the manufacture and sale of hats, not the manufacture of equipment used to make hats, and this equipment sale was an isolated one.[117] An auctioneer at a Kansas cattle auction was a merchant, according to the court, which reasoned that because he auctioned as many as 2,000 head a week, he was knowledgeable in the sale of cattle and therefore fit the definition of merchant in Section 2-104(1).[118] This of course does not mean that all auctioneers are treated as merchants; they are typically hired professionals who act on behalf of the seller and may not have any special knowledge of the goods being sold. However, professional auctioneers of particular goods such as cattle or tobacco may find themselves treated as merchants with respect to the auctioned goods. Of interest to all hospitals and their patients is a recent decision holding a hospital to be a merchant for items used in surgery.[119] A pharmacist is usually a merchant of nonprescription drugs, but not of prescription drugs. The reasoning is that in the latter instance, the purchaser relies on the physician's skill in selecting and prescribing the correct medication, and the pharmacist only follows the physician's directions.[120]

---

[116] Titus v. Polan, 72 Wis. 2d 23, 240 NW2d 420 (1976).

[117] Kates Millinery, Ltd. v. Benay-Albee Corp., 114 Misc. 2d 230, 450 NYS2d 975 (1982), aff'd, 120 Misc. 2d 429, 467 NYS2d 348 (1983). Similarly, a fire department was not a merchant for the sale of a used pumper truck. Village of Chatham v. Board of Fire Comm'rs, 90 AD2d 860, 456 NYS2d 494 (1982); see also Jatco, Inc. v. Charter Air Center, Inc., 527 F. Supp. 314 (SD Ohio 1981).

[118] Powers v. Coffeyville Livestock Sales Co., 665 F2d 311, 32 UCC Rep. 766 (10th Cir. 1981).

[119] Skelton v. Druid City Hosp. Bd., 459 So. 2d 818 (Ala. 1984).

[120] See, e.g., McLeod v. WW Merrell Co., 174 So. 2d 736 (Fla. 1965); Bichler v. Willing, 58 AD2d 331, 397 NYS2d 57 (1977); Batiste v. American Home Prods. Corp., 32 NC App. 1, 231 SE2d 269 (1977). There also is a question of whether there is a sale by the physician to the patient, thus causing the provisions of Section 2-314 to apply to the doctor. The pharmacist is still subject to the implied warranty that he has filled the prescription correctly.

[b] Requirement That Transaction Involve the Sale of Goods

The implied warranty of Section 2-314 applies to goods where there is a contract for their sale. This requirement imposes two conditions. First, the warranty only applies to sales of goods. Second, it only comes into play where there is an actual sale. "Goods" are defined in Section 2-105 to include movable chattels, unborn young of animals, growing crops, and identified things attached to realty that are severable from the realty.[121] Section 2-106 defines "contract for sale" and "sale" as:

> "Contract for sale" includes both a present sale of goods and a contract to sell goods at a future time. A "sale" consists in the passing of title from the seller to the buyer for a price (Section 2-401). A "present sale" means a sale which is accomplished by the making of the contract.

Section 2-102 is one of the general governing provisions of Article 2. This section limits the application of Article 2 to transactions in goods, a somewhat broader concept than simply a sale of goods. There is support for the argument that the sale limitation of Section 2-314 should be read in the context of the general definition of coverage in Section 2-102.[122] This is not a universally held opinion, however, and several courts have given a rather narrow reading to the sale requirement of Section 2-314. The different approaches have been especially evident in cases involving equipment leases. Some courts have said that because a lease is a lease and not a sale, Section 2-314 does not apply.[123] Other courts

---

[121] The drafters of the UCC had in mind things such as minerals. Section 2-107 discusses what may be severable from realty.

[122] 2 *Hawkland UCC Series* § 2-314:03 (1982) (hereinafter cited as Hawkland). Professor Hawkland also relies on the language in Section 2-313, Official Comment 2, suggesting a fairly broad understanding of the coverage of the warranty section of Article 2.

[123] See, e.g., R&W Leasing v. Mosher, 636 P2d 832 (Mont. 1981); see also Miller Auto Leasing Co. v. Weinstein, 189 NJ Super. 543, 461 A2d 174 (1983), aff'd, 193 NJ Super. 328, 473 A2d 996 (1984) (financer is not a seller); Staco Energy Prods. Co. v. Driver-Harris Co., 578 F. Supp. 700 (SD Ohio 1983) (a manufacturer's agent is not a seller). But cf. Smith v. Fiat-Roosevelt Motors, Inc., 556 F2d 728 (5th Cir. 1977).

have held precisely the opposite.[124] In an equipment lease, the lessee usually has virtually all the attributes and responsibilities of ownership. The lessor often is a merchant seller of the same goods (e.g., an automobile dealer who sells and leases new cars). The consumer commonly decides to lease rather than to buy for reasons unrelated to the quality of the equipment (e.g., to deduct lease payments from current taxable income). It seems more sensible to treat long-term equipment leases of automobiles, computers, or office machines as functionally equivalent to sales and within the coverage of the warranty provisions of the UCC. For all practical purposes, the transaction is the same as a sale.[125]

The sale of goods requirement has given rise to several cases that involve medical treatments. During the course of an operation in a hospital, is a blood transfusion a ''sale'' of blood to the patient, or is it the provision of a service that is incidental to the patient's overall care? If the transfused blood is tainted and gives the patient hepatitis, the answer to this question is critical in determining whether the patient has any realistic claim against the hospital for damages. It may be difficult to prove negligence or medical malpractice, but if transfused blood that has been warranted by the hospital either expressly or impliedly[126] is tainted, strict liability exists.

In a 1975 decision, the Supreme Court of West Virginia determined that a blood transfusion was not covered by UCC warranties because it was an incidental transfer of personal property in con-

---

[124] See, e.g., Pisano v. American Leasing, 146 Cal. App. 3d 194, 194 Cal. Rptr. 77 (1983); Barco Auto Leasing Corp. v. PSI Cosmetics, Inc., 125 Misc. 2d 68, 478 NYS2d 505 (1984).

[125] This is particularly true in connection with automobiles. Leasing is a marketing tool that is used not only with businesses but also with private consumers because a lease may present an easier financial package for the consumer than a purchase. The lessee might be able to lease a car for sixty months at a fairly modest monthly rental charge and then decide whether to keep the car by making a balloon payment or whether to turn it in and take a new one on a similar basis. The transaction is the same as a purchase, except the consumer never has to tie up a significant amount of capital. The car is covered by the standard manufacturer's warranty, the consumer acquires insurance in the same way, and the car is registered in the consumer's name.

[126] Of course, there may be a question whether there is an implied warranty that all blood used in transfusions is good. See McMichael v. American Red Cross, 532 SW2d 7 (Ky. 1975).

nection with a contract for the provision of professional services.[127] However, a New Jersey court had no difficulty at all in deciding that a blood transfusion was a sale covered by the UCC, although it rejected the plaintiff's claim of a breach of the implied warranty of merchantability and said that the plaintiff had to prove breach of an express warranty (or negligence on his tort count).[128] A similar case held that the failure of a heart-lung machine during open-heart surgery was not a breach of the implied warranty of Section 2-314 because there was no sale of the machine.[129] In two other cases, neither a radiological technician nor a hospital was the merchant of a patient's radiation treatments,[130] but a hospital was held to be a merchant subject to the coverage of the UCC for equipment used during the patient's operation.[131]

No clear pattern emerges in these medical cases. They raise questions of fact common to many other cases in which a court must determine whether the principal purpose of a contractual agreement is to provide services or to transfer title to goods.[132]

[c] Requirement That Goods Be Merchantable

Even if a buyer proves all the other elements of an action under Section 2-314, he still may fail to recover if he cannot show that the goods bought were not merchantable. The UCC applies a general market definition of merchantability. The buyer's satisfaction and the suitability of the goods to his particular needs are not the keys to this definition; rather, the test is whether the goods are of the kind and quality normally expected in the trade. To this end,

---

[127] Foster v. Memorial Hosp. Ass'n, 159 W. Va. 147, 219 SE2d 916 (1975), and see Jennings v. Roosevelt Hosp., 83 Misc. 2d 1, 372 NYS2d 277 (1975); see also Schuchman v. Johns Hopkins Hosp., 9 UCC Rep. 637 (Md. Super. Ct. 1971) (hospital not a merchant); McMichael v. American Red Cross, 532 SW2d 7 (Ky. 1975) (implied warranty of merchantability inapplicable because of difficulty in policing quality of blood).

[128] Jackson v. Muhlenberg Hosp., 96 NJ Super. 314, 232 A2d 879 (1967), rev'd on other grounds, 53 NJ 138, 249 A2d 65 (1969).

[129] Redwine v. Baptist Gen. Convention, 681 P2d 1121 (Okla. Ct. App. 1982).

[130] Nevauex v. Park Place Hosp., Inc., 656 SW2d 923 (Tex. Ct. App. 1983).

[131] Skelton v. Druid City Hosp. Bd., 459 So. 2d 818 (Ala. 1984).

[132] See supra ¶ 4.03[1].

Section 2-314 lists six general standards of quality.[133] These standards are not exhaustive, and other implied warranties may arise from the course of dealing between the seller and buyer or from the usages of the trade.[134] The burden is on the buyer to prove the existence and the breach of the implied warranty,[135] although he need not prove his actual reliance on the warranty.[136] The existence of breach in merchantability cases is usually determined by a jury's examination of the circumstances.[137]

There are hundreds of reported opinions on the subject of merchantability, and they are as varied as the cases themselves. The following rules seem to apply generally in merchantability cases:

(1) The warranty is satisfied if the goods are suitable for ordinary use even if they are not perfect.[138]

---

[133] UCC § 2-314(2) states:

"Goods to be merchantable must be at least such as

"(a) pass without objection in the trade under the contract description; and

"(b) in the case of fungible goods, are of fair average quality within the description; and

"(c) are fit for the ordinary purposes for which such goods are used; and

"(d) run, within the variations permitted by the agreement, of even kind, quality and quantity within each unit and among all units involved; and

"(e) are adequately contained, packaged, and labeled as the agreement may require; and

"(f) conform to the promises or affirmations of fact made on the container or label if any."

See also UCC § 2-314, Official Comments 6, 7, 8, 9. Official Comment 6 says, for instance, that "the intention is to leave open other possible attributes of merchantability."

[134] UCC § 2-314(3).

[135] See, e.g., RG Moeller Co. v. Van Kampen Constr. Co., 57 Mich. App. 308, 225 NW2d 742 (1975).

[136] See, e.g., El Fredo Pizza, Inc. v. Roto-Flex Oven Co., 199 Neb. 697, 261 NW2d 358 (1978).

[137] See, e.g., Ploof v. BIM Truck Serv., Inc., 53 AD2d 750, 384 NYS2d 521 (1976).

[138] See, e.g., Nassau Suffolk White Trucks, Inc. v. Twin County Transit Mix Corp., 62 AD2d 982, 403 NYS2d 322 (1978).

(2) There is no breach if the defects in the product are minor and repairable by the seller.[139]

(3) If the buyer refuses to allow the seller to try to repair the defects, he may forfeit his remedy for breach of warranty.[140]

(4) Negligent installation by the buyer is not a defense to a warranty action if the defect existed in the goods before they were installed (this may create difficulties in proving damages).[141]

(5) After the goods are tendered, the buyer must either give the seller reasonable notice of the alleged breach of warranty under Section 2-607(3)(a) or waive the breach by accepting the nonconforming goods.[142]

(6) If the seller is to be allowed to exercise his right to cure under Section 2-508, he must have notice of the problem.

(7) When the buyer gives notice of defects and the seller elects to attempt to cure them by repairing the merchandise, the statute of limitations is tolled while the seller is working on the goods.[143]

(8) If the buyer inspects the goods before they are delivered and finds they are acceptable, he may waive any subsequent right to claim a breach of warranty.[144]

---

[139] See, e.g., Tallmadge v. Aurora Chrysler Plymouth, Inc., 25 Wash. App. 90, 605 P2d 1275 (1979); see also UCC § 2-508 on the seller's right to cure; ¶ 5.04[7].

[140] See, e.g., Pronti v. DML of Elmira, Inc., 103 AD2d 916, 478 NYS2d 156 (1984). This case involved an express warranty that furniture would be delivered "in perfect condition." The same reasoning should apply to an implied warranty case.

[141] See, e.g., Duff v. Bonner Bldg. Supply, Inc., 103 Idaho 432, 649 P2d 391 (1982), aff'd, 105 Idaho 123, 666 P2d 650 (1983).

[142] This may not be too onerous if the defects are not obvious. In a case involving defects in insulation, a court ruled that filing a lawsuit one year after discovery of the defects complied with the reasonable-notice requirements of Section 2-607(3)(a). Shooshanian v. Wagner, 672 P2d 455 (Alaska 1983).

[143] Colorado-Ute Elec. Ass'n v. Envirotech Corp., 524 F. Supp. 1152 (D. Colo. 1981).

[144] See, e.g., Hummel v. Skyline Dodge, Inc., 41 Colo. App. 572, 589 P2d 73 (1978); Consolidated Supply Co. v. Babbitt, 96 Idaho 636, 534 P2d 466 (1975).

Beyond these fairly broad rules, other factors come into play, as several cases illustrate. A mobile home with formaldehyde-based insulation was not merchantable because the formaldehyde caused the buyers to suffer allergic reactions.[145] However, the purchaser of a nonprescription topical analgesic suffered a severe allergic reaction but had no claim for breach of an implied warranty.[146] These different results at case law clearly indicate the meaning of merchantability. Formaldehyde causes allergic reactions in many people and the health hazards of its use are well-known. Although it may not be as dangerous as asbestos, for instance, its use in a home can render the home uninhabitable for a significant percentage of the population. The topical analgesic in the second case, however, is used regularly and safely by thousands of people with no side effects, and it must be assumed that the plaintiff's reaction was extremely unusual. The implied warranty of merchantability is not a warranty of freedom from all defects, nor is it a basis for asserting strict product liability. It is only a warranty that the goods conform to the general standards of the trade and that they are fairly useful for their intended purposes.[147]

The customs of the local trade also are important. For example, a buyer who ordered sheetrock expected to receive a certain type and quality of the material. The seller delivered laminated sheetrock, which was not what the buyer had in mind. The buyer was unable to make a case for breach of the implied warranty, however, because in the local trade the term "sheetrock" typically included laminated as well as other types of sheetrock, and the delivered goods were generally suitable for their intended use.[148] A seller lost in another case in which the buyer ordered steel without designating the quality required, because the buyer was able to

[145] Tiderman v. Fleetwood Homes of Wash., 102 Wash. 2d 334, 684 P2d 1302 (1984).

[146] Griggs v. Combe, Inc., 456 So. 2d 790 (Ala. 1984).

[147] A good example of a consumer products case is Virgil v. Kash N' Karry Serv. Corp., 61 Md. App. 23, 484 A2d 652 (1984). When the plaintiff added milk to hot coffee that she had poured into a thermos, the thermos imploded, causing injury to the plaintiff. This was a breach of the implied warranty of merchantability because the product failed in the course of normal and expected use.

[148] Tracor, Inc. v. Austin Supply and Drywall Co., 484 SW2d 446 (Tex. Civ. App. 1972).

show that the local trade usage implied that steel so ordered would be of "commercial quality."[149]

In some cases, the performance of the goods in use determines the question of a breach of warranty. Linoleum that turned yellow shortly after it was installed did not measure up to the standard of merchantability.[150] Building studs that warped, buckled, and bowed were not of "fair, average quality" within the meaning of Section 2-314.[151] A buyer who contracted trichinosis after eating pork tried to prove a breach of the implied warranty that pork sold for human consumption is free of disease-causing microbes. The plaintiff lost because the seller showed that it is impossible to contract trichinosis if pork is cooked properly.[152] At first, this case seems to apply a standard of contributory negligence, but it is simply an application of the general standards of Section 2-314. Heating pork to a certain temperature removes any danger of trichinosis and it is fairly common knowledge that even the most carefully handled fresh pork may carry trichinosis. Thus, meat that is safe for consumption if properly cooked is merchantable. Interestingly, the standard is different for beef because many people consume beef that is quite rare or even raw.

[4] Implied Warranties of Fitness for a Particular Purpose: Section 2-315

The implied warranty of fitness for a particular purpose focuses on the agreement between the buyer and the seller rather than on external standards of suitability. A product that meets all the requirements of Section 2-314 may not satisfy Section 2-315 if the seller has agreed to produce according to the buyer's specifications.[153] There may be an express warranty, but the seller can be held under Section 2-315 for warranting goods to meet the buyer's

---

[149] Ambassador Steel Co. v. Ewald Steel Co., 33 Mich. App. 495, 190 NW2d 275 (1971).

[150] Mindell v. Raleigh Rug Co., 14 UCC Rep. 1124 (Mass. Hous. Ct. 1974).

[151] Jetero Constr. Co. v. South Memphis Lumber Co., 531 F2d 1348 (6th Cir. 1976).

[152] Huebner v. Hunter Packing Co., 59 Ill. App. 3d 563, 16 Ill. Dec. 766, 375 NE2d 873 (1978).

[153] Warranties are cumulative. See UCC § 2-315, Official Comment 2; UCC § 2-317; infra ¶ 4.04[6].

request even if he does not expressly warrant them. Section 2-315 reads:

> Where the seller at the time of contracting has reason to know any particular purpose for which the goods are required and that the buyer is relying on the seller's skill or judgment to select or furnish suitable goods, there is unless excluded or modified under the next section an implied warranty that the goods shall be fit for such purpose.

There are two operative requirements for the implied warranty of fitness: (1) the seller must have reason to know at the time of contracting (not later) that the buyer is purchasing for a particular purpose; and (2) the buyer must rely on the seller to provide satisfactory goods. Unlike other UCC warranties, the implied warranty of fitness explicitly requires a showing of the buyer's reliance, although the reliance is on the seller's skill or judgment rather than on the seller's affirmations of fact about the quality of the goods.

Cases under Section 2-315 often center on the communications between buyer and seller. The buyer must inform the seller by some means of his requirements. Alternatively, the circumstances of the transaction must be such that it can be reasonably inferred that the seller is familiar with the buyer's needs.[154] A seller is not expected to anticipate every use of his goods,[155] but he must reasonably anticipate the buyer's requirements. For example, a seller who knew that his buyer was an inexperienced farmer was liable for a violation of the Section 2-315 warranty for selling unsatisfactory farm equipment.[156] The seller must let the buyer know of any potential problems he foresees. It is not enough for the seller to say that he is reluctant to sell the goods for the buyer's intended use — only to make the sale nonetheless — without specifying the reasons for his reluctance.[157]

---

[154] See, e.g., Myers v. Montgomery Ward & Co., 253 Md. 282, 252 A2d 855 (1969).

[155] Section 2-315 does not provide general "lemon protection." See, e.g., Royal Lincoln-Mercury Sales, Inc. v. Wallace, 415 So. 2d 1024 (Miss. 1982).

[156] Massey-Ferguson, Inc. v. Evans, 406 So. 2d 15 (Miss. 1981). A seller who knew that a farmer wanted a hay baler capable of handling a 3,000-pound bale was in breach of the Section 2-315 warranty for providing a baler that only handled an average 1,400-pound bale. Agar v. Kysar, 628 P2d 1350 (Wyo. 1981).

[157] Addis v. Bernardin, Inc., 226 Kan. 241, 597 P2d 250 (1979).

[5] Exclusion and Modification of Express and Implied Warranties: Section 2-316

Despite the treatment of warranties under Sections 2-314 and 2-315, Section 2-316 allows the seller to protect himself from warranty liability by excluding or limiting both express and implied warranties either by words or actions. Some specific rules follow, however, and Section 2-316(1) presents a significant catch that negates "unreasonable" limitations:

> Words or conduct relevant to the creation of an express warranty and words or conduct tending to negate or limit warranty shall be construed wherever reasonable as consistent with each other; but subject to the provisions of this Article on parol or extrinsic evidence (Section 2-202), negation or limitation is inoperative to the extent that such construction is unreasonable.

The principal purpose of Section 2-316(1) is to protect the unsuspecting buyer from standard form agreements that exclude all warranties where the language of the agreement is inconsistent with the representations made by the seller during the course of negotiations.[158] If the agreement contains both an express warranty and a disclaimer, the warranty prevails.[159]

Section 2-316(2) sets forth specific rules for the exclusion of implied warranties. To exclude the implied warranty of merchantability, the seller must specifically use the word merchantability in the exclusion and any writing must be conspicuous. Similarly, the warranty of fitness for a particular purpose can be excluded only by a writing that is conspicuous. Section 2-316(2) suggests that the following sentence successfully excludes the implied warranty of

---

[158] In the words of the UCC drafters: "It seeks to protect a buyer from unexpected and unbargained language of disclaimer by denying effect to such language when inconsistent with language of express warranty and permitting the exclusion of implied warranties only by conspicuous language or other circumstances which protect the buyer from surprise." UCC § 2-316, Official Comment 1. A good example is Gladden v. Cadillac Motor Car Div., Gen. Motors Corp., 83 NJ 320, 416 A2d 394 (1980). The warranty accompanying the tires for an automobile limited the buyer's remedy for a breach of warranty to replacement of the tires. The court refused to enforce this limitation because the seller's general representations about the quality of the automobile, including the tires, were much broader. This case should be read in connection with Section 2-302 and the cases on unconscionability. See Chapter 12.

[159] See, e.g., Wenner v. Gulf Oil Corp., 264 NW2d 374 (Minn. 1978).

fitness for a particular purpose: "There are no warranties which extend beyond the description on the face hereof."[160] Such a sentence still does not exclude the implied warranty of merchantability, however, because it does not contain the word merchantability.[161] The point is clear enough. To exclude the implied warranties of Sections 2-314 and 2-315, the seller must be straightforward and the language of exclusion cannot be hidden in the fine print on the back of an invoice.[162]

Section 2-316(2) does not stand alone. It is modified by Section 2-316(3), which states that warranties may be excluded or limited by any of the following: (1) descriptive phrases in the agreement such as "with all faults" or "as is";[163] (2) the buyer's prior inspection of the goods if an examination would have revealed defects in merchandise he later could complain of;[164] (3) the course of the sales agreement between the parties to the sale; or (4) the customs of the trade.[165] Usually, the burden is on the seller to prove a course of dealing that negates an implied warranty, and simply using a standard form invoice over and over again is insufficient to show a trade custom.[166] Exclusion by common phrases such as "with all faults" may be ineffective, however, if other clauses of a written agreement are inconsistent or if the seller has made representations of quality during the negotiations that have become part of the basis of the bargain.[167] Furthermore, the buyer's inspection must be more than a cursory glance. The drafters of the UCC had in mind the buyer's meaningful examination of goods before entering into the contract, not simply an inspection upon

---

[160] UCC § 2-316(2).

[161] See, e.g., Insurance Corp. of N. Am. v. Automatic Sprinkler Corp. of Am., 62 Ohio St. 2d 91, 423 NE2d 151 (1981).

[162] See, e.g., Pennington Grain and Seed, Inc. v. Tuten, 422 So. 2d 948 (Fla. Dist. Ct. App. 1982) (failure of seeds to produce any crop was a breach of the implied warranties of merchantability and fitness for a particular purpose; limitation of liability clause was inoperative because it "had not been bargained for").

[163] UCC § 2-316(3)(a).

[164] UCC § 2-316(3)(b).

[165] UCC § 2-316(3)(c). Section 2-316(4) refers to Sections 2-718 and 2-719 on the limitation of remedies for breach of warranty.

[166] See, e.g., Hartwig Farms, Inc. v. Pacific Gamble Robinson Co., 28 Wash. App. 539, 625 P2d 171 (1981).

[167] See, e.g., Sires v. Luke, 544 F. Supp. 1155 (SD Ga. 1982); Knipp v. Weinbaum, 351 So. 2d 1081 (Fla. Dist. Ct. App. 1977), cert. denied, 357 So. 2d 188 (Fla. 1978).

delivery. They expressly rejected the application of the doctrine of caveat emptor as a rationale for the general exclusion of warranties.[168]

[6] Cumulation and Resolution of Conflicting Warranties: Section 2-317

Section 2-317 outlines the rules that apply where more than one express or implied warranty exists in an agreement and where there are actual or potential conflicts among the warranties. The predominant rule of interpretation is to construe warranties as consistent with one another or, if that is impossible, to ascertain the intentions of the parties. To determine the intentions of the parties, Section 2-317 provides three rules of construction: (1) exact or technical specifications prevail over general language or an inconsistent model; (2) a sample from the bulk prevails over general descriptive language; and (3) express warranties prevail over inconsistent implied warranties, except the implied warranty of fitness for a particular purpose.[169] This section continues the tendency to favor the existence of warranties over vague and general attempts to exclude them. In case law, for example, statements about the speed of a computer made in the machine's specifications prevailed over a general disclaimer clause in the sales contract.[170]

[7] Privity and Third-Party Beneficiaries: Section 2-318

Section 2-318 maintains the general trend away from the strict common-law doctrine of privity. The purpose of Section 2-318 is to extend the coverage of a seller's warranty to people who may be expected to use a product even if they are not in privity with the seller. The UCC suggests three alternatives for states to consider. The first covers people in the buyer's family or household and guests in the buyer's home as long as it is reasonable to expect these people to "use, consume or be affected by the goods." The

---

[168] UCC § 2-316, Official Comment 8. For a discussion of the examination standards, see, e.g., Holm v. Hansen, 248 NW2d 503 (Iowa 1976); Twin Lakes Mfg. Co. v. Coffey, 222 Va. 467, 281 SE2d 864 (1981).

[169] UCC §§ 2-317(a)–2-317(c). There may be a disclaimer of implied warranties and an effective express warranty. See, e.g., Delhomme Indus., Inc. v. Houston Beechcraft, Inc., 669 F2d 1049 (5th Cir. 1982).

[170] Consolidated Data Terminals v. Applied Digital Data Sys., Inc., 708 F2d 385 (9th Cir. 1983).

second alternative goes farther and extends coverage to "any natural person who may reasonably be expected to use, consume or be affected by the goods." Both these alternatives are limited to claims for personal injury,[171] and the seller cannot exclude or limit the operation of either alternative. The third alternative covers the same class of people as the second but extends coverage to claims for any injury. Under this alternative, the seller cannot exclude or limit liability for personal injury; presumably, however, other UCC provisions on the limitation of liability apply to other kinds of injuries. Although the first alternative has been the most popular choice of the states, a substantial number of jurisdictions have opted for the more extensive coverages of the second and third alternatives.[172]

Whichever alternative a state chooses, it still must deal with the issue of reasonable expectation. This was at the heart of an Indiana circuit court case. The owners of an above-ground swimming pool had no further use for it and gave it to a neighbor, who set it up in his back yard. Unfortunately, the neighbor dived into the four-feet-deep water, suffered a broken back, and became paralyzed. The hapless diver brought suit against the swimming pool manufacturer for breach of an implied warranty of fitness for the usual purposes of swimming and diving but was denied standing because he had no privity under Section 2-318. Indiana had adopted the first privity alternative, and the neighbor was not a member of the buyer's family or household. The court could not stretch the facts enough to find him to be a guest, even though the original buyers had given him the pool as a friendly gesture.[173] In comparison, Section 2-318 is most commonly used in automobile cases in which it is reasonable to assume that the family car is used to transport all members of the family as well as occasional guests.

---

[171] See, e.g., Pronti v. DML of Elmira, Inc., 103 AD2d 916, 478 NYS2d 156 (1984), citing Miller v. General Motors Corp., 99 AD2d 454, 471 NYS2d 280 (1984), aff'd, 64 NY2d 1081, 479 NE2d 249, 489 NYS2d 904 (1985).

[172] See generally Hawkland § 2-318.

[173] Corbin v. Coleco Indus., Inc., 748 F2d 411, 39 UCC Rep. 1242 (7th Cir. 1984). Even if the neighbor were a guest, he would still have to show reasonable expectation that the pool could be used as a diving pool and that there was an implied warranty that included use for diving by adults, which would be problematic at best.

CHAPTER 5

Conditions

¶ 5.01 CONDITIONS AND COVENANTS

[1] Distinction Between Conditions and Covenants

Every contract involves covenants, which are promises between the parties to the contract about their mutual obligations. The breach of one of these promises is a breach of the contract, and the nonbreaching party has a right to seek the remedies available for a breach.[1] Whether the breach is material enough to be a repudiation[2] or whether it is insignificant varies, depending on the facts of the particular transaction and the intentions of the parties.

The failure of a condition, however, has altogether different ramifications. A condition is an uncertain event external to the contract that may or may not occur.[3] The passage of time is not a condition because it is certain to occur. Weather, health, and the actions of third parties are examples of common conditions. Although one of the parties to the agreement may be able to influence the occurrence of a condition,[4] its incidence ultimately is a matter of fate or of the decision of one or more third parties. In comparison, covenants are almost always within the control of the contracting parties.[5] If a failure of a condition occurs, no performance is due. If the failure of a condition predates performance,

---

[1] The available remedies are numerous, as discussed in Chapters 6 through 12.

[2] See ¶ 3.02[2].

[3] In the language of the second Restatement, a condition is "an event, not certain to occur, which must occur, unless occurrence is excused, before performance under a contract becomes due." Restatement (Second) of Contracts § 224 (1981).

[4] See infra ¶¶ 5.03[1], 5.03[2] for a discussion of the obligation to satisfy conditions.

[5] At least the parties make that tacit assumption when they enter into their agreement. For a consideration of what happens when intervening circumstances remove a party's ability to control a contract promise, see Chapters 8 and 9.

the contract never comes into existence. If the condition fails to occur after performance has begun, the contract ceases to exist.[6]

Conditions may be express or implied. An express condition is either agreed upon by the parties, who then make it a part of the contract, or it is imposed on the agreement as a matter of law. An implied condition arises either from the actions of the parties or from the court's interpretation of the meaning of the covenants contained in the agreement. Implied conditions are related to the general duty of good faith.[7] The failure of a condition defeats the contract, and by implying one a court may defeat the purpose of the parties to have an agreement if the implied condition does not occur. Implying a covenant does not have such a radical effect. The breach of an implied covenant does not defeat the contract; it is merely a breach for which normal contract remedies are available.

[2] Source of Conditions: Defeasible Bonds at Common Law

The modern theory of conditions has its roots in the use of defeasible bonds in cases dating from fourteenth-century England. Defeasible bonds were a common corollary to debt transactions. If George borrowed a sum from Henry, he often executed a bond for a larger sum due on a date certain after the date for the repayment of the loan. This gave Henry the security of a bond as well as a claim sounding in debt if George was to default on the debt. It also provided an incentive for George to repay the debt to avoid the larger and absolute obligation of the bond. A suit on the bond was procedurally more simple and more certain in its outcome for

---

[6] A condition is an event not certain to occur that must occur, unless its nonoccurrence is excused, before performance under the contract becomes due. First Nat'l Bank of DeKalb County v. National Bank of Ga., 249 Ga. 216, 290 SE2d 55 (1982); Wolverine Ins. Co. v. Sorrough, 122 Ga. App. 556, 177 SE2d 819 (1970). "In technical legal usage the term 'condition' has gradually taken on the meaning of something so fundamental to the object of the contract that its failure to occur effects a release from contractual obligation or a discharge of the contract." Kessler & Gilmore, *Contracts* 813, 814 (2d ed. 1970).

[7] See infra ¶ 5.03.

Henry than a suit on the debt.[8] Language of defeasance in the bond rendered it null and void if George paid his debt to Henry on time. Nonpayment of the bond was the condition to its enforcement, and if payment occurred, the bond was worthless. Similarly, performance nullified bonds that were used to secure performance in land transactions or in contracts involving mutual covenants.[9]

[3] Shift From Independent to Dependent Covenants at Common Law

At common law, covenants in bilateral agreements were regarded as independent — that is, the obligation of one party to perform did not depend on performance by the other party. In *Nicholas v. Raynbred,* a famous seventeenth-century case, the contract at issue was for the purchase of a cow.[10] In an action for the price, the seller was not required to plead and prove tender and delivery of the cow. It was enough to show an exchange of promises. The buyer was not entirely out of luck, however. Although he could not defend against the action for the price by averring nondelivery of the cow, he was free to bring his own action on the seller's promise to deliver. Presumably, the damages for the two breaches would even out.[11]

This cumbersome approach was reformed in 1773, when Lord Mansfield adopted the more commonsensical idea of treating many covenants as dependent. As a result of this approach, breach problems could be handled in one action, and the defendant could offer an excuse for nonperformance based on the plaintiff's own failure to perform. Mansfield's opinion in *Kingston v. Preston* established a common-law basis for dependent covenants:

> There are three kinds of covenants: 1. Such as are called mutual and independent, where either party may recover dam-

---

[8] The transaction that forms the basis for Shakespeare's *The Merchant of Venice* was almost exactly like this, although the average bond was not for a pound of flesh cut nearest the heart.

[9] See generally Simpson, *A History of the Common Law of Contract* 90, 91 (1975).

[10] Nicholas v. Raynbred, 80 Eng. Rep. 238 (KB 1615).

[11] See, e.g., Pordage v. Cole, 85 Eng. Rep. 449 (KB 1669).

> ages from the other, for the injury he may have received by a breach of the covenants in his favour, and where it is no excuse for the defendant to allege a breach of the covenants on the part of the plaintiff. 2. There are covenants, which are conditions and dependent, in which the performance of one depends on the prior performance of another, and therefore, till this prior condition is performed, the other party is not liable to an action on his covenant. 3. There is also a third sort of covenants, which are mutual conditions to be performed at the same time; and, in these, if one party was ready, and offered, to perform his part, and the other neglected, or refused, to perform his, he who was ready, and offered, has fulfilled his engagement, and may maintain an action for the default of the other; though it is not certain that either is obliged to do the first act.[12]

The independent covenant approach that allowed a party in breach to sue on the covenants of the other party without proving his own performance created anomalies and was inefficient. However, the introduction of the notion of dependent covenants in which performance of one party becomes a condition for performance of the other created its own problems. When the condition for performance is wholly external (e.g., performance depends on the weather), matters of proof are fairly simple and there is little question about good faith. But conditions for performance are more often within the control of the parties to a covenant. When a covenant that is a condition is breached, a court must decide whether the parties have acted in good faith and whether the covenant has been fulfilled or at least has been performed to the point of satisfying the condition. Of course, the court first must decide whether a particular covenant should be treated as a condition.[13] For instance, is nonpayment of one installment of a long-term debt obligation a failure of a condition that occasions a default and an acceleration of the entire obligation? Although Lord Mansfield's sensible analysis altered the notion of independent obligation, it also initiated issues that continue to be important in the interpretation of mutual obligations of performance in a contract.

---

[12] Kingston v. Preston, 99 Eng. Rep. 437 (KB 1773).

[13] For a discussion of this issue, see generally Grieg, "Condition — Or Warranty?" 89 LQ Rev. 93 (1973).

[4] Conditions as a Form of Wager

There is no reason why the parties to an agreement cannot make almost anything that is not illegal or unconscionable a condition to their performance. It is simply a part of the freedom of contract to choose to make performance conditional on identified contingencies. This means that contracts on conditions may come close to being wagering contracts. In a classic nineteenth-century case, *Gray v. Gardner,*[14] the defendant agreed to pay the plaintiff the sum of $5,198.87

> [O]n the condition that if a greater quantity of sperm oil should arrive in whaling vessels at Nantucket and New Bedford, on or between the first day of April and the first day of October of the present year, both inclusive, than arrived at said places, in whaling vessels, on or within the same term of time the last year, then this obligation [is] void.

The whole case hinged on the question of whether one vessel arrived at Nantucket on October 1. Even though the vessel appeared in Nantucket Roads on October 1, the court did not consider this to be an arrival within the meaning of the contract, which could only occur when the ship moored or dropped anchor in the harbor. That did not occur until after the specified date.

The decision in *Gray* established two principles that continue to govern cases decided today. First, nothing is inherently wrong in using conditions to set up agreements that are essentially bets on the likelihood of a contingency.[15] Freedom of contract overcomes whatever reluctance there might be in giving public approval to wagers. Second, the question of the occurrence or nonoccurrence of a condition is essentially one of contract interpretation and is subject to the normal rules of interpretation. The intention of the parties manifested in the written agreement and in their own actions is given effect by the court, which must untangle ambiguities in the meaning of the contract terms.

---

[14] Gray v. Gardner, 17 Mass. 188 (1821).

[15] "Both parties put themselves upon a nice point in this contract; it was a kind of wager as to the quantity of oil which should arrive at the ports mentioned before a certain period. They must be held strictly to their contract, there being no equity to interfere with the terms of it." Id. at 190.

¶ 5.02 REMEDIAL CONSEQUENCES

[1] Conditions Precedent and Subsequent

In *Gray v. Gardner,*[16] the court placed the burden of proof on the party seeking discharge because of the failure of a condition. This made sense; the party who should have performed but who claimed an excuse should bear the burden of proving his excuse. That has not always been so clear, however. Courts traditionally have distinguished between conditions precedent and conditions subsequent. Simply put, a condition precedent must occur before there is an obligation to perform, whereas a condition subsequent is something that occurs after performance has begun that removes the obligation to perform and returns the parties to the status quo before performance began. Although the second Restatement of Contracts eschews the distinction between precedent and subsequent conditions and speaks only in terms of conditions,[17] courts, commentators, and practitioners continue to make the distinction, and it is useful to be aware of the differences in pleading and proving one or the other.

If a condition precedent fails to occur, no obligation ripens. For example, if Sam agrees to cut Tom's hay tomorrow "if it does not rain," a rainless day is a prerequisite, or condition precedent, to Sam's obligation to perform. If there is rain, then there is no contract.[18] It is not always this clear, however. What if there is a light drizzle, or if it rains early in the morning when Sam is getting ready for work, but stops in time for him to cut the hay?[19] Who decides what is "rain" within the meaning of the contract, and who has the burden of proving whether or not the condition was met?

The general rule is that the plaintiff has the burden of proof for

---

[16] See supra ¶ 5.01[4].

[17] Restatement (Second) of Contracts § 224 (1981).

[18] Compare, e.g., a promise to cut Tom's hay on the next day without rain. There is a condition — a rainless day — but the contract is not extinguished by one, two, or more rainy days. The obligation to perform does not ripen until there is a rainless day, but the covenant to perform when there is a rainless day continues from day to day. Of course, if there is an unusually rainy season, the parties may run into the question of what is a reasonable time for the covenant to continue to hold.

[19] Of course, the hay may be too wet to cut anyway, but assume that it is not.

a condition precedent and the defendant has the burden for a condition subsequent. Thus, if Sam does not perform and cites rain as the reason for his nonperformance, Tom must prove that it was not raining and that the condition to Sam's obligation to perform had been satisfied. This burden of proof may not be too onerous, however. Rule 9(c) of the Federal Rules of Civil Procedure allows a plaintiff to allege generally that all conditions precedent have been performed or have occurred, and the onus then shifts to the defendant to plead the nonoccurrence of a condition.[20] In a federal action or in a state with rules of procedure similar to those of the federal courts, the problem of proof thus may not be critical in the early stages of litigation. A general plea will probably survive a motion to dismiss, but at some point the plaintiff will have to tender evidence that supports the allegations in the complaint, however general they may be.

Conditions subsequent are more likely to occur in property transactions as conditions on a deed, although they also appear occasionally in ordinary contract situations. For example, a father might promise a settlement and an annuity if his daughter and her affianced get married. The subsequent marriage thus is both the consideration for the father's promise and the condition to his obligation.[21]

Some insurance policies are written in terms of conditions subsequent even though the conditions are not so designated. Consider the following general condition in an animal insurance policy: "The insured shall file with the Company a detailed sworn proof of loss within sixty days after the death of the animal."[22] The policy also commits the company to pay a stated sum for the death or injury of identified animals that results from various categories of accidents and illnesses. The insurance company's obligation to pay ripens when an insured animal dies as a result of one of the risks against which it is insured, but the obligation to pay may be discharged if the insured does not file a proof of loss within sixty days of the animal's death. Filing the proof of loss thus becomes a

---

[20] Lumbermens Mut. Ins. Co. v. Bowman, 313 F2d 381 (10th Cir. 1963). See generally Murphy & Speidel, *Studies in Contract Law* 820 n.2 (2d ed. 1977).

[21] See, e.g., DeCicco v. Schweizer, 221 NY 431, 117 NE 807 (1917).

[22] This condition comes from a livestock mortality policy of the American Bankers Insurance Company of Florida.

condition subsequent to the liability of the insurer. In practice, this means that the burden of pleading and proving the failure of the condition subsequent — the giving of notice — falls on the company. Rule 8(c) of the Federal Rules of Civil Procedure makes the nonoccurrence of a condition subsequent an affirmative defense.[23] The obligation to file proof of loss can be stated in terms of a condition precedent — for example, "There is no obligation on the part of the company until the insured files a claim and any such claim must be filed within sixty days of the incident giving rise to the claim." The initial burden of proof is thus on the insured rather than the insurance company.

Professor Farnsworth, the chief architect of the second Restatement, has stated that one of the reasons for the Restatement's failure to distinguish between conditions precedent and subsequent was to avoid the mechanistic allocation of the burden of proof. In his view, the burden of proof should be on the party who has the principal interest in the condition or who is in the better position to proffer evidence on the issue. He gives the example of a contract for the painting of a house to the owner's satisfaction. The burden should be on the owner to prove or disprove the condition of satisfaction rather than on the painter to try to prove why his work should be satisfactory.[24] However, the second Restatement has not been published long enough to discern any trends, and it is also not clear whether courts will change their precedents on matters of proof as a result of the American Law Institute's approach to the question.[25]

[2] Forfeiture

Courts disfavor what they refer to as forfeiture. In the context of conditions, this means that courts prefer to interpret an agreement in a way that gives effect to the apparent agreement rather than to interpret it in a way that removes the obligation to perform

---

[23] See also Title Guar. & Sur. Co. v. Nichols, 224 US 346 (1912).

[24] Farnsworth, *Contracts* § 8.2, at 542, 543 (1982) (hereinafter cited as Farnsworth).

[25] There is the further question whether the second Restatement should be read as a "restatement" of the prevailing currents of the common law or as a statement of the drafters' idea of what the law should be.

by finding a condition, as opposed to a covenant, that has not been performed.[26] It is difficult for a court to overlook an express condition, but there may be enough ambiguity to support an interpretation that preserves the contract and the obligation to perform. In *Gray v. Gardner,* for instance, there was an express condition, but there was no definition of "arrival" in the contract.[27] If the court construed "arrival" to mean heaving to in sight of the harbor, the condition would have been satisfied. Many other cases present much closer questions. If the condition is implied rather than express, a court has even greater flexibility in fashioning a way to preserve the contract.

The general rule is that there must be strict compliance with express conditions, and, as in *Gray,* there are several examples of adherence to this rule.[28] For the rule to apply, however, the condition must be clear and unambiguous.[29] As another commentator has stated:

> American courts clearly tend in practice to insist on strict and literal fulfillment of express conditions only when they are apparently material to the agreement of the parties and the risks created thereby. Conditions which are merely "technical" — i.e., asserted solely for the purpose of defeating the plaintiff's claim, but not related in substance to the defendant's real reason for nonperformance — [are] found to be generally excused under various theories, including waiver, estoppel, repudiation, reasonable satisfaction, and the like.[30]

---

[26] See generally Restatement (Second) of Contracts § 227 comment b, § 229 comment b (1981).

[27] See supra ¶ 5.01[4].

[28] See, e.g., Inman v. Clyde Hall Drilling Co., 369 P2d 498 (Alaska 1962) (employment contract provided that discharged employee was to give written notice of any claim within thirty days of discharge and was not to sue on any such claim before six months or after twelve months; discharged employee did not file written notice and also filed suit within six months; held, the filing of a suit was not "written notice" and the conditions were not met, and the employer won summary judgment); Whelchel v. Smith, 155 Ga. App. 901, 273 SE2d 619 (1980) (agreement of a sublessee to pay rents based on a percentage of gross income conditional only on creation of accounts receivable, not dependent on their collection).

[29] See, e.g., Sasser & Co. v. Griffin, 133 Ga. App. 83, 210 SE2d 34 (1980).

[30] Knapp, *Problems in Contract Law* 834 (1976), citing Childres, "Conditions in the Law of Contracts," 45 NYU L. Rev. 33 (1970).

Reliance and restitution are common ways to avoid the injustice that may seem to occur as the result of the invocation of the theory of conditions. For instance, it may be a condition of payment for services rendered that all the services be completed or that the recipient of the services have received payment from some third party. Someone may have been hired to paint a house or plow a field for a definite term of one month. The employer may contend that it is a condition of the obligation to pay that the house be painted completely, or that the whole field be plowed, or that the employee work the entire month. Although the employer's contention may be justified, if the employee paints most of the house, plows most of the field, or works twenty-five days of the month, the employer still receives work of value, and a court may decide that he should pay the fair value of the services rendered even though the condition for the contractual obligation to pay has not been satisfied.[31]

Another way to deal with the same problem is to treat the condition as unreasonable. For example, if the contract required one month's work to accomplish a defined series of tasks but the employee completed the tasks in a shorter amount of time, a court would probably find that the condition had been satisfied because strict adherence to the contractual time requirement would not be substantially related to the fundamental subject matter of the agreement.[32] A court also might take an expansive view of what constitutes satisfaction of the condition. An antenuptial contract between two New Yorkers was upheld even though their subsequent marriage was void for violation of the New York rules of consanguinity because the marriage would have been valid in some states.[33]

When payment or performance is conditional on an action by a third party (e.g., payment of a subcontractor is contingent upon the owner's full payment of the general contractor or the architect's issuance of the final certificate), courts sometimes read the condition simply as a way to designate a convenient time for payment

[31] The classic reliance/restitution case in an employment situation is Britton v. Turner, 6 NH 481 (1834).

[32] See, e.g., Jackson v. Richards, 433 A2d 888 (Pa. Super. Ct. 1981).

[33] See, e.g., In re Estate of Simms, 26 NY2d 163, 257 NE2d 627, 309 NYS2d 170 (1970) (bride was the niece by the half-blood of the groom).

and not as a condition of payment.[34] This is certainly not a universal approach, however, and a number of courts strictly apply the condition of the owner's payment to the general contractor or the architect's issuance of the final certificate.[35] If the owner withholds payment unreasonably or the architect unreasonably refuses to issue the final certificate, courts often are willing to excuse the condition and require payment of the subcontractor, especially if the delay is the result of a dispute with the general contractor.[36]

[3] Waiver

Perhaps the most common excuse for a condition is waiver by the party who seeks to avoid performance and to assert the failure of a condition. Waiver is only applied to the party who benefits from the condition.[37] In a typical house sale transaction, the buyer agrees to purchase subject to financing. Although the buyer can waive the financing condition and pay cash, the seller cannot waive the financing condition.[38]

The waiver doctrine tends to be applied when the condition is technical or relatively minor, unless it has been clearly modified. Nevertheless, it has been an important factor in reducing the number of cases that apply conditions strictly and cause a forfeiture of the principal purpose of the agreement.[39] Silent acquiescence in a party's failure to perform a condition or to cause a condition to

---

[34] See, e.g., Dancy v. William J. Howard, Inc., 297 F2d 686 (7th Cir. 1961); Midland Eng'g Co. v. John A. Hall Constr. Co., 398 F. Supp. 981 (ND Ind. 1975).

[35] See, e.g., Jerome Distribs., Inc. v. BLI Constr. Co., 142 Ga. App. 776, 237 SE2d 13 (1977); DI Corbett, Inc. v. Venture Constr. Co., 140 Ga. App. 586, 231 SE2d 536 (1976); Mascioni v. Miller, Inc., 261 NY 1, 184 NE 473 (1933).

[36] See, e.g., Anthony P. Miller, Inc. v. Wilmington Hous. Auth., 179 F. Supp. 199 (D. Del. 1959); Laurel Race Course v. Royal Constr. Co., 274 Md. 142, 333 A2d 319 (1975); Frankfort Distilleries v. Burns Bottling Mach. Works, 174 Md. 12, 197 A 599 (1938); Terminal Constr. Corp. v. Bergen County, 18 NJ 294, 113 A2d 787 (1955).

[37] See, e.g., CPD Chem. Co. v. National Car Rental Sys., Inc., 148 Ga. App. 756, 252 SE2d 665 (1979).

[38] See, e.g., Huntington Mining Holdings, Inc. v. Cottontail Plaza, Inc., 79 AD2d 647, 433 NYS2d 824 (1980).

[39] Farnsworth § 8.5, at 565, citing Restatement (Second) of Contracts § 84(1)(a) (1981).

occur may be a waiver of the right to rely on the condition so that the party asserting it may be estopped from doing so.[40] Even an antiwaiver provision may be waived,[41] and waiver may be implied from conduct as well as from express statements.[42] For example, it is an implied, if not express, condition of an agreement to marry that the parties be legally competent to marry. An antenuptial contract for the division of property upon the termination of the marriage typically is conditional on both the marriage and its legality.[43] If a man and woman enter into an antenuptial agreement knowing that their marriage will be invalid (e.g., one or both is still married to another or one is underage and does not have parental consent), each will be estopped to assert the condition of marriage in an action on the antenuptial contract subsequent to their purported marriage.[44]

[4] Estoppel

A party who asserts the failure of a condition may be prevented from doing so by the doctrine of estoppel even if he has not acted in such a way as to waive the condition. Estoppel is a means to prevent injustice. When a court says that a party is estopped from asserting a condition, what it is really saying is that it would be unfair to allow the party to do so. There may have been no waiver or modification, and there may be no question that the condition has not occurred, but for some reason the assertion of

---

[40] See, e.g., Barton v. Chemical Bank, 577 F2d 1329 (5th Cir. 1978).

[41] See, e.g., JEM Enters., Inc. v. Taco Pronto, Inc., 145 Ga. App. 573, 244 SE2d 253 (1978).

[42] See, e.g., Royal Atlanta Dev. Corp. v. MD Hodges Enters., Inc., 141 Ga. App. 838, 234 SE2d 676 (1977); Crawford v. First Nat'l Bank of Rome, 137 Ga. App. 294, 223 SE2d 488 (1976).

[43] Some states refuse to enforce antenuptial agreements for the division of property upon the subsequent dissolution of a marriage because they are said to be in contemplation of divorce and therefore in derogation of marriage. The trend, however, is to recognize and to enforce such agreements. Courts are not blind to the social and cultural changes in the institution of marriage and to the fact that many marriages are no longer permanent. Antenuptial agreements can be useful estate-planning tools for both parties.

[44] See, e.g., Szlauzis v. Szlauzis, 255 Ill. 314, 99 NE 640 (1912); Knollenberg v. Meyer, 151 Kan. 768, 100 P2d 746 (1940). See generally Annot., 46 ALR3d 1403 (1972).

the condition's failure is tainted. Perhaps the party knew that the condition could not be fulfilled at the time of the agreement — for example, a man who signs an antenuptial agreement knowing that he is still married to another woman and that he cannot legally marry the woman who joins him in the antenuptial contract.[45] Perhaps the party who seeks discharge should have undertaken to try to bring the condition about but did nothing — for instance, a buyer of a house subject to financing who makes no real effort to apply for and to obtain financing.[46] Or perhaps in an agreement contingent upon one party's satisfaction, the party to be satisfied has been unreasonable in his demands.[47]

A breach also may cause an estoppel. The breach may be of an express or implied covenant to try to bring about the occurrence of the condition, or it might be an act that has the effect of preventing the other contracting partner or a third party from satisfying the condition. Generally, there is a good-faith obligation not to interfere with the other party's performance, and this includes the obligation not to do anything calculated to prevent the occurrence of a condition.[48]

¶ 5.03 EXPRESS AND IMPLIED CONDITIONS AND THE DUTY OF GOOD FAITH

Difficult problems often arise in connection with implied conditions. Should there be an implied condition, and, if so, what should it be? Judicial treatment of implied conditions goes hand in hand with the concept of good faith in the performance of contrac-

---

[45] See, e.g., American Sur. Co. v. Conner, 251 NY 1, 166 NE 783 (1929); Broadrick v. Broadrick, 25 Pa. Super. 225 (1904).

[46] See, e.g., Beekay Realty Corp. v. Cayre, 256 So. 2d 539 (Fla. Dist. Ct. App. 1972); Schroeder v. Morris, 20 So. 2d 437 (La. Ct. App. 1945).

[47] See generally Farnsworth § 8.4, at 556, 557 (1982); Burton, "Breach of Contract and the Common Law Duty to Perform in Good Faith," 94 Harv. L. Rev. 369 (1980); Note, 43 U. Pitt. L. Rev. 375 (1981).

[48] For a consideration of the relationship between a breach and the occurrence or nonoccurrence of a condition, see Restatement (Second) of Contracts §§ 245, 295 (1981).

tual obligations. Both the second Restatement[49] and the UCC[50] state that there is a duty of good faith implied in every contractual undertaking.[51] This duty arises most commonly in cases that involve an implied duty to bring about a condition or to exercise discretion in a reasonable way.

[1] Good-Faith Duty to Satisfy Implied Conditions

Even if a contract does not contain any express conditions, it may have one or more implied conditions. The existence and identity of these conditions are determined by examining all the circumstances surrounding the agreement, including the course of dealing between the parties, their overall intentions, and the customs of the trade. A common practice alone does not create a condition. In commercial real estate projects, for instance, it is common to close the transaction for the permanent financing upon the completion of the structure and to use the proceeds to pay off the construction loan, among other things. Completion of the construction of all improvements, however, may not be a condition to the closing of the permanent loan. Whether the completion of construction is a condition depends on the mutual understanding of the parties and their intentions as evidenced by their written agreement and their dealings with one another. There may be many reasons for construction delays and there may not be any good reasons to delay the closing of the permanent financing simply because some construction remains to be done.[52] If the permanent lender does not want to close before the construction is completed,

---

[49] "Every contract imposes upon each party a duty of good faith and fair dealing in its performance and its enforcement." Restatement (Second) of Contracts § 205 (1981).

[50] UCC § 1-203.

[51] On good faith, see generally Braucher, "Interpretation and Legal Effect in the Second Restatement of Contracts," 81 Colum. L. Rev. 13 (1981); Summers, "The General Duty of Good Faith — Its Recognition and Conceptualization," 67 Cornell L. Rev. 810 (1982).

[52] See, e.g., Morgan Guar. Trust Co. of NY v. Atlanta Nat'l Real Estate Trust, 149 Ga. App. 118, 253 SE2d 774 (1979); Baker Mortgage Co. v. Hugenberg, 145 Ga. App. 528, 244 SE2d 56 (1978). Of course, in a market of rapidly increasing interest rates, the permanent lender certainly might want to avoid a below-market loan commitment.

he can always negotiate an express condition in the loan commitment.

[2] Good-Faith Duty to Satisfy Express Conditions

In comparison, it is the custom in private house sales that closing is expressly conditional on the buyer obtaining a mortgage.[53] This raises the question of whether there is an implied covenant to bring about the express condition. If the buyer agrees to purchase a house subject to the condition of obtaining financing,[54] what is his duty, if any, to seek appropriate financing? In most instances, it is a practical condition as well as a legal one because few people have enough ready cash to buy a house. Courts and commentators all agree that the buyer cannot sit on his hands even if the contract is silent about his duty to seek a loan. To hold otherwise does not make sense, the courts reason, because the parties entered into an agreement for the sale of a house and if the buyer must obtain financing to be able to perform, it is assumed that he will try to do so.[55]

---

[53] If after a good-faith effort the buyer is unsuccessful, the contract is void. Stan Weber & Assocs., Inc. v. Goodlett, 402 So. 2d 745 (La. Ct. App. 1981).

[54] Typically, a contract specifies some of the particulars of the contemplated financing, such as maximum interest rate, number of years of installment payments, and the minimum amount of financing. Some are even more specific and identify the particular lending institution and the precise terms of the loan. Others also make the purchase contingent on the sale of the buyer's current home. The degree of specificity is a matter of negotiation between the seller and the buyer. In the absence of clarity about interest rates and other terms, a court is likely to look at the average for similar sales in the community to determine what would have been a reasonable satisfaction of the condition. For an interesting empirical analysis of house sales and the terms of typical contracts in the area around Madison, Wisconsin, see Raushenbush, "Problems and Practices With Financing Conditions in Real Estate Purchase Contracts," 1963 Wis. L. Rev. 566 (1963). The changes in market conditions since the early 1960s have no doubt made such contracts more complicated than they were when Raushenbush did his study, but it is still a useful analysis of illustrative agreements. See also Aiken, " 'Subject to Financing' Clauses in Interim Contracts for Sale of Realty," 43 Marq. L. Rev. 265 (1960) (hereinafter cited as Aiken).

[55] See, e.g., Kirya v. Bulls, 404 So. 2d 58 (Ala. Ct. App. 1981); Smith v. Evans, 620 SW2d 627 (Tex. Civ. App. 1981); Manning v. Bleifus, 272 SE2d 821 (W. Va. 1980).

What does satisfy a buyer's good-faith requirement? If a buyer makes inquiries and is told that no bank or savings and loan association in the area will make a loan on the terms specified in the contract, he may not have to make a formal application because the law will not require him to perform a useless act.[56] However, an informal inquiry, such as a single telephone call to a loan officer, is not satisfactory.[57] If the buyer does apply for a loan and is turned down he may be excused, but not if it appears that credit has loosened sufficiently since the application to allow him to qualify,[58] or if the seller has attempted to arrange financing but the buyer has not followed through.[59] Sometimes a single formal application satisfies the good-faith requirement,[60] but not always.[61] Two applications usually suffice,[62] but again, not always.[63] In cases holding that multiple applications do not satisfy the buyer's good-faith requirement, there is almost invariably a problem with the applications or their presentation. A buyer may have filed them late or provided insuffícent information, and even though he made some effort, it was not the kind of effort expected from someone acting in good faith. Moreover, there is a difference between "good faith" and "best efforts." The buyer does not have to go to extraordinary

---

[56] See, e.g., Management, Inc. v. Masterson, Inc., 616 P2d 356 (Mont. 1980); Saltzman v. McCombs, 71 Nev. 93, 281 P2d 394 (1955).

[57] See, e.g., Beekay Realty Corp. v. Cayre, 256 So. 2d 539 (Fla. Dist. Ct. App. 1972).

[58] See, e.g., Fry v. George Elkins Co., 162 Cal. App. 2d 256, 327 P2d 905 (1958).

[59] See, e.g., Smith v. Vernon, 6 Ill. App. 3d 434, 286 NE2d 99 (1972).

[60] See, e.g., Luttinger v. Rosen, 164 Conn. 45, 316 A2d 757 (1972); Antonini v. Thrifty-Nifty Homes, Inc., 76 So. 2d 564 (La. Ct. App. 1955); Lynch v. Carroll, 24 Wash. App. 667, 604 P2d 510 (1979).

[61] See, e.g., Brewster v. Yockey, 153 So. 2d 489 (La. Ct. App. 1963); Bushmiller v. Schiller, 35 Md. App. 1, 368 A2d 1044 (1977); Anaheim Co. v. Holcombe, 246 Ore. 541, 426 P2d 743 (1967).

[62] See, e.g., Lach v. Cahill, 138 Conn. 418, 85 A2d 481 (1951); Hanover, Ltd. v. Fields, 568 P2d 751 (Utah 1977).

[63] See, e.g., Fry v. George Elkins Co., 162 Cal. App. 2d 256, 327 P2d 905 (1958); Ray v. Peeples, 387 So. 2d 1303 (La. Ct. App. 1980).

lengths; he simply must make a reasonable effort. As long as he does so, it avails the seller nothing to show that with a strenuous effort the buyer might have been able to obtain financing.[64] The issue of what satisfies good faith is essentially a factual issue that a jury must determine by taking into account all the surrounding circumstances.[65] It is not a proper subject for disposition on a motion for summary judgment.[66] This leads to some uncertainty, which might be removed by carefully drafting the original agreement or, perhaps, by using option contracts.[67]

Many other circumstances involve express conditions and the implied agreement of one of the parties to try to bring about the occurrence of the condition.[68] House sales cases, however, are

---

[64] For a discussion of the notion of best efforts, see Farnsworth, "On Trying to Keep One's Promises: The Duty of Best Efforts in Contract Law," 46 U. Pitt. L. Rev. 1 (1984). Because most of these cases involve the question of whether the broker is entitled to a commission, there is sometimes an issue of the seller's good faith or best efforts. The seller is obligated to pay the commission if the closing would have occurred but for some wrongful act or breach of good faith on his part. See e.g., Shear v. National Rifle Ass'n, 606 F2d 1251 (DC Cir. 1979). If the buyer breaches, however, the seller is under no duty to sue for specific performance so that the broker can collect his commission. See, e.g., Beattie-Firth v. Colebank, 143 W. Va. 740, 105 SE2d 5 (1958); Amies v. Wesnofske, 255 NY 156, 174 NE 436 (1931). Section 2-306(2) imposes a best-efforts obligation on the parties to an exclusive dealing agreement. See infra ¶ 5.04[3]. For an application of this best-efforts provision, see, e.g., Bloor v. Falstaff Brewing Corp., 601 F2d 609 (2d Cir. 1979).

[65] See, e.g., Manning v. Bleifus, 272 SE2d 821 (W. Va. 1980).

[66] See, e.g., Osten v. Shah, 104 Ill. App. 3d 784, 60 Ill. Dec. 497, 433 NE2d 294 (1982).

[67] Option contracts are the approach favored by one commentator. See Aiken 265.

> "The argument is that buyers will refuse to pay for options, if not solidly confident of their ability to finance; and that sellers will not give options except for substantial consideration, without present assurance that buyers actually will buy. The reply is that sellers now give for nothing what are effectively options, without assurance that buyers actually will buy; and that buyers risk in deposits (and often lose, by negotiation or by litigation) far more substantial sums than they would be called upon to pay for equivalent options."

Id. at 300.

[68] The Automobile Dealers' Day in Court Act, 15 USC §§ 1221 et seq., has been the source of a number of cases. It includes an express good-faith provision:

good examples of the general problem, and the approaches used by courts in these cases apply to other situations as well. What constitutes good faith is essentially a question of common sense in the particular circumstances. The past relationships of the parties, the customs of the trade, and the parties' own statements of intention are equally important in ascertaining good faith.

[3] Requirements and Outputs Contracts

Contracts for the requirements or the output of an enterprise provide opportunities to consider the issues of implied conditions and the duty of good faith. Is there an implied condition that there be requirements or an output, or is there simply an implied covenant to that effect? What is the good-faith duty, if any, of a party to have requirements or outputs? What is a reasonable amount of either? How is this to be determined? What if a party can expend his energies more profitably doing something else?

The question of whether requirements or outputs are implied conditions or implied covenants is critical, in determining appropriate remedies, as illustrated in the following scenarios. In the first situation, the buyer agrees to purchase the seller's total output of widgets for the next fiscal year if the seller decides to manufacture any widgets, but the seller expressly reserves the right to decide whether to manufacture any widgets. The buyer gambles that the seller will have an output of widgets for the year. If there are no widgets, there is no contract, and the buyer has no grounds for complaint because he has left the decision about production

---

> "The term 'good faith' shall mean the duty of each party to any franchise, and all officers, employees, or agents thereof to act in a fair and equitable manner toward each other so as to guarantee the one party freedom from coercion, intimidation, or threats of coercion or intimidation from the other party: *Provided,* that recommendation, endorsement, exposition, persuasion, urging or argument shall not be deemed to constitute a lack of good faith."

15 USC § 1221(e). For a consideration of this provision, see, e.g., David R. McGeorge Car Co. v. Leyland Motors Sales, Inc., 504 F2d 52 (4th Cir. 1974), cert. denied, 420 US 992 (1975); Fabert Motors, Inc. v. Ford Motor Co., 355 F2d 888 (7th Cir. 1966).

expressly to the seller.[69] The buyer has no claim for a breach of contract, because no contract ever comes into existence. Indeed, there may be an argument that the contract is void for indefiniteness.[70]

In a second scenario, the buyer simply agrees to purchase the seller's total output of widgets for the next fiscal year. The seller and buyer have not done business together before. Although the seller has manufactured widgets in the past, he has produced them only intermittently.

The buyer in this situation is in a somewhat better position than the buyer in the first example. The fact that the seller has manufactured widgets in the past indicates that he can do so and that he might have made money from them. It is not unreasonable to suppose that the seller might manufacture widgets during the year in question. Indeed, a court might imply a covenant to manufacture at least some widgets. The implied covenant could be justified as required by the doctrine of good faith and the policy against forfeiture. If the parties went to the trouble to make a contract, there must have been some intention to trade in widgets, and courts prefer to find substance in an agreement rather than to apply the theory of conditions literally and find that there is no agreement. In addition, the agreement of the seller to sell his output of widgets coupled with a history of manufacture suggests that, in good faith, it might be expected that he would manufacture some widgets. Thus, if the seller decides not to manufacture widgets, the condition of purchase will fail, but a court may excuse the condition by implying the good-faith covenant to manufacture widgets

---

[69] Although it may be unlikely, there is the possibility that the buyer may have some cause for complaint if the seller decides not to produce widgets for the purpose of damaging the buyer in some way. A court might read a good-faith requirement into the seller's obligation and say that only a good-faith exercise of the discretion to manufacture widgets or not is acceptable.

[70] At one time courts were reluctant to recognize requirements or outputs contracts for just this reason — there was not a definite subject matter. See, e.g., Bailey v. Austrian, 19 Minn. 535 (1873). Businessmen liked these contracts too much, however, and courts were faced with so many of them that they began to read into them an implied covenant to have outputs or requirements in order to supply the necessary definiteness. See, e.g., Lima Locomotive & Mach. Co. v. National Steel Castings Co., 155 F 77 (6th Cir. 1907). Section 2-306 implies a covenant of good faith in all such contracts covered by Article 2. See discussion infra at note 72.

and to avoid forfeiture. If so, the buyer would have an action for breach of contract — the breach of the implied covenant to have an output of widgets. Of course, the difficult question of how much output satisfies the implied covenant still remains, and the seller could defend by proving that the decision not to have an output was made in good faith for sound business reasons.[71]

In the third case, the buyer and seller have done business together for five years. During this time, the buyer has purchased an average of 10,000 widgets per year from the seller or about 90 percent of the seller's total widget production. The buyer and seller enter into a purchase agreement in which the buyer will take all of the seller's widget output for the next fiscal year. This situation presents the best case for the buyer because a definite business relationship and history of dealing exist so that a court can project a reasonable expectation of an output for the year in question. The facts more strongly support the implication of a covenant to have outputs of a fairly determinable amount. Again, the seller may be able to overcome this implied covenant by showing good-faith extenuating circumstances, but the basic discussion would center on whether there was a breach of a covenant within the agreement, not whether there was an agreement at all.

Most commercial contracts that involve outputs or requirements fall under UCC coverage and are subject to the explicit good-faith provision of Section 2-306(1):

> A term which measures the quantity by the output of the seller or the requirements of the buyer means such actual output or requirements as may occur in good faith, except that no quantity unreasonably disproportionate to any stated estimate or in the absence of a stated estimate to any normal or otherwise comparable prior output or requirements may be tendered or demanded.

---

[71] Going out of business (or perhaps out of the widget business) would generally be a good-faith defense. See, e.g., Fort Wayne Corrugated Paper Co. v. Anchor Hocking Glass Corp., 130 F2d 471 (3d Cir. 1942). Whether going into bankruptcy or corporate reorganization is a legitimate, good-faith way to avoid onerous contractual obligations such as collective bargaining agreements is an issue of some currency. See, e.g., NLRB v. Bildisco and Bildisco, 104 S. Ct. 1188, 79 L. Ed. 2d 482 (1984).

Section 2-306 was partially intended to do away with the argument that a requirements or outputs contract lacked mutuality of obligation and, therefore, was void for vagueness.[72] That end is achieved by reading a reasonable quantity term into each agreement. The UCC also makes explicit the practice of implying a covenant of good faith to have requirements or outputs.[73] The UCC drafters did recognize that there could be legitimate excuses for not having any production or needs, but these excuses must be considered in light of the general obligation of good faith, a duty that is not expressly defined but relates to the relationship of the parties and the customs of the trade.[74]

A buyer who has had requirements in the past sometimes may be able to avoid any contractual obligations by having no requirements at all, despite the language of Section 2-306, which seems to imply a good-faith duty to have *some* requirements (except perhaps in extremely unusual circumstances). For example, the National Parks Service entered into an agreement with a general contractor for work that included paving a specified area. The contract contemplated a need for a substantial amount of crushed limestone. The subcontractor for the paving made an agreement with a limestone supplier for the necessary amount of limestone. After all these contracts were made, the National Parks Service and the general contractor modified the agreement to make the limestone unnecessary. Even though this left both the subcontractor and his supplier out on a limb, the Court of Appeals for the District of

---

[72] UCC § 2-306, Official Comment 2; City of Louisville v. Rockwell Mfg. Co., 482 F2d 159 (6th Cir. 1973).

[73] This duty of good faith must be read together with Section 2-103(1)(b), which states: " 'Good faith' in the case of a merchant means honesty in fact and the observance of reasonable commercial standards of fair dealing in the trade." See also Massachusetts Gas & Elec. Light Supply Corp. v. V-M Corp., 387 F2d 605 (1st Cir. 1967).

[74] UCC § 2-103, Official Comment 2, states in part:

> "A shutdown by a requirements buyer for lack of orders might be permissible when a shutdown merely to curtail losses would not. The essential test is whether the party is acting in good faith. Similarly, a sudden expansion of the plant by which requirements are to be measured would not be included within the scope of the contract as made but normal expansion undertaken in good faith would be within the scope of this section."

Columbia found that the changes were made in good faith. The limestone supplier had no grounds for complaint.[75]

Changes in market conditions that result in a substantial difference between the contract price and the market price of the goods that are the subject matter of the transaction generally do not excuse a decision not to have requirements (or suddenly to double or triple requirements) or to refuse to deliver any output. The great increase in oil prices that followed the Arab oil embargo in 1973 was not an excuse for Gulf Oil to avoid its contractual obligations to supply fuel to Eastern Airlines, nor for Gulf to seek a modification of the price term.[76]

Homestake Mining Co. v. Washington Public Power Supply System[77] presented an interesting problem. Homestake agreed to supply the utility with 1.5 million pounds of uranium oxide for the core of a nuclear reactor. The contract contained an option for the buyer to order up to 10 percent more uranium. Washington Public Power exercised the option, but the seller said that it would deliver only if the utility could show that it had a legitimate need for the additional 150,000 pounds for its own use and was not buying on speculation. The price of uranium had risen dramatically in the time between the negotiation of the agreement and its performance. In an action to determine whether the contract was for the requirements of the buyer or whether it was simply a contract for the sale of 1.5 million pounds of uranium oxide with an option to purchase another 150,000 pounds, the court concluded that it was a

---

[75] Weaver & Assocs., Inc. v. Asphalt Constr., Inc., 587 F2d 1315 (DC Cir. 1978). The supplier argued that the contract should be construed as one for the fixed amount of limestone because there was an estimate in the original agreement that established a reasonably definite amount. The court disagreed and treated the case as one involving a requirements contract. There was an estimate, but the contract was for paving an area and using whatever amount of limestone might be required for the completion of the job. This put the buyer in a better position because of the provision in Section 2-306 that there may be no requirements if the buyer operates in good faith. But cf. Copylease Corp. of Am. v. Memorex Corp., 397 F. Supp. 853 (SDNY 1975) (contract specifying a quantity during its "initial" term was not a requirements contract but was one for a minimum stated amount).

[76] Eastern Airlines, Inc. v. Gulf Oil Corp., 415 F. Supp. 429 (SD Fla. 1975). This case, and a number of others similar to it, also raises questions of commercial impracticability.

[77] Homestake Mining Co. v. Washington Pub. Power Supply Sys., 476 F. Supp. 1162 (ND Cal. 1979).

requirements contract governed by Section 2-306. The buyer had to show a justifiable need for the extra 150,000 pounds based on its own requirements in order to demand delivery. The court relied on a combination of factors in its determination. The parties did state maximum and minimum amounts (such a statement is consistent with either a requirements agreement or an agreement simply for the sale of goods regardless of needs), but they also couched the contract in language that related to the buyer's needs for its new nuclear reactor. The evidence indicated that neither party intended the contract to be used for the buyer's speculation in the uranium market. The 10 percent option was a "fudge factor" in case the parties did not accurately estimate how much uranium oxide would be necessary for the reactor core.

The implication of a good-faith obligation to have requirements or outputs adds some certainty to these agreements. The parties can avoid this implied duty by expressly negotiating a contract that is conditional on output or requirements. That leaves the buyer or the seller with the discretion, respectively, to have requirements or outputs. Most people, however, do not go to the trouble of entering into formal agreements that leave the other party with so much discretion. The implied good-faith covenant that the buyer will have reason to buy and that the seller will have reason to sell comports with reality and with common sense. The good-faith standard is ambiguous, but by tying it to commercial standards, the UCC and the courts put it in a context in which one contract can be compared with others that involve similar situations.

[4] Contracts That Require Obligee's Satisfaction

Some contracts require that performance be completed to the satisfaction of its recipient or to a third party, such as an architect who must issue a certificate of satisfaction on a building. If the satisfaction of the obligee or his designated agent is a condition of the obligation to pay, is there any good-faith duty to be reasonable in deciding whether performance is satisfactory? Generally, yes, although what constitutes reasonableness varies greatly with the nature of the performance. The obligee may be allowed to be demanding and even eccentric if, for example, the contract is with a tailor for a new suit of clothes. More objective standards of reasonableness apply when the contract is for something like a satisfactory heating system.[78]

Judicial treatment of satisfaction is related to the general disregard for the perfect tender rule. At least since the 1921 opinion of Judge Benjamin Cardozo in *Jacob & Youngs, Inc. v. Kent*[79] the obligee has been held to a standard of objective reasonableness in determining whether the tender satisfies the requirements of the contract. Judge Cardozo wanted to avoid forfeiture of a construction contract because the contractor used a brand of pipe that was different from the brand specified in the agreement, although of a similar quality. Despite explicit language in the agreement that strict adherence to every term, including specifications about types of materials, was a condition to the obligation of the owner to pay for the construction, the court construed the agreement to allow minor deviations that did not affect basic quality or the central purpose of the agreement.[80]

A party to a contract often becomes dissatisfied with the agreement before it is completed. The market may have changed in an unexpected way or the party may conclude that the agreement was an unwise commitment. Unhappiness or dissatisfaction with the terms of the agreement or with the facts that were known to the parties when they contracted is no excuse for nonperformance. If the obligee's satisfaction is to be a condition, it must relate entirely to the quality of the performance, not to other aspects of the agreement.[81] Third parties (most often architects) must generally adhere to a standard of reasonable, honest satisfaction based on commer-

---

[78] See, e.g., Simpson, *Handbook of the Law of Contracts* § 149, at 309, 310 (1965).

[79] Jacob & Youngs, Inc. v. Kent, 230 NY 239, 129 NE 889 (1921).

[80] Section 2-601 is that statute's version of the perfect tender rule, but it must be read in connection with Section 2-508, which gives the seller time to cure a nonconforming tender. See infra ¶ 5.04[11].

[81] See generally Farnsworth § 8.4, at 557, citing at note 38 DeVoine Co. v. International Co., 151 Md. 690, 136 A 37 (1927) (buyer agreed to take cherries of "quality satisfactory" and was not excused when his business slacked off and he decided to use his own supply because he conceded that the quality of the seller's cherries was satisfactory).

cial expectations.[82] If the third party is unreasonable, the court may ignore the condition altogether.[83]

¶ 5.04 UCC PROVISIONS AFFECTING GENERAL RULES OF CONDITIONS

[1] Scope of UCC Relationship to Conditions

No single provision of the UCC deals with the question of conditions; more than a dozen sections of Article 2 involve issues relevant to whether a condition exists, whether it has been satisfied or excused, and what is to be done if it has not been satisfied.[84] Although an exhaustive analysis of the UCC and its provisions is beyond the scope of this work, the effect of its provisions on common-law rules and their relationship to the general rules that apply to conditions cannot be ignored.

[2] Section 2-301: Obligations of Buyers and Sellers

Section 2-301 states the basic obligations of the parties in deceptively simple language: "The obligation of the seller is to transfer and deliver and that of the buyer is to accept and pay in accordance with the contract." What the section fails to do is to identify when these obligations ripen and to state whether the obligations are independent or mutually dependent. Is the buyer's obligation to accept and to pay conditional on the seller's transfer and delivery, or is it an independent covenant?[85] What constitutes a delivery? Is

---

[82] Compare, e.g., Laurel Race Course v. Royal Constr. Co., 274 Md. 142, 333 A2d 319 (1975) with Frankfort Distilleries v. Burns Bottling Mach. Works, 174 Md. 12, 197 A 599 (1938).

[83] See, e.g., Anthony P. Miller, Inc. v. Wilmington Hous. Auth., 179 F. Supp. 199 (D. Del. 1959); Terminal Constr. Corp. v. Bergen County, 18 NJ 294, 113 A2d 787 (1955).

[84] Other sections also come into play, but the following UCC sections in Article 2 are particularly relevant: §§ 301, 306, 308, 310, 503, 504, 507, 508, 511, 512, 513, 601, 605, 612.

[85] In language that is certainly less than crystal clear, the drafters explain Section 2-301 as follows: "This section uses the term 'obligation' in contrast to the term 'duty' in order to provide for the 'condition' aspects of delivery and payment insofar as they are not modified by other provisions of this Article such as those on cure of tender." UCC § 2-301, Official Comment.

the obligation to transfer and to deliver conditional on payment? For the answers to these questions, it is necessary to refer to other sections of Article 2, to the common law, and to "usage of trade, course of dealing and performance, and the general background of circumstances."[86]

A case involving a delay in the delivery of an executive airplane illustrates the interplay among sections of the UCC and between the UCC and common-law principles.[87] In controversy was the contract between the manufacturer of the aircraft and the buyer/middleman who was being sued by the ultimate purchaser for nondelivery. The manufacturer, concerned about possible delays caused by technical complexities encountered in building the airplane, included a clause in the agreement that excused liability for anything other than return of the deposit for delays in delivery.[88] Despite the buyer's willingness to pay for the airplane, the seller's obligation to deliver never ripened because it was conditional upon his own ability to perform in a timely fashion. The buyer was limited to a recovery of the deposit and no question of good faith was involved.[89] Apparently, the manufacturer tried to comply because a court almost certainly would imply a good-faith duty to try to deliver the airplane on time in such a situation. The buyer might have gained some protection from a best-efforts provision.

[3] Section 2-306: Requirements, Outputs, and Exclusive Dealing Contracts

Section 2-306 deals with requirements, outputs, and exclusive dealing contracts.[90] It implies a good-faith duty to have requirements or outputs on the parties to such contracts and also assures

---

[86] Id.

[87] Dow Corning Corp. v. Capital Aviation, Inc., 411 F2d 622 (7th Cir. 1969).

[88] The clause stated, in part, that there would be no liability for "failure or delay in making delivery for any cause whatever. If delivery of the products covered by this order is not made within 30 days . . . purchaser may cancel this order and have the full deposit refunded."

[89] The court found this limitation of remedies under Section 2-719 to be valid because it was a freely negotiated limitation clause and not punitive.

[90] See supra ¶ 5.03[3].

some certainty in determining quantities by referring to past practices and trade usage.[91]

[4] Section 2-308: Place for Delivery

Section 2-308 specifies the place for delivery if the parties have not identified the place in their agreement.[92] This assists in determining when the seller has made delivery as required by Section 2-301 and therefore helps to identify when the buyer's obligation to pay ripens. Again, an ambiguity exists. If there is no agreement on delivery at another location,[93] is the duty to deliver at the place specified in Section 2-308 a condition to the buyer's obligation to pay, or is it a covenant that, if breached, would not necessarily excuse the buyer from the obligation to pay? The buyer may have an action for breach, but if the place of delivery is not a condition, he may be in breach if he does not pay. Of course, there may be instances in which the buyer cannot reasonably know of his obligation to pay without delivery or at least notice of it. The seller has an obligation to inform the buyer that the goods are available.

[5] Section 2-310: Timing of Payment

Section 2-310 identifies the time when payment becomes due in the absence of an express agreement about the time for payment.

---

[91] See generally City of Louisville v. Rockwell Mfg. Co., 482 F2d 159 (6th Cir. 1973); Massachusetts Gas & Elec. Light Supply Corp. v. V-M Corp., 387 F2d 605 (1st Cir. 1967).

[92] Section 2-308 reads:

"Unless otherwise agreed

"(a) the place for delivery of goods is the seller's place of business or if he has none his residence; but

"(b) in a contract for sale of identified goods which to the knowledge of the parties at the time of contracting are in some other place, that place is the place for their delivery; and

"(c) documents of title may be delivered through customary banking channels."

[93] Surrounding circumstances, usages of the trade, and course of dealing between the parties may establish an express agreement otherwise even if the contract is silent. UCC § 2-308, Official Comment 4.

In general, payment is due either upon receipt,[94] after inspection for goods shipped under reservation,[95] or upon the buyer's receipt of documents when delivery is made by documents.[96] When a sale is on credit, the credit period begins to run from the time of shipment or, if the invoice is postdated, from the time of the invoice date.[97] Reading Section 2-310 together with Section 2-301, the obligation for full payment ripens immediately upon delivery at the place of delivery.[98] This means, for instance, that if delivery is to occur at the seller's place of business, the buyer must be prepared to make full payment at that location. These provisions may be overcome not only by express agreement of the parties, but also by trade practices and course of dealing.[99] Sections 2-512 and 2-513 also affect the applicability of Section 2-310.[100] Subject to various qualifications, they protect the buyer's right to inspect goods before paying for them to ensure that they conform to the agreement, but they do not necessarily excuse the buyer from the obligation to pay immediately upon receipt (or in advance) if there is an agreement to do so, whether the agreement is express or customary.

[6] Section 2-503: Acceptable Tender of Delivery

Section 2-503 goes into great detail about what constitutes acceptable tender of delivery. The seller is generally required to do what is reasonable to put the goods in the hands of the buyer. This

---

[94] UCC § 310(a). This provides the buyer with an opportunity to inspect. Delivery may occur at the seller's place of business, but the buyer does not have to pay until receipt, which means that he can look at the goods before paying, although he may already bear the risk of loss (delivery has occurred) or the credit period may have begun to run. UCC § 2-310, Official Comment 1.

[95] UCC § 310(b). The seller is protected because even if the buyer has a right of inspection, the seller does not have to surrender possession until payment is made unless there has been a prior agreement for a sale on credit. UCC § 2-310, Official Comment 2.

[96] UCC § 310(c).

[97] UCC § 310(d).

[98] See, e.g., Lewis v. Hughes, 276 Md. 247, 346 A2d 231 (1975); Southwest Eng'g Co. v. Martin Tractor Co., 205 Kan. 684, 473 P2d 18 (1970).

[99] See, e.g., Cooper Alloy Corp. v. EBV Sys., Inc., 111 RI 756, 306 A2d 837 (1973) (trade practice was to require cash in advance).

[100] See UCC § 2-310, Official Comment 3.

includes giving notice to the buyer that is sufficient to allow him to act. This section is intended to supplement the provisions of Section 2-301 on the seller's general obligation of tender and delivery and the provisions of Section 2-507 that define the effect on the buyer of the seller's tender.[101] As used in Section 2-507, the term "tender" means "such performance by the tendering party as puts the other party in default if he fails to proceed in some manner."[102]

It might appear that the seller's failure to comply with his obligations of tender would excuse the buyer altogether because there would be a failure of a condition precedent to his obligation to perform. The tender obligation, however, tends to be treated more as a covenant than as a condition. If the seller fails to comply, the buyer may be excused from compliance with the payment terms of the agreement, but the contract may not be discharged.[103] Although UCC language may seem to make proper tender a condition to payment, the decision to treat a failed tender as a breach is consistent with the policy against forfeiture and with the policy in favor of giving effect to the apparent intention of the parties to have a contractual relationship.

[7] Section 2-504: Shipment of Goods

Section 2-504 expands the description of what constitutes tender by outlining the approach to be used when the contract authorizes the seller to ship the goods. The parties may agree on a specific mode of carriage and may identify when delivery actually occurs for purposes of establishing the risk of loss. This section only applies when they have not done so, when it is also contemplated that the seller *will* ship the goods. Any form of shipment is acceptable as long as it meets a test of commercial reasonableness and the seller gives notice to the buyer of the selected mode of shipment.[104] Notice normally occurs when the invoice or a bill of lading is sent, but particular circumstances may require a more

---

[101] UCC § 2-503, Official Comment 2.

[102] UCC § 2-503, Official Comment 1.

[103] See, e.g., Kingston 1686 House, Inc. v. BSP Transp., Inc., 121 NH 93, 427 A2d 9 (1981).

[104] UCC § 2-504, Official Comment 3.

rapid form of communication.[105] In the absence of an agreement to the contrary, delivery occurs when the goods are put in the hands of a common carrier.[106]

[8] Section 2-507: Seller's Reclamation Rights

Section 2-507 is one of the few UCC provisions that explicitly deals with the question of conditions. It states:

> (1) Tender of delivery is a condition to the buyer's duty to accept the goods and, unless otherwise agreed, to his duty to pay for them. Tender entitles the seller to acceptance of the goods and to payment according to the contract.
>
> (2) Where payment is due and demanded on the delivery to the buyer of goods or documents of title, his right as against the seller to retain or dispose of them is conditional upon his making the payment due.

Section 2-507(1) clarifies the obligations of Section 2-301 by adopting Lord Mansfield's view that the major covenants of delivery and payment are mutually dependent. The covenants are not independent, and the buyer cannot be held liable for nonpayment unless it is shown that the seller tendered. This makes explicit what is implicit in Section 2-301: The major obligations are conditions one for the other.[107]

Section 2-507(2) protects the seller's interest in the goods until the buyer has made payment. This has given rise to a number of bad-check cases. Unless otherwise agreed, payment by check usu-

---

[105] UCC § 2-504, Official Comment 5.

[106] See, e.g., Electric Regulator Corp. v. Sterling Extruder Corp., 280 F. Supp. 550 (D. Conn. 1968) (contract for delivery FOB Norwalk, Ct. was a shipment contract within the meaning of Section 2-504 and risk of loss passed to the buyer when goods were passed to the common carrier in Norwalk). The shift in risk of loss from seller to buyer depends on the seller making a proper contract of carriage and notifying the buyer of the shipment. Sheinberg-Kellerei GMBH v. Vineyard Wine Co., 281 SE2d 425 (NC Ct. App. 1981).

[107] This does not mean that the seller can escape liability by failing to fulfill the condition of tender and delivery, because there is also an implied duty of good faith to bring about this condition. Failure to deliver would be a breach; the contract would not be extinguished unless the agreement explicitly provided otherwise.

ally satisfies the buyer's obligation of payment. If the seller delivers upon receipt of the buyer's check, can he reclaim the goods if the check fails to clear on the theory that there has been a failure of a condition to his obligation to deliver? The answer is a highly qualified yes.[108]

Section 2-507(2) does not include a time limitation applicable to the seller's reclamation rights, but the Official Commentary, by making a cross-reference to Section 2-702(2), suggests that the seller has ten days in which to reclaim from a credit buyer who is found to be insolvent.[109] Several courts have followed the Official Commentary and have grafted the ten-day limitation of Section 2-702(2) onto Section 2-507(2).[110] This can place the seller in a difficult position. Sometimes ten days or more pass between receipt of a check and notice of dishonor. One court has held that the time period runs from delivery of the goods rather than from notice of dishonor, which puts the seller in a particularly awkward position, especially if he does not receive notice of dishonor until eleven days after delivery.[111] Of course, if the buyer keeps the goods for more than ten days, the seller runs a substantial risk that they will have been resold, processed, damaged, or destroyed.

If the seller does not assert his reclamation rights within the proper time period, he waives them. The tight time limit, especially if it runs from delivery and not from notice, can work against attempts at a mutually agreeable compromise. The buyer may have made a good-faith mistake in issuing a bad check. The seller usually prefers to have his money, even if it is late, than to retake the goods, but if he does not act promptly to reclaim, he may waive that right and be in an even worse predicament if the buyer's second check also fails to clear. Of course, he may demand payment by certified or cashier's check, but this might be awkward if the buyer and seller have done business together before and contemplate a continuing relationship that, of necessity, must be

---

[108] See, e.g., Lawrence v. Graham, 29 Md. App. 422, 347 A2d 271 (1975).

[109] UCC § 2-507, Official Comment 3.

[110] See, e.g., Sorrels v. Texas Bank & Trust Co. of Jacksonville, Tex., 597 F2d 997 (5th Cir. 1979); Stoners v. Mahon, 526 F2d 1238 (5th Cir. 1976); Holiday Rambler Corp. v. Morris, 32 UCC Rep. 1222 (D. Kan. 1981).

[111] Szabo v. Vinton Motors, 630 F2d 1 (1st Cir. 1980).

founded on mutual trust. The seller always has an action for the price,[112] but that may not be worth much if the buyer keeps bouncing checks. There are also delays and substantial transaction costs associated with bringing a lawsuit for the price. If the seller learns of dishonor before he has completed delivery (the goods may be in transit, delivery having taken place when the goods were passed to a common carrier), he can stop delivery.[113]

The trade practices of a particular industry may also affect the seller's ability to exercise his reclamation rights. For example, Oregon loggers sought to reclaim their logs from a sawmill that failed to pay for them. The evidence showed that the practice was to pay on the twenty-fifth of each month for logs delivered between the first and the fifteenth of that month. Because payment was not due on delivery according to the trade practice, there was no reclamation right under Section 2-507(2). The loggers were in the position of sellers on credit and were left with their claim for money damages for nonpayment but no right of reclamation.[114]

Delays can cause other problems for the seller. Between the time of delivery and notice of dishonor of the payment check, the buyer may have used the goods as collateral for a loan from a bank or another third party. As a general rule, an intervening security interest prevails over the seller's right of reclamation under Section 2-507(2).[115] After reclamation the seller is in a good position in a bankruptcy proceeding because reclamation is not a voidable preference.[116] This makes sense because the right of reclamation under Section 2-507(2) derives from the theory of conditions. The failure of the condition of payment on delivery excuses the seller's obligation to deliver and returns the parties as closely as possible to the status quo ante, in which possession and title were in the seller and not in the buyer. The goods, therefore, should not be

---

[112] See UCC § 2-709.

[113] Clock v. Missouri-Kansas-Texas RR Co., 407 F. Supp. 448 (ED Mo. 1976). The seller must follow the rules of Section 2-705 on stoppage of delivery in transit.

[114] Stumbo v. Paul B. Hult Lumber Co., 251 Ore. 20, 444 P2d 564 (1968).

[115] See, e.g., United States v. Wyoming Nat'l Bank of Caspar, 505 F2d 1064 (10th Cir. 1974); Guy Martin Buick, Inc. v. Colorado Springs Nat'l Bank, 32 Colo. App. 235, 511 P2d 912 (1973).

[116] Peck v. Augustin Bros. Co., 203 Neb. 574, 279 NW2d 397 (1979).

subject to attachment to satisfy the buyer's creditors. However, if the buyer has already gone into bankruptcy and the goods have been levied upon, the seller cannot reclaim them and stands as an unsecured creditor.[117]

[9] Section 2-508: Seller's Cure of Nonconforming Tender or Delivery

Section 2-508 establishes an exception to the perfect tender rule set forth generally in Section 2-601 because it allows the seller to cure a nonconforming tender or delivery. The cure must occur within the original time for performance and the seller must give the buyer seasonable notice of his intention to cure.[118] The seller may have additional time beyond the original term of the agreement to cure if "the buyer rejects a nonconforming tender which the seller had reasonable grounds to believe would be acceptable."[119] The buyer is in breach if he does not allow the seller to cure after the seller gives notice,[120] which is one of the most significant departures from the perfect tender rule as well as from the general notion of dependent covenants. This approach is consistent, however, with the policy disfavoring forfeitures and favoring an interpretation of the relationship that will support the existence of a contract.

The seller does not have unbridled discretion to decide what is an appropriate cure, nor what is a reasonable time in which to effect a cure. The time for cure is subject to external, objective standards of reasonableness that depend on the particular facts of the transaction.[121] In deciding what constitutes a satisfactory cure, the seller may have to take the buyer's desires into account. For instance, in cases involving new cars that were "lemons," the courts have been sympathetic to consumers and have essentially said that the seller can cure only by substituting another similar car

---

[117] Mullen v. Sweetheart Cup Corp., 15 UCC Rep. 828 (SD Fla. 1974).

[118] UCC § 2-508(1).

[119] UCC § 2-508(2).

[120] JOC Oil USA, Inc. v. Consolidated Edison Co. of NY, Inc., 107 Misc. 2d 376, 434 NYS2d 623 (1980).

[121] See, e.g., Ramirez v. Auto-Sport, 88 NJ 277, 440 A2d 1345 (1982); Jorgenson v. Pressnall, 274 Ore. 285, 545 P2d 1382 (1976).

and not by trying to fix the "lemon."[122] These cases have involved cars that had extremely serious defects; the results might be different if the defects were relatively minor. Even so, the courts also had to overlook warranty and remedy limitations to repair or replacement of defective parts to find that anything short of total substitution was an ineffective cure.

[10] Section 2-511: Tender of Payment

As a complement to Section 2-310, Section 2-511 establishes tender of payment as a condition to the seller's duty to tender and to deliver goods.[123] The parties can decide what constitutes tender of payment and make it a part of their agreement, or they can rely on the custom of the trade to determine what qualifies as tender of payment.[124] For example, the seller cannot suddenly demand payment in cash or by certified check if the custom is to make payment by ordinary check,[125] unless there is some good reason for his demand, such as the previous dishonor of the buyer's bad check.

Section 2-511(3) presents an interesting problem concerning the interplay between it and Sections 2-507(2) and 2-702(2). It states, in part, that "payment by check is conditional and is de-

---

[122] See, e.g., Zabriskie Chevrolet, Inc. v. Smith, 99 NJ Super. 441, 240 A2d 195 (1968) (car would not even run 2.5 miles from dealer's showroom to buyer's house because of defective transmission and other problems); Bayne v. Nall Motors, Inc., 12 UCC Rep. 1139 (Iowa 1973) (differential froze after 406 miles, causing axle to lock; new differential ineffective cure because of likelihood of other problems associated with differential freeze-up).

[123] Section 2-511(1) reads: "Unless otherwise agreed tender of payment is a condition to the seller's duty to tender and complete any delivery."

[124] Section 2-511(2) reads: "Tender of payment is sufficient when made by any means or in any manner current in the ordinary course of business unless the seller demands payment in legal tender and gives any extension of time reasonably necessary to procure it." The Official Commentary describes the "essence" of this provision as the avoidance of commercial surprise. UCC § 2-511, Official Comment 3.

[125] Chrysler Credit Co. v. Barnes, 126 Ga. App. 444, 191 SE2d 121 (1972). On the other hand, the acceptance of a check does not transform a cash sale into a credit sale, the time for the ostensible extension of credit being the time between the delivery of the check and its collection. In re Helms Veneer Corp., 287 F. Supp. 840 (WD Va. 1968). A postdated check, however, is an instrument of credit, and the relationship becomes that of creditor and debtor. UCC § 2-511, Official Comment 6.

feated as between the parties by dishonor of the check on due presentment."[126] This ties in to the reclamation rights of the seller under Section 2-507(2) because the condition to make tender and delivery under Section 2-511(1) is conditional on payment, which, if made by check, means that it is conditional on the honor of the check upon presentment. Section 2-511(3) does not state any time limits, but at least one court has said that the ten-day period of Section 2-702(2), which applies to sales on credit where the seller learns of the buyer's insolvency, also applies to Sections 2-511(3) and 2-507(2).[127] The seller again faces a problem if a bank is slow to provide notice of dishonor. If the buyer is insolvent and goes into bankruptcy before the check is dishonored and the goods have been subjected to levy by the trustee, the seller stands as an unsecured creditor.[128]

[11] Section 2-513: Inspection of Goods

Section 2-513 establishes the buyer's right to inspect goods before payment or acceptance. It therefore places another limitation on the ripening of the obligation to pay when the condition of tender and delivery is satisfied. Inspection may occur after delivery if the contract provides for shipment by the seller to the buyer.[129] The buyer does not have the right of prior inspection when the contract provides for COD delivery or for payment on documents of title.[130] Inspection must take place within a reason-

---

[126] This language seems tq suggest something approaching a sale on credit despite the holding in the *Helms* case, supra note 125.

[127] In re Helms Veneer Corp., 287 F. Supp. 840 (WD Va. 1968).

[128] Mullen v. Sweetheart Cup Corp., 15 UCC Rep. 828 (SD Fla. 1974).

[129] Section 2-513(1) reads:

> "Unless otherwise agreed and subject to subsection (3), where goods are tendered or delivered or identified to the contract for sale, the buyer has a right before payment or acceptance to inspect them at any reasonable place and time and in any reasonable manner. When the seller is required or authorized to send the goods to the buyer, the inspection may be after their arrival."

See also Performance Motors v. Allen, 280 NC 385, 186 SE2d 162 (1972).

[130] UCC § 2-513(3). The buyer must bear the costs of inspection. UCC § 2-513(2). If the contract provides for a method of inspection, that method is presumed to be exclusive. UCC § 2-513(4).

able time and manner at the buyer's discretion,[131] and reasonableness is determined by trade usage, customs in the area, or past practices between the parties.[132]

[12] Section 2-601: Acceptance or Rejection of Nonconforming Goods

If the buyer is not happy with the inspection that he conducts in accordance with Section 2-513, what can he do? Section 2-601 provides that if the goods tendered are nonconforming,[133] the buyer may reject the whole,[134] accept the whole, or accept any "commercial unit or units" and reject the remainder.[135] The buyer's options are essentially those that a party has where there is a failure of a condition, as opposed to a breach of a covenant. It is as if the contract were void ab initio and the buyer has the option to walk

---

[131] UCC § 2-513, Official Comment 3; G&H Land & Cattle Co. v. Heitzman & Nelson, Inc., 102 Idaho 204, 628 P2d 1038 (1981); Michael M. Berlin & Co. v. T. Whiting Mfg., Inc., 5 UCC Rep. 357 (NY Sup. Ct. 1968).

[132] UCC § 2-513, Official Comment 3; EPN-Deleval, SA v. Inter-Equip, Inc., 542 F. Supp. 238 (SD Tex. 1982).

[133] In general, courts look to the written agreement rather than to extrinsic oral discussions to determine whether goods conform. Webb v. Chevy Chase Cars, Inc., 259 Md. 330, 269 A2d 810 (1970). The standard parol evidence rule applies, however, and extrinsic evidence may be admissible to explain ambiguities.

[134] The "whole" may include accessories to the principal object of the contract. In Ford Motor Credit Co. v. Harper, 671 F2d 1117 (8th Cir. 1982), the court allowed a farmer to reject delivery of a large disc harrow along with his rejection of a nonconforming tender of a tractor because the tractor was necessary to pull the disc harrow.

[135] Section 2-601 reads:

> "Subject to the provisions of this Article on breach in installment contracts (Section 2-616) and unless otherwise agreed under the sections on contractual limitations of remedy (Sections 2-718 and 2-719), if the goods or the tender of delivery fail in any respect to conform to the contract, the buyer may
>
> "(a) reject the whole; or
>
> "(b) accept the whole; or
>
> "(c) accept any commercial unit or units and reject the rest."

The insistence that a partial acceptance be of a commercial unit is to protect the interest of the seller in the remainder and to avoid a bad-faith partial rejection that substantially diminishes the value of the goods retained by the seller. UCC § 2-601, Official Comment 1.

away from the deal or to excuse the failure of the condition and to accept the performance as tendered.[136] The one difference arises in connection with the option to accept part of the performance and to reject the rest. If there are several tenders and one is nonconforming, the contract may be divisible into a series of separate agreements for each delivery, and a nonconforming tender in one delivery is a failure of the condition necessary to the buyer's obligation to pay for that delivery. If the contract is not divisible, however, the buyer's option to accept a commercial unit and reject the rest means that the buyer can impose a modification upon the seller. The contract is not void in its entirety, but may be kept alive in part at the buyer's option.

The buyer's right to reject nonconforming goods can run into the seller's right to cure a nonconforming tender under Section 2-508. There may be other problems in reconciling the buyer's rejection rights with an agreement to limit remedies pursuant to the provisions of Sections 2-718 or 2-719. The consumer who buys a lemon from an automobile dealer is likely to have these problems. Consider the unhappy buyer who traded his old car in on a new Rambler that would not make it home because it kept stalling. He returned the car to the dealer the next day and received a new carburetor to cure the stalling problem. He never had a chance to test the quality of the new carburetor, however, because the next day the transmission broke. This was enough for the buyer, who returned the ill-fated Rambler and demanded his money and his old car back. He exercised his Section 2-601 right to reject the whole and to demand rescission. The seller countered by claiming his right to cure under Section 2-508. He had provided a new carburetor and he stood ready to remedy the transmission problem. Furthermore, the seller pointed out that the contract contained a provision limiting the buyer's remedies for a breach of warranty to the repair or the replacement of a defective part. The court was not moved by the seller's arguments and held for the unhappy purchaser of the lemon.[137] Whether the court would have reached a

---

[136] See supra ¶ 5.01[1].

[137] Menard & Holmberg Rambler, Inc. v. Shea, 8 UCC Rep. 167 (Mass. 1967).

similar result had the contract been between two merchants or for a less complicated and less dangerous chattel is open to debate.[138]

[13] Section 2-605: Buyer's Statement of Rejection

If the buyer is not careful to state his reasons for rejection, he may waive the defects and, pursuant to the provisions of Section 2-605, he may not be able to rely on the defects as justification for his rejection in a subsequent action by the seller.[139] One of the objects of Section 2-605 is to give the seller adequate notice of the defects so that he can cure. Indeed, a rejection without a statement of objections may be evidence of commercial bad faith and an attempt by the buyer to avoid what has become an unprofitable transaction.[140] Simply complaining about a delivery may not amount to a rejection. The buyer must be specific about what he is doing and why.[141]

[14] Section 2-612: Individual Treatment of Each Installment in Installment Contracts

A perennial problem is whether breach of one part of an installment contract constitutes a default on the whole. The general

---

[138] Judges do seem somewhat unsympathetic to car dealers in disputes with consumers. In the case of Jakowski v. Carole Chevrolet, Inc., 180 NJ Super. 122, 433 A2d 841 (1981), the buyer had specified undercoating and a polymer finish for his new car. It was delivered with neither and the buyer would not accept delivery. The dealer agreed to cure, but before the cure was complete, the car was stolen from the dealer's lot. Which insurance company bore the risk of loss, the buyer's or the seller's? The risk of loss fell on the seller, said the court, because the delivery was nonconforming and could not be complete until the seller made a satisfactory cure. Considering that undercoating and a polymer finish are relatively inexpensive and hardly central to the operation of an automobile, this was a somewhat strict application of the perfect tender rule, but it was not unreasonable to cast the risk of loss on the dealer because he did have possession and control of security for the automobile.

[139] Section 2-605(1) reads: "The buyer's failure to state in connection with rejection a particular defect which is ascertainable by reasonable inspection precludes him from relying on the unstated defect to justify rejection or to establish breach." Sections 2-602, 2-603, and 2-604 describe the procedures the buyer must follow upon making a rejection and his responsibilities and rights in connection with rejected goods in his possession.

[140] UCC § 2-605, Official Comment 2.

[141] See, e.g., Phil Jacobs, Inc. v. Mifflin, 23 Ill. App. 3d 999, 320 NE2d 329

trend of the common law is to treat installment contracts as divisible and to say that the failure to make a delivery or a payment is a breach of the contract but not a default.[142] Breach of part of an installment contract thus is a broken covenant but not a failed condition. The UCC makes this trend explicit in Section 2-612 for transactions governed by Article 2.[143] In practical effect, each installment becomes a separate contract for which the buyer has a right of rejection and the seller has a right of cure.[144] Nonconformity of one installment amounts to a default only where the nonconformity "substantially impairs the value of the whole contract."[145] Even then the contract is reinstated if the aggrieved party accepts another nonconforming installment "without seasonably notifying of cancellation," brings an action only for past breaches, or makes a demand for performance of future installments.[146] The clear purpose of Section 2-612 is to support the continued existence of a contractual relationship between the parties despite a breach or other failure of one performance in a series of performances. It cannot be read in a vacuum, however; Section 2-612 must be considered together with other UCC sections, including Section 2-609, which provides that a party may "demand adequate assurance of due performance" when he has reasonable grounds for insecurity.

(1974). But cf. Fenton v. Contemporary Dev. Co., 12 Wash. App. 345, 529 P2d 883 (1974).

[142] Of course, the parties can provide otherwise. Loan agreements typically provide that upon nonpayment of an installment when due (perhaps after a grace period), the creditor can accelerate the note and demand payment in full. Failure to insist on an acceleration clause may result in a waiver of the right to treat a late payment or a nonpayment as a default on the whole.

[143] See, e.g., Kirkwood Agri-Trade v. Frosty Land Foods Int'l, Inc., 650 F2d 602 (5th Cir. 1981); Laredo Hides Co. v. H&H Meat Prods. Co., 513 SW2d 210 (Tex. Civ. App. 1974).

[144] Section 2-612(2) provides:

> "The buyer may reject any installment which is nonconforming if the nonconformity substantially impairs the value of that installment and cannot be cured or if the nonconformity is a defect in the required documents; but if the nonconformity does not fall within subsection (3) and the seller gives adequate assurance of its cure the buyer must accept that installment."

[145] UCC § 2-612(3).

[146] Id.

[15] Other UCC Provisions

Other UCC sections relate to the issue of conditions versus covenants. Sections 2-703 (the seller's general remedies), 2-711 (the buyer's general remedies), 2-718 and 2-719 (limitations of remedies), and 2-606, 2-607, and 2-608 (the components, effect, and revocation of acceptance) may be relevant in determining how to sort out a transaction that has gone awry. If there is one unifying theme in all these sections, it is that the drafters of the UCC preferred an analysis that supported the existence of an agreement rather than an analysis likely to result in the avoidance of an agreement. That is, given a choice, the UCC prefers covenants to conditions and breaches to forfeitures. Wherever there is a statement in the UCC of what appears to be a condition (e.g., the obligation to pay ripens upon the condition of tender and delivery), other sections limit the buyer's or the seller's ability to plead a failure of a condition to avoid an obligation. This is consistent with both the common-law preference for constructions that avoid forfeitures and the notion that if the parties have made a contract of sale they probably intend it to have substance and not to be a wager on whether an external event will occur. It is also consistent with the buyer's and the seller's good-faith obligations to bring their respective contractual obligations to fruition.

CHAPTER 6

Equitable Remedies

¶ 6.01 EQUITABLE VS. LEGAL REMEDIES

[1] Historical Distinctions Between Law and Equity

One of the bewildering complexities of Anglo-American law is the continuing distinction between law and equity. There are fundamental differences in the justifying principles of the two systems. This disparity created enough problems when the two systems were separate. Now that law and equity have been merged in almost all American jurisdictions, a single judge must decide whether to act as a chancellor in equity or as a common-law judge.

The distinctions between the systems are primarily apparent in the remedies available. A plaintiff in one contract action can recover only money damages as a substitute for the performance for which he bargained, but in another case a plaintiff can demand specific performance, or precisely what he bargained for with no substitutions. These differences reflect different conceptual approaches to the law of contracts and several hundred years of English and American legal history.

The civil-law jurisdictions on the European continent prefer the remedy of specific performance to award of damages in contract actions. The civil-law courts assume that promises are to be enforced and that the promisor should not be free to choose breach and substituted performance and pay money damages for the consequences of a failed promise. If there are significant hardships or if an award of specific performance would be an exercise in futility, the civil-law courts provide for a substitute, but such cases are the exception rather than the rule.[1] Although some commentators have argued that there is a moral basis to contract and that the underlying presumption of contract law should be in favor of a requirement that contract promises be enforced according to their terms,[2] En-

---

[1] See Dawson, "Specific Performance in France and Germany," 57 Mich. L. Rev. 495 (1959).

[2] See, e.g., Fried, *Contract as Promise* (1981).

glish and American common-law courts have favored substitutional relief.

There are many reasons for the differences in the two approaches, but there is no question that the common-law courts have never considered it their duty to require a defaulting promisor to perform except in what the courts have characterized as unusual circumstances. Common-law judges have been reluctant to become too closely involved in the private law-making of the parties and have limited their role to economic umpires. They sort out the pieces of a failed transaction in order to soften the loss to the nondefaulting party, but they are reluctant to try to reconstruct the particulars of the transaction and to give it new life.[3]

[2] Development of Equity in Courts of Chancery

[a] Redress of Grievances in Extraordinary Circumstances

Over several generations, English common-law courts developed different forms of action to fit various kinds of disputes. These were not always satisfactory because they did not cover all the kinds of disputes that arose in private transactions. In the English monarchy, as in many other monarchies, a citizen could petition the king directly for a redress of grievances if the citizen was unable to obtain satisfaction from one of the king's appointed servants. This was true in legal disputes as well as in other matters. The king was supposed to do justice among his subjects even if it meant bypassing or overruling the ordinary structures and institutions of his own government. The chancellor received these petitions and acted as the king's delegate in acting upon them. Of course, the king could always overrule his chancellor,[4] but in the normal course a chancellor who was generally in the king's favor wielded enormous political power. Because the chancellor could not handle all the petitions himself and also perform his other duties, he set up his own bureaucracy, known as the Courts of Chancery, to rule on the petitions of redress.

---

[3] See, e.g., Farnsworth, "Legal Remedies for Breach of Contract," 70 Colum. L. Rev. 1145, 1152, 1153 (1970) (hereinafter cited as Farnsworth); Huston, *The Enforcement of Decrees in Equity* 7 (1915).

[4] The king's response to his chancellor could be even more drastic, as Henry VIII's was to Thomas More.

[b] Differences of Emphasis and Procedure in Chancery and Common-Law Courts

Because most chancellors were also clerics, the style of their secular courts and bureaucracies followed the style of the ecclesiastical courts. The chancellor's courts approached promissory transactions from a perspective based on the traditions of petitions to the king to do justice and the emphasis on justice and fairness in the ecclesiastical courts. Common-law judges were reluctant to bring the power of the state to bear on the personal relationships created by contracting parties and limited their intrusion to requiring a substitute for performance. Judges of the Courts of Chancery, on the other hand, were willing to become intimately involved in the parties' affairs in order to reach a fair, just, and equitable result. The tendency of the Courts of Chancery was to make a defaulting party perform his promise. The moral element was clearly apparent and no doubt reflected the religious background of most of the chancellors.[5]

There were also procedural differences between the king's common-law courts and the Courts of Chancery. The equity courts (Courts of Chancery) took evidence on written depositions, although they later heard oral testimony. There was no cross-examination and no juries (although a chancellor could empanel an advisory jury to assist him in a case). The chancellor was both fact-finder and judge and had the discretion to issue a wide range of remedies and to tailor them to each situation. Judges sitting in equity also tended to be somewhat more lenient than their common-law counterparts about the introduction of evidence.

The common-law courts were more formal than the Courts of Chancery. They used juries and the jurors became the principal fact-finders. Judges decided the law but deferred to the jury's determination of factual disputes. Testimony was oral and there was

---

[5] The Courts of Chancery did not attempt to accomplish justice in a generalized public sense. Their purpose was to provide equity between the petitioner and the respondent, which meant that the court could take into account all the particulars of the relationship between the parties. The same result might not be reached in a similar case because the parties may have treated each other somewhat differently. In comparison, one of the goals of the common-law courts was to develop rules of general application that would ensure predictable, uniform treatment among similar cases.

cross-examination, although in time written depositions were allowed in limited circumstances, as is the case today. The usual remedy was money damages, which was enforced differently in each court. If a defendant in a legal action failed to pay the judgment, the common-law court issued an order to the sheriff to seize the defendant's property and to sell it in order to pay the judgment. In comparison, the chancellor's remedies were personal, and if the respondent (the chancery defendant called upon to respond to the petition) failed to obey the order, he could be held in contempt and jailed. Thus, the maxim developed that law acts in rem and that equity acts in personam.

[c] Deference of Chancery Courts to Common-Law Courts

Every lawyer is familiar with the statement that equity defers to law and that equity does not intervene if there is an adequate remedy at law. There may be a question about what is an adequate remedy at law, but the general rule holds. Of the many historical reasons for the deference of the Courts of Chancery to the common-law courts, the simplest and perhaps most compelling is that the Courts of Chancery developed in order to deal with extraordinary cases that could not be handled at law. Because the Chancery petitioner could not get a remedy elsewhere, he appealed to the king's sense of justice and fair dealing. If there were a means for the petitioner to obtain redress elsewhere, there was then no reason for the chancellor to intervene on the king's behalf.[6] No doubt most of the English chancellors were also careful not to extend their practical powers through their bureaucracies beyond what was acceptable to the monarch and to Parliament.

The petitioner had to come into the Courts of Chancery with "clean hands" and he himself had to "do equity" in order to receive equity. The petitioner asked the king through the chancellor to go outside the bounds of normal judicial processes and governmental operations because he had an extraordinary need for justice in a particular case. In order to justify the invocation of state power on the side of a particular petitioner's demand for

[6] Farnsworth 1154.

justice, the Courts of Chancery demanded that the petitioner be deserving, a rule that still applies.

The Courts of Chancery were also reluctant to try to enforce an agreement that was vague and susceptible to different interpretations. If it was difficult to determine the equities of a particular case, the Courts of Chancery did not want to intervene. They also did not want to become involved in trying to enforce decrees that were themselves vague or that involved oversight of complicated undertakings over an extended period of time. Some modern courts reflect this tendency by generally refusing to issue decrees that require action, such as the construction of a building.[7] The Courts of Chancery also refused most petitions that required the respondent to perform a personal service because of the severity of the sanction for failure to comply (jail and a fine) or the difficulty in determining whether a personal service was properly performed (e.g., did the opera singer sing as well as she should have?).[8] Some courts have equated an order of specific performance for a personal service to a form of state-sanctioned slavery.

[3] Contemporary Differences Between Law and Equity

Judges continue to have wide discretion in fashioning equitable decrees, but they usually can order nothing more than the payment of money in a law case. The contempt sanction applies to recalcitrant respondents in equity, but a defendant who defaults on a money judgment in law is subject only to a sheriff's levy and execution on his property. Equity courts sometimes issue decrees that require the payment of money, as in a suit for an accounting or occasionally in a suit for specific performance of a contract to lend money.[9] There is the distinct possibility, therefore, that a debtor (one who does not abide by an equitable decree to pay money) may find himself in jail for contempt.[10]

Even with the merger of law and equity, many of these distinc-

---

[7] But see discussion infra at ¶ 6.06.

[8] Lumley v. Wagner, 42 Eng. Rep. 687 (1852).

[9] See infra ¶ 6.04.

[10] There is a certain irony in this because at least one of the English colonies, Georgia, was founded as a haven for the inmates of debtors' prisons.

tions continue. The seventh amendment to the United States Constitution preserves the right of trial by jury in actions for twenty dollars or more that would have been tried in the English common-law courts.[11] Sometimes it is difficult to decide what is a legal issue and what is an equitable issue, especially if the claim for relief is based on a right developed after the ratification of the seventh amendment.[12] The Supreme Court has decided that legal issues should be tried first to a jury even if the case is first filed as an equity action and that when there is a question of whether the issue is a matter of equity or a legal issue, the presumption is that the issue is a legal one and that the parties are entitled to a jury trial.[13] This reflects the traditional deference of equity to law and the Supreme Court's concern to protect a constitutional interest in jury trials.

With some slight variations, most of these rules apply in determining whether a complainant in a contract case is entitled to an equitable or a legal remedy. Perhaps the most significant change of the past generation has been a growing willingness to employ equitable remedies. Although judges still adhere to the rule that equity defers to law unless the legal remedy is inadequate, the inadequacy of some legal remedies is being demonstrated more creatively today than in the past.[14]

Primarily for the historical reasons discussed previously,[15] the preferred remedies for contract breaches are substitutional and not specific. The disappointed party is able to claim the monetary equivalent of performance to the extent that it can be calculated

---

[11] The seventh amendment to the United States Constitution provides that "in suits at common law, where the value in controversy shall exceed twenty dollars the right of trial by jury shall be preserved, and no fact tried by a jury shall be otherwise reexamined in any Court of the United States, than according to the rules of the common law."

[12] See, e.g., Ross v. Bernhard, 396 US 531 (1970); 9 Wright & Miller, *Federal Practice and Procedure* § 2302 (1971).

[13] See, e.g., Dairy Queen, Inc. v. Wood, 369 US 469 (1962); Beacon Theatres, Inc. v. Westover, 359 US 500 (1959).

[14] See, e.g., Linzer, "On the Amorality of Contract Remedies — Efficiency, Equity, and the Second Restatement," 81 Colum. L. Rev. 111 (1981) (hereinafter cited as Linzer); Van Hecke, "Changing Emphases in Specific Performance," 40 NCL Rev. 1 (1961).

[15] See supra ¶ 6.01[2].

with any degree of certainty,[16] but he is rarely able to demand that the defaulting party actually perform his part of the bargain. This means that the great bulk of contract actions are handled in the law courts or, since the merger of law and equity, by judges applying the principles of the common-law courts rather than those of the courts of equity.

When a case is brought in equity, however, the usual equitable defenses apply. The petitioner must have clean hands and must have performed in a fair and just manner himself. This does not mean that a defaulting petitioner is automatically out of court; the equities may still be on the side of one who is technically in default if he can assure the court that he will perform.[17] The petitioner must act promptly to assert his rights or he may be barred by the doctrine of laches. The contract itself must be fairly definite, reasonable, and legal in its terms,[18] and there can be no hint of unconscionability.[19]

Although there still is a strong presumption in favor of substitutional remedies, the merger of law and equity into one system and the growing tendency of some courts to fashion more creative remedies may lead to a wider use of equitable principles in connection with legal remedies. In addition, the inclusion of arbitration clauses in a wide range of contracts and the willingness of arbitrators to issue awards that are essentially the same as decrees in equity may have the result of expanding further the practical availability of equitable remedies.[20]

---

[16] See ¶ 7.01.

[17] See infra ¶ 6.02[3][d] for a discussion of cases involving defaulting purchasers under installment sales contracts for the purchase of land.

[18] At one time, the petition itself had to describe with particularity the provisions of the contract to be sure that it met basic requirements of consideration, definiteness, and fairness. See, e.g., Georgia Money Corp. v. Monteleone Apartments, Inc., 223 Ga. 418, 156 SE2d 39 (1967); Banks v. Harden, 220 Ga. 266, 138 SE2d 320 (1964); Bauermeister v. Sullivan, 87 Ind. App. 628, 160 NE 105 (1928); Linse v. Zastrow, 63 Mont. 241, 207 P 119 (1922). Under modern pleading rules it is not as important to include all such allegations in the complaint itself, but at trial the substantive issues remain. See generally Annot., 100 ALR2d 551 (1965).

[19] See ¶ 10.03[2] for a discussion of the unconscionability defense.

[20] See infra ¶ 6.06.

¶ 6.02 LAND SALES CONTRACTS

[1] Basis for Equitable Remedies for Breach of Land Sale Contracts

Contracts for the sale of land have always been treated differently from other kinds of contracts in determining whether equitable remedies should be available. Contrary to the general rule, the presumption is that equity and not law should enforce contracts for the sale of land. The justification is that each tract of land is unique and that money damages can never be an adequate remedy for the failure to deliver a parcel of real estate. This justification itself reflects the importance of land in feudal English society.[21]

Today it is difficult to argue with any credibility that every interest in land is unique. Surely the distinctions among the lots in suburban subdivisions or condominium units in high-rise buildings are minimal and would not be significant enough to support an action in equity if the subject matter were something other than land. Nonetheless, the presumption remains, and with rare exceptions courts of equity take jurisdiction of cases that involve the breach of a contract to convey land.[22]

[2] Specific Performance in Realty Sales

The argument that specific performance should be available in a real estate transaction because each tract of land is unique applies more to the buyer than to the seller. The buyer presumably is more interested in a particular tract, house, leasehold, or apart-

---

[21] See generally 11 *Williston on Contracts* § 1418A (3d ed. 1968) (hereinafter cited as Williston); 5A *Corbin on Contracts* § 1143 (1964) (hereinafter cited as Corbin).

[22] See Calamari & Perillo, *The Law of Contracts* § 16-2, at 582 (2d ed. 1977) (hereinafter cited as Calamari & Perillo). For a rare case to the contrary, see Suchan v. Rutherford, 90 Idaho 288, 410 P2d 434 (1966). One court did find high-rise condominiums to be indistinguishable one from the other and considered legal remedies to be adequate for breach of a contract to convey a condominium. Centex Homes Corp. v. Boag, 128 NJ Super. 385, 320 A2d 194 (1974).

ment.[23] The seller can be made whole by an award of damages equivalent to the difference between the contract price and the market price at the time of closing or the resale price if he is fortunate enough to find another buyer.[24]

Although specific performance applies more to buyers, sellers have been equally successful in obtaining it, which has been justified by mutuality of remedy. This doctrine holds that if the buyer is entitled to specific performance by the seller, the seller should expect no less.[25] Today, however, mutuality of remedy is a doctrine most often observed in the breach and is hardly considered an adequate justification for a legal rule. There is also the argument that the seller's proof of market value is speculative, but it only says that no other parcel is truly comparable in value because each parcel of realty is unique.[26] Considering how often courts accept evidence of comparable values and expert testimony to determine the worth of property for a variety of purposes (e.g., condemnation hearings and tax valuations), the argument that specific performance for the seller is the only appropriate remedy because it is difficult for the seller to prove the economic value of his land rests on a thin reed. The real problem most sellers face is that they are land poor. If a buyer breaches the contract and the seller receives money damages for the difference in value between the contract price and the market value of the land, the seller still may be short of cash. In fact, if the contract was negotiated at arm's length in a fairly stable market, it is the best evidence of fair market value and there may be no damage. The real value to the seller of specific

---

[23] This is not necessarily true if the buyer is a dealer in real estate who is only interested in resale. For a rare case in which a court denied a buyer's request for specific performance because he was buying for resale only and could be made whole by money damages, see Watkins v. Paul, 95 Idaho 499, 511 P2d 781 (1973). See generally Thompson & Sebert, *Remedies: Damages, Equity and Restitution* 11-2 (1983).

[24] See Chapter 8.

[25] See, e.g., Richman v. Seaberg, 353 Mass. 757, 231 NE2d 380 (1967); Belilove v. Reich, 102 RI 250, 229 A2d 775 (1967).

[26] See Restatement (Second) of Contracts § 360 comment e (1981).

performance is usually the ability to transform land into liquid assets.[27]

[3] Remedies for Specific Breaches of Realty Contracts

Failed land transactions often involve factors other than a simple refusal to convey. The seller may not have good title, or one party may be in default on one provision of the contract. Because an equity court has broad discretion to fashion remedies appropriate to the specific case, the result may be a decree that is for specific performance plus some other relief by way of reformation, partial rescission, or money damages.

[a] Remedies for Seller's Breach of Implied Warranty of Title

A contract for the sale of an interest in land contains an implied warranty that the seller has good and marketable title to the interest being sold. Lack of clear title is a breach of the contract sufficient to justify the buyer's rescission with no further obligation.[28] If the buyer is willing to waive the defects in title, the seller may not interpose them as a defense to his nonperformance.[29] If the buyer still wants the property and is unwilling simply to waive the defects in title, a court of equity can order specific performance with an abatement in price to take into account the diminished value caused by the cloud on title.[30] This remedy closely resembles reformation, and the effect is the same as if the court reformed the price term of the contract and then enforced it. In fact, courts merge specific performance and damages. The breach of the war-

---

[27] A seller might be able to sue for the price, which amounts to the same thing as specific performance from his perspective, but at least it is a more forthright approach than justifying an equitable decree on the basis of a worn-out principle of equity or a spurious argument about the difficulties of proof. See, e.g., Trachtenburg v. Sibarco Stations, Inc., 477 Pa. 517, 384 A2d 1209 (1978).

[28] See generally 7 Williston § 923; Sutton v. Ford, 215 Ark. 269, 220 SW2d 125 (1949). Whether the title is marketable is a matter of property law, not contract law.

[29] Lawton v. Byck, 217 Ga. 676, 124 SE2d 369 (1962).

[30] See 11 Williston § 1436; 5A Corbin § 1160; Langley v. Norris, 141 Tex. 405, 173 SW2d 454 (1943).

ranty of good title gives rise to a claim for money damages. Rather than have two actions, one to enforce the contract and another for damages arising from the breach of warranty, the remedy of specific performance coupled with an abatement accomplishes both purposes in a single decree.[31] However, a court will not order specific performance with an abatement in price for defects in the title if the buyer knew of the defects when he entered the contract[32] or if the defects are so serious that the only interest that can be conveyed is substantially different from the interest described in the contract (e.g., a life estate instead of a fee).[33]

[b] Combining Remedies of Specific Performance and Money Damages

The question sometimes arises whether a petitioner in equity can receive both money damages and specific performance or some other equitable remedy. Cases that do not involve decrees requiring the respondent to pay damages to the petitioner cannot provide an answer because they simply involve the enforcement of contracts by the modification of the price term.[34] When the question of receiving money damages and other equitable remedies was put directly to the English Court of Appeal in *Capital and Suburban Properties, Ltd. v. Swycher,*[35] the court responded in the negative because the two remedies were mutually exclusive. Having chosen to proceed in equity, the petitioner could not demand a legal remedy as well. In *Swycher,* the seller of an interest in real estate had been successful in obtaining a decree for specific perfor-

---

[31] This approach is consistent with the arguments advanced by some that the petitioner in an equity action should generally be entitled to damages for injuries sustained by virtue of the breach even if the main remedy sought is specific performance. See, e.g., Dawson, "Damages After Specific Performance," 93 LQ Rev. 232 (1977) (hereinafter cited as Dawson).

[32] See, e.g., Hughes v. Hadley, 96 NJ Eq. 467, 126 A 33 (1924).

[33] In re Estate of Hayhurst, 478 P2d 343 (Okla. 1970); see also Reid v. Allen, 216 Va. 630, 221 SE2d 166 (1976). There is also some question of whether a seller can demand specific performance with an abatement for a defect in title if the buyer does not want to proceed with the transaction but would prefer to rescind or simply to receive money damages for the warranty breach. See Dobbs, *Remedies* 862 (1973).

[34] Such cases are cited supra at ¶ 6.02[3][a] ns. 28–30, 32, 33.

[35] Capital and Suburban Properties, Ltd. v. Swycher, [1976] Ch. 319.

mance against the recalcitrant buyer, but the buyer had refused to abide by the decree. In order to protect himself as much as possible, the seller sold the property to a third party for less than the contract price and then sought to collect as damages the difference between the contract and the resale. The court refused to allow him to do so.

The *Swycher* case has been the subject of harsh criticism,[36] and it is inconsistent with English precedents.[37] There is some logic in *Swycher,* however. If the means for the enforcement of a decree in equity is the contempt sanction,[38] it may be inappropriate to use legal remedies in substitution. On the other hand, it seems sensible for a seller to do just what the seller in *Swycher* did, which is to dispose of the property to someone else and then to seek the difference in money damages. This approach generally is less costly for all than putting a recalcitrant (and perhaps insolvent) buyer in jail for failure to comply with the decree. *Swycher* is also a case in which the specific performance decree was probably an inappropriate remedy in the first place. The seller was obviously interested in a sale and transfer of land for liquid assets. He could have accomplished his whole purpose by selling to a third party and collecting the difference from the defaulting buyer. The presumption that equity should intervene just because land was involved was of little use.

American courts have been more willing to allow an equity petitioner to recover both money damages and specific performance or some other equitable remedy. This more liberal approach is consistent with the concept of discretionary relief that is available in equity. The chancellor is supposed to fashion a decree that

---

[36] Dawson 232.

[37] Dawson cites Griffiths v. Vezey, [1906] 1 Ch. 796, and Austins of East Ham, Ltd. v. Macey, [1941] Ch. 338, and argues

> "It is respectfully submitted that the true position is as suggested by Sir Wilfrid Greene, M.R. in *Austins of East Ham, Ltd v. Macey, viz.* that the defaulting party's failure to comply with the decree gives the innocent party a further right to obtain the normal remedies available for wrongful repudiation — to treat himself as discharged and bring an action on the contract for damages or to rescind the contract and seek *restitution in integrum.*"

Dawson 238.

[38] See supra ¶ 6.01[3].

does justice between the parties and is not supposed to be limited by strictly formal rules of remedies in doing so. Furthermore, the whole notion of mutuality of remedies is of little consequence in modern American courts. Most courts seem to consider it to be a vestige of the old forms of action and to have little meaning under current rules of practice and procedure.[39]

[c] Damages for Seller's Delay in Closing

A fairly common problem in land sales transactions is the seller's delay in closing the deal. In an inflationary market, this may result in higher financing costs for the buyer. American courts usually have allowed a buyer who brings a specific performance action against a tardy seller to recover the difference in the costs of financing between the time that closing should have occurred and the time that the decree is issued. These costs have been characterized as reasonably foreseeable under the standards of *Hadley v. Baxendale,*[40] which is an interesting melding of legal and equitable remedial principles.[41]

There are two ways of measuring damages in such a case. The first focuses directly on the difference in financing costs. The interest rates at the time that closing should have occurred and the time of the decree are compared over the life of the loan and discounted to present values. The present discounted difference in cost between the two results from this comparison. The second measure of damages focuses on the underlying real estate, and the buyer can recover any reduction in market value caused by interest rate increases during the interim.[42] In *Rekki v. Olasson,*[43] the defendant argued that the petitioner's damages for an increase in financing costs should be offset by the property's increase in market value during the period between the time when the closing should have occurred and the issuance of the decree of specific performance

[39] See generally Calamari & Perillo 588.

[40] Hadley v. Baxendale, 9 Ex. 341, 156 Eng. Rep. 145 (1854); see Chapter 7.

[41] See, e.g., Hutton v. Gliksberg, 128 Cal. App. 3d 240, 180 Cal. Rptr. 141 (1982); Annot., 11 ALR4th 891 (1982).

[42] Stratton v. Tejani, 139 Cal. App. 3d 204, 187 Cal. Rptr. 231 (1982).

[43] Rekki v. Olasson, 28 Wash. App. 751, 626 P2d 513 (1981).

against the seller.[44] The court sensibly rejected that argument because the increased value really belonged to the purchaser, who would have had that increase if the deal had closed as planned.

In addition to the increased cost of financing, courts also have allowed petitioners in delay cases to recover extra moving expenses that result from the decree. This does not include the moving expenses that would have been necessary in any event, but only additional expenses, such as the costs of moving furniture into a warehouse and back out again.[45] In a fairly strict application of the *Hadley* doctrine of foreseeability, several courts have refused to allow petitioners in delay cases to recover rents paid in the interim, apparently on the grounds that the petitioners would have had space costs of some kind no matter what.[46] Business losses during the interim may be recoverable if they are susceptible of reasonably certain proof and if they were reasonably foreseeable as a result of the seller's delay.[47]

Sometimes the damages available to a buyer in an action for specific performance against a tardy seller are described as "rents and profits." The petitioner must be careful to understand what is meant by this term and to present evidence consistent with it. The damages are for the lost yield on the property during the period of delay — the profit that would have been made by renting the premises. The term does not relate to the buyer's own costs for alternative premises during the interim.[48]

[d] Remedy of Specific Performance for Buyer in Default

Most real estate transactions involve mortgage financing in which the lender holds a security interest in the land but the bor-

---

[44] Rising interest rates do not always mean that real estate values go down, because land may be a good hedge against inflation.

[45] See, e.g., Regan v. Lanze, 47 AD2d 378, 366 NYS2d 512, rev'd on other grounds, 40 NY2d 475, 354 NE2d 818, 387 NYS2d 79 (1975); Bush v. Cathey, 598 SW2d 777 (Tenn. Ct. App. 1979).

[46] See, e.g., Smith v. Schrader, 80 Cal. App. 478, 251 P 967 (1926); Baker v. Puffer, 299 Ill. 486, 132 NE 429 (1921); Sterne v. Benbow, 151 NC 460, 66 SE 445 (1909).

[47] See, e.g., White v. Felkel, 225 SC 453, 82 SE2d 813 (1954). But cf. Jacob v. Miner, 67 Ariz. 109, 191 P2d 734 (1948).

[48] Walker v. Benton, 407 So. 2d 305 (Fla. Dist. Ct. App. 1981).

rower holds the title. If the borrower defaults on the mortgage note, the lender may foreclose on the mortgage, but the borrower still has an equity interest in the property to the extent that its value exceeds the remaining debt.[49] Some land sales, however, are by installment sales contracts without mortgages. They are classic unilateral contracts in which the buyer agrees to pay a certain amount for the property in installments, usually with interest, over an extended period. The seller retains title until the final payment is made. Thus, if the buyer defaults, the seller has title to the property without having to go through foreclosure. These contracts often contain forfeiture clauses, which provide that upon a default the seller not only retains title to the property but keeps all the payments made on the contract to date. Obviously there is little security for the buyer.

When faced with the enforcement of these kinds of contracts in equity actions, courts have been quite creative and have managed to transform many of them into de facto mortgage transactions. *MacFadden v. Walker,* an en banc decision of the California Supreme Court, is a good example.[50] The buyer was an elderly woman who had made timely payments for ten years on an installment sales contract for the purchase of a tract of land. There was a misunderstanding and dispute between her and the seller about credit for timber harvested from the land, and she set off the timber value against the contract payments. This put her into default under the terms of the agreement, which contained a typical forfeiture clause. The seller sued to quiet title. She counterclaimed for specific performance and tendered the entire balance due with interest into court. Despite her default and the seller's arguments about unclean hands, the California Supreme Court ruled in favor of the buyer, reasoning that forfeiture would amount to an unjust enrichment of the seller that was disproportionate to any injury that he had suffered. The court said:

> [A]llowing the defaulting vendee to cure his default and per-

---

[49] On the other hand, the borrower may also be liable for any deficiency, which is the amount that remains on the mortgage note after the property is sold and the proceeds of the sale are used to pay the note.

[50] MacFadden v. Walker, 5 Cal. 3d 809, 488 P2d 1353, 97 Cal. Rptr. 537 (1971).

form the contract may often be the fairest solution, for the unjust enrichment of the vendor that is precluded by restitution of the excess of part payments over the damages caused by the breach may bear little or no relation to the forfeiture imposed on the vendee if his right to perform the contract is terminated.[51]

The great majority of American courts have followed the same approach as the *MacFadden* court, especially where the equities are in favor of the buyer (e.g., the buyer has made substantial payments or the default is more technical than substantive) and the seller is able to get the benefit of his original bargain.[52] The fact that the buyer in *MacFadden* was able to pay into court the entire balance due was undoubtedly an important factor in the outcome because the seller would recover precisely what he bargained for. If the buyer defaults and makes no indication that he is able or willing to perform, he generally will lose.[53] A buyer who wins a decree of specific performance may lose his right to claim the benefits of the decree if he then fails to tender payment and take title within a reasonable time.[54] In *Commonwealth v. Pendleton,*[55] for example, the buyer lost because he had been in default for a year and only became interested in curing the default because the value of the land increased dramatically.[56]

The seller's own actions may prevent him from enforcing the forfeiture provisions of an installment sales contract for land and

---

[51] Id. at 1356. See also Barkis v. Scott, 34 Cal. 2d 116, 208 P2d 367 (1949).

[52] See, e.g., H&L Land Co. v. Warner, 258 So. 2d 293 (Fla. Dist. Ct. App. 1972); Rothenberg v. Follman, 19 Mich. App. 383, 172 NW2d 845 (1969); Williams Plumbing Co. v. Sinsley, 53 Cal. App. 3d 1027, 126 Cal. Rptr. 345 (1975); Kaiman Realty, Inc. v. Carmichael, 65 Hawaii 637, 655 P2d 872 (1982); Allabastro v. Wheaton Nat'l Bank, 77 Ill. App. 3d 359, 32 Ill. Dec. 831, 395 NE2d 1212 (1979). Contra Ellis v. Butterfield, 98 Idaho 644, 570 P2d 1334, reh'g denied, 98 Idaho 663, 572 P2d 509 (1977).

[53] See, e.g., Nix v. Clary, 640 P2d 246 (Colo. Ct. App. 1981).

[54] Lancaster v. Simmons, 621 SW2d 935 (Mo. Ct. App. 1981).

[55] Commonwealth v. Pendleton, 480 Pa. 107, 389 A2d 532 (1978).

[56] A seller is not precluded from curing a default just because the value of the property increases. The problem in this case was as much one of laches as anything else. The buyer had done nothing but sit on his hands for a year and then had called on a court of equity to help him because it looked as if the deal had turned into a good one.

may open him to a defaulting buyer's suit for specific performance. If the seller's conduct contributes to the buyer's default or delay, the buyer may be entitled to specific performance.[57] The seller's acceptance of late payments may be a waiver of his right to demand strict adherence to the terms of the contract and amount to a de facto modification.[58] The significance of the default is also a factor. In *Cook v. Rezek,*[59] the court did not consider a delay of seventeen days in the payment of $500 on a total contract of $112,000 to be enough of a breach to cause a default under the contract.

[4] Necessity of Definite Terms in Commercial Realty Contracts

The general requirement that a contract must be clear and definite in its terms in order to be enforced by a court of equity has caused some problems in commercial real estate sales. In a typical transaction, the seller agrees to subordinate his purchase money mortgage to the security interest taken by the construction lender. When the contract for the sale of the property to the developer is negotiated, the construction loan often has not been negotiated. Therefore, the subordination clause in the purchase money mortgage may be general and vague, especially with respect to the terms and conditions of the anticipated construction loan. Some courts have refused to enforce options to buy or agreements to sell because the subordination clause is too vague and ambiguous.[60]

---

[57] See, e.g., Daley v. Earven, 131 Ariz. 182, 639 P2d 372 (Ariz. Ct. App. 1981) (seller did not show up to receive check from buyer); Hochard v. Deiter, 219 Kan. 738, 549 P2d 970 (1976) (buyer did not make final payment because seller did not tender merchantable title).

[58] See, e.g., Dean v. Tutor, 566 SW2d 301 (Tex. Civ. App. 1978); Sawin v. Carr, 114 NH 462, 323 A2d 924 (1974). This waiver results even if the contract contains a time-is-of-the-essence clause. Aden v. Alwardt, 76 Ill. App. 3d 54, 31 Ill. Dec. 514, 394 NE2d 716 (1979); Endres v. Warriner, 307 NW2d 146 (SD 1981); Tanner v. Baadsgaard, 612 P2d 345 (Utah 1980). Usually the seller is required to give notice of his intention to demand strict adherence to the terms of the contract and to assert his right to forfeiture before the courts will entertain his claim. Three-O-Three Indus., Inc. v. Moffitt, 622 SW2d 736 (Mo. Ct. App. 1981).

[59] Cook v. Rezek, 89 SD 667, 237 NW2d 18 (1975).

[60] See, e.g., Troj v. Chesebro, 30 Conn. Supp. 30, 296 A2d 685 (1972); Lawrence v. Shutt, 269 Cal. App. 2d 749, 75 Cal. Rptr. 533 (1969).

Other courts have been somewhat more lenient. Subordination to any "FDIC insured lending institution" was sufficiently clear to be enforced by an Alaskan court.[61] Participation in the negotiations for the construction financing or an ownership interest in the developer may estop a seller from asserting that the subordination clause is too vague to be enforced.[62]

¶ 6.03 PERSONALTY SALES CONTRACTS

[1] Use of Equity Remedies in Contracts for Sales of Unique or Difficult-to-Value Personalty

It is presumed that equity courts do not entertain actions for the specific enforcement of contracts involving the sale or exchange of personalty. Unlike real estate, personalty is presumed to be relatively fungible, and substitutional relief at law is adequate. A classic exception to this rule involves the sale of a family heirloom or some other unique, irreplaceable object. Although these cases are rare, the uniqueness argument has found its way into a number of situations that involve property for which there are few adequate substitutes or that is difficult to value. Thus, courts have granted specific performance of a contract to transfer a patent,[63] a copyright,[64] shares of stock in a closely held corporation,[65] shares sufficient to gain control of a publicly held corporation,[66] an entire business,[67] and a private franchise.[68] Even the tax consequences

---

[61] Stenehjem v. Kyn Jin Cho, 631 P2d 482 (Alaska 1981).

[62] Woodworth v. Redwood Empire Sav. and Loan Ass'n, 22 Cal. App. 3d 347, 99 Cal. Rptr. 373 (1971); see also Annot., 26 ALR3d 855 (1969).

[63] Conway v. White, 9 F2d 863 (2d Cir. 1925).

[64] Benziger v. Steinhauser, 154 F 151 (CCSDNY 1907).

[65] Owen v. Merts, 240 Ark. 1080, 405 SW2d 273 (1966).

[66] Armstrong v. Stiffler, 189 Md. 630, 56 A2d 808 (1948).

[67] Leasco Corp. v. Taussig, 473 F2d 777 (2d Cir. 1972); Cochrane v. Szpakowski, 355 Pa. 357, 49 A2d 692 (1946). The courts reasoned that the goodwill of each business was unique unto that business and there could be no adequate substitute.

[68] Hogan v. Norfleet, 113 So. 2d 437 (Fla. Dist. Ct. App. 1957); DeBauge Bros. v. Whitsitt, 212 Kan. 758, 512 P2d 487 (1973); Annot., 82 ALR3d 1102 (1978).

peculiar to a transaction may make it appropriate for enforcement by an equity court.[69]

[2] Use of Equity Remedies When Legal Remedies Are Inadequate

Well before the UCC was adopted, courts began to decide that the remedies at law were inadequate for several ordinary chattel contracts because of the difficulty in effecting cover or otherwise protecting the nonbreaching party from significant harm. The focus had begun to shift from the uniqueness of the chattel to the question of whether the legal remedy was indeed a reasonable substitute. In the language of one court, in order to be adequate the remedy at law had to be as "certain, prompt, complete and efficient to attain the ends of justice as a decree of specific performance."[70] Courts were especially ready to overlook the presumption against the use of equity in personalty contract cases when an element of the public interest was at issue (e.g., a case involving a public utility), even if issuing a decree of specific performance would involve the court's long-term oversight. "While a court may refuse to grant specific performance where such a decree would require constant and long-continued court supervision, this is merely a discretionary rule of decision which is frequently ignored when the public interest is involved."[71]

The standards for determining inadequacy have varied over the years, and courts have begun to apply a fairly broad inadequacy standard. This is particularly apparent in chattel transactions governed by the UCC. Legal remedies have been found to be inadequate not simply where the goods are unique, identified to the contract, otherwise unavailable and critical to the plaintiff, but also

---

[69] See Calamari & Perillo § 16-3, at 584, citing an unreported decision discussed in Note, 22 Vand. L. Rev. 416 (1969).

[70] National Marking Mach. Co. v. Triumph Mfg. Co., 13 F2d 6, 9 (8th Cir. 1926); and see Snip v. City of Lamar, 239 Mo. App. 824, 201 SW2d 790 (1947).

[71] LaClede Gas Co. v. Amoco Oil Co., 522 F2d 33, 39 (8th Cir. 1975), citing Joy v. St. Louis, 138 US 1 (1891); Western Union Tel. Co. v. Pennsylvania Co., 129 F 849 (3d Cir. 1904); Municipal Gas Co. v. Lone Star Gas Co., 259 SW 684 (Tex. Civ. App. 1924), aff'd, 117 Tex. 331, 3 SW2d 790 (1928).

where cover is difficult, economically unwise, or less satisfactory than the original contract. The test has really become one of comparative adequacy in many cases rather than a test of total inadequacy. In the words of Professor Linzer:

> A survey of recent decisions suggests that the courts' traditional reluctance to grant specific relief, manifested in the prerequisite that legal remedies be inadequate, is being replaced, in some circles, with approaches displaying greater flexibility toward equitable remedies. Overall, the courts display great variety in their approaches to pleas for specific relief. While some courts grant and deny specific performance on the basis of pigeonholing, others use the traditional analysis adopted by the second *Restatement's* black-letter text. Most significant, some courts have even used a comparative adequacy approach.[72]

[3] Remedy of Specific Performance Under Section 2-716

Section 2-716 of the UCC provides that specific performance is an appropriate remedy when the goods covered by the contract are unique or in "other proper circumstances."[73] The draftsmen of the UCC intended to expand the availability of specific performance beyond that allowed under the Uniform Sales Act in similar situations.[74] Unique items have some special personal or sentimental value, and in this regard the UCC does not change the common understanding of the equity courts. The UCC, its commentators, and the courts, however, have also included within the category of unique goods those "that have a particular market significance, such as goods covered by an output contract or which are being

---

[72] Linzer 126.

[73] The pertinent provisions of Section 2-716 provide that: "(1) Specific performance may be decreed where the goods are unique or in other proper circumstances, and (2) The decree for specific performance may include such terms and conditions as to payment of the price, damages, or other relief as the court may deem just."

[74] See Uniform Sales Act § 68; UCC § 2-716, Official Comment 1; 3 *Williston on Sales* § 603 (rev. ed. 1948); 3 *Hawkland Uniform Commercial Code Series* § 2-716:02 (1982) (hereinafter cited as Hawkland).

specially manufactured for the buyer."[75] Furthermore, the clause "other proper circumstances" in Section 2-716(1) has provided the courts with an opportunity to expand their discretionary use of equitable remedies in disputes over the sale of goods.[76]

Courts have granted specific performance in contracts for custom-made environmental protection equipment,[77] a personally designed audio system,[78] a custom-built yacht,[79] and restaurant and bar equipment.[80] In comparison, specific performance has been denied in cases involving contracts for the sale of a mobile home,[81] an automobile,[82] and a pickup truck.[83] The purchaser of a Rolls Royce fared better, however, than the purchaser of a run-of-the-mill automobile, even though the Rolls Royce was not unique — the company sold about 100 units of the model in the United States each year.[84]

The case involving the Rolls Royce is a good example of the operation of the "other proper circumstances" clause. The buyer made a $3,500 down payment on the car and waited almost a year

---

[75] 3 Hawkland § 2-716:03, at 410, citing RL Kimsey Cotton Co. v. Ferguson, 233 Ga. 962, 214 SE2d 360 (1975); Gay v. Seafarer Fiberglass Yachts, Inc., 14 UCC Rep. 1335 (NY Sup. Ct. 1974). Note that it is not necessary to identify the goods to the contract to obtain specific performance as compared with the remedy of replevin available under Section 2-716(3). This section provides that

> "The buyer has a right of replevin for goods identified to the contract if after reasonable effort he is unable to effect cover for such goods or the circumstances reasonably indicate that such effort will be unavailing or if the goods have been shipped under reservation and satisfaction of the security interest in them has been made or tendered."

[76] See generally Axelrod, "Specific Performance of Contracts for Sales of Goods: Expansion or Retrenchment in the 1980's," 7 Vt. L. Rev. 249 (1982).

[77] Colorado-Ute Elec. Ass'n v. Envirotech Corp., 524 F. Supp. 1152 (D. Colo. 1981).

[78] Cumbest v. Harris, 363 So. 2d 294 (Miss. 1978).

[79] Gay v. Seafarers Fiberglass Yachts, Inc., 14 UCC Rep. 1335 (NY Sup. Ct. 1974).

[80] Gerwin v. Southeastern Cal. Ass'n of Seventh Day Adventists, 14 Cal. App. 3d 209, 92 Cal. Rptr. 111 (1971).

[81] Pierce-Odom, Inc. v. Evenson, 5 Ark. App. 67, 632 SW2d 247 (1982).

[82] In re Basson, 432 F. Supp. 1013 (D. Conn. 1977).

[83] Paloukos v. Intermountain Chevrolet Co., 99 Idaho 740, 588 P2d 939 (1978).

[84] Schweber v. Rallye Motors, Inc., 12 UCC Rep. 1154 (NY Sup. Ct. 1973).

for delivery while the seller retained the deposit. The seller then convinced the buyer to rescind the transaction because the model in the style and color he wanted would not be available for a long time. A few days later, the dealer had an identical model in the showroom and when the buyer went to claim it, the seller stood by the rescission and refused the sale. The court was no doubt swayed in the buyer's favor by the seller's apparent misrepresentations, his retention of the deposit for a year, and perhaps by the intimation that he hoped to get a better deal on a sale to someone else.

The most interesting change in the application of equitable remedies in chattel transactions has occurred in connection with long-term contracts or contracts for the output or requirements of one of the parties.[85] The modern rule seems to be that specific performance is proper in output or supply-type contracts when cover is not reasonably available or when there is a concern for the public welfare, as in a contract for the supply of fuel to a public utility. In *LaClede Gas Co. v. Amoco Oil Co.*,[86] the buyer was able to cover in the short term with acceptable contracts, but was unable to obtain a satisfactory long-term contract for propane gas that would substitute for the contract that was in default. The court was concerned not only with the buyer's problems in assuring a supply of propane gas but also with the buyer's customers, who needed the gas for their domestic and industrial uses.[87]

The public interest, however, is not always critical. *Copylease Corp. of America v. Memorex Corp.*[88] involved a long-term agreement for the supply of toner for copying machines, and the buyer was able to get another contract for the supply of toner. The problem was that the buyer contended that the seller's toner was the best on the market. The court thus ordered a hearing on the quality of toner and said that the buyer should obtain specific performance

---

[85] For a discussion of requirements and outputs contracts, see ¶ 5.03[3].

[86] LaClede Gas Co. v. Amoco Oil Co., 522 F2d 33 (8th Cir. 1975).

[87] See also United Nuclear Corp. v. General Atomic Co., 96 NM 155, 629 P2d 231 (1980), cert. denied, 451 US 901, reh'g denied, 452 US 932 (1981); Orange and Rockland Util., Inc. v. Amerada Hess Corp., 67 Misc. 2d 560, 324 NYS2d 494 (1971).

[88] Copylease Corp. of Am. v. Memorex Corp., 408 F. Supp. 758 (SDNY 1976).

if his contention was true because in that event cover would not be available.[89] *Copylease* and *LaClede* also indicate courts' greater willingness to police long-term agreements.

Even if cover is reasonably available, the transaction costs of covering may be a sufficient reason for ordering specific performance. That was the court's reasoning in *Gerwin v. Southeastern California Association of Seventh Day Adventists,*[90] a case that involved the sale of restaurant equipment. The buyer could obtain similar equipment on the market, but only at prices he could not afford. The usual legal remedy would be to provide the buyer with the difference between the contract price and the cost of the substituted goods. Although this remedy usually is sufficient to make the buyer whole and to finance the additional expenses, some buyers cannot finance the substitute purchase in the interim. They do not have the resources to cover and then to wait for the result of a lawsuit to make them whole again. The seller is not usually burdened with the financial shortcomings of his buyer, but if the seller knows of the buyer's position, a court may focus as much on the quality of the deal as on the identity of the goods and the possibility of cover in the market. This was the approach taken in *Gerwin*.

A court may also take into account the effect that a breach will have on the buyer's customers, even if the buyer is not a public utility. The critical point in the buyer's favor in *RN Kelly Cotton Merchant, Inc. v. York,*[91] a case involving a contract for the purchase of cotton, was that the buyer had already entered into resale contracts with its customers, and they in turn had entered into resale contracts with their customers. The court found that the third-party customers would be irreparably harmed by the seller's breach because of their reliance on the deliveries. This justified an

---

[89] See also Eastern Airlines, Inc. v. Gulf Oil Corp., 415 F. Supp. 429 (SD Fla. 1975); Kaiser Trading Co. v. Associated Metals and Minerals Corp., 321 F. Supp. 923 (ND Cal. 1970).

[90] Gerwin v. Southeastern Cal. Ass'n of Seventh Day Adventists, 14 Cal. App. 3d 209, 92 Cal. Rptr. 111 (1971).

[91] RN Kelly Cotton Merchant, Inc. v. York, 379 F. Supp. 1075 (MD Ga. 1973), aff'd, 494 F2d 41 (5th Cir. 1974).

award of specific performance.[92]

If a product is generally available on the market, courts still adhere to the rule that there is an adequate remedy at law.[93] A contract price lower than the market average is not enough to justify specific performance.[94] There must be something more, as there was in *Gerwin* — a showing of an overall financial inability to effect cover at market rates.

¶ 6.04 LOAN CONTRACTS

A contract to lend money seems at first to be enforceable only at law. In any event, the remedy for breach is money damages, and money is certainly a fungible good generally available in the market. If the borrower has to pay a higher interest rate or additional closing costs, it is simple enough to award him the difference in the cost between the original loan contract and a substitute.[95] Never-

---

[92] This was one in a series of cases involving cotton contracts. When the market suddenly rose dramatically, sellers tried to get out of their contracts in order to take advantage of the better market prices. In RL Kimsey Cotton Co. v. Ferguson, 233 Ga. 962, 214 SE2d 360 (1975), the court specifically ruled that the increase in market price was not a reason to refuse specific performance.

[93] See, e.g., Weathersby v. Gore, 556 F2d 1247 (5th Cir. 1977); Tower City Grain Co. v. Richman, 232 NW2d 61 (ND 1975); Marion Mfg. Co. v. Long, 588 F2d 538 (6th Cir. 1978); Columbia Gas Transmission Corp. v. Larry H. Wright, Inc., 443 F. Supp. 14 (SD Ohio 1977). Even a poorly pleaded complaint may support an action at law if the case is inappropriate for equity. The case of Ziebarth v. Kalenze, 238 NW2d 261 (ND 1976), was an action for the specific performance of a contract for the sale of cattle. Because the seller sold the cattle to a third party in the meantime, specific performance would have been impossible. Even though the complaint did not request legal relief, the court reasoned that with the merger of law and equity the presumption was that if relief were unavailable in equity it would be available in law (or vice versa) whether or not the complaint stated claims in the alternative.

[94] Duval and Co. v. Malcom, 233 Ga. 784, 214 SE2d 356 (1975); Missouri Pub. Serv. Co. v. Peabody Coal Co., 583 SW2d 721 (Mo. Ct. App. 1979), cert. denied, 444 US 865 (1980); Hilmor Sales Co. v. Helen Neushaefer Div. of Supronics Corp., 6 UCC Rep. 325 (NY Sup. Ct. 1969). When the market is reversed, the same holds true for the seller.

[95] This is certainly the general rule. See, e.g., Turley v. Ball Assoc., Ltd., 641 P2d 286 (Colo. Ct. App. 1981); Kent v. Walter E. Heller & Co., 349 F2d 480 (5th Cir. 1965); Mehr & Kilgore, "Enforcement of the Real Estate Loan Commitment: Improvement of the Borrower's Remedies," 24 Wayne L. Rev. 1011 (1978).

theless, several courts have been willing to employ the specific performance remedy and to compel a lender to close a loan transaction. All the cases thus far have been by borrowers against lenders; there is no reported case of a successful suit for specific performance by a lender, which stands to reason. Lenders can usually find borrowers, and they are likely to be hesitant about the creditworthiness of a borrower who decided to renege on a loan transaction. It is better to lose a little interest than to run the risk of losing the principal as well.

In *First National State Bank v. Commonwealth Federal Savings and Loan Association,*[96] the court determined that the loan contract was "unique" in that the evidence showed that similar financing was not available elsewhere and that it would be difficult to measure the economic injury to the petitioner with certainty. Other cases have focused on the borrower's reliance more than on the particulars of the loan agreement. For instance, the lender was ordered to perform in *McErlean v. Union National Bank*[97] because the borrower had substantially changed his position in relying upon the lender's promise to make a construction loan.[98] Courts also have been influenced by rising interest rates and the financial disaster that may follow if the permanent financing on a real estate development falls through after a construction loan comes due.[99]

The lender's knowledge of the borrower's intentions and position may be important. Another important factor is whether the agreement is construed to be for a single loan or for a series of loans. Both these factors figured significantly in *Cuna Mutual In-*

---

[96] First Nat'l State Bank v. Commonwealth Fed. Sav. and Loan Ass'n, 610 F2d 164 (3d Cir. 1979).

[97] McErlean v. Union Nat'l Bank, 90 Ill. App. 3d 1141, 46 Ill. Dec. 406, 414 NE2d 128 (1980).

[98] See also Jacobson v. First Nat'l Bank, 129 NJ Eq. 440, 20 A2d 19, aff'd, 130 NJ Eq. 604, 23 A2d 409 (1941); Leben v. Nassau Sav. and Loan Ass'n, 40 AD2d 830, 337 NYS2d 310, aff'd, 34 NY2d, 312 NE2d 180, 356 NYS2d 46 (1972).

[99] See Vandeventer v. Dale Constr. Co., 271 Ore. 691, 534 P2d 183 (1975); Selective Builders, Inc. v. Hudson City Sav. Bank, 137 NJ Super. 500, 349 A2d 564 (1975); Draper, "The Broken Commitment: A Modern View of the Mortgage Lender's Remedy," 59 Cornell L. Rev. 418 (1974); Groot, "Specific Performance of Contracts to Provide Permanent Financing," 60 Cornell L. Rev. 718 (1975).

surance Society v. Dominguez,[100] in which a credit union agreed to lend a total of $4,114 to a husband and wife to help them purchase a home. The credit union paid $614 on the agreement and was to pay the remainder to the couple in a series of biweekly installments. When the husband died, the credit union refused to make any more advances. The court gave specific performance to the widow because it construed the agreement to be for a loan of $4,114, not for a series of loans, and the credit union was estopped to deny the agreement because the borrower relied on the loan to purchase a house, and the lender was aware of this reliance.[101]

Another element often arises in credit union cases. A typical credit union is more of a service organization than a commercial bank, and its relationship to its members is of a fiduciary nature. A credit union, therefore, might be treated somewhat differently from a commercial bank or a savings and loan association.

¶ 6.05 PERSONAL SERVICE CONTRACTS

It is a cardinal rule that courts of equity do not order specific performance of a personal service contract. It is said that to do so amounts to a form of slavery in violation of the thirteenth amendment to the United States Constitution, that it is not the role of the courts to force people to do things they find to be distasteful, that it is impossible to police such a decree, and that the remedy would not be useful for the complainant because there is no way to expect that an unhappy person's performance will be as satisfactory as the expected performance at the time of the bargain.[102]

Some courts follow this rule as rigidly as others follow the rule that specific performance is the correct remedy for the breach of a

---

[100] Cuna Mut. Ins. Soc'y v. Dominguez, 9 Ariz. App. 172, 450 P2d 413 (1969).

[101] Although it really should not make any difference, the court seemed to be swayed somewhat by the fact that the money was to be used to purchase real estate. The court almost seemed to treat the case as one falling under the presumption in favor of specific performance for contracts involving the sale of real estate.

[102] See generally Calamari & Perillo § 16-5; Restatement (Second) of Contracts § 367 (1981).

contract for the transfer of an interest in land.[103] In a surprising number of cases, however, courts do order specific performance of personal service contracts, although they rarely discuss the issue in terms of contract law. Most of these are reinstatement or tenure decisions in employment cases, and they are based either on a collective bargaining agreement or some standards of public law.[104] Some of these cases represent legislative decisions about remedies for certain kinds of injuries, and others reflect the deference to collective bargaining as a means to organize the labor force, even at the expense of individual interests in private contract. Nevertheless, these cases do show that the hard-and-fast rule against the specific enforcement of personal service contracts is not really that hard and fast.

Despite the traditional refusal of equity courts to order the specific performance of employment agreements, they have often

---

[103] See, e.g., Linzer 111, 128, citing Gage v. Wimberly, 476 SW2d 724 (Tex. Civ. App. 1972); Bussard v. College of Saint Thomas, Inc., 294 Minn. 215, 200 NW2d 155 (1972); Sprunt v. Board of Trustees, 223 Tenn. 210, 443 SW2d 464 (1969); Zannis v. Lake Shore Radiologists, Ltd., 73 Ill. App. 3d 901, 392 NE2d 126 (1979). The *Zannis* decision emphasized the need for a close personal working relationship among a group of doctors as one of the reasons for denying specific performance. Similar arguments, including one based upon the constitutional right of association, were made by the Atlanta law firm of King & Spalding in response to a sex discrimination suit by a former associate who argued that she had been denied partnership because of her sex. That suit was based on Title VII of the Civil Rights Act of 1964, which prohibits racial and sexual discrimination in employment. Although the Supreme Court opinion in that case only dealt with the question of whether the complainant had stated a cause of action under Title VII, the Court did dismiss the associational argument as any barrier to the maintenance of a sex discrimination lawsuit. Hishon v. King & Spalding, 104 S. Ct. 2229 (1984); see also Lucido v. Cravath, Swaine & Moore, 425 F. Supp. 123 (SDNY 1977). One of the Title VII remedies is reinstatement, which amounts to a form of specific performance. Thus, the *Zannis* rationale may fall before other competing social policies.

[104] See, e.g., Linzer 111, citing Madison County Bd. of Educ. v. Wigley, 288 Ala. 202, 259 So. 2d 233 (1972); Endress v. Brookdale Community College, 144 NJ Super. 109, 364 A2d 1080 (1976); AAUP v. Bloomfield College, 129 NJ Super. 249, 322 A2d 846 (1974), aff'd, 136 NJ Super. 442, 346 A2d 615 (1975). There may be a greater concern with removing artificial barriers to employment or to participation in commerce than with maintaining traditional distinctions between law and equity. See generally note, "Tenure and Partnership as Title VII Remedies," 94 Harv. L. Rev. 457 (1980); Hunter, "The Constitutional Status of Academic Freedom in the United States," 19 Minerva 519, 545–554 (1981).

enjoined the defaulting party from engaging in another competitive activity. The most famous of such cases is *Lumley v. Wagner*.[105] Miss Johanna Wagner, a German cantatrice, agreed to perform for three months at a theater in London leased and managed by Mr. Lumley. She also agreed not to perform in any other theater during the term of the engagement. Mr. Gye, the manager of a competing London theater subsequently persuaded Miss Wagner to break her contract with Lumley and sing at his own theater. Although the court agreed that Lumley could not force Wagner to adhere to her contract and sing for him, it said that Lumley could enjoin her from singing anywhere else in London during the term of her original engagement. The Lord Chancellor said:

> It was objected that the operation of the injunction in the present case was mischievous, excluding the Defendant J. Wagner from performing at any other theatre while this Court had no power to compel her to perform at Her Majesty's Theatre. It is true that I have not the means of compelling her to sing, but she has no cause of complaint if I compel her to abstain from the commission of an act which she has bound herself not to do, and thus possibly cause her to fulfil her engagement.[106]

Lumley is still the leading precedent for the exercise of the equity court's power of restraint in personal service cases. Miss Wagner is also the model for many of the defendants, because these kinds of cases usually involve sports and entertainment figures. In the business world, the most common problem is the enforcement of restrictive covenants in employment agreements. Generally, these are subject to a rule-of-reason test and are enforced only to the extent that they do not unduly interfere with the defendant's ability to pursue his livelihood and are not anticompetitive.[107] There is some support for the argument that specific performance should be the preferred remedy for the enforcement

---

[105] Lumley v. Wagner, 42 Eng. Rep. 687 (1852).

[106] Id. at 693; see also Lumley v. Gye, 2 E&B 216, 118 Eng. Rep. 749 (1853).

[107] See ¶ 8.03[2] for a discussion of restrictive covenants.

of restrictive covenants (in practice, this is more likely to be in the form of an injunction of a breach of the covenant) because it is more efficient than trying to assign a monetary value to the plaintiff's interest in having the defendant adhere to the covenant.[108] The more widely accepted approach is to examine restrictive covenants for substantive fairness between the parties. The tendency is to lean toward legal rather than equitable remedies.[109]

¶ 6.06 ARBITRATION AWARDS

Because arbitration is a popular method of resolving disputes, arbitration clauses appear in a wide range of contracts. A question that sometimes arises is whether arbitrators are bound by the same limitations as judges in fashioning remedies. That is, must an arbitrator favor legal remedies over equitable remedies as a general rule, or is he free to ignore the historical distinctions between law and equity that bind judges? The answer to this question depends upon whether one views the arbitrator as an agent of the parties who is bound by their agreement or as an agent of the state who is bound by rules of general application as well as by the particular contract at issue.

State and federal laws regulate arbitration, and courts usually enforce arbitration awards.[110] This state involvement supports the argument that arbitrators are agents of the state, at least in part, and their actions thus are circumscribed by public concerns, including the substantive remedial limitations generally imposed on courts. The prevailing rule, however, is that arbitrators derive their

---

[108] See Kronman, "Specific Performance," 45 U. Chi. L. Rev. 351, 362 (1978).

[109] See Yorio, "In Defense of Money Damages for Breach of Contract," 82 Colum. L. Rev. 1365 (1982); Note, "Economic and Critical Analysis of the Law of Covenants Not to Compete," 72 Geo. LJ 1425 (1984).

[110] The federal law is codified at 9 USC §§ 1 et seq. For a discussion of the general application of federal law, see Moses H. Cone Memorial Hosp. v. Mercury Constr. Corp., 460 US 1 (1983).

authority solely from the contract,[111] and, as long as it is legal,[112] they are not limited in their discretion concerning remedies by the precedents that bind courts. If the contract specifies a preference for equitable remedies or allows the arbitrator to make up his own mind, he need not be bound by the precedents that prevent judges from issuing equitable decrees in a variety of cases.[113]

> [The] mandate clearly is that in interpreting [an] agreement and in fashioning a remedy in accordance with that agreement, an arbitrator is given broad latitude and discretion. His remedy need not be specifically authorized by the agreement. And, so long as his remedy represents a fair solution to the dispute, the remedy awarded should be affirmed. Reviewing courts should be extremely reluctant to substitute their interpretation of the agreement for that of the arbitrator. . . . [H]is awards should be upheld so long as he does not disregard or modify plain and unambiguous provisions of [the] agreement.[114]

Courts usually refuse to compel performance of construction contracts because they are difficult to supervise and they are, in one sense, personal service contracts.[115] In comparison, arbitrators

---

[111] See, e.g., Ruppert v. Egelhofer, 3 NY2d 576, 148 NE2d 129, 170 NYS2d 785 (1958). The federal law is especially liberal. All doubts are to be construed in favor of the arbitrator's authority, especially with respect to remedies, "for it is essential that arbitrators have a great deal of flexibility in fashioning remedies if the national policy favoring the settlement of disputes by arbitration is to have any real substance." Willoughby Roofing and Supply Co. v. Kajima Int'l, Inc., 598 F. Supp. 353, 357 (MD Ala. 1984), citing United Steelworkers v. Enterprise Wheel and Car Corp., 363 US 593 (1960); Mogge v. District 8, Int'l Ass'n of Machinists, 454 F2d 510 (7th Cir. 1971); Local 369, Bakery and Confectionery Workers IU v. Cotton Baking Co., 514 F2d 1235 (5th Cir. 1975), cert. denied, 423 US 1055 (1976).

[112] See, e.g., In re Silverberg, 75 AD2d 817, 427 NYS2d 480 (1980) (law partnership agreement specified a remedy that could not be awarded because it violated the Code of Professional Responsibility).

[113] Of course, the contract may prohibit some remedies. See, e.g., United Elec. Radio & Mach. Workers v. Honeywell, Inc., 522 F2d 1221 (7th Cir. 1975).

[114] General Tel. Co. v. Communications Workers of Am. 648 F2d 452, 457 (6th Cir. 1981).

[115] See, e.g., Northern Del. Indus. Dev. Corp. v. EW Bliss Co., 245 A2d 431 (Del. Ch. 1968); 5A Corbin § 1172. But cf. City Stores Co. v. Ammerman, 266 F. Supp. 766 (DDC 1967), aff'd, 394 F2d 950 (DC Cir. 1968).

regularly order specific performance of construction contracts. Despite some concern about whether courts should enforce arbitration awards granting remedies that the courts would not have granted in the first instance, the prevailing rule is that an arbitrator's award of specific performance in a construction contract case will be upheld.[116]

Arbitration awards of equitable remedies have also been upheld in cases involving the reinstatement and back pay for an employee,[117] enforcement of the terms of a union contract,[118] enforcement of a lease agreement,[119] injunction of solicitation of former employer's customers,[120] and restrictive covenants in employment agreements.[121] The deference of courts to awards made by arbitrators indicates a growing willingness to approve alternative means of dispute resolution, as well as general respect for the parties' own agreement about what is most suitable for them. If contracts are to be treated as matters of private law-making, then it only stands to reason that courts should respect the private law of remedies chosen by the parties as well as the substantive negotiated provisions of the transactions.

---

116 The leading case is Grayson-Robinson Stores, Inc. v. Iris Constr. Corp., 7 AD2d 367, 183 NYS2d 695 (1959), aff'd, 8 NY2d 133, 168 NE2d 377, 202 NYS2d 303 (1960).

117 William J. Burns Int'l Detective Agency, Inc. v. New Jersey Guards Union, Inc., 64 NJ Super. 301, 165 A2d 844 (1960); Staklinski v. Pyramid Elec. Co., 6 NY2d 159, 160 NE2d 78, 188 NYS2d 541 (1959).

118 District No. 2, Marine Eng'rs Beneficial Ass'n v. Isbrandtsen Co., 36 Misc. 2d 617, 233 NYS2d 408 (1962).

119 Suffolk Dev. Corp. v. Pat-Plaza Amusement Corp., 236 NYS2d 71 (1962).

120 Utility Laundry Serv., Inc. v. Sklar, 300 NY 255, 90 NE2d 178 (1949).

121 Young v. Deschler, 202 Misc. 811, 110 NYS2d 220 (1952); Linwood v. Sherry, 16 Misc. 2d 488, 178 NYS2d 492, aff'd, 7 AD2d 757, 181 NYS2d 772 (1958).

CHAPTER 7

General Rules of Damages for Breach of Contract

¶ 7.01 MONEY DAMAGES VS. SPECIFIC PERFORMANCE TO REMEDY BREACH

In a perfect world, the perfect remedy for a breach of contract would be specific performance because each party would get exactly what he bargained for. As a practical matter, however, specific performance is often impossible. For example, the performing party may have gone bankrupt, the principal may have died, or, as often happens, neither party wants the contract carried out as originally planned. Furthermore, an unhappy performing party may not hold up his end of the bargain very well, and courts are reluctant to enforce contract performance except in limited circumstances.[1] Although some critics argue that the specific performance remedy should be used more often to strengthen the theoretical and moral basis of contract law,[2] the remedy available to most contract litigants is money damages.

At the close of the nineteenth century, Oliver Wendell Holmes wrote, "The duty to keep a contract at common law means a prediction that you must pay damages if you do not keep it — and nothing else."[3] This idea is central to the concept of efficient breach and to the measurement of damages in contract actions.

---

[1] See ¶ 6.01[1].

[2] See, e.g., Fried, *Contract as Promise* (1981) (hereinafter cited as Fried).

[3] Holmes, "The Path of the Law," 10 Harv. L. Rev. 457, 462 (1897).

The point is simple: The law of the contract is the law that the parties themselves have created for their transaction. To be sure, there are public-law aspects. Courts do not enforce contracts for illegal purposes, nor do they require incompetents (e.g., children, the mentally deranged) to abide by their undertakings. They are also reluctant to require the specific performance of most contracts. Instead, courts award damages that are the monetary equivalent, as well as can be established, of full performance. The agreement itself is the key, not a publicly imposed notion of what constitutes reasonable damages. The purpose is to compensate the plaintiff for his lost expectancy, but not to overcompensate him.

A well-established school of thought holds that the limitations on contract damages serve the goal of economic efficiency by allowing the parties to make economically rational choices without fear of unknown consequences, thereby assisting in the efficient allocation of goods and services.[4] The commentators do not unanimously subscribe to this concept. Some believe that the limitations are too strict and result in chronic undercompensation, thereby undermining the goal of economic efficiency.[5] Others question the normative values implied by the selection of economic efficiency as a goal of contract law.[6]

---

[4] See Posner, *Economic Analysis of the Law* 88–90 (1977); Barton, "The Economic Basis of Damages for the Breach of Contract," 1 J. Legal Studies 277 (1972); Birmingham, "Breach of Contract, Damage Measures, and Economic Efficiency," 24 Rutgers L. Rev. 273 (1970); Goetz & Scott, "Liquidated Damages, Penalties and the Just Compensation Principle: Some Notes on an Enforcement Model and a Theory of Efficient Breach," 77 Colum. L. Rev. 554 (1977).

[5] See Farber, "Reassessing the Economic Efficiency of Compensatory Damages for Breach of Contract," 66 Va. L. Rev. 1443 (1980) (hereinafter cited as Farber); Leff, "Injury, Ignorance and Spite—The Dynamics of Collective Coercion," 80 Yale LJ 1 (1970).

[6] Professor Fried has challenged the basic premise of Holmes' view that there is nothing fundamentally wrong with breaking a contract because the nonbreaching party can be made whole with money and, updating the comment to include an economic analysis, because it may be better for all involved if someone breaks an inefficient agreement in favor of a more efficient agreement. In Fried's view,

> "There exists a convention that defines the practice of promising and its entailments. This convention provides a way that a person may create expectations in others. By virtue of the basic Kantian principles of trust and respect, it is wrong to invoke that convention in order to make a promise, and then to break it."

Whatever the debate among scholars, the fact remains that the recovery of damages in a contract case is subject to limiting principles that try to prevent the nonbreaching party from receiving anything more than he would have received on full performance but that also try to make him whole. Three of these principles are central to an understanding of damages. First, the damages must be foreseeable as a consequence of the breach itself. Second, an actual or implied understanding of the risk of these damages must be apparent from the facts. Third, proof must be certain concerning the fact of damage and reasonably certain about the amount.

¶ 7.02 ELEMENTS OF THE DAMAGE REMEDY

[1] Purpose and Applications of Damage Remedies

The fundamental goal of the damage remedy is straightforward: The nonbreaching party should be placed in the same position he would have enjoyed if the breach had not occurred. The idea is to provide the plaintiff with the monetary equivalent of specific performance, and this goal is universally accepted as the guiding principle of contract remedies. The difficulty in many cases is figuring out what would have been the nonbreaching party's position at the end of the transaction. This may often amount to speculation about the future that has little basis in the circumstances. The avoidable consequences rule, or the principle of mitigation, also applies, and a court not only must guess what the future might have held for the plaintiff but also must decide whether the plaintiff did all that he reasonably could to help himself after the breach occurred. Another limiting factor is the principle that the defendant should not be punished for a breach and the plaintiff must not be better off as a result of a litigation recovery than he would have been with full performance.[7]

Fried 17. Somewhat less fundamental criticisms are contained in Linzer, "On the Amorality of Contract Remedies — Efficiency, Equity, and the Second Restatement," 81 Colum. L. Rev. 111 (1981); Michelman, "Norms and Normativity in the Economic Theory of Law," 62 Minn. L. Rev. 1015 (1978); Moineil, "Efficient Breach of Contract: Circles in the Sky," 68 Va. L. Rev. 947 (1982).

[7] For further discussion of the punishment notion in contract cases, see Chapter 11.

The problem is simplest where one party has fully performed and all that remains is the other party's payment of the contract price. If there is no question of performance, the remedy is the contract amount, the oldest and most elementary of contract recoveries. The modern action derives from the old common-law writ of general assumpsit (that is, an action of assumpsit brought upon the contract and founded on an implied promise).[8] The only difficulty might be in calculating the contract price if it were unliquidated.

More commonly, a breach occurs when the contract is still in the executory stage. The common-law writ for breach after partial performance was for special assumpsit (that is, an action of assumpsit brought upon an express contract).[9] The plaintiff was entitled to recover for his "injury," an ambiguous term. Did that mean the costs he had incurred to date, his anticipated profit, his anticipated profits on other deals that depended on the performance of the first contract, his losses on other deals that could be traced back to the failure of the first, or some combination of all these? These are the kinds of questions that courts continually face in contract cases.

[2] The Expectancy Remedy

There are three generally recognized remedies in contract recoveries: expectation, reliance, and restitution.[10] The expectancy remedy usually consists of the value of the profit the nonbreaching

---

[8] See, e.g., UCC § 2-709 (action for the price); Calamari & Perillo, *Contracts* § 14-1, at 518, 519 (2d ed. 1977) (hereinafter cited as Calamari & Perillo).

[9] Id.

[10] See Fuller & Perdue, "The Reliance Interest in Contract Damages (Parts 1 and 2)," 46 Yale LJ 52, 53 (1936) (hereinafter cited as Fuller & Perdue). For almost fifty years this article has guided the discussion of damage recoveries in contract cases. Fuller and Perdue identified these three remedies in contract recoveries. Id. at 53, 54. As a matrix for the analysis of damage claims, the article has had far-reaching effect and is especially helpful to lawyers who must decide how to present evidence of injury and what to emphasize in seeking a recovery. Section 344 of the second Restatement follows the outline of the article with no significant variations. See also Hudec, "Restating the 'Reliance Interest,' " 67 Cornell L. Rev. 704, 707, 708 (1982) (hereinafter cited as Hudec). Hudec suggests

party would have made on the contract. It is the most common measure of damages and is what is usually meant by the "benefit of the bargain." This recovery most closely approximates the goal of satisfying the promisee in the same way as if there had been full performance. Consider the following two situations.

> **EXAMPLE 1.** Brown agrees to sell 100 widgets to Green for \$100. When Brown presents the widgets for delivery, Green reneges. Brown thus has an action against Green for \$100. The recovery will give Brown his full expectancy; that is, the amount he agreed to accept in return for full performance. Since Brown must pay his expenses from this amount, his net will be his profit on the transaction.[11]

> **EXAMPLE 2.** Brown agrees to sell 100 widgets to Green for \$100. Green reneges after Brown has manufactured only 50 widgets. Because Brown must spend \$.50 to manufacture each widget, he has spent \$25 when Green reneges. Brown thus has a claim against Green for \$75, because that amount gives him his full expectancy of a \$50 net profit.

These examples illustrate that the expectancy recovery in a situation involving a typical executory breach must be calculated from the contract price. The nonbreaching party's interest is not the contract price, but that portion of the contract price that affords the same net profit he would have had on full performance. The expectancy is calculated as if the contract had indeed been completed. Many litigants face the frustration of finding that the expectancy does not actually make them whole because the trans-

---

that many of the cases that specifically rely on the Fuller and Perdue article are leading cases in the field. Id. at 705. The method of analysis in the Fuller and Perdue article seems to permeate opinions even when the participants have no conscious awareness of the authors' approach. See Danzig, *The Capability Problem in Contract Law* 5-43 (1978), for a discussion of Sullivan v. O'Connor, 363 Mass. 579, 296 NE2d 183 (1973), in which the lawyers and the trial judge applied the reliance interest principles discussed by Fuller and Perdue apparently in total ignorance of their commentary.

[11] Of course, Brown might not get his \$100 if he sells the widgets to another buyer in the meantime or if he fails to comply with the mitigation principle. The example assumes that he attempted to mitigate but could not.

action costs associated with the breach were not taken into account.[12]

[3] The Reliance Remedy

Sometimes it is impossible to prove what a party's profit would have been on a contract. The breach might have occurred so early that future success would be only speculative. The plaintiff might be a new company that has not been in operation long enough to make a reasonable estimate of its profitability. Sometimes it is not in the plaintiff's best interests to pursue an expectancy recovery because he merely stands to break even or perhaps to lose money on the deal. The best course might be to seek recovery of the nonbreaching party's reliance expenditures. The goal of this remedy is to return the plaintiff to the status quo ante as if the contract had never existed. Conceptually, this goal is fundamentally different from the expectancy recovery. The idea is not to reach the monetary equivalent of specific performance and thereby to recreate the contract, but to reach the position that would have existed for the plaintiff if there had not been a transaction. The expectancy recovery affirms the existence of a contract; the reliance recovery tries to deny it.

As a general rule, reliance damages are easier to prove than expectancy in an executory contract. Consider, for example, a situation where a contractor agrees to build a house for $100,000. When he is half-finished, the buyer reneges. The contractor's reliance damages are the costs of labor and materials to date. These costs are relatively easy to compute because the contractor has cancelled checks, receipts, invoices, purchase orders, personnel records, and tax records that reflect his expenditures. However, this simple concept becomes more complicated in application, for if the contractor is paid for all his expenses to date, he is not returned to exactly the same position he was in before the agreement. Restitution of the status quo ante does not take into account lost opportunities and other consequential losses. There are addi-

---

[12] These costs include attorneys' fees and miscellaneous expenses associated with the disruption of a breach. See Farnsworth, "Legal Remedies for Breach of Contract," 70 Colum. L. Rev. 1145, 1147 n.11 (1970).

tional problems in deciding whether certain kinds of fixed costs should be attributed to a contract as part of the reliance expenditures.[13]

[4] The Restitution Remedy

The goal of the restitution remedy in a contracts case is to put the breaching party back into the position he was in before the agreement. As such, it is the opposite of the reliance remedy. Restitution is appropriate where the breaching party has been unfairly enriched by the acts of the nonbreaching party. Its purpose is to cause the breaching party to give up his unfair gains. In situations that involve a restitutionary recovery, courts usually find an offense against fair dealing. The restitution remedy attempts to do justice in a general sense rather than merely sorting out the economics of the parties' private agreements.

The measure of recovery is the defendant's gain, not the plaintiff's loss or expectancy. Consider the following situation.

> **EXAMPLE 3.** Gray agrees to hold $10,000 in escrow for White. The money is intended as the down payment on a house whose closing is due to occur in thirty days. Until closing, Gray uses the $10,000 to purchase shares of stock in a publicly traded company. At closing, however, the money is not available, and, as a result, the closing does not take place. White has several possible actions against Gray, including actions sounding in tort. He certainly has a cause of action for breach of contract. White's contract damages are at least $10,000, his basic reliance expenditure. In addition, White suffers a loss of expectancy if he is unable to buy the house and will have to purchase a more expensive one or he loses the chance to profit from the purchase of the first house at a price below current market. He may also recover as consequentials some of the transaction costs surrounding the failed deal. He also has a claim in restitution, which may be his most valuable cause of action, especially if he can close on the house with minimal disruption. White can recover the full value of the investment Gray made with his money because

[13] See infra ¶ 7.04.

Gray breached the contract by misusing White's money. If the stock appreciates in value, Gray must turn that profit over to White, in restoration of the ill-gotten gains.

An entire body of law exists on the subject of restitution. In contract cases, it is a means to measure damages in certain situations. As a means of measurement, however, the use of a restitutionary remedy brings into play many of the concepts of fairness and justice central to the whole theory of restitution.[14] Courts use the principles of restitution in fashioning contract recoveries where the expectancy and reliance approaches are not adequate to do justice. Nevertheless, the purpose of restitution is altogether different from more traditional contract remedies. The expectancy approach tries to approximate the result of a fully performed contract. The reliance approach tries to make the plaintiff whole, to put him in the status quo ante. In contrast, the restitution approach focuses on the defendant, not the plaintiff, and makes him relinquish an unfair gain.

¶ 7.03 PROOF OF THE NONBREACHING PARTY'S EXPECTANCY

[1] Problems of Proving Expectation Damages

Although expectation damages are the most common form of recovery in contract cases, they can be difficult to prove. Contract litigants do not have the advantage of the fairly open-ended approaches to proof available in tort actions. A contract plaintiff must prove not only the fact of injury but also its amount and foreseeability as a risk assumed by the breaching party as part of the agreement. Offers of proof must be presented carefully and must be tailored to the particular contract. Although these limitations may make proof somewhat more difficult than in an average tort case, the rules of proof give the litigant an advantage. They assist in deciding what evidence to present and how to present it by defining in advance the boundaries of permissible recoveries. Furthermore, courts do not require mathematical precision in calculating the expectancy, just reasonable certainty. The Supreme Court of Wisconsin outlined the general requirements:

---

[14] See generally Chapter 9.

Damages for breach of contract are recoverable only to the extent that the evidence permits the loss to be established to a reasonable degree of certainty. However, such damages need not be ascertainable with absolute exactness or mathematical precision. The evidence is sufficient if it enables the trier of fact to make a fair and reasonable approximation. The plaintiff bears the burden of establishing reasonably certain damages.[15]

[2] Proximate Cause and Fact of Damages

Although it is couched in language similar to the tort rule, the contract rule of proximate cause is quite different. A clear connection must exist between the breach of contract and the fact of damage. The exact amount of the damage suffered need not be proved to establish proximate causation, but it must be proved that the breach was itself the motivating factor — not that it *could* have been a factor, but that it *was* the factor. In the words of the United States Supreme Court, "Certainty in the fact of damages is essential. Certainty as to the amount goes no further than to require a basis for a reasoned conclusion."[16] For instance, the Minnesota Supreme Court refused to allow a contract plaintiff to recover because the evidence did not prove with certainty that the losses he suffered were the result of the breach. The evidence showed that the losses may have been the result of market forces independent of the defendant's actions.[17]

Proximate cause is a question of fact for a jury. It may be shown by both circumstantial and direct evidence.[18] Whatever the specific evidence, it must be sufficient to show that some loss did occur, that it flowed directly from the breach, and that there is a rational basis from which the amount of damage can be calculated.[19]

---

[15] Thorp Sales Corp. v. Gyuro Grading Co., 107 Wis. 2d 141, 319 NW2d 879, 884 (1982).

[16] Palmer v. Connecticut Ry. & Lighting Co., 311 US 544, 561 (1941).

[17] Polaris Indus., Inc. v. Plastics, Inc., 299 NW2d 414 (Minn. 1980).

[18] General Supply & Equip. Co. v. Phillips, 490 SW2d 913 (Tex. Civ. App. 1972).

[19] Lakota Girl Scout Council, Inc. v. Havey Fund Raising Management, Inc., 519 F2d 634 (8th Cir. 1975); and see Paper Mach. Corp. v. Nelson Foundry Co.,

In many instances courts presume nominal damage upon proof of a breach, but this is not very helpful; it only provides a basis for recovering court costs. If there are any significant losses, the plaintiff must be able to meet a strict standard of causation as the first step in the proof process.

[3] Foreseeability of Damages

[a] Standards in Contract Law vs. Standards in Tort

The rules of foreseeability truly set contract cases apart from cases in tort. A plaintiff's recoverable damage must have been a foreseeable result of a breach of the contract. It is not enough to show that damage followed naturally from the breach, which is sufficient proof in a tort case. There must be a more direct connection between the damage and the risks actually assumed by the parties when they entered into the agreement. The foreseeability rule is consistent with the underlying theory of the enforcement of contracts at common law. A tort involves a public duty imposed equally upon everyone, and a breach of that duty exposes an individual to liability for all the consequences of the breach in the ordinary course of affairs. Because a contract is private law created by the parties, it does not involve the community concerns and obligations central to tort. The parties' agreement forms the fundamental law of the case, and it is the basis for determining liability for damages caused by breach.

The distinction between foreseeability standards in tort and contract is particularly clear in some statutes. In California contract actions, for example, a plaintiff can recover "for all the detriment proximately caused thereby, or which, in the ordinary course of things, *would be likely to result therefrom.*"[20] In a tort case, the successful plaintiff can recover an amount "which will compensate for all the detriment proximately caused thereby, *whether it could have been anticipated or not.*"[21]

---

108 Wis. 2d 614, 323 NW2d 160 (1982); Reiman Assoc., Inc. v. R/A Advertising, Inc., 102 Wis. 2d 305, 306 NW2d 292 (1981).

[20] Cal. Civil Code § 3300 (1972) (emphasis added).

[21] Id. § 3333 (emphasis added).

[b] Standards of General and Specific Damages: The *Hadley v. Baxendale* Rule

The leading case in establishing the foreseeability rule is *Hadley v. Baxendale.*[22] This 1854 English case is read by every first-year contracts student and is cited in thousands of decisions. Despite such widespread familiarity, it is useful to review *Hadley* to see exactly what it said about the recovery of damages in contract actions.

The scenario of the case is as follows: The crankshaft that ran a mill broke; the millers engaged the defendants to take the broken shaft to another town to be repaired and then to return it to the mill. The parties thus entered into an ordinary contract of carriage. The evidence indicated that the millers let the carters know that the matter was urgent and that the defendants said they could quickly deliver the broken crankshaft to and from the town in which the repair shop was located. However, the defendants did not deliver as rapidly as they promised; consequently, there was a substantial delay in getting the shaft repaired and back to the mill. The plaintiffs did not have a spare shaft, and the mill was shut down the entire time that the shaft was in transit and in the shop. Because the defendants did not live up to their promises of speedy delivery, the plaintiffs sought to recover from them the profits they lost for the time that the mill was closed. In refusing to allow the recovery of lost profits, the court established a formula that has been used in case after case throughout common-law jurisdictions. The formula states:

> Where two parties have made a contract which one of them has broken, the damages which the other party ought to receive in respect of such breach of contract should be such as may fairly and reasonably be considered either arising naturally, i.e., according to the usual course of things, from such breach of contract itself, or such as may reasonably be supposed to have been in the contemplation of both parties, at the time they made the contract, as the probable result of the breach of it.[23]

---

[22] Hadley v. Baxendale, 9 Ex. 341, 156 Eng. Rep. 145 (1854).

[23] Id.

This standard set up a two-part test. Some kinds of damages, often called general damages, flow naturally from a breach. Although not directly addressed in *Hadley,* this would have been the cost of carriage for the shaft. Other damages, often called special damages, are peculiar to the transaction, and the breaching party is not liable for them unless he expressly assumed their risk or unless both parties contemplated their probability when they entered into the contract. Lost profits fall in the category of special damages. They could not be recovered in *Hadley* because the proof did not show that the defendants assumed the risk of liability for lost profits or that the defendants knew the plaintiff's particular circumstances. The statement that the matter was urgent was insufficient evidence to show that the carters assumed the risk of lost profits if they were slow in delivery. The court commented that in the ordinary course of events millers are likely to have spare crankshafts to avoid the need to shut down if one breaks. Furthermore, the court noted that a loss of profits can result from many different influences, regardless of the status of the crankshaft. Finally, the evidence did not show that the plaintiffs told the defendants that the broken crankshaft was their only crankshaft and that the mill would be out of business for the time it took to transport and repair it. Thus, the defendants did not specifically undertake any risk other than the general risk of carriage.

Two points about *Hadley* are especially important in understanding its influence. First, the decision was a reaction to the virtually unbridled discretion of juries that had been the rule before the case. The English judges wanted control over the award of damages by jurors who might be swayed more by emotion than by reason,[24] suggesting that the decision was meant to be a reasonable principle of limitation, not an exclusion of remedies. Second, the opinion did not prevent the recovery of special or consequential damages; it simply made claims for these damages subject to more stringent standards of proof.

---

[24] See, e.g., Corbin, 5 *Contracts* § 1019 (1964) (hereinafter cited as Corbin); McCormick, "The Contemplation Rule as a Limitation Upon Damages for Breach of Contract," 19 Minn. L. Rev. 497 (1935).

[c] Tacit Agreement Rule

Soon after *Hadley,* the English courts took *Hadley* one step further and added an additional restriction to the recovery of special or consequential damages. The *Hadley* court said that peculiar circumstances that might give rise to special damages had to be made known to a contracting party in order for him to be held to the risk. Subsequent cases said that there must be more than a communication — the defendant must have both knowledge and acceptance of the special circumstances and their attendant risks in order to be held liable.[25] This came to be known as the tacit agreement rule and was followed in 1903 by Justice Holmes' decision in the well-known case of *Globe Refining Co. v. Landa Cotton Oil Co.*[26] Some state courts also followed the tacit agreement rule, but they were few.[27]

The tacit agreement rule has now been abandoned in England, and the foreseeability standard of *Hadley* has been somewhat loosened. In a 1967 decision of the House of Lords, Lord Reid restated the *Hadley* rule in this modern version:

> In cases like *Hadley v. Baxendale* or the present case it is not enough that in fact the plaintiff's loss was directly caused by the defendant's breach of contract. It clearly was so caused in both. The crucial question is whether, on the information available to the defendant when the contract was made, he should, or the reasonable man in his position would, have realised that such loss was sufficiently likely to result from the breach of contract to make it proper to hold that the loss flowed naturally from the breach or that loss of that kind should have been within his contemplation.[28]

This is a far cry from the tacit agreement rule, and it broadens the

---

[25] Horne v. Midland RR, LR, 7 CP 583 (1872); British Columbia Saw-Mill Co. v. Nettleship, LR, 3 CP 499 (1868).

[26] Globe Ref. Co. v. Landa Cotton Oil Co., 190 US 540 (1903).

[27] See, e.g., Hawkins v. Delta Spindle of Blytheville, 245 Ark. 830, 434 SW2d 825 (1968); Keystone Diesel Engine Co. v. Irwin, 411 Pa. 222, 191 A2d 376 (1963).

[28] The Heron II (Kaufos v. C. Czarnikow, Ltd.) [1967] 3 All ER 686 (HL); and see Victoria Laundry (Windsor), Ltd v. Newman Indus., Ltd., 1 All ER 997; [1949] 2 KB 528.

Hadley rule, despite Lord Reid's disclaimer, a "reasonable man" standard based on knowledge with or without agreement.[29]

For the most part, American courts have rejected the tacit agreement rule. Commentators have criticized it sharply,[30] the drafters of the first Restatement of Contracts rejected it,[31] and the UCC repudiates it in Section 2-715. Despite a few diehards,[32] the rule has little current influence. American courts instead follow the rule of *Hadley,* although the facts of a particular case are so important in deciding the question of foreseeability that the rule only serves as a general guideline. It does impose limitations, however, that are not imposed in tort cases, and if contract litigants are not aware of them, they may find it very difficult to prove a case. Either the foreseeability rule or the requirement of reasonable certainty in proof of special damages[33] can be a convenient means to deny a claim that appears excessive.

[d] Foreseeability of Lost Profits as Consequential Damages in Commercial Contexts

One line of American cases, exemplified by *Masterson v. Mayor of Brooklyn,*[34] differs from the decision reached in *Hadley* and exists parallel to the *Hadley* line. In the mid-nineteenth century, the city of Brooklyn, New York (then separate from New York City) ordered a substantial quantity of cut marble to be used in the construction of a city hall. The supplier fulfilled his bargain, but the city reneged and left him with a large pile of cut marble for which there was little salvage value. The supplier sued successfully for various consequential damages, and the New York court said that in a commercial-type contract, lost profits, as consequential damages, would be presumed to be foreseeable. The plaintiff did

---

[29] Id.

[30] See, e.g., Williston, 11 *A Treatise on the Law of Contracts* § 1357 (10th ed. 1967); Corbin § 1010.

[31] See Restatement (First) of Contracts § 330 comment a (1932).

[32] See Keystone Diesel Engine Co. v. Irwin, 411 Pa. 222, 191 A2d 376 (1963), which was a UCC case. The decision is anomalous and is probably of questionable value.

[33] See infra ¶ 7.03[4].

[34] Masterston v. Mayor of Brooklyn, 7 Hill (NY) 61 (1845).

not have to prove actual or reasonable foreseeability.[35] Although the decision in *Masterson* was published in 1845, nine years before *Hadley,* it is still cited for the proposition that lost profits, as consequential damages, are presumed to be foreseeable in commercial contexts.[36] Some cases similar to *Masterson* use language that seems inconsistent with the *Hadley* rule of foreseeability, but the facts are nonetheless consistent with a *Hadley* approach. In a commercial situation in which the subject matter of the contract is clearly mutual profit, lost profits that result from a breach are more like general damages that flow naturally from the breach than like special damages.

A 1980 Colorado case that involved a breach of warranty on farm equipment aptly illustrates the application of the *Hadley* rule in a commercial context. A farmer sued for crop losses because the farm equipment he purchased failed to work as warranted. The defendant argued that the damages were too remote and were not within the reasonable contemplation of the parties. The case fell within UCC coverage, and the court applied the language of Section 2-715, which holds a seller responsible for "any loss resulting from general or particular requirements and needs of which the seller at the time of contracting had reason to know." In rejecting the defendant's arguments and allowing the claim for the crop losses, the court said:

> The statutory "reason to know" standard, in our view, triggers liability for consequences that may not have been actually foreseen but which were foreseeable. . . . A manufacturer knowing that its products will be used for crop production reasonably can be expected to foresee that defects in those products may cause crop losses.[37]

---

[35] Id.

[36] The cases are collected in Dunn, *Recovery of Damages for Lost Profits* § 1.10, at 22, 23 (1978) (hereinafter cited as Dunn). Among the more recent cases cited by Dunn are Rivenbark v. Finis P. Ernest, Inc., 37 Ill. App. 3d 536, 346 NE2d 494 (1976); Nelson v. Reisner, 51 Cal. 2d 161, 331 P2d 17 (1958); M&R Contractors & Builders v. Michael, 215 Md. 340, 139 A2d 350 (1958).

[37] Prutch v. Ford Motor Co., 618 P2d 657, 662 (Colo. 1980), citing Lewis v. Mobil Oil Corp., 438 F2d 500, 510 (8th Cir. 1971).

[e] Current Modifications of the *Hadley* Foreseeability Standard

The *Hadley* rule still may undergo modifications that will be more significant than current decisions establishing certain presumptions about damages in particular kinds of cases. Section 351 of the second Restatement indicates the possible direction of these changes:

> (1) Damages are not recoverable for loss that the party in breach did not have reason to foresee as a probable result of the breach when the contract was made.
>
> (2) Loss may be foreseeable as a probable result of a breach because it follows from the breach
>
> (a) in the ordinary course of events or
>
> (b) as a result of special circumstances beyond the ordinary course of events, that the party in breach had reason to know.
>
> (3) A court may limit damages for foreseeable loss by excluding recovery for loss of profits, by allowing recovery only for loss incurred in reliance, or otherwise if it concludes that in the circumstances justice so requires in order to avoid disproportionate compensation.

Sections 351(1) and 351(2) of the second Restatement are a slightly modernized version of the *Hadley* rule. The presumption of consequential damages in certain cases can be justified under either section: Either lost profits or some other consequential damage naturally flow from the breach, or the damage can be expected (e.g., crop losses due to failure of agricultural equipment). The average farmer, unlike the average miller, may not have a spare set of equipment. However, Section 351(3) is a departure from *Hadley*. It suggests that a court can simply ignore the *Hadley* rule (and any others, for that matter) if it thinks that the plaintiff asks for too much in damages. In lieu of the ordinary rules of common law, a court can fall back on its sense of justice and allow reliance damages or whatever else it considers appropriate. The court is only limited by the requirement that it avoid "disproportionate compensation," which in this context must be interpreted as a method for putting a cap on plaintiffs' recoveries in contract actions.

The limitation in Section 351 of the second Restatement was probably a reaction to excessive recoveries that occurred in an expanding, inflationary economy. In addition, the language of the *Hadley* rule can be manipulated to favor either plaintiffs or defendants, and it has been repeated so many times that it resembles a ritual incantation that lacks substance. Whether the drafters of the second Restatement have done any better, however, is problematic at best.[38] The limitation in Section 351(3) may have the effect of limiting plaintiffs to reliance recoveries in many cases in which they traditionally would have been allowed to recover their expectancy, measured by lost profits. If this is the result, contract plaintiffs may be even more severely undercompensated than some commentators think they are.[39] On the other hand, Section 351 of the second Restatement and other similar sections that enlarge upon the reliance damage aspects of remedies[40] may allow courts to be more creative in providing plaintiffs with recoveries that are truly adequate to compensate them for breaches without simultaneously ruining defendants.[41] It seems clear that the second Restatement goes beyond the case law and suggests a system in which judges have enormous leeway to make their own decisions about what is just compensation. Of course, judges have always had the power to apply the *Hadley* rule to the facts of a case in ways that are sensitive to principles of fairness, but Section 351(3) is far more open-ended. Thus, the future of the foreseeability standard of *Hadley* is now somewhat uncertain.

[4] Lost Profits as Consequential Damages

[a] Valuation of Damages Caused by Lost Profits

In the business world, lost profits are the most common measure of consequential damages and lost expectancy when a contract breach occurs. Even if the plaintiff can demonstrate both the

---

[38] See Harvey, "Discretionary Justice Under the Restatement (Second) of Contracts," 67 Cornell L. Rev. 666, 673 (1982).

[39] See Farber 1443; Young, "Half Measures," 81 Colum. L. Rev. 19 (1981).

[40] See, e.g., Restatement (Second) of Contracts §§ 87, 90, 97, 344, 349 (1982).

[41] This is certainly the view of Professor Farnsworth but as Reporter for the second Restatement and one of its principal draftsmen, one would expect him to defend the work product. See Farnsworth, "Ingredients in the Redaction of the Restatement (Second) of Contracts," 81 Colum. L. Rev. 1 (1981).

fact of damage and a clear causal link with the breach, it still may be difficult to prove the amount of damage. Although the value of lost profits and other consequential damages do not have to be proven with precision, the proof must be solid enough to justify a reasonable approximation by the trier of fact. Thus, rules of certainty and foreseeability apply both to proof of damage and to fact of damage. The basic formula for calculating lost profits is simple: Contract price − expenses incurred and expected = net profit. The defendant should receive credit for payments made, and the plaintiff should not recover for avoided expenses.[42]

[b] Foreseeability of Lost Profits vs. Conjecture

To recover lost profits, a plaintiff must prove that they were the foreseeable result of a breach and are not a matter of conjecture or speculation. A recent opinion of the Court of Appeals for the First Circuit, applying Massachusetts law, contained a statement of the standard: Lost profits are recoverable

> [w]here it appears that the loss was the natural, primary and probable consequence of the breach, that the profits arising from the performance of the contract or the loss likely to result from its nonperformance were within the contemplation of the parties, and that the profits are not so uncertain or contingent as to be incapable of reasonable proof.[43]

Although lost profits may be presumed to be the natural consequence of the breach of a commercial agreement, the plaintiff still must be able to show that he would have made a profit. It is not enough to show that the contract was entered into for the purpose of making a profit. For example, a distributor was able to recover for the profits lost on orders received before his distributorship was wrongfully terminated that he could not fill because of the termination. He could not recover for anticipated orders, because the projections were speculative. The plaintiff's case concerning anticipated orders was weak because his projections of orders greatly

---

[42] For a standard formulation, see, e.g., Advance Constr. Co. v. Dunn, 263 Ark. 332, 563 SW2d 888 (1978), which indicates the rule in construction contract cases can be slightly different. For a discussion of such cases, see Chapter 4.

[43] Knightsbridge Mktg. Servs., Inc. v. Promociones y Protectos, SA, 728 F2d 572, 575 (1st Cir. 1984).

exceeded any prior experience.[44] Another plaintiff was able to recover for the profits lost on anticipated jobs, proven by evidence of oral orders, that could not be completed because of the breach of a contract to deliver a machine tool.[45]

One of the best ways to prove lost profits on a contract is to show a history of profitability, especially in similar kinds of transactions. If a supplier breaches a contract of supply, the purchaser can introduce evidence of past profits on previous supply agreements. A movie exhibitor, for instance, can demonstrate its experience with other movies before the breach.[46] The more specific the evidence, the better its chances of success. Documentary evidence usually is superior to oral testimony, especially by interested parties such as the principals of the enterprise seeking relief.[47] One court even suggested that failure to produce documentary proof of a business' operations and profitability and reliance on the oral testimony of interested people justifies a presumption that the documentary evidence was damaging to the plaintiff's case. ''Where more certain and satisfactory evidence is available to a party who instead produces evidence of a weaker and inferior nature, a presumption arises against him for withholding the evidence.''[48]

[c] Proof of Costs

It is impossible to prove profits without first proving costs. Failure to produce satisfactory cost evidence dooms a lost profits claim to failure, because the trier of fact has no basis on which to

---

[44] Vigano v. Wylain, Inc., 633 F2d 522 (8th Cir. 1980).

[45] Stephan's Mach. & Tool, Inc. v. D&H Mach. Consultants, 65 Ohio App. 2d 197, 417 NE2d 579 (1979). This case is also a good example of the presumptions that apply in modern commercial relationships. There was no serious question in the case about the kinds of reasonable expectations that the defendant might have had about the consequences of his failure to deliver the machine tool according to the contract as there was in *Hadley*. Of course, the contract in *Hadley* was for carriage, and in this case it was for supply of a piece of equipment.

[46] See, e.g., Eastern Fed. Corp. v. Avco-Embassy Pictures, Inc., 326 F. Supp. 276 (ND Ga. 1970).

[47] See, e.g., Snow v. CIT Corp. of the South, Inc., 278 Ark. 554, 647 SW2d 465 (1983); Comtrol, Inc. v. H-K Corp., 134 Ga. App. 349, 214 SE2d 588 (1975).

[48] Consolidated Eng'g Co. of Ga., Inc. v. UIR Contractors, Inc., 136 Ga. App. 923, 222 SE2d 692, 693 (1975).

compute profits. *Robertson v. Ceola,*[49] a 1973 decision of the Arkansas Supreme Court, is an extreme example, but it illustrates the problem clearly. The plaintiff in *Robertson* had a small tile-setting business, and the case was based on a breach of a tile-setting contract on which he had completed a substantial amount of work. He proved the cost of materials and of his unskilled laborers; he did not, however, introduce evidence of the value of his own services as a skilled tile-setter. As a result, insufficient data were available to calculate the profit factor in the contract. In a business so small that the principal was himself a laborer, he probably considered his own income from the contract to be part of the profits, but the point is that his labor was a cost, not an element of profit. The total recovery should have included the value of his labor as a cost as part of the reliance recovery, but the recovery could not be calculated without taking his own labor value into account.

The injured party must also relate the proof of costs to the particular transaction at issue. Proof of general costs and profits usually does not suffice; direct costs must be established. This can create difficulties for a large enterprise that uses consolidated financial statements and does not regularly do unit- or product-line cost studies.[50] The necessity of ascertaining the costs associated with a particular agreement raises the question of whether fixed overhead should be included in the costs. Consider the following situation.

> **EXAMPLE 4.** Green, a merchant, agrees to buy 1,000 units of a new line of television sets at $300 per unit from wholesaler White. In anticipation of delivery, Green spends $10,000 advertising the new line in the local newspapers. The sets are advertised at $459.99. After White delivers half of the sets and Green pays for them, White breaches. In preparing Green's financial statements for the past ten years, his accountants have allocated 25 percent of Green's total fixed overhead to the home appliance department of his store. Green's accountants and internal bookkeeper will testify that about 10 percent

---

[49] Robertson v. Ceola, 255 Ark. 703, 501 SW2d 764 (1973).

[50] See, e.g., Silco, Inc. v. Gwinnett County Hosp. Auth., 151 Ga. App. 634, 260 SE2d 758 (1979).

of the overhead allocated to household appliances should be attributed to TV sets. Green has average sales of 5,000 sets a year for each of the last five years.

What costs should be attributed to the Green-White contract to determine Green's lost profit? Assume that the retail markup was reasonable and that Green sells 500 sets at $459.99 per set. The first part of the calculation of costs is easy: Green's gross profit on the 500 sets that were not delivered would have been 500 × $459.99, or $229,995. Green's direct cost is 500 × $300, or $150,000, the total wholesale price. Because the additional advertising was directly related to the new line of sets, it should be treated as an item of direct variable overhead and should be attributed to the contract as a cost item. In this instance, a 50 percent allocation of the advertising expense seems fair, or $5,000. The defendant can argue that the profit that Green would have finally realized on the transaction would have been less than the gross profit minus direct costs and direct variable overhead because Green would have had to pay salaries, utilities, taxes, leases, and a host of other items. Green's net out-of-pocket loss, therefore, is his anticipated gross profit minus direct costs and all fixed and variable overhead.

In line with the principle of compensating plaintiffs in contract actions only for their actual net losses, White would argue that fixed overhead should be subtracted from the gross profit to avoid overcompensation. Green would argue in turn that the only way to guarantee a profit at the end of the year is to have an aggregate of contracts that provide for income that exceeds all fixed and variable expenses. Fixed costs do not vary with each transaction and must be paid regardless of circumstances. If they are subtracted from the recovery claimed for a breach of contract, there will be insufficient income to cover the fixed expenses at the end of the year.

Green's argument is valid, and fixed expenses should not be subtracted in calculating net profits. All in all, this argument has prevailed in the courts, although the refusal to consider fixed overhead has been sometimes justified by claiming that it is too difficult or conjectural to allocate a portion of fixed overhead to a single transaction.[51]

[d] Evidence of Comparable Transactions

In order to establish lost profits more carefully, a claimant may introduce evidence of comparable transactions (either its own or those of closely similar enterprises) and expert testimony. *Chung v. Kaonoki Center Co.,*[52] a 1980 decision of the Hawaii Supreme Court, provides a good example. Chung entered into a lease for space at a new shopping center to run a Chinese fast-food restaurant. The shopping center broke the agreement and leased the space to another restaurant, which also specialized in Chinese fast food. To prove lost profits, Chung hired an expert witness who compiled the actual experience of the replacement restaurant in the shopping center, the experience of similar fast-food establishments in the area, and industry averages to provide a projected net income stream for Chung's enterprise. He than capitalized this income stream over the ten-year period of the broken lease and reduced it to a present cash value. The court approved this approach and sustained Chung's $175,000 jury verdict.[53]

[e] Liability for Losses on Collateral Contracts

The profit that a nonbreaching party hopes to make on a transaction may result from a resale or a collateral transaction. A pur-

---

[51] See, e.g., Buono Sales, Inc. v. Chrysler Motors Corp., 449 F2d 715 (3d Cir. 1971), citing Vitex Mfg. Corp. v. Caribtex Corp., 377 F2d 795, 799 (3d Cir. 1967), where the court said: "[I]t is apparent that the fixed expenses of a business must be paid from the profits remaining after all direct costs have been paid. Unless damages restore the latter amount to plaintiff, it will not be fully compensated for the breach." See also UCC § 2-708, Comment 2.

[52] Chung v. Kaonoki Center Co., 62 Hawaii 594, 618 P2d 283 (1980).

[53] In Polaris Indus. v. Plastics, Inc., 299 NW2d 414 (Minn. 1980), the court rejected the use of industry averages in projecting lost profits, although the defendant made a good showing that the averages were suspect figures. They came from trade association records, and the evidence showed that many members of the association did not report their profit figures to the association and that there was no way to verify the accuracy of the figures that were reported. And see, e.g., approving the use of expert witnesses to prove lost profits, Knightsbridge Mktg. Servs., Inc. v. Promociones y Protectos, SA, 728 F2d 572 (1st Cir. 1984); United Roasters, Inc. v. Colgate-Palmolive Co., 649 F2d 985 (4th Cir. 1981); City Welding & Mfg. Co. v. Gidley-Eschenheimer Corp., 16 Mass. App. 372, 451 NE2d 734 (1983).

chaser may buy real estate for immediate resale and not as a long-term investment. Similarly, the performance of a second contract might depend on the successful completion of the first contract. To what extent is a party in breach liable for the loss on a collateral contract? The general rule is simply a variation on *Hadley*. If the collateral contract and its relationship to the principal contract are known at the time of contracting, the breaching party may be liable for losses the nonbreaching party sustains on the collateral agreement.[54] Some states, such as Pennsylvania, have more restrictive approaches and require a showing that is virtually equivalent to the breaching party's express assumption of risk for losses sustained on collateral transactions.[55] Other jurisdictions are not so restrictive and merely require proof of reasonable contemplation based upon the context.[56]

[f] Burden of Evidentiary Proof

The requirements of foreseeability and certainty are evidentiary tests. The plaintiff cannot simply prove a breach and then testify off the cuff.[57] He has to be able to show the nature of his business operation, a reasonable basis for determining the costs

---

[54] See, e.g., Texas Power & Light Co. v. Barnhill, 639 SW2d 331, 336 (Tex. Civ. App. 1982), "Lost profits from collateral contracts, however, are recoverable only if such collateral contracts are known to or are within the contemplation of the parties at the time they enter into the contract which is subsequently breached." See also Scott S. Div. Employees Credit Union v. Loftin, 50 Ala. App. 571, 281 So. 2d 283, 285, 286 (1973) (lost profits on collateral contract recoverable if reasonably contemplated and if the contract was in existence at the time the principal agreement was reached; lost profits on collateral contracts entered into after the principal contract are too remote and speculative). And see Automatic Poultry Feeder Co. v. Wedel, 213 Cal. App. 2d 509, 28 Cal. Rptr. 795 (1963); Wentworth & Irwin, Inc. v. Sears, 153 Ore. 201, 56 P2d 324 (1936); Arkwright Mills v. Clearwater Mfg. Co., 217 SC 530, 61 SE2d 165 (1950).

[55] Macchia v. Megow, 355 Pa. 565, 50 A2d 314 (1947).

[56] See, e.g., Dunn § 1.12, at 36, citing, e.g., Mechanical Wholesale, Inc. v. Universal-Rundle Corp., 432 F2d 228 (5th Cir. 1970); Childress v. Cook, 245 F2d 798 (5th Cir. 1957); Beatty v. Oakland Sheet Metal Supply Co., 111 Cal. App. 2d 53, 244 P2d 25 (1952); Larsen v. Waldon Plywood Co., 65 Wash. 2d 1, 390 P2d 677 (1964).

[57] See, e.g., Tri-State Sys., Inc. v. Village Outlet Stores, Inc., 135 Ga. App. 634, 260 SE2d 758 (1979) (estimate that business lost $40,000 because contract to erect billboards along interstate highway was breached was guess by principal in company unsubstantiated by any documentary or expert proof or analysis).

associated with the contract, and some rational means for projecting the profits that would have resulted if the breach had not occurred. In fact, the plaintiff does not have to show that he would have made a profit on the specific deal if he can show that his losses would have been less if the transaction were completed.[58] If the claimant does present reasonable evidence, courts often resolve doubts about certainty against the breaching party even if the amount of injury cannot be precisely determined.[59] In the words of the Missouri Supreme Court

> [t]here are cases in which the experience of mankind is convincing that a substantial pecuniary loss has occurred, while at the same time it is of such a character that the amount in money is incapable of proof. In these cases the defendant usually has reason to foresee this difficulty of proof and should not be allowed to profit by it. In such cases, it is reasonable to require a lesser degree of certainty as to the amount of the loss, leaving a greater degree of discretion to the jury.[60]

[g] Valuation of Lost Profits and Costs in New Businesses

New or unestablished businesses often have difficulty proving their costs and lost profits because they have no history from which to construct a database for projections. For this reason, some courts have held that a new business cannot recover lost profits because the proof is necessarily speculative.[61] Recently, however, courts have become more liberal in allowing new busi-

---

[58] United Roasters, Inc. v. Colgate-Palmolive Co., 649 F2d 985 (4th Cir. 1981).

[59] See, e.g., Lorenz Supply Co. v. American Standard, Inc., 100 Mich. App. 600, 300 NW2d 335 (1980); Cardinal Consulting Co. v. Circo Resorts, Inc., 297 NW2d 260 (Minn. 1980).

[60] Coach House of Ward Parkway v. Ward Parkway Shops, 471 SW2d 464, 471 (Mo. 1971), citing Restatement (First) of Contracts § 331 (1932); and cited with approval in Vigano v. Wylain, Inc., 633 F2d 522, 528 (8th Cir. 1980).

[61] See Comment, "Remedies — Lost Profits as Contract Damages for an Unestablished Business: The New Business Rule Becomes Outdated," 56 NCL Rev. 693 (1978). This comment collects virtually every case that even touches upon the subject and is an especially helpful research tool.

nesses to seek lost profits.[62] The UCC also appears to eliminate the limitation on recovery by unestablished businesses, although it does so in an offhand comment to Section 2-708.[63] Case law in Iowa and California illustrates this trend. The original rule in Iowa was fairly strict and made it virtually impossible for a new business to prove lost profits.[64] Its approach has evolved into a rule of reasonable certainty essentially no different from the ordinary rules that apply in lost profits cases.[65] Over the past fifty years, California courts have made a similar change in standards.[66]

If a new business is allowed to seek lost profits in a contracts case, how can it prove those profits without a history? Three ways have met with success. First, if the plaintiff has prior experience in a similar business or has other outlets (i.e., the plaintiff's business is part of a chain), that experience may be used as evidence of profitability.[67] Second, the plaintiff may be able to use the experience of other similar enterprises in analogous situations. For example, the relative success or failure of a Chinese fast-food restaurant

---

[62] Id. at 695; see Dunn § 4.2, at 113–119. Florida continues to buck the trend and does not allow a lost profits recovery for a new business. A&P Bakery Supply & Equip. Co. v. Hawatmeh, 388 So. 2d 1071 (Fla. Dist. Ct. App. 1980).

[63] Section 2-708 deals with the seller's damages for nonacceptance or repudiation. Comment 2 says, in part,

> "This section permits the recovery of lost profits in all appropriate cases, which would include all standard priced goods. The normal measure there would be list price less cost to the dealer or list price less manufacturing cost to the manufacturer. It is not necessary to a recovery of 'profit' to show a history of earnings, especially if a new venture is involved."

[64] See City of Corning v. Iowa-Nebraska Light & Power Co., 225 Iowa 1380, 282 NW 791 (1938).

[65] "The fact that plaintiff's business was relatively new would not, in and of itself, require that evidence of lost profits be excluded since such profits may be awarded where evidence demonstrates its feasibility." Mid-Country Meats, Inc. v. Woodruff-Evans Constr. Co., 334 NW2d 332, 337 (Iowa Ct. App. 1983), citing Lakota Girl Scout Council, Inc. v. Havey Fund-Raising Management, Inc., 519 F2d 634 (8th Cir. 1975).

[66] Compare California Press Mfg. Co. v. Stafford Packing Co., 192 Cal. 479, 221 P 345 (1923), with S. Jon Kreedman & Co. v. Meyer Bros. Parking-W. Corp., 58 Cal. App. 3d 173, 130 Cal. Rptr. 41 (1976).

[67] See, e.g., Smith Dev. Corp. v. Bilow Enters., Inc., 112 RI 203, 308 A2d 477 (1973) (breach involving a new McDonald's franchise; evidence of the experience of other McDonald's franchises was allowed); see also Fera v. Village Plaza, Inc., 396 Mich. 639, 242 NW2d 372 (1976).

in a shopping center may indicate the possibility of success for another Chinese fast-food restaurant in a comparable shopping center.[68] Third, the plaintiff may use an expert witness to make a prediction based on as much information as he can gather,[69] although simple pro forma projections in a business plan do not suffice.[70] In addition, courts sometimes allow evidence of a new-business principal's prior success as an employee in a related enterprise together with evidence of his subsequent success, despite the failed contract.[71] Although this kind of evidence can hardly prove the lost profits of the new business with certainty, it does tend to prove the reliability of the plaintiff and his business acumen. If it is connected with proof of a ready market for the new business' product or service, it has greater probative value.[72]

[5] Damages to Goodwill

A loss of profits may not be the only consequence of a failed transaction. For example, a plaintiff may suffer losses in attempting to recover on a breached collateral contract.[73] Although the *Hadley* rule and related evidentiary rules prevent claimants from recovering for all the consequences that flow from a breach of contract, some elements of consequential damage other than lost profits may be awarded to the nonbreaching party in addition to or in lieu of lost profits.

Despite the fact that the concept of goodwill is ephemeral, no one doubts its importance in the successful operation of a business. A business that is unable to satisfy its customers because one of its suppliers fails to deliver or because the products it receives are faulty faces a host of problems. It is not uncommon to see a claim

---

[68] See, e.g., Chung v. Kaonoki Center Co., 62 Hawaii 594, 618 P2d 283 (1980); see also supra ¶ 7.03[4][d].

[69] Id.; Knightsbridge Mktg. Servs., Inc. v. Promociones y Protectos, SA, 728 F2d 572 (1st Cir. 1984).

[70] MacDonald v. Hawkes, 11 Mass. App. 869, 420 NE2d 923 (1981).

[71] See, e.g., El Fredo Pizza, Inc. v. Rob-Flex Oven Co., 199 Neb. 697, 261 NW2d 358 (1978).

[72] See, e.g., Alliance Tractor & Implement Co. v. Lukens Tool & Die Co., 204 Neb. 248, 281 NW2d 778 (1979).

[73] See supra ¶ 7.03[4][e].

for damages to goodwill included in a breach of contract action. A few courts have dismissed goodwill claims as speculative, but most have applied the standard rules of foreseeability and certainty derived from *Hadley*.[74] Although neither the text of Section 2-715 on consequential and incidental damages nor its accompanying commentary addresses the issue of goodwill, a few decisions have interpreted the section as a bar to a goodwill recovery.[75] This is inconsistent with the language of Section 2-715 and with the commentary. As one of the comments notes, "Any seller who does not wish to take the risk of consequential damages has available the section on contractual limitation of remedy."[76]

[6] Scope of Recovery for Consequential Damages

Neville Chemical Co. v. Union Carbide Corp.[77] illustrates the possible scope of recovery for consequential damages in a contract case. Union Carbide sold chemicals to Neville, which used them to prepare a resin that was used by other manufacturers in producing shoe soles and floor tiles. Unfortunately, the resin gave off a noxious odor, and the finished products could not be sold. Retailers claimed against their suppliers on up the line to Neville, which paid all the claims and incurred all the expenses of researching the odor's origin. The research paid off because the source was in the chemicals supplied by Union Carbide, and Neville obtained a full recovery against Union Carbide for all the claims and costs.

Sometimes plaintiffs do get carried away. In the amusing case

---

[74] Dobbs, *Remedies* § 12.3, at 813 (1973) (hereinafter cited as Dobbs); and see Pemberton v. OvaTech, Inc., 669 F2d 533 (8th Cir. 1982) (dictum); Stott v. Johnson, 36 Cal. 2d 864, 229 P2d 348 (1951); Sol-O-Lite Laminating Corp. v. Allen, 223 Ore. 80, 353 P2d 843 (1960); Sherwin-Williams v. Perry, 424 SW2d 940 (Tex. Civ. App. 1968) (dictum); Note, "Consequential Damages: The Loss of Goodwill," 23 Baylor L. Rev. 106 (1971).

[75] See, e.g., Kassah v. Central Soya, 432 Pa. 217, 246 A2d 848 (1968); Harry Rubin & Sons v. Consolidated Pipe Co., 396 Pa. 506, 153 A2d 472 (1959); cf. Neville Chem. Co. v. Union Carbide Corp., 422 F2d 1205 (3d Cir. 1970).

[76] UCC § 2-715, Comment 3. The reference is to Section 2-719. In addition, the contract-market formulas for buyers and sellers under the UCC, as well as the section on cover contracts, contemplate the possible recovery of additional consequential damages. See UCC §§ 2-708, 2-712, 2-713.

[77] Neville Chem. Co. v. Union Carbide Corp., 422 F2d 1205 (3d Cir. 1970).

of *Newsome v. Western Union Telegraph Co.,*[78] the plaintiff was not as successful. He sent a telegram ordering that four gallons of corn whiskey be sent to the crew on a timber raft. Apparently, the crew refused to take the raft downstream without a good supply of liquor. Western Union garbled the message and it did not get through. The crew refused to make the trip; the river subsided, making it impossible to navigate the raft; and the market fell by the time the plaintiff finally got his timber downstream. He sued for the difference in the timber's market value, the additional costs of paying the salaries of the crew while they waited for the whiskey to arrive, plus a few other odds and ends. Although three separate juries found for the plaintiff, they were reversed on appeal each time because there was an insufficient causal connection between Western Union's failure to send an order for whiskey and the plaintiff's failure to get his timber to market when it would yield the best price.

¶ 7.04 PROOF OF RELIANCE DAMAGES

[1] Essential and Incidental Reliance

If the nonbreaching party is unable to prove with reasonable certainty what he would have gained if no breach had occurred, the next best result is to recover the costs associated with the failed transaction. This at least puts the plaintiff back where he was before the agreement, the basic theory of reliance damages. In fact, a reliance recovery may be better than an expectancy recovery if the contract appears to be a losing proposition.

A claimant must be able to present proof of reliance damages with as much certainty and clarity as in a suit for the recovery of expectancy damages. Documentary evidence of actual expenses and other evidence directly connecting these expenses to the contract are equally important. The critical point of proof centers on the requirement that the breached contract must have been the inducement for the expenditure claimed; there must be a direct causal connection between the two.[79]

---

[78] Newsome v. Western Union Tel. Co., 153 NC 153, 69 SE 10 (1910).

[79] See, e.g., Restatement (Second) of Contracts § 349 (1982); Hudec 721.

The traditional distinction between essential and incidental reliance was first clearly articulated by Fuller and Perdue.[80] Essential reliance includes the costs specifically induced by the contract and the representations made in connection with it. Incidental reliance includes all other expenditures, which may or may not be directly related to the failed agreement. There may even be a plausible causal connection between these expenditures and the agreement, but they are not necessary to performance and generally the claimant cannot recover them. Consider, for instance, the example of a young law student in New Haven who applies for and accepts a position as an associate with a law firm in Atlanta. It is essential that she move to the city in which the law firm has its offices. Therefore, her reasonable moving expenses are essential reliance expenditures. A new car and wardrobe fall in the category of incidental reliance expenditures. If, however, the firm tells her that she will need a car to visit its satellite offices and that it must be sufficiently impressive to her clients, the new associate could probably justify reasonable expenditure for the car as an item of essential reliance. The same would hold true for the new wardrobe if the law firm is specifically concerned about her appearance.

This situation illustrates the dichotomy between essential and incidental reliance. Professor Hudec has criticized the terminology as unclear and has suggested substituting a "direct/consequential" distinction.[81] Hudec's language hardly seems an improvement; if there is sometimes a lack of clarity, it is more often than not the result of imprecision in the parties' respective understanding. The distinction between essential and incidental reliance is consistent with the basic goal of compensation without overcompensation. The plaintiff should be returned to his status quo ante, but not made better off than he was before the transaction. In recovering his actual losses, he cannot hold the breaching party responsible for his own extravagance or for the risks of expenditures that were not reasonably among the risks assumed when both parties entered into the agreement.

---

[80] See Fuller & Perdue 53, 54.

[81] Hudec 724, 725.

[2] Valuation of Opportunities Lost as a Result of Breach

Proof of actual costs in reliance cases is usually a fairly simple matter. At worst, it is no more complicated than proving the costs of performance as a basis for calculating projected net profits.[82] A strong and subjective element of fairness is also involved, which requires that a party who is out of pocket because of another party's breach of contract should be made whole. A much more difficult element in reliance cases involves lost opportunities. Fuller and Perdue included foregone opportunities as part of their formula for calculating reliance losses.[83] It is difficult to prove that the cost of a lost performance may be the subsequent loss of another opportunity. Furthermore, the question arises whether a lost opportunity falls under the foreseeability doctrine. Did the non-breaching party assume the risk of liability for the other party's foregone business chances? As is so often the case, the facts are critical.

Consider again the New Haven law student who has accepted a position in an Atlanta firm.[84] After moving to her new home, she learns on the first day of work that the law firm has decided that her services are not needed. Assuming the existence of a valid employment contract, she clearly has a claim for moving expenses and perhaps for her new car and some of her clothes. She also can claim for lost income from the job subject to mitigation by income from a comparable job she may subsequently obtain.[85] Her expectancy recovery thus may suffice to cover her damages. Assume further that she also received a job offer from a firm in Houston, but turned it down to take the job in Atlanta. In the interim, the Houston firm filled the position. The young lawyer spends six months searching for another job and several thousand dollars in travel expenses for interviews before she finally is hired in Denver. She will not be whole unless she can recover these expenses plus

---

[82] See supra ¶ 7.03[4][g].

[83] Fuller & Perdue 53, 54.

[84] See supra ¶ 7.04[1].

[85] See infra ¶ 7.07.

the marginal cost of her move to Denver.[86] What if a colleague who took a job with the Houston firm tells her that after six months the firm gives all first-year associates a $3,000 bonus and that business was so good that the period required for consideration for partnership was reduced from eight to seven years? Does the new lawyer have a claim based on her lost opportunity to work for the Houston firm measured by the bonus and the chance for earlier consideration for partnership? What if the average share of the partners in Houston is larger than their counterparts in Denver? Does she have a lost opportunity claim based on the lost potential for income throughout her productive life? Although contract lawsuits often raise similar questions as lawyers try to get the best possible recovery for their clients, courts tend to reject such claims as too speculative.

A 1955 Connecticut case illustrates the problem of dealing with lost opportunities. In *Fisher v. Jackson,*[87] a baker left the bakery where he was employed to take a job as a reporter with a newspaper in New Haven. According to the evidence, the reporter's job came with the promise of regular raises of a certain amount and indications that it would continue indefinitely. When the newspaper later fired the reporter, one of his claims for damages was based on the lost wages from his job as a baker. The court refused to allow any claim based on the lost opportunities of the baker's job because, the court reasoned, the plaintiff could not be both a baker and a reporter. When he decided to take the newspaper job, he had to give up the baker's job. Giving up the job was a risk he assumed that was necessary to his performance as a reporter. He could not complain because he made a knowing choice that turned out to be disappointing.

This differs from the example of the disappointed law firm

---

[86] The marginal cost of the Denver move is the difference between the cost of a move from New Haven to Denver and the cost of a move from New Haven to Atlanta to Denver. If the lawyer took a job anywhere outside New Haven, she would have moving expenses, which would be essential to performance of her employment contract. In this example, the proper allocation of risk places the marginal cost of unwanted moves on the breaching party. The Denver firm assumes the risk of the cost of the Atlanta-to-Denver move when it makes the offer of employment. The additional cost incurred by the lawyer uncompensated by the expectancy (a salary) is the extra moving cost, not all the moving costs.

[87] Fisher v. Jackson, 142 Conn. 734, 118 A2d 316 (1955).

applicant. The unhappy reporter in *Fisher* had a job with the newspaper for some time and his employment was at will rather than for a specified term. Thus, the newspaper did perform. The Atlanta law firm, however, reneged before the lawyer began to work.[88] The court's point in *Fisher* was simple and applies regardless of circumstances. Contract damages are not meant to compensate for "might have beens." People always must choose among opportunities, and if their options are mutually exclusive, choosing the wrong one does not permit recovery to compensate for the mistake.[89] In addition, the lawyer's lost opportunities for a bonus, an earlier partnership, and a more lucrative partnership at the Houston firm are speculative claims. There is no assurance that the lawyer would have lasted the six months necessary to earn the bonus, and there certainly is no assurance that she would have lasted long enough to be considered as a partner, that if considered she would have made it, and that if promoted the firm would have continued to be more prosperous than the Denver firm.

¶ 7.05 THE CONTRACT-MARKET FORMULA FOR MEASURING DAMAGES

[1] Origin in Market Speculation

One of the most common methods to determine the damage recovery in a contract action is the contract-market formula,[90] which simply measures the difference between the contract price to be paid and the market value of the chattel, land, or service at

[88] Nevertheless, it is likely that a newspaper's offer of employment is an offer of employment at will and not for a term. Thus it cannot be said in most cases that there is an expectation of employment for any specific time, and a dismissal need not be based on poor work quality or habits. There are laws against invidious discrimination but not against firing employees at will for other reasons, whether based on work performance or not.

[89] Of course, if it can be shown that the breaching party never intended to perform, there might be a claim for fraud in the inducement.

[90] See generally McCormick, *Handbook on the Law of Damages* § 48, at 184, 185 (1935); Dobbs § 3.2-3, at 139–150; Peters, "Remedies for Breach of Contracts Relating to the Sale of Goods Under the Uniform Commercial Code: A Road Map to Article Two," 73 Yale LJ 199 (1963).

the time that performance was to occur.[91] It only applies if there is a market for the material of the transaction. The formula builds in a recovery for a consequential damage that resembles damages for lost profits.

The rule dates from the late eighteenth and early nineteenth centuries. Previously, contract law tended to be a formal mechanism for the passage of title. That is, the contract was an agreement for the exchange of a particular good or a parcel of real estate at an agreed-upon price, and its usefulness lay in the expression of the mutual promises of good title, willingness to buy, and consideration. The contract was not a mechanism for risk allocation in a speculative market, and if specific performance were unavailable, the standard remedy was rescission plus restitution of any down payment.[92] In 1776, this approach reached its high-water mark in *Flureau v. Thornhill,* which involved a failed real estate transaction in London.[93] Although the London market was fueled by inflation and speculation, the court allowed the disappointed buyer to recover only his earnest money. He could not recover any "damages for the fancied goodness of the bargain, which he supposes he has lost."[94]

By the early nineteenth century, stock and commodities mar-

---

[91] This has been the rule at least since Gainsford v. Carroll, 2 B&C 624, 107 Eng. Rep. 516 (KB 1828). Determining the time that performance should have occurred can be critical in a rapidly changing market. See, e.g., Segall v. Finley, 245 NY 61, 156 NE 97 (1927), in which the difference between the contract price and the market price varied from $22,400 to $106,400, depending on which date was identified as the proper measurement date. The court in *Segall* decided that the day that title to the commodity in question (sugar) should have passed was the date to use. Unfortunately for the defendant, sugar then was at the highest point of the market. Under the UCC, the date of cover controls, if cover is made, even if that date is different from the date of performance under the original contract. UCC § 2-712. This serves the mitigation principle and also adds some certainty to the process. If the contract-cover rule had applied in *Segall,* the plaintiff's recovery would probably have been $50,400, or less than half the contract-market recovery.

[92] The older cases are considered at length in Horwitz, "The Historical Foundations of Modern Contract Law," 87 Harv. L. Rev. 917 (1974).

[93] Flureau v. Thornhill, 2 Black., W. 1078, 96 Eng. Rep. 635 (CP 1776).

[94] Id., cited in Simon & Novack, "Limiting the Buyer's Market Damage to Lost Profits: A Challenge to the Enforceability of Market Contracts," 92 Harv. L. Rev. 1395, 1398 (1979) (hereinafter cited as Simon & Novak).

kets, roughly similar to their modern counterparts, were well-developed in both England and the United States. In these markets, contracts were more than static formalities for the gentlemanly exchange of land and goods; they were mechanisms to allocate risk and to wager on the future. The contract-market formula developed as a means to settle differences in a failed transaction in which the subject matter was not so much the specific commodity being exchanged as it was the parties' respective bets on the direction of the market. This formula reflected the reality of the transactions and imposed order and predictability on a volatile situation.[95] It soon became a standard method of damage measurement in many other contexts.[96]

[2] Problems in Application

Three problems arise in applying the contract-market formula. First, because it developed in connection with stock and commodity exchanges in which there was an active market, it was relatively easy to fix the market value of a specific good at a specific time. Outside these markets, however, there is rarely such a ready reference for determining market value. Indeed, the contract price should itself be the best indicator of value if the contract is the result of arm's-length bargaining between knowledgeable parties. Second, the formula can be difficult to apply if the contract is for a

---

[95] See generally Kessler & Gilmore, *Contracts* 1041–1043 (2d ed. 1970).

[96] The contract-market formula is codified as part of the sales law in UCC §§ 2-708(1) and 2-713. *Flureau* was rejected in most jurisdictions years ago, and the approach in land sales contracts is virtually the same as in chattel sales contracts governed by the UCC. See generally 5 Corbin § 1098; McCormick, *Handbook on the Law of Damages* § 177 (1935). A century ago the Georgia Supreme Court stated the rule for land sales contracts in language that continues to apply: "The measure of damages in such a case would be the difference between the price agreed to be paid and the value of the land when the contract was broken by the refusal of the vendor to comply with it." Irvin v. Askew, 74 Ga. 581 (1885). See also Solomon v. Western Hills Dev. Co., 110 Mich. App. 257, 312 NW2d 428 (1981); George E. Shepard, Inc. v. Kim, Inc., 52 NC App. 700, 279 SE2d 858 (1981). The *Flureau* or "English" rule is still followed in a few jurisdictions if the vendor breaches because of a defect in title. See, e.g., Large v. Gregory, 417 NE2d 1160 (Ind. Ct. App. 1981); Long v. Brown, 593 SW2d 371 (Tex. Civ. App. 1979). Others have refused to follow the "English" rule even in that limited situation. See, e.g., Smith v. Warr, 564 P2d 771 (Utah 1977).

series of performances over time, especially if the performing party has some discretion in choosing the time of performance (e.g., delivery within thirty days). Third, the formula may be inconsistent with the general goal of contract remedies if it results in a recovery greater than the lost expectancy of the disappointed party.

The first of these problems is essentially a matter of proof. Outside established exchanges or active markets the best solution is to offer proof of expert appraisals or comparable transactions in order to reach an approximation of the value of the contract's subject matter. There is no reason not to take the contract itself into account as evidence probative of value, but it may not be finally determinative because parties often have good reasons for buying or selling above or below the market.[97]

A multiple-performance contract simply may not be susceptible to the contract-market formula because of its conjectural nature. If there is a ready and ongoing market, the problem may be only one of arithmetic, but if there is already some difficulty in proving a market, the problem may be insurmountable if the case requires proof of a series of markets over time. The plaintiff then should resort to proof of lost profits or, if that is too conjectural, to proof of reliance expenditures.

Perhaps the most difficult problems arise when the contract-market formula promises to reward the nonbreaching party with a recovery greater than his actual damage. The formula sometimes works to the plaintiff's considerable advantage, as illustrated in the following situation.

> **EXAMPLE 5.** Gray agrees to sell 100 shares of stock to Brown at $10 per share. On the date of delivery, the stock is trading at $8 and Brown reneges. Under the contract-market formula, Gray is entitled to damages of $200 ($10 − $8 × 100). This is true even if Gray does not sell the stock at $8 but holds it until the market goes back up to $12 or more. Gray suffers no real economic injury except the short-term loss on his bal-

---

[97] See infra ¶ 7.06 for a further discussion of proof of value.

ance sheet,[98] but he can keep the stock in a rising market, get his $200, and later sell the stock at a further advantage.[99]

This result at first seems to be inconsistent with the general rule of limiting a contract recovery to an amount that does not overcompensate the plaintiff. In this example, it appears as if the nonbreaching party gets to eat his cake and keep it too. The traditional explanation, however, is that Gray suffers a lost opportunity. If he had sold 100 shares at $10 when the shares were trading at $8, he could have reinvested his $1,000 in 125 shares, and when the market went back up he could have netted an additional profit.[100] On the other hand, the market might have dropped even more. Brown left Gray holding the stock when it was worth $8 and it may have continued to fall in value to $5 or less. Gray then would have had a clear economic loss, and $200 would not have made him whole. The point of holding Brown to the contract-market formula when the market rises is to protect Gray when the market drops with a rule that fixes the gamble as the parties made it, regardless of subsequent events.

The standard contract-market formula has the advantages of reasonable objectivity, uniformity, simplicity, and predictability, but some courts have been reluctant to apply it where the evidence discloses that the plaintiff's actual loss is less than the difference between the contract price and current market price. "Under this view, the plaintiff should not be granted a windfall, since the purpose of contract damages is solely to indemnify for actual loss, not to deter breach."[101] More commonly, however, the standard con-

---

[98] This might affect his ability to do something in the meantime — e.g., obtain a loan of more than $800 using the stock as collateral — but assume that Gray did nothing and planned to do nothing but await a more favorable market.

[99] For similar hypotheticals see the illustrations to Restatement (First) of Contracts § 329 (1932) and Simon, "A Critique of the Treatment of Market Damages in the Restatement (Second) of Contracts," 81 Colum L. Rev. 80, 87 (1981) (hereinafter cited as Simon). Simon notes that the illustration is missing from the companion provision in the second Restatement. In his opinion, this may signal a shift toward a requirement of proving actual loss. Id.

[100] Of course, this is mere speculation. Gray might have reinvested in a stock that went down.

[101] Simon 85, citing, e.g., Nobs Chem., USA, Inc. v. Koppers Co., 616 F2d 212 (5th Cir. 1980); Coast Trading Co. v. Cudahy Co., 592 F2d 1074 (9th Cir. 1979).

tract-market formula is used for the reasons discussed previously.[102] Furthermore, it is often difficult to ascertain the nonbreaching party's actual loss, because any such inquiry involves a subjective evaluation of his state of mind.

Sometimes, using a more subjective approach that tries to approximate actual loss may benefit the plaintiff more than mechanically applying the contract-market formula. A good case in point is *Madison Funds, Inc. v. The Charter Co.*[103] The defendant was supposed to make a shelf registration of the plaintiff's restricted stock on December 3, 1971, but failed to do so until August 31, 1972. The plaintiff argued that the damage recovery should be determined by ascertaining the highest value of the stock between December 3 and August 31. The defendant responded that the court should only take into account the market prices on those two dates because there was no proof that the plaintiff would have sold in between. Furthermore, if a sale had occurred between the two dates, it might have been at a lower figure because the value of the stock rose and fell, making any definite calculation impossible. The court reasoned that the risk of conjecture properly falls on the defendant as the breaching party, but that the defendant should not have to bear the risk of the highest possible price between December and August. The court compromised by using the earliest reasonable time after December 3, 1971 that the plaintiff could have disposed of the stock without depressing the market and selected the highest price within that period.[104]

[3] Use With Resale Contracts

Should a resale contract determine market value? For instance, a real estate investor may have a contract of resale on a parcel of land when he buys the property. If the price in the resale contract is higher than the market price determined by expert testi-

---

[102] Simon 85, citing, e.g., United States v. Burton Coal Co., 273 US 337 (1927); Kaufman v. Diversified Indus., Inc., 460 F2d 1331 (2d Cir. 1972); Brightwater Paper Co. v. Monadnock Paper Mills, 161 F2d 869 (1st Cir. 1947); and see Simon & Novack 1421–1425.

[103] Madison Funds, Inc. v. The Charter Co., 427 F. Supp. 597 (SDNY 1977) (applying Florida law).

[104] Id. at 609, see also Simon & Novack 1425, 1426.

mony and comparable sales, which price governs? In such a case the contract-market rule probably should not be used. Instead, the parties should look to the rules of foreseeability that apply to lost expectancy cases.[105] The loss of the resale opportunity is really a loss of consequential profits peculiar to the particular plaintiff rather than a form of market damages that would have more general application. Whether the difference between the contract price and the resale price should govern is essentially a matter for determination under the rule of *Hadley v. Baxendale* and its progeny.[106]

In some instances the absence of a resale contract may be fatal to the plaintiff's case if a problem arises in proving the certainty of a market price. For example, a public relations firm produced and sold radio jingles and other promotional materials to a radio station for which the station agreed to pay cash plus a number of one-minute advertising spots. The producer apparently intended to resell the radio spots to various advertisers. When the radio station breached the agreement, the producer sued for both the cash payments and the value of the advertising spots. The court only allowed a recovery in the amount of the cash, because the producer failed to prove that it had resold or that it could have resold the advertising spots to third parties. In addition, there was insufficient proof of the prices at which such resales might occur.[107] The dissenting judge argued that there was a market for radio advertising spots and the value of the spots could be determined by reference to that market. In his opinion, there should have been no requirement that the plaintiff prove actual or possible resales.[108]

---

[105] See supra ¶ 7.03[3].

[106] See supra ¶ 7.03[4][b]. Cohen v. Lovitz, 255 F. Supp. 302 (DDC 1966), is an interesting illustration. There was a contract to purchase a parcel of commercial real estate at a price of $1 million. The vendee had in hand a contract of resale for $1.8 million. The vendor breached and the vendee sued for specific performance. The vendee was successful, but only after two years of litigation. By then the contract of resale had long since lapsed, but the property had a fair market value of only $1.4 million. The vendee also wanted the difference between the current market value of the property and the resale contract price, or $355,000. This was treated as an item of special damage subject to the *Hadley* rule of foreseeability.

[107] William B. Tanner Co. v. WIOO, Inc., 528 F2d 262 (3d Cir. 1975).

[108] Id. at 274 (Seitz, CJ, dissenting).

[4] UCC Application Provisions

In general, UCC application of the contract-market formula is closely tied to the principle of mitigation and to the rules applicable to consequential damages. Section 2-708(1) sets forth the contract-market formula for the seller when the buyer breaches,[109] although it also acts with other UCC sections. Section 2-708(2), for example, allows courts the discretion to employ a lost-profits measure (including reasonable overhead) if the contract-market formula "is inadequate to put the seller in as good a position as performance would have done." In any event, the seller has an action for the price under Section 2-709 less the proceeds of any resale. According to the Official Commentary, however, "The action for the price is now generally limited to those cases where resale of the good is impracticable except where the buyer has accepted the goods or where they have been destroyed after risk of loss has passed to the buyer."[110]

The buyer's contract-market formula is set out in Section 2-713, which specifically allows the recovery of additional consequential damages less expenses saved by reason of the breach.[111] This section must be read together with Section 2-712, which allows the buyer to recover the difference between the contract price and any cover contract price plus incidental transactional costs. A cover contract is a reasonable substitute for the original contract.[112] The contract-market formula of Section 2-713 applies *only* when

---

[109] The seller gets the difference between the contract price and the market price "at the time and place for tender" plus incidental damages as defined in Section 2-710 but less expenses saved in consequence of the breach. The buyer receives credit for any payments made to date on the contract price.

[110] UCC § 2-709, Comment 2.

[111] UCC § 2-713(1). The buyer's consequential damages are defined in Section 2-715(2), which states:

> "Consequential damages resulting from the seller's breach include (a) any loss resulting from general or particular requirements and needs of which the seller had reason to know and which could not reasonably be prevented by cover or otherwise; and (b) injury to person or property proximately resulting from any breach of warranty."

[112] UCC § 2-712(1). Comment 2 to that section states, in part, "The test of proper cover is whether at the time and place the buyer acted in good faith and in a reasonable manner, and it is immaterial that hindsight may later prove that the method of cover used was not the cheapest or most effective."

the buyer has not covered. Comment 5 to Section 2-713 states, "The present section provides a remedy which is completely alternative to cover under the preceding section and applies only when and to the extent that the buyer has not covered."

¶ 7.06 PROOF OF ENTERPRISE VALUE

The study of the general principles of contract damages does not usually include a consideration of valuation problems, which are more often in the province of studies on evidence or taxation where such practical problems are centrally important. Nevertheless, a lawyer advising a client on a contract matter or handling a contracts case should be aware of some of the principles of enterprise valuation because they may affect the calculation and recovery of damages.

The question of enterprise value is most likely to arise in the context of an agreement for the disposition of all or a part of a closely held business. The principals in small businesses often have buy-out agreements that come into play on the death, retirement, or withdrawal of one of the principals. Although many of these agreements contain formulas to calculate the value of an interest in the business, there may be disagreements about the application of the formula. In some instances, the determination of value may be a fairly wide-open proposition. In addition, sales of businesses and business interests sometimes go awry, necessitating a reasonable determination of the whole enterprise's value.

The valuation of a business requires the consideration of at least the following factors:

(1) Economic conditions, including general trends, specific characteristics of the sector of the economy in which the enterprise operates, and possible future developments.

(2) Size of the enterprise compared to the size and number of its competitors.

(3) Number of owners of the enterprise. Control is a key factor, and the value of an interest depends in part on whether it is a minority interest with little or no control over the direction of the business or whether the owner of the inter-

est can influence the enterprise's operation and management.[113]

(4) Earnings history of the enterprise.

(5) Short- and long-term assets and liabilities of the enterprise.

(6) Quality of the enterprise's management and labor force.

(7) Special problems, such as sensitivity to regulation.

(8) Special attributes, such as the availability of tax advantages.

None of these factors can be considered in a vacuum because market values are relative values. The appraiser must take into account the value the market gives to enterprises of a particular sort and the valuations afforded by people who have choices of investments in order to weigh the relative value of different firms as investment opportunities. If no ready market exists for interests in the business, a common method of valuation is to look at comparable enterprises for which there is a ready market, such as businesses whose stock is traded on an exchange or over the counter. A recent acquisition or merger of a similar business may also provide useful information to use in determining value. As a check against comparisons with other businesses, it is also possible to examine the value of the assets to calculate the enterprise's net asset value,[114] which should be roughly equivalent to a value based on a comparison with other enterprises.[115]

Once a database is established, determining enterprise value requires additional calculations. For instance, the enterprise's me-

---

[113] For a discussion of discounts for minority interests and the like in the context of taxation, see, e.g., Comment, "Estate and Gift Valuation: Discounts of Partnership Interests," 59 Neb. L. Rev. 737 (1980).

[114] If the enterprise is an operating company rather than a holding company (i.e., one involved in the production of goods for sale or the provision of services rather than one involved in holding assets for appreciation), the IRS requires that in most cases the appraiser should "accord primary consideration to earnings." Rev. Rul. 59-60, 1959-1 CB 237. See, e.g., Estate of Martha B. Watts, TC Memo. 1985-595.

[115] For a good discussion of the basic principles of appraisal, see Pratt, *Valuing a Business: The Analysis and Appraisal of Closely Held Companies* (1981).

dian average earnings and the median average price of multiple earnings of comparable publicly traded companies can be used to estimate value.[116] The cash flow of the business can be capitalized using a discount factor determined by an examination of the cash-flow history of comparable companies. The relationship between cash flow or earnings and the company's asset value, adjusted properly for liabilities and for comparison with other companies, also can be examined. If the appraiser uses an assets-valuation approach, he must consider the time that it would require to sell the assets, either as part of an ongoing business or separately in a liquidation, together with the costs of selling them.[117]

Contracts lawyers need not be experts in valuation, but they should at least be aware of the principles that apply to the valuation of enterprises for which there is no ready market. It is often useful to employ an adviser — an investment banker or professional appraiser, for example — to study the company in question.[118]

¶ 7.07 THE MITIGATION PRINCIPLE

One of the oldest principles of contract damages is that the complaining party must mitigate his loss. He cannot sit idly by and allow damages to accrue or the situation to worsen if he has a

---

[116] The median average usually provides a truer result than the mean average because it discounts numbers that are skewed upward or downward. The numbers 17, 6, 5, 4, and 3 add up to 35. Their mean average is 7 (35 divided by 5), but the median is 5, and 5 is more representative of the group of numbers than 7, because it is close to four of them and 17 is the extraordinary number. The distinctions are not always so clear, and the mean may be more accurate in some cases, but more often than not, the median is a better number to use.

[117] Valuation is an important factor in taxation, and a number of Treasury Regulations, Revenue Rulings, and cases set out the general principles and apply them in specific contexts. They provide useful guidelines for enterprise valuation in general even if no tax question is involved. See, e.g., Treas. Reg. § 20.2031-3; Rev. Ruls. 59-60, 1959-1 CB 237, 65-192, 1965-2 CB 259, 68-609, 1968-2 CB 327; True, Jr. v. United States, 82-2 USTC ¶ 13,503 (D. Wyo. 1982); Internal Revenue Service Appellate Conference Valuation Training Program No. 6126-01 (4-67).

[118] The valuation of services may sometimes present similar difficulties, but usually there is a market for services so that some comparisons can be made.

reasonable opportunity to minimize the damage.[119] At trial, the burden of proof is usually on the defendant to show that the plaintiff failed to minimize damages,[120] but the burden of actually doing so is on the nonbreaching party as soon as the breach occurs. Thus, the disappointed party must not only bear the brunt of the breach, but must also try to remedy the situation as best he can. Of course, this is usually consistent with the nonbreaching party's best interests and does not involve anything that does not make good business and common sense. The mitigation principle, however, is another example of the workings of the overall goal of avoiding overcompensation. It is consistent with the notion of efficient breach because the breaching party does not bear the risk of the entire loss but only the loss that the nonbreaching party is unable to mitigate.[121]

The key to the mitigation principle is the concept of reasonableness. There is no requirement that the nonbreaching party expend any extra effort or do anything extraordinary to minimize loss. For example, if an employment agreement is breached, the employee does not have to take any work that is available; he may refuse jobs that are outside his area of interest or expertise or that

---

[119] "The fundamental basis is thus compensation for pecuniary loss naturally flowing from the breach; but this first principle is qualified by a second, which imposes upon a plaintiff the duty of taking all reasonable steps to mitigate the loss consequent on the breach, and debars him from claiming any part of the damage which is due to his neglect to take such steps." British Westinghouse Elec. & Mfg. Co. v. Underground Elec. Ry. Co. of London, [1912] AC 673, 689. Although the UCC does not have a specific provision on mitigation, the requirements of good faith and commercial reasonability imply the obligation to minimize damages. See, e.g., Bache & Co. v. International Controls Corp., 339 F. Supp. 341 (SDNY 1972); Wurlitzer Co. v. Oliver, 334 F. Supp. 1009 (WD Pa. 1971); Oloffson v. Coomer, 11 Ill. App. 3d 918, 296 NE2d 871 (1973); Fessler & Loiseaux, *Contracts* 723, 724 (1982); see also Restatement (First) of Contracts § 336 (1932); Restatement (Second) of Contracts § 350 (1982).

[120] Stark v. Shell Oil Co., 450 F2d 994 (5th Cir. 1971); Sandler v. Lawn-A-Mat Chem. & Equip. Corp., 141 NJ Super. 436, 358 A2d 805 (1976); Davis v. Small Business Inv. Co., 535 SW2d 740 (Tex. Civ. App. 1976). In response, the plaintiff only has to show that what he did was reasonable, not that it was what the defendant would have done or that it was the best thing to have done. Eazor Express, Inc. v. International Brotherhood of Teamsters, 520 F2d 951 (3d Cir. 1975).

[121] However, the breaching party may be liable for costs incurred in seeking to minimize damages. Spang Indus., Inc. v. Aetna Cas. & Sur. Co., 512 F2d 365 (2d Cir. 1975); Mr. Eddie, Inc. v. Ginsberg, 430 SW2d 5 (Tex. Civ. App. 1968).

require him to move to another location.[122] The disappointed buyer in a case governed by the UCC does not have to take any cover contract, but only one that involves the same or similar goods and that is reasonable in terms and time. Thus, it may be misleading to refer to a duty to mitigate. In fact, the nonbreaching party does not have to do anything. He just may not be able to recover for damages that he could have avoided. The choice is between present action and the possibility of a smaller recovery at an indefinite time in the future.[123]

If the nonbreaching party does mitigate, he may be hard pressed to recover more than minimal damages even if he argues that he lost an opportunity — that he could have had both the breached contract and the contract in mitigation. For example, in *Sierra Wine & Liquor Co. v. Heublein., Inc.,*[124] a franchise termination case, the plaintiff's claim for lost profits was reduced by the profits from a replacement franchise because the plaintiff could not have held both franchises at the same time. In *Copenhaver v. Berryman,*[125] the plaintiff operated a laundry complex in the basement of an apartment building pursuant to a contract with the defendant. After the defendant breached the contract, the plaintiff removed the washers and dryers and within six months had all the machines in operation at other locations. Although the plaintiff argued that he could have had the contract machines as well as all the others in operation if the breach had not occured, the court did not find that likely and reduced the damage claim by the revenues from the substituted locations.[126]

---

[122] See, e.g., Ballard v. El Dorado Tire Co., 512 F2d 901 (5th Cir. 1975); Redman v. Department of Educ., 519 P2d 760 (Alaska 1974); Parker v. Twentieth Century Fox Film Corp., 3 Cal. 3d 176, 474 P2d 689, 89 Cal. Rptr. 737 (1970); Ryan v. Superintendent of Schools of Quincy, 373 NE2d 1178 (Mass. 1978); Harrison, "Wrongful Discharge: Toward a More Efficient Remedy," 56 Ind. LJ 207 (1981).

[123] See generally Thompson & Sebert, *Remedies: Damages, Equity and Restitution* § 2.03, at 2-64 (1983).

[124] Sierra Wine & Liquor Co. v. Heublein, Inc., 626 F2d 129 (9th Cir. 1980).

[125] Copenhaver v. Berryman, 602 SW2d 540 (Tex. Civ. App. 1980).

[126] On similar facts involving vending machines, see Macke Co. v. Pizza of Gaithersburg, Inc., 259 Md. 479, 270 A2d 645 (1970).

CHAPTER 8

Damages and Other Remedies for Breach of Contract in Specific Situations

¶ 8.01 DAMAGES FOR BREACH OF LAND SALES CONTRACTS

Although specific performance is the preferred remedy for the breach of a contract to convey real property,[1] sometimes it may be an impossible or undesirable option. The alternative is money damages.

The so-called English rule of damages follows the decision in the eighteenth-century case of *Flureau v. Thornhill*.[2] Thornhill, the seller, reneged on a contract for the sale of a parcel of London real estate during a period of heavy speculation. Flureau, the buyer, was upset at the loss of a good opportunity to purchase a parcel of land he believed would increase substantially in value. He sought to recover the difference between the agreed-upon price and the market price at closing, but the court refused to grant that relief. Instead, the court ruled that Flureau's only remedy was rescission plus restitution of his earnest money. The disappointed party was returned to his status quo ante, but he did not recover the expected benefit of the bargain.[3]

Although some courts in the United States have followed the *Flureau* opinion, it is definitely the minority rule.[4] Most jurisdictions apply a contract-market formula to determine damages in

---

[1] See ¶ 6.02.

[2] Flureau v. Thornhill, 2 Black., W. 1078, 96 Eng. Rep. 635 (CP 1776). See ¶ 7.05[1].

[3] The court said that the plaintiff could not recover any "damages for the fancied goodness of the bargain, which he supposes he has lost." Flureau v. Thornhill, 96 Eng. Rep. 635 (CP 1776).

[4] See, e.g., Long v. Brown, 593 SW2d 371 (Tex. Civ. App. 1979); Junk v. Barnard, 99 Ind. 137 (1884).

land sales disputes.[5] The recovery for the buyer includes not only a return of the earnest money but also the difference between the contract price and the fair market value of the property as of the date of closing.[6] If the buyer breaches (often because the market has fallen), the formula is the same — the contract price less fair market value as of the date of closing.[7]

In an arm's-length transaction, the contract price and the fair market value are often almost identical. The most that the average litigant can expect is a return to his status quo ante plus recovery of some transaction costs. The contract-market formula obviously is more important to the buyer in a rising market and to the seller in a falling market because it fixes the risk as the parties agreed in their contract. It approximates, as closely as possible, specific performance for the investor or seller. Of course, it does not satisfy nonobjective personal preferences, such as an emotional attachment to a parcel of land, nor is it of much help to a land-poor seller who needs the cash from the sale. His balance sheet may be the same afterwards, but his liquidity will not be what it would have been had the sale gone through.

Fair market value can be an elusive concept. In the real estate market there usually are comparable transactions, and brokers often can present expert testimony about the value of real property.[8] Property tax assessments also may be used as evidence of value, although their credibility is suspect. If the buyer has a contract of resale, it should indicate fair market value if it is also an arm's-length transaction. It may not be decisive, however, because the resale contract may be evidence of consequential damages or lost

---

[5] See discussion of the contract-market formula at ¶ 7.05.

[6] See, e.g., Corbin, 5 *Corbin on Contracts* § 1098 (1964) (hereinafter cited as Corbin); McCormick, *Handbook on the Law of Damages* § 177 (1935); Smith v. Warr, 564 P2d 771 (Utah 1977).

[7] See, e.g., Soloman v. Western Hills Dev. Co., 110 Mich. App. 257, 312 NW2d 428 (1981); George E. Shepard, Jr., Inc. v. Kim, Inc., 52 NC App. 700, 279 SE2d 858 (1981).

[8] See ¶ 7.03[4][b]. The owner may also be allowed to present opinion testimony about value. See, e.g., Croft v. Kamens, 171 Ga. App. 105, 318 SE2d 809 (1984).

profits and thus subject to the foreseeability limitations of the *Hadley* rule.[9]

A subsequent resale of the same property may be the best evidence either of fair market value or of changes in market value since the date on which closing should have occurred. *Croft v. Kamens,*[10] a recent Georgia decision, provides a good example. Croft agreed to buy a house from Kamens for $235,000. She was unable to close for two reasons: First, she could not sell her house, and second, mortgage interest rates had increased dramatically between the time of contracting and the time set for closing. Within five days of the original closing date, Kamens entered into another contract of sale for $200,000, which subsequently closed. Kamens sued Croft for the difference in price. At trial, three witnesses testified about the market value of the house as of the date set for the original closing. Croft's husband gave his opinion that the house was worth $235,000, the contract price, and that Kamens sold below market value. A real estate appraiser testified that the fair market value of the house was between $220,000 and $230,000. Kamens himself testified that the value was only $200,000, the price at which he was able to strike a deal. His opinion was based on his own purchase price several years earlier ($130,000), the cost of repairs and renovations during his ownership ($40,000), offers when the house was first on the market (the contract with Croft and another offer of $232,500 rejected in favor of Croft's offer), and changes in the market brought on by the great increase in mortgage interest rates during the period between the signing of the contract and the closing date. The jury returned a verdict of $30,000 for Kamens, and the Georgia Court of Appeals affirmed.

One difficulty that arises in many land sales cases is translating the contract terms into cash-equivalent terms. If the seller finances the sale, the purchase money mortgage must be adjusted to a present cash value in order to determine the contract price. In the case of an ordinary house sale financed by a commercial lender, the contract purchase price is just as it is stated on the contract. If

---

[9] See ¶ 7.03[3][e]. On this point, see, e.g., Cohen v. Lovitz, 255 F. Supp. 302 (DDC 1966) aff'd sub nom., Wolf v. Cohen, 379 F2d 477 (DC Cir. 1967), Bush v. Cathey, 598 SW2d 777 (Tenn. Ct. App. 1979).

[10] Croft v. Kamens, 171 Ga. App. 105, 318 SE2d 809 (1984).

two parties negotiate a privately financed sale, however, the stated price may be a factor of the negotiations on terms. Consider the following terms of sale:

(1) White agrees to sell a parcel of land to Brown for $10,000 cash at closing.
(2) White agrees to sell the land to Brown for $10,000, to be paid $1,000 cash at closing and the remainder in 120 equal monthly installments of principal and interest with interest on the unpaid principal balance at the rate of 10 percent per year.

In each of these sales the contract price for the land is $10,000, but the two transactions may have quite different values to the parties. A great deal depends on the prevailing interest rates, the parties' respective needs for liquidity or cash flow, their respective tax situations,[11] and their respective interests in pursuing other investment opportunities. For purposes of simplicity, a court may be inclined to treat these two transactions as equivalent in value because the purchase price is the same, but the terms of sale make the two transactions fundamentally different, and a proper valuation should take these differences into account.

Sometimes the prevailing party may be able both to recover damages and benefit from the remedy of specific performance.[12] This usually occurs when the nonbreaching party loses an investment or resale opportunity as a result of the breach and the party in default had reason to know that the additional loss would be a consequence of the breach. This is a mechanism for giving the nonbreaching party his full expectancy, although it does impose a significant additional cost on the defendant. The defendant does not suffer a total loss, however, because the buyer who obtains specific performance still must pay the contract price and the seller who prevails still must turn over the property.

---

[11] If the seller stands to reap a large capital gain on the sale of the property, he may prefer to take payment in installments to spread out the tax liability over time. The maximum rate for capital gains is now 20 percent, which is not particularly burdensome, but income tax rates go up to 50 percent and the interest on the purchase money note is taxed at ordinary income rates. The buyer can deduct the interest to receive a tax advantage.

[12] See ¶ 7.01.

¶ 8.02 DAMAGES FOR BREACH OF CHATTEL SALES CONTRACTS GOVERNED BY THE UCC

[1] General Principles and Relation to Common Law

Agreements for the sale and purchase of chattels usually fall within the coverage of the UCC, which has been adopted by every state. There are minor state variations in some of the provisions of the UCC, but the main clauses are essentially the same from state to state. The UCC approach to remedies for broken agreements involving the sale of chattels is not fundamentally different from the common law. A seller can recover the entire price of the chattels or its unpaid portion, reduced by the value of any goods he retains. A buyer can recover the contract-market differential; that is, the difference between the contract price and the cost of substituted goods. If the goods in question are custom-made or identified to the contract, the buyer may have an action in replevin similar to the action at common law for the recovery of a unique chattel.[13] Both seller and buyer may be able to recover incidental damages. A seller may have an action for his expected profit or, in some instances, for the price. A buyer may recover consequential damages subject to the normal contract rules of foreseeability.[14] In short, there are few departures from the general thrust of common law, although there are enough variations and opportunities for choice to consider the available remedies with some particularity.

[2] Seller's Remedies

Sections 2-703 through 2-710 of the UCC outline the options available to a seller when a buyer breaches. Section 2-703 is simply an outline of the remaining substantive sections, but it is a handy reference for a seller's possible choices in a given circumstance.[15]

---

[13] See generally Dobbs, *Remedies* § 2.5 (1973).

[14] See ¶ 7.03[3][d].

[15] Section 2-703 states:

"Where the buyer wrongfully rejects or revokes acceptance of goods or fails to make a payment due on or before delivery or repudiates with respect to a part or the whole, then with respect to any goods directly affected and if the breach is of the whole contract . . . , then also with respect to the whole undelivered balance, the aggrieved seller may

[a] Section 2-704: Completion of Goods for Resale

Section 2-704 is typical of the "reasonability" approach of the UCC.[16] When a seller learns of a breach or a repudiation, he may identify goods in his possession as conforming to the contract and may decide whether to manufacture the rest of the goods under the contract or to cease production.[17] This decision must be based on reasonable commercial judgment, which should preclude manufacture simply to increase damages.[18] The object is to allow an aggrieved seller to complete a line for resale because resale is his primary practical remedy. If the goods cannot be resold, they still may have residual value that can be set off against their price. A seller also has an advantage if he can identify goods to the contract; by so doing, he provides the necessary factual basis for an action for the price.

"(a) withhold delivery of such goods;

"(b) stop delivery by any bailee as hereinafter provided (Section 2-705);

"(c) proceed under the next section respecting goods still unidentified to the contract;

"(d) resell and recover damages as hereafter provided (Section 2-706);

"(e) recover damages for nonacceptance (Section 2-708) or in a proper case the price (Section 2-709);

"(f) cancel."

One of the critical issues under this section is whether there has been a breach or a repudiation that triggers the remedial sections. For further discussion of this point, see ¶ 2.02.

[16] Section 2-704 provides:

"(1) An aggrieved seller under the preceding section may

"(a) identify to the contract conforming goods not already identified if at the time he learned of the breach they are in his possession or control;

"(b) treat as the subject of resale goods which have demonstrably been intended for the particular contract even though those goods are unfinished.

"(2) Where the goods are unfinished an aggrieved seller may in the exercise of reasonable commercial judgment for the purpose of avoiding loss and of effective realization either complete the manufacture and wholly identify the goods to the contract or cease manufacture and resell for scrap or salvage value or proceed in any other reasonable manner."

[17] As to what constitutes identification, see UCC §§ 2-401, 2-501.

[18] Reasonable commercial judgment is closely related to the concept of good faith. See Northern Helex Co. v. United States, 207 Ct. Cl. 862, 524 F2d 707, cert. denied, 429 US 866 (1975); Anderson, 4 *Uniform Commercial Code* § 2-704:7, at 343 (3d ed. 1983) (hereinafter cited as Anderson).

[b] Section 2-705: Stoppage of Delivery

Section 2-705 is a self-help provision tied closely to the concept of relief from the obligation to perform where the other party repudiates the contract.[19] It allows a seller to stop delivery of goods in transit or in the possession of a bailee, such as a warehouseman, when the seller learns of the buyer's breach or repudiation or when the buyer is insolvent.[20] The seller may also halt delivery temporarily if he has good reason to feel insecure about the buyer's ability to perform. Some risk is involved, however, because an improper stoppage is a breach by the seller.[21]

---

[19] Section 2-705 provides:

"(1) The seller may stop delivery of goods in the possession of a carrier or other bailee when he discovers the buyer to be insolvent . . . and may stop delivery of carload, truckload, planeload or larger shipments of express or freight when the buyer repudiates or fails to make a payment due before delivery or if for any other reason the seller has a right to withhold or reclaim the goods.

"(2) As against such buyer the seller may stop delivery until

"(a) receipt of the goods by the buyer; or

"(b) acknowledgement to the buyer by any bailee of the goods except a carrier that the bailee holds the goods for the buyer; or

"(c) such acknowledgement to the buyer by a carrier by reshipment or as a warehouseman; or

"(d) negotiation to the buyer of any negotiable document of title covering the goods.

"(3)(a) To stop delivery the seller must so notify as to enable the bailee by reasonable diligence to prevent delivery of the goods.

"(b) After such notification the bailee must hold and deliver the goods according to the directions of the seller but the seller is liable to the bailee for any ensuing charges or damages.

"(c) If a negotiable document of title has been issued for goods the bailee is not obliged to obey a notification to stop until surrender of the document.

"(d) A carrier who has issued a nonnegotiable bill of lading is not obliged to obey a notification to stop received from a person other than the consignor."

[20] If the buyer was insolvent at the time of the sale and the seller knew of this insolvency, he may be estopped from relying on insolvency as a reason for stopping delivery. 4 Anderson § 2-705:11, at 352, 353.

[21] Section 2-705, Official Comment 1 states, in part: "Improper stoppage is a breach by the seller if it effectively interferes with the buyer's right to due tender under the section on manner of tender of delivery. However, if the bailee obeys an unjustified order to stop he may also be liable to the buyer."

[c] Section 2-706: Resale of Goods

A seller may resell goods covered by the contract when a buyer breaches, and Section 2-706 sets forth the mechanics for accomplishing the resale.[22] In a resale made "in good faith and in a commercially reasonable manner,"[23] a seller may recover from a

---

[22] Section 2-706 states:

"(1) Under the conditions stated in Section 2-703 on seller's remedies, the seller may resell the goods concerned or the undelivered balance thereof. When the resale is made in good faith and in a commercially reasonable manner the seller may recover the difference between the resale price and the contract price together with any incidental damages allowed under the provisions of this Article . . . , but less expenses saved in consequence of the buyer's breach.

"(2) Except as otherwise provided in subsection (3) or unless otherwise agreed, resale may be at public or private sale including sale by way of one or more contracts to sell or of identification to an existing contract of the seller. Sale may be as a unit or in parcels and at any time and place and on any terms but every aspect of the sale including the method, manner, time, place and terms must be commercially reasonable. The resale must be reasonably identified as referring to the broken contract, but it is not necessary that the goods be in existence or that any or all of them have been identified to the contract before the breach.

"(3) Where the resale is at private sale the seller must give the buyer reasonable notification of his intention to resell.

"(4) Where the resale is at public sale

"(a) only identified goods can be sold except where there is a recognized market for a public future sale of futures in goods of the kind; and

"(b) it must be made at a usual place or market for public sale if one is reasonably available and, except in the case of goods which are perishable or threaten to decline in value speedily, the seller must give the buyer reasonable notice of the time and place of the resale; and

"(c) if the goods are not to be within the view of those attending the sale the notification of the sale must state the place where the goods are located and provide for their reasonable inspection by prospective bidders; and

"(d) the seller may buy.

"(5) A purchaser who buys in good faith at a resale takes the goods free and clear of any rights of the original buyer even though the seller fails to comply with one or more of the requirements of this section.

"(6) The seller is not accountable to the buyer for any profit made on any resale. A person in the position of a seller . . . or a buyer who has rightfully rejected or justifiably revoked acceptance must account for any excess over the amount of his security interest, as hereinafter defined (subsection (3) of section 2-711)."

[23] For a discussion of commercial reasonableness in this context, see Bache & Co. v. International Controls Corp., 339 F. Supp. 341 (SDNY), aff'd, 469 F2d 696 (2d Cir. 1972).

buyer the difference between the contract price and the proceeds of the resale plus incidental damages "but less expenses saved in consequence of the buyer's breach." This provides a seller with his full expectancy and is also consistent with the mitigation principle: The buyer is not punished beyond the risk he assumes in the contract.[24] A seller must identify the goods to the contract before he can invoke the remedy of resale,[25] and he has the burden of proving the breach that justified the resale.[26] On the other hand, if a breach occurs, a seller has a duty to mitigate damages by disposing of the goods on reasonable terms.[27]

Section 2-706 contains a list of requirements for the resale of goods designed to ensure that the resale is handled fairly and reasonably. For instance, the buyer must be given notice so that he can attend and bid for the goods. Resale may be either public or private. A private sale is negotiated between the parties as opposed to a sale through an established market or by bid. The buyer is entitled to notice in either event, although the seller does not have to notify the buyer of the time and place of a private sale. It is enough to inform the buyer that there will be a private sale in sufficient time, depending on the urgency of the matter, in order for the buyer to consider whether to make an offer or to cure the breach.[28]

A good-faith purchaser at resale is in the same position as a typical bona fide purchaser for value. Even if the seller has failed to comply with the requirements of Section 2-706, the resale purchaser takes title to the goods free and clear of any claims by the original buyer.[29] If the seller does not conform to the provisions of Section 2-706, he loses his right to claim against the buyer for any deficit resulting from the resale.[30]

---

[24] See ¶ 7.07.

[25] Action Time Carpets, Inc. v. Midwest Carpet Brokers, Inc., 271 NW2d 36 (Minn. 1978).

[26] Bacon's Estate, 18 Bucks Co. LR 39 (1982).

[27] Industrial Leasing Corp. v. Thomason, 96 Idaho 574, 532 P2d 916 (1974).

[28] See UCC § 2-706, Official Comment 8.

[29] UCC § 2-706(5). Official Comment 10 suggests that this is a departure from the old Uniform Sales Act.

[30] See, e.g., Foster v. Colorado Radio Corp., 381 F2d 222 (10th Cir. 1967); Lee Oldsmobile, Inc. v. Kaiden, 32 Md. App. 556, 363 A2d 270 (1976); Anheuser

A seller has a distinct advantage under Section 2-706: If the resale turns out to be more profitable than the contract, he may keep the excess. He does not have to account to the buyer for any profits beyond the original contract price.[31]

[d] Section 2-708: Formulas for Calculation of Damages

The next substantive remedial provision is contained in Section 2-708. Section 2-707 merely defines an agent "in the position of a seller" who can invoke the remedies of Sections 2-705, 2-706, and 2-710 on behalf of a seller.[32] Section 2-708 states the basic formulas for the calculation of damages in a suit by a seller.

Section 2-708(1) sets forth the UCC version of the traditional contract-market formula.[33] "[T]he measure of damages for non-acceptance or repudiation by the buyer is the difference between the market price at the time and place for tender and the unpaid contract price together with any incidental damages, . . . but less expenses saved in consequence of the buyer's breach."[34] For all intents and purposes, the resale price under Section 2-706 is the market price for the calculation of damages in accordance with the contract-market formula, as long as the resale is commercially

---

v. Oswald Refractories Co., 541 SW2d 706 (Mo. Ct. App. 1976); Acuri v. Figliolli, 91 Misc. 2d 831, 398 NYS2d 923 (1977).

[31] UCC § 2-706(6), Official Comment 11.

[32] Section 2-707 states:

> "(1) A 'person in the position of a seller' includes as against a principal an agent who has paid or become responsible for the price of goods on behalf of his principal or anyone who otherwise holds a security interest or other right in goods similar to that of a seller.
>
> "(2) A person in the position of a seller may as provided in this Article withhold or stop delivery (Section 2-705) and resell (Section 2-706) and recover incidental damages (Section 2-710)."

[33] For a discussion of the contract-market formula, see ¶ 7.05.

[34] Time and place of tender are to be determined from the agreement read in light of UCC provisions defining terms such as FOB. See UCC §§ 2-307–2-310, 2-319–2-322. Section 2-708, Official Comment 1 further provides:

> "In the event that there is no evidence available of the current market price at the time and place of tender, proof of a substitute market may be made under the section on determination and proof of market price. Furthermore, the section on the admissibility of market quotations is intended to ease materially the problem of providing competent evidence."

reasonable.[35] Nevertheless, it is not conclusive evidence of market value.[36]

There are few complications in the application of Section 2-708(1) by itself, because the UCC remedy does not differ from the common-law contract market remedy. However, Section 2-708(1) is tied to Section 2-708(2), which provides the following:

> If the measure of damages provided in subsection (1) is inadequate to put the seller in as good a position as performance would have done then the measure of damages is the profit (including reasonable overhead) which the seller would have made from full performance by the buyer, together with any incidental damages . . . due allowance for costs reasonably incurred and due credit for payments or proceeds of resale.

The purpose of Section 2-708(2) is not clear, and it has been the subject of sharp criticism.[37] The Official Commentary says that its purpose is "to eliminate the unfair and economically wasteful results arising under the older law when fixed price articles were involved."[38] The drafters seemed to have in mind a situation like the following: The seller and buyer contract for the sale and purchase of 1,000 widgets at a unit price of $1. Widgets are common goods and the contract price is the same as the standard market price for widgets. Upon a breach by the buyer, the seller resells widgets identified to the contract at a unit price of $1. The application of the contract-market formula or the contract-resale formula results in no recovery because there is no loss. But what if the resale is to a regular customer who was going to order widgets

---

[35] See, e.g., President Container, Inc. v. Patimco, 82 AD2d 879, 440 NYS2d 313 (1981); Buchsteiner Prestige Corp. v. Abraham & Strauss, 107 Misc. 2d 327, 433 NYS2d 972 (1980). For an example of the result when the resale was not commercially reasonable, see Coast Trading Co. v. Cudahy Co., 592 F2d 1074 (9th Cir. 1979).

[36] Acuri v. Figliolli, 91 Misc. 2d 831, 398 NYS2d 923 (1977).

[37] See, e.g., Harris, "A Radical Restatement of the Law of Seller's Damages: Sales Act and Commercial Code Results Compared," 18 Stan. L. Rev. 66 (1965) (hereinafter cited as Harris).

[38] UCC § 2-708, Official Comment 2.

anyway? The seller then may argue that he has lost the opportunity for two sales, one to the breaching buyer and one to his regular customer. The widget unit price may have been constant at $1, but he has not sold as many widgets as he would have if the breach had not occurred. Section 2-708(2) allows a recovery based on this lost volume theory because the seller can claim for the profits on the contract, the differential between the $1 unit price and his unit cost.[39] This puts the seller in "as good a position as performance would have done."

Consider a seller who is not seeking to dispose of standard items but who enters into a contract to provide custom goods or component parts of some other product. If the buyer breaches, the seller may be left with goods for which there is no ready market and no reasonable opportunity for resale. Unless the requirements of Section 2-709 are met,[40] the seller may not have an action for the price. Section 2-708(2) allows this seller to sue for the profit on the transaction,[41] and he can even recover the anticipated profit on goods not yet manufactured.[42] A jobber is in a similar position.[43]

Lost-volume sellers of standard-priced goods, custom-components manufacturers, and jobbers are not the only sellers covered by Section 2-708(2). The UCC makes no such distinctions, but makes the lost profits remedy available to all sellers when the contract-market formula is insufficient to put the seller in as good a position as performance. This means that any seller may be able to

---

[39] The hypothetical lost-volume seller derives from Harris. See Snyder v. Herbert Greenbaum and Assocs., Inc., 38 Md. App. 144, 380 A2d 618 (1977); Famous Knitwear Corp. v. Drug Fair, Inc., 493 F2d 251 (4th Cir. 1974); Neri v. Retail Marine Corp., 30 NY2d 393, 285 NE2d 311, 334 NYS2d 165 (1972).

[40] See infra ¶ 8.02[2][e].

[41] See, e.g., Snyder v. Herbert Greenbaum and Assocs., Inc., 38 Md. App. 144, 380 A2d 618 (1977).

[42] See, e.g., Anchorage Centennial Dev. Co. v. Van Wormer & Rodrigues, Inc., 443 P2d 596 (Alaska 1968).

[43] See generally White & Summers, *Handbook of the Law Under the Uniform Commercial Code* §§ 7-8–7-13, at 225–238 (1972); Peters, "Remedies for Breach of Contracts Relating To the Sale of Goods Under the Uniform Commercial Code: A Roadmap for Article Two," 73 Yale LJ 199 (1963).

avail himself of this remedy.[44] The standard measure is the difference between the list price of the goods in question and the cost to the dealer/seller or the manufacturing cost to the manufacturer/seller. Because there is no need to show a history of profitability, a new-business seller is at no disadvantage.[45]

[e] Section 2-709: Suit for the Price of Goods

If a buyer fails to pay the price of the merchandise when it becomes due, Section 2-709 allows a seller to sue for the price. However, an action for the price is available only for goods accepted by the buyer, for conforming goods lost or damaged within a commercially reasonable time after the passage of risk of loss to the buyer, or for goods identified to the contract that the seller cannot resell at a reasonable price.[46] This does not include nonresellable goods that have not been completely manufactured (e.g., custom-made goods). In such a case, a seller's remedy is for damages on a repudiation under Section 2-708.[47] If a seller chooses to sue for the price, he must hold goods identified to the contract in his possession for the buyer, provided, however, that he can resell them prior to judgment and that he credit the proceeds of resale to the buyer's account.[48] When the buyer pays the judgment, he is

---

[44] Some commentators have suggested that virtually all sellers fall within the coverage of Section 2-708(2). See Childres & Burgess, "Seller's Remedies: The Primacy of UCC 2-708(2)," 48 NYU L. Rev. 833 (1973). Others have challenged the idea that many, if not most, sellers have a lost-volume argument. See Goetz & Scott, "Measuring Seller's Damages: The Lost Profits Puzzle," 31 Stan. L. Rev. 323 (1979); Shanker, "The Case for a Literal Reading of UCC Section 2-708(2) (One Profit for the Reseller)," 24 Case W. Res. L. Rev. 697 (1973); *but* challenging the challengers, see Sebert, "Remedies Under Article Two of the Uniform Commercial Code: An Agenda for Review," 130 U. Pa. L. Rev. 360 (1981).

[45] UCC § 2-708, Official Comment 2. For a discussion of "new-business" sellers, see ¶ 7.03[4][g].

[46] UCC §§ 2-709(1)(a), 2-709(1)(b). These are meant to be the only instances in which there can be an action for the price. See UCC § 2-709, Official Comment 6. For a collection of the cases on the subject of actions for the price under Section 2-709, see Annot., 90 ALR3d 1141 (1979).

[47] See, e.g., Rowland Meledandi, Inc. v. Kohn, 7 UCC Rep. 34 (NY Civ. Ct. 1969).

[48] UCC § 2-709(2).

entitled to goods remaining in the seller's possession.[49] If the seller does not qualify for a recovery of the price, Section 2-709 expressly provides that he can seek recovery under Section 2-708 either for the contract-market differential or for his profit.[50]

[f] Section 2-710: Recovery of Incidental Damages

In addition to the basic remedies available, a seller also can recover incidental damages under Section 2-710.[51] This section compensates a seller for the additional transactional costs he incurs as a result of the breach so that he can be made whole. The illustrations of recoverable items in Section 2-710 are not exhaustive, and any commercially reasonable expense directly resulting from the breach may be recovered. The kinds of incidental damages that may be recovered include additional storage costs for goods,[52] telephone charges resulting from conversations about the breach,[53] additional insurance or finance charges on goods,[54] transportation charges for removing goods,[55] and similar items.[56] Incidental damages do not include consequential damages.[57] In this respect the UCC treats buyers and sellers differently, for there is no express provision for the recovery of consequential damages by a seller as there is for a buyer.[58]

---

[49] Id.

[50] UCC § 2-709(3).

[51] Section 2-710 states: "Incidental damages to an aggrieved seller include any commercially reasonable charges, expenses or commissions incurred in stopping delivery, in the transportation, care, and custody of goods after the buyer's breach, in connection with return or resale of the goods or otherwise resulting from the breach."

[52] Cohn v. Fisher, 118 NJ Super. 286, 287 A2d 222 (1972).

[53] Quattlebaum v. Schutt, 5 UCC Rep. 370 (1968).

[54] Intermeat, Inc. v. American Poultry, Inc., 575 F2d 1017 (2d Cir. 1978); Neri v. Retail Marine Corp., 30 NY2d 393, 285 NE2d 311, 334 NYS2d 165 (1972).

[55] Cesco Mfg. Corp. v. Norcross, Inc., 7 Mass. App. 837, 391 NE2d 270 (1979).

[56] GNP Commodities, Inc. v. Walsh Heffernan Co., 95 Ill. App. 3d 966, 51 Ill. Dec. 245, 420 NE2d 659 (1981); Servbest Foods, Inc. v. Emessee Indus., Inc., 82 Ill. App. 3d 662, 37 Ill. Dec. 945, 403 NE2d 1 (1980).

[57] Nobs Chem., USA, Inc. v. Koppers Co., 616 F2d 212 (5th Cir. 1980).

[58] See infra ¶ 8.02[3][d] for a discussion of Section 2-715, which allows buyers to recover consequential damages. This difference in treatment has been the subject of some criticism. See, e.g., 4 Anderson § 2-710, at 414, 415.

[3] Buyer's Remedies

A buyer's principal remedies upon a seller's breach or repudiation are contained in Sections 2-711 through 2-717. Section 2-711 catalogs the available remedies under the succeeding sections.[59] In general, a buyer has two categories of remedies: He may either seek damages, which are generally determined from the difference between the contract price and the market or "cover" price plus consequentials,[60] or he may seek a form of specific relief by replevying goods identified to the contract.[61]

[a] Section 2-712: Contract-Cover Recovery

Section 2-712 establishes the basic contract-cover recovery. A buyer may substitute another contract for the one broken and treat it as a cover contract if it is made in good faith and within a reasonable time after the breach.[62] The buyer may then claim the

---

[59] Section 2-711 states:

"(1) Where the seller fails to make delivery or repudiates or the buyer rightfully rejects or justifiably revokes acceptance then with respect to any goods involved, and with respect to the whole if the breach goes to the whole contract . . . the buyer may cancel and whether or not he has done so may in addition to recovering so much of the price as has been paid

"(a) 'cover' and have damages under the next section as to all the goods affected whether or not they have been identified to the contract; or

"(b) recover damages for nondelivery as provided in this Article (Section 2-713).

"(2) Where the seller fails to deliver or repudiates the buyer may also

"(a) if the goods have been identified recover them as provided in this Article (Section 2-502); or

"(b) in a proper case obtain specific performance or replevy the goods as provided in this Article (Section 2-716).

"(3) On rightful rejection or justifiable revocation of acceptance a buyer has a security interest in goods in his possession or control for any payments made on their price and any expenses reasonably incurred in their inspection, receipt, transportation, care, and custody and may hold such goods and resell them in like manner as an aggrieved seller (Section 2-706)."

[60] UCC §§ 2-712, 2-713, 2-715.

[61] UCC § 2-716.

difference between the cost to him of the original agreement and the cover contract plus incidental and consequential damages, but less expenses saved in consequence of the breach. Although a cover contract is consistent with the goal of minimizing damages, the buyer is under no duty to cover, and failure to do so does not bar him from any other remedy.[63] Normally, a buyer seeks a cover contract in his own self-interest, but if the principal agreement is for special goods a cover may not be possible.

A cover contract need not be identical to the principal agreement. The Official Commentary to Section 2-712 expressly recognizes that the substituted contract may differ from the original contract in any number of significant points. The key is that the buyer must act reasonably to obtain goods that will satisfy his needs. The Official Commentary to Section 2-712 provides the following:

> The definition of "cover" . . . envisages a series of contracts or sales, as well as a single contract or sale; goods not identical with those involved but commercially usable as reasonable substitutes under the circumstances of the particular case; and contracts on credit or delivery terms differing from the contract in breach, but again reasonable under the circumstances. The test of proper cover is whether at the time and place the buyer acted in good faith and in a reasonable manner, and it is immaterial that hindsight may later prove that the method of cover used was not the cheapest or most effective.[64]

---

[62] Section 2-712 states:

"(1) After a breach within the preceding section the buyer may 'cover' by making in good faith and without unreasonable delay any reasonable purchase of or contract to purchase goods in substitution for those due from the seller.

"(2) The buyer may recover from the seller as damages the difference between the cost of cover and the contract price together with any incidental or consequential damages as hereinafter defined (Section 2-715), but less expenses saved in consequence of the seller's breach.

"(3) Failure of the buyer to effect cover within this section does not bar him from any other remedy."

[63] UCC § 2-712(3). The mitigation principle comes into play in the buyer's claim for consequential damages because they are limited to what could not have been avoided by a covering contract. See UCC § 2-712, Official Comment 3.

[64] UCC § 2-712, Official Comment 2.

A covering contract becomes the buyer's yardstick for measuring damages. He can only recover the difference between the original contract price and the cover contract price, regardless of the market. The cover contract is not evidence of market value for the calculation of damages; it is determinative.[65] This means that the breaching seller may gain the advantage of the buyer's good fortune in covering below the contract price. In such a circumstance, there are no damages other than incidentals and any consequentials that the buyer might be able to prove.

[b] Section 2-713: Contract-Market Differential Recovery

If a buyer does not cover, he can claim the contract-market differential under Section 2-713. The market price should be determined when the buyer learns of the seller's breach or repudiation, and the market location is the place for tender. If the buyer rightfully rejects the goods after they have arrived, the market location is the place of arrival.

Section 2-713 essentially restates the long-standing contract-market formula and marks no significant change from the common law, except in the time for measuring damages.[66] The Official Commentary notes that the market price to be used in the formula is the "price for goods of the same kind and in the same branch of trade."[67] If this is difficult to prove, the buyer may introduce

---

[65] See, e.g., Cooper v. Kruse-Reed, Inc., 554 SW2d 45 (Tex. Civ. App. 1977); Kiser v. Lemco Indus., Inc., 536 SW2d 585 (Tex. Civ. App. 1976); RN Kelly Cotton Merchant, Inc. v. Cox, 295 Ala. 94, 323 So. 2d 426 (1976).

[66] Some states applied a time of performance test rather than a time of breach test. See, e.g., Henderson v. Otto Goedecke, Inc., 430 SW2d 120 (Tex. Civ. App. 1968).

[67] UCC § 2-713, Official Comment 2. Section 2-713 states:

"(1) Subject to the provisions of this Article with respect to proof of market price (Section 2-723), the measure of damages for nondelivery or repudiation by the seller is the difference between the market price at the time when the buyer learned of the breach and the contract price together with any incidental and consequential damages provided in this Article (Section 2-715), but less expenses saved in consequence of the seller's breach.

"(2) Market price is to be determined as of the place for tender or, in cases of rejection after arrival or revocation of acceptance, as of the place of arrival."

evidence of comparable market prices or spot sales.[68] If it is impossible to prove a market price, the Official Commentary suggests that this may be evidence of shortages that would make specific performance under Section 2-716 an appropriate remedy.[69] The buyer has the burden of proof on the various elements of damage.[70]

The purpose of Section 2-713 is not simply to restate the common law, but also to provide symmetry with Section 2-712[71] and with the seller's remedies under Section 2-708.[72] The cover price and the market price may not always be the same, but if a buyer recovers the contract-cover or contract-market differential, his economic position should be the same whether he can help himself by covering or must instead depend on the market. Section 2-713 also provides a check against a buyer who fails to act promptly. For Section 2-712 to apply, the buyer must obtain cover without unreasonable delay. This ties the damage remedy to the time of the breach. The same holds true under Section 2-713, because the time for measuring the contract-market differential is the time when the buyer learned of the breach and thus could have begun to help himself. Neither section allows the buyer to recover more by delaying in a rising market. (On the other hand, if the market falls and the buyer was unable to cover, he recovers at the price that was current when the breach occurred, not at the later lower market price.) Furthermore, the allowance of consequential damages under Section 2-715[73] gives the buyer the opportunity to claim for lost profits, although the buyer's claim for relief is not as explicitly stated in terms of profits as it is for the seller in Section 2-708(2).[74]

---

[68] Section 2-724 expressly provides that reports of market quotations in newspapers or other publications are admissible evidence of the market price of commodities traded in an established market. For discussion of proof of a substitute market for an uncommon product (in this instance a pace car used at a racetrack), see Chappell Chevrolet, Inc. v. Strickland, 4 Ark. App. 108, 628 SW2d 25 (1982).

[69] UCC § 2-713, Official Comment 3.

[70] See, e.g., Willametz v. Goldfield, 171 Conn. 622, 370 A2d 1089 (1976); Fort Hill Lumber Co. v. Georgia-Pacific Corp., 261 Ore. 431, 493 P2d 1366 (1972).

[71] See supra ¶ 8.02[3][a].

[72] See supra ¶ 8.02[2][d].

[73] See infra ¶ 8.02[3][d].

[74] See supra ¶ 8.02[2][d].

A common difficulty under Section 2-713 is establishing the time when the buyer learned of the breach for purposes of setting the market price. Is there any free play in this determination? For example, can the buyer wait to give the seller a chance to cure a breach or to change his mind on a repudiation? If so, what is a reasonable waiting period? If Section 2-712 offers any guidance, the waiting period might be characterized as commercially reasonable under the circumstances. A buyer has the option to delay somewhat in seeking cover, which obviously reflects the practical difficulties in shifting business affairs to take care of a failed transaction. If the buyer is unable to cover, should he be able to claim the most advantageous market figure during the commercially reasonable period that was available for cover? At least one court has so construed Section 2-713.[75] The more common approach, however, is to apply Section 2-713 as it is written and to use the time of actual breach as the time for measurement.[76] If negotiations about the possible breach continue between the seller and the buyer, the usual time for measurement is the date when the negotiations break down and the threatened breach actually occurs.[77] If there is an anticipatory repudiation by the seller, the determination of the correct time for measurement can be somewhat more difficult. The tendency is to use the time when the buyer learns of the repudiation.[78]

[c] Section 2-714: Claim for Breach of Contract Obligations

If a buyer accepts goods and subsequently discovers that they do not conform to his expectations under the contract, Section 2-714 provides him with the right to sue for the difference in value between what he contracted for and what he received. In essence,

---

[75] See Carson v. Mulnix, 263 NW2d 701 (Iowa (1978).

[76] See, e.g., First Nat'l Bank of Chicago v. Jefferson Mortgage Co., 576 F2d 479 (3d Cir. 1978); Carl Wagner & Sons v. Appendagez, Inc., 485 F. Supp. 762 (SDNY 1980); Palmer v. Idaho Peterbilt, Inc., 102 Idaho 800, 641 P2d 346 (Idaho Ct. App. 1982).

[77] DR Curtis Co. v. Mathews, 103 Idaho 776, 653 P2d 1188 (Idaho Ct. App. 1982).

[78] See, e.g., Cosden Oil & Chem. Co. v. Karl O. Helm Aktiengesellschaft, 736 F2d 1064 (5th Cir. 1984). For a general discussion of anticipatory repudiation, see Chapter 3.

this is a claim for a breach of warranty, but it can include a claim for any failure of the seller to perform his obligations under the contract.[79] A buyer may also recover incidental and consequential damages under Section 2-714. The difference in value is measured at the time and place of acceptance, "unless special circumstances show proximate damages of a different amount."[80] This section carries forward the distinction of the Uniform Sales Act between warranty damages and ordinary contract damages.[81]

One of the most critical distinctions between Section 2-714 and other UCC provisions is that it refers to the *value* of goods, not just to the price of goods under the contract or in the market. The decision in *Chatlos Systems, Inc. v. National Cash Register Corp.*[82] graphically illustrates this distinction. The buyer purchased a computer system for a contract price of $46,020. The system did not perform satisfactorily, and the buyer brought suit. At trial the buyer won more than $57,000 in damages for breach of warranty (the difference in value represented and received) plus another $63,500 in consequential damages. The Court of Appeals for the Third Circuit reversed the consequential damages award and remanded the case for another calculation of the warranty damages under Section 2-714. On remand, the district court found that the direct damages were actually $200,000. On the second appeal the seller argued that the contract price had to be the maximum recovery for direct damages, but the court of appeals affirmed the $200,000 award on the theory that this represented the buyer's

---

[79] UCC § 2-714, Official Comment 2. Section 2-714 states:

"(1) Where the buyer has accepted goods and given notification . . . he may recover as damages for any non-conformity of tender the loss resulting in the ordinary course of events from the seller's breach as determined in any manner which is reasonable.

"(2) The measure of damages for breach of warranty is the difference at the time and place of acceptance between the value of the goods accepted and the value they would have had if they had been as warranted, unless special circumstances show proximate damages of a different amount.

"(3) In a proper case any incidental and consequential damages under the next section may also be recovered."

[80] UCC § 2-714(2).

[81] For a criticism of this distinction in the Uniform Sales Act, see 3 *Williston on Sales* § 615 (rev. ed. 1948).

[82] Chatlos Sys., Inc. v. National Cash Register Corp., 670 F2d 1304 (3d Cir.), cert. dismissed, 457 US 1112 (1982).

benefit of the bargain. Because the computer system did not meet the contract expectations, the seller lost the value in his deal in excess of the contract price, and this could be recovered under Section 2-714.

The outcome in *Chatlos* is extreme, but it is not inconsistent with the reasoning in other cases. For instance, the return of the purchase price was not a satisfactory measure of damages in a suit for breach of warranty in connection with the sale of a hay baler.[83] On the other hand, return of the down payment was determined to be a sufficient recovery when a buyer who had made no other payments refused to accept farm equipment that did not meet contract specifications.[84]

A more common problem under Section 2-714 arises in determining whether the cost of repair is a satisfactory measure of recovery. *Tarter v. MonArk Boat Co.* is a leading case.[85] A boat sold for $160,000 did not meet the contract requirements, and the evidence showed that its fair market value as delivered was only about $80,000. Other evidence showed that repairs totaling $37,000 had been made and that these put the boat into good condition in accordance with the contract. The court held that the proper measure of damages was the cost of repair, because this gave the buyer what he had bargained for — a boat worth about $160,000. Theoretically, the cost of repair or replacement is not the same as the difference in value between what the seller represented and what the buyer received. Courts have used the repair or replacement cost, however, in a variety of circumstances, no doubt because evidence of repair or replacement costs is fairly easy to ascertain and reasonably certain.[86] Even if such evidence is not conclusive as to the difference in value, it is useful as probative evidence.

If the buyer uses the nonconforming goods before he has them

---

[83] Agar v. Kysar, 628 P2d 1350 (Wyo. 1981). But see Bendix Home Sys., Inc. v. Jessop, 644 P2d 843 (Alaska 1982).

[84] Massey-Ferguson, Inc. v. Evans, 406 So. 2d 15 (Miss. 1981).

[85] Tarter v. MonArk Boat Co., 430 F. Supp. 1290 (ED Mo. 1977), aff'd, 574 F2d 984 (8th Cir. 1978).

[86] See, e.g., City of NY v. Pullman, Inc., 662 F2d 910 (2d Cir. 1981), cert. denied, 454 US 1164 (1982); Custom Automated Mach. v. Penda Corp., 537 F. Supp. 77 (ND Ill. 1982); District Concrete Co. v. Bernstein Concrete Corp., 418 A2d 1030 (DC Ct. App. 1980).

repaired, the seller should be credited with the depreciation in value occasioned by the buyer's use. This assumes that the buyer preserves his right to complain of the nonconformity, because acceptance and use may estop him from later complaining about the quality of the goods. There are common instances in which it may not be feasible for a buyer to have the repairs made immediately. He may not have the cash, or he may be uncertain about what course of action to pursue. If he does use the goods, the seller should not be held accountable for any diminution in value that results from the buyer's use.[87]

[d] Section 2-715: Recovery of Incidental and Consequential Damages

Section 2-715 provides a buyer with the opportunity to recover both incidental and consequential damages resulting from the breach.[88] The buyer's incidental damages include essentially the same elements as the seller's incidentals[89] and are not usually a matter of much controversy.[90] More difficult problems arise in determining consequential damages.

The definition of consequential damages in Section 2-715(2)(a) is similar to the definitions found in *Hadley v. Baxendale* and the

---

[87] See, e.g., Chrysler Corp. v. Wilson Plumbing Co., 132 Ga. App. 435, 208 SE2d 321 (1974).

[88] Section 2-715 states:

"(1) Incidental damages resulting from the seller's breach include expenses reasonably incurred in inspection, receipt, transportation and care and custody of goods rightfully rejected, any commercially reasonable charges, expenses or commissions in connection with effecting cover and any other reasonable expense incident to the delay or other breach.

"(2) Consequential damages resulting from the seller's breach include

"(a) any loss resulting from general or particular requirements and needs of which the seller at the time of contracting had reason to know and which could not reasonably be prevented by cover or otherwise; and

"(b) injury to person or property proximately resulting from any breach of warranty."

[89] See supra ¶ 8.02[2][f].

[90] Section 2-715(1) describes the kinds of damages that may be called "incidental," but Official Comment 1 makes it clear that this list is illustrative and not exhaustive.

second Restatement of Contracts.[91] Most courts agree that the UCC rejects the tacit agreement test[92] and only requires that damages be foreseeable, not that they actually be foreseen.[93] The normal rules of remoteness and conjecture apply,[94] and the buyer must also comply with the mitigation principle in order to pursue his claim for consequential damages.[95] If the buyer uses the goods, there may be a question whether that use is a legitimate attempt to mitigate or whether it amounts to an acceptance of the goods that precludes a suit for damages. This is a factual issue that must be determined case by case.[96] The buyer should be careful to make known his dissatisfaction with the goods and should preserve his right to claim damages by clearly informing the seller that if he uses the goods, it is only for the purpose of mitigation and is not an acceptance of nonconforming goods.

Section 2-715(2)(b) makes it clear that the seller is liable for personal injuries that result from his breach of warranty. This removes any privity problems that might have existed if the buyer were sued for damages by a third party who suffered injury as a result of the seller's breach of warranty. The test under Section 2-715(2)(b) is the tort standard of foreseeability—proximate cause — rather than the *Hadley* standard of foreseeability used to determine whether contract damages for consequential injury are available. On the issue of proximate cause, the Official Commentary states:

---

[91] See ¶ 3.02[1][b].

[92] See ¶ 7.03[3][c].

[93] See, e.g., Troxler Elec. Laboratories, Inc. v. Solitron Devices, Inc., 722 F2d 81 (4th Cir. 1983); Frank B. Bozzo, Inc. v. Electric Weld Div., 283 Pa. Super. 35, 423 A2d 702 (1980), aff'd, 495 Pa. 617, 435 A2d 176 (1981); Cook Assocs., Inc. v. Warnick, 664 P2d 1161 (Utah 1983), cf. J&J Farms, Inc. v. Cargill, Inc., 693 F2d 830 (8th Cir. 1982).

[94] For a discussion of the prohibition against the recovery of conjectural damages, see ¶ 7.03[4][b].

[95] See, e.g., AES Technology Sys., Inc. v. Coherent Radiation, 583 F2d 933 (7th Cir. 1978); Baden v. Curtiss Breeding Serv., 380 F. Supp. 243 (D. Mont. 1974).

[96] See, e.g., Can-Key Indus., Inc. v. Industrial Leasing Corp., 286 Ore. 173, 593 P2d 1125 (1979).

Where the injury involved follows the use of goods without discovery of the defect causing the damage, the question of "proximate" cause turns on whether it was reasonable for the buyer to use the goods without such inspection as would have revealed the defects. If it was not reasonable for him to do so, or if he did in fact discover the defect prior to his use, the injury would not proximately result from the breach of warranty.[97]

[e] Section 2-716: Remedy of Specific Performance

Specific performance is an unusual remedy; the common law has long given preference to damages, especially in cases that involve the sale and exchange of chattels.[98] Exceptional cases have involved unique items for which money is no real substitute. Section 2-716 allows a buyer to demand specific performance of the contract not only when the goods are unique, but also "in other proper circumstances."[99] Furthermore, the buyer can replevy goods identified to the contract if cover is not a reasonable alternative.[100] The Official Commentary to Section 2-716 indicates that the UCC drafters intended a departure from the common law in making equitable remedies more freely available as a means to assist the free flow of commerce. The tone of the commentary suggests that it is more efficient and in the best interests of all parties if the buyer can obtain the goods, or some of them, and go on about his business. A current partial performance may be superior to the

---

[97] UCC § 2-715, Official Comment 5.

[98] See generally ¶ 6.03[1].

[99] UCC § 2-716(1). The section provides in full:

"(1) Specific performance may be decreed where the goods are unique or in other proper circumstances.

"(2) The decree for specific performance may include such terms and conditions as to payment of the price, damages, or other relief as the court may deem just.

"(3) The buyer has a right of replevin for goods identified to the contract if after reasonable effort he is unable to effect cover for such goods or the circumstances reasonably indicate that such effort will be unavailing or if the goods have been shipped under reservation and satisfaction of the security interest in them has been made or tendered."

[100] UCC § 2-716(3).

recovery of a future money judgment. The remedies of Section 2-716 thus are consistent with the encouragement of cover in Section 2-712.[101]

What is an "other proper circumstance" within the meaning of Section 2-716? If the goods are unique, Section 2-716 does nothing more than the common law, but if the goods are not unique, what triggers the specific performance remedy?[102] Courts have taken a rather broad view and have tended to equate the difficulty of effecting cover with "other proper circumstances." The availability of a money damage remedy is not dispositive. Similarly, the possibility of cover does not preclude specific performance if it would be difficult to obtain the cover. This approach seems to have particular credence in cases that involve long-term requirements contracts, even for products that have an established market, such as oil and gas.[103] If cover is readily available but the buyer has financial problems that make it difficult for him to take advantage of the opportunity to cover, that may also be a "proper" circumstance for specific performance.[104] Even though cover has been the benchmark for most of the cases to date, the language of Section 2-716(1) is so open-ended that a court is free to take into account any number of possible reasons for using the specific performance remedy.

In order to demand replevin, a buyer must be able to identify the goods to the contract. As a result, it is not an option when the

---

[101] See supra ¶ 8.02[3][a].

[102] There is not always agreement on what is unique. One court found a Corvette to be unique; another did not. Compare Sedmak v. Charlie's Chevrolet, Inc., 622 SW2d 694 (Mo. Ct. App. 1981) with Scholl v. Hartzell, 20 D&C2d 304 (Pa. Ct. Com. Pl. 1981).

[103] LaClede Gas Co. v. Amoco Oil Co., 522 F2d 33 (8th Cir. 1975), is a good example. The buyer won specific performance of a long-term contract for the supply of propane gas even though cover for at least his short-term needs was available. The court was concerned that the market for propane gas would not remain steady enough during the term of the broken contract for the buyer to be reasonably certain of cover. Of course, by ordering specific performance, the court also avoided the problem of calculating projected damages over the life of a long-term contract in a fluctuating market. But cf. Weathersby v. Gore, 556 F2d 1247 (5th Cir. 1977) (cotton buyer could not get specific performance because cotton was readily available on the market).

[104] See, e.g., Gerwin v. Southeastern Cal. Ass'n of Seventh Day Adventists, 14 Cal. App. 3d 209, 92 Cal. Rptr. 111 (1971).

contract goods are fungible and undifferentiated among the seller's various contracts (e.g., 10,000 barrels of oil in a storage tank) or when the goods have not been manufactured. If the goods are identified to the contract, replevin is a useful remedy because it is simple and direct. The buyer gets exactly what he wanted, and he does not have to deal with the equitable defenses that might be asserted in a suit for specific performance. Replevin is a legal remedy, and if the buyer meets the requirements of Section 2-716, he can obtain virtually immediate possession of the goods. In addition to identifying the goods to the contract, the buyer also must show that cover is not possible.[105]

When a court enters a decree for specific performance, Section 2-716 allows the court to amend the terms and conditions "as to payment of the price, damages, or other relief" as may seem "just."[106] This does not mean that the court can reform the contract without limitation; for example, it cannot change the actual price agreed upon. This provision simply allows the court to make minor adjustments in the performance and payment terms to conform to the practicalities of the situation.[107] If there has been a breach, presumably there has been a change either in the position of one of the parties, the parties' relationship to each other, or market conditions. Section 2-716(2) gives the court the flexibility to write the decree in a way that provides the buyer with performance but that also makes the performance reasonably possible under the changed circumstances. Equity courts have a great deal of discretion in fashioning decrees, and Section 2-716 simply reflects that discretion.

[f] Section 2-717: Deduction of Damages From Price Due on Contract

Section 2-717 is a short but useful self-help provision. It provides in full: "The buyer on notifying the seller of his intention to do so may deduct all or any part of the damages resulting from any

---

[105] See, e.g., Tatum v. Richter, 280 Md. 332, 373 A2d 923 (1977); Putnam Ranches, Inc. v. Corkle, 180 Neb. 533, 203 NW2d 502 (1973).

[106] UCC § 2-716(2).

[107] See, e.g., Iowa Elec. Light & Power Co. v. Atlas Corp., 467 F. Supp. 129 (ND Iowa 1978).

breach of the contract from any part of the price still due under the same contract."

When a buyer accepts goods, he becomes liable for their price.[108] Section 2-717 makes it possible for the buyer to accept goods, notify the seller of their nonconformity and his claim for damages, and withhold payment without triggering a default and subjecting himself to liability for breach because of his nonpayment. This can be a powerful tool, because it puts the burden of pursuing legal action on the seller. If the seller knows or suspects that he himself may be in breach, he may just accept the buyer's deduction. The buyer gains the significant advantage of being able to keep the money rather than paying it and then suing to get some or all of it back at an indefinite time in the future.[109]

The buyer must act in good faith by giving notice to the seller of his intention to withhold all or a portion of his payment, and he can only deduct payments on the breached contract. For example, if the buyer has three contracts with the seller and is only dissatisfied with the goods under one contract, he can only deduct payments on that contract and not on either of the other two.[110]

¶ 8.03 DAMAGES FOR BREACH OF EMPLOYMENT AGREEMENTS

[1] General Principles

Although the treatment of employment agreements does not differ significantly from the treatment of other kinds of contracts, there is an underlying concern for the sale of human capital.[111]

---

[108] UCC § 2-607(1).

[109] The seller does not have to accept the buyer's tender of less than the full amount due and owing, or he may accept and reserve rights under Section 1-207. For examples of the application of Section 2-717, see, e.g., Hughes Tool Co. v. Max Hinrichs Seed Co., 112 Cal. App. 3d 194, 169 Cal. Rptr. 160 (1980); Shreve Land Co. v. J&D Fin. Corp., 421 So. 2d 722 (Fla. Dist. Ct. App. 1982).

[110] See, e.g., CR Bard, Inc. v. Medical Elecs. Corp., 529 F. Supp. 1382 (D. Mass. 1982).

[111] For a discussion of the concept of human capital, see Becker, *Human Capital* (1975); Fleisher & Kniesner, *Labor Economics* (1980); Thurow, *Dangerous Currents* (1983).

Courts look upon the enforcement of a personal service agreement as akin to involuntary servitude, and therefore disfavor using the specific performance remedy in actions to enforce employment agreements. This attitude carries over to actions for damages, because liability for significant damages may be as coercive as an equitable remedy. With that caveat, however, the enforcement of personal service agreements involves considerations similar to those involved in the enforcement of other contracts.

Employees who do not work under contract are employed at will — their employers can fire them at will. Other employees are subject to a master contract such as a collective bargaining agreement that governs their employment rights. Usually they cannot be dismissed at will, but only for cause. Some employees have individual contracts for a specified term. Those who are subject to contracts, whether individual or master agreements, usually have a right to claim damages for a wrongful termination, unlike employees hired at will.

The standard measure of damages for a discharged employee with an employment contract is the present discounted value of his anticipated salary over the life of the contract reduced by the salary received from subsequent employment.[112] If the salary is not fixed for the full term of the agreement or is based on a commission schedule, the court entertains evidence of the discharged employee's past raises, sales experience, prior commissions, or evidence from other similarly situated employees. The object is to consider evidence that makes it possible to project with some degree of certainty the employee's likely income over the remaining term of the contract. Obviously, this task is more difficult early in the term.[113] The mitigation principle does not require that the employee take noncomparable work or that he move to another location, but if the claimant fails to take an opportunity for similar work, the court acts as if he had taken the job and reduces his claim accordingly. This gives full weight to the mitigation principle and prevents the accumulation of unnecessary damages. Recovery of

---

[112] See 5 Corbin § 1095.

[113] The problem is analogous to that of proving lost profits for a newly established business. See ¶ 7.03[4][g].

the discharged employee's unearned salary also gives him the full expectancy of his employment contract.[114]

Sometimes a court goes a little farther and awards an element of reliance damages in addition to the lost expectancy. The most common claim of this sort includes the additional costs incurred in seeking substitute employment.[115]

If the employee breaches the agreement, the employer can recover the difference between the cost of hiring a replacement and the contract salary of the breaching employee for the term of the agreement. Aside from relatively small transaction costs, this means that the employer has no damage recovery unless he has to pay the replacement a higher salary. The employer has no basis for recovery unless he does replace the departed employee.[116]

[2] Covenants Not to Compete

One of the most common terms in an employment agreement is a covenant not to compete.[117] The employee agrees that after he

---

[114] Because courts usually award damages in a lump sum, the income stream must be reduced to a lump-sum present value. Nonetheless, there really is no fundamental impediment to an award requiring the defendant to pay the plaintiff a salary, according to the terms of the agreement, over the life of the contract. Courts probably eschew such remedies to avoid subsequent enforcement problems and to ensure some finality to the case.

[115] See, e.g., Wyatt v. School Dist. No. 104, Fergus County, 148 Mont. 83, 417 P2d 221 (1966). The plaintiff, a wrongfully discharged schoolteacher, recovered the value of her salary for the school year, reduced by the salary from her subsequent substituted job, plus the value of free living quarters that were part of her contracted consideration, plus the cost of traveling to seek a new job and moving to that job. (Her claim for moving expenses to take the teaching job was denied because those costs were a necessary part of her preparation to perform.) The value of the living quarters was part of her normal expectancy. The court treated the cost of seeking a new job as an item of reasonably foreseeable consequential damage.

[116] The net effect is that an irreplaceable employee may leave with virtual impunity but the more fungible employee may have to pay some damages.

[117] Covenants not to complete have been the subject of an enormous amount of academic commentary. See, e.g., Blake, "Employee Agreements Not to Compete," 73 Harv. L. Rev. 625 (1960); Closius & Schaffer, "Involuntary Nonservi-

leaves the employer's business (for whatever reason) he will not compete with the employer in a certain area, or with respect to a certain product, service, or business, or for a certain period of time. The object of the covenant is obvious. An employee is privy to the confidential business plans and practices of his employer. If he joins a competing business, this information can be used to the former employer's detriment. An employer can reasonably expect and can require that a full-time employee devote his working energies solely to his employer's business and that he not appropriate any of the employer's property interests to his own benefit. This is consistent with the fundamental principles of agency law. Thus, if an employee solicits his employer's customers for himself or for a rival business, or provides competitive information to a rival business during his employment, he can be held liable in damages and dismissed for cause.[118] The covenant not to compete simply tries to extend the employee's duty beyond the termination date of the employment contract.[119]

Courts are reluctant to enforce covenants not to compete in personal service contracts. One of the basic reasons is pragmatic. An individual's ability to make a living depends on his ability to sell his own services to others. If a contract prevents him from doing so

---

tude: The Current Judicial Enforcement of Employee Covenants Not to Compete — A Proposal for Reform," 57 S. Cal. L. Rev. 531 (1984) (hereinafter cited as Closius & Schaffer); Handler & Lazaroff, "Restraint of Trade and the Restatement (Second) of Contracts," 57 NYU L. Rev. 669 (1982); Hutter, "Drafting Enforceable Employee Non-Competition Agreements to Protect Confidential Business Information: A Lawyer's Practical Approach to the Case Law," 45 Alb. L. Rev. 311 (1981).

[118] See, e.g., Restatement (Second) of Agency § 393 (1957); Arnold's Ice Cream Co. v. Carlson, 330 F. Supp. 1185 (EDNY 1971); Foley v. D'Agostino, 21 AD2d 60, 248 NYS2d 121 (1964); Lowndes Prod., Inc. v. Brower, 259 SC 322, 191 SE2d 761 (1972).

[119] Nonenforcement of a covenant not to compete may create a disincentive on the part of the employer to share confidential business information with the employee. See Sullivan, "Revisiting the 'Neglected Stepchild': Antitrust Treatment of Postemployment Restraints of Trade," 1977 U. Ill. LF 621, 636 (hereinafter cited as Sullivan). The Georgia Supreme court found a way to deal with this problem in Nolan v. Meyners-Robinson Co., 246 Ga. 49, 246 SE2d 656 (1980), by deciding to enforce a nondisclosure clause even though the companion covenant not to compete was unenforceable.

or severely limits his options, it may border on unconscionability.[120] Furthermore, a limitation on an individual's freedom to sell his services is a restraint on free trade of those services, and courts have treated such restraints as anticompetitive and inefficient.[121] Finally, some courts seem to treat covenants not to compete as if they were contracts of adhesion imposed on the employee by the employer.[122] This correlates with the unconscionability argument. There may be an element of adhesion in many contracts, but in many others the restrictive covenant is a negotiated clause. The prevailing rule is that covenants not to compete are subject to strict scrutiny and are construed against the former employer.[123] Some states even limit the enforceability of such covenants with specific legislation.[124]

Restrictive covenants usually cover the identity of competitive activity, the geographic area of restricted employment, and the length of time competition is restricted. There are literally thousands of cases interpreting the provisions of various covenants not to compete.[125] The common theme among them is that no restriction will be enforced unless it is reasonable.[126] Because reasonabil-

---

[120] For a general discussion of the topic of unconscionability, see Chapter 12.

[121] The opposing argument of those who favor freedom of contract is that a person should be allowed freely to trade limitations on his ability to sell his services in return for a negotiated consideration as long as the transaction is neither fraudulent nor illegal.

[122] See, e.g., Restatement (Second) of Contracts § 188 comment g (1982).

[123] See, e.g., Alexander & Alexander, Inc. v. Wohlman, 19 Wash. App. 670, 578 P2d 530 (1978); National Homes Corp. v. Lester Indus., Inc., 293 F. Supp. 1025 (WD Va.), modified, 404 F2d 225 (4th Cir. 1968); Williston, 14 *A Treatise on the Law of Contracts* § 1636 (3d ed. 1967, supp. 1983).

[124] NC Gen. Stat. § 75-2 (1981) (covenants invalid under general state antitrust law); La. Rev. Stat. Ann. § 23.921 (West 1964); Wis. Stat. Ann. § 103.46.5 (1979–1980) ("unreasonable" covenants invalid); Ala. Code § 8-1-1 (1984); Cal. Bus. & Prof. Code §§ 16600–16602 (West 1964); Fla. Stat. § 542.33 (1983); Mont. Code Ann. §§ 28-2-703–28-2-705 (1984); ND Cent. Code 9-08-06 (1975); Okla. Stat. tit. 15, §§ 217–219 (1981); Ore. Rev. Stat. § 653.295 (1983); SD Codified Laws Ann. §§ 53-9-8–53-9-11 (1980) (foregoing declare covenants invalid with some exceptions; e.g., in connection with the sale of a business).

[125] For a collection of many of the cases, see Annot., 61 ALR3d 397 (1975).

[126] One Note states:

"Under the common law of contracts, covenants not to compete are enforce-

ity is not self-defining and varies with the circumstances of each case, the determination of enforceability is largely ad hoc. Nevertheless, courts' hostility to restrictive covenants is so great that it is unlikely that any covenant will survive if it extends for more than a short time (probably a few months, possibly a year), covers a large geographic area (one that would force the former employee to move), or defines the restricted activities too broadly (preventing the manager of a fast-food restaurant from running a competing fast-food restaurant may be acceptable, but preventing him from engaging in the restaurant business is not). The number of cases suggests that employers continue to insert unenforceable restrictive covenants in employment agreements. The purpose is unclear, although a clause may have an in terrorem effect, and the employee may not want to take the chance that a court would find it to be reasonable.

It has been suggested that covenants not to compete simply be done away with as useless because employers can protect their interests adequately through the rules of agency law and master-servant relationships.[127] The employer's know-how and trade information is part of his property. If an employee appropriates this information or know-how, he violates his fiduciary duty as an agent and also engages in what amounts to a taking of the employer's property. The unhappy employer can rely on the law of agency, property, and torts to accomplish what seems difficult to

---

> able if, and to the extent that, they are reasonable. To be deemed reasonable, a covenant must meet three criteria. First, the covenant must be necessary for the protection of the promisee. Courts recognize that a promisee has a legitimate interest in protecting business goodwill and trade secrets, but courts will invalidate or reform a covenant that is broader than is necessary to protect those interests. Second, the covenant must not be oppressive to the promisor. Courts are particularly hesitant to validate employee covenants because of the harsh effects on employees who have nothing but their labor to sell. Finally, the covenant must not be injurious to the public. Although courts recognize a public policy favoring freedom of contract, they are reluctant to enforce covenants that prevent competition and deprive the community of needed goods or services."

Note, "Economic and Critical Analyses of the Law of Covenants Not to Compete," 72 Geo. LJ 1425, 1427, 1428 (1984) (citations omitted).

[127] See generally Closius & Schaffer.

accomplish through contract law. Although this point is well-taken, courts might be as reluctant to impose liability on a former employee under agency, property, or tort principles as they are under explicit contract provisions if the imposition of liability would hurt the individual's chances to make a living or would have an anticompetitive effect. Whether the enforcement of covenants not to compete would be anticompetitive is a question that is beyond the scope of this work.[128]

Some courts have applied the "blue-pencil" theory to covenants not to compete and have simply rewritten them to make them enforceable or have stricken some portions and enforced others.[129] The prevailing and more modern view, however, is that if a covenant fails for one reason, the whole covenant fails.[130] The first Restatement accepted the blue-pencil theory, but fifty years later the drafters of the second Restatement rejected it as "contrary to the weight of authority."[131] The blue-pencil theory is now more frequently used in connection with restrictions ancillary to the sale of a business.[132]

¶ 8.04 DAMAGES FOR BREACH OF DISTRIBUTOR AGREEMENTS

[1] Basic Interests of Distributor and Manufacturer

Manufacturers that are not vertically integrated often depend upon a system of distributors to bring their products to market. The manufacturer wants to sell as many products as it can produce at a

---

[128] See Sullivan 621.

[129] See, e.g., Timenterial, Inc. v. Dagata, 29 Conn. Supp. 180, 277 A2d 512 (1971); Solari Indus., Inc. v. Malady, 55 NJ 571, 264 A2d 53 (1970); Sidco Paper Co. v. Aaron, 465 Pa. 586, 351 A2d 250 (1976).

[130] See, e.g., Rector-Phillips-Morse, Inc. v. Vroman, 253 Ark. 750, 489 SW2d 1 (1973); Purcell v. Joyner, 231 Ga. 85, 200 SE2d 363 (1973).

[131] See Restatement of Contracts § 518 (1932); Restatement (Second) of Contracts § 184, Reporter's note (1981).

[132] Compare, e.g., Jenkins v. Jenkins Irrigation, Inc., 244 Ga. 95, 259 SE2d 47 (1979), with Redmond v. Royal Ford, Inc., 244 Ga. 711, 261 SE2d 585 (1979), and see Note, "Validity of Covenants Not to Compete: Common Law Rules and Illinois Law," 1978 U. Ill. LF 249.

price that will net a reasonable profit. The manufacturer also wants to maintain its distinct image and to establish a recognizable product identity. Sometimes the manufacturer's focus is on volume production and maximum sales at small unit profit margins; sometimes the emphasis is on more limited production with a higher markup. The manufacturer often pursues a policy between these options. Whatever the manufacturer's policy, he is naturally interested in seeing that his distributors follow suit. For example, a mass-volume discounter does not want his distributor to adopt a marketing strategy of high markups, low volume, and appeal to an upscale market segment. The opposite is just as true. To put it simply, the approach to selling Volkswagens is different from the approach to selling Jaguars.

The distributor has the same basic interest as the manufacturer — profitability — and wants to be able to pursue a course of business that ensures success. As long as the distributor's interest is consistent with the manufacturer's interest no problems arise, but when the distributor's local approach changes to suit his own profit goals, thus affecting the manufacturer's overall marketing strategy, problems almost invariably develop. In order to meet the needs of both parties, the typical distributor agreement contains restrictions that apply to each party. Because of the laws that prohibit contracts in restraint of trade and some of the fairness principles of the common law, these restrictions have not always been sustained by the courts. The cases do, however, provide some guidelines, and it is possible to predict with some degree of certainty what kinds of restrictions are acceptable and what kinds will not be enforced. The determination of enforceability involves greater stakes in this area than in others because an invalid restraint in a distribution agreement may violate the federal antitrust laws and subject the manufacturer (and sometimes the distributor) to severe civil and criminal penalties.[133]

Because they are so pervasive and such an important part of the American economy, automobile dealerships provide a wealth of examples for the study of distributor agreements. Consider the following situation.

---

[133] The penalty provisions are contained in the Clayton Act, § 4, 15 USC § 15 (1973).

EXAMPLE 1. White wants to become a Ford dealer in Atlanta, and Ford believes that the market is ripe for another dealership. In addition to the usual concerns of any two contracting parties (e.g., financial strength, good faith, and ability to perform), White and Ford both have specific, identifiable concerns. For example, if White invests a substantial amount of capital in setting up the dealership (e.g., acquiring land, constructing a showroom and service area, hiring mechanics, salespeople, and managerial personnel, advertising, and financing the inventory), he does not want Green to set up a Ford dealership across the street, especially if Green runs a stripped-down operation that only does new car sales and has no other services. Green would be a classic "free rider." He would rely on White's efforts to attract buyers to the area and then seek to lure them across the street. In short, White wants a fair chance to recoup his investment without giving someone else the benefit of his advertising and location. White also wants to be sure that he can get an adequate supply of cars and that he does not have to buy more cars from Ford than he can sell. He wants to be able to price the cars to make a sale at a profit, which means that he might want to sell some cars for which there is a high demand at a large markup and sell others as loss leaders. If Ford's stock or reputation falls, White wants to be free to sell other makes of automobile, foreign as well as domestic. Finally, White would prefer that other Ford dealers not be allowed to undercut his prices, especially on popular models.

Ford wants to sell as many cars as possible in Atlanta, and it wants its dealers to be financially sound and to uphold the company's quality identity. It is costly to Ford when a dealer goes bankrupt and reflects badly on the whole Ford enterprise. Similarly, Ford wants to ensure that its customers have services and parts available for their cars. Ford also has to be sure that its dealer's profit interests and marketing programs are consistent with its own interests. For example, a dealer may be happy selling 100 cars a month at a profit of $500 per car, but Ford might prefer that he sell 200 cars a month at a unit profit of $250 per car. Ford therefore may want to put a maximum resale price on its automobiles or to require the dealer to undertake more local advertising or increase his hours of operation. In addition, Ford may impose quotas and penalties for not meeting the quotas. To protect the solvency of its dealers and to project an image of quality or respectability, Ford may want to avoid deep discounting and loss leaders by setting a minimum resale price or by establishing a unit profit goal and penalizing dealers who fail to meet it. Because Ford does not want its efforts (e.g., advertising, point-of-sale signs, banners, and financial support for the dealer) to inure to the benefit of its competitors, it may want to prohibit the dealer from selling any other makes of automobile. Ford also wants to retain some flexibility in appointing its dealers and therefore may not want to be limited in its choice of dealership locations.

One way for Ford to accomplish its goals is to integrate operations from manufacture to retail sale. This has become a common practice in recent years, especially in the oil industry. The costs of vertical integration, however, are enormous, and it probably does not make sense for a large national manufacturer with an established pattern of sales through distributors suddenly to adopt a vertically integrated marketing scheme. The same is true of a newer industry; the costs may not be worth the results.[134] Thus, the question becomes the extent to which Ford can use the rules of contract to approximate a system of complete vertical integration.

White, the Ford dealer, has at his disposal all the usual contract defenses to Ford's attempt to enforce provisions he considers to be onerous. He could make the arguments applicable to contracts of adhesion, and he could raise the unconscionability defense. The extent to which either of these would be of assistance is problematic. As a businessman, White's invocation of the unconscionability defense probably will not receive as sympathetic a hearing as one that might be given to an ordinary consumer.[135] The adhesion argument might be

---

[134] Indeed, the profits and efficiencies of dealer or franchisee operations may be much greater than the profits of a vertically integrated operation run by a hired manager. At least that was the conclusion of one study of restaurants in a chain. See Shelton, "Allocative Efficiency vs. 'X-Efficiency': Comment," 57 Am. Econ. Rev. 1252 (1967).

[135] See Chapter 12.

more productive, depending on the extent to which the terms of any deal between Ford and White are negotiated and not simply imposed as a take-it-or-leave-it proposition.[136] The real test of enforceability comes under the applicable trade regulation laws and cases. Although much of the case law derives from an application of the federal antitrust laws, there are several state trade regulation statutes, including a significant number that impose specific limitations on the terms of distributor agreements.[137]

[2] Resale Price Maintenance

In 1911, the United States Supreme Court ruled that a manufacturer could not set the prices at which a distributor resold its products. The Court held in *Dr. Miles Medical Co. v. John D. Park & Sons Co.*[138] that a resale price maintenance provision was illegal per se under the Sherman Antitrust Act. Although the manufacturer in *Dr. Miles* had established an agency/consignment arrangement so that the distributor never had formal title to the products, the Court found that this was a sham and that title actually passed to the distributor. Once title passed, the seller/manufacturer could no longer control the price of resale. The Supreme Court has con-

---

[136] Two noted contract authorities have used automobile dealer agreements as examples of the use of status concepts as opposed to freedom-of-contract concepts. See Kessler & Gilmore, *Contracts* ch. 18 (2d ed. 1970) (hereinafter cited as Kessler & Gilmore).

[137] Many of these statutes are written to apply to franchising, but they also have an effect on ordinary distributor contracts. The lawyer should be especially careful about some statutes' treatment of franchise-type contracts as securities. State laws that affect distributor contracts include: Ark. Stat. Ann. § 70-809 (1979); Cal. Corp. Code §§ 31000–31104 (West 1977); Conn. Gen. Stat. § 42-133e (1981); Ill. Rev. Stat. ch. 121½ § 703 (1983); Md. Ann. Code art. 56, § 345 (1957); Ore. Rev. Stat. § 650.005 (1983); RI Gen. Laws § 19-28-3 (1982); Va. Code § 13.1-559 (1978); Wis. Stat. §§ 553.01–553.78 (1979, 1980); Wash. Rev. Code § 19.100.010 (1983); Hawaii Rev. Stat. § 482E (1976); Minn. Stat § 80C.01 (1982); Mo. Rev. Stat. § 407.400 (1978); NJ Rev. Stat. Ann. § 56:10.3 (West Supp. 1985); SD Codified Laws Ann. § 37-5A-6 (1977); NY Gen. Bus. Law § 681 (McKinney 1984); Mich. Comp. Laws § 445.1502 (1979).

[138] Dr. Miles Medical Co. v. John D. Park & Sons Co., 220 US 373 (1911).

sidered a number of price maintenance cases since *Dr. Miles,*[139] but the principle remains the same: Once title passes, the seller cannot control the price. The manufacturer can suggest resale prices but cannot impose them on the distributor. It does not matter whether the manufacturer sets a minimum or a maximum price,[140] even though the latter may sometimes provide the consumer with protection from price-gouging.[141]

[3] Other Vertical Restrictions

The Supreme Court has vacillated on other types of vertical restrictions on distributors, such as area or market limitations. The leading case for a number of years was *United States v. Arnold, Schwinn & Co.,*[142] in which the Court seemed to treat a wide range of vertical restraints on distributor activities as illegal per se under the antitrust laws. The Court changed its tack in *Continental TV,*

---

[139] United States v. Colgate & Co., 250 US 300 (1919) (in apparent contradiction to *Dr. Miles,* the Court sustained the unilateral termination of a dealer who failed to adhere to the manufacturer's suggested resale price); United States v. General Elec. Co., 272 US 476 (1926) (Court said that a vertical price restriction would be legal if title to the goods never left the manufacturer, but the distributor was simply an agent-consignee); United States v. Parke, Davis & Co., 362 US 29 (1960) (Court limited the influence of the *Colgate* decision by ruling that the manufacturer could do nothing more than announce a suggested resale price and refuse to deal with noncompliers); Simpson v. Union Oil Co., 377 US 13 (1964) (Court ruled that Union Oil could not terminate a service station dealer who failed to adhere to Union's resale price requirements, even though Union had set up an agency/consignment scheme in apparent accord with the *General Electric* case). For a discussion of the standard of proof necessary to show an illegal price-fixing restraint, see Monsanto Co. v. Spray-Rite Serv. Corp., 104 S. Ct. 1464 (1984).

[140] See, e.g., Albrecht v. Herald Co. 390 US 145 (1968); Kiefer-Stewart Co. v. Joseph E. Seagram & Sons, Inc., 340 US 211 (1951).

[141] Debate continues on this point and on the effects of vertical restraints in general. See, e.g., Blair & Kaserman, "The *Albrecht* Rule and Consumer Welfare: an Economic Analysis," 33 Fla. L. Rev. 461 (1981); Easterbrook, " Maximum Price Fixing," 48 U. Chi. L. Rev. 886 (1981); and see generally Posner, "The Chicago School of Antitrust Analysis," 127 U. Pa. L. Rev. 925 (1979); Nelson, "Comments on a Paper by Posner," 127 U. Pa. L. Rev. 949 (1979).

[142] United States v. Arnold, Schwinn & Co., 388 US 365 (1967).

Inc. v. GTE Sylvania, Inc.[143] and applied a "rule of reason"[144] to vertical restraints that do not involve prices. Thus, each case must be analyzed on the basis of its particular facts. Consider again the protagonists from the previous example.[145] A location clause that limits White to one place for his dealership but that also prohibits Ford from awarding another dealership near White is likely to be upheld unless it is too broad. For instance, if White were prohibited from having any other Ford dealerships anywhere else in the country or from dealing in any other makes of cars anywhere else, these restrictions probably would be invalid. Ford has a legitimate interest in seeing that White devote his energy and time to the Ford dealership originally awarded him, but prohibiting him from business expansion is not the only way to accomplish this goal. A "best efforts" clause and reasonable quotas or goals may bring about the same end. If White is successful with the first dealership, the principles of open competition require that he be allowed to try his hand at other enterprises, subject to his contractual duty of good faith to Ford.

A similar analysis applies in considering other restrictions. Ford may prohibit White from selling new Chevrolets at the same

---

[143] Continental TV, Inc. v. GTE Sylvania, Inc., 433 US 36 (1977).

[144] In antitrust law, some activities, such as price fixing, are illegal per se. Customer allocations by competitors on the same level (horizontal competitors) is also illegal. However, other illegal activities or agreements are not illegal on their face and are subject to a rule of reason analysis; that is, the court examines the facts of the particular case and the effect of the restraint in question to determine whether it is, in fact, anticompetitive, procompetitive, or neutral. Justice Brandeis described and justified the rule of reason in Chicago Bd. of Trade v. United States, 246 US 231, 238 (1918):

> "The true test of legality is whether the restraint imposed is such as merely regulates and perhaps thereby promotes competition. To determine that question the court must ordinarily consider the facts peculiar to the business to which the restraint is applied; its condition before and after the restraint was imposed; the nature of the restraint and its effect, actual or probable. The history of the restraint, the evil believed to exist, the reason for adopting the particular remedy, the purpose or end sought to be attained, are all relevant facts."

This approach is so hallowed in antitrust law that the Rule of Reason often appears thus, with initial capital letters. See, e.g., Butler, "Restricted Distribution Contracts and the Opportunistic Pursuit of Treble Damages," 59 Wash. L. Rev. 27 (1983).

[145] See supra ¶ 8.04[1].

location, may require White to do a certain amount of advertising, or may demand that White provide a specific number of service bays and mechanics in the shop. Ford also may limit White's ability to strip a car or to load it with dealer options. This is a thin line, because Ford cannot control all the dealer's practices for products he buys and sells, although it can act reasonably to protect its own reputation and the integrity of the automobiles it manufactures. Ford may not be concerned with the dealer's installations of radios or air conditioners, but it may have a legitimate quality control concern with the dealer's manipulations of the computers in many of the new cars. Finally, as a creditor of the dealer, Ford may impose reasonable financial restrictions on the dealer in order to protect its own security.

The grant of an exclusive territory or an exclusive right to distribute a particular product may cause a problem at two levels. First, if the area of exclusivity is too great, a third party may claim that it presents an unreasonable barrier to entry and amounts to an attempt to monopolize a market.[146] Second, if there are several distributors who communicate among themselves as well as with the manufacturer, a third party may claim illegal territorial or customer allocation. Horizontal competitors may not divide territories or customers among themselves. That is a per se violation of the federal antitrust laws.[147] The intent to allocate territories or customers may be inferred from patterns of conduct, which may include communications from distributors to the manufacturer who acts as a de facto conduit for horizontal communication.[148]

[4] Contract Drafting Guidelines

The contract drafter can write a document that suits the parties and that may be consistent with all the common-law require-

---

[146] On barriers to entry, see, e.g., Bain, *Barriers to New Competition,* (1956); Kessler & Stern, "Competition, Contract and Vertical Integration," 69 Yale LJ 1 (1959); Lockhardt & Sacks, "The Relevance of Economic Factors in Determining Whether Exclusive Arrangements Violate Section 3 of the Clayton Act," 65 Harv. L. Rev. 913 (1952).

[147] See, e.g., United States v. Topco Assocs., Inc, 405 US 596 (1972).

[148] See, e.g., Eiberger v. Sony Corp. of Am., 459 F. Supp. 1276 (SDNY 1978), aff'd, 622 F2d 1068 (2d Cir. 1980).

ments and still find that it runs afoul of a trade regulation law. The drafter should carefully draft distributor agreements, therefore, because what may appear to be an innocuous clause that is agreeable to both parties may turn out to be the basis for a treble damage action under the antitrust laws. The following guidelines are helpful:

(1) Do not include any provisions that set minimum or maximum resale prices. Suggested prices are acceptable, but the manufacturer cannot set the resale price of a product after title passes to the distributor.
(2) Limit exclusive territories and exclusive rights to products to what the distributor can reasonably handle and to what will give him a fair competitive opportunity. The distributor will want as much exclusivity as he can get, and a manufacturer entering a new market may be tempted to grant an aggressive salesman nationwide or worldwide rights.[149] Both parties should avoid these temptations and define areas of responsibility consistent with their respective capacities that leave them each the flexibility to respond to changes in the market.
(3) Provide distributors with the freedom to make incidental sales outside their defined areas. A distributor may need to be able to service a customer who has a small demand outside the exclusive zone, or he may have an opportunity to make an occasional sale elsewhere. As long as these rights are reciprocal (shared by all distributors), they tend to support the reasonability of the whole scheme and to comport with common sense.
(4) Use a best efforts clause with at least some defined goals. This is a means to keep the distributor's attention and energy devoted to the project. On the other hand, it is also a tool the distributor can use in demanding appropriate support and a dependable supply.

[149] One way to avoid the problem of horizontal per se illegality is to have a provision for an area of primary responsibility rather than strict exclusive rights. This may still be read as a horizontal exclusive right if the primary responsibility provision is a sham to hide territorial restraints among distributors. Compare Hobart Bros. v. Malcolm T. Gilliland, Inc., 471 F2d 894 (5th Cir.), cert. denied, 412 US 923 (1973), with Superior Bedding Co. v. Serta Assocs., Inc., 353 F. Supp. 1143 (ND Ill. 1972).

(5) If the manufacturer is also a distributor, the agreements with other distributors must be carefully drafted because the manufacturer acts at the same level of competition as the distributors. What may be a reasonable vertical restriction can quickly become an illegal horizontal agreement.

(6) Check the laws of the states in which the distributor is to do business for statutes applicable to distributor agreements that affect the drafting.

¶ 8.05 DAMAGES FOR BREACH OF FRANCHISE AGREEMENTS

Almost the entire preceding discussion of distributor agreements applies equally to franchise agreements.[150] There is a similar concern in franchise agreements with the influence and effect of the antitrust laws and other trade regulation statutes, and a number of state statutes also deal with franchising. In fact, some of the concerns in distribution arrangements assume a greater urgency in franchise contexts because the relationship of the parties is somewhat different. The grant of a franchise is akin to the sale of a property interest, and some courts have suggested that for the term of the franchise there is a quasifiduciary relationship between the parties, who are like partners in a joint enterprise.[151] The sale of a franchise (this is the common description of the agreement) may be the sale of a security within the meaning of the securities laws, and the careful lawyer must be sure that his client is either exempt or has complied with the applicable securities laws.[152] The method of attracting potential franchisees also may be subject to Federal Trade Commission regulation.[153]

---

[150] See supra ¶ 8.04.

[151] See, e.g., Atlantic Richfield Co. v. Razumic, 480 Pa. 366, 390 A2d 736 (1978); Sergmiller v. Western Men, Inc., 20 Utah 2d 353, 437 P2d 892 (1968); Brown, "Franchising — A Fiduciary Relationship," 49 Tex. L. Rev. 650 (1971).

[152] This can be onerous; it may entail the filing of an extensive registration statement with the SEC, and if the federal laws apply, the franchisor must be careful to follow the regulations or he may find himself in serious legal trouble. In addition, a myriad of state securities laws may apply, and many of them carry stiff penalties for noncompliance. See generally Cavitch, *Business Organizations* § 240.03 (1984).

[153] See 16 CFR 436 (1985).

Because the transfer of a franchise is, by its nature, the transfer of a property interest in the franchisor's business, defined areas of exclusivity are customary. A McDonald's franchisee is assured that there will not be a competing McDonald's across the street, although the area of exclusivity varies with the franchise's location and local population density. There is, therefore, a presumption that a franchise agreement defines areas and products, a presumption of exclusivity that may not be so great in connection with a distribution agreement.

The tendency to treat franchisors and franchisees as if they were in a quasifiduciary relationship in which the franchisor is, in some sense, responsible for the franchisee means that any attempt by the franchisor to enforce the terms of the agreement may be met with more scrutiny than an attempt to enforce the terms of another type of contract. Of course, no court will prevent Holiday Inns from demanding that a franchisee meet the cleanliness and quality control standards of the company or any other standard reasonably designed to protect the franchisor's name and reputation.

The determination of damages in a case involving the wrongful termination of a franchise can include some difficult calculations. The principle is the same as in any other contract: The nonbreaching party should receive his expectancy. In a franchise situation, however, this may require determining the present value of a franchise over a ten-, fifteen-, or twenty-year period. Future streams of income can be estimated from past profits. If the business is new, evidence of the business success of comparable franchisees or expert testimony may be necessary.[154]

Many franchise agreements contain a clause that allows the franchisor to terminate the agreement upon notice, with or without cause. The franchisor may argue that the agreement is worth no more than the projected profits from the termination period (e.g., thirty or sixty days). However, in cases involving terminations without cause courts have tended to construe the franchise agreement as the conferral of a right for the term of the agreement,

---

[154] See ¶ 7.03[4][g].

which may be a number of years.[155] Thus, property and fiduciary concepts take precedence over the specific language of the agreement. Results have been similar where the evidence shows that even though a franchise may have a term of one year, renewable at the franchisor's discretion, the custom is to renew the contract for a substantial number of years. A court may treat the contract as if it were for ten years, for instance, rather than for one year with a possibility of renewal.

If the franchisee wrongfully terminates, the damages for the franchisor are equally difficult to calculate if the franchise has a number of years to run. The franchisor should receive the present value of the expected stream of royalty payments over the remaining term of the agreement. If he obtains a substitute franchisee, the mitigation rules apply to reduce the recovery. (The same mitigation rule applies to the franchisee, but it may be more difficult to obtain a substitute franchise than a substitute franchisee.[156]) A common way to avoid difficult calculation problems is to include a liquidated damages clause in the franchise agreement.[157]

¶ 8.06 DAMAGES FOR BREACH OF CONSTRUCTION CONTRACTS

A typical commercial construction contract contains provisions that deal with the remedies available upon a breach, such as an arbitration clause and a liquidated damages clause. It also usually contains a retainage clause that gives the owner some leverage over a contractor who cannot complete the job and conditions the contractor's final payment on the owner's satisfaction. Although questions may arise about the enforceability of remedies speci-

---

[155] Several state statutes, specify the respective responsibilities of the franchisor and franchisee upon termination. See, e.g., Ark. Stat. Ann. § 70-810 (1979); Conn. Gen. Stat. § 142-133(f) (1981); Del. Code Ann., tit. 6, § 2552 (1975); Hawaii Rev. Stat. § 482E-6(2) (1976); Ill. Rev. Stat., ch. 121½, § 704.4 (1983); Mich. Comp. Laws § 445.527(f) (1979); Miss. Code Ann. § 75-77-3 (Supp. 1984); Wash. Rev. Code § 19.100.180(2)(j) (1983); Wis. Stat. § 135.045 (1979, 1980).

[156] For one thing, the terminated franchisee may still be subject to a covenant not to compete.

[157] See Chapter 9.

fied by contract clauses,[158] the nonbreaching party can usually recover in accordance with ordinary rules of damages.

Problems most often arise where there is a breach before performance is complete. If performance has not begun or is complete, the calculation of damages is simpler. The greatest difficulty occurs when the contract is a losing proposition for one or both parties. Courts then must decide whether to retain the risk allocation of the contract as written, which may result in a loss to the nonbreaching party, or to undertake a reallocation of the risk in order to provide the nonbreaching party with a fair recovery. Consider the following situations.

> **EXAMPLE 2.** Contractor Black agrees to build a house for owner Brown for $50,000. Black anticipates a net profit of $5,000 on the project. Before Black has made any expenditures, Brown breaches. Black's recovery is $5,000. If he had made any expenditures in preparation, Black could have recovered $5,000 plus the expenditures (provided they were reasonable and were directly related to the project), less any salvage value in materials acquired through the expenditures.

> **EXAMPLE 3.** Black agrees to build a home for Brown for $50,000, but breaches before doing anything. Brown can recover the difference between $50,000 and the cost, if it is higher, of a contract with another builder for the same project, plus any incidental transaction costs.

> **EXAMPLE 4.** Black agrees to build a house for Brown for $50,000. Brown breaches the agreement after Black has completed the job. Black's recovery is his net profit, calculated by reference to the contract price: He can recover any installments Brown still owes up to $50,000.[159]

---

[158] See ¶ 9.01.

[159] Two different formulas can be applied to reach essentially the same result. One is actual cost incurred plus anticipated profit; the other is unpaid contract price less cost to complete. Both aim to give the contractor a recovery of reliance expenditures and his expectancy, the profit. Thompson & Sebert, *Remedies: Damages, Equity and Restitution* § 11.03, at 11-27 (1983).

EXAMPLE 5. Black agrees to build a $50,000 house for Brown, who subsequently breaches after Black is halfway through with the work. However, Black underestimated the job and had already spent $30,000 in direct reliance expenses when Brown breached. If he were to finish the job, Black would have to spend another $30,000, resulting in a net loss of $10,000 on the project. Should Black recover half his contract price ($25,000) or his reliance expenses ($30,000)? Should he get any credit for the value of his services even if that would include a profit figure he would not have had on full performance? Or should the court simply give effect to the contract that the parties made and let the risk of loss fall where it may?

One approach to the problems raised in Example 5 follows the reasoning of *Kehoe v. Mayor of Rutherford,*[160] an 1893 decision of the New Jersey courts, and only allows a recovery based upon a rateable share of the contract consideration. If the contractor has completed half the project, he gets half the contract price; if that does not give him a profit recovery, it is simply a matter of poor risk allocation in the original agreement. In the words of the *Kehoe* court, "What is done was done under the contract, and should be paid for accordingly."[161]

Most jurisdictions, however, have rejected the *Kehoe* approach and allow the plaintiff in such a case to recover "off" the contract on a restitutionary theory for the fair market value of the goods and services provided. In other words, the contract price does not operate as a ceiling on the recovery.[162] The justification for this approach was set forth in the 1911 case of *City of Philadelphia v. Tripple*[163] and has been followed consistently. The defendant gives up any right to rely on the contract as a limitation when he breaches because the breach amounts to a repudiation, and the

---

[160] Kehoe v. Rutherford, 56 NJL 23, 27 A 912 (1893).

[161] Id. at 914.

[162] Leading cases include Unites States v. Algernon Blair, Inc., 479 F2d 638 (4th Cir. 1973); Scaduto v. Orlando, 381 F2d 587 (2d Cir. 1967); United States ex rel. Susi Contracting Co. v. Zara Contracting Co., 146 F2d 606 (2d Cir. 1944); Acme Process Equip. Co. v. United States, 347 F2d 509 (Ct. Cl. 1965), rev'd on other grounds, 385 US 138 (1966).

[163] City of Philadelphia v. Tripple, 230 Pa. 480, 79 A 703 (1911).

defendant cannot repudiate the contract for one purpose and rely on it for another.[164] This rule appeared in both the first and second Restatements: "[O]n a breach by nonperformance that gives rise to a claim for damages for total breach or on a repudiation, the injured party is entitled to restitution for any benefit that he has conferred on the other party by way of part performance or reliance."[165]

Neither the contract price nor the value of the services or goods to the defendant generally operates as a limitation on the recovery, although both may be evidence of value.[166] Certainly the contract price has some probative worth as an indication of value determined through a process of negotiation.[167] There must have been some benefit conferred, although the determining factor is not the value to the particular breaching party but the value of the benefit in the market.[168]

Oddly enough, if performance is complete and all that remains is payment of a sum certain of money, the remedy for breach is the contract price and not a restitutionary recovery off the contract.

---

[164] The court stated:

> "[T]he owner, who finds himself in this position of advantage, voluntarily puts an end to his contract rights in the premises. This in legal effect he does if he himself breaks the contract or discharges the builder from his obligation to perform it. The situation which then presents itself is one in which the builder has in good faith expended money in the course of work done for the benefit of the owner, and has, in the absence of contract, an equitable claim to be reimbursed. The owner, on the other hand, has deprived himself of the legal right which would have sufficed to defeat the equity. He accordingly stands defenseless in the presence of the builder's claim."

Id. at 706.

[165] Restatement (Second) of Contracts § 373(1) (1981). For the treatment given the subject in the earlier Restatement, see Restatement of Contracts § 348 (1932).

[166] There is some authority for using the contract as a ceiling on recovery, e.g., Johnson v. Bovee, 40 Colo. App. 317, 574 P2d 513 (1978), but this is not consistent with a restitutionary recovery in which the measure is supposed to be the fair market value objectively determined.

[167] As Judge Clark of the Second Circuit said in an often-cited case, "The contract may be important evidence of the value of the performance to the defendant as may also the cost of labor and materials." United States ex rel. Susi Contracting Co. v. Zara Contracting Co., 146 F2d 606, 611 (2d Cir. 1944).

[168] See, e.g., Restatement (Second) of Contracts § 373 comment d (1981); and see Perillo, "Restitution in the Second Restatement of Contracts," 81 Colum. L. Rev. 37 (1981).

The second Restatement says, "The injured party has no right to restitution if he has performed all of his duties under the contract and no performance by the other party remains due other than the payment of a definite sum of money for that performance."[169] Why the breaching party can rely on the contract as a limiting factor when performance is complete but cannot do so when the breach occurs in an executory stage is a mystery to which there is no good answer.

Indeed, this whole area of the law has an air of mystery about it. In the average breach case, the contract is the measuring device, and a breach does not amount to a repudiation of the whole. The defendant usually can invoke the terms of the agreement in defense to the plaintiff's damage claims.[170] There are many instances in which a quantum meruit recovery is allowed, such as in quasicontract disputes or in situations that do not involve any definite payment terms. If the parties have agreed upon a consideration, however, courts usually look to that consideration as the guideline for awarding damages. Executory breaches of construction contracts are an anomaly. Courts may be trying to take into account the possibility of consequential damages that would not otherwise be recoverable, but the approach is rather complicated if that is the goal.

There is an additional anomaly. The injured party has no incentive to seek damages off the contract unless the contract is a losing proposition for him or unless it is substantially below market rates. The transactional costs of proving fair market value (e.g., testimony from third parties, discovery disputes, evidentiary disputes, the greater likelihood of appealable error) are such that it does not make sense to seek a restitutionary recovery unless there is a significant chance of higher damages. In comparison, it is a simple matter to prove the contract. In most of these cases the owner gets a good deal, and it does not make economic sense for him to breach the agreement. The question of breach itself, there-

---

[169] Restatement (Second) of Contracts § 373(2) (1982).

[170] There are breaches and there are breaches, however. Sometimes the breach is not significant enough to justify the other party's nonperformance. At other times the breach amounts to a repudiation and the nonbreaching party is relieved of further duty to perform. For further discussion of this point, see Chapter 2.

fore, may be problematic in these cases, which means that it often makes little sense to treat them as fundamental repudiation cases. Professors Kessler and Gilmore offer a biting description of the typical situation:

> The situation is that *A* has entered into a contract with *B* under which *A* for a price of $10,000, has agreed to do work which it becomes clear as the job progresses, will cost $20,000. Everyone agrees that, except for the remote possibility of reformation for mistake or something of the sort, *A*, if he completes the job, gets only $10,000. *B* merely has to sit tight, meanwhile punctiliously performing his own obligations under the contract, to get $20,000 worth of work for half its cost. Under such circumstances is it plausible that *B* would ever lapse into a default which would allow *A* to get off the hook by "rescinding" the contract and bringing his quantum meruit action for restitution? Yet, in case after case of this type, we are solemnly assured by the court that *B* did in fact "default." One possible explanation is . . . the actual situation is complicated and confused, there are mutual recriminations, each party accuses the other of bad faith, misconduct and faulty performance; until the judicial dice have been rolled, no one has the least idea of which side is in breach and which is not. Most opinions in litigation of this sort, however, become extremely cryptic at the point of explaining exactly what *B*'s mysterious default consisted of.[171]

The owner may have an incentive to breach if the project is a loser for him, but he finds himself in a quandry. If he is going to lose money on the contract as it is written, it may make sense for him to cut his losses by terminating the deal, but he runs the risk of not being able to estimate his liability exposure unless he is certain that the contract is a good one for the contractor. If the contractor also stands to lose, the owner may lose even more if the contractor seeks a restitutionary recovery. This makes his determination of what constitutes an efficient breach all the more difficult. One commentator has suggested a loss allocation measure of damages. If the total loss of both parties will be $15,000, of which one will

---

[171] Kessler & Gilmore 1060. For a sharp criticism of this whole approach, see Childres & Garamella, "The Law of Restitution and the Reliance Interest in Contract," 64 Nw. UL Rev. 433 (1969).

lose $10,000 and the other $5,000 the expenses to the date of breach should be reallocated so that two-thirds of the net losses go to one and one-third to the other.[172] Although this makes some sense and is consistent with the notion of enforcing the private law of the agreement as the parties have made it, there is little likelihood that any court will adopt such an approach. It involves too many complications and difficulties of proof in what is already a complicated area. In addition, it removes completely the notion of fault, which, however faint, does continue to play some role in contract remedies.

In the case of a breach by the contractor, the owner's usual remedy is the cost to complete. He gets the monetary equivalent of substitutional relief, the difference between the contract price and what it now will cost him to have the project completed. There usually is a difference if for no other reason than that the new contractor must add in his start-up costs and a profit factor. This does not fully account for all the consequential damages that may accrue from delays in bringing the project to completion, but the recovery of any additional damages depends upon the owner's ability to satisfy the requirements of the *Hadley v. Baxendale* rule.[173]

The owner may not do as well in some cases if the dispute is over whether there has been compliance with the contract to the owner's satisfaction. In the well-known case of *Jacob & Youngs, Inc. v. Kent,*[174] Judge Benjamin Cardozo set out what is known as the substantial performance rule.[175] In constructing a house, the defendant used a different brand of pipe from the brand specified in the contract. Cardozo agreed that although there was a technical breach, the pipe used was of similar quality to the pipe specified. The contractor, therefore, was in substantial compliance with the terms of the agreement and the proper measure of recovery was the difference in the value of the house with the pipe as installed

---

[172] See Dobbs § 12.24, at 912–924.

[173] One way for the owner to protect himself is to include a liquidated damages clause.

[174] Jacob & Youngs, Inc. v. Kent, 230 NY 239, 129 NE 889 (1921).

[175] For further discussion of Jacob & Youngs and the rule of substantial performance, see ¶ 2.02[1].

and the value with the pipe as specified. This difference was nominal, if anything. The alternative was the cost to repair (or to complete the contract according to its terms), but this would have involved the removal of walls and the substitution of functionally identical pipe. This offended Cardozo's common sense and was economically wasteful. Thus, the unhappy owner was essentially without a remedy.[176]

The result in *Jacob & Youngs* certainly does not seem irrational. If the brands of pipe were fungible, it makes little difference which was used, and there is little to be gained from tearing up the house to put in new pipes while taking out perfectly good ones. However, other cases may involve more difficult or subtle questions of performance, and the difference in recovery between the disappointed party's subjective interest in strict adherence to the contract and an objective determination of relative economic value can be quite great.[177]

Two cases are often cited as illustrations of the differing results of such situations: *Groves v. John Wunder Co.*[178] and *Peevyhouse v. Garland Coal & Mining Co.*[179] In *Groves,* the defendant breached an agreement for the use of property as a quarry by not refilling the quarry and reclaiming the land. The evidence showed that the cost to reclaim according to the terms of the agreement was $60,000, but that even if reclamation were accomplished, the total value of the real estate in question would be only slightly more than $12,000. Nevertheless, the court allowed a recovery of

---

[176] For a discussion of whether a breach has occurred when there is substantial performance within the meaning of Cardozo's opinion, see ¶ 2.02[1].

[177] What if the dispute were not over the brand of pipes in the walls but over the color of the living room and dining room? Unless the contractor used some garish color, there probably would be virtually no difference in market value between a house with a light blue living room and a white dining room compared with green and yellow. The owner's interest might be very different, however. In addition to an aesthetic preference for blue and white (or green and yellow), the color scheme affects the suitability of rugs, furniture upholstery, curtains, and other decorative items. A court would probably say that the owner could demand strict adherence to the color stated in the agreement. For comparison, see, e.g., cases involving tailor-made clothes, such as Brown v. Foster, 113 Mass, 136 (1873).

[178] Groves v. John Wunder Co., 205 Minn. 163, 286 NW 253 (1939).

[179] Peevyhouse v. Garland Coal & Mining Co., 382 P2d 109 (Okla. 1962).

the cost to complete despite the fact that it was grossly disproportionate to the diminution in value. On almost identical facts, the *Peevyhouse* court reached the opposite result and only allowed a recovery of the difference in value before and after the defendants began a strip-mining operation.[180] The *Peevyhouse* court agreed that the normal measure of recovery is the cost to complete according to the terms of the agreement, but

> where the contract provision breached was merely incidental to the main purpose in view, and where the economic benefit which would result to [plaintiff] by full performance of the work is grossly disproportionate to the cost of performance, the damages which [plaintiff] may recover are limited to the diminution in value resulting to the premises because of the nonperformance.[181]

The second Restatement follows a rule similar to that set forth in *Peevyhouse*.[182]

The result of these various opinions is that there is no symmetry in the treatment of breaches by the performing and the paying parties in construction contracts. This creates difficulties in damage estimations and in offers of proof at trial. It also presents some inconsistencies with the overall goals of contract remedies. The

---

[180] Reclamation would have cost $29,000. The jury made an award of $5,000, which was itself more than the total value of the land in question, even if reclaimed, and the Oklahoma Supreme Court reduced this to $300, which the court found to be the reasonable diminution in the land's value.

[181] Id. at 114.

[182] See Restatement (Second) of Contracts § 348 comment c (1981), which says in part,

> "If an award based on the cost to remedy the defects would clearly be excessive and the injured party does not prove the actual loss in value to him, damages will be based instead on the difference between the market price that the property would have had without the defects and the market price of the property with the defects. This diminution in market price is the least possible loss in value to the injured party, since he could always sell the property on the market even if it had no special value to him."

This leaves little room for sentimental attachment to property.

moral may be that the best way to assure some predictability and certainty in a construction contract is to include provisions that establish remedies in advance or that set forth the procedures to be followed in determining an appropriate remedy.

CHAPTER 9

Quasi-Contracts and Restitutionary Remedies

¶ 9.01 QUASI-CONTRACTS AND THE THEORY OF RESTITUTION

[1] Intent of Restitution in Promissory Relationships

The interplay between restitution and contract law can be complex and uncertain; damage theories in contract and restitutionary theories complement or contradict one another.[1] The greatest difficulty arises in distinguishing restitution as a body of law distinct from contract and tort on the one hand and restitution as a description of a group of remedies available in contract actions on the other hand. The intent of restitution is to do justice through an equitable approach to remedies for persons who have conferred benefits on others. Restitution covers a wide range of relationships, many of which involve fraud, duress, or other wrongdoing. This chapter examines the narrow portion of restitution that is most closely connected with promissory relationships.

[2] Quasi-Contracts as Bridge Between Contract and Tort

The modern law of restitution dates from sixteenth- and seventeenth-century common law.[2] It was developed to cover cases that fit neither into contract nor tort but that nonetheless demanded some form of relief. These cases usually involved some form of enrichment that was unjust in that the enriched party had not, but should have, paid for a benefit. To make these cases fit within the forms of pleading then in use, courts created a fictional promissory relationship and imposed a duty, in law, on the defendant to pay for the benefit conferred.

Restitution connotes a restoration — a return to the plaintiff of property wrongfully or mistakenly taken by another. If a thief steals a priceless family heirloom, the victim can sue him in tres-

---

[1] See Chapter 8 for an introduction to the concept of restitutionary recovery. For comprehensive treatments of restitution, see Palmer, *Law of Restitution* (4 vols.) (1978) (hereinafter cited as Palmer) and Goff & Jones, *The Law of Restitution* (2d ed. 1978). The American Law Institute published the Restatement of Restitution in 1937.

[2] See generally Simpson, *A History of the Common Law of Contract* 489–505 (1975).

pass for damages (the value of the heirloom) or can seek to recover the heirloom itself (restitution of stolen property). Similarly, if a party mistakenly delivers property to another, he may be able to rescind the transaction and recover. Although the precise factual patterns may present problems, the category of cases that involve the restoration of benefits wrongfully or mistakenly obtained is relatively simple to understand. More difficult cases generally fall within the category of quasi-contract. As Professor Simpson has written:

> The term "quasi-contract" was known to common lawyers, and borrowed by them as a label to describe situations where liability for breach of promise was imposed and made remediable by action of assumpsit although the promise sued upon was in some sense implied or fictional, or at least need not be proved by the plaintiff. . . . In particular it is not possible to unify the case law in terms of the principle against unjust enrichment; first, because there is no contemporary evidence of the conscious adoption of such a principle, and second, because some of the situations in which a promise was implied by law — for example, implied mutual promises to perform the award of arbitrators — are not explicable in terms of such a principle.[3]

Quasi-contract, that portion of the law of restitution most closely related to promissory transactions, thus developed to fill a void between contract and tort. Like tort, it includes an element of public law and a strong justice component. The defendant has to pay money or restore property because it is wrong, a violation of a duty, for him to retain a benefit or its value. The question of justice does not relate solely to the relationship between the parties, but also involves common understandings of what is fair. Like contract, restitution involves a concept of promise, albeit one created by intellectual construct rather than one developed from the parties' own communications. Courts treat the relationship as if the parties had made mutual promises and then base their remedies on

---

[3] Id. at 489.

this fictional agreement, whether the parties had an intention to agree or not.[4]

[3] Quasi-Contracts and Implied Contracts

The use of fictonal promises in quasi-contract has led to confusion between quasi-contracts (or contracts implied in law) and implied contracts (or contracts implied from factual situations). The theoretical difference between the two is great. The law imposes liability on a defendant in a quasi-contract because it serves justice to do so. The intentions of the parties are not irrelevant and may be important in determining whether the defendant's enrichment was unjust. Did the plaintiff really intend to make a gift, but later changed his mind?[5] Did the plaintiff act officiously and thrust an unrequested or even unwanted benefit on the defendant who would be unreasonably inconvenienced if he had to make restoration?[6] The critical inquiry, however, is whether justice requires that the defendant restore property or pay money to the plaintiff. In comparison, an implied-in-fact contract does not differ theoretically from an express contract. The parties have acted as if there were an agreement, but they have not clarified various portions of the contract. The law does not impose a relationship on them; rather, it gives effect to the relationship they have created by their actions. The technical distinction between quasi-contract and implied contract, therefore, is that the "former is an intellectual construct while the latter is a factual description."[7]

---

[4] "Contracts implied in law . . . are obligations imposed by law for the purpose of bringing about justice without reference to the intentions of the parties." Wall & Childres, "The Law of Restitution and the Federal Government," 66 Nw. UL Rev. 587, 599 (1971) (hereinafter cited as Wall & Childres).

[5] For example, a doting uncle may pay his nephew's college tuition but later become upset at his nephew's chosen profession (or bad grades or social life) and demand repayment. Is it unjust for the nephew to retain the benefit? Probably not, if he reasonably expected that his uncle's tuition payments were gifts.

[6] For example, if an enterprising teenager mows the lawn while a neighbor is out of town for the weekend, it is not unjust for the neighbor to refuse to pay the teenager. After all, he was a trespasser, and the neighbor did not request the service. The situation might be different if the neighbor was at home, saw the teenager approach, and watched him cut the grass, especially if the neighbor knew that the teenager did yard work to earn his spending money.

[7] Wall & Childres 598.

[4] Concepts of Public Law and Justice, Unjust Enrichment, and Receipt of Benefit

Much of the common law of quasi-contract came from family law cases. These illustrate the public-law aspects of the concept. At common law the husband was responsible for the necessities of his spouse and children. If necessary goods or services were provided to his wife or minor children by a third party, the law made the husband answerable to the provider for the value of the goods or services. The husband could not legally refuse to provide necessities to his wife and children and thus was bound by status to a public-law duty. If someone else performed a portion of this duty, the husband could not justly retain the value of the benefit conferred because he could not legally avoid the duty. These cases were treated as quasi-contract cases, and, although it might have been preferable to have put them into a special category of family law, they illustrate the public-law and justice aspects of quasi-contract theory.[8]

During the late nineteenth century, legal scholars embarked on a series of attempts to classify the law and to bring unity to contracts, torts, and other categories by identifying their dominant general principles. Quasi-contract was not left out. In 1893, Keener published his famous book, *A Treatise on the Law of Quasi-Contracts*. In addition to collecting and trying to reconcile the many cases, Keener's thesis was that quasi-contract, as an outgrowth of restitutionary principles, was wholly independent of contract. It was a body of law based upon legal duty and the concept of justice. Contract, on the other hand, had its basis solely in private agreement. Keener's thesis found favor with Professor Arthur Corbin[9] and became the dominant view in American law.[10]

Keener argued from the principle of unjust enrichment. The purpose of the law was to force the defendant to give up a gain that he had acquired wrongfully or that would be wrongful for him to keep without payment. Some twenty years later, Woodward pub-

---

[8] See generally Atiyah, *The Rise and Fall of Freedom of Contract* 182, 183 (1979) (hereinafter cited as Atiyah).

[9] Corbin, "Quasi-Contractual Obligations," 21 Yale LJ 533 (1912).

[10] Dawson, *Unjust Enrichment* 21, 22 (1951); Perillo, "Restitution in a Contractual Context," 73 Colum. L. Rev. 1208, 1209 (1973).

lished his equally well-known treatise on the subject and expanded the concept of quasi-contract to include cases that involved the receipt of a benefit that was neither wrongful to receive nor wrongful (in any general public sense) to keep and that did not enrich the defendant's estate.[11] The draftsmen of the first Restatement of Contracts tended to follow this more expansive view and focused on the concept of benefit receipt.[12] The second Restatement borrows from both works and seems to mold the two concepts into a more general approach.[13] Some simple illustrations may clarify the distinctions.

In the famous case of *Cotnam v. Wisdom,*[14] the court established the principle that an injured or sick person impliedly promises to pay the reasonable charges of a doctor or other medical professional who comes to his aid even if the victim is unconscious or otherwise mentally incompetent. This fictional agreement serves several purposes. It encourages doctors, nurses, and other medical professionals to come to the aid of a person in distress.[15] Although the law imposes no duty to be a good Samaritan, there is a commonsense expectation that a doctor or nurse will assist an injured person, and the law does not want to discourage that expectation.[16] The rule further recognizes that the average person would seek to have such aid if he were competent to request it, and that doctors and other medical professionals are in the business of providing medical services for pay. In *Cotnam,* the victim was thrown from a streetcar. A witness summoned Dr. Wisdom, who also called in Dr. Abel, a surgeon, to assist. The victim suffered

---

[11] Woodward, *The Law of Quasi-Contracts* (1913).

[12] Perillo, "Restitution in the Second Restatement of Contracts," 81 Colum. L. Rev. 37, 38 (1981) (hereinafter cited as Perillo).

[13] "The Restatement (Second) ignores the conflict between the rationales of 'unjust enrichment' and 'receipt of benefit,' frequently basing its rhetoric upon the former while grounding its operative rules primarily on the latter. When a proper case for restitution is advanced, the Restatement (Second) usually allows recovery for benefits conferred whether or not the defendant has been enriched in estate." Id. at 38 (footnotes omitted).

[14] Cotnam v. Wisdom, 83 Ark. 601, 104 SW 164 (1907).

[15] The promise of a reward may offset the fear of a suit for malpractice or negligence if things go amiss.

[16] Even though the law may not impose such a general duty on a physician, the ethics of the medical profession may do so.

severe head injuries and despite the efforts of the two doctors he died soon after the accident, never having regained consciousness. The doctors successfully sued the victim's estate for "reasonable compensation for the services rendered."

The benefit conferred by the doctors was the value of their services while treating the victim. He was unconscious throughout the ordeal, and his enjoyment of the benefit was certainly de minimis. Yet it was a benefit received even if the result was foreordained by the severity of the injuries. The decedent's estate was not enriched; the doctors' services did not improve his financial situation, nor was there a transfer of any property (except in the abstract sense of services as a form of transferable personal property). There was nothing belonging to the plaintiff to be "restored" from the decedent's estate. Instead, the question was one of payment for a beneficial, although not enriching, service. The decedent had not acted in any way that was unjust. Indeed, he was merely the unconscious object of the whole transaction.[17]

The equally celebrated case of *Britton v. Turner*[18] illustrates the unjust enrichment principle. The plaintiff, a laborer, had agreed to work for the defendant for one year for a total consideration of $120. The plaintiff, however, worked just short of ten months and quit. He sought to recover the value of the services he had performed, but the defendant denied any liability for wages because the plaintiff was in breach and had not worked the entire year. The court allowed the plaintiff to recover upon a count in quantum meruit for the reasonable worth of his labor.[19] In contrast to *Cotnam,* the defendant had agreed expressly to pay for the plaintiff's work, although his promise was to pay for one year's work, not ten months' work. The plaintiff's unexcused breach arguably destroyed the contract, and ample authority existed for the proposi-

---

[17] The administrators of Cotnam's estate were not unjust in their questioning of the bill submitted by the doctors. They were bound as fiduciaries to be careful in the administration of the estate and when the case arose the law was certainly not clear on the subject of liability to the doctors.

[18] Britton v. Turner, 6 NH 481 (1834).

[19] The jury awarded him $95, which was almost precisely his rateable share under the contract.

tion that a defaulting party could not recover in restitution.[20] Nevertheless, the court reasoned that the defendant had been enriched. He had received almost ten months of labor for which he had been willing to pay, and it would be unjust to allow him to enjoy the fruits of that labor for free.[21] In contrast to *Cotnam,* the defendant in *Britton* received a benefit that enriched his estate and for which he had already agreed to pay in principle. Both cases involved services and a duty to pay for them. The intent of the parties and the subsequent effect on their respective balance sheets were different. In *Britton,* a benefit was conferred (ten months of labor) that presumably enriched the employer by improving the operation of his farm. In addition, the employer already had some expectation of liability. In *Cotnam,* a benefit also was conferred (the doctors' medical attentions), but it was fruitless and the victim was innocent of any participation in the process.

An even clearer case of unjust enrichment would be one in which a buyer orders grade-A widgets but the seller mistakenly delivers grade-AA widgets. If the buyer can return the widgets for

---

[20] See, e.g., Giles v. Edwards, 7 TR 181, 101 Eng. Rep. 920 (1797); Stark v. Parker, 19 Mass. 267 (1824). Contra Hayward v. Leonard, 25 Mass. 180 (1828). English courts still tend to be somewhat reluctant to reward the breaching party. See generally Jones, "The Recovery of Benefits Gained From a Breach of Contract," 99 LQ Rev. 443 (1983) (hereinafter cited as Jones), citing and discussing, e.g., Tito v. Waddell (No. 2) [1977] Ch. 106, 332; Radford v. De Froberville, [1977] 1 WLR 1262; Joyner v. Weeks [1891] 2 QB 31 (CA). Moreover, the orthodox view in England is still one of antipathy to the "principle of reversing unjust enrichment"; Burrows, "Contract, Tort and Restitution — A Satisfactory Division or Not?" 99 LQ Rev. 217, 232, 233 (1983) (hereinafter cited as Burrows), citing Orakpo v. Mason Invs. [1978] AC 95. There is authority to the contrary. Id. at 232 n.58, citing, e.g., The Fibrosa [1943] AC 32, 64 (Lord Wright); Government of India v. Taylor [1955] AC 491, 513 (Lord Keith); Nissan v. Attorney-General [1968] 1 QB 286, 352 (Winn, LJ); Greenwood v. Bennett [1973] 1 QB 195, 202 (Lord Denning); BP Exploration (Libya) v. Hunt [1979] 1 WLR 783 (Goff, J.); Barclays Bank v. WJ Simms Son & Cooke (Southern) Ltd. [1980] QB 677.

[21] On its face, the outcome is common sense. The laborer had worked for almost a year. He quit at the end of December, and it clearly seemed unfair to the jury to cast him out into the New Hampshire winter without a dime. But, as Professors Kessler and Gilmore have noted, the salary was small even for the times and most likely the plaintiff was a typical hired hand who received free room and board, some clothing, and other odds and ends in addition to his small salary. Thus, it would be unfair to say that he had not been compensated at all for his work. Kessler & Gilmore, *Contracts* 878 n.4 (2d ed. 1970). The $120 in wages may have been intended as a bonus to encourage the plaintiff to stay for the full year.

a nominal cost and the seller is ready to deliver grade-A widgets in return and to compensate the buyer for his transaction costs, it would be unjust for the buyer to retain the higher quality widgets and to refuse to pay any more than the grade-A quality price.[22]

One of the more common benefit received but no unjust enrichment scenarios involves a defaulting contractor or a defaulting owner.[23] If a contractor has performed half of a construction job, the work product may be worth less than the sum of its parts (labor and materials) and less than half of the value of the completed project. Indeed, a half-completed job may add little or nothing to and might even detract from the value of the underlying real estate. The contractor has provided the owner with tangible property (e.g., lumber, bricks, and nails) and services as the laborer did in *Britton*. The owner rightfully received all this and may rightfully keep it. But if his estate is not enriched, should he have to pay? Generally speaking, the answer is yes, even though his balance sheet may tell him that he is paying for something of no value.[24]

[5] Quasi-Contracts and Ordinary Contracts

Even though all the cases and illustrations cited previously are quasi-contract cases that thus involve the imposition of legal obligations, they all bear a close resemblance to ordinary contract cases. In *Britton,* as in the hypothetical widget transaction or the construction agreement, there was a preexisting express agreement. It was the breach or the failure of that agreement that provided the factual basis for a consideration of restitutionary con-

---

[22] This problem also can be handled as a mistake case. See UCC §§ 2-508, 2-513, 2-601–2-609.

[23] For a discussion of damages in construction contracts, see ¶ 8.05.

[24] The general rule is that the owner can recover from the defaulting contractor the difference between the cost to complete the project and the original contract price. The contractor is entitled, nonetheless, to credit for work done, although measurement problems may be somewhat troublesome. This approach is not new. For an example at common law, see Planche v. Colburn (1831) 8 Bing. 14, 131 Eng. Rep. 305 (defendants engaged plaintiff to write a book; defendants went out of business and plaintiff was able to recover in quantum meruit for work done on the book even though he did not finish it and defendants obviously had no use for it); see also Chandler v. Boswell [1904] 1 KB 493.

cepts. In *Cotnam,* one party could never have agreed to anything, but it is not farfetched to posit a hypothetical agreement between a provider of services and a person in need of those services.[25] The only open question is the one of fees, and courts regularly take evidence to decide reasonable charges for various services.

Despite the continuing distinction between quasi-contract, implied contract, and express contract, some contend that they are simply variants of a single species. In Professor Perillo's words:

> Cases in which restitution is sought involve predominately either tortious conduct or performance under a failed agreement. In the latter instance, contractual policies should underlie the remedial rules readjusting the parties' economic relations. Among these policies are honoring the allocation of risks agreed to by the parties and recognizing customary understandings of suitable risk allocations, relative fault, and elementary fairness. Prevention of unjust enrichment is also a contractual policy, but it is not preeminent.[26]

Certainly, many quasi-contract cases arise from failed consensual transactions. In such situations, courts should not be reluctant to look to contract rules for guidance and to fashion a remedy in accordance with basic contract principles. Courts do not stop at the lines drawn by pure contract approaches, however. If they did, plaintiffs in cases such as *Britton* would have more difficulty because a court's central mission in a contract case is to determine the intent of the parties and to give it effect. If the parties intended to require full performance as a condition to payment, then if a court orders payment on something less than full performance it has already overstepped the boundaries of pure contract and has imposed on the parties a public definition of their relationship and their duties to one another.[27] There is clearly a close relationship

---

[25] A favorite question on law school exams is: What is the result if the victim in *Cotnam* was religiously opposed to the use of doctors? Or if he had been given a blood transfusion while unconscious and he was a devout Jehovah's Witness?

[26] Perillo 42, 43.

[27] If the parties have agreed to something illegal, that is one thing. The point here is that a court may step in and reorder the parties' relationship not because it is illegal but because it does not accord with the court's definition of justice.

between quasi-contract and restitution on the one hand and contract on the other. It may be almost impossible to decide whether a particular pattern of facts fits better in one than in another, but there remains a formidable conceptual difference between the two that cannot be overcome simply by noting that many cases of restitution are, at heart, breach of contract cases. The difference lies in the source of the applicable law and the aims of the law. The source of the law in the contract case is the parties' agreement, subject of course to the governing rules of relevant statutes such as the UCC. The purpose of the law is to enforce the agreement either specifically or with money damages. In quasi-contract, the source of the law is in the public legal definition of justice and the purpose of the courts is to do justice, not simply to help private parties put back together the pieces of a failed bargain. This allows courts to exercise much broader discretionary authority in fashioning remedies.

[6] Restitution and Tort vs. Restitution and Contract

One of the greatest confusions comes from the failure to distinguish between restitution as a theoretical source of legal rights and obligations and restitution as a shorthand description of a group of remedies that may be available in a wide range of actions. As a general rule, "in contractual contexts other than total breach, the law of restitution is a source of remedial (secondary) rights rather than a source of primary rights."[28] The term "restitution" may be used loosely to describe a particular remedy, or a case may be classified as one in quasi-contract because the remedy is restitutionary. That, however, does not make the case truly one in restitution unless the reason for granting a remedy derives from some publicly defined duty or relationship and not from a relationship created by the parties themselves. Again, some illustrations may clarify the problem, although they may not solve all the dilemmas.

---

[28] Perillo, "Restitution in a Contractual Context," 73 Colum. L. Rev. 1208, 1215 (1973).

EXAMPLE 1. White steals a valuable painting from Green, a tortious act for which Green has at least two remedies. First, he can sue in trespass for damages equal to the value of the painting;[29] second, he can sue in restitution to recover the painting itself.[30] Green also has a third remedy that has its roots in contract law. He can sue on an implied assumpsit for the monetary value of the painting as if White had agreed to purchase it but had failed to tender the price. Because White is a tortfeasor and Green did not set out to sell the painting, it would stretch credibility past the breaking point to characterize this as an implied-in-fact contract. There never was any consensus ad idem nor any interest on the part of White or Green in creating a consensual transaction. If there is an assumpsit action, it is because the law imposes a duty on White to pay Green for what he has unjustly taken from him. White was wrong both to take and to keep. Green's right to sue on an implied assumpsit derives from the breach of the same public duty that justifies his right to sue in trespass. As a practical matter, a lawyer probably would prefer to sue in trespass in a simple case such as this because tort law allows greater flexibility in proving consequential damages[31] and because punitive damages might be available in a tort action.[32] A contract plaintiff, however, has the advantage of a strict liability standard that is not available in most tort actions, and with the flexible rules of modern pleading a careful lawyer likely would include separate counts in trespass, restitution, and assumpsit in the complaint.

---

[29] He can also recover consequential damages that may cover his transaction costs, and if the tort was willful, he may be able to get punitive damages.

[30] This may be an action in trover, or he may impose a constructive trust on the painting. If the painting has been sold to an innocent third party, Green may not be able to recover the painting but he may be able to trace the proceeds into other property (e.g., White sells the painting for $10,000 and then buys a car with the cash).

[31] See Chapter 7.

[32] In some jurisdictions it may be possible to sue in contract for damages and, if the facts support a claim in tort, to sue for punitive damages on that basis. There is a trend toward greater allowance of extracontractual damages where a contract breach is closely tied with tortious conduct. See Chapter 11.

EXAMPLE 2. While Gray is at work, ABC Department Store mistakenly delivers a new television set to her home. Gray's weekly maid service happens to be there when the delivery is made, and the cleaners accept delivery assuming it to be correct. By the time Gray arrives, ABC has discovered the error and has delivered another set to the person who ordered one. ABC requests that Gray allow its deliverymen to return and pick up the set. If Gray decides to keep the set, most people would agree that she should pay for it, even though she did not order it. Gray did nothing wrongful in obtaining the set, but it would be unjust for her to retain it without a fair payment.[33] The genesis of this problem was in ABC's mistake. Although the law does not provide remedies for all mistakes, both the law and common sense recognize that a mistake such as this is not unusual in the commercial world and that the error can be cured simply and without cost to anyone except the mistaken party. (Indeed, the whole problem could have been avoided if Gray had been at home.) Furthermore, ABC is a commercial enterprise in the business of selling goods, and there is no suggestion that there was any gratuitous intention on the part of ABC. As in Example 1, ABC may sue in tort for the value of the television or (possibly) seek the return of the chattel.[34] ABC also may sue on an implied assumpsit for the value of the set. This assumpsit action drifts slightly closer to an implied-in-fact contract, because Gray knowingly retains a chattel that is meant to be in commerce. Nevertheless, it again strains credibility to treat this as a voluntary, consensual transaction. ABC did not intend to make a contract with Gray, nor did she intend to buy a television set. If she decides to keep the television, she simply profits from ABC's mistake. The law, therefore, imposes on her the duty to pay, and

---

[33] This need not be the price marked on the set; however, it should be a reasonable price in the appropriate market.

[34] The latter remedy is unlikely because there is nothing unique about a television set and ABC may be fully compensated by money damages.

this case fits most easily within the quasi-contract category.[35] Gray's wrongful retention of the property is a public wrong.

EXAMPLE 3. ABC Department Store again delivers a television set. In this case, however, the television set is delivered at the request of Gray's Uncle George. Although Gray may not have wanted a new television set, if she decides to keep this one the law probably will not require her to pay her uncle. There is a presumption of a gratuity because the transfer is intrafamily.

Example 3 is a simple case, but it illustrates the public nature of the quasi-contract situation. That is, the law makes certain assumptions about relationships and imposes duties or liabilities on the basis of those assumptions. In neither Example 2 nor Example 3 did Gray set out to buy a television. She arrived home to find a new television in her house, and she liked it well enough that she did not want to go to even the minimal inconvenience necessary to return it. On the other hand, she did not like the television well enough to part with money as a condition to keeping it. In Example 2, Gray has to pay; in Example 3, she probably does not. The different results have nothing to do with Gray's preference. Instead, they relate to the different statuses of the parties conferring the benefits. One is a commercial enterprise, the other is a friendly uncle. The law assumes a paying relationship for the former and a gratuitous relationship for the latter. Thus, the differences are not related to any variations in a consensual relationship, but result from differences in the public law applied to the two situations.

---

[35] This case should be distinguished from the one in which it is difficult or impossible to return the benefit conferred or unjustly acquired. If for example, a teenager cuts his neighbor's grass while the neighbor is away, the teenager's time can hardly be restored to him, nor can he restore to his neighbor the grass clippings as unmown lawn. Unless there is some reason for expecting payment to be made (e.g., the teenager has cut the neighbor's lawn in the past for pay), the law will probably treat the teenager as a gratuitous, officious meddler and the neighbor will not have to pay for the service even though he has a gain (a trimmed lawn) and the teenager has a loss (time, wear and tear on the mower, and gasoline).

EXAMPLE 4. Black and Brown have a contract and Brown breaches after Black has completed a portion of his performance. Black can recover the expectancy (his net profit on the deal),[36] his expenditures (reliance),[37] or, in certain circumstances, the value of services performed or goods provided to the date of the breach.[38] If Black recovers on the third remedy, most courts would characterize the recovery as one in restitution. However, Black does not recover because Brown owes him a public duty; he recovers because Brown breached a contract. Restitution is only a shorthand way to describe the method of calculating damages for the breach of contract. In fairness, some courts may characterize Brown's breach as a repudiation of the contract and then create the fiction that both parties are strangers and that Black has enriched Brown, who cannot justly retain the benefit without payment.[39] This approach, however, is an intellectual fiction. The relationship of the parties was created in the first place by the parties themselves, and the dispute is the result of a breach of contract, not the result of the failure of one party to adhere to a publicly defined standard of behavior.

The four preceding examples certainly do not exhaust the range of possibilities between pure tort and pure contract that might support an action in quasi-contract or that might justify the award of a restitutionary remedy. They simply illustrate that quasi-contract does indeed cover a separate body of cases that fall between contract and tort. One situation may involve wrongdoing or reprehensible conduct and thus be closer to the tort side, while another might be closer to a simple contract breach and involve no wrongful or unjust behavior. It is important, nevertheless, to keep in mind the great conceptual difference between a contract action

---

[36] See ¶ 7.02[2].

[37] See ¶ 7.02[3].

[38] See ¶ 7.02[4].

[39] See, e.g., Boomer v. Muir, 24 P2d 570 (Cal. Dist. Ct. App. 1933); see generally Childres & Garamella, "The Law of Restitution and the Reliance Interest in Contract," 64 Nw. UL Rev. 433 (1969); Palmer, "The Contract Price as a Limit on Restitution for Defendant's Breach," 20 Ohio St. LJ 264 (1959); Perillo 44, 45. See infra ¶ 9.02[4].

and a quasi-contract action. The former affirms the private law created by the parties and the latter vindicates public-law interests without limitation by the parties' private-law interests.

Despite the close relationship between restitution and tort on one hand and restitution and contract on the other, Professor Corbin and other commentators of the early twentieth century were correct in segregating quasi-contract, as a part of restitution, from the general law of contracts.[40] The movement toward a marriage between contract and quasi-contract is probably more of a reflection of the expanding use of reliance and benefit principles for the justification of contracts than of any fundamental flaw in the separate classification of quasi-contract. In the late twentieth century, contract itself has more of a social face than it had during the nineteenth century. As contract has moved closer to public law, it is not surprising that the overlaps with quasi-contract and even with tort have seemed to expand.[41]

¶ 9.02 RESTITUTIONARY REMEDIES

[1] Recoveries In Quantum Valebant and In Quantum Meruit

In principle, restitutionary remedies provide the complaining party either with specific relief (e.g., return of the chattel wrongfully taken or retained) or with the monetary value of the goods or services provided. In the latter instance, courts usually speak of a recovery in quantum valebant (as much as the goods are worth) or in quantum meruit (as much as the plaintiff deserves); sometimes the action is said to be one in quantum meruit or one in quantum valebant. This shorthand description may be useful, but it can also be misleading. Quantum valebant or meruit is nothing but a method of measurement, and neither provides a standard of liability. A plaintiff may recover in quantum meruit for services provided under an express contract if the agreement is silent or ambiguous as to the price. On the other hand, quantum meruit is the method commonly used to put a value on the services for which payment should be made in a quasi-contract case.

---

[40] In support of this argument, see, e.g., Burrows 217.

[41] See generally Atiyah 764–770.

[2] Determining Value of Recoverable Service or Product

[a] Objective Fair Market Standard

It is one thing to say that a plaintiff should recover the reasonable value of a service or a product, but another to affix a specific cash amount to that value. The usual approach attempts to determine the objective fair market value of the service or the product.[42] If there is a ready market, proof may be simple; more often than not however the plaintiff must proffer evidence of a range of values in similar circumstances to provide an adequate database for a reasonable estimate. Determination of the actual value is usually a matter of fact for a jury.[43] Failure to present objective evidence of value other than the plaintiff's own estimate may be fatal to the case.[44] The plaintiff must also be sure that his evidence is from the correct market (e.g., wholesale or retail).[45]

[b] Focus on Defendant's Gain

The use of an objective market standard has the advantage of reasonable certainty and relative simplicity of proof. It is not, however, the only standard used nor is it necessarily consistent with the underlying principles of quasi-contract or restitution in general. In their famous article on contract damages, Fuller and Perdue said that the goal of restitution was to take away from the defendant an unjustly acquired or retained gain.[46] The expectancy recovery and

---

[42] See generally Douthwaite, *Attorney's Guide to Restitution* § 8.2, at 327–331 (1977) (hereinafter cited as Douthwaite), and see, e.g., Peaney v. Pellandini, 97 Idaho 655, 551 P2d 610 (1976); Huff v. Thornton, 287 NC 1, 213 SE2d 198 (1975). Although most quasi-contract actions fall outside the coverage of the UCC, the UCC takes a sensible approach to the admission of market quotations and other evidence of market value that should be useful in almost any situation. See UCC §§ 2-723, 2-724.

[43] See, e.g., Bernini v. Zylka, 51 AD2d 689, 379 NYS2d 104 (1976) (attorneys' fees).

[44] See Development Corp. of Ga. v. Berndt, 131 Ga. App. 277, 205 SE2d 868 (1974).

[45] For a classic example of the necessity to prove the correct market, see Charles St. Garage Co. v. Meyer Kaplan, 312 Mass. 624, 45 NE2d 928 (1942); see also UCC § 2-713, Official Comment 2.

[46] Fuller & Perdue, "The Reliance Interest in Contract Damages (Part I)," 46 Yale LJ 52, 53, 54 (1936); see also Henderson, "Promises Grounded in the Past: The Idea of Unjust Enrichment and the Law of Contracts," 57 Va. L. Rev. 1115, 1141 (1971).

the reliance recovery both focus on the plaintiff's loss — his lost bargain or his out-of-pocket expenses. The restitutionary recovery, in comparison, focuses on the defendant's gain whether or not there is an equivalent loss by the plaintiff. The injustice of the gain triggers liability. If this principle of liability is carried through to the measurement of recovery, the proper approach would be to restore to the plaintiff the value of the defendant's gain. When the plaintiff obtains specific recovery that is essentially what happens, but if the recovery is in money, an objective market value approach may or may not approximate the defendant's gain.

[c] Combination of Plaintiff's Loss and Defendant's Gain

In many instances there is not an even balance between a loss on the plaintiff's side and a gain on the defendant's side. Indeed, one party may have only an insignificant gain or loss compared to the other or to objective market standards. A half-completed building provides a common example; the builder may have made expenditures that far exceed the value of the unfinished building.

The often-cited case of *Matarese v. Moore-McCormack Lines, Inc.*[47] is a good example of another circumstance in which the plaintiff has no out-of-pocket loss but only a lost opportunity. The plaintiff in *Matarese* was an uneducated worker who came up with an idea to save time and money and to promote safety in loading and unloading cargo on the docks. He discussed it with the defendant's agent, who promised the plaintiff one-third of any savings made by the defendant if it adopted his idea. The defendant did use the idea, but paid nothing to the plaintiff. The defendant said that the agent had no authority to make such a promise and, furthermore, that the plaintiff's advice was vague and officiously given. The court disagreed and found that the advice was given with a reasonable expectation of payment and that the defendant had used the plaintiff's knowledge, thus depriving him of the opportunity to capitalize on his own inventiveness.

To measure the recovery, the court instructed the jury to consider both the value of the plaintiff's idea as used by the defendant (its cost savings) and the reasonable value of the plaintiff's services. The court seemed to be making an attempt to measure both

---

[47] Matarese v. Moore-McCormack Lines, Inc., 158 F2d 631 (2d Cir. 1946).

the plaintiff's loss (his time and services) and the defendant's gain (savings from the use of the plaintiff's idea).

The plaintiff only spent the time necessary to describe his idea to the agent. What he lost was the opportunity to sell the idea to the defendant at a fair value. The defendant's cost savings were certainly evidence that the idea was valuable, but the defendant would not have been likely to pay an amount for the idea equal to the sum of any cost savings that might result since there would be no incentive to do so (hence, the one-third of savings offer by the agent). In the "market" for the idea, its present value should have been something less than its total value over time to the defendant. By focusing on evidence of both the plaintiff's loss and the defendant's gain, the court was trying to cause the defendant to disgorge the benefit received or its unjust enrichment, even though the fair market value of the idea on an open market sale probably would have been less than the sum of the savings and the value of the plaintiff's services.[48]

Matarese involved competing principles. The parties and the court could have treated the case as an implied-in-fact contract. The agent and the plaintiff entered into an express agreement despite the vagueness of some of the details. If the agent acted with apparent authority, there was no strong reason to treat the circumstances as anything other than a case ex contractu, albeit with an ambiguous price term. The plaintiff's expectancy was one-third of the defendant's cost savings, and the only problem was to prove the amount of the savings. By treating the case as one of quasi-contract, the court shifted the emphasis from the plaintiff's expectancy to the defendant's gain. The goal was to make the defendant give up an unjust gain even if that caused the plaintiff to be better off than if the contract had proceeded as planned.

The result in *Matarese* demonstrates the importance of the conceptual basis of an action and the continuing distinction between quasi-contract and pure contract. Because the two bodies of law have different goals and justificatory principles, it should not be surprising that the results in two cases with similar factual circumstances will differ if one case is tried in contract and the other

---

[48] The jury awarded a recovery of $40,000, which was affirmed by the Court of Appeals for the Second Circuit.

in quasi-contract. The measurement standard in *Matarese* included elements of reliance (the plaintiff's loss — the value of his time and services) and elements of unjust enrichment (the defendant's gain — its cost savings). This approach illustrates another aspect of quasi-contract — the discretion available to a court to measure the remedy in a way that takes into account general principles of justice. Although the underlying theory may be to do justice by causing a defendant to give up an ill-gotten gain, this pattern may not fit every situation. Instead, the focus may be on the value of the plaintiff's loss or, as in *Matarese,* on some combination of loss and gain. This open-ended approach makes the classification of quasi-contract cases virtually impossible, and it means that the formulation of general rules is a Sisyphean task.

Despite these concerns, the more favored valuation approach focuses on the objective fair market value of what was transferred (products, services, ideas) from the plaintiff to the defendant. In a given case, a court might determine that justice is served by a more particularized, subjective consideration of loss or gain,[49] but most of the time an objective market approach serves the interests of the plaintiff as well as the administration of justice by promoting efficiency and simplicity in the order of proof and the trial of a case. The plaintiff contractor, for instance, is protected from the recalcitrant builder who decides in the middle of a project that a Turkish bath will not be worth the cost of his investment and that it will not enhance the value of the underlying real estate.[50]

[3] Restoration of Benefits Received by the Defaulting Party

Two of the most common reasons to breach a contract are to save money or to make more money by doing something else. In

---

[49] If the plaintiff's loss exceeds the defendant's gain or the fair market value of his performance, the plaintiff might choose to sue in reliance rather than in restitution. See Restatement (Second) of Contracts §§ 158, 272, 371 (1981). Comment b to section 371 says that there can be no reliance recovery in a restitution action unless there has also been a benefit conferred. It is unlikely that there will be many restitution cases in which there is no benefit conferred. See Perillo 39, 40. The Restatement (Second) § 349 also allows a plaintiff to choose between reliance and expectancy approaches to damages. See Chapter 7.

[50] On somewhat similar facts, see, e.g., Vickery v. Ritchie, 202 Mass. 247, 88 NE 835 (1909).

such a circumstance, should the nonbreaching party be allowed to sue in restitution or for a restitutionary remedy that results in an award determined by reference to the savings made by the breaching party or the opportunity gained by the defaulter? The famous case of *Groves v. John Wunder Co.*[51] provides one answer. In *Groves,* the defendant operated a quarry on land leased from the plaintiff. One of the requirements of the lease was that the land be returned in its original condition fully reclaimed. The defendant did not reclaim the land, and the plaintiff successfully sued for the cost of reclamation even though the diminished value of the land was substantially less than the cost of the reclamation.

The English case of *Joyner v. Weeks*[52] helped to establish the precedential basis for *Groves*. In *Joyner,* a tenant failed to leave the leased premises in good order at the conclusion of the lease. The plaintiff recovered the cost of repairs rather than the damage to the reversion. The court reasoned that this method had the virtue of simplicity (proof of repair costs was more straightforward than proof of the before-and-after values of the leasehold) and that the defaulting party should not benefit by virtue of his default. Other cases have followed the general pattern established in *Joyner.*[53]

There are at least two ways of analyzing cases such as *Groves* and *Joyner*. First, from a contract perspective, all the courts did was to demand strict adherence to the terms of each contract. But this argument overlooks the principle that the courts do not demand strict adherence to the letter of the contract if it would be economically wasteful to do so.[54] In *Joyner* the degree of the difference between the cost of repair and damage to the reversion may not have been great, but it was enormous in *Groves*. The property owner in *Groves* received payment for the use of the quarry. His

---

[51] Groves v. John Wunder Co., 205 Minn. 163, 286 NW 235 (1939). For a discussion of Groves, see ¶ 8.06. But contra see Peevyhouse v. Garland Coal & Mining Co., 382 P2d 109 (Okla. 1962).

[52] Joyner v. Weeks, [1891] 2 QB 31 (CA).

[53] See, e.g., Arbutus Park Estates, Ltd. v. Fuller, 74 DLR (3d) 257 (BC 1976); Samson and Samson, Ltd. v. Proctor [1975] 1 NZLR 655.

[54] Jacob & Youngs, Inc. v. Kent, 230 NY 239, 129 NE 889 (1921). For a discussion of *Jacob & Youngs,* see ¶ 2.02[1].

loss was the damage to the reversion, but the court awarded him several times his loss by requiring the defendant to restore his gain in not paying the cost of reclamation. Of course, it can be argued that the plaintiff would have charged more for the lease or would not have leased the property at all if the defendant had not agreed to the reclamation clause and that his expectancy was a reclaimed reversion.

Nevertheless, the *Joyner* and *Groves* cases are probably better understood from a second line of analysis that focuses on restitution. The point of the damage awards was to make each defendant give up an enrichment he had acquired unjustly. Although the injustice lay in the contract breach and not in the breach of a general public duty, the notion that the defendant got something he should not have was the key to each case.

The common law, however, does not favor results that are economically wasteful or impracticable under the prevailing circumstances. Thus, some English courts have limited the application of *Joyner* to cases in which the plaintiff proves that he has done or will do whatever the defendant has failed to do.[55] Although this approach has met with some criticism,[56] it is an attempt to deal with both the principle of avoiding waste and the principle of restoring the parties in a restitution case to the status quo ante.[57] If the plaintiff holds property simply as an investment and does not plan to do anything with it in the near future, his balance sheet can be made whole by an award that equals the damage to the reversion.[58] On the other hand, his interests may go beyond a balance sheet analysis, and if he intends to make the repairs,

---

[55] See, e.g., Tito v. Waddell (No. 2) [1977] Ch. 106, 332–334; Radford v. DeFroberville [1977] 1 WLR 1262.

[56] See, e.g., Jones 450, 451.

[57] See, e.g., Douthwaite 323, citing, e.g., Lobdell v. Miller, 114 Cal. App. 2d 328, 250 P2d 357 (1952); Bodenhamer v. Patterson, 278 Ore. 367, 563 P2d 1212 (1977).

[58] This is consistent with the limitation in many tort actions to a recovery no greater than the value of the property before the tort, regardless of the cost of repairs. See, e.g., Rutledge v. Glass, 125 Ga. App. 549, 188 SE2d 261 (1972); Darrah v. Womack, 123 Ga. App. 766, 182 SE2d 518 (1971).

he certainly has a good claim for compensation in most circumstances.[59]

Sometimes a party breaches a contract not to save money but to make more money on a better deal. In that event, should the default be treated as a repudiation and the nondefaulting party be allowed to recover the value of the defaultor's gain on the new transaction, or should the nondefaulting party be limited to a normal contract damage recovery? This issue was at the heart of *The Siboen and The Sibotre,*[60] a charter party case. The owner of the two ships withdrew them from a charter party contract with the complainants because the ships could be put into service on another contract at a much more profitable rate of return. The complainants sought to recover the profits made by the defaulting owners on the new contract. In essence, their argument was that the new profits were a form of unjust enrichment. The injustice arose from the contract breach and the owners should have to give up their wrongfully acquired gain. The court, however, rejected this argument and said that the circumstances were a simple case of contract breach and the charterers could be made whole by an award of damages that would compensate them for the difference in cost between the broken contract and a substitute charter party contract plus normal, provable transaction costs. Even though the owners were in breach solely for the purpose of taking a better opportunity, that was not the kind of wrong that was necessary to support a claim of unjust enrichment.

The result in *The Siboen and the Sibotre* was sensible and consistent with the general approach to contract damages traditionally followed by common-law courts. It was certainly consistent with the theory of efficient breach.[61] The owners elected to make a more efficient use of the ships they owned. The law could make the nondefaulting parties whole by awarding them the difference in cost between the breached contract and a substitute contract or the market cost of similar vessels.[62] This was a predictable,

---

[59] That is, if the repairs are of damage to the property. There may be other concerns, as in the *Jacob & Youngs* case, if there is no diminution in objective value but only a subjective desire to use a particular brand of product.

[60] The Siboen & The Sibotre, [1976] 1 LR 293.

[61] See ¶ 7.01.

[62] See ¶ 7.02[1].

reasonably ascertainable risk that the owners could calculate in advance, and this made it possible for them to make an economically rational decision about the use of their vessels. If the court had adopted the complainants' damage theory, the owners would have been punished for an economically efficient decision and would have received a disincentive to the pursuit of the most efficient use of their vessels.

The complainants' damage theory also required the court to conclude that there was something wrong, in a public-law sense, in the contract breach. Arguments have been made that the conscious breach of a contract is morally wrong,[63] and there are cases in which courts have found a breach to be a public wrong because of special circumstances.[64] The overwhelming weight of judicial authority and scholarly comment, however, has been to the contrary.[65] There is no moral wrong and no breach of a public duty involved in the breach of a private, consensual agreement. The defaulting party may be held to his performance or its monetary equivalent, but no more. Thus, in a case such as *The Siboen and The Sibotre,* the defendant clearly gains in the opportunity to reap higher profits, but it is not an unjust gain that requires the intervention of the judicial system.

At first glance, *The Siboen and The Sibotre* may appear to share similarities with cases such as *Joyner* and *Groves*. The latter two cases both involved simple breaches, but the plaintiffs were able to recover the value of the cost savings attributable to the breach. Certainly the courts in *Joyner, Groves,* and similar cases seemed to have been influenced by the notion that the defendants profited from a conscious wrong, and the tenor of the opinions leans toward restitutionary justifications. There is a significant difference, however, in that the awards were related directly to terms of the contracts. The agreement to reclaim the land in *Groves* may

---

[63] See Fried, *Contract as Promise* (1981).

[64] E.g., breach of fiduciary duty, breach of a publicly imposed obligation such as breach by an insurer of an insurance contract, or breach with knowledge that it will cause immediate and undue hardship. For a discussion of cases of this type in which a contract breach is treated as the equivalent of a tort, see Chapter 11.

[65] See generally ¶ 1.03.

have been unwise or inefficient, but it was a freely made agreement. The risk of that cost was a part of the transaction. In comparison, the owners in *The Siboen and The Sibotre* did not make future opportunities a part of the risk allocation in their deal. Their risk was the cost of performing or paying a monetary equivalent to the value of their performance and nothing more.

[4] Contract Price as a Cap on Recovery

Because many restitution cases arise from failed contractual relationships, courts often have to decide whether the contract price should limit the recovery. If the market value of the performance in question is roughly equivalent to the contract price, there is little difficulty. Problems arise when the nondefaulting party is in a bad or losing contract. If he can recover "off" the contract for the market value of his performance, the default by the other party may turn into a windfall for him. The basic policy question is whether courts should respect the private law negotiated by the parties or whether they should treat the contract as a nullity because the defaulting party has repudiated it and assess damages by reference to external standards. On the whole, courts have followed the latter approach even though it seems inconsistent with many of the basic principles of contract law.

The focus of the restitution remedy is to put the defendant in the status quo ante. As Professor Farnsworth has written:

> The objective is not to put the *injured* party in as good a position as he would have been in if the contract had been performed, nor even to put the *injured* party back in the position he would have been in if the contract had not been made; it is rather, to put the party *in breach* back in the position he would have been in if the contract had not been made.[66]

These kinds of cases therefore present two problems. As mentioned, the first is whether the contract should be respected or ignored. The second is whether the remedy simply returns the

---

[66] Farnsworth, *Contracts* 905 (1982) (hereinafter cited as Farnsworth) (emphasis in the original).

defendant to the status quo ante or actually punishes him while providing the plaintiff with a windfall. Consider the three following situations.

> **EXAMPLE 5.** Black, a hunter, builds a small lodge on a tract of mountain property owned by Gray without Gray's knowledge or permission. Black spends $5,000 for materials, pays two laborers $5,000 to help him, and expends time, energy, and resources of his own worth $5,000. His total investment is $15,000. Gray is outraged when she discovers the lodge because to her it is worthless; indeed, it detracts from the property because she planned to use it in its natural state for primitive camping as a refuge from the fast life of the city. Before doing anything, she employs two experts: one advises her that the lodge, as built, enhances the land's value by about $10,000 and the other advises her that the residual salvage value of the materials net of all costs of razing the structure is about $2,000.

> **EXAMPLE 6.** Gray knows that Black is building the lodge on her land, that he owns an adjoining tract, and that he is mistaken about the property line. Despite this knowledge, Gray consciously refuses to tell Black that he is building on the wrong property until Black has finished the lodge.

> **EXAMPLE 7.** Black agrees to build the lodge for Gray for a total contract price of $10,000. Black seriously underestimates the costs involved in transporting materials and obtaining labor for construction in this remote site. When he is about 75 percent finished with the construction and has incurred expenses or provided services worth about $12,000, Gray breaches the contract and tells Black to stop.

In Example 5, Gray owes Black nothing because Black was a trespasser who built at his own risk. There was a benefit conferred on Gray of at least $2,000, but the law will not reward the conscious trespasser. If anything, Gray has an action against Black.

In Example 6, however, Black has a quasi-contract action against Gray because Gray consciously accepted the receipt of a benefit in a context that was not intended to be gratuitous.[67] But what should Black receive? The total value of the materials and labor, or $15,000? The value of the enhancement to the real estate, or $10,000? Some other figure? Because Gray consciously let Black proceed with the project, it can be assumed that she intends to keep the lodge and not to tear it down, so the net salvage value figure may be irrelevant. Gray's balance sheet gain is $10,000. If the only purpose of a restitutionary remedy is to return Gray to her status quo ante, the proper recovery is $10,000. However, that would leave Black with a $5,000 loss. The standard approach in this circumstance is to award the defendant's gain plus an amount sufficient to restore the plaintiff to his status quo ante, in this case a total of $15,000. Courts describe this in terms of awarding the plaintiff the market value of his performance, but in fact it amounts to a combined total of the defendant's gain and the plaintiff's loss. The focus is on what the plaintiff lost, not on what the ultimate value of that performance is to the recipient.[68]

Example 7 is the most difficult situation. If the contract had been fully performed, Black would have been entitled to no more than $10,000 and he would have had to incur a $5,000 loss because of his bad judgment. Furthermore, courts in similar circumstances have consistently held that if Black had completed his performance and Gray breached by refusing to make the contract payment, Black's only action would be for the price.[69] However, Gray breached when 75 percent of the performance was completed. Should Black then get 75 percent of the contract price plus incidental damages or the fair market value of his performance to date

---

[67] The situation might be different if Black were merely a mistaken improver; that is, if he had built the lodge on the wrong property by mistake and without Gray's knowledge. Courts have been reluctant to make the recipients of such mistakenly bestowed benefits pay for them if they cannot be readily returned. See generally Dobbs § 11.5.

[68] On the other hand, if the value of Gray's land was increased by $20,000, Black might argue for a recovery of that amount because Gray's total gain was unjust, regardless of the market value of Black's materials and services. Any windfall should go to the innocent performer rather than to the wrongful beneficiary. Most courts, however, reject this argument and leave Black to his quantum meruit claim.

[69] See, e.g., United States v. Americo Constr. Co., 168 F. Supp. 760 (D. Mass. 1958); Restatement (Second) of Contracts § 373 (1981).

(i.e., 75 percent of $15,000, or $12,000)? Most courts would award Black $12,000, even though that is $2,000 more than he would have received on full performance if no breach had occurred.[70] This also seems to be the approach favored by the second Restatement, although its position is not totally clear.[71]

The justification for going off the contract and awarding damages based on a fair market value analysis is that by breaching the defaulter repudiated the contract, which can no longer be relied on to define the relationship between the parties.[72] The opposing argument is that courts should not ignore the parties' risk allocation and should respect their negotiated transaction. To do otherwise is to ignore the private law the parties created when they first entered into the agreement. As Perillo has noted:

> Restitution for breach is a contractual remedy; consequently, it seems inappropriate to ignore the parties' allocation of the risks. Should a plaintiff who would have lost on the contract receive an amount that not only spares him from further loss

---

[70] In the example, it is obviously economically irrational for Gray to breach because she has a favorable deal, although this sort of case arises surprisingly often. People in Gray's position, for example, may run into financial troubles or have other personal problems. In more complicated construction projects, it may not be clear to either party that the deal is skewed; the imbalance may only become apparent after the fact when the economics of the transaction are scrutinized. From Black's perspective, performing even at a loss may be better than getting the reputation of a defaulter. In addition, if Black has employees on a permanent payroll, some income is better than none.

[71] See Restatement (Second) of Contracts § 373(2) (1981). One of the earlier drafts of the second Restatement rejected this approach and would have set the contract price as a cap on recovery. Tentative draft number 14, § 387(2) (1979). There is some apparent inconsistency between the second Restatement § 373 and comment b to § 374. The latter seems to suggest a contract price cap on recovery in cases of this type. See Perillo 44, 45. See generally 1 Palmer 389. Interestingly, the Reporter for the second Restatement has said that the Restatement is neutral on this issue. Farnsworth 913 n.22.

[72] Leading cases include United States v. Algernon Blair, Inc., 479 F2d 638 (4th Cir. 1973); Scaduto v. Orlando, 381 F2d 587 (2d Cir. 1967); United States ex rel. Susi Contracting Co. v. Zara Contracting Co., 146 F2d 606 (2d Cir. 1944); City of Philadelphia v. Tripple, 230 Pa. 480, 79 A 703 (1911). See Boomer v. Muir, 24 P2d 570 (Cal. Dist. Ct. App. 1933) (contractor recovered $250,000 in restitution even though his contract claim would have amounted to no more than $20,000). For a discussion of what constitutes a total breach that is the equivalent of a repudiation, see Seepersad, "Restitution and Total Failure of Consideration," 123 New LJ 435 (1973).

> but also compensates him as if he had made a profitable bargain? Perhaps, on the erroneous assumption that the restitutionary action is divorced from the contract upon which the performance was based, that a contractual breach necessarily involves fault, or that the defendant is profiting from his own breach if he uses the contract to shield against greater liability. This last thought ignores the fact that the defendant's profit, if any, stems from the parties' bargain and not from any subsequent wrongdoing.[73]

This entire approach seems even more anomalous if a defaulting party has been making installment payments. The breach then is not of the whole contract, but only of the executory promise to continue installments until the project is complete. The restitutionary off the contract approach may be of significant value in a complex situation where it is difficult to predict with any degree of certainty the expectancy of the nonbreaching party and where the calculation of actual reliance expenses to date may be time-consuming and complicated. Restitution in such a case may be a useful shorthand approach to providing a reliance cost recovery while casting any doubts in favor of the nonbreaching party and against the defaulter.[74] Beyond that, there really is little reason to maintain the fiction of a breach/repudiation scenario that allows a court to ignore a negotiated contract in favor of a remedy that has its roots in the duty to do justice in a general, public sense where there has been a wrongful taking or retention of a benefit. A few courts have adopted this view and have looked to the contract price as a limitation on recovery.[75]

When the sides are reversed, these kinds of cases are especially interesting. In Example 7, if Black had breached, Gray could have sued for the difference in the contract price and the cost of getting the job completed by someone else.[76] Thus, Black would have been liable to Gray for the market value of goods and services necessary to compete the project in excess of the contract price. There is a great difference in the recoveries for the two different

---

[73] Perillo 44, 45.

[74] See, e.g., Farnsworth 909–913.

[75] See, e.g., Johnson v. Bovee, 40 Colo. App. 317, 574 P2d 513 (1978); Wuchter v. Fitzgerald, 83 Ore. 672, 163 P 819 (1917).

[76] See ¶ 4.06.

breaches. If Gray defaults, Black can recover from Gray whatever is necessary to give him a total payment of $12,000. This is $4,500 more than 75 percent of the contract price. If Black breaches at a similar point, Gray can recover only $1,250. The formula for calculating the recovery is as follows: The total market value of the materials and labor is $15,000, and 25 percent of the project remains to be built. The market value of the materials and labor for the remainder should be 0.25 × $15,000, or $3,750. If Gray has paid Black for the work to the date of the breach, she has spent $7,500, and she now must spend another $3,750 for a total of $11,250, or $1,250 more than she bargained for. Her recovery, therefore, is $1,250, which gives her exactly her bargain, a completed lodge for a net cost of $10,000.

The result is obvious: The more work that Black does, the less is his risk of liability exposure on a breach to Gray, but the loss he actually suffers increases. That is, if he breaches before starting, his exposure is $5,000. If he breaches almost at the end of the performance, his liability exposure to Gray is negligible, but he has already absorbed most of the $5,000 loss. The opposite holds true for Gray. The more that Black does, the greater her possible exposure for additional payments if she breaches. If Gray waits until Black finishes, her liability is no more than the contract.

[5] Contracts Unenforceable by Reason of the Statute of Frauds

Although the statute of frauds is easy to satisfy,[77] contracts occasionally run afoul of its provisions. If there has been performance and the conferral of a benefit, should the complaining party be able to obtain relief in restitution when relief in contract is barred by the statute of frauds? The cases are far from consistent.

The general rule is that restitution is not available when performance is complete and all that remains is the payment of the contract price by the recipient of the performance. If a contract

[77] The purpose of the Statute of Frauds is to make the parties reduce to writing their agreements on certain kinds of transactions, such as land sales contracts or contracts that cannot be completed within one year. The writing requirement can be easily satisfied, however, and there are numerous exceptions to the full influence of the Statute. See, e.g., Crabtree v. Elizabeth Arden Sales Corp., 305 NY 48, 110 NE2d 551 (1953).

action is barred because of the statute of frauds, the question is whether this rule should apply. Fortunately, the problem is simple in many such cases because full performance removes the cases from provisions of the statute of frauds. This is generally true for contracts that cannot be fully performed in a year and contracts for the sale of chattels or real estate.[78] The complainant thus has a cause of action in contract, and, presumably, in restitution if the context supports the alternative theory. If the action in contract is barred, however, it seems only fair for the party who has fully performed to have some remedy, and restitution should be available.[79]

The purpose of the statute of frauds is to prevent overreaching, deceit, and similar problems in the negotiation and formation of an agreement. Its purpose is not to prevent a fair recovery for the value of services performed and accepted. Indeed, it is contrary to the underlying purpose of the statute of frauds to employ it as a shield against liability for a nongratuitous benefit.

The same reasoning should apply to partial performance cases, even though the statute may be fully in force. The issue of the availability of restitution arises outside the framework of contract.[80] Whether there is a cause of action in restitution should not depend on whether there is a cause of action in contract because of a technical question.[81]

¶ 9.03 RESTITUTION AGAINST THE FEDERAL GOVERNMENT

The court of claims has jurisdiction over contract claims against the United States, whether the claims arise from express or

[78] See generally Farnsworth § 6.9, at 420–425.

[79] In support of this point, see Farnsworth 914; see also 2 Palmer § 6.4; Restatement (Second) of Contracts § 375 comment b (1981).

[80] See, e.g., Douthwaite § 8.2, at 330, 331; Jeanblanc, "Restitution Under the Statute of Frauds: Measurement of the Legal Benefit Unjustly Retained," 15 Mo. L. Rev. 1 (1950); Jeanblanc, "Restitution Under the Statute of Frauds: What Constitutes A Legal Benefit," 26 Ind. LJ 1 (1950).

[81] This does not mean that the contract question should be ignored. It may be that policy should require the enforcement of a contract rather than the use of restitution or that the contract should set some limits on the damages available.

implied-in-fact contracts.[82] The federal district courts share concurrent jurisdiction over claims that meet jurisdictional amount requirements.[83] The jurisdiction of these courts derives from explicit statutory waivers of sovereign immunity. The courts have consistently read these statutes as waivers of immunity only for express or implied-in-fact contracts and not for quasi-contracts.[84] Nevertheless, there are a few exceptions. Restitution may be appropriate where there is a mutual mistake[85] or when the United States has committed a "material breach."[86] In addition, the courts have sometimes stretched the facts to create an implied-in-fact contract when there is nothing more than a quasi-contract.[87]

---

[82] 28 USC § 1491 (Supp. 1981).

[83] 28 USC § 1346(a)(2) (Supp. 1981).

[84] See, e.g., Algonac Mfg. Co. v. United States, 192 Ct. Cl. 649, 428 F2d 1241 (1970).

[85] Chris Berg, Inc. v. United States, 192 Ct. Cl. 176, 426 F2d 314 (1970).

[86] Acme Process Equip. Co. v. United States, 171 Ct. Cl. 324, 347 F2d 509 (1965), rev'd on other grounds, 385 US 138 (1966).

[87] See Thompson & Sebert, *Remedies: Damages, Equity and Restitution* 4-57, 4-58 (1983); Wall & Childres 587.

CHAPTER 10

Agreed Remedies for Breach

¶ 10.01 PRIVATE POWER VS. PUBLIC POLICY: PREDETERMINATION OF DAMAGES AND REMEDIES

If the theory of freedom of contract is carried to its logical conclusion, it seems reasonable that the parties to a private agreement should be able to determine the sanctions that follow from a breach as well as the scope of the agreement itself. When two parties negotiate a contract, one of their greatest interests is to allocate risks rationally. Predictability is an important factor in risk allocation: A party wants to know not only what his risk is but how likely he is to incur it and under what circumstances it is probable. However, if the resolution of disputes on breach is left entirely up to the public judicial process, there is always an element of uncertainty. Even where the remedial rules are simple, there is always the unknown risk of a third-party review by a judge or a jury. The parties to a contract can reduce this uncertainty by deciding upon remedies in advance.

Nevertheless, courts have consistently limited the power of contracting parties to decide in advance the types of remedies that will be awarded if a breach occurs. The reasons for this policy all relate to the basic power of contracting partners to affect the public-law aspects of their private agreements. Although contract law is the quintessential private law, the enforcement of sanctions against a breaching party brings into play the entire power of the state and thus is replete with public-law implications. Courts are reluctant to allow private parties to intrude too far into the domain of judges and legislators.

Three common measures are used in contracts to determine in advance either the nature of the remedy that will be available to a nondefaulting party or the procedure for settling a dispute. The first is a liquidated damage clause, which is a mechanism used to calculate damages when the injury is difficult to measure or the damages are uncertain. These contract clauses may have a penal or in terrorem effect, and if they do, they are rarely enforced. A second means to limit risks involves the use of exclusions and limitations on remedies. Exclusion and limitation clauses reduce the possibility of risk by excluding certain kinds of damages, such as consequentials, from the available catalog of remedies. Finally, the contracting parties may wish to avoid the costs and problems of litigation by submitting their disputes to arbitration.

In principle, courts enforce these agreements as they enforce other provisions of a contract, subject to limitations imposed by law or public policy. However, courts are often unwilling to enforce privately agreed remedial claims if they are substantially different from those the court would itself consider without a remedial provision in the contract. This reluctance is most evident in liquidated damage clause cases, where the old common-law principle against the enforcement of forfeiture or penalty clauses continues to be influential. The courts also display a concern for substantive fairness measured by external standards in cases involving limitations on remedies, such as the exclusion of consequential damages. Interestingly, the courts look favorably on arbitration clauses, and state and federal law generally encourages the use of arbitration as a procedure to resolve disputes. In fact, courts allow arbitrators to award remedies that they themselves would not award and probably would not enforce if the parties included them in a remedial clause in their contract. Although this deference to arbitrators may seem anomalous, it is consistent with the common-law tradition of leaving matters of private agreement to private parties. The courts are hesitant only when a party directly calls upon the judicial authority to aid in enforcing a private agreement or when arbitrators make awards that exceed the awards normally available in judicial proceedings. Once again, the issue is the balance between private power and public policy.

¶ 10.02 LIQUIDATED DAMAGE CLAUSES

[1] Judicial Criteria of Enforceability

The principal purpose of a liquidated damage clause is to avoid the problem of calculating damages after there has been a dispute between parties to a contract. The use of such clauses in a contract serves the goals of efficiency and predictability and makes it easier for a party to balance the anticipated costs of performance against the risk exposure of breach. Despite the fact that the parties may agree to the use of liquidated damage clauses and their undeniable efficiency in the context of individual circumstances, these clauses have never been favored by courts. Older common-law decisions were almost invariably hostile, because courts considered liquidated damage provisions to be the same as penalties.[1]

The rule against the enforcement of penalty clauses originated in equity as a means to deal with unfairness and overreaching in the bargaining process and was later carried over into the law courts.[2] The English approach crossed the Atlantic and was adopted, with some modifications, by all American jurisdictions except Louisiana, which has remained true to its civil-law tradition by not sharing the common-law hostility to liquidated damage clauses.[3] More recently, courts have reluctantly begun to enforce liquidated damage clauses. The tests they apply to determine whether a particular clause is worthy of enforcement or whether it is an unenforceable penalty that results in unfair overcompensation reflect the judicial hesitance to approve liquidated damage clauses.[4] The standard test applies three criteria. First, the parties must have intended the clause to be a means to calculate damages, not a penalty or forfeiture. Second, the contract must be one in which it will be difficult to calculate damages or in which it was impossible to preestimate damages with any certainty at the time of contracting. Third, damages figured according to the damage clause in the contract must be reasonable in terms of what they would be if they were measured by the standard rules of common law.[5] This last criterion is by far

---

[1] See Note, "Liquidated Damages Recovery Under the Restatement (Second) of Contracts," 67 Cornell L. Rev. 862 (1982) (hereinafter cited as Note, "Liquidated Damages Recovery"); Note, "Penalties and Damages," 92 LQ Rev. 20 (1976) (hereinafter cited as Note, "Penalties and Damages"). Liquidated damage clauses must be distinguished from penal bonds, which have an altogether different history. Today they usually arise in connection with public works contracts in which a substantial public interest raises policy questions different from those involved in private agreements. For a historical study of the penal bond, see, e.g., Loyd, "Penalties and Forfeitures," 29 Harv. L. Rev. 117 (1915).

[2] Calamari & Perillo, *Contracts* § 14-31, at 564 (2d ed. 1977) (hereinafter cited as Calamari & Perillo). See, e.g., Lowe v. Peers (1768) 4 Burr. 2225, discussed in Note, "Penalties and Damages" 21.

[3] See Pembroke v. Gulf Oil Corp., 454 F2d 606 (5th Cir. 1971) and see Lowry, "Penalty Clauses and Breach of Contract," 131 The New LJ 306 (1981) (hereinafter cited as Lowry).

[4] Some of the discussions in the cases are similar to those in the opinions that refuse to award punitive damages for breaches of contract. The purpose is to compensate, not to punish the defendant and reward the plaintiff. For a discussion of punitive damages, see ¶ 11.03.

[5] Calamari & Perillo 565.

the most important of the three. Courts simply do not enforce agreements that provide for damages that are grossly out of line with what the law provides, especially if the value of the contract remedy is higher.[6]

The court's decision in the Ohio case of *Welch v. K-Beck Furniture Mart, Inc.*[7] illustrates the emphasis it placed on the reasonableness factor:

> Damages for breach by either party may be liquidated in the agreement but only at an amount which is reasonable in the light of the anticipated or actual harm caused by the breach, the difficulties of proof of loss and the inconvenience or non-feasibility of otherwise obtaining an adequate remedy. A term fixing unreasonably large liquidated damages is void as a penalty.[8]

Welch also provides a good example of the general principle of fairness at work. Welch bought a set of furniture on a layaway plan. The retail installment sales contract he signed provided that he had to pay about 40 percent of the total purchase price before he was entitled to possession. A default by Welch in any payment triggered a forfeiture of all payments made to date and discharged the furniture store from any further obligation to perform. Welch paid $413 on a total purchase price of $1,763 and then defaulted. The furniture store kept his money and all the furniture pursuant to the terms of the contract. The court intervened and said that the forfeiture clause was an unenforceable penalty because it had no substantial relation to the actual damages suffered by the store as a consequence of Welch's breach.[9]

---

[6] Id. at 566. See Simpson, *Contracts* § 198, at 399–401 (2d ed. 1965); Burnham, "Contract Damages in Montana Part I: Expectancy Damages," 44 Mont. L. Rev. 41–42 (1983).

[7] Welch v. K-Beck Furniture Mart, Inc., 3 Ohio App. 3d 171, 444 NE2d 48 (1981).

[8] Id. at 49. The court indicated that reasonableness could be judged either as of the time of contracting or as of the time of breach. The older rule was that the time for considering reasonableness was the time of contracting, but the UCC and the second Restatement both suggest that the time of breach is also appropriate.

[9] Welch v. K-Beck Furniture Mart, 3 Ohio App. 3d 171, 444 NE2d 48, 50 (1981).

[2] UCC Criteria of Enforceability

The UCC follows the pattern of the common law. Section 2-718 establishes a three-part test for the validity of liquidated damage clauses. There are, however, some significant differences between the common-law tests and the UCC approach. Under the UCC, a liquidated damage clause is valid if the amount stipulated is reasonable in light of the actual damages suffered, if the problems of proof are difficult, and if the plaintiff would otherwise find himself without an adequate remedy.[10] The UCC does not consider the intent of the parties; rather, the focus is on an objective determination of the reasonableness of the remedy and its use as a substitute for normal rules of damage determination. In this sense the UCC and the common-law approaches are similar. The problem is in deciding whether the remedy that the parties have agreed upon is fair or reasonable in light of what public law would otherwise impose upon the breaching party. There is a critical difference in timing between the two approaches. Common-law courts usually look at the time of contracting to determine fairness unless the

---

[10] Section 2-718 states:

"(1) Damages for breach by either party may be liquidated in the agreement but only at an amount which is reasonable in the light of the anticipated or actual harm caused by the breach, the difficulties of proof of loss, and the inconvenience or nonfeasibility of otherwise obtaining an adequate remedy. A term fixing unreasonably large liquidated damages is void as a penalty.
(2) Where the seller justifiably withholds delivery of goods because of the buyer's breach, the buyer is entitled to restitution of any amount by which the sum of his payments exceeds

(a) the amount to which the seller is entitled by virtue of terms liquidating the seller's damages in accordance with subsection (1), or

(b) in the absence of such terms, twenty percent of the value of the total performance for which the buyer is obligated under the contract or $500, whichever is smaller.

(3) The buyer's right to restitution under subsection (2) is subject to offset to the extent that the seller establishes

(a) a right to recover damages under the provisions of this Article other than subsection (1), and

(b) the amount or value of any benefits received by the buyer directly or indirectly by reason of the contract.

(4) Where a seller has received payment in goods their reasonable value or the proceeds of their resale shall be treated as payments for the purposes of subsection (2); but if the seller has notice of the buyer's breach before reselling goods received in part performance, his resale is subject to the conditions laid down in this Article on resale by an aggrieved seller (Section 2-706)."

contract damages are so grossly disproportionate to those that would otherwise be awarded that the clause is unconscionable. The UCC, however, allows the court to examine fairness both at the time of contracting and at the time of breach. A figure for damages that may have seemed too high when the agreement was reached may be valid if it reasonably approximates damages when breach occurs.[11]

[3] Standard of Reasonability

Whether a case arises under the UCC or is simply an ordinary common-law contract case, the only significant question is the relationship between the damages that would be awarded without a liquidated damage clause and the damages that such a clause provides. Although courts may from time to time discuss other issues, the only one that consistently seems to make a difference is the issue of reasonableness. Even then, it is more often than not reasonableness from the perspective of the party in breach than from the perspective of the plaintiff. For instance, a clause that provides for damages that exceed what the law would normally allow is often struck down as an unenforceable penalty, but a clause that provides for less than the law would allow is often upheld.[12] Of course, there are some limits. If the damages calculated according to the contract are extremely low, the clause may be struck as an unconscionable attempt to limit remedies.[13]

[4] Standard of Express Agreement

The question of what constitutes a reasonable attempt to determine and to fix damages is essentially factual and is normally established case by case. The courts have discussed a few guidelines that at least provide a clue to the enforceability of a particular contract provision.

---

[11] See generally 3 *Hawkland UCC Series* § 2-718:01-04, at 425–431 (1982) (hereinafter cited as Hawkland).

[12] See, e.g., Widnes Foundry, Ltd. v. Cellulose Acetate Silk Co. [1931] 2 KB 393 (on appeal [1933] AC 20); Note, "Penalties and Damages," 20, 24, 25 (1976).

[13] Hawkland § 2-718:02, at 428.

A common statement in cases at common law is that both parties must expressly agree to a liquidated damage clause before it is enforceable.[14] In effect, this says little more than that courts are careful about what may appear to be adhesion contracts or agreements that involve questionable negotiation procedures. In this sense, liquidated damage provisions are not treated any differently from any other substantive portions of a contract, although there may be somewhat more solicitude for a party who seeks to avoid the clause because of the traditional hostility to such provisions. Occasionally, a judge refuses to enforce a damage clause in the contract because he decides that actual damages are easy to prove with certainty.[15] More often than not, there is some other good reason for not giving effect to the parties' agreement, such as disproportion between the agreed damages and the actual damages, but if the actual injury is simple to prove, then one of the justifications for a liquidated damage clause is absent.

[5] Standard of Compensation for vs. Deterrence of Breach

A flat fee that is akin to a fine for the breach of a covenant within an agreement may be unenforceable as a penalty if the court decides that its purpose was to deter a breach rather than to compensate the nonbreaching party for costs incurred as a result of a breach. The Supreme Court of Mississippi refused to enforce a rule in the articles of association of a trade group that imposed a monetary fine on members who violated the rules. The court reasoned that the fine was a deterrent in the nature of a punishment and was not related to any actual injury suffered by the association or its members as a result of one member breaking a rule.[16] For essentially the same reasons, the California Supreme Court invalidated a late-charge provision in a loan agreement. The court said that the

---

[14] See, e.g., Dessert Seed Co. v. Drew Farmers Supply, Inc., 248 Ark. 858, 454 SW2d 307 (1970).

[15] See, e.g., Lee Oldsmobile, Inc. v. Kaiden, 32 Md. App. 556, 363 A2d 270 (1976).

[16] Continental Turpentine & Rosin Co. v. Gulf Naval Stores Co., 244 Miss. 465, 142 So. 2d 200 (1962).

purpose was to coerce timely payments, not to compensate the lender for costs associated with missed or late payments.[17]

Late-charge provisions do not always fare so poorly, however. In *Grumman Flxible Corp. v. City of Long Beach,*[18] a federal court applying New York law upheld a late fee of $35 per bus per day for delinquent payments on a bus order. The court decided that the late fee served the dual purpose of compensating the seller/lender for lost interest on the delinquent payments and for other "risks attendant to late receipt of the purchase price."[19] In another New York case, the appeals court considered a provision in a sales contract that required the defaulting buyer to pay attorneys' fees to the seller in an amount equal to 30 percent of the face amount of the contract. Although the court remanded the case for further findings on whether the 30 percent figure was reasonably related to the actual damages likely to be suffered by the seller, it did not consider the fee to be unenforceable on its face.[20]

A case from North Carolina, *Knutton v. Cofield,*[21] and one from Texas, *Speedi Lubrication Centers, Inc. v. Atlas Match Corp.,*[22] illustrate the most common problem of trying to relate actual damages to those figured in accordance with the contract. Speedi Lubrication ordered a substantial number of matchbook covers from Atlas Match. The contract provided that the buyer would pay liquidated damages in the amount of 50 percent of the contract price for matchbook covers ordered but not paid for. Even though the seller could retain the goods that the buyer ordered but did not pay for, the damage fee was reasonable; matchbook covers imprinted with Speedi Lubrication's logo are not valuable to anyone else. *Knutton* involved a jukebox instead of matchbook covers, but the result was similar. The plaintiff placed a jukebox in the

---

[17] Garrett v. Coast & S. Fed. Sav. & Loan Ass'n, 9 Cal. 3d 731, 511 P2d 1197, 108 Cal. Rptr. 845 (1973).

[18] Grumman Flxible Corp. v. City of Long Beach, 505 F. Supp. 623, 626 (EDNY 1980).

[19] Id.

[20] Equitable Lumber Corp. v. IPA Land Dev. Corp., 38 NY2d 516, 344 NE2d 391, 381 NYS2d 459 (1976).

[21] Knutton v. Cofield, 273 NC 355, 160 SE2d 29 (1968).

[22] Speedi Lubrication Centers, Inc. v. Atlas Match Corp., 595 SW2d 912 (Tex. Civ. App. 1980).

defendant's restaurant, and the parties agreed to split the gross receipts fifty/fifty over a rental term of five years. After seventy-two weeks, the defendant unplugged the plaintiff's machine and installed another that belonged to a competitor. The plaintiff successfully invoked a liquidated damage clause that provided him with a recovery equal to the number of weeks remaining on the original term (188) times the average weekly receipts for the weeks elapsed divided by two.

These two cases illustrate both courts' general concern with the reasonableness and fairness principles and the utility of a carefully drawn liquidated damage clause. In *Speedi Lubrication Centers,* the seller could have sued the buyer for the purchase price less the salvage value of the matchbooks or the difference in value between the contract and any cover the seller might have been able to effect. The 50 percent of contract price figure avoided any concern with overcompensation in terms of the original agreement and also took into account the mitigation principle and the possibility of a cover contract, however remote the possibility might have been for the plaintiff. In *Knutton,* the formula used reflected the common-law rule for calculating damages in similar cases, and sufficient data existed from which to make a reasonable projection of future earnings from the jukebox. A question of mitigation could have arisen in *Knutton;* the plaintiff could have removed the jukebox and placed it somewhere else. There could also have been some concern about the length of the projections (188 weeks) in relation to the time elapsed to breach (72 weeks). These concerns, however, were probably overcome by the simplicity and certainty of the formula, and the court did not address the mitigation and speculation issues. In both cases, the contract terms made it possible to avoid litigation about damages with all the attendant problems of proof and time costs. Efficiency and certainty are certainly two of the strongest reasons for enforcing an agreed-upon formula for the calculation of damages.

The North Carolina and Texas courts probably took into account the fact that the parties were commercial entities that could reasonably be expected to possess the business knowledge to watch out for their own interests. There might have been greater concern for the protection of the defendant if he had been a consumer who had not negotiated the terms of the contract but who simply had accepted them as presented. The principles of fairness used to protect consumers, however, are applied in the commercial arena if a court decides that a provision is substantively unconscionable and is not to be sanctioned by the state, no matter what the parties may have agreed and no matter who or what they are.[23]

[6] Validity as Exclusive Remedies and Absent Damages

Two additional interesting questions arise in liquidated damage cases: First, is the clause meant to be the exclusive remedy? Second, can the clause ever be enforced if there is no actual damage although a breach clearly occurs? In answer to the first question, if the parties take the time and expend the effort to negotiate a damage clause, it is not unreasonable to assume that they intended it to provide the remedy for a breach and that they wanted to avoid the uncertainties of leaving their respective remedies to the judgment of a court or a jury. Partly from a continuing hostility to remedies clauses[24] and partly from a desire to ensure that there is no substantive unfairness, courts have more often than not held liquidated damage clauses to be optional and not exclusive remedies.[25] This means that there is often little substance to a liquidated damage clause unless both parties agree about its purpose and effect. If the clause is optional, the plaintiff can simply decide which offers him the better chance for a good recovery — the common law (or the UCC, if applicable) or the contract itself. This does not mean that the plaintiff has the upper hand, because the damage clause in the contract will not be enforced if it substantially overcompensates him.

The second question of whether a damage clause is valid if there has been no damage brings into play the issue of reasonableness. Many older cases refused to consider the question of actual harm because the time for testing the validity of a clause was at the

---

[23] See, e.g., Hertz Commercial Leasing Corp. v. Dynatron, Inc., 37 Conn. Supp. 7, 427 A2d 872 (1980).

[24] For a more general discussion of limitations on remedies, see ¶ 7.03.

[25] See, e.g., Ralston Purina Co. v. Hartford Accident & Indem. Co., 540 F2d 915 (8th Cir. 1976).

time of contracting, not at the time of breach.[26] One of the leading cases setting forth what is known as the no-harm rule was *McCarthy v. Tally,*[27] decided by the California Supreme Court in 1955. When *Tally* was decided, California statutory law imposed two requirements on liquidated damage clauses: First, at the time of contracting it must have been difficult to preestimate damages with any degree of certainty, and second, the parties must have intended the damages formula in the contract to be a reasonable estimate of compensation for loss to the nonbreaching party and must not have intended that the clause have the deterrent effect of a penalty.[28] The court held that no evidence of the absence of loss at the time of breach should be considered because the time for determining the validity of the contract provision was the time at which the parties entered into the agreement. If it met the test of reasonableness at the time of contracting the clause was valid, notwithstanding the fact that there was no actual injury upon a breach. The same problem cannot arise in a UCC case because Section 2-718 expressly provides that the reasonableness of a liquidated damage clause is to be considered both at the time of contracting and at the time of breach.[29]

The modern version of the no-harm rule developed from several government contract cases. The best known is *United States v. Bethlehem Steel Co.,* decided by the United States Supreme Court in 1907.[30] Bethlehem Steel agreed to build gun carriages for the Spanish-American War, and the contract provided that Bethlehem would pay a fee of $35 per day per gun carriage for each day of delay in delivering the carriages. The war was over before the first performance was due, and although Bethlehem was late in performing it argued that it should not have to pay the late fee because the government suffered no harm; the war had ended and there was no pressing need for the gun carriages. Nevertheless, the Supreme Court upheld the penalty clause and justified its decision in an

---

[26] Note, "Liquidated Damages Recovery" 862, 867 n.38.

[27] McCarthy v. Tally, 46 Cal. 2d 577, 297 P2d 981 (1955).

[28] Cal. Civil Code, §§ 1670, 1671 (West 1955); Comment, "Liquidated Damages and the 'No Harm Rule,' " 9 Stan. L. Rev. 381 (1957).

[29] See Note, "Liquidated Damages Recovery" 862, 871, 872.

[30] United States v. Bethlehem Steel Corp., 205 US 105 (1907).

opinion that reflected its great concern at the time for the concept of freedom of contract. However, *Bethlehem Steel* is not a good precedent for private contracts. It involved a government contract entered into in wartime for war supplies, thus creating a high level of concern for the public interest that would not exist in a usual private agreement. In fact, decisions in similar government contract cases have not always been consistent, and defendants have sometimes been allowed to introduce evidence showing the absence of actual injury.[31]

The first Restatement of Contracts was somewhat unclear about the no-harm issue. The black-letter provision stated that the validity of a liquidated damage clause was to be determined as of the time of contracting.[32] This meant that the provision might be enforced even if there was no damage as long as it was a reasonable preestimate of damages at the time of contracting and was not unconscionable. The comments to the black letter, however, added a note of ambiguity. Comment e to Section 339 indicated that evidence showing the absence of harm should be admissible and that in the absence of injury, a liquidated damage clause should not be enforced. Courts have decided in both ways. Some followed the black letter and tested the validity of liquidated damage provisions as of the time of contracting, while others relied on the reasoning of the comment to allow defendants to introduce evidence showing no harm.[33]

The second Restatement tries to solve the ambiguity problem by adopting the language of the UCC. It provides that the parties may agree on "an amount that is reasonable in the light of the anticipated or actual loss caused by the breach and the difficulties of proof of loss."[34] This approach makes a great deal of sense because it takes into account the fallibility of the parties' projections. Although there is less certainty than with a rule that sets one

---

[31] Compare Massman Constr. Co. v. City Council of Greenville, 147 F2d 925 (5th Cir. 1945) (penalty clause voided because no harm from delay) with Bethlehem Steel Corp. v. City of Chicago, 350 F2d 649 (7th Cir. 1965) (penalty clause enforced; absence of damage irrelevant).

[32] Restatement of Contracts § 339 (1932).

[33] See Note, "Liquidated Damages Recovery" 869, 870.

[34] Restatement (Second) of Contracts § 356 (1981).

time for testing the reasonableness of a provision, allowing the parties to introduce evidence of reasonableness both at the time of contracting and at the time of breach serves the purposes of the principles of fairness and of compensatory damages. Because it avoids the anomaly of rewarding the plaintiff when the defendant's breach has not caused any damage, it is also consistent with the long-established rule against the enforcement of purely penal clauses.

The determination of the enforceability of a liquidated damage clause is generally a matter for a judge, not for a jury.[35] Despite the necessity of a case-by-case factual analysis, judges can generally decide the question with reasonable alacrity and efficiency. There is not a wide range of results in cases of this sort, which one might expect from jury considerations of varying circumstances.

[7] Debate Among Commentators: Are Liquidated Damage Clauses Enforceable?

There has not been a large number of liquidated damage clause cases, at least in comparison with cases that involve other issues of contract interpretation and application. This is probably the result of two factors. First, if the parties have truly agreed to a remedy in advance, their contracting purpose is served by adhering to that agreement without involving the courts. Second, the reluctance of common-law courts to enforce remedial clauses no doubt has deterred many potential litigants from even raising the issue. Leaving aside the question of unconscionability, there has been nonetheless a fair amount of academic comment on the enforceability of liquidated damage clauses. Freedom of contract should support the power of the parties to agree to whatever provisions they want, as long as they are not fraudulent or illegal, but even while repeating the importance of freedom of contract courts have struck down liquidated damage clauses because they do not comport with the courts' own determinations of appropriate damages. Is there an anomaly, or is the reluctance to enforce such clauses consistent with the general principles underlying the common law of private

---

[35] See, e.g., Pasquale Food Co. v. L&H Int'l Airmotive, Inc., 51 Ala. App. 127, 283 So. 2d 438 (1973).

agreement? This is the specific question that has intrigued several scholars.

In a leading article on the topic, Professors Goetz and Scott argued that the presumption should favor the enforcement of liquidated damage clauses.[36] Giving effect to the parties' allocation of risks and choice of remedies would promote efficiency, and problems of unfairness or aberrations in the bargaining process could be handled adequately through the doctrine of unconscionability. The Goetz and Scott thesis was based on two assumptions. First, the parties' choice of a liquidated damage clause is evidence that they consider the costs of negotiation to be less than the expected costs of litigation upon a breach. Second, by agreeing upon a remedy in advance, the parties minimize the "error costs" to the promisee who might otherwise be unable to recover "non-provable idiosyncratic value." That is, the promisee who has no measureable injury may be able to protect his subjective interests through prior negotiation of a remedy, and this promotes efficiency in the contracting process.[37] Other commentators have reached similar conclusions but have based their arguments on a more straightforward application of the concept of freedom of contract — if the parties agree to a provision after fair negotiation and it is not illegal, courts should not disturb their private allocation of risk.[38] The most compelling point made by these commentators is that damage provisions reduce the time and complexity of litigation and thus benefit other users of the courts as well as the litigants themselves.

There have been just as many articles taking the opposite position and generally supporting the common-law and UCC rules. One of the arguments in support of the limited enforceability of remedy clauses seems at first to be a bootstrap argument — because the presumption against such clauses has been in use for a long time and has been consistently applied by common-law

---

[36] Goetz & Scott, "Liquidated Damages, Penalties and the Just Compensation Principle: Some Notes on an Enforcement Model and a Theory of Efficient Breach," 77 Colum. L. Rev. 554 (1977) (hereinafter cited as Goetz & Scott).

[37] Goetz & Scott 578.

[38] See, e.g., Beale, *Remedies for Breach of Contract* 52–62 (1980); Lowry 306, 307; Sweet, "Liquidated Damages in California," 60 Calif. L. Rev. 84, 89, 145 (1972); Note, "A Critique of the Penalty Limitation on Liquidated Damages," 50 S. Cal. L. Rev. 1055 (1977).

courts, it must make sense. Although this argument may not seem to prove much, it cannot be dismissed out of hand. There is some merit to the suggestion that if a rule were clearly inefficient the common-law courts would have dismissed it or modified it years ago.[39] Instead, court after court in jurisdictions throughout the United States and the British Commonwealth has consistently limited the enforceability of liquidated damage clauses to those that do not overcompensate the plaintiff and do not have any earmarks of substantive or procedural unfairness.

In a thoughtful essay, Professor Rubin argued that the common-law courts have been correct in maintaining that the rule against the enforcement of liquidated damage clauses that are substantially different from ordinary remedies is efficient, contrary to the thesis of Professors Goetz and Scott.[40] Rubin argued that the interests of third parties as well as those of the contracting principals must be taken into account in determining efficiency. In normal situations, the rules for calculating damages should result in a rough equivalence between the costs of breach and the costs of performance to the promisor. Similarly, the promisee should be in the same economic position after a damage recovery that he would have been in after full performance. Although the dynamics of the marketplace make a consistent result impossible, there is an attempt at symmetry. There is neither a reward for performance nor a punishment for nonperformance beyond the limits of the contract itself. Neither party has an incentive to breach, to perform, or to retard performance greater than that of the other party, except in situations in which there is a significant unexpected change in market conditions or in the condition of one of the parties.[41]

Rubin argued that liquidated damage clauses that provide remedies substantially different from those provided by the common

---

[39] See, e.g., Clarkson, Miller, & Muris, "Liquidated Damages v. Penalties: Sense or Nonsense?" 1978 Wis. L. Rev. 351, 390 (1978).

[40] Rubin, "Unenforceable Contracts: Penalty Clauses and Specific Performance," 10 J. Legal Studies 237 (1981) (hereinafter cited as Rubin).

[41] For a good discussion of just such a situation, see Note, 53 NCL Rev. 579 (1975) (discussing the cotton market in North Carolina in 1973 when prices tripled between the time farmers entered into futures contracts for their crops and the time of harvest).

law skew the balance between the costs of performance and breach. If the damage clause sets a high figure, the promisee has an incentive to seek a breach either by making it difficult for the promisor to perform (although the promisor may be able to invoke the doctrine of good faith) or by challenging the quality of performance in a lawsuit.[42] By the same token, if the remedy is excessive, the promisor may perform when nonperformance would be more efficient in a situation in which he might have chosen to breach if the common-law rule of damage calculation were to apply. The same kinds of problems would result if the contract remedy were lower than the common-law remedy. The promisor would have an additional incentive to breach, and the promisee might be compelled to seek judicial assistance to prevent a breach or might make inefficient concessions as an inducement for performance. By refusing to enforce contract provisions that are unreasonably disproportionate to normal contract recoveries under the common law, Rubin argues that courts reestablish symmetry and minimize the possibilities of additional litigation.[43]

Professor MacNeil reached the same conclusion as Rubin in a seminal article published in 1962,[44] but for substantially different reasons. He distinguished two aspects of freedom of contract. The first is freedom from restraint in the bargaining process. Parties are free to negotiate and agree upon whatever they want. The second is the power of contract, which involves the ability to enforce an agreement by calling upon the state to apply its sanctions to the recalcitrant party.[45] When a party seeks the assistance of the state in enforcing a private agreement, the state has the authority to determine the extent to which it will exercise its power. It is not a matter for the parties to decide. Thus, a court will not enforce an agreement that is illegal (a contract to fix prices) or that is against public policy (a racially restrictive covenant in a deed). When a court does enforce an agreement, there is an implied statement that

---

[42] Rubin 237.

[43] See also Telser, "A Theory of Self-Enforcing Agreements," 53 J. Bus. L. 27 (1980).

[44] MacNeil, "Power of Contract and Agreed Remedies," 47 Cornell LQ 495–506 (1962) (hereinafter cited as MacNeil).

[45] Id.

the agreement and the remedy are consistent with law and policy and are entitled to the full sanction of the state. Therefore, if the parties agree to a remedy that is significantly out of line with one that a court would award, MacNeil argues that courts are well within the bounds of their traditional authority in refusing to enforce the parties' remedy.[46] The parties have the freedom to choose a remedy, and as long as they keep the matter to themselves, the state will not interfere. However, when a party goes to court and seeks the state's assistance, he does not have the power to dictate the scope of the state's authority, which is a matter for courts to decide. Thus, limits on the power of contract are defined both by law and public policy.

The debate among the commentators helps in understanding the basis of the common-law and UCC rules. Without much more careful and thorough study, it is impossible to determine whether the approach advocated by Goetz and Scott is more or less efficient than the approach advocated by Rubin. MacNeil's argument, however, is consistent with the approach of courts to the general enforcement of contracts and therefore has the advantage of consistency with the prevailing authorities. Courts take a jaundiced view of liquidated damage clauses and, despite arguments in favor of their use in minimizing problems of proof at trial, are unlikely to change their views radically. For cases that arise under the UCC, courts continue to be bound by the strictures of Section 2-718, and the general principles of Section 356 of the second Restatement apply in most common-law cases. The critical inquiry in each instance involves the reasonableness of the contract remedy in light of what the plaintiff could obtain under standard principles of measurement. The one point on which courts and commentators all seem to agree is that liquidated damage clauses are most useful where damages are difficult or impossible to calculate with any certainty. The clause then provides a mechanism for the enforcement of a remedy that otherwise might not have been available, subject always to concerns about fairness.[47]

---

[46] Id. at 496–498.

[47] Id. at 506.

¶ 10.03 EXCLUSIONS OF CONSEQUENTIAL DAMAGES AND LIMITATIONS OF REMEDIES

[1] Contractual Modification of Remedies and Judicial Reactions

A liquidated damage clause is only one specialized means a party can use to predetermine the remedy he can obtain (or for which he will be liable) upon a breach. Contracts often contain provisions that limit damages or that specify certain kinds of recoveries. Among the most common are exclusions of consequential damages and limitations of liability on warranties to the repair or replacement of a defective product. Sometimes an agreement specifies that specific performance is the preferred remedy or excludes equitable remedies. Many of the same arguments advanced in favor of or against liquidated damage clauses apply equally to other provisions that affect remedies.[48] Enforcing contractual limitations advances the idea of freedom of contract[49] and permits parties to allocate risks as they see fit.[50] On the other hand, a limitation clause may provide insufficient protection for the nonbreaching party if he is not put in as good a position as he would have enjoyed with full performance. This raises the question of whether a court should lend its aid to enforcing a contract that is inconsistent with the general principles of statutory and common law.[51] The approach of the courts to the enforcement of contractual modifications of remedies has been similar to the approach in liquidated damage clause cases: Aberrational or unfair modifications are not enforced; those that are consistent with rules of general application tend to fare better.

---

[48] See supra ¶ 10.01.

[49] Hawkins Constr. Co. v. Matthews Co., 190 Neb. 546, 209 NW2d 643 (1973).

[50] Schroeder v. Fageol Motors, Inc., 12 Wash App. 161, 528 P2d 992 (1974); rev'd on other grounds, 80 Wash. 2d 256, 544 P2d 20 (1975).

[51] See, e.g., UCC § 1-106; Soo Line RR Co. v. Fruehauf Corp., 547 F2d 1365 (8th Cir. 1977); American Elec. Power Co. v. Westinghouse Elec. Corp., 418 F. Supp. 435 (SDNY 1976); Conte v. Dwan Lincoln-Mercury, Inc., 172 Conn. 112, 374 A2d 144 (1976). See generally Zaretsky, "Contractual Modification or Limitation of Remedy," in *Breach of Contract Under the UCC: Litigation and Settlement* 89, 92 (1979).

[2] UCC Qualifications of Contractual Modification of Remedies

Most of the recent decisions have involved the UCC. Section 2-719 explicitly approves private modifications of remedies, but with some limitations. There are two important qualifications: First, if a limitation or modification fails in its essential purpose, it will not be enforced; and second, if a limitation on consequential damages is unconscionable, it will not be enforced.[52] A limitation on consequential damages for personal injury is prima facie unconscionable.[53] The UCC also presumes that limitations are optional unless there is an express agreement to make them exclusive.[54] The courts construe limitations and modifications most strongly against the drafter.[55]

The dual concerns of the authors of the UCC are apparent in the Official Commentary. The drafters wanted to heighten the negotiating freedom of the parties, but at the same time they wanted to ensure that adequate sanctions would be available for breach.

> Under this section parties are left free to shape their remedies to their particular requirements and reasonable agreements limiting or modifying remedies are to be given effect.
>
> However, it is of the very essence of a sales contract that at least minimum adequate remedies be available. If the parties intend to conclude a contract for sale within this Article they must accept the legal consequence that there be at least a fair quantum of remedy breach of the obligations or duties outlined in the contract.[56]

[3] The Repair-or-Replacement Limitation

Many cases have involved the repair-or-replacement limitation. Sellers of goods commonly include a provision in the sales agreement, acknowledgment of sale form, invoice, or product label

---

[52] UCC §§ 2-719(2), 2-719(3).

[53] UCC § 2-719(3).

[54] UCC § 2-719(1)(b).

[55] Farmers Union Grain Terminal Ass'n v. Nelson, 223 NW2d 494 (ND 1974).

[56] UCC § 2-719, Official Comment 1.

that limits the seller's liability to the repair or replacement of a defective product in lieu of other remedies that would be available under the UCC. In many instances this works to the advantage both of the seller and the buyer. The buyer wants a product that works in accordance with his reasonable expectations. Unsatisfactory goods that can be fixed quickly or replaced are usually satisfactory — indeed, far more satisfactory than a lawsuit for damages. In addition, the seller gains the advantage of excluding other risks.[57] Problems develop when the seller is slow to respond to the buyer's complaint about unsatisfactory goods, is unable to correct the defect, or continues to make repairs instead of providing the buyer with substitute goods. A court may conclude in such cases that the repair-or-replacement option failed, and the buyer will be able to sue for any remedy provided by the UCC.[58]

Timing is the critical element in determining the effectiveness of a repair-or-replacement limitation. The buyer need not show the seller's bad faith or negligence; he simply must demonstrate that the product was defective and that it was not fixed or replaced within a reasonable time. "The detriment to the buyer is the same whether the seller diligently but unsuccessfully attempts to honor his promise or acts negligently or in bad faith."[59] One of the most common complaints is the inability to get a lemon fixed by an automobile dealer. Courts have demonstrated a definite sympathy for a consumer who makes repeated trips to the dealership for redress and who still does not have a satisfactory car.[60]

Many contracts contain both a repair-or-replacement clause and a separate exclusion of consequential damages. If the repair-or-replacement clause fails in its essential purpose, does that mean that the limitation on consequential damages also fails and that the

---

[57] See, e.g., Beal v. General Motors Corp., 354 F. Supp. 423 (D. Del. 1973); Ford Motor Co. v. Gunn, 123 Ga. App. 550, 181 SE2d 694 (1971).

[58] See, e.g., Kohlenberger, Inc. v. Tyson's Foods, Inc., 256 Ark. 584, 510 SW2d 555 (1974); Jacobs v. Metro Chrysler-Plymouth, Inc., 125 Ga. App. 462, 188 SE2d 250 (1972).

[59] Chatlos Sys., Inc. v. National Cash Register Corp., 635 F2d 1081, 1085 (3d Cir. 1980), relying on SM Wilson & Co. v. Smith Int'l, Inc., 587 F2d 1363, 1374, 1375 (9th Cir. 1978).

[60] See, e.g., Riley v. Ford Motor Co., 442 F2d 670 (5th Cir. 1971); Ehlers v. Chrysler Motor Corp., 88 SD 612, 226 NW2d 157 (1975).

plaintiff can recover all damages allowed by the UCC? The argument in favor of the plaintiff is straightforward. The purpose of the limitation is to induce the seller to make certain that the buyer gets a satisfactory product in a timely fashion. If the seller cannot do so, he should not obtain the benefits of the contractual limitations on liability, because the essential bargain has failed. The seller might respond, however, by saying that the failure of one clause — the repair-or-replacement provision — should not invalidate the entire contract, including an exclusion of consequential damages. The buyer could have protected himself by making the exclusion conditional on the performance of the repair-or-replacement provision, or he could have refused to agree to an exclusion of consequentials. In responding to these arguments, courts have split between buyers and sellers. Generally, they have been more solicitous of consumers who have not negotiated a sale but who have simply bought a product at retail, but they have also examined closely a number of contracts between commercial parties.

In the case of *Lewis Refrigeration Co. v. Sawyer Fruit, Vegetable and Cold Storage Co.,*[61] the Court of Appeals for the Sixth Circuit, applying Washington law, held that the failure of a repair-or-replacement clause does not necessarily invalidate a separate exclusion of consequential damages that is otherwise acceptable under Section 2-719.[62] However, another federal court, applying Illinois law, ruled that a buyer could seek all remedies available under the UCC in similar circumstances and that the contractual exclusion of consequential damages would not be enforced.[63] Courts in North Carolina, New York, and South Dakota have followed the same line as *Lewis*.[64] On the other hand, courts in Delaware, Hawaii, and Michigan have concluded in specific cases that an exclusion of consequential damages fails if the repair-or-re-

---

[61] Lewis Refrigeration Co. v. Sawyer Fruit, Vegetable and Cold Storage Co., 709 F2d 427 (6th Cir. 1983).

[62] Id. at 434, 435.

[63] Custom Automated Mach. v. Penda Corp., 537 F. Supp. 77 (ND Ill. 1982); and see Adams v. JI Case Co., 125 Ill. App. 2d 388, 261 NE2d 1 (1970).

[64] American Elec. Power Co. v. Westinghouse Elec. Corp., 418 F. Supp. 435 (SDNY 1976); Stutts v. Green Ford, Inc., 47 NC App. 503, 267 SE2d 919 (1980); Johnson v. John Deere Co., 306 NW2d 231 (SD 1981).

placement clause fails.[65]

The essential legal problem was identified in the South Dakota case of *Johnson v. John Deere Co.*[66] Whether a repair-or-replacement clause fails in its essential purpose is a factual question. A judge or a jury decides the issue after the fact. Whether an exclusion of consequential damages is enforceable is a legal question of unconscionability. A judge determines that issue as a matter of law.[67] Legally, the issues may present separate problems — one may be decided by a jury, the other by a judge — but they both become bound to the particular facts of a case.[68] For instance, in *Lewis* the court suggested that the buyer's identity was crucial. If the buyer was a consumer, an exclusion of consequential damages would be prima facie unconscionable if the contract failed in its essential purpose. If the buyer was a commercial entity, however, there would be no presumption of unconscionability. Similarly, the wording of an agreement may be decisive. There is a rebuttable presumption that contractual modifications of remedies are in addition to those available at common law or under the UCC and that they are not exclusive.[69] This presumption can be overcome either by evidence showing that the trade practice or the parties' conduct indicated that the modifications were understood to be exclusive remedies [70] or by the express language of the agreement itself.[71]

---

[65] Beal v. General Motors Corp., 354 F. Supp. 423 (D. Del. 1973); Earl M. Jorgenson Co. v. Mark Constr. Inc., 56 Hawaii 466, 540 P2d 978 (1975); Fargo Mach. & Tool Co. v. Kearney & Trecker Corp., 428 F. Supp. 364 (ED Mich. 1977).

[66] Johnson v. John Deere Co., 306 NW2d 231 (SD 1981).

[67] Id. at 237, 238.

[68] In KKO, Inc. v. Honeywell, Inc., 517 F. Supp. 892 (ND Ill. 1981), the court stated that it could not be determined as a matter of law that failure of a repair-or-replacement clause would invalidate an exclusion of consequential damages.

[69] Lewis Refrigeration Co. v. Sawyer Fruit, Vegetable and Cold Storage Co., 709 F2d 427, 435 (6th Cir. 1983).

[70] See, e.g., Dow Corning Corp. v. Capitol Aviation, Inc., 411 F2d 622 (7th Cir. 1969).

[71] The language must be conspicuous (Insurance Co. of N. Am. v. Automatic Sprinkler Corp. of Am., 67 Ohio St. 2d 91, 423 NE2d 151 (1981)), and it must be brought to the attention of and explained to the buyer, especially if he is a con-

[4] Standards of Enforceability

Regardless of the success or failure of a repair-or-replacement clause, an exclusion of consequential damages must meet the unconscionability standard of Section 2-719(3). Exclusion clauses are not often found to be unconscionable in a commercial context, but they sometimes run afoul of the general requirement of Section 2-719 that there be a "fair quantum of remedy."[72] Although the question of whether a contract provision is unconscionable or fails to provide a fair quantum of remedy is one of law to be decided by a court,[73] courts usually require a hearing and do not decide the matter simply on the pleadings or on brief.[74]

One of the most extensive discussions of the standards for the enforcement of an exclusion of consequential damages occurred in a series of opinions in *Hill v. BASF Wyandotte Corp.*,[75] a case brought by a South Carolina farmer against the manufacturer of a herbicide. The farmer had purchased the herbicide for use on his soybean crop. It was different from what he had used in the past, but he said that he relied on the salesman's representations that the product was equally as effective, and it was less expensive. Unfortunately, the herbicide did not perform as well as the farmer expected, and his soybean crop was much smaller than normal because the plants were crowded by weeds. The weeds also caused cultivation and harvesting problems. The farmer sued for lost profits and other consequential damages. The cans of herbicide had labels that contained language expressly limiting the manufacturer's warranty and excluding liability for "consequential, special, or indirect damages." The plaintiff argued that the salesman's representations about quality should control and override any limi-

---

sumer (A&M Produce Co. v. FMC Corp., 135 Cal. App. 3d 473, 186 Cal. Rptr. 114 (1982); Gladden v. Cadillac Motor Car Div., 83 NJ 320, 416 A2d 394 (1980)).

[72] 3 Hawkland § 2-719:04, at 453 (1982).

[73] See, e.g., KKO, Inc. v. Honeywell, Inc., 517 F. Supp. 892 (ND Ill. 1981); Phillips Mach. Co. v. LeBlond, Inc., 494 F. Supp. 318 (ND Okla. 1980).

[74] See, e.g., Frank's Maintenance & Eng'g, Inc. v. CA Roberts Co., 86 Ill. App. 3d 980, 408 NE2d 403 (1980); Haugen v. Ford Motor Co., 219 NW2d 462 (ND 1974).

[75] Hill v. BASF Wyandotte Corp., 696 F2d 287 (4th Cir. 1982).

tations written on the cans' labels. Furthermore, the exclusions did not allow for a fair recovery in light of the damages the farmer actually suffered. The Court of Appeals for the Fourth Circuit, applying South Carolina law, disagreed and said that the labels controlled. The plaintiff conceded that he had notice of the content of the labels, and the salesman's oral representations could not override the express written terms of the agreement as stated on the labels.

On remand from the Court of Appeals for the Fourth Circuit, the district court certified the question of damage calculation to the South Carolina Supreme Court for guidance. Because the labels excluded any consequential damages, the problem was to determine how to figure direct damages. The South Carolina court said:

> [T]he measure of actual damages . . . is the value the crop would have had if the product had conformed to the warranty less the value of the crop actually produced, less the expense of preparing for market the portion of the probable crop prevented from maturing. If the measure of damages we have adopted includes an element of lost profits, such inclusion is merely coincidental as the measure covers the direct loss resulting in the ordinary course of events from the alleged breach of warranty.[76]

The defendant argued that the recovery should be limited to the cost of the herbicide, the monetary equivalent of the repair-or-replacement remedy. Obviously, the South Carolina court was not willing to lean that far in the seller's favor. The allegations of the complaint set out a prima facie case that the warranties, whether express or implied, had failed because the product did not control weeds in a satisfactory manner. The buyer could not be made whole because the crop had already been planted, cultivated, and harvested. Any repair-or-replacement remedy had already failed in its essential purpose.

The Florida Court of Appeals reached the same result in another herbicide case and held that the exclusion of liability for

---

[76] Hill v. BASF Wyandotte Corp., 280 SC 174, 311 SE2d 734 (1984).

consequential damages on the cans' labels was effective.[77] Although it might seem somewhat strange to give so much weight to a label, the cans in question were large and contained five gallons of the herbicide. The information on the labels was prominently displayed, and there was no question of notice. The courts seemed reluctant to allow farmers, experienced in the ways of managing agricultural businesses, to be treated as if they were ordinary consumers. If an average consumer bought a product off the shelf that he had not used before and the product failed, a court might show more solicitude for the buyer, because the label does not represent a negotiated deal. The South Carolina farmer, on the other hand, could have protected himself on his fairly large purchase by attempting to formalize the salesman's representations. In the words of another court, the UCC "holds the merchant to a higher standard than a consumer. And although a commercial setting does not necessarily bar a claim of unconscionability, 'it is the exceptional commercial setting where a claim of unconscionability will be allowed.' "[78]

Business experience and the use of counsel are important factors in deciding whether to employ the unconscionability doctrine in exclusion of remedy cases. The Pennsylvania Supreme Court, for instance, upheld an exclusion of consequential damages in a contract that had been negotiated over a period of six months with Westinghouse by a businessman and his lawyer.[79] In another case involving two commercial entities that maintained a business relationship for thirteen years, a federal court enforced a prohibition of the recovery of lost profits and said, "It would be improper to borrow, without differentiation, concepts developed to protect consumers and employ them in favor of one commercial party over another."[80]

---

[77] Monsanto Agricultural Prods. Co. v. Edenfield, 426 So. 2d 574 (Fla. Dist. Ct. App. 1982).

[78] Jamestown Farmers Elevator, Inc. v. General Mills, Inc., 413 F. Supp. 764, 772 (DND 1976), citing County Asphalt, Inc. v. Lewis Welding & Eng'g Corp., 323 F. Supp. 1300, 1308 (SDNY 1970). And see Hi Neighbor Enters., Inc. v. Burroughs Corp., 492 F. Supp. 823 (ND Fla. 1980).

[79] K&C, Inc. v. Westinghouse Elec. Corp., 437 Pa. 303, 263 A2d 390 (1970).

However, what appears to be a commercial relationship may more closely resemble a relationship between an accomplished businessman and an inexperienced consumer. In *Johnson v. Mobil Oil Corp.*,[81] the court refused to enforce the limitation on consequential damages contained in the retail dealer franchise contract between Johnson and Mobil Oil. There was nothing substantively wrong with the contract; the court indicated that it might be fully enforceable in many situations. There was no informed consent to the provision, however. The dealer was functionally illiterate and could not read or understand the contract. Even though Johnson did not tell Mobil's representative that he could not read and there was no evidence of any overreaching or unfair bargaining procedures by Mobil, the court did not believe that an exclusionary clause should be enforced without clear and knowing consent. Indeed, the court imposed a duty on Mobil that was close to that of a fiduciary.

> [B]efore a contracting party with the immense bargaining power of the Mobil Oil Corporation may limit its liability vis-à-vis an uncounseled layman, as it seeks to do in this case, to "difference money damages," it has an affirmative duty to obtain the voluntary, knowing assent of the other party. This could easily have been done in this case by explaining to plaintiff in laymen's terms the meaning and possible consequences of the disputed clause.[82]

In what was closer to a purely commercial setting, the Illinois Court of Appeals refused to enforce a damage limitation clause that

---

[80] Stanley A. Klopp, Inc. v. John Deere Co., 510 F. Supp. 807, 810 (ED Pa. 1981); see also Cryogenic Equip., Inc. v. Southern Nitrogen, Inc., 490 F2d 696 (8th Cir. 1974); Wyatt Indus., Inc. v. Publicker Indus. Inc., 420 F2d 454 (5th Cir. 1969); US Fibres, Inc. v. Proctor & Schwartz, Inc., 358 F. Supp. 449 (ED Mich. 1972), aff'd, 509 F2d 1043 (6th Cir. 1975); County Asphalt, Inc. v. Lewis Welding & Eng'g Corp., 323 F. Supp. 1300 (SDNY 1970), aff'd, 444 F2d 372 (2d Cir.), cert. denied, 404 US 939 (1971).

[81] Johnson v. Mobil Oil Corp., 415 F. Supp. 264 (ED Mich. 1976).

[82] Id. at 269.

appeared on a seller's acknowledgment form.[83] The immediate question is: Why should a label on a herbicide can be effective, while a provision in a seller's acknowledgment form is not? Despite some language in the Illinois court's opinion about the buyer's reasonable expectations and the unfairness of exclusion clauses, the key to the case seems to have been notice. The exclusion was in an inconspicuous location on the seller's form in the midst of a great deal of other boilerplate language and was not brought to the buyer's attention.[84] The farmers who bought the disappointing herbicides conceded that they had notice of the limiting provisions. If notice exists and the buyer is capable of looking out for his own interests, courts generally are willing to enforce damage limitation or exclusion clauses even if the resulting recovery is fairly small,[85] as long as it does not grossly violate the fair quantum of recovery standard of Section 2-719.

Courts follow a similar pattern for other kinds of modifications to ordinary remedies. If these modifications are bargained for, understood, and consistent with general principles of fairness, they will be enforced. Courts are reluctant, however, to enforce provisions that provide remedies greater than or fundamentally different from those available at common law or under the UCC. It is unlikely, for instance, that a contract provision that calls for specific performance as the preferred remedy will be enforced unless the contract is one for which the specific performance remedy would normally be available. In short, courts allow parties to agree to accept less than they might otherwise get, but are reluctant to allow parties to demand more than their usual legal or equitable remedial rights. This approach is consistent with the liquidated damage cases and with MacNeil's thesis that it is the province of

---

[83] Frank's Maintenance & Eng'g, Inc. v. CA Roberts Co., 86 Ill. App. 3d 980, 408 NE2d 403 (1980).

[84] Id. at 410, 411. But at least two other courts have said that the limitation clause does not have to be conspicuous. Flintkote Co. v. WW Silkinson, Inc., 220 Va. 564, 260 SE2d 229 (1979); Orrox Corp. v. Rexnord, Inc., 389 F. Supp. 441 (MD Ala. 1975).

[85] See, e.g., Cardinal Stone Co. v. Rival Mfg. Co., 669 F2d 395 (6th Cir. 1982); Firemen's Fund Am. Ins. Co. v. Burns Elec. Sec. Servs., Inc., 93 Ill. App. 3d 298, 417 NE2d 131 (1980).

courts to determine the boundaries of enforcement and sanctions for promissory transactions.[86]

¶ 10.04 ARBITRATION CLAUSES

[1] Benefits and Problems

When a contract fails or the parties have a dispute, the resolution of their differences can be costly. Litigation is time-consuming, lawyers are expensive, and the adversary process tends to exacerbate differences, often resulting in hard feelings. Litigation also imposes costs on society, both directly through burdens on the judicial process and indirectly through increased prices for products and other services sold or provided by the litigants. All in all, litigation is rarely a happy experience for the participants. If the parties to a contract want to maintain fairly good relations because they may continue business in the future, they have a strong additional incentive to avoid a court proceeding.

One of the most common ways to ensure an adequate means to resolve disputes and to minimize costs is to include an arbitration clause in a contract. These clauses have long-established precedent in labor law, and both courts and legislatures have reacted very favorably toward their use in all types of contracts. Indeed, a federal statute on arbitration covers all commercial agreements involving interstate commerce.[87] Many states have adopted the Uniform Arbitration Act,[88] and in others the common law supports

---

[86] MacNeil 495. MacNeil argues that the parties should be allowed to agree to the remedy of specific performance if that is the only remedy that will give adequate protection to the nonbreaching party's interest. Id. at 521. This position really just restates the traditional rule that equity intervenes when law does not provide an adequate remedy.

[87] 9 USC 1743 (1970).

[88] Twenty-nine states and the District of Columbia have adopted the Uniform Arbitration Act. They are: Alaska, Arizona, Arkansas, Colorado, Delaware, Idaho, Illinois, Iowa, Kansas, Louisiana, Maine, Maryland, Massachusetts, Michigan, Minnesota, Missouri, Nevada, New Mexico, New York, North Carolina, Oklahoma, Oregon, Pennsylvania, Rhode Island, South Carolina, South Dakota, Texas, Washington, Wyoming, and the District of Columbia. Seven states have arbitration statutes that are similar to the Uniform Arbitration Act.

the concept of arbitration.[89]

Problems in arbitration cases usually center around a few questions. Is the arbitration clause exclusive, or is it an optional means of dispute resolution? Does it cover all disagreements, or only certain ones? What is the scope of the arbitrator's remedial authority? Is the arbitration award fully enforceable according to its terms? What is the reviewing authority of a court? Careful drafting avoids many of these difficulties, but some of them raise fundamental questions about the role of arbitrators as substitutes for judges and the extent to which they are bound by public law and public policy rather than the private law of an individual contract.

If the parties are satisfied to send their disputes to arbitration, the process can start without a problem. If there is a disagreement about whether the dispute is arbitrable, however, the first question is: Who decides? Some courts have said that an arbitrator cannot decide the question of arbitrability because it is a jurisdictional issue that is a matter of law and therefore in the exclusive province of courts.[90] The majority of courts, however, have said that the arbitrator may determine the question of arbitrability.[91] This approach is more consistent with the encouragement of arbitration as a means to settle disputes. It is also more efficient. There would be a great deal of wasted time and expense if the parties had to go to court only to be told that they should go to arbitration.[92]

These include: Connecticut, Florida, Georgia, Indiana, Ohio, Utah, and Wisconsin. See *Am. Jur. 2d Desk Book* Item No. 124 (Supp. 1984).

[89] See, e.g., Vernon v. Drexel Burnham & Co., 52 Cal. App. 3d 706, 125 Cal. Rptr. 147 (1975); McRae v. Superior Court of Los Angeles County, 221 Cal. App. 2d 166, 34 Cal. Rptr. 346 (1963); New Jersey Mfr. Ins. Co. v. Haran, 128 NJ Super. 265, 319 A2d 768 (1974). Some states have a confusing mixture of common law and statutory law. See, e.g., OC Ga. A 9-9-133 (1982); Sturges & Reckson, "Common Law and Statutory Arbitration: Problems Arising From Their Coexistence," 46 Minn. L. Rev. 819 (1962); Note, "Commercial Arbitration," 12 Ga. L. Rev. 323 (1978).

[90] See, e.g., Cruger v. Allstate Ins. Co., 162 So. 2d 690 (Fla. Dist. Ct. App. 1964); Safeway Ins. Co. v. Parker, 105 Ill. App. 2d 208, 245 NE2d 75 (1969).

[91] See, e.g., United Steelworkers of Am. v. American Mfg. Co., 363 US 564 (1960); Morris v. Zuckerman, 69 Cal. 2d 686, 446 P2d 1000, 72 Cal. Rptr. 880 (1968); Layne-Minn. Co. v. Regents of Univ. of Minn., 266 Minn. 284, 123 NW2d 371 (1963).

[92] See generally Dobbs, *Remedies* § 12.27, at 943, 944 (1973) (hereinafter cited as Dobbs).

Even if a contract contains an arbitration clause that appears to be valid, either the arbitrator or a court may still rule that arbitration is inappropriate if there is, in reality, no contract on which to base the arbitration (e.g., it is void ab initio for some reason),[93] if the dispute concerns a matter outside the coverage of the arbitration clause,[94] or if the contract is illegal.[95] Some issues are not subject to arbitration for reasons of public policy regardless of the will of the parties, such as the interpretation and application of the Securities Act of 1933,[96] the Seamen's Wage Act,[97] and the Commodity Exchange Act.[98] Occasionally, the facts may show that one of the parties has waived the right to demand an arbitration[99] or that there really is not an express agreement to arbitrate so that the disappointed party has the option to proceed at law.[100]

[2] Arbitration of Damages Resulting From Fraud

One of the more interesting issues is whether matters of fraud are subject to arbitration. If fraud exists, the complaining party has a cause of action in tort that exists separate and apart from the contract. If the plaintiff proceeds in tort and succeeds, the contract no longer is viable. When a contract is void by reason of fraud, the consensus is that arbitration is not available. The basis for arbitration — the contract itself — is without life and cannot support the agreed remedial procedure. Fraud in the inducement raises a somewhat more difficult question. The contract itself is not fraudulent;

---

93 See, e.g., Interocean Shipping Co. v. National Shipping & Trading Corp., 462 F2d 673 (2d Cir. 1972), no appeal from remand, 523 F2d 527 (1975), cert. denied, 423 US 1054 (1976).

94 See, e.g., Rosenthal v. Emanuel, Deetjen & Co., 516 F2d 325 (2d Cir. 1975).

95 See, e.g., Durst v. Abrash, 22 AD2d 39, 253 NYS2d 351 (1964), aff'd, 17 NY2d 445, 213 NE2d 887, 266 NYS2d 806 (1965).

96 Wilko v. Swan, 346 US 427 (1953).

97 U.S. Bulk Carriers, Inc. v. Arguelles, 400 US 351 (1971).

98 Bache-Halsey Stuart, Inc. v. French, 425 F. Supp. 1231 (DDC 1977).

99 See, e.g., American Locomotive Co. v. Chemical Research Corp., 171 F2d 115 (6th Cir. 1948), cert. denied, 336 US 909 (1949); Carcich v. Nordie, 389 F2d 692 (2d Cir. 1968).

100 See, e.g., Matter of Marlene Indus. Corp., 45 NY2d 327, 380 NE2d 239, 408 NYS2d 410 (1978).

rather, the acts that induced one party to enter the contract were fraudulent. The complaining party may avoid the contract in the same way as in an ordinary fraud action. Practically, the contract is just as dead. For this reason, some courts have held that fraud in the inducement is not an arbitrable issue.[101] The majority, however, have followed the lead of the United States Supreme Court in *Prima Paint Corp. v. Flood & Conklin Manufacturing Co.*[102] and have held that fraud in the inducement is an arbitrable matter because the arbitration clause is severable from the contract as a whole. It is a separate contract on remedial matters that does not fall with the contract in chief.[103] If the arbitration clause itself was fraudulently induced, arbitration will not be available.[104]

The rule adopted by the Supreme Court and most other courts allowing the arbitration of fraud in the inducement is a good example of the favorable attitudes of courts toward arbitration. The support for arbitration as a remedial procedure is also evident in cases that deal with appeals from judicial decisions that either denied or granted a party's request to compel arbitration. In the first place, an order from a court to compel arbitration in accordance with a contract is equivalent to an order for specific performance of that portion of the contract. It therefore represents a deviation from the principle that equity intervenes only where the legal remedy is inadequate. In most instances, the party seeking to compel arbitration could recover money damages for noncompliance. By requiring arbitration, a court recognizes either that money is inadequate compensation for failure to comply with an

---

[101] See, e.g., George Engine Co. v. Southern Shipbuilding Corp., 350 So. 2d 881 (La. 1977); Annot., 11 ALR4th 774, 778 (1982).

[102] Prima Paint Corp. v. Flood & Conklin Mfg. Corp., 388 US 395 (1967).

[103] See, e.g., National Camera, Inc. v. Love, 644 P2d 94 (Colo. Ct. App. 1982); Fairways Plaza Assocs. v. Commercial Constr. Corp., 419 So. 2d 1197 (Fla. 1982); Weinrott v. Carp, 32 NY2d 190, 298 NE2d 42, 344 NYS2d 848 (1973).

[104] See, e.g., Schoenamsgruber v. Hamburg-Am. Line, 294 US 454 (1935); Roeder v. Huish, 105 Ariz. 508, 467 P2d 902 (1970); Graham v. Scissor-Tail, Inc., 28 Cal. 3d 807, 623 P2d 165, 171 Cal. Rptr. 604 (1981); Harris v. State Farm Mut. Auto Ins. Co., 283 So. 2d 147 (Fla. Dist. Ct. App. 1973); Bellaire City Schools Bd. of Educ. v. Paxton, 59 Ohio St. 2d 65, 391 NE2d 1021 (1979). Contra Cajun Elec. Power Coop., Inc. v. Louisiana Power & Light Co., 334 So. 2d 554 (La. Ct. App. 1976); Merrill Lynch, Pierce, Fenner & Smith, Inc. v. Griesenbeck, 21 NY2d 688, 234 NE2d 456, 287 NYS2d 419 (1967).

agreed-upon procedure for the efficient settlement of disputes or that there is peculiar merit in nonjudicial means for dealing with disagreements.

[3] Appeal and Review of Arbitration Awards

When a court decides that a provision for arbitration should be enforced, the usual rule is that no appeal will lie until after the arbitration is complete and the arbitrator has made his award. The order compelling arbitration is an interlocutory order.[105] On the other hand, an order denying arbitration may be treated as a final order that is immediately appealable.[106]

Courts show a similar deference in reviewing arbitration awards. Most adhere to the rule that the scope of review is more limited than in an appeal from the decision of a lower court.[107] Courts generally do not overturn arbitrators' awards unless there are gross errors of fact or law.[108] Even a mistake in choosing the method of the calculation of a damage award is not necessarily a sufficient reason to reverse an award.[109] There is not unanimity, however. Out of a concern for the increasing scope of arbitrators' remedial powers, the Court of Appeals for the Third Circuit, for instance, has adopted a test of "fundamental rationality" to apply to the review of awards.[110]

---

[105] I.e., not final, provisional, temporary — something intervening between the commencement and the end of a suit which decides some matter, but is not a final decision of the whole controversy.

[106] See, e.g., Merrill Lynch, Pierce, Fenner & Smith, Inc. v. Haydu, 637 F2d 391 (5th Cir. 1981) (applying Florida law).

[107] See, e.g., Seither & Cherry Co. v. Illinois Bank Bldg. Corp., 95 Ill. App. 3d 191, 50 Ill. Dec. 672, 419 NE2d 940 (1981); Garver v. Ferguson, 76 Ill. 2d 1, 27 Ill. Dec. 773, 389 NE2d 1181 (1979); Annot., 22 ALR4th 366 (1983).

[108] See, e.g., Fisher v. Gause, 236 Ga. 663, 225 SE2d 2 (1976); Bituminous Casualty Corp. v. United Servs. Auto Ass'n, 158 Ga. App. 739, 282 SE2d 198 (1981). Del Bianco & Assocs. v. Adam, 6 Ill. App. 3d 286, 285 NE2d 480 (1972), cert. denied, 410 US 955 (1973); Dobbs § 12.27, at 941–943 (1973). But see Graham v. Scissor-Tail, Inc., 28 Cal. 3d 807, 623 P2d 165, 171 Cal. Rptr. 604 (1981); Note, "Unconscionability of Presumptively Biased Arbitration Clauses Within Adhesion Contracts," 70 Calif. L. Rev. 1014 (1982).

[109] See, e.g., William B. Lucke, Inc. v. Spiegel, 131 Ill. App. 2d 532, 266 NE2d 504 (1970).

[110] Swift Indus., Inc. v. Botany Indus., Inc., 466 F2d 1125 (3d Cir. 1972).

[4] Powers of the Arbitrator

An issue that may generate significant controversy is the question of the scope of the remedies available to the arbitrator. Obviously, the contract itself may define the limits of the arbitrator's power, and there is usually no question about the power of an arbitrator to make a monetary award even if the claim is unliquidated.[111] The most common problems arise when the arbitrator tries to exercise equitable powers. Some courts reason that arbitrators derive their authority from the judiciary and that they are bound by the same substantive rules as judges. If a judge cannot issue an equitable order, neither should an arbitrator.[112] Others argue that private parties, not courts, delegate power to arbitrators and that a contract is the only limitation on their powers.

The two leading cases upholding the authority of an arbitrator to exercise equitable powers a court would not exercise in a similar situation are both from New York. The first, *Staklinski v. Pyramid Electric Co.,*[113] involved a long-term employment contract that included a provision for termination upon disability. The company said that the employee (the president) was disabled, but he disputed that determination and demanded arbitration. The arbitrator found that the president was not disabled and ordered reinstatement. The court of appeals approved the award even as it noted that it would not have required reinstatement because that would have amounted to specific performance of an employment contract. The terminated employee could have recovered monetary damages for wrongful termination that would have been the financial equivalent of reinstatement. In the following year, the court approved an arbitration award that compelled specific performance of a building construction contract in *Grayson-Robinson Stores, Inc. v. Iris Construction Corp.*[114] Again, a court probably

---

[111] See, e.g., Bankers & Shippers Inc. Co. v. Gonzalez, 234 So. 2d 693 (Fla. Dist. Ct. App. 1970).

[112] Carr v. Kalamazoo Vegetable Parchment Co., 354 Mich. 327, 92 NW2d 295 (1958).

[113] Staklinski v. Pyramid Elec. Co., 6 NY2d 159, 160 NE 2d 78, 188 NYS2d 541 (1959).

[114] Grayson-Robinson Stores, Inc. v. Iris Constr. Corp., 8 NY2d 133, 168 NE2d 377, 202 NYS2d 303 (1960); see also Ruppert v. Egelhofer, 3 NY2d 576, 148 NE2d 129, 170 NYS2d 785 (1958).

would not have granted specific performance because of the problems of oversight and the availability of substantial monetary damages as compensation.

The New York approach prevails, and as a result, arbitrators may be able to issue a wider range of awards than their brethren on the bench.[115] Of course, there are some limits. As a general rule, an arbitrator cannot make an award of punitive damages.[116] Dicta in several cases suggest that punitive damages may be awarded if the contract expressly allows the arbitrator to consider them,[117] but they are against the weight of authority that holds for strong policy reasons against the award of punitive damages in contract cases.[118]

Arbitration continues to be a favored procedural device. It saves judicial time and often makes it possible for parties to reach a more informal resolution of their dispute at substantial savings. Approving the use of arbitration is consistent with freedom of contract, and as long as the courts retain reviewing authority to police awards for gross mistakes or violations of public policy, there is no concern with private infringements of public responsibilities. In the words of MacNeil,

---

[115] In some instances an arbitrator may even be able to make an award that a statute prohibits a court from ordering, although the award cannot be fundamentally inconsistent with the general policy of the statute. See Boys Markets, Inc. v. Retail Clerk's Union, Local 770, 398 US 235 (1970); New Orleans SS Ass'n v. General Longshore Workers, ILA Local Union No. 1418, 389 F2d 369 (5th Cir. 1968). The Uniform Arbitration Act § 12(a)(5) provides, "The fact that the relief was such that it could not or would not be granted by a court of law or equity is not ground for vacating or refusing to confirm the award."

[116] Garrity v. Lyle Stuart, Inc., 40 NY2d 354, 353 NE2d 793, 386 NYS2d 831 (1976).

[117] See, e.g., Refinery Employees Union v. Continental Oil Co., 268 F2d 447 (5th Cir.), cert. denied, 361 US 896 (1959); International Union of Operating Eng'rs Local No. 450 v. Mid-Valley, Inc., 347 F. Supp. 1104 (SD Tex. 1972).

[118] See Chapter 11. It has been indicated that punitive damages may be allowed in a labor dispute; at least they are not illegal under federal labor law. Sheetmetal Workers Int'l Assoc. v. Helgesteel Corp., 335 F. Supp. 812 (WD Wis. 1971). Several courts, however, have rejected awards of punitive damages in labor cases. See, e.g., Baltimore Regional Joint Bd. v. Webster Clothes, Inc., 596 F2d 95 (4th Cir. 1979); Safeway Stores, Inc. v. Int'l Assoc. of Machinists, Lodge No. 1486, 534 F. Supp. 638 (D. Md. 1982); School City of E. Chicago v. East Chicago Fed'n of Teachers, 422 NE2d 656 (Ind. Ct. App. 1981). Labor law is so regulated and specialized that labor cases can rarely be used as analogies in common-law or UCC disputes.

As long as the parties are seeking only the procedural advantages of arbitration or substantive advantages which do not change the basic nature of contract, it is an infringement of the power of contract to refuse whatever sanctions are needed to enforce their agreement, and that fact should be considered by the court when making its decision to withhold or grant enforcement.[119]

---

[119] MacNeil 527.

CHAPTER 11

Extracontractual Damages

¶ 11.01 GENERAL PROBLEMS IN RECOVERY OF EXTRACONTRACTUAL DAMAGES

Every potential litigant faces the problem of the high costs of lawyers, witnesses, and other services associated with judicial proceedings. The substantial costs of litigation deter many claimants, and in the absence of a statute or a specific contractual provision, the average litigant in a contract action can recover only the relatively modest court costs, even if he wins the case. As a result, compensatory damages may not actually compensate the plaintiff. He may be vindicated, and the defendant may have to pay substantial damages, but it is likely that the plaintiff will never be returned to the same economic position he would have enjoyed if the defendant had performed.

Plaintiffs in tort actions can soften the effect of the American presumption against the recovery of attorneys' fees by recovering punitive or substantial consequential damages for such amorphous injuries as mental anguish or emotional distress. The black-letter principles on contract law hold that neither punitive nor mental distress damages can be recovered for breach of contract. These damages do not flow from the private law and the private expectations of the parties; rather, they represent recoveries for conduct that violates some social obligation. As is true with so many black-letter rules, however, there are exceptions, and the cases indicate that there are many ways to avoid this rule.

Although courts in most jurisdictions do not permit the recovery of punitive damages in contract actions without proof of an independent tort, some do allow punitive damages for conduct accompanying the breach that is *almost* tortious, even though it does not fit into a specific tort category. Others treat the breach as a tort if the manner in which the breach occurs is reprehensible. In addition, special rules govern particular kinds of contracts, such as those between insureds and insurers or those that involve a fiduciary relationship. Even in states with a strict independent tort requirement, claims for punitive damages have caused some shifts in the rules on elections of remedies. The same set of operative facts may support a recovery of compensatory damages for breach of contract and punitive damages for a tort. The plaintiff thus recovers in contract and partially in tort without having to elect between remedies ex contractu and in delicto.

Some courts also allow the recovery of subjective mental anguish damages. This occurs either because the contract is a peculiar one (e.g., a promise to marry or a contract for embalming and funeral services) or because the breach is more likely to cause distress than any clearly definable economic loss. Leaving aside the special cases of marriages, funerals, and fiduciary relationships, courts seem to be influenced by the degree to which the plaintiff expects nonpecuniary benefits (e.g., a happy holiday trip) or by the degree to which the plaintiff relies on the expertise of the performing party (e.g., the construction of a new house). There are fewer of these cases than others that involve punitive damage claims, but they can roughly be fit into the theory of foreseeability that follows from *Hadley v. Baxendale*.[1] They open the way for fairly substantial recoveries in certain kinds of cases beyond the apparent economic effect of the agreement.

The willingness of courts to entertain claims for extracontractual damages is consistent with the observation of Professor Atiyah that more and more relationships are governed by considerations of public law than by simple reference to the parties' expressed

---

[1] Hadley v. Baxendale, 9 Ex. 341, 156 Eng. Rep. 145 (1854). For a discussion of the Hadley foreseeability rule, see ¶ 7.03[3][b].

agreement: "I suggest that there is today a growing recognition that, even where a transaction is a result of some voluntary conduct, the resulting rights and duties of the parties are, in large part, a product of the law and not of the parties' real agreement."[2] The following discussion of extracontractual damages illustrates the gray areas of distinction between contracts and torts that exist where the facts of a particular transaction do not fit neatly in a clearly defined category.

¶ 11.02 RECOVERY OF ATTORNEYS' FEES

[1] General Rule: Denial of Award to Prevailing Party

A typical contracting party who suffers damages caused by breach wants performance to satisfy his claim, not a suit to obtain a monetary substitute for performance, and for good reason.[3] A breach of contract usually causes the aggrieved party some inconvenience and often has serious consequences. Although nothing can fully substitute for performance, the plaintiff can be partly satisfied if he recovers a damage award that puts him in an economic position similar to that he expected from full performance. This certainly is the goal of contract law. The often-stated principle of remedies is to put the plaintiff in as good a position as he would have enjoyed without the breach.[4] Unfortunately, the nonbreaching party rarely achieves this goal. He may recover the benefit of his lost bargain, but in the process he is likely to incur substantial expenses that he cannot shift to the breaching party. Attorneys' fees are often the largest single item of the nonbreaching party's unexpected and unwanted expense.

Courts in the United States do not usually award attorneys' fees to the prevailing party in a trial, contrary to the practice of most western legal systems, including the English. Court costs, in comparison, are often charged to the losing party, although they rarely amount to a substantial sum. The rule in this country has

---

[2] Atiyah, *The Rise and Fall of Freedom of Contract* 734 (1978).

[3] In rare circumstances an aggrieved party may actually benefit from breach (e.g., when the contract is a losing proposition and the breach allows a suit "off" the contract in restitution).

[4] See, e.g., UCC § 1-106(1).

been a topic of considerable discussion and criticism over the years.[5] After paying all the costs of litigation and waiting for his case to wend its way through the judicial system, the successful plaintiff in a contract action may have a better understanding of the meaning of a Pyrrhic victory. The rationale for the general refusal of American courts to make the losing party pay the winner's legal fees is unclear. One reason suggested by the commentators is that the risk of having to pay attorneys' fees could discourage poor plaintiffs from pursuing meritorious claims for fear that they might lose.[6] This reasoning does not make a great deal of sense; the fear of losing and having to pay the defendant's lawyers might dissuade some plaintiffs who have claims of little merit but who sue in hopes of a nuisance settlement. It seems more likely that the problem of paying his own attorney without any hope of recovering those costs is a greater deterrent to litigation by the claimant with a good claim but little money than the risk that he might have to pay an unspecified amount sometime in the future if the outcome is not favorable. In any event, judges are competent to monitor fee awards to prevent them from being unreasonable. Whatever the rationale, the presumption against fee shifting remains strong, and there is little likelihood of any radical change.[7] The successful litigant in most cases still must satisfy his lawyer's bill from his own pocket.

[2] Statutory and Contractual Fee-Shifting Provisions

There are some common exceptions to the American rule against charging legal fees to the losing party. For the litigant in a

---

[5] See, e.g., Berger, "Court Awarded Attorneys' Fees: What Is 'Reasonable'?" 126 U. Pa. L. Rev. 281 (1977); Kuenzel, "The Attorneys' Fee: Why Not a Cost of Litigation?" 49 Iowa L. Rev. 75 (1963); McLaughlin, "The Recovery of Attorneys' Fees: A New Method of Financing Legal Services," 40 Fordham L. Rev. 761 (1972); Sands, "Attorneys' Fees as Recoverable Costs," 63 ABA J. 510 (1978); Note, 17 Wake Forest L. Rev. 457 (1981); Project, "Recent Developments in Attorneys' Fees," 29 Vand. L. Rev. 685 (1976).

[6] Calamari & Perrillo, *The Law of Contracts* § 14-36, at 569 (1977), citing Note, "Attorneys' Fees: Where Shall the Ultimate Burden Lie?" 20 Vand. L. Rev. 1216 (1967).

[7] There may be some incremental change toward a slightly more liberal approach to fee shifting, but the trend is evolutionary in character, not revolution-

contract case, two exceptions are important. First, a statute may provide for fee shifting; second, the agreement in dispute may contain a fee-shifting provision. Other exceptions may come into play in certain special cases. For instance, some jurisdictions allow a court to charge fees against a bad-faith litigant who is stubbornly litigious or who asserts frivolous defenses for the purpose of delay.[8] In addition, a case may arise ex contractu that results in the creation or preservation of a common fund from which the successful plaintiff may be awarded attorneys' fees, but such a case is more likely to develop in a situation that involves fiduciary or trust relationships.[9] There is also a limited exception in some jurisdictions (but not in the federal courts) that allows fee shifting in favor of a litigant who acts as a private attorney-general in creating or protecting a right or interest of significant public concern.[10]

---

ary. See generally 1 Speiser, *Attorneys' Fees* § 12:7 (1973) (hereinafter cited as Speiser).

[8] See generally Note, "Attorney Fees: Exceptions to the American Rule," 25 Drake L. Rev. 717, 732, 733 (1976); Roadway Express, Inc. v. Piper US Hall v. Cole, 412 US 1 (1973); Huechner v. Milburn, 538 F2d 1241 (6th Cir. 1976); Rolax v. Atlantic CLRR, 186 F2d 473 (4th Cir. 1951); Cleveland v. Second Nat'l Bank, 149 F2d 466 (6th Cir. 1945). A few states impose a penalty on unsuccessful appellants if the appeal is not meritorious or is frivolous. Fla. Stat. Ann. § 59.33 (1969); OC Ga. A. § 5-6-6 (1982); La. Code Civ. Proc. Ann. art. 59.33 (1969); Miss. Code Ann. § 11-3-23 (Supp. 1982); Mass. Gen. Laws Ann. ch. 211, § 10 (Supp. 1982). Rule 38 of the Federal Rules of Appellate Procedure allows a court to impose single or double costs for a frivolous appeal. See generally Comment, "Mandatory Assessment of Damages Against an Unsuccessful Appellant: A Constitutional Analysis," 53 Miss. LJ 281 (1983); Comment, "Mandatory 10-Percent Penalty on Unsuccessful Appeals of Money Judgements in Alabama — Constitutional and Policy Considerations," 32 Ala. L. Rev. 197 (1980).

[9] See generally 1 Speiser § 11.1 and see, e.g., Central RR Banking Co. v. Pettus, 113 US 116 (1885).

[10] The United States Supreme Court disavowed the private attorney-general exception in Alyeska Pipeline Serv. Co. v. The Wilderness Soc'y, 421 US 240 (1975). In response to the *Alyeska* decision, Congress passed the Civil Rights Attorney's Fee Awards Act of 1976, 42 USC § 1988 (1981), which allows an award of attorneys' fees to the prevailing party in a federal civil rights action. For a discussion of the availability of fees in one state for a private attorney-general action, see Serrano v. Priest, 20 Cal. 3d 25, 569 P2d 1303, 141 Cal. Rptr. 315 (1977). Attorneys' fees sometimes may be included in the fine for a civil contempt. Toledo Scale Co. v. Computing Scale Co., 261 US 399 (1923). If the plaintiff's success established, as a matter of law, the rights of members of a discernible class to collect on similar claims, there is also authority for an award of attorneys' fees. Sprague v. Taconic Nat'l Bank, 307 US 161 (1939).

Scores of statutes address fee shifting in different kinds of cases, and the provisions of these statutes vary greatly in their requirements and in the discretion allowed trial judges. For instance, more than seventy-five federal laws authorize fee shifting in private litigation. These include twenty-eight statutes that regulate business practices, six that involve environmental protection, four that protect civil rights, and three that provide remedies for patent or copyright infringement.[11]

Most jurisdictions approve allocations or awards of attorneys' fees that are provided for by contract.[12] Provisions for attorneys' fees are most common in notes and other evidences of indebtedness, and some jurisdictions limit the enforcement of fee-shifting provisions to contracts that involve debts.[13] A few jurisdictions refuse to enforce contract provisions for attorneys' fees because they are against public policy unless a specific statute authorizes a fee-shifting provision in the specific kind of contract at issue.[14] There may be a slight tendency in minority-rule jurisdictions toward a more liberal interpretation of the underlying policy and applicable statutes that could lead to more frequent fee shifting. For instance, a North Carolina statute allows fee shifting only if it is provided for in "any note, conditional sale contract, or other evidence of indebtedness."[15] The North Carolina Supreme Court construed the phrase "other evidence of indebtedness" to include an equipment lease in the case of *Stillwell Enterprises, Inc. v. Interstate Equipment Co.*[16] Although an equipment lease involves the payment of money, it is certainly not a debt in the traditional understanding of that term, and the *Stillwell* decision seems to indicate a desire to give effect to the parties' contractual choice of remedy rather than to adhere strictly to statutory law.[17]

---

[11] Note, 17 Wake Forest L. Rev. 457, 465 (1981).

[12] 2 Speiser § 15:3.

[13] Id.; Annot., 17 ALR2d 288 (1951).

[14] See generally 2 Speiser § 15:5.

[15] NC Gen. Stat. § 6-212 (1969).

[16] Stillwell Enters., Inc. v. Interstate Equip. Co., 300 NC 286, 266 SE2d 812 (1980).

[17] See generally Note, 17 Wake Forest L. Rev. 457 (1981).

Fee-shifting provisions in notes and similar instruments usually favor the creditor. A standard provision might call for a fee of 10 to 15 percent of the amount due on a note if the debtor fails to pay and the creditor has to bring suit. In at least one state, provisions of this type are reciprocal, even if they are written in favor of only one party; that is, in an action on a note a successful defendant could claim attorneys' fees even if the note only provided for fees to be paid to the creditor's lawyer.[18]

[3] Recovery of Incidental and Consequential Damages Under the UCC

The UCC provides for the recovery of incidental and consequential damages by sellers in Section 2-713 and by buyers in Section 2-715.[19] Section 1-106 also provides that remedies are to be "liberally construed" so that the plaintiff is in a position that is as good as his position would have been if full performance had occurred, "but neither consequential or special nor penal damages may be had except as specifically provided in this Act or by other rule of law."[20] Litigants have tried to recover attorneys' fees under these UCC provisions, but they generally have had little success.

A successful plaintiff who must pay substantial legal fees to vindicate his rights is not in as good a position as he would have been with full performance. Therefore, plaintiffs have argued that Section 1-106 requires an award of attorneys' fees. Courts have consistently rejected this argument and have construed Section 1-106 to refer only to traditional common-law rules for determining compensatory damages. Furthermore, they have read the section

---

[18] Mont. Code Ann. § 28-3-704 (1981); Diehl & Assocs., Inc. v. Houtchins, 180 Mont. 48, 588 P2d 1014 (1979); Burnham, "Contract Damages in Montana Part I: Expectancy Damages," 44 Mont. L. Rev. 1, 47 (1983).

[19] See ¶ 8.02 for a discussion of sellers' and buyers' recovery of incidental and consequential damages.

[20] Interestingly, this portion of Section 1-106 is not included in the Louisiana statute. The comment to the Louisiana code states that it would be contrary to existing Louisiana law. La. Rev. Stat. Ann. § 10:1-106, comment (a) (1983).

as a restatement of existing remedies, not as a statutory expansion of remedies.[21]

Litigants have also asserted that attorneys' fees are incidental or consequential damages within the meaning of Sections 2-713 or 2-715. These arguments have occasionally been successful, although the weight of authority clearly is to the contrary.[22] The successful cases have involved warranty defenses by good-faith buyers against third-party claimants. For example, in *Universal CIT Credit Corp. v. State Farm Mutual Insurance Co.*,[23] a 1973 Missouri case, a good-faith buyer won attorneys' fees from his seller after giving the seller notice of a third-party claim against title and of his intention to defend against the claim. The buyer in *De La Hoya v. Slim's Gun Shop*[24] found himself in a particularly embarrassing predicament. He bought a gun from Slim's in good faith, but the gun turned out to be stolen property, and the buyer was arrested for possession of stolen property. In an action against Slim's based on a breach of the warranty of title, he won the fees his lawyer charged to extricate him from his trouble with the police.

These cases are somewhat unusual, and the attorneys' fees fall more easily within the category of damages that would reasonably be foreseeable upon a breach. A seller presumably has better knowledge of title than anyone else, and if he sells a chattel to a

---

[21] See generally 1 *Hawkland UCC Series* § 1-106:01, at 95, 96 (1982) (hereinafter cited as Hawkland), citing Perkins State Bank v. Connally, 632 F2d 1306 (5th Cir. 1980); Florida Nat'l Bank at Gainesville v. Alfred & Ann Goldstein Found., Inc., 327 So. 2d 110 (Fla. Dist. Ct. App. 1976); Merrimack Farmers Exch., Inc. v. Elliott, 111 NH 121, 276 A2d 258 (1971); Neri v. Retail Marine Corp., 30 NY2d 393, 285 NE2d 311, 334 NYS2d 165 (1972).

[22] See generally 2 *Anderson on the Uniform Commercial Code* § 2-715:50, at 536 (3d ed. 1983) (hereinafter cited as Anderson), citing numerous cases; and see, e.g., Nick's Auto Sales, Inc. v. Radcliffe Auto Sales, Inc., 591 SW2d 709 (Ky. Ct. App. 1979); Jacobs v. Rosemount Dodge-Winnebago S., 310 NW2d 71 (Minn. 1981); DeVore v. Bostrom, 632 P2d 832 (Utah 1981); Murray v. Holiday Rambler, Inc., 83 Wis. 2d 406, 265 NW2d 513 (1978).

[23] Universal CIT Credit Corp. v. State Farm Mut. Ins. Co., 493 SW2d 385 (Mo. Ct. App. 1973).

[24] De La Hoya v. Slim's Gun Shop, 80 Cal. App. 3d, 146 Cal. Rptr. 68 (1978). Other less dramatic cases include Chemco Indus. Applicators Co. v. EI DuPont, 366 F. Supp. 278 (ED Mo. 1973); Cady v. Dick Loehr's, Inc., 100 Mich. App. 543, 299 NW2d 69 (1980).

good-faith purchaser who has no knowledge of an adverse claim, shifting the cost of defending the title back to the seller is really an allocation of a cost of performance, not a shifting of postbreach expenses external to the contract. If the evidence tends to suggest that the seller knew of the adverse claim at the time of sale, the warranty breach also bears earmarks of misrepresentation, and courts may be inclined to be somewhat more liberal in fashioning remedies because the conduct is close to being tortious.[25]

An Oklahoma court awarded attorneys' fees to the successful party as costs in a breach of contract case governed by the UCC.[26] There was no discussion, and this apparently is the only case that has characterized fees as costs. In another attempt to reward the winning party, a trial court in Utah included an award of attorneys' fees as an element of punitive damages in a contract case. This award was reversed by the Utah Supreme Court because no independent tort existed on which to base an award of punitive damages, regardless of the elements used to calculate them.[27] This case points up one of the major differences between plaintiffs in tort cases and in contract cases. Tort plaintiffs generally have more latitude in proving consequential damages, and in willful tort cases they may be able to recover punitive damages. This provides tort plaintiffs with a cushion for the payment of costs and fees not available to contract plaintiffs.[28]

No cases exist that treat attorneys' fees as incidental damages under either Section 2-713 or Section 2-715. Incidental damages under these UCC sections have been limited to such expenses as transportation and storage costs for rightfully rejected goods and other costs directly related to the incident that caused the litigation.[29]

---

[25] See generally Annot., 4 ALR3d 270 (1965).

[26] Osboren v. Bendix Home Sys., Inc., 613 P2d 445 (Okla. 1980).

[27] Jorgensen v. John Clay & Co., 660 P2d 229, 232, 233 (Utah 1983).

[28] In a case involving expert witnesses, the contracts plaintiff has another uncompensated cost; expert witness fees are not consequential damages under the UCC. See, e.g., Winchester v. McCullock Bros. Garage, Inc., 388 So. 2d 927 (Ala. 1980).

[29] See generally 4 Anderson §§ 2-715:4, 2-715:64.

[4] General Guidelines to Ensure Recovery

The approach of American courts to awards of attorneys' fees seems to be moving away from the traditional presumption against fee shifting, but the movement is slight and most contract litigants will continue to bear the costs of their own lawyers and other professional advisers. In many cases, this means that the nonbreaching party's net recovery will be substantially less than the compensatory damages calculated by the judge or the jury. Although some cases may fall within the coverage of specific statutes, the best way to assure a recovery of some of the attorneys' fees and other costs is to include a fee-shifting provision in the contract. Most states enforce these provisions if they are reasonable and not penal; in the states that do not regularly enforce fee-shifting clauses, statutes often exist that allow fee awards in particular kinds of cases, especially those that involve debts or other extensions of credit.

¶ 11.03 RECOVERY OF PUNITIVE DAMAGES

[1] Allowance of Punitive Damages

Punitive damages (sometimes called exemplary damages) serve many purposes in willful tort cases. They are intended to punish the defendant, to deter others from engaging in similar conduct, and to express community outrage at the defendant's antisocial behavior. They can also serve the silent purpose of compensating the plaintiff for the costs he incurs as a result of the defendant's conduct. Because punitive damages are, in one sense, a fine for antisocial behavior that violates public law, the cardinal rule is that they are not available in contract actions. Professor Farnsworth stated this rule as follows:

> [N]o matter how reprehensible the breach, damages that are punitive, in the sense of being in excess of those required to compensate the injured party for his lost expectation, are not ordinarily awarded for breach of contract. . . . [C]ontract law is, in its essential design, a law of strict liability, and the

accompanying system of remedies operates without regard to fault.[30]

Commentators have criticized rules that allow the award of punitive damages in tort cases because their standards are so vague that the results are often capricious and unfair.[31] In contrast, one writer has rejected the traditional limitations on contract recoveries as too narrow and inconsistent with economic realities. He has argued that the typical plaintiff in a contract action is undercompensated and that "supercompensatory damages" are justified.[32] Whatever arguments scholars have made, courts have consistently rejected the argument for punitive damages in what they characterize as "pure" contract cases while carving out a number of exceptions for specific kinds of contracts and for cases that seem to involve some elements of tort liability. Indeed, in the opinion of one writer, the exceptions seem at times to be swallowing the rule.[33] The number of ex contractu cases in which the plaintiff seeks punitive damages has increased substantially in recent years,

---

[30] Farnsworth, *Contracts* § 12.8, at 842 (1982). For a good judicial discussion of this point, see Battista v. Lebanon Trotting Ass'n, 538 F2d 111 (6th Cir. 1976). Both the first and the second Restatements have said that punitive damages are not available in contract cases. Restatement of Contracts § 342 (1932); Restatement (Second) of Contracts § 355 (1981).

[31] See, e.g., Ellis, "Fairness and Efficiency in the Law of Punitive Damages," 56 S. Cal. L. Rev. 1, 52, 53 (1982): "In summary, the law of punitive damages is characterized by a high degree of uncertainty that stems from the use of a multiplicity of vague, overlapping terms and the extraordinary deference accorded to juries who receive little meaningful guidance." And see Ghiardi, "The Case Against Punitive Damages," 8 Forum 411 (1972, 1973). See, e.g., Hawes Office Sys., Inc. v. Wang Laboratories, Inc., 537 F. Supp. 939 (EDNY 1982); Lowell v. Massachusetts Bonding & Ins. Co., 313 Mass. 257, 47 NE2d 265 (1943).

[32] Farber, "Reassessing the Economic Efficiency of Compensatory Damages for Breach of Contract," 66 Va. L. Rev. 1443, 1476–1478 (1980). For much the same reasons, another author has argued for the availability of punitive damages in consumer actions. Rice, "Exemplary Damages in Private Consumer Actions," 55 Iowa L. Rev. 307 (1969).

[33] Note, "Punitive Damages in Contract Actions — Are the Exceptions Swallowing the Rule?" 20 Washburn LJ 86 (1980); and see Sullivan, "Punitive Damages in the Law of Contract: The Reality and the Illusion of Legal Change," 61 Minn. L. Rev. 207 (1977) (hereinafter cited as Sullivan); Note, "The Expanding Availability of Punitive Damages in Contract Actions," 8 Ind. L. Rev. 668 (1975).

and in a surprising number of these cases the plaintiff has been successful despite the reiteration of the presumption against punitive damages.

Courts have allowed punitive damages for many years in cases that involve three categories of breach: (1) breach of a promise to marry;[34] (2) breach of a contract whose performance is a public duty (e.g., a breach by a public utility or common carrier);[35] and (3) breach of a fiduciary duty.[36] In several recent cases, litigants have included claims for punitive damages because either an independent tort accompanied the breach of contract, or the breach was coupled with fraudulent conduct, or the breach itself amounted to a tort. These cases often are confusing because the facts vary greatly and the opinions fail to distinguish between what is in delicto and what is ex contractu. They fall into what one critic has called a "twilight zone" between "mere breach and obvious tort."[37] It is essential to examine carefully the facts of these various types of cases to determine whether there is in fact any shift toward the award of punitive damages for breach of contract or whether courts are engaged in reworking tort liability under the rubric of contract.

[2] Punitive Damages in Breach of Marriage Cases

The marriage cases are the simplest. Changes in social mores, statutes, and the common law have virtually eliminated actions for breach of the promise to marry. Significant damage questions in quarrels between former lovers are more likely to arise in "palimony" cases, including those that involve promises to make a

---

[34] See, e.g., Goldstein v. Young, 156 Fla. 500, 23 So. 2d 730 (1945); Coryell v. Colbaugh, 1 NJL 77 (1791); Simpson, *Contracts* § 195, at 394 (1965) (hereinafter cited as Simpson).

[35] See, e.g., Trout v. Watkins Livery & Undertaking Co., 148 Mo. App. 621, 130 SW 136 (1910).

[36] See, e.g., PSG Co. v. Merrill Lynch, Pierce, Fenner & Smith, Inc., 417 F2d 659 (9th Cir. 1969), cert. denied, 397 US 918 (1970) (breach by stockbroker); Brown v. Coates, 253 F2d 36 (DC Cir. 1958) (breach by real estate broker).

[37] Sullivan 235.

will.[38] Even so, older cases that awarded punitive damages bore the earmarks of tort more than those of contract. Although the action may have arisen from a broken promise, the damage award more often than not was related to the manner in which the engagement was broken. For example, humiliating the bride by failing to show up for the wedding was worse than a quiet, private revocation. The manner of the breach, not the breach itself, was the driving force behind the damage award.[39] Many decisions came close to creating a separate tort action for humiliation, and a suit today might be brought for the intentional infliction of emotional distress rather than for a simple breach of contract.[40]

[3] Punitive Damages in Breach of Public Duty Cases

[a] Public Utility and Common Carrier Cases

The public utility and common carrier cases also resemble tort actions more than they do straightforward contract actions. Punitive damages are justified because the defendant has violated a public obligation. It may be that the operative fact is the breach of a private agreement with the plaintiff, but unlike ordinary contracting parties, public utilities and common carriers are under a public duty not to breach a contract. This duty limits their freedom to choose not to perform because the contract is inefficient; that is, because performance will be more expensive than the damages occasioned by breach. In some instances, the defendant has held a government-licensed monopoly, as in the case of a telegraph company or a waterworks, and the court has treated a breach of con-

---

[38] See, e.g., Marvin v. Marvin, 18 Cal. 3d 660, 557 P2d 106 (1976). See generally Hunter, "An Essay on Contract and Status, Race, Marriage and the Meretricious Spouse," 64 Va. L. Rev. 1039 (1978); McWalter, "Marriage as Contract: Towards a Functional Redefinition of the Marital Status," 9 Colum. JL & Soc. Probs. 607 (1973); Weitzman, "Legal Regulation of Marriage: Tradition and Change," 62 Calif. L. Rev. 1169 (1974).

[39] See, e.g., Osman v. Winter, 30 Ore. 177, 46 P 780 (1982).

[40] See ¶ 11.04.

tract as an abuse of the public trust.[41] More commonly, the defendant has been a member of a regulated industry that is considered to be of significant public importance. Most of the recent cases in this area have involved insurance companies.

[b] Insurance Cases

Several themes run through insurance cases. First, there is the general principle that insurance agreements are to be read and construed more strongly against the insurer because the average consumer is less able to understand the implications of the technical aspects of an insurance policy than the author of the policy.[42] Second, there is the notion that an insurance policy is something more than a simple contract: It is a means for socializing the costs of a variety of risks and, as such, is invested with elements of the common good as well as the interests of the particular insurer and insured.[43] The breach of an insurance contract by an insurer also may be a breach of a publicly imposed duty rather than a simple breach of the privately created relationship between the insured and the insurer. Although the action may be characterized as one in contract, the argument that the breach is of a public rather than a

---

[41] See, e.g., Birmingham Waterworks Co. v. Keiley, 2 Ala. App. 629, 56 So. 838 (1911); Woodbury v. Tampa Waterworks, 57 Fla. 243, 49 So. 556 (1909); Woody v. National Bank, 194 NC 549, 140 SE 150 (1927). Important public policy may be a factor in some cases. A worker who was discharged for trying to organize fellow workers pursuant to the federal Railway Labor Act was allowed to sue for back pay, emotional distress, injury to reputation, and punitive damages. Brown v. World Airways, Inc., 539 F. Supp. 179 (SDNY 1982).

[42] See, e.g., Gaunt v. John Hancock Mut. Life Ins. Co., 160 F2d 599 (2d Cir. 1947).

[43] Classic articles on the dual nature of insurance contracts include: Funk, "The Duty of an Insurer to Act Promptly on an Application," 75 U. Pa. L. Rev. 207 (1927); Kessler, "Contracts of Adhesion — Some Thoughts About Freedom of Contract," 43 Colum. L. Rev. 629 (1943); Shultz, "The Special Nature of the Insurance Contract: A Few Suggestions for Further Study," 15 Law & Contemp. Probs. 376 (1950). The authors of a well-known contracts casebook treat insurance as an example of "status" rather than "contract." See Kessler & Gilmore, *Contracts* 1336–1376 (2d ed. 1970); see also Holmes, "Is There Life After Gilmore's Death of Contract? — Inductions From a Study of Commercial Good Faith in First-Party Insurance Contracts," 65 Cornell L. Rev. 330 (1980).

private duty means that the action has the basic characteristic of one in tort.[44]

Most of the insurance cases in which courts have awarded punitive damages have involved bad-faith refusals or delays in paying valid claims. The Indiana case of *Rex Insurance Co. v. Baldwin*[45] is typical. The insurance company refused to pay the amount due on a life insurance policy. The company argued that the decedent had made material misrepresentations on his application, but the incontestability period had passed before the insured died and the company knew that its legal position was indefensible. The appeals court upheld the trial court's punitive damage award because the company's refusal to pay was in bad faith. The same court sustained another award of punitive damages for an unwarranted delay in paying on a fire insurance policy.[46] Another insurance company, however, was able to show that its delay in payment resulted from a good-faith investigation of possible arson, and it did not have to pay punitive damages.[47]

The Indiana Court of Appeals made explicit the connection between the insurance cases and tort concepts in its 1982 decision in *Nationwide Mutual Insurance Co. v. Neville*.[48] The court discussed the general rules that govern punitive damage awards and said that punitive damages may be available when a serious wrong that is tortious in nature has been committed that does not fit conveniently into a tort category.[49] The court concluded that some evidence must exist of "fraud, gross negligence or oppression."[50] Even though the performance of an insurance contract may be a public responsibility, the insurer's breach is not always a breach of a public duty that justifies punitive damages. The plaintiff still must show some oppressive action. The Indiana Court of Appeals indi-

---

[44] "The special relationship between the insurer and the insured illustrates the public policy considerations that may support exemplary damages in cases such as this." Egan v. Mutual of Omaha Ins. Co., 24 Cal. 3d 809, 820, 598 P2d 452, 457, 157 Cal. Rptr. 482, 487 (1979).

[45] Rex Ins. Co. v. Baldwin, 163 Ind. App. 308, 323 NE2d 270 (1975).

[46] Vernon Fire & Casualty Co. v. Sharp, 264 Ind. 599, 349 NE2d 173 (1976).

[47] Hoosier Ins. Co. v. Mangino, 419 NE2d 978 (Ind. Ct. App. 1981).

[48] Nationwide Mut. Ins. Co. v. Neville, 434 NE2d 585 (Ind. Ct. App. 1982).

[49] Id. at 593.

[50] Id.

cated what it considered to be oppressive acts that justify punitive damages in *Riverside Insurance Co. v. Pedigo.*[51] The insurance company rejected numerous claim forms under a fire policy for technical reasons. The insured, who became exasperated and filed suit, did not learn until the litigation began that the real reason for the delay was an ongoing arson investigation. The court characterized the insurance company's refusal to inform the insured of the investigation and its refusal to process his claim as deceitful and therefore allowed a claim for punitive damages.

Some courts have been explicit about treating the breach of an insurance contract (or at least the breach of the implied duty of good faith) as an independent tort. This appears to be the rule, for instance, in Alabama,[52] Mississippi,[53] Montana,[54] North Dakota,[55] Oklahoma,[56] and Vermont.[57] The Mississippi courts have established an odd limitation. Although the breach of the implied duty of good faith in an insurance contract may be tortious and may support a claim for both punitive and compensatory damages, Mississippi does not allow compensatory damages to exceed the policy limits.[58] Thus, the action for breach of the insurance contract sounds in tort and compensatory damages may be calculated up to a point in accordance with tort principles of liability, but the plaintiff's recovery and the defendant's liability are limited by the terms of the contract. Of course, by allowing recovery of punitive damages, Mississippi provides a means for the jury to circumvent the limitations imposed by the policy.

The confusing intermixture of tort and contract principles in Mississippi illustrates the difficulties courts have experienced in trying to classify these cases. In a 1968 decision, the North Caro-

---

[51] Riverside Ins. Co. v. Pedigo, 430 NE2d 796 (Ind. Ct. App. 1982).

[52] Chavers v. National Sec. Fire & Casualty Co., 405 So. 2d 1 (Ala. 1981).

[53] Standard Life Ins. Co. v. Veal, 354 So. 2d 239 (Miss. 1977).

[54] Jardine, Stephenson, Blewett & Weaver v. USF&G Co., 91 FRD 284 (D. Mont. 1981).

[55] Corwin Chrysler-Plymouth, Inc. v. Westchester Fire Ins. Co., 279 NW2d 638 (ND 1979).

[56] McCorkle v. Great Atl. Ins. Co., 637 P2d 583 (Okla. 1981).

[57] Phillips v. Aetna Life Ins. Co., 473 F. Supp. 984 (NH 1979).

[58] Travelers Indem. Co. v. Wetherbee, 368 So. 2d 829 (Miss. 1979).

lina Supreme Court refused to allow a punitive damage recovery in a case that involved an insurance company's refusal to defend a claim against its insured. The court characterized the breach as "willful," "intentional," and in "wanton disregard of the rights of plaintiff," but the breach did not amount to a tort because it was nothing more than an intentional refusal to perform a contract.[59] Although North Carolina courts have since become somewhat more tolerant of punitive damage claims in similar cases,[60] their refusal to extend tort principles to cover insurance cases that involve breaches of the implied duty of good faith is evidence of the continuing strength of contract principles and the inconsistencies that result when, in examining virtually the same set of facts, one court looks through contract lenses and the other looks through tort lenses.

The California courts have shown as much or more ingenuity as any others in classifying breaches of insurance contracts in ways that justify the recovery of damages measured by the standards of tort law rather than contract law. A California statute specifically limits punitive damage awards to actions for breach of noncontractual obligations if the plaintiff proves that the defendant acted with malice, oppressively or fraudulently.[61] Thus, a breach of contract does not support an award of punitive damages even if the contract is of a special nature, such as a contract between an insured and an insurer. Beginning with the 1967 case of *Crisci v. Security Pacific Insurance Co.,*[62] California courts have fashioned a rule that allows plaintiffs to avoid the limitations of contract recoveries. The courts have reasoned that an independent duty of good faith exists that may be broken when the insurance company breaches the contract. When that happens, the contract breach can be treated as an oppressive breach of the independent duty and, for all intents and purposes, as a tort that might support an award of punitive damages.

---

[59] King v. Insurance Co., 273 NC 396, 159 SE2d 891, 893 (1968). To the same effect, see Girard Trust Bank v. Easton, 165 SE2d 252 (NC Ct. App. 1965).

[60] See, e.g., Newton v. Standard Fire Ins. Co., 291 NC 105, 229 SE2d 297 (1976); Murray v. Allstate Ins. Co., 51 NC App. 10, 275 SE2d 195 (1981).

[61] Cal. Civil Code § 3294 (1980).

[62] Crisci v. Security Pac. Ins. Co., 66 Cal. 2d 425, 426 P2d 173, 58 Cal. Rptr. 13 (1967).

The leading California case is *Gruenberg v. Aetna Insurance Co.,*[63] decided in 1973. Gruenberg's business was destroyed by fire. It was insured for $35,000 by three different insurance companies. At the scene of the fire, Gruenberg became involved in a heated argument with an arson investigator, and he was arrested. An insurance claim adjuster informed the police that Gruenberg had excess coverage on the premises. The implication of this conversation was that he had a motive for setting the fire, and the authorities subsequently charged Gruenberg with arson. While these charges were pending, the lawyer for the insurers demanded that Gruenberg appear in his office and respond under oath to questions. He refused, on the advice of his lawyer, as long as the police investigation continued. Eventually, the charges against Gruenberg were dropped for insufficient evidence, and he agreed to answer the questions of the insurance lawyer, but the insurers asserted that the coverage was void because Gruenberg had refused to show up for questioning the first time. In the ensuing lawsuit, the court said that if Gruenberg's allegations were true, the defendants had violated their duties of good faith and fair dealing. Gruenberg only had to allege and prove unreasonable or malicious behavior by the insurance companies in order to establish a cause of action for a breach of a noncontractual obligation for which punitive damages might be available.

Gruenberg was especially significant in California because the cases since *Crisci* had required plaintiffs to allege and prove the elements of a separate, identifiable tort, such as the intentional infliction of emotional distress,[64] in order to recover punitive damages. The proof of the various elements of a separate tort could create difficulties for a plaintiff. The emotional distress tort, for instance, required a showing of extreme or outrageous conduct. After *Gruenberg,* a plaintiff only had to show that there was a breach accompanied by unreasonable or malicious behavior. The breach of the good-faith duty, not the nature of the accompanying activity, became the key. *Gruenberg* thus transformed a certain

[63] Gruenberg v. Aetna Ins. Co., 9 Cal. 3d 566, 510 P2d 1032, 108 Cal. Rptr. 480 (1973).

[64] See, e.g., Fletcher v. Western Nat'l Life Ins. Co., 10 Cal. App. 3d 376, 89 Cal. Rptr. 78 (1970); see also Merlo v. Standard Life & Assurance Ins. Co., 59 Cal. App. 3d 5, 130 Cal. Rptr. 416 (1976).

kind of contract breach into a tort. *Gruenberg,* however, was decided simply on the pleadings. The next year the California Court of Appeals clarified *Gruenberg* and held that the plaintiff would have to prove that the defendant breached the duty of good faith with the specific intent to injure the plaintiff in order to make out a case for punitive damages.[65]

Neal v. Farmers Insurance Exchange[66] is an example of what California courts considered to be malice after *Gruenberg*. The insured was seriously injured by an uninsured motorist in an automobile accident. His policy included uninsured motorist coverage up to $15,000. The insured's lawyer tried to reach a prompt settlement because his client was in poor financial condition due partially to other family health problems. When the insurer countered with an offer of $5,000, the parties reached an impasse. The claim went to arbitration and the arbitrator awarded the $15,000 policy limit to the insured. In a subsequent action for bad-faith dealing, it came out that the insurer had a company policy of delaying payments to financially insecure policy holders in order to force settlements favorable to the insurer. This satisfied the malice requirement. The jury returned an undifferentiated verdict of $15 million for compensatory and punitive damages. The trial judge reduced the award to $750,000 and the court of appeals sustained the judgment.

Some states have statutory remedies or penalties for bad-faith dealing by insurance companies. In these jurisdictions, courts sometimes have held that the statutory remedy is exclusive.[67] That has not always been the case, especially where the plaintiff has alleged a special injury beyond those contemplated by the statute.[68]

Insurance cases might be considered to be in a special category along with other public duty cases and to have little or no

---

[65] Silberg v. California Life Ins. Co., 11 Cal. 3d 452, 113 Cal. Rptr. 711 (1974).

[66] Neal v. Farmers Ins. Exch., 21 Cal. 3d 910, 148 Cal. Rptr. 389 (1978).

[67] See generally McCarthy, *Punitive Damages in Bad-Faith Cases* § 1.2, at 4, 5 (3d ed. 1983).

[68] Id., citing Continental Re-Ins. Co. v. Spanton, 667 F2d 1289 (9th Cir. 1981); Baker v. American States Ins. Co., 428 NE2d 1342 (Ind. Ct. App. 1981); Bob Godfrey Pontiac, Inc. v. Orloff, 291 Ore. 318, 630 P2d 840 (1981).

effect on contract law in general, but many of the opinions do not differentiate insurance cases from others. There is apparent in some of the opinions a concern for the protection of the weaker party in a bargain. Although the decisions are not explicit, many opinions have overtones of paternal concern for the consumer or the weaker, less competent contracting party. For instance, in *Sweet v. Grange Mutual Casualty Co.*,[69] a 1975 Ohio decision, the court made much of the fact that the plaintiff was a disabled Vietnam War veteran whose only means of transportation was his automobile, which had been destroyed in an accident. The insurance company's refusal to pay full value for the automobile was bad faith, no matter who the plaintiff might have been, but the court's solicitude for the disabled veteran indicated a special awareness of the plaintiff's identity that could have influenced its ultimate handling of the case. In addition, many courts have written their opinions in language that is not confined to insurance cases and that may apply more generally.[70]

[4] Punitive Damages in Breach of Fiduciary Duty Cases

The final identifiable group of decisions that can be segregated from general contract cases involve the breach of a fiduciary duty.[71] These cases are not altogether different from the public duty cases because the public law defines fiduciary relationships and there is a community interest in assuring that certain kinds of

---

[69] Ashland County Court of Appeals No. 607, Unreported, June 30, 1975, cited in Battista v. Lebanon Trotting Ass'n, 538 F2d 111, 117 (6th Cir. 1976).

[70] See Note, "The Expanding Availability of Punitive Damages in Contract Actions," 8 Ind. LJ 668, 680 (1975). See generally Birnbaum & Wrubel, "Extracontractual Damages Against Insurers: An Overview" in *Extracontractual Damages* 1 (Groves, ed. 1983).

[71] See, e.g., PSG Co. v. Merrill Lynch, Pierce, Fenner & Smith, Inc., 417 F2d 659 (9th Cir. 1969), cert. denied, 397 US 918 (1970); International Bhd. of Boilermakers v. Braswell, 388 F2d 193 (5th Cir. 1968), cert. denied, 391 US 935 (1968); Hess v. Jarboe, 201 Kan. 705, 443 P2d 294 (1968); Brown v. Coates, 253 F2d 36 (DC Cir. 1958); Harper v. Interstate Brewery Co., 168 Ore. 26, 120 P2d 757 (1942). In one odd dictum, the Court of Appeals for the Fifth Circuit noted that the concept of fiduciary duty originated in equity. The court reasoned that because courts of equity do not award punitive damages, none is available for breaches of equitable duties. Carter Equip. Co. v. John Deere Indus. Equip. Co., 681 F2d 386, 396 (5th Cir. 1982).

trusts are maintained properly.[72] Nevertheless, the fiduciary cases often do not involve heavily regulated industries (with the obvious exceptions of banks, brokerage houses, real estate brokers, and other financial institutions) and may involve highly private agreements that have little effect on the rest of the world.

Nonfeasance may be as reprehensible in a fiduciary case as malfeasance. The marriage cases and the bulk of the public duty and insurance cases involve malfeasance: The defendant not only breached the contract, but he did so in a malicious or oppressive manner. For example, an insurer, knowing that its insured was in desperate straits, may have refused to pay a claim even though there was no legal basis for the refusal; a prospective groom may have renounced his promise to marry on the eve of the wedding and cast aspersions on the virtue of his betrothed. Few, if any, of these cases have involved simple nonfeasance, which certainly may be a breach of contract but which may not contain those elements of bad faith that seem to justify tortlike recoveries. In a fiduciary relationship, however, nonfeasance can be as bad as malfeasance because the nature of the relationship places a heavy burden on the person who is the fiduciary. What might be a simple breach in another context may be a more serious offense in a fiduciary relationship.

The well-known trial lawyer Percy Foreman was the central figure in a fiduciary duty case that should be of interest to most lawyers.[73] A Mrs. Singleton retained Foreman to represent her in a divorce proceeding. During the course of the proceedings, Mrs. Singleton decided that she wanted to settle and to halt the case. According to Mrs. Singleton, Foreman "exploded," refused to settle, and said that he would "ruin" both her and her husband if she tried to settle. Mrs. Singleton sued Foreman, who won a judgment on the pleadings. The Court of Appeals for the Fifth Circuit reversed because the complaint alleged facts that were sufficient to make out a prima facie case for breach of Foreman's fiduciary duty as counsel to Mrs. Singleton or for the intentional infliction of emotional distress. The court said that Mrs. Singleton was entitled to a day in court and if she were to prove what she alleged she

---

[72] See, e.g., Sullivan 226–229.

[73] Singleton v. Foreman, 435 F2d 962 (5th Cir. 1970).

might be entitled to punitive damages. Too much should not be made of the Foreman case because it did involve allegations that clearly established a prima facie tort action, but the opinion describes the high standard of care that a fiduciary must meet.

Brown v. Coates[74] was a more typical fiduciary duty case. The plaintiff contracted with the defendant, a real estate agent, to exchange his home for one listed by the defendant. The defendant was to sell the plaintiff's home and apply the net proceeds to the purchase of the other house. The agent sold the plaintiff's house but did not apply the proceeds properly, in breach of the agency agreement. The court stated that the defendant "held himself out to the public as a person in whom the public could place trust and confidence in real estate transactions."[75] The defendant's actions were not only in breach of the contract but were also in violation of the trust that the plaintiff reposed in him, and the court awarded both compensatory and punitive damages.

The 1979 decision of the Kansas Supreme Court in *Henderson v. Hassur*[76] is especially significant because it involved two businessmen in a commercial setting, albeit one that involved a relationship of trust. The plaintiff owned a chain of restaurants and wanted to expand into Mexico. He engaged the defendant to select and to purchase suitable locations in return for a stated fee for each purchase. The plaintiff later discovered that the defendant made a secret profit of $32,000 on one of the transactions. The court found this to be a breach of the defendant agent's fiduciary obligation of disclosure and fair dealing and allowed a claim for punitive damages as well as restitution of the secret profit.

Banks have had to pay punitive damages for wrongfully dishonoring a depositor's check. A wrongful dishonor, however, is closely akin to a slander of credit, and the relationship of the bank to its depositors entails both fiduciary obligations and public responsibilities.[77] Thus, it is difficult to separate wrongful dishonor

---

[74] Brown v. Coates, 253 F2d 36 (DC Cir. 1958).

[75] Id. at 38.

[76] Henderson v. Hassur, 594 P2d 650 (Kan. 1979).

[77] See, e.g., Yacht Club Sales and Serv., Inc. v. The First Nat'l Bank of N. Idaho, 101 Idaho 852, 623 P2d 464 (1980); Winkler v. Citizens State Bank, 89 Kan. 279, 131 P 597 (1913); Simpson § 195, at 394.

cases from fiduciary, public duty, and insurance cases. Interestingly, it has been held that the statutory remedies of the UCC for wrongful dishonor are not exclusive and do not preclude a claim for punitive damages.[78]

[5] Punitive Damages in Contract Cases: Remedies in Tort and in Contract

Many cases involve neither special relationships nor public duties. The question in these cases is to what extent the black-letter prohibition of punitive damages for contract breaches applies. These are the most confusing cases, because although courts have consistently reiterated the presumption against punitive damages, many have sought assiduously to avoid that limitation by one means or another. The result is a hodgepodge of decisions that borrow reasoning from the fiduciary and public duty cases to create new tort actions or to create actions that are somewhere between tort and contract but do not fit comfortably in either. Perhaps the most interesting aspect of these cases is the marriage of different theories through one set of operative facts. Every law student learns the basic principle that a given set of facts might make out a case ex contractu or in delicto. Modern pleading rules

---

[78] Siegman v. Equitable Trust Co., 267 Md. 309, 297 A2d 758 (1972). Section 4-402 provides:

> "A payor bank is liable to its customer for damages proximately caused by the wrongful dishonor of an item. When the dishonor occurs through mistake liability is limited to actual damages proved. If so, proximately caused and proved damages may include damages for an arrest or prosecution of the customer or other consequential damages. Whether any consequential damages are proximately caused by the wrongful dishonor is a question of fact to be determined in each case."

Thus, Section 4-402 establishes a tort standard of foreseeability for damages and seems to treat a wrongful dishonor as if it were a tort. There is no mention of punitive damages. Section 1-106(1) provides that remedies "shall be liberally administered" but goes on to prohibit "special or penal damages . . . except as specifically provided in this Act or by other rule of law." The *Siegman* court said that the omission of punitive damages from the language of Section 4-402 could not be construed as a prohibition when read together with the "liberal administration" provision of Section 1-106(1). *Siegman* should be compared with Waters v. Trenckmann, 503 P2d 1187 (Wyo. 1982), which interpreted Section 1-106(1) to prohibit punitive damage recoveries in UCC cases. See 1 Hawkland § 1-106:04, at 104 (approving *Siegman* and disapproving *Waters*).

allow a plaintiff to set out the facts in support of two separate counts, but sometime between the filing of the complaint and the completion of his presentation the plaintiff's lawyer must decide whether to pursue a remedy in tort or in contract. He cannot recover in both. This time-honored principle, which has its roots deep in the common law, is repeatedly ignored in the series of cases that try to fit contract breaches into categories that allow the recovery of punitive damages. As a result, a plaintiff who elects to proceed ex contractu may obtain a remedy that sounds in tort as well as in contract.[79]

[a] The South Carolina Rule

The South Carolina courts have given the most consideration to punitive damage recoveries in contract cases.[80] The landmark South Carolina case was *Welborn v. Dixon,*[81] decided in 1904. The plaintiff borrowed money from the defendant and conveyed certain real property as security for the note. The defendant agreed to reconvey the property upon payment of the note but breached the agreement by selling the land to a third party. The plaintiff was able to recover both compensatory and punitive damages. *Welborn* established the "South Carolina" rule that punitive damages may be awarded where a fraudulent act accompanies a breach of contract.

The South Carolina rule has been applied most often in cases between insureds and insurers. The 1974 decision in *Wright v. Public Savings Life Insurance Co.*[82] is a good example. The insured plaintiff was an elderly domestic servant who had two policies with the defendant, a life policy and a health and accident policy. She paid weekly premiums, sometimes directly at the field office in one city, other times by mail to the company's home office in another city. She received receipts for her payments from the field office but never received any acknowledgments from the

---

[79] See, e.g., Life Ins. Co. of Va. v. Murray Inv. Co., 646 F2d 224 (5th Cir. 1981).

[80] See Note, "Punitive Damages for Breach of Contract in South Carolina," 10 SCLQ 444 (1958); Note, "Punitive Damages for Breach of Contract," 11 NCL Rev. 160 (1933).

[81] Welborn v. Dixon, 70 SC 108, 49 SE 232 (1904).

[82] Wright v. Public Sav. Life Ins. Co., 262 SC 285, 204 SE2d 57 (1974).

home office. The home office cancelled her policies for nonpayment. Someone later forged the plaintiff's name to a form saying that the policies were cancelled properly. The court found the actions of the insurance company to have been both in breach of the contract and fraudulent. The plaintiff was entitled to seek punitive damages. The definition of "fraudulent act," however, was nebulous: "Courts are compelled to content themselves with comparatively few general rules for its discovery and defeat, and allow the facts and circumstances peculiar to each case to bear heavily upon the conscience and judgment of the court or jury in determining its presence or absence."[83]

Although *Wright* was an insurance case and numerous applications of the *Welborn* doctrine have involved litigation with insurance companies, the South Carolina rule has been applied in all types of cases. The special relationship between insured and insurer may ease the plaintiff's burden of proof, but that relationship is not the key to the rule.[84]

[b] The Texas Rule

Texas also has developed an independent tort rule.[85] Punitive damages may be recovered if a contract breach is accompanied by an independent tort of the type that would normally justify an award of punitive damages. At first glance, the South Carolina and the Texas rules may seem to be two ways of saying the same thing, but there are striking differences between them. The Texas rule requires that the plaintiff allege and prove the elements of a tort separate and apart from the breach of contract. The facts must

---

[83] Id. at 285, 204 SE2d at 59.

[84] See, e.g., Sullivan v. Calhoun, 117 SC 137, 108 SE 634 (1923) (landlord breached contract with sharecropper, ran him off the premises, and took his crops). But cf. Holland v. Spartanburg Herald-Journal Co., 166 SC 454, 165 SE 203 (1932) (plaintiff sold his interest in defendant company on the condition that he would be employed for three years at a stated salary, but he was fired; held, that allegations of breach by willful and malicious discharge were insufficient to support a claim for punitive damages).

[85] See, e.g., Briggs v. Rodriguez, 236 SW2d 510 (Tex. Civ. App. 1951); National Fin. Co. v. Abernathy, 66 SW2d 358 (Tex. Civ. App. 1934); Morgan v. Sternberg, 23 SW2d 527 (Tex. Civ. App. 1929); Hooks v. Fitzenreiter, 76 Tex. 277, 13 SW 230 (1890).

support two separate and identifiable claims for relief. The South Carolina rule, on the other hand, only requires that the breach be fraudulent, which is a relatively loose concept as described in *Wright*. There is no need to prove the elements of a specific tort. The Texas rule may be somewhat broader in that any kind of independent tort suffices as long as it is of a type reprehensible enough to support a demand for punitive damages. In South Carolina, any breach of contract suffices if it is accomplished in a manner that is offensive to the "conscience and judgment of the court or jury." Thus, the South Carolina rule more radically departs from traditional common-law approaches.[86]

The case of *Schepp v. Giles* [87] provides a good example of the Texas rule. The plaintiff alleged that he was wrongfully discharged from his job and that the defendant had falsely called him a liar. The wrongful discharge was a contract breach. Calling the plaintiff a liar was slander, which was a tort that would justify an award of punitive damages under Texas Law. Therefore, the plaintiff could seek normal contract damages for the breach and punitive damages for the slander. This really was little more than two separate actions handled in one proceeding, and it did not even raise any election of remedies problems. Firing the plaintiff and slandering him were two separate acts, either of which could have supported an action.

The Texas rule was restated in 1981 in *Amoco Production Co. v. Alexander*.[88] The owners of the royalties on an oil field sued the lessee of the field, Amoco Production Company, alleging that Amoco's imprudent performance resulted in the field being drained without proper recovery. The plaintiffs wanted compensatory and punitive damages, but the court held that the breach of the implied covenant in the lease to prevent drainage was simply a contract breach and the defendant's negligence did not amount to a tort that would support a demand for punitive damages. In comparison, a

---

[86] See Note, "Punitive Damages for Breach of Contract in South Carolina," 10 SCLQ 444–446 (1958).

[87] Schepp v. Giles, 222 SW 348 (Tex. Civ. App. 1920); see also Dallas Hotel Co. v. McCue, 25 SW2d 902 (Tex. Civ. App. 1930) (in discharging hotel clerk, manager rudely took hold of her and shoved her into a public room).

[88] Amoco Prod. Co. v. Alexander, 420 SW2d 317 (1981).

claim for punitive damages was upheld in *Palmer v. Fuqua,*[89] a fifth circuit decision applying Texas law, because the contract breach also constituted a breach of the fiduciary relationship among business partners.[90]

[c] Applications of the South Carolina and Texas Rules in Other Jurisdictions

The Texas rule has been followed more often than the South Carolina rule, although there are significant variances among state jurisdictions that illustrate the vagueness of the descriptive terms courts use in many of these cases. The inconsistencies among the cases can be appreciated only by examining a number of them. In the following discussion, states that are not mentioned either have not addressed the problem or have simply copied the approach of another state without adding anything to the debate.

[i] Arizona. Arizona courts follow the Texas rule, at least in form. The 1981 opinion in *Miscione v. Bishop,*[91] held that punitive damages were not available without proof of a separate identifiable tort. Furthermore, the court indicated that the plaintiff had to prove some actual damage beyond nominal damages. *Miscione* did not clarify the dictum in *Lerner v. Brettschneider,*[92] decided two years earlier, that an "aggravated, outrageous, malicious or wanton" breach of contract itself might be a tort.[93] Thus, Arizona requires an independent tort, but the breach itself may be a tort. If the contract breach were treated as a tort for purposes of the independent tort rule, Arizona would be closer to the South Carolina rule. It would also come closer to abolishing the election problem by creating two causes of action from one set of facts and perhaps allowing recovery on both.

---

[89] Palmer v. Fuqua, 641 F2d 1146 (5th Cir. 1981).

[90] In Texas, partners are fiduciaries one to another. Johnson v. Peckham, 132 Tex. 148, 120 SW2d 786 (1938). *Fuqua* involved an alleged breach by the managing general partner of the duty he owed to the limited partners in a limited partnership.

[91] Miscione v. Bishop, 130 Ariz. 371, 636 P2d 149 (1981).

[92] Lerner v. Brettschneider, 123 Ariz. 152, 598 P2d 515 (1979).

[93] Id. at 152, 598 P2d at 519.

[ii] Arkansas. The Arkansas approach follows that of Texas but with a bow in the direction of South Carolina. There must be a "a willful or malicious act in connection with" the breach of a contract to support a claim for punitive damages.[94] As in Texas, there is an independent act requirement, but as in South Carolina, the act must be connected directly to the breach, and it is not clear that the act must constitute a tort that would sustain a separate action. However, it is not enough merely to allege fraud,[95] and Arkansas does not have the same rather open-ended appeal to the conscience found in South Carolina.

[iii] Florida. Although Florida follows the Texas rule in theory, cases in this state present a truly ambiguous picture. For instance, *Guthertz v. Lewis*[96] involved a landlord who wrongfully overcharged his tenants. The landlord refused to return the rents and deposits he wrongfully collected and attempted to conceal his actions by filing false statements with the federal agency that guaranteed the mortgage on the property. This conduct was not only in breach of the leases, but was also criminal.[97] Yet the Florida Court of Appeals held that there was no independent tort and that the only issue was a straightforward breach of contract. In another case, a young physician who was starting out in practice was dismayed when for two years in a row the telephone company left him out of the yellow pages even though he had entered into a contract for a listing each year. Although the Florida Court of Appeals in *Hanftt v. Southern Bell Telephone and Telegraph Co.*[98] reiterated the independent tort rule, it also said, "The negligent performance of a contractual duty properly supports a tort action."[99] On the one hand, lying, wrongfully taking and retaining money, and crimi-

---

[94] Curtis v. Partain, 614 SW2d 671, 673 (Ark. 1981).

[95] Id.

[96] Guthertz v. Lewis, 408 So. 2d 600 (Fla. Dist. Ct. App. 1982).

[97] Id. at 603 n.5.

[98] Hanftt v. Southern Bell Tel. & Tel. Co., 402 So. 2d 453 (Fla. Dist. Ct. App. 1981).

[99] Id. at 456, citing Gallichio v. Corporate Group Serv., Inc., 227 So. 2d 519 (Fla. Dist. Ct. App. 1969). This decision went further than even South Carolina has been willing to go; South Carolina courts still require a contemporaneous fraudulent act. A willful breach, even with fraudulent intent, is not enough. See Survey, "Business and Insurance Law," 34 SCL Rev. 19, 35 n.107 (1982).

nal behavior are insufficient to satisfy the independent tort requirement; on the other hand, a clerical error in omitting a name from a telephone directory is sufficient to support a claim for tort damages in an action arising ex contractu. In attempting to apply Florida law, the Court of Appeals for the Fifth Circuit decided that a flagrant breach of contract (not simply negligent performance) was not enough to justify punitive damages.[100] Instead, the breach had to be so wanton, malicious, and outrageous as to be a tort.[101] The best that can be said is that the Florida rule is unclear.

[iv] Georgia. Although Georgia courts and a state statute expressly prohibit the recovery of punitive damages in actions that arise ex contractu,[102] the rule has in fact been bent. Georgia allows punitive damages in contract cases if there is evidence of fraud on the theory that the tort of fraud supports the claim for punitive damages.[103] *Clark v. Aenchbacher,*[104] decided by the Georgia Court of Appeals in 1977, is a good case in point. *Clark* was a suit against a builder for improper construction of a house in violation of the construction contract. There was sufficient evidence of fraud because the defects in the house were latent and there were implications of willful omissions by the builder. For instance, there were no ties between the brick veneer and the wood frame of the house, there was an inadequate bearing wall in the garage, and there was inadequate support for the front wall and porch.

Albert Properties, Inc. v. Watkins,[105] another 1977 decision, was an example of an independent tort case. In a dispossessory

---

[100] Splitt v. Deltona Corp., 662 F2d 1142 (5th Cir. 1981).

[101] Id. at 1146, 1147, relying on Griffith v. Shamrock Village, 94 So. 2d 854 (1957), and see American Int'l Land Corp. v. Hanna, 323 So. 2d 567 (1976). For an attempt to make some sense of the Florida law, see Coleman, "Punitive Damages for Breach of Contract: A New Approach," 11 Stetson L. Rev. 250 (1982).

[102] See Combined Contractors, Inc. v. Welch, 160 Ga. App. 790, 288 SE2d 229 (1982); Hospital Auth. of Charlton Country v. Bryant, 157 Ga. App. 330, 277 SE2d 322 (1981); Nestle Co. v. JH Ewing & Sons, 153 Ga. App. 328, 265 SE2d 61 (1980); Traders Ins. Co. v. Mann, 118 Ga. 381, 45 SE 426 (1903). O.C.Ga.A. § 13-6-0 (1982).

[103] See, e.g., Rosenberg v. Moseman, 140 Ga. App. 694, 231 SE2d 417 (1976); Diana v. Monroe, 132 Ga. App. 669, 209 SE2d 70 (1974).

[104] Clark v. Aenchbacher, 143 Ga. App. 282, 238 SE2d 442 (1977).

[105] Albert Prop., Inc. v. Watkins, 143 Ga. App. 184, 237 SE2d 670 (1977).

action, the tenant counterclaimed for malicious interference with his possession of the premises when the landlord removed the door to the tenant's apartment. The court allowed $100 for actual damages and $500 for punitive damages and said that punitive damages will be allowed where the evidence shows "an intentional disregard of the rights of another."[106] In this instance, the landlord's removal of the door was an intentional trespass upon the tenant's property interest in the premises that was not justified by the tenant's own breach of the lease agreement.

[v] Idaho. The leading case, *Linscott v. Ranier National Life Insurance Co.,*[107] involved an insurer's refusal to pay a claim, but the opinion did not limit the holding to cases between insurers and insureds. The court approved the award of punitive damages in breach of contract actions where the plaintiff proves "outrageous conduct" undertaken with "evil intent" in "conscious disregard of the rights of another."[108] The language ("outrageous conduct," "evil intent") suggests a tort standard of liability, but the court was unclear whether there must be an independent tort, such as fraud or trespass, or whether the manner in which the breach occurs supports a claim for punitive damages. The use of the phrase "conscious disregard of the rights of another" is also ambiguous, because it is not clear whether the court had in mind the public rights of the plaintiff (those that a tortfeasor might violate) or the private rights of the plaintiff derived from the contract. If punitive damages are available only for conduct that violates the public rights of a person, *Linscott* does nothing but expand Idaho's concept of tort liability, but if the court had in mind the private, contractual rights of the plaintiff, the punitive damage liability would flow directly from the contract breach, not from the breach of a public duty. Although the *Linscott* opinion is not limited to insurance cases, it is

---

[106] Id. at 185, citing Gilman Paper Co. v. James, 235 Ga. 348, 219 SE2d 447 (1975). Georgia does not allow the recovery of punitive damages when no other damages are recovered. Horne v. Drachman, 247 Ga. 802, 280 SE2d 338 (1981); Haugabrook v. Taylor, 225 Ga. 317, 168 SE2d 162 (1969). In comparison, Florida allows punitive damages upon a showing of liability that justifies nominal damages. Guthertz v. Lewis, 408 So. 2d 600, 602 n.4 (Fla. Dist. Ct. App. 1982), citing Lassiter v. International Union of Operating Eng'rs, 349 So. 2d 622 (Fla. 1977).

[107] Linscott v. Ranier Nat'l Life Ins. Co., 100 Idaho 854, 606 P2d 958 (1980).

[108] Id. at 854, 606 P2d at 965.

likely that the special responsibilities of insurers had an effect on the court's reasoning, and it could be misleading to read too much into *Linscott*.[109]

[vi] Illinois. Illinois courts require proof of an independent tort plus proof of malice, wanton disregard of the rights of others, or oppression. There may be some lack of clarity in the definitions of malice, wantonness, and oppression, but it is clear that a breach of contract, even if willful and reprehensible, does not support an award of punitive damages.

The 1981 decision in *St. Ann's Home for the Aged v. Daniels*[110] provides a good example. A nursing home sued the husband, son, and granddaughter of a resident for their refusal to pay for health care provided to the resident. At trial, the evidence showed that the son was the person primarily responsible for his mother's affairs, and the court allowed punitive damages against him for willful refusal to pay, despite his knowledge of the nursing home's limited financial resources. The appellate court reversed the award of punitive damages because there was no proof of an independent tort. The appellate court went on to say:

> It is not so much the tort committed as the motive and conduct in committing it that is the basis of awarding punitive damages. While Joseph A. Daniels' breach caused a hardship to St. Ann's and he knew that the home was in great financial need, we do not believe his conduct can properly be characterized as wanton, malicious, or oppressive.[111]

---

[109] In a wrongful dishonor case, the same court said that punitive damages would be available whether the dishonor was classified as a tort or as a contract. The liability in that case stemmed from the special responsibility of a bank to its depositors and thus fits better within the fiduciary duty category. Yacht Club Sales and Serv., Inc. v. The First Nat'l Bank of N. Idaho, 101 Idaho 852, 623 P2d 464 (1980); see also Boise Dodge, Inc. v. Clash, 92 Idaho 902, 453 P2d 551 (1969).

[110] St. Ann's Home for the Aged v. Daniels, 95 Ill. App. 3d 576, 51 Ill. Dec. 64, 420 NE2d 478 (1981).

[111] Id. at 576, 420 NE2d at 482. In Hutchinson v. Brotman-Sherman Theatres, Inc., 94 Ill. App. 3d 1066, 50 Ill. Dec. 422, 419 NE2d 530 (1981), the plaintiff, who was the assignee of exclusive telecast rights for the heavyweight championship fight between Muhammad Ali and George Foreman in Zaire, was

[vii] Indiana. Recent cases from Indiana indicate that this jurisdiction may become the leader in developing a theory for the recovery of punitive damages in cases that arise ex contractu. Most of the published opinions have involved disputes between insurers and insureds, but courts have not limited their decisions to insurance cases. On the contrary, they have indicated that the principles apply to all kinds of contract cases, although if one party, such as an insurance company, has certain public responsibilities, these special characteristics obviously will affect the outcome.

The most extensive treatment of the issue came in the 1982 case of *Riverside Insurance Co. v. Pedigo,*[112] which involved allegations of the insurer's unreasonable delay, deceit, and bad faith in responding to an insured's claim under a fire policy. The court stated that a plaintiff can recover punitive damages in an action based on a breach of contract under two circumstances: (1) When the proof shows that the conduct in breach of the contract independently amounted to a common-law tort; or (2) When the evidence indicates that a serious wrong, tortious in nature, occurred, but the conduct does not conveniently fit into a tort category.[113] The first category simply restates the Texas rule. The second category goes beyond the South Carolina rule in that it establishes that under certain circumstances a breach of contract may be of a nature that justifies penal damages even if there is no breach of a clearly defined public duty. The court did not go so far as to suggest that any breach of contract would support a claim for punitive damages; there must be some allegations and proof of fraudulent, grossly negligent, or oppressive conduct.[114] Despite this requirement, Indi-

---

able to show an independent tort of fraud in his contract action against the promoters. See also McIntosh v. Magma Sys., Inc., 539 F. Supp. 1185 (ND Ill. 1982); Garman v. New York Life Ins. Co., 501 F. Supp. 51 (ND Ill. 1980); Sabath v. Mansfield, 60 Ill. App. 3d 1008, 18 Ill. Dec. 8, 377 NE2d 161 (1978); McGrady v. Chrysler Motors Corp., 46 Ill. App. 3d 136, 360 NE2d 818 (1977).

[112] Riverside Ins. Co. v. Pedigo, 430 NE2d 796 (Ind. Ct. App. 1982). For additional discussion of this case, see supra ¶ 11.03[3][b].

[113] Riverside Ins. Co. v. Pedigo, 430 NE2d 796, 804 (Ind. Ct. App. 1982).

[114] Id., citing Nationwide Mut. Ins. Co. v. Neville, 434 NE2d 585, 593 (Ind. Ct. App. 1982); cf. Hibschman Pontiac, Inc. v. Batchelor, 266 Ind. 310, 362 NE2d 845 (1977). The court also cited Jones v. Abriani, 350 NE2d 635 (Ind. Ct. App. 1976), in which a seller refused to return a deposit upon a buyer's rightful rejection

ana has stepped beyond the traditional limitation on damages in contract cases, albeit very cautiously. The Indiana Court of Appeals said in a 1980 opinion:

> The promisor's motive for breaking a contract is generally regarded as irrelevant because the promisee will be compensated for all damages proximately resulting from the promisor's breach. Where the facts surrounding the promisor's breach indicate substandard business conduct, the promisee may also enjoy a limited sense of requital in taking his business elsewhere in the future, but he is not entitled to mulct the promisor in punitive damages. Something more than a state of mind described as heedless disregard of the consequences is required for the imposition of punitive damages in breach of contract cases. Actual malice, or wantonness from which the law can imply malice, must be shown. The word "reprehensible" is used, as where there is conscious and deliberate conduct. Deceit is involved. Negligent conduct or incompetence is insufficient.[115]

[viii] Iowa. This jurisdiction follows the Texas rule: Punitive damages are available only where the conduct breaching a

---

of a defective mobile home, and Joseph Schlitz Brewing Co. v. Central Beverage Co., 359 NE2d 566 (Ind. Ct. App. 1977), in which a brewer terminated a distributor in violation of an Indiana statute as well as the distributorship agreement. *Jones* can be put into the first category because the retention of the deposit after a rightful rescission could have been a conversion. *Central Beverage* can be characterized as a public duty case in that the brewer violated a public law when it breached the private distributor agreement. The stated rule of New Mexico is similar to Indiana's: Punitive damages are available in a breach of contract case if there is a showing of malice or of reckless or wanton disregard of the plaintiff's rights. However, because the leading decisions involve insurance companies, there is some question as to the breadth of the rule. Curtiss v. Aetna Life Ins. Co., 90 NM 105, 560 P2d 169 (1976); State Farm Gen. Ins. Co. v. Clifton, 86 NM 757, 527 P2d 798 (1974).

[115] Harper v. Goodin, 409 NE2d 1129, 1133 (Ind. Ct. App. 1980); see also Hoosier Ins. Co. v. Mangino, 419 NE2d 978 (Ind. Ct. App. 1981) (no punitive damages allowed when there was a delay in paying on fire insurance claim based on good-faith investigation of arson); Vernon Fire & Casualty Ins. Co. v. Sharp, 264 Ind. 599, 349 NE2d 173 (1976) (punitive damages justified by unwarranted delay in paying fire insurance claim); Rex Ins. Co. v. Baldwin, 163 Ind. App. 1308, 323 NE2d 270 (1975) (punitive damages allowed for bad-faith refusal to pay life insurance claim).

contract is also an intentional tort. An intentional breach is not enough; there must also be wrongful conduct and malice, which means willful or reckless disregard of the rights (in a public sense) of another.[116] The breach of an insurance company's duty to defend its insured is a tort that supports a claim for punitive damages.[117] Similarly, mishandling an insurance claim may constitute the tort of intentional infliction of emotional distress.[118] The insurance cases are consistent with those in other jurisdictions and do not change the prevailing Iowa rule that requires an independent tort.[119]

[ix] Maryland. In Maryland, a plaintiff cannot recover punitive damages for a "pure" breach of contract,[120] even if the breach is intentional and malicious. Damages are recoverable, however, "in tort actions arising out of contractual relationships where actual malice is present."[121] Despite Maryland courts' apparent disapproval of punitive damages for a breach of contract,

---

[116] Muchmore Equip., Inc. v. Grover, 315 NW2d 93, 100 (Iowa 1982); Pringle Tax Serv., Inc. v. Knoblauch, 282 NW2d 151, 153 (Iowa 1979).

[117] Koozman v. Farm Bureau Mut. Ins. Co., 315 NW2d 30 (Iowa 1982).

[118] Higgins v. Blue Cross of W. Iowa, 319 NW2d 232 (Iowa 1982); Amsden v. Grinell Mut. Re-Ins. Co., 203 NW2d 252 (Iowa 1972).

[119] Kansas, Kentucky, Maine, Mississippi, North Dakota, New York, and Tennessee follow essentially the same line as Iowa. See, e.g., Atkinson v. Orkin Exterminating Co., 5 Kan. App. 2d 739, 625 P2d 505 (1981) (a wanton and willful breach of contract is not a tort and does not justify punitive damages); Ford Motor Co. v. Mayor, 575 SW2d 480 (Ky. 1978) (a breach of warranty that was also unlawful under the Kentucky Consumer Protection Act was not tortious and did not support a claim for punitive damages); Forbes v. Wells Beach Casino, Inc., 490 A2d 646 (Me. 1979) (in the absence of an independent tort, court will not allow a claim for punitive damages); Gulf Guar. Life Ins. Co. v. Kelley, 389 So. 2d 920 (Miss. 1980) (punitive damages not available in contract action unless attendant conduct is an intentional wrong that amounts to an independent tort); Corwin Chrysler-Plymouth, Inc. v. Westchester Fire Ins. Co., 279 NW2d 638 (ND 1979) (there must be an independent, willful tort for damages to be awarded; breach of an insurer's good-faith duty will suffice); Garrity v. Lyle Stuart, Inc., 40 NY2d 354, 353 NE2d 783, 386 NYS2d 831 (1976) (no punitive damages allowed in a contract case because only a transgression of a private right has occurred); BF Myers & Son of Goodlettsville, Inc. v. Evans, 612 SW 912 (Tenn. Ct. App. 1980) (reward of punitive damages requires a separate showing of fraud, malice, gross negligence, oppression, or similar misconduct).

[120] General Motors Corp. v. Piskor, 281 Md. 627, 381 A2d 16 (1977).

[121] Sims v. Ryland Group, Inc., 37 Md. App. 470, 378 A2d 1,4 (1977).

even with evil intent, the Court of Appeals for the Fourth Circuit interpreted Maryland law to allow punitive damages where the defendant "maliciously" breaches a contract and defined malice as "an evil or rancorous motive influenced by hate; the purpose being to deliberately and willfully injure the plaintiff."[122] This statement appeared in an insurance case and, therefore, might reflect judicial concern for the special obligations of insurers rather than a general statement of contract principles.

[x] Michigan. One of the peculiarities of Michigan law is its distinction between punitive and exemplary damages. Punitive damages are to punish the defendant for malicious, reckless, or outrageous antisocial conduct. They are not awarded in ordinary contract cases without proof of an independent tort "except under special circumstances rarely present."[123] On the other hand, exemplary damages compensate the plaintiff for hurt feelings and humiliation. They may be available in certain personal contract cases as a form of compensatory damages on the theory that the breaching party reasonably should have expected hurt feelings or humiliation to follow from his breach.[124]

[xi] Missouri. In theory, Missouri follows the Texas rule, but the 1981 decision in *Budget Rent-A-Car of Missouri, Inc. v. B&G Rent-A-Car, Inc.*[125] suggests that Missouri might be leaning toward the approaches taken by courts in South Carolina and Indiana. In *Budget Rent-A-Car of Missouri, Inc.*, the plaintiff was a franchisor who sued former franchisees for breaches of the covenants not to compete in their franchise agreements. The defendants set up sham companies and made various assignments to them,

---

[122] Wiggins v. North Am. Equitable Life Assurance Co., 644 F2d 1014, 1018 n.2 (4th Cir. 1981).

[123] American Cent. Corp. v. Stevens Van Lines, Inc., 103 Mich. App. 507, 303 NW2d 234, 237 (1981). To the same effect, see Van Marter v. American Fidelity Fire Ins. Co., 114 Mich. App. 171, 318 NW2d 79 (1982); Kewin v. Massachusetts Mut. Life Ins. Co., 409 Mich. 401, 295 NW2d 50 (1980); Caradonna v. Thorious, 17 Mich. App. 41, 169 NW2d 179 (1969).

[124] Fletcher v. Aetna Casualty & Sur. Co., 80 Mich. App. 439, 264 NW2d 19 (1978).

[125] Budget Rent-A-Car of Mo. v. B&G Rent-a-Car, Inc., 619 SW2d 832 (Mo. Ct. App. 1981).

apparently to avoid obligations to the franchisor. The Missouri court said that the plaintiff's claim for punitive damages was supported because "The evidence shows appellants' breach to have been willful and without just cause or excuse, and the same was sought to be concealed."[126] The conduct of the franchisees was close to fraud or deceit, and there may have been sufficient evidence to support a separate action in tort, but the language of the opinion indicates an inclination to allow a claim for punitive damages upon a showing of deceitful or reprehensible conduct in connection with a breach, even if the conduct does not constitute a separate tort.

[xii] New Jersey. New Jersey courts have been especially strict about the requirements for punitive damages. For instance, punitive damages are not available in a commercial contract action, regardless of the nature of the breach or the conduct accompanying the breach.[127] The definition of a commercial contract is not absolutely clear, but it presumably includes the great bulk of all agreements that involve the exchange of goods or services for money or for other goods or services. Personal contracts presumably include those agreements in which the principal consideration is something other than money or a good or service, the value of which may be represented by money.

The strictness of the New Jersey approach was apparent in *Pierce v. Ortho Pharmaceutical Corp.*[128] The plaintiff alleged that he was wrongfully discharged from his job because he refused to perform certain acts that he knew violated the law, regulations, or public policy affecting the drug industry. The court said that the discharge was either a breach of contract or a tort and that the plaintiff in such a case had to elect whether to proceed in contract or in tort. If he chose to seek recovery in contract, he could not claim punitive damages. This decision was consistent with common-law rules on elections of remedies, and it illustrated the difference between a traditional approach and one favored by a jurisdic-

---

[126] Id. at 838.

[127] Sandler v. Lawn-A-Mat Chem. & Equip. Co., 141 NJ Super. 437, 358 A2d 805 (1976).

[128] Pierce v. Ortho Pharmaceutical Corp., 84 NJ 58, 417 A2d 505 (1980).

tion such as South Carolina. A South Carolina plaintiff may choose to proceed in contract to take advantage of the strict liability principles of contract law, and he still may be able to obtain the advantage of a tortlike damage recovery if he can prove fraudulent conduct connected with the breach. In New Jersey, the decision to proceed in contract eliminates the possibility of a recovery of any tort damages.

[xiii] North Carolina. North Carolina courts long have followed the independent tort rule, but have also required an element of aggravation in the tortious conduct that accompanies the breach. One of the earliest decisions was made in *Purcell v. Richmond & Danville Railroad Co.,*[129] an 1891 case. A train failed to stop at a station as scheduled and left the plaintiff standing on the platform. This amounted to a breach of the contract to carry the plaintiff; it was negligent conduct; and it was a breach of the duty of a common carrier to provide a public service.[130]

Generally, North Carolina courts have been intolerant of contract plaintiffs who seek to recover extracontractual damages,[131] although this approach has loosened slightly. For instance, in *Oestreicher v. American National Stores, Inc.,*[132] the North Carolina Supreme Court said that breach of contract damages could include more than compensatory damages governed by the agreement

---

[129] Purcell v. Richmond & Danville RR Co., 108 NC 414, 12 SE 954 (1891).

[130] Although characterized as a punitive damage case, this action could have been handled as a case for nonpecuniary damages based on inconvenience under a mental distress theory.

[131] See, e.g., King v. Insurance Co. of N. Am., 273 NC 396, 159 SE2d 891 (1968); Davis v. North Carolina State Highway Comm'n, 271 NC 405, 156 SE2d 685 (1967); Swinton v. Savoy Realty Co., 236 NC 723, 73 SE2d 785 (1953); Murray v. Allstate Ins. Co., 51 NC App. 10, 275 SE2d 195 (1981); Mesimer v. Stancil, 45 NC App. 533, 263 SE2d 32 (1980); Comment, "Extra-Contractual Remedies for Breach of Contract in North Carolina," 55 NCL Rev. 1125 (1977) (hereinafter cited as Comment, "Extra-Contractual Remedies"); Note, "Recovery of Punitive Damages for Fraud and Deceit," 31 NCL Rev. 473 (1953). Pennsylvania is just as strict (and perhaps even more strict) as North Carolina. See, e.g., Adams Assocs., Inc. v. Ruintach Publishing, Inc., 429 A2d 726 (Pa. Super. Ct. 1981); Argo Welded Prods., Inc. v. JT Ryerson Steel & Sons, Inc., 528 F. Supp. 583 (ED Pa. 1981).

[132] Oestreicher v. American Nat'l Stores, Inc., 290 NC 118, 225 SE2d 797 (1976).

when the breach "smacks of tort because of the fraud and deceit involved."[133] During the same term, the North Carolina Supreme Court dispensed with the aggravation requirement and said that punitive damages might be available where the trial judge finds "actionable fraud."[134] Although this did not change the independent tort requirement, it did relax one of the proof requirements the plaintiff must satisfy.

Language in the decision in *BB Walker Co. v. Ashland Chemical Co.,*[135] a 1979 federal court decision applying North Carolina law, suggests a more radical departure from the traditional approach. The court said that the defendant's breach and subsequent conduct were "willful, malicious, reckless and unfair,"[136] entitling the plaintiff to punitive damages. The court's language almost went so far as to characterize the breach of contract as itself a tort, although the case was in fact an unfair competition case. The defendant cut off the plaintiff's source of supply under a supply contract and then tried to solicit the plaintiff's customers, knowing that the plaintiff was having difficulty meeting their demands because of its own contract breach. Although there was clearly a breach, the whole scheme was tortious in nature, and the court probably reacted more to the overall conduct than to the specific contract breach.

[xiv] Oklahoma. Oklahoma courts have avoided the independent tort problem by simply declaring that a contract breach is itself a tort if it is onerous and malicious.[137] In fact, an Oklahoma statute allows punitive damages for breach of contract where the breach is "willful, designed to injure, intentional, purposeful or malicious."[138]

---

[133] Id. at 118, 225 SE2d at 807–809.

[134] Newton v. Standard Fire Ins. Co., 291 NC 105, 229 SE2d 297 (1976), and see Comment, "Extra-Contractual Remedies" 1126, 1127; see also Burger Chef Sys., Inc. v. Melfred Co., 547 F2d 786 (4th Cir. 1976).

[135] BB Walker Co. v. Ashland Chem. Co., 474 F. Supp. 651 (MDNC 1979).

[136] Id. at 664, 665.

[137] See, e.g., Lilly v. St. Louis & SF Ry. Co., 31 Okla. 521, 122 P 509 (1912); Hobbs v. Smith, 27 Okla. 830, 115 P 347 (1911); Storck v. Cities Servs. Garage Co., 634 P2d 1319, 1323 (Okla. Ct. App. 1981) (dictum).

[138] 23 OS 1971 § 9; see also Morris v. Barton, 200 Okla. 4, 190 P2d 451 (1947); Leigh v. Wadsworth, 361 P2d 849 (Okla. 1961).

[xv] Virginia. Virginia cases are not remarkable in themselves; the courts have consistently reiterated the Texas rule and have said that punitive damages are available only if there is an independent tort and proof of "malice, fraud or criminal indifference."[139] They are remarkable, however, in that they formed the background for one of the more significant cases in this area of damage theory, *United States v. Snepp*.[140]

Frank Snepp was a former CIA agent who wrote a book about his activities as an agent. In the book he made a number of disclosures of confidential information that the CIA considered to be harmful. Snepp also failed to comply with an agreement he had signed when he joined the CIA to submit any writings about his CIA work for Agency clearance prior to publication. The government sued Snepp for breach of contract. The district court generally held for the government on the contract claim and imposed a constructive trust in favor of the government on all royalties produced by Snepp's book. The court reasoned that Snepp had violated a fiduciary duty of trust, which justified the imposition of a constructive trust. Furthermore, the court thought that a constructive trust would be appropriate because damages would be difficult to calculate. The court would have to project the royalties to be derived in the future from sales of a book not yet released and reduce them to a present value, an exercise that was too conjectural in the district court's opinion.[141]

On appeal, the fourth circuit reversed the decision to impose a constructive trust. The appellate judges concluded that Snepp's contract had not created a fiduciary relationship. Thus, there was no basis on which to issue an order in equity. In addition, the court did not think that compensatory damages were too speculative to be determined. But the most intriguing suggestion the court made was that, on remand, the government should amend its complaint

---

[139] See, e.g., Wright v. Everett, 197 Va. 608, 90 SE2d 855 (1956); Vickhouse v. Fidelity Bond & Mortgage Co., 508 F. Supp. 1096 (ED Va. 1981); Material Handling Indus., Inc. v. Eaton Corp., 391 F. Supp. 977 (ED Va. 1975); Matney v. First Protection Life Ins. Co., 73 FRD 696 (WD Va. 1977).

[140] United States v. Snepp, 595 F2d 926 (4th Cir. 1979).

[141] United States v. Snepp, 456 F. Supp. 176 (ED Va. 1978).

and ask for punitive damages.[142] The government lawyers had not included any request for punitive damages, apparently because they framed the complaint as a straightforward breach of contract. Judge Winter, writing for the majority, recognized that punitive damages are not ordinarily available in contract actions and that this case did not fit any of the normal exceptions. In fact, he excluded one possible theory by deciding that Snepp had no fiduciary duty to the government. However, Judge Winter thought that punitive damages should be allowed because Snepp's actions had "implications of a tort" and because compensatory damages were hard to prove with certainty, although not impossible to prove.[143]

The majority partially relied on three Virginia cases, but none really stood for the proposition advanced in *Snepp*. The first, *Matney v. First Protection Life Insurance Co.*,[144] was a suit for bad-faith failure to pay a claim under a health insurance policy. It fit easily within the general line of insurance cases and, therefore, was similar to the public duty and utility cases. The second, *Material Handling Industries, Inc. v. Eaton Corp.*,[145] was an action by a retailer against a manufacturer for breach of contract and violations of the antitrust laws. The conduct alleged to be in violation of the antitrust laws made *Material Handling Industries* a case that was essentially grounded in tort. The third case, *National Homes Corp. v. Lerter Industries, Inc.*,[146] involved the question of whether bankruptcy discharged a punitive damage award; it had nothing to do with the correctness of the award in the first place.[147] Judge Winter's opinion thus created out of whole cloth a new right to claim punitive damages in contract cases. A plaintiff merely had to allege that a defendant's actions had implications of tort and that compensatory damages would be hard to measure precisely.

---

[142] United States v. Snepp, 595 F2d 926, 935 n.7 (4th Cir. 1979).

[143] Id. at 936–938.

[144] Matney v. First Protection Life Ins. Co., 73 FRD 696 (WD Va. 1977).

[145] Material Handling Indus., Inc. v. Eaton Corp., 391 F. Supp. 977 (ED Va. 1972).

[146] National Homes Corp. v. Lerter Indus., Inc., 336 F. Supp. 644 (WD Va. 1972).

[147] United States v. Snepp, 595 F2d 926, 939, 940 n.2 (4th Cir. 1979) (Hoffman, J., dissenting).

Although this new standard is open-ended and may have far-reaching implications, it is of limited precedential value. The United States Supreme Court reversed the decision of the court of appeals and reinstated the constructive trust remedy of the trial court.[148] In addition, the appeals court's distaste for Snepp and his disregard of the CIA contract was obvious. There was a thinly veiled interest in seeing him brought to justice even at the cost of bending legal doctrines. The *Snepp* case, however, is a good example of the flexibility that some courts are willing to employ to fashion remedies they find to be appropriate for the redress of plaintiffs' grievances, no matter whether cases orginally are brought as contract actions or tort actions.

[6] UCC Regulation of Punitive Damages

In any discussion of remedies, it would be shortsighted to overlook the influence of the UCC because of the vast number of agreements governed by that statute. By its terms the UCC largely leaves the question of punitive damages to the common law. Section 1-106 prohibits penal damages in UCC actions "except as specifically provided in this Act or by other rule of law." Some courts have read Section 1-106 as a general bar to punitive damages,[149] but others have reached exactly the opposite conclusion.[150] Professor Hawkland seems to be of the opinion that the latter courts are correct; Section 1-106 does not prohibit punitive damages.[151] His position has merit, especially in light of the admonition in Section 1-106 that remedies are to be liberally administered, but the Official Commentary to Section 1-106 indicates general disap-

---

[148] United States v. Snepp, 444 US 507 (1980).

[149] See, e.g., First Sec. Bank of Utah v. Turkey Growers, Inc., 610 P2d 329, 332 (Utah 1980); Waters v. Trenckmann, 503 P2d 1187, 1191 (Wyo. 1972).

[150] See, e.g., Clayton v. Crossroads Equip. Co., 655 P2d 1125 (Utah 1982); Siegman v. Equitable Trust Co., 267 Md. 309, 297 A2d 758 (1972); Grandi v. Le Sage, 74 NM 799, 399 P2d 285 (1965).

[151] 1 Hawkland § 1-106:04, at 103, 104. Hawkland does recognize that Section 1-106 can act as a limitation on remedies by its stricture that the plaintiff not be made better off than he would have been in the event of full performance. Id. § 1-106:02, at 11.

proval of punitive damages in cases that arise under the UCC: "Subsection (1) is intended . . . to make it clear that compensatory damages are limited to compensation. They do not include consequential or special damages, or penal damages; and the Act elsewhere makes it clear that damages must be minimized. Cf. Sections 1-203, 2-706(1), and 2-712(2)." [152]

Section 2-721 provides plaintiffs with some relief from the election of remedies problem: "Remedies for material misrepresentation or fraud include all remedies available under this Article for nonfraudulent breach. Neither rescission or a claim for rescission of the contract for sale nor rejection or return of the goods shall bar or be deemed inconsistent with a claim for damages or other remedy." Thus, a plaintiff who rightfully rescinds can also seek damages and need not limit his claim to restitution.[153]

One statement can be made with reasonable certainty: The definition of consequential damages under the UCC does not include punitive damages. Consequential damages are compensatory, and they are not intended to include a punitive element.[154]

[7] General Conclusions

The preceding discussion has considered only a small number of the contract actions in which the complaining party has asserted a claim for punitive damages. Despite the black-letter law that says such damages are not available in suits arising ex contractu, litigants continue to seek them and are often successful. In some instances the results are not surprising. The breach of the promise to marry cases are a species apart from ordinary contract actions. Public utilities, insurance companies, and common carriers have certain public responsibilities imposed on them by law and their contracts with consumers are not altogether private; rather, they

---

[152] UCC § 1-106 Official Comment 1.

[153] See, e.g., Fousel v. Ted Walker Mobile Homes, Inc., 124 Ariz. 126, 602 P2d 507 (1979) (plaintiff rescinded a mobile home purchase contract because of seller's breach and also recovered punitive damages for the seller's wanton and malicious conduct), and see 5 Anderson § 2-721:13, at 60.

[154] See, e.g., Overseas Equip. Co. v. Aceros Arquitectonicas, 374 So. 2d 537 (Fla. Dist. Ct. App. 1979); 4 Anderson § 2-715:32.

are invested with public obligations of good faith and fair dealing. The conduct surrounding a breach may be tortious. Allowing the recovery of punitive damages in a contract suit on the basis of an independent tort is really a means for dealing with an election of remedies problem. It does not alter basic tort and contract theories but simply allows the plaintiff a remedy he might have had anyway if he had filed a complaint for a tortious injury.

The cases that cross the border between contract and tort are those that characterize certain breaches as torts, that allow punitive damages if the breach is accompanied by malice or evil intent, or that simply say the conduct of the defendant has tort implications even though it does not fit within a recognized tort category. The facts of each case are particularly important, because no plaintiff has won a punitive damage claim merely because the defendant breached a contract. The manner in which the breach occurred and its effect on the plaintiff, especially if the defendant knew that the breach would cause serious problems, are the key factors. The plaintiff's case is easier if a special relationship of trust or public obligation exists or if the plaintiff is a consumer with relatively little bargaining power. In a purely commercial setting, courts are almost invariably intolerant of claims for punitive damages.[155]

¶ 11.04 RECOVERY OF DAMAGES FOR MENTAL DISTRESS

[1] General Disallowance in Contract Cases

Many contracts do not involve a consideration that can be translated easily into money. They are often personal in nature and there is no real substitute for performance.[156] Courts have two basic problems in trying to determine appropriate damage awards for breaches of contracts such as these. First, there is the difficult task of translating the lost expectancy of a personal service into a monetary sum. Second, the real injury suffered by the plaintiff is

---

[155] See, e.g., Burger Chef Sys., Inc. v. Melford Co., 547 F2d 786 (4th Cir. 1976); Lubrication and Maintenance, Inc. v. Union Resources Co., 522 F. Supp. 1078 (SDNY 1981).

[156] There are few instances in which a court would order specific performances for the reasons discussed at ¶ 7.01.

mental distress or unhappiness as a consequence of the breach, not an economic loss that is the immediate result of the breach. For example, when a couple arrives at a resort hotel for a long-awaited vacation and finds that their room is not available because of overbooking, the economic loss is easy to handle (restitution of any deposit, plus difference in cost between the defendant hotel and another hotel, plus incidentals), but the real injury comes from inconvenience and disappointment. Should the hotel be required to pay damages for inconvenience or disappointment? If so, on what theory? How are those damages calculated? Although there are many variables, there is authority for the proposition that the hotel should pay because it is reasonable to assume that disappointment follows as a natural, foreseeable consequence of overbooking holiday reservations. Many of the cases establishing the authority for this proposition and for similar results in other disappointment cases have been heard in the courts of the British Commonwealth, but some of the authority comes from courts in the United States.

The traditional rule is similar to that for the recovery of punitive damages: Recovery for mental distress, disappointment, and anguish is inappropriate in contract actions for four reasons: (1) it is not directly related to the economic effect of the breach; (2) it is open to speculation; (3) it may be the subject of frivolous claims; and (4) it is not reasonably within the contemplation of the breaching party.[157] However, the drafters of the second Restatement of Contracts noted that there are two major exceptions to the rule. First, mental distress damages are available if the breach is wanton or reckless and causes bodily injury. Second, the defendant may have to pay mental distress damages if he "had reason to know when the contract was made that the breach would cause mental suffering for reasons other than pecuniary loss."[158]

[2] Allowed Recoveries in Bodily Injury and Physical Trauma Cases

Bodily injury cases bear a close resemblance to tort cases. They eliminate the concern that some courts have expressed about

---

[157] See generally Riley, "Contracts: In Appropriate Cases There May Be Recovery of Mental Distress, Absent Physical Trauma, Arising out of Breach of Contract," 26 Drake L. Rev. 215 (1979) (hereinafter cited as Riley).

[158] Restatement (Second) of Contracts § 341 (1981).

the subjective nature of mental distress because an actual injury provides a tangible example of harm from which a court and jury can work. On the other hand, a plaintiff's mere testimony that he was upset without any proof of discernible injury obviously leaves open a wide range of speculative possibilities.

The California decision in *Chelini v. Nieri*[159] is often cited as a leading example of bodily injury or physical trauma cases. The plaintiff entered into a contract with a funeral home to handle his mother's burial. The plaintiff's mother had had a terrible fear of insects and water during her lifetime, and Chelini wanted to be certain that her body was carefully embalmed and sealed in a casket to protect it from insects and water damage. Nieri, the defendant, assured Chelini that the embalming procedures, together with a hermetically sealed casket, would preserve his mother's body. Some time after the funeral, the plaintiff began to doubt the defendant's representations. Chelini had the grave opened, and found that his mother's body had deteriorated substantially. He was so upset that his blood pressure became abnormally high, he suffered fainting spells, and he had to reduce his level of work. The trial court awarded damages for mental distress resulting from the breach of contract, and the appellate court sustained the award:

> Whenever the terms of a contract relate to matters which concern the comfort, happiness or personal welfare of one of the parties, or the subject matter of which is such as directly to affect or move the affection, self-esteem, or tender feelings of that party, he may recover damages for physical suffering or illness proximately caused by its breach.[160]

The court in *Chelini* noted that the defendant's actions were consistent with the tort of deceit in that he knowingly made representations he would be unable to perform. This may have affected the court's readiness to allow a mental distress recovery. The court was unwilling to sustain a claim for punitive damages because the plaintiff elected to try the case on a contract theory.[161]

---

[159] Chelini v. Nieri, 32 Cal. 2d 480, 196 P2d 915 (1948).

[160] Id. at 480, 196 P2d at 916.

[161] Id. at 480, 196 P2d at 919.

The discussion of the tortious aspects of the defendant's conduct in *Chelini* left open the question of whether a plaintiff could recover mental distress damages without proving conduct that was tortious in nature. This question was partially answered in *McDowell v. Union Mutual Life Insurance Co.,*[162] a 1975 decision of a federal court based on California law. The suit was for mental anguish damages and the complainant alleged that the defendant insurer had refused to pay a disability claim in bad faith. The plaintiff's wife suffered a nervous breakdown as a result of unsuccessful efforts to obtain the insurance payments. The immediate legal problem was the statute of limitations. Unless the longer statute for contract actions applied, the plaintiff was out of court. In determining the applicable statute of limitations, the court ruled that the case arose from contract and that contract actions could support claims for mental distress damages. Although the court's language seemed to eliminate any specific requirement of tortlike conduct, the court did note that an insurance company's bad-faith refusal to pay a legitimate claim is similar to a tort. Furthermore, the special relationship of insureds and insurers means that an insurance case may not be solid authority for a rule of general application.

Stewart v. Rudner,[163] a 1957 Michigan decision, is another good example of a physical trauma case. While she was pregnant, the plaintiff asked her doctor to deliver her child by Cesarean section because she already had had two stillborn children during normal childbirth and she feared another because of the difficulty she had experienced in normal childbirth. Although the doctor agreed, when she went into labor he decided not to do a Cesarean but to proceed with an ordinary birth. Unfortunately, the baby died. The doctor's failure to fulfill his promise was the kind of contract breach, the court said, that "would naturally give rise to mental distress as the inevitable and foreseeable result and so may be compensated."[164]

---

[162] McDowell v. Union Mut. Life Ins. Co., 404 F. Supp. 136 (CD Cal. 1975).

[163] Stewart v. Rudner, 349 Mich. 459, 84 NW2d 816 (1957).

[164] Id. at 459, 84 NW2d at 824; see also Davis v. Aetna Casualty & Sur. Co., 169 Ga. App. 825, 314 SE2d 913 (1984) (delay in providing family medical care in workers' compensation care is misfeasance in performance of a contractual obligation that is tortious and supports claim for pain and suffering damage).

[3] Allowed Recoveries for Reasons Other Than Pecuniary Loss

If the defendant's conduct causes a physical injury to the plaintiff, the resulting action more often than not will sound in tort. Thus, there are relatively few mental distress contract cases involving physical trauma. The majority of mental distress cases have not involved bodily harm, but have involved emotional problems that have arisen either from a failure to perform a contract or from negligent or callous behavior in performance. In many of these situations the plaintiff has suffered little if any economic injury, and the question is whether courts will countenance any recovery for hurt feelings in the absence of a hurt pocketbook.

[a] Personal Contract vs. Commercial Contract Standard

Courts have drawn a sharp line between personal contracts and commercial contracts. Mental distress damages often have been allowed in personal contract cases but not in commercial ones. In *Meyer v. Nottiger,*[165] the court defined personal contracts as those that involve "rights we cherish, dignities we respect and emotions recognized as both sacred and personal."[166] The plaintiff in *Meyer* sued for breach of a contract to perform burial services, and courts generally have been solicitous of people who have difficulties with morticians and funeral homes. In fact, California has adopted a standard of care for mortuaries that effectively creates a tortlike action for a failure to perform.[167] Aside from burial cases, courts have characterized as personal contracts: (1) agreements to deliver personal messages,[168] and (2) contracts that are "so coupled with matters of mental concern or with the sensibilities of the parties to whom the duty is owed that their breach can reasonably be expected to result in mental anguish."[169] One court suggested that the amount of money exchanged in an agreement could be critical to its classification as a personal contract: If little or no

---

[165] Meyer v. Nottiger, 241 NW2d 911 (Iowa 1976).

[166] Id.

[167] Allen v. Jones, 104 Cal. App. 3d 207, 163 Cal. Rptr. 445 (1980).

[168] Mentzer v. Western Union Tel. Co., 62 NW 1 (1895).

[169] Robertson v. Dale, 464 F. Supp. 680, 684 (MDNC 1979).

money was involved, the contract probably was personal, not commercial.[170]

Contracts that involve highly personal matters may nevertheless be treated as commercial contracts. When they are, the plaintiff ordinarily is unsuccessful in seeking mental distress damages. For instance, the North Carolina Supreme Court held that a separation agreement between estranged spouses was not a personal agreement.[171] The Michigan Supreme Court said that a disability income protection insurance policy was a commercial contract and the plaintiff could recover no more than the pecuniary value of the contract plus legal interest for late payments despite the personal stress he suffered as a result of difficulties involved in obtaining payments from the insurer.[172]

[b] Foreseeability of Damages Standard

The most widely adopted approach in dealing with mental distress damages attempts to avoid the dichotomy between personal and commercial contracts. The second Restatement speaks instead in terms of foreseeability:

> In awarding damages, compensation is given for only those injuries that the defendant had reason to foresee as a probable result of his breach when the contract was made. If the injury is one which follows the breach in the usual course of events, there is sufficient reason for the defendant to foresee it; otherwise it must be shown specifically that the defendant had reason to know the facts and to foresee the injury.[173]

This approach puts mental distress damages in the ordinary category of compensatory damages and ties the cases directly to the

---

[170] Laurns v. Shingleton, 231 NC 10, 55 SE2d 810 (1949); and see Riley 216.

[171] Stanback v. Stanback, 297 NC 181, 254 SE2d 611 (1979).

[172] Kewin v. Massachusetts Mut. Life Ins. Co., 409 Mich 401, 259 NW2d 50 (1980); and see Note, 27 Wayne L. Rev. 1357, 1358 (1981). But cf. Note, "The Expectation of Peace of Mind: A Basis for Recovery of Damages for Mental Suffering Resulting From Breach of First-Party Insurance Contracts," 56 S. Cal. L. Rev. 1345 (1983); Holmes, "A Contextual Study of Commercial Good Faith: Good-Faith Disclosure in Contract Formation," 39 U. Pitt. L. Rev. 381 (1981).

[173] Restatement (Second) of Contracts § 330 (1981).

Hadley v. Baxendale rule of foreseeability.[174] Properly applied, there should be no formal distinction between personal and commercial contracts, but it stands to reason that emotional distress is more likely to follow from a negligently performed burial service than from the breach of a contract for the sale of chattels. Many problems, including anxiety, may follow from the failure of a debtor to pay a note when it is due, but the creditor can be made whole with money damages. For all their foreseeability, mental distress damages also have a punitive effect. Someone who is upset with a funeral home may get some or all of his money back and something extra to compensate for his emotional trauma. This "something extra" is more than mere compensation and has some of the earmarks of tort damages.

Louisiana stands out as the American jurisdiction that has developed most fully the concept of emotional distress damages in contract cases. The seminal case was *Lewis v. Holmes,*[175] decided in 1903. The defendant agreed to make the plaintiff's wedding gown and four other bridal dresses. The bride's gown was too short, however, and the defendant never made the other four dresses. The plaintiff did not discover that the gown was unsatisfactory and that the other dresses were not sewn until the eve of her wedding. This naturally was the cause of considerable distress, and the plaintiff won damages for humiliation and disappointment.

> When the contract has for its object the gratification of some intellectual enjoyment, whether in religion, morality, or taste, or some convenience or other legal gratification, although these are not appreciated in money by the parties, yet damages are due for their breach. A contract for a religious or charitable foundation, a promise of marriage, or an enjoyment for a work of some of the fine arts, are objects and examples of this rule.[176]

Lewis was partially based on a Louisiana statute that allowed damages for the breach of a contract to confer a benefit on the plaintiff that could not be measured in money.[177] The "intellectual

---

[174] See ¶ 7.03[3][b].

[175] Lewis v. Holmes, 109 La. 1030, 34 So. 66 (1903).

[176] Id. at 1030, 34 So. at 67.

[177] La. Civ. Code art. 1934(3) (1903).

gratification'' standard of *Lewis* continues to apply in Louisiana courts apart from its original statutory basis. For instance, in *Melson v. Woodruff,*[178] the plaintiffs won mental anguish damages when they agreed to buy a new house, but the seller failed to close on time. As a result, the plaintiffs had to move out of their former home and find temporary accommodations while waiting for the seller to convey.[179] The court characterized the contract as noncommercial and reasoned that disappointment and inconvenience were the natural, foreseeable consequences of the seller's failure to perform on time. There was a similar result in *Arquemborg v. Bourgue*.[180] The seller in that case closed the deal, but failed to convey possession in accordance with the contract because he had taken another month's rent from the current tenant. As a particularly distasteful consequence, the disappointed purchasers had to live in the guest room of the leprosarium in which the husband worked.

One opinion in a case involving defective houses allowed mental distress damages on reasoning similar to that in *Clark v. Aenchbacher,*[181] in which the plaintiff recovered punitive damages for breach of a contract to build a house because of latent structural defects.[182] The Alabama Supreme Court in *B&M Homes v. Hogan*[183] concluded that fear and apprehension were foreseeable consequences of defective construction that should have been within the reasonable contemplation of the contractor. In both these cases, the courts expressed a concern for the protection of the expectations of consumers who put their trust in a builder's exper-

---

[178] Melson v. Woodruff, 23 So. 2d 364 (La. Ct. App. 1945).

[179] This inconvenience factor made *Melson v. Woodruff* very much like cases from common-law jurisdictions in which distress damage claims have been successful because of the physical inconvenience that has resulted from the breach. See, e.g., Hobbs v. London and SW Ry. Co. (1875) 10 QB 111 (train stopped at wrong station on a cold, wet night with result that plaintiff and wife had to walk some distance to reach their home). See generally Note, 11 Melb. UL Rev. 593–595 (1978). See also discussion of *Hobbs* and similar cases infra at ¶ 11.04[3][c].

[180] Arquemborg v. Bourgue 243 So. 2d 92 (La. Ct. App. 1971).

[181] Clark v. Aenchbacher, 143 Ga. App. 282, 238 SE2d 442 (1977).

[182] For a discussion of the punitive damages awarded in *Clark,* see supra ¶ 11.03[5][c][iv].

[183] B&M Homes v. Hogan, 376 So. 2d 667 (Ala. 1979); Hill v. Sereneck, 355 So. 2d 1129 (Ala. Ct. App. 1978).

tise. The plaintiffs were making large financial commitments, and they at least expected to receive houses that were structurally sound and safe for habitation. Although each plaintiff could have been made whole in a strictly economic sense by recovering the reasonable costs of repair, they were allowed an extra measure of damage, either as punishment for the defendant's poor performance or as a means to soothe their anger.

Not every court has been as solicitous of plaintiffs' concerns, however. In another defective house case, the Texas Court of Civil Appeals denied a claim for mental distress damages:

> As a general rule, mental suffering does not constitute an element of damages that may be recovered in an action either for a breach of contract or for a tort founded in a right growing out of a breach of contract [citations omitted]. The foregoing rule, however, is qualified to the extent that in some instances a recovery can be had where it is shown that the mental perturbation was more than ordinary regret or annoyance but is of the type commonly denominated as mental anguish; provided, however, the mental anguish must be shown to have been within the contemplation of the defendant at the time the contract was made.[184]

In this particular case the court did not believe that the defendant reasonably could have foreseen that the breach of its contract to sell a home free of material defects would cause the plaintiff to suffer mental anguish.

[c] British Commonwealth Cases

The most serious discussion of mental distress damages in recent years has occurred in cases heard in various courts in the British Commonwealth. Although these decisions have no direct precedential value in the United States, opinions in English, Canadian, Australian, and New Zealand courts on common-law issues often influence American judges indirectly. The continuing vitality

---

[184] Rogowicz v. Taylor & Gray, Inc., 498 SW2d 352, 355 (Tex. Civ. App. 1973).

of *Hadley v. Baxendale* is the most obvious example.[185] Furthermore, many of these Commonwealth cases rely on *Lewis v. Holmes,*[186] the 1903 Louisiana decision, as the starting point for analysis and have developed it into a doctrine of more general application.

The courts of England and other Commonwealth nations long have adhered to the basic principle that mental distress damages are not available in actions for breach of contract. The case most often cited for this proposition is *Addis v. Gramophone Co.,*[187] decided by the House of Lords in 1909. The plaintiff was discharged from his employment, and the courts rejected his claim for damages arising from hurt feelings, loss of reputation, and difficulty in finding new employment. The only damages allowed directly flowed from the terms of the plaintiff's employment contract. One leading commentator has argued that the *Addis* decision and the rule that developed from it resulted from a misunderstanding of the differences between punitive and compensatory damages. The latter may include consequential injuries that follow naturally from a breach: "The rule results from a failure to distinguish between exemplary damages (which are meant to be punitive) and damages from injured feelings (which are meant to compensate the plaintiff for a loss though it is not a pecuniary one)."[188]

Two major exceptions developed to the *Addis* rule, one for contracts related to marriages and one for contracts in which the breach caused a physical inconvenience. In *Mills v. Harris,*[189] for instance, a disappointed bride won a damage award of £150 sterling because when her fiance broke the engagement, her "feelings were hurt in a deliberately rough and unmannerly way."[190] In another

---

[185] Hadley v. Baxendale, 9 Ex. 341, 156 Eng. Rep. 145 (1854). For further discussion of *Hadley,* see ¶ 7.03[3][b].

[186] See supra ¶ 11.04[3][b].

[187] Addis v. Gramophone Co. [1909] AC 488.

[188] Treitel, *The Law of Contract* 659 (4th ed. 1975), cited in Note, 11 Melb. UL Rev. 593, 594 (1978).

[189] Mills v. Harris [1963] WAR 145.

[190] Id. at 149. This kind of damage recovery was done away with by statute. See Law Reform (Miscellaneous Provisions) Act of 1970 § 1 (England and Wales); Marriage Act 1961–1976 § 111A (Australia). See generally Clarke, "Damages in Contract for Mental Distress," 52 Australian LJ 626, 627 (1978) (hereinafter cited as Clarke).

instance the photographer failed to show up at a wedding, and the newlyweds were able to recover against him for the emotional distress of disappointment at having no wedding photographer.[191] This case was hardly different in its reasoning from *Lewis v. Holmes*.

The 1875 case of *Hobbs v. London and South Western Railway Co.*[192] is the leading Commonwealth physical inconvenience decision. A train stopped at the wrong station and the plaintiff and his wife had to walk some distance to get home on a cold, wet night. This case and the marriage cases share a reasonable expectation that a breach will result in something more than mere economic loss. The breaching party is not held to a risk beyond what an ordinary person would have assumed to be part of the contracted bargain.

More recent opinions have begun to apply the reasoning of the marriage and physical inconvenience cases to other situations. The most common applications have been in cases involving problems with vacation arrangements or breaches of employment contracts.

The principal "holiday" case is *Jarvis v. Swans Tours, Ltd.*,[193] in which the plaintiff was able to recover compensation for disappointment in his vacation trip because it was not of the quality promised by the defendant. The critical victory for the plaintiff was the acceptance of his damage proof in a contract action. Disappointment damages might be available in a tort action based on misrepresentation, but if a plaintiff can claim the same damages in a contract action, proof of liability is simpler because of the strict liability standard in contract. There is no need to prove negligence or any of the other elements of a tort. Prior to *Jarvis*, some courts allowed distress or disappointment damages to unhappy travelers by applying the rationale of the physical inconvenience cases,[194] but *Jarvis* opened wider possibilities of recovery.[195] Perhaps the

---

[191] Diesen v. Samson [1971] SLT 49 (Sheriff's Court Reports).

[192] Hobbs v. London and SW Ry. Co. [1875] 10 QB 111.

[193] Jarvis v. Swans Tours, Ltd. [1973] 1 QB 233.

[194] See, e.g., Athens-MacDonald Travel Serv. Party, Ltd. v. Kazis [1970] SASR 264.

[195] See, e.g., Elder v. Koppe [1975] 53 DLR (3d) 705. Recovery is available only for the plaintiff's personal loss. In Jackson v. Horizon Holidays, Ltd. [1975]

best example of the potential for recovery in post-*Jarvis* cases was the 1974 decision in *Keks v. Esquire Pleasure Tours, Ltd.*[196] The defendant promised accommodations suitable for the plaintiff's family and housekeeper. Although the rooms were superior to those agreed upon, no accommodations were available for the housekeeper and the family had to take their meals in restaurants. The plaintiff's recovery included the difference in cost between restaurant meals and meals that would otherwise have been prepared by the housekeeper plus a separate sum for disappointment in the arrangements.

Unhappy travelers have had some limited success in recovering mental distress damages in the United States. The plaintiff in *Harris v. Waikane Corp.*[197] and a group of his friends made arrangements for a ten-day sailing vacation aboard a yacht anchored in Hawaii. When they arrived in Hawaii, they found that the yacht was unavailable, and they had to spend their vacation in a crowded hotel. The court allowed mental distress damages because the disappointment was a reasonably foreseeable result of the breach of the yacht charter. The court seemed to believe that relief from the contract obligation, return of any deposits, and ten days at a crowded hotel did not sufficiently make up for the lost expectancy of ten days of sailing on a yacht in Hawaiian waters.[198]

In the area of employment contracts, the most important recent case is *Cox v. Philips Industries, Ltd.*,[199] decided in 1976. The defendant assigned the plaintiff to a new position within the firm. Although his pay remained the same, he had fewer duties and

---

1 WLR 1468, the plaintiff recovered for his own mental distress plus that of his wife and children, who accompanied him on vacation. This result was disapproved by the House of Lords in Albacruz v. Albazero [1977] AC 774, which denied recovery on an agency theory. Perhaps a spouse or children could sue on a third-party beneficiary theory.

[196] Keks v. Esquire Pleasure Tours, Ltd. [1974] 3 WWR 406.

[197] Harris v. Waikane Corp., 484 F. Supp. 372 (D. Hawaii 1980).

[198] See also Dold v. Outrigger Hotel, 54 Hawaii 18, 501 P2d 368 (1972) (mental anguish damages allowed in hotel overbooking case). Hawaii follows a rule of allowing mental distress damages when the conduct of the defendant is wanton or reckless and has implications of a tort. See, e.g., Chung v. Kaonohi Center Co., 62 Hawaii 594, 618 P2d 283 (1980); Hall v. American Airlines, Inc., 1 Hawaii App. 258, 617 P2d 1230 (1980).

[199] Cox v. Philips Indus., Ltd. [1976] 1 WLR 638.

responsibilities. The lateral move apparently was a way either of easing the plaintiff out of his job or at least removing him from the ladder of upward progression. As a result, the plaintiff became depressed and physically ill. Assuming that the move was a breach of the plaintiff's employment contract, the court concluded that mental distress damages were available because depression, illness, and mental anguish reasonably could be expected to follow from breach of an employment contract by the employer. The same reasoning was used in *Tippett v. International Typographical Union, Local 226*[200] to uphold a mental distress award for wrongful expulsion of a union member. The expulsion was a breach of the worker's contract of membership, and as a result of the breach he became a social outcast among his peers. At least one commentator has argued that *Cox* effectively overruled *Addis* and that the rule is now one of general applicability — mental distress damages may be recovered whenever they are a reasonably contemplated consequence of the breach.[201]

The influence of *Jarvis* outside vacation cases is evident in two decisions in cases brought by disappointed clients against their lawyers. *Cook v. Swinfen,*[202] a 1967 decision, was an action by a client for negligent representation in a divorce proceeding. The court treated the case as one arising ex contractu and did not allow recovery for the plaintiff's anxiety, even though it eventually resulted in a nervous breakdown. "[T]he Court of Appeal decided that no damages could be awarded for this because, on the facts of the case, it was not a reasonably foreseeable consequence of the defendant's negligence that the plaintiff would suffer nervous shock and a breakdown in health."[203] Nine years later the reasoning of *Cook v. Swinfen* was rejected in *Heywood v. Wellers (A*

---

[200] Tippett v. International Typographical Union, Local 226 (1977) 71 DLR (3d) 146.

[201] Lawson, "Damages: Some Recent Developments — I," 128 New LJ 600, 602 (1978) (hereinafter cited as Lawson); and see Note, 11 Melb. UL Rev. 593, 597 (1978) (arguing that most of the cases can be fit within the rule of *Hadley v. Baxendale*).

[202] Cook v. Swinfen [1967] 1 WLR 457.

[203] Clarke 630.

Firm),[204] in which it was held, on the basis of *Jarvis,* that a client *could* recover for mental distress when a solicitor breached his contract of representation. Even though *Jarvis,* a holiday case, was the basis for *Heywood,* it might be a mistake to rely too heavily on *Heywood* in other kinds of actions. The relationship between a lawyer and his client involves a fiduciary trust, and the breach of that trust has both public and private implications. The same caution is necessary as is required in the use of insurance or fiduciary cases to argue for an award of punitive damages.

The mental distress cases have all involved some personal feelings or close relationships (e.g., marriage, the expected pleasure of a vacation, a lawyer's representation), and there is a serious question whether these opinions have, or should have, any application in commercial contexts. Breach of an employment contract or wrongful expulsion from a union is closer to a commercial than to a purely personal relationship. The results of the breach are primarily economic, unlike the breach of an agreement to prepare a trousseau. Nevertheless, there may be a great deal of personal identity and professional pride involved in a job, and union membership may be critical to social acceptance in a working-class neighborhood. These kinds of contracts, therefore, may have strong personal characteristics that go beyond their economic purposes. Generally, attempts to apply the reasoning of cases such as *Jarvis* to situations that do not involve significant personal, noneconomic interests have been unsuccessful.[205]

One case that tried to bridge the gap between commercial and personal contracts was *Newell v. Canadian Pacific Airlines, Ltd.*[206] The defendant breached a contract for the carriage of goods by failing to transport two dogs safely. As a result, one died and the other was taken seriously ill. The plaintiffs were able to recover

---

[204] Heywood v. Wellers (A Firm) [1976] 1 QB 446. In addition, the language of a majority indicated that the approach applied to all types of cases, not just to those that involved solicitors and their clients.

[205] See, e.g., Falko v. James McEwan & Co. Pty, Ltd. [1977] VR 447 (breach of contract to install water heater); British Guiana Credit Corp. v. Da Silva [1965] 1 WLR 248 (credit case). See generally Note, 11 Melb. UL Rev. 593, 597, 598 (1978). But cf. Lawson 600, 601.

[206] Newell v. Canadian Pac. Airlines, Ltd. [1977] 74 DLR (3d) 574.

mental distress damages because their anguish was within the *Hadley* test of foreseeability for a breach of the contract. Although the court described the contract as commercial, the facts were consistent with classification as a personal contract. The plaintiffs were an elderly couple and the dogs were their special pets that they were taking on their vacation. The average person would not have taken a long airplane trip with pets, which seemed to indicate the plaintiffs' unusual affection for the dogs.

CHAPTER 12

Excuses for Nonperformance

¶ 12.01 SCOPE AND TYPES OF EXCUSES FOR NONPERFORMANCE

The discussions in preceding chapters focus on the remedies available to the nondefaulting party when a breach occurs. Sometimes, however, the breaching party has a good reason for failing to perform and may be excused from further performance. This chapter examines the excuses a defaulting party may offer, their treatment in the contract relationship, and their effect on both parties to a contract.

First among the defaulting party's excuses for nonperformance are the interrelated doctrines of mutual mistake, impossibility, and frustration of purpose. All three involve the question of whether a performing party should be excused from his obligation to perform because of a misunderstanding or the occurrence of a supervening event. Of course, excused performance is an exception to the general theory of strict liability in contracts, and although a court of equity may not require a party to perform an impossible or useless task, a court of law may treat the problem of nonperformance as a simple breach and make the nonperforming party answer in damages. Largely as a result of this tendency to apply a theory of strict liability for contract obligations, common-law courts have been reluctant to allow the performing party to be excused except in the most extreme circumstances. Courts today are somewhat more lenient, but it is still necessary for the party who claims an excuse to carry a heavy burden of proof that performance should not be required or that damages as a substitute should not be awarded.

In general, the excuse of mistake is available only where (1) the mistake is mutual, and (2) the mistake concerns a basic assumption of the contract. The mistake must be about facts that existed (or did not exist) when the parties entered into the contract. This may include a mistaken assumption that certain facts will continue to exist or hold true. If only one party is mistaken, a court usually does not grant relief unless the nonmistaken party is also guilty of reprehensible conduct, such as fraud. Mistakes in performance often may be corrected under appropriate provisions of the UCC unless the nonmistaken party or a third party has acted in reliance on the error to his detriment.

Impossibility is the second in the first set of overlapping excuses. If performance is objectively impossible (e.g., a governmental regulation renders it illegal, the subject matter of the contract is destroyed, or the performing party dies), courts usually excuse performance unless it appears that the performing party assumed the risk of the event that caused impossibility. If the subject matter of the transaction is not identified to the contract, the performing party may not be able to escape liability for his performance, even if the contract goods are destroyed by an external event such as fire.

If performance is possible, the performing party may be able to avoid liability through the doctrine of frustration of purpose or, where the UCC applies, through the doctrine of commercial impracticability under Section 2-615. For the frustration defense to apply, the fundamental purpose of the contract must have become frustrated or rendered useless by a supervening event. In some situations performance may not be impossible, but it may be useless. Increased costs or a bad deal are not frustration excuses. Something unexpected, whose risk was not assumed by the performing party, must occur to essentially defeat the purpose of the agreement and the intentions of the parties.

When the performing party is excused because of a successful plea of mistake, impossibility, or frustration, neither party has further obligations. Whether a court attempts to sort out the parties' risk allocation as it existed when the event occurred that occasioned the excuse depends primarily on the facts of the case. Sometimes the court cannot, or should not, do any more than relieve the parties from future obligations to one another and leave them where they are. More often courts attempt to return the parties to their status quo ante, unless to do so would work an injustice on third parties. Sometimes a court grants the remedy of reformation to modify the agreement in accordance with the new set of facts. This unusual remedy is commonly used to correct scriveners' errors or similar technical mistakes.

Mistake, impossibility, and frustration of purpose all involve a fundamental failure of understanding or a change in expected circumstances. A second set of excuses, which includes waiver, accord, and unconscionability, involves different problems. The defenses of waiver and accord are essentially variations on modification. Although there may not have been a formal contract modification, the excuse arises from the parties' mutual agreement or from their course of dealing during the term of the agreement, not from some misunderstanding at the outset or from a fundamental change in circumstances occasioned by unexpected developments. If the performing party pleads unconscionability as an excuse for nonperformance, he raises issues about fundamental fairness that may go to the heart of the agreement (Is it enforceable at all?) or its method of negotiation (Did the plaintiff abuse his position or engage in deceptive practices?).

There are great conceptual differences between the defenses of waiver or accord and the defense of unconscionability. In practice, however, the factual circumstances that support each of these defenses may be quite similar. A consumer installment credit transaction provides a common example. Unless the creditor carefully requires strict adherence to the payment schedule and does not tolerate late payments, he may find that he has waived the right to demand timely payment. Through his lateness, a slow-paying debtor may end up with a de facto modification of his original installment agreement.[1] If a creditor tries to enforce an installment agreement according to its terms, he may run into an unconscionability defense if the real interest rates (including fees for services, insurance, and so forth, coupled with the scope of the security interest (e.g., liens on previously acquired chattels and on those purchased on credit), are considered to be onerous or if they were inadequately explained to the debtor.[2] The interest in many of these cases is to protect a consumer from sharp practices or onerous terms imposed by a standard form contract on a take-it-or-leave-it basis. In one instance, a court may follow an approach based on a notion of waiver, while another court may approach the unfairness issue directly by using the doctrine of unconscionability. These defenses and excuses are used most often to protect the interests of consumers, although they also are employed in commercial contexts. The excuses of waiver or accord are more common in commercial contexts than unconscionability.

The interrelationship of the problem of excuse and the question of remedies is central to an understanding of excuses for nonperformance. The basic purpose of most contract remedies is to give the nondefaulting party either his original bargain or its mone-

---

[1] The creditor, of course, normally prefers a late payment to a default and a lawsuit for the deficiency.

[2] See, e.g., Williams v. Walker-Thomas Furniture Co., 350 F2d 445 (DC Cir. 1965) (furniture store retail installment purchase plan called for security interest in previously acquired furniture as well as goods bought subject to agreement); American Home Improvement Co. v. MacIver, 105 NH 435, 201 A2d 886 (1964) (high real interest rates inadequately understood).

tary equivalent. If the contract is breached and the defendant asserts that he should be excused for mistake or some other reason, two separate problems immediately arise. First, is the excuse good? Should the defendant be permitted to avoid further performance? Second, what, if anything, should be done with the parties? If they simply are left as they are, their risk of loss may be allocated disproportionately. A court might try to return the parties to their status quo ante or to reform the agreement to fit the new circumstances, but neither of these alternatives may be realistic. As a result, the problem of excuse is often bound up in the question of remedies and is, at heart, a remedial problem as well as an issue of the substantive law of contracts. When an agreement fails, a court must find a way to deal with the failure and the parties' expectations without imposing liability on the nonperforming party. As can be expected, the results are not always consistent. Almost invariably one party suffers a disproportionate risk of loss.

Thus, although the facts of a case are important in all aspects of contract law, few principles are so closely related to fact questions as those that deal with excuses for nonperformance. Questions about issues such as materiality, basic assumption, risk assumption, frustration, and mutual intentions cannot be decided in the abstract. It is often difficult to predict with certainty the outcome of a case or series of cases involving assertions of excuse for mistake, impossibility, frustration, waiver and accord, or unconscionability.

¶ 12.02 MISTAKE

[1] Mistake in Formation vs. Mistaken Performance

There are two categories of mistake cases. The first involves a misunderstanding of some material portion of the agreement itself. For example, it may be that no agreement actually exists because the parties had two different things in mind when they entered into the contract; there never was a consensus ad idem. Cases such as these are commonly called mistake in formation cases. The second category of mistake cases includes those in which there has been an error in performance, such as an arithmetic mistake on a bid form, an overpayment, or an improper delivery. Cases that involve mistakes in formation more often result in excuse than mistaken performance cases because they fit more easily into the traditional doctrine of mutual mistake. The greatest difficulty in both categories is to determine the mental intentions of the parties at the time they entered into the contract.

[2] Mutual vs. Unilateral Mistakes

Common-law courts long have recognized a distinction between mutual and unilateral mistakes. Mutual mistake usually suffices as an excuse, although it must relate to an important (material) aspect of the agreement. In addition, the party claiming the excuse must show that both parties were mistaken at the time of contracting and that the disappointed party did not bear the risk of loss from the mistake. Section 294 of the second Restatement of Contracts reads in part:

> Where a mistake of both parties at the time the contract was made as to a basic assumption on which the contract was made has a material effect on the agreed exchange of promises, the contract is voidable by the adversely affected party unless he bears the risk of the mistake.[3]

Unilateral mistake is usually insufficient to excuse performance unless the mistaken party can also show fraud, overreaching, or other artifice on the part of the other party. Although there have been exceptions to these general rules and the distinctions are sometimes unclear, more often than not courts grant relief in mutual mistake cases and deny relief when only one party is mistaken.[4] In mutual mistake cases it can be argued that there never was a contract, but in unilateral mistake cases it can be said that the mistaken party simply should have been more careful. One of the difficulties in almost all mutual mistake cases, however, is proving that the mistake was indeed mutual. Although the parties initially may agree on that point and only dispute the remedies for

---

[3] The Restatement (Second) of Contracts § 293 defines "mistake" as a "belief not in accord with the facts."

[4] See generally Calamari & Perillo, *The Law of Contracts* § 9-26, at 299, 300 (2d ed. 1977) (hereinafter cited as Calamari & Perillo); Rabin, "A Proposed Black Letter Rule Concerning Mistaken Assumptions in Bargain Transactions," 45 Tex. L. Rev. 1273 (1967).

nonperformance, one party often denies mistake or materiality and tries to hold the other party to the bargain. The evidence can thus become highly subjective.

[3] Categories of Formation Mistakes

There are four fundamentally different kinds of formation mistakes: (1) The parties never enter into an agreement because they never reach a consensus ad idem; (2) The language that the parties use in their agreement has a different meaning for each of them, causing different understandings of the same term; (3) The parties understand each other, but the subject of their discussions is different from the expectations of either; and (4) Only one of the parties is in fact mistaken. Several classic cases illustrate these categories and reveal the confusions that can arise in dealing with formation mistakes.

[a] No Consensus ad Idem

The famous case of the good ship *Peerless, Raffles v. Wichelhaus,*[5] illustrates the mistake that occurs when the parties to a contract have different things in mind when they enter into an agreement. The plaintiff agreed to sell the defendant Indian cotton, which was to be shipped from Bombay to Liverpool on the ship *Peerless*. Unfortunately, there were two ships of the same name. One was due to sail in October and the other in December. The buyer had in mind the ship that would sail in October, but the seller shipped on the *Peerless* that left Bombay in December. When the cotton arrived in Liverpool two months later than expected, the buyer refused to take delivery. The seller alleged a contract and sued for breach, but the buyer prevailed because the court reasoned that there was never an agreement. The parties had failed to reach a consensus on one of the critical elements of the transaction, the identity of the vessel carrying the cotton.

Raffles seems deceptively simple. Certainly the problem could have been avoided by the use of more explicit language. The troublesome aspect of the decision, and of other similar mistake cases, is well illustrated by the almost equally famous "switch." What if

---

[5] Raffles v. Wichelhaus, 2 Hurl. & C. 906, 159 Eng. Rep. 375 (Ex. 1864).

there had been no cotton on either ship? Could the buyer have sued the seller for breach, or could the seller have avoided the contract because there was no agreement about the vessel of carriage? Twelve professors of contract law responded to these questions and split evenly: Six maintained that there was a contract and a good action for breach, and six said that a contract never existed because there was never an express meeting of the minds.[6]

The inability of a panel of law professors to agree on the outcome of a hypothetical contracts case may not be surprising, but it does indicate the importance of the issue of materiality. Those who conclude that there is an enforceable agreement either in *Raffles* or the hypothetical variant discussed in the preceding paragraph must focus on the admitted agreement to buy and to sell cotton. They must conclude that the parties intended to do business and to trade in cotton and that although important, the identity of the transport vessel was not central to the transaction. Those who hold to the contrary see the agreement as a cohesive whole in which time, identity of carrier, mode of delivery, and price are all essential items of agreement. Failure to reach a consensus on one is equivalent to a failure to reach an agreement on the whole. It is as if one portion of the agreement (the identity of the ship) is a condition to the remainder of the agreement.[7]

Another relevant factor in cases such as *Raffles* is the nature of the market that is involved. Even if the parties do not specify the importance of time, a court may assume its importance if the transaction involves a commodity in a volatile market or if there exists a normal and expected chain of transactions that all depend on the others. There may have been a substantial difference in the market price of cotton in Liverpool between the time the first *Peerless* arrived and the arrival of the second *Peerless*.[8] If the buyer expected the cotton to arrive on the first vessel, he may have made commitments to third-party purchasers, and when there was no

---

[6] Kessler & Gilmore, *Contracts* 711 (2d ed. 1970).

[7] For a discussion of the importance of certain aspects of an agreement to the enforceability of the whole, see, e.g., the opinion of Judge Benjamin Cardozo in The Sun Printing and Publishing Ass'n v. Remington Paper and Power Co., 235 NY 338, 139 NE 470 (1923).

[8] For an interesting discussion of the risks of delay in a volatile market, see, e.g., The Heron II (Kaufos v. C. Czarnikow, Ltd.) [1967] 3 All ER 686 (HL).

cotton on the ship he would be embarrassed and out of pocket. Evidence about the nature of the markets involved thus could greatly influence a court's determination of materiality. In comparison, a purchaser in a stable market who is buying for long-term investment may not complain about a brief delay in delivery, even if the parties differed in their understanding about the ship that was to carry the goods.

Another classic case that is often used as an example of mutual mistake in the sense of the absence of any consensus ad idem is *Sherwood v. Walker.*[9] The seller agreed to sell a barren cow for the price of beef on the hoof, but when the buyer arrived to collect the cow and tendered the agreed-upon price, the seller reneged. Since he entered the agreement he discovered that the cow was pregnant, and as breeding stock she was worth about ten times her value as beef, not to mention the expected value of the calf. The buyer sought to replevy the cow upon his tender, but the court held for the seller on a theory of mutual mistake. Although both the buyer and seller had the same cow in mind, their agreement contemplated a barren cow, not one capable of calving.

Like *Raffles, Sherwood* seems simple but really is not. In *Raffles,* when the buyer and seller each spoke of *Peerless,* they presumably thought that there was but one such ship, although in fact there were two. The agreement seemed clear when it was not. In *Sherwood* there was never any question about which cow was involved. The question was whether both the buyer and the seller thought that she was suitable only for beef or whether the buyer hoped he could make a good deal in buying the cow for a beef price while in fact getting a cow that could breed.[10] It might have been possible for the court to have treated *Sherwood* as a difference in value case rather than as a difference in understanding case. The normal rule is that any difference in the market value of the exchanged goods from what is expected is a normal risk of doing business. It is not the purpose of courts to try to balance the values of all exchanges. *Sherwood* could also fit into the third category of

---

[9] Sherwood v. Walker, 66 Mich. 568, 33 NW 919 (1887).

[10] Extrinsic evidence could be helpful here. If the buyer had already contacted a slaughterhouse, that would support an argument that he was buying the cow for beef, not for breeding.

formation mistake cases in which the parties agree on the object, but its nature turns out to be something different from what either party assumed at the outset.[11]

In a case such as *Sherwood,* the parties may testify to very different intentions and understandings. The court must either choose sides in a swearing contest of mutual intentions,[12] rely on extrinsic evidence, or resort to the application of a justice principle (e.g., refuse to enforce an agreement because the exchange is unfair).

[b] Different Understandings of the Same Term

Sometimes the parties to an agreement use a word that has a different meaning for each. To use two amusing examples of cross-cultural misunderstandings: What is a "chicken" and what kind of bean is a "feverole"? In *Frigaliment Importing Co. v. BNS International Sales Corp.,*[13] Judge Friendly stated the problem: "The issue is, what is chicken? Plaintiff says 'chicken' means a young chicken, suitable for broiling and frying. Defendant says 'chicken' means any bird of that genus that meets contract specifications on weight and quality, including what it calls 'stewing chicken' and plaintiff pejoratively terms 'fowl.' "[14]

When he thought of chicken, the Swiss buyer in *Frigaliment* had in mind small young birds suitable for delicate preparations. The American seller, however, thought that the contract called for a wide range of sizes and ages and that it was satisfactory to ship birds that were suitable for stewing but not for simple broiling. Yet both parties used exactly the same word and the contract even specified the sizes of the birds. The seller won, as a matter of contract interpretation, because his understanding was consistent with the normal trade expectations in the American market. There

---

[11] See discussion, especially of *Wood v. Boynton,* infra at ¶ 12.02[3][c].

[12] This is one reason why the issue of materiality is usually a question for the jury. See, e.g., Gust v. Consolidated Rail Corp., 116 Mich. App. 90, 321 NW2d 852 (1982).

[13] Frigaliment Importing Co. v. BNS Int'l Sales Corp., 190 F. Supp. 116 (SDNY 1960).

[14] Id. at 117.

was no question that American law, specifically the law of New York, applied to the interpretation of the agreement.

Although the plaintiff in *Frigaliment* affirmed the contract by suing for a breach of warranty, the case illustrates the problem that can arise when the parties to a contract have a subjective misunderstanding, despite what appears to be a valid and clear objective agreement. In his opinion, Judge Friendly quoted Justice Holmes' statement that "the making of a contract depends not on the agreement of two minds in one intention, but on the agreement of two sets of external signs — not on the parties having *meant* the same thing but on their having *said* the same thing."[15] By that reasoning a contract did exist, because both parties said the same thing, but the difficulty with a strictly objective approach is that what appears to be an objective statement of fact may have quite different meanings to different people. In *Sherwood* there was no question whatsoever about the identity of the cow; there was a difference of understanding in the court's opinion between the subject matter of the transaction (a sterile cow) and the reality (a pregnant cow), although the parties both looked at the same cow.[16] In short, what appears to be objective may not be, and courts may have to rely on extrinsic evidence to determine what a word or a phrase actually meant to the parties. The objective approach, however, is helpful as a check against postagreement changes in the parties' understandings because the deal has not worked out well. The court was able to decide *Frigaliment* through a process of contract interpretation without resorting to the doctrine of mistake because the buyer agreed to be bound by New York law and, by implication, the understanding of the word "chicken" in New York commercial law.[17] The buyer also wanted to hold the seller to the agreement as he understood it; he was not seeking to avoid the contract.

An English case involving international misunderstandings of the word "feverole," a kind of North African bean, deals more directly with the doctrine of mistake. The buyer and the seller were both brokers. The buyer had an inquiry from an Egyptian principal

---

[15] Id.

[16] See supra ¶ 12.02[3][a].

[17] In another case a year later, Judge Friendly suggested that mistake might have been a better way to approach *Frigaliment*. See Dadourian Export Co. v. United States, 291 F2d 178, 187 n.4 (2d Cir. 1961).

for a quantity of "Moroccan horsebeans," or "feveroles." The buyer communicated this inquiry to the seller and asked him what kind of beans these were and also inquired about their availability and price. The seller advised him that feveroles were indeed horsebeans, and after some negotiation they reached an agreement for a shipment. The seller delivered horsebeans grown in Tunisia and Algeria. Unfortunately, these turned out to be "feves," a somewhat different variety of horsebeans from what the Egyptian principal meant by "feveroles." The buyer's principal wanted a slightly smaller and finer bean, and this led to a suit for reformation for mutual mistake. The question was whether the English word "horsebeans" used in the contract included both feves and feveroles. Although the evidence tended to show that both brokers thought that only feveroles qualified as horsebeans, the fact that the class of horsebeans was larger and did include feves convinced the English court that heard the case to deny relief. The objective manifestation of the contract governed despite the different subjective understanding.[18]

The outcome in the horsebean case seems incorrect. The evidence tended to show that the parties both had in mind the same kind and quality of bean even though the language they used was susceptible to a broader meaning. The suit was for reformation, not avoidance, and the risk of business loss on the seller's side, while not insignificant, was not disastrous. It could be argued that there was never a real agreement since the language was too vague to meet the standards of certainty.[19] If so, the case should be treated as one like *Raffles,* although that also seems a bit harsh. The buyer and seller both wanted a deal for horsebeans, and the suit for reformation affirmed their intention to have a business transaction. Neither wanted to avoid doing business with the other; they simply wanted to straighten out one aspect of the transaction. Strict adherence to an objective interpretation, however, took away whatever flexibility the court might have had in trying to reach some reasonable accommodation.

---

[18] Frederick E. Rose (London), Ltd. v. William H. Pim, Jr. & Co. [1953] 2 QB 450, 2 All ER 739 (CA). This case, and others similar to it, are discussed in detail in Fuller, "Mistake and Error in the Law of Contracts," 33 Emory LJ 41 (1984).

[19] Id. 44.

[c] Subject of Agreement Differs From Parties' Expectations

A buyer or seller may learn to his chagrin that what appeared to be a good deal at the time of contracting was not one at all. For example, a seller may unload something he thinks has little value, only to learn that his buyer subsequently resold it for a nice profit. On the other hand, a buyer may think that goods he purchased are valuable but later find that they are practically worthless. In such situations, if one party has acted fraudulently, the unhappy contracting partner usually has a claim for relief.[20] If the negotiations have proceeded in good faith, however, the risk of loss usually falls on the disappointed party as an expected risk of doing business. Mistake as to the real value of a transaction is not generally a good excuse for nonperformance.[21]

Perhaps the most often cited case in this category of formation mistakes is *Wood v. Boynton*.[22] While walking along a road in a small Wisconsin town, Mrs. Wood found a small, pretty stone, which she picked up and kept. She apparently thought that it was a topaz or something similar. When she went to a jeweler to have a pin repaired, she asked him what he thought the stone might be, and he agreed that it might be a topaz. He said that he would give a dollar for it because it was pretty, but Mrs. Wood decided to keep it for the time being. Two or three months later, Mrs. Wood was short of money, returned to the jeweler, and sold the stone to him for a dollar. It later turned out that the stone was an uncut diamond with a value of about $700. Mrs. Wood tendered back the dollar plus a dime in interest and tried to have the transaction undone on the ground of mutual mistake. She was unsuccessful. There was no evidence of sharp dealing, and the court said:

---

[20] If, of course, he can get jurisdiction over the other party, is willing to invest the resources necessary to pursue a lawsuit, and can collect his judgment when he finally gets one.

[21] As one court said, "We will not allow a party to a contract to escape a bad bargain merely because it is burdensome." Neal-Cooper Grain Co. v. Texas Gulf Sulphur Co., 508 F2d 283, 293, 294 (7th Cir. 1978). If it is unconscionable to require performance, the court may allow avoidance, but that is by reason of the application of a justice principle, not by reason of the application of the doctrine of mistake.

[22] Wood v. Boynton, 64 Wis. 265, 25 NW 42 (1885).

> If she chose to sell it without further investigation as to its intrinsic value to a person who was guilty of no fraud or unfairness which induced her to sell it for a small sum, she cannot repudiate the sale because it is afterwards ascertained that she made a bad bargain.[23]

There are several ways of distinguishing *Wood* from *Sherwood*. The usual distinction is that there was never a meeting of the minds about the identity of the cow at issue in *Sherwood,*[24] whereas there was never any mistake about the identity of the stone in *Wood*. This only tells half of the story, however. In neither instance did the seller or the buyer know at the time of contracting the *true* identity of the subject of the transaction. The pregnant cow in *Sherwood* was worth about ten times the agreed-upon price because it was pregnant. The stone in *Wood* was actually worth 700 times its price because both parties were ignorant of its true identity. A clearer distinction treats *Wood* as a case that involves a mistake about value. Both the buyer and seller gambled on the stone's value. If it were not a topaz, it probably was not even worth one dollar, and the jeweler would have lost something. It turned out the other way around, and the court treated the matter as just the ordinary risk of an ordinary transaction.[25] The agreement was to transfer a stone of unknown value and uncertain identity for an agreed price, not to transfer a cow *known* to be barren for the price of beef on the hoof.

Perhaps one of the most telling differences in the two cases is timing. The seller in *Sherwood* learned of the error before the transaction was closed. The loss to the buyer amounted to disappointment and some of his time. In *Wood,* the seller initiated the transaction and the true value of the stone did not become known to the buyer until several months later. The transaction had long

---

[23] Id. at 265, 25 NW at 44.

[24] See supra ¶ 12.02[3][a].

[25] Although one might expect a jeweler to have superior knowledge and might therefore expect him to be held to a somewhat higher standard, perhaps including some duty of disclosure, the evidence showed no indication of overreaching or lack of fairness on his part. In addition, one must assume that finding a valuable uncut diamond on a dusty road in a small Wisconsin town is not a normal event and was not one a century ago. The jeweler probably never even thought in terms of diamonds.

since been closed. Thus, in *Sherwood* the court had to decide whether to require the parties to go forward with an agreement that the court knew was unfair in terms of the consideration; in *Wood,* however, the court would have been forced to undo a closed transaction in which there had been no duress, misrepresentation, or other reprehensible behavior. That would have been contrary both to the general doctrine of repose and to the notion of strict liability in contracts.

Like *Raffles,* these two cases have been the subject of voluminous commentary. What can be gleaned from both is that mutual mistake cases rest very heavily on the facts peculiar to each transaction. The general rule that a court will assist in rectifying the problems caused by a mutual mistake does not really lead very far. The court still must decide whether the mistake was mutual, whether it was material to the transaction, whether there was any knowledge on either side that undercut their relative positions, and whether anything can be done that will not cause more injustice than has resulted from the error of the parties.

A case involving famous violins and violinists helps to clarify some of these problems while raising even more.[26] George Smith, an octogenarian, was a collector of rare violins. Efrem Zimbalist, the famous violinist, was interested in purchasing two of the violins in Smith's collection. They agreed upon a total purchase price of $8,000; $2,000 was to be tendered as a down payment and the balance was due in monthly installments of $1,000. Zimbalist was to take immediate possession. The critical part of the agreement was contained in a memorandum signed by Zimbalist, which read as follows:

> I hereby acknowledge receipt of one violin by Joseph Guarnerius and one violin by Stradivarius dated 1717 purchased by me from George Smith for the total sum of Eight Thousand Dollars toward which purchase price I have paid Two Thousand Dollars the balance I agree to pay at the rate of one thousand dollars on the fifteenth day of each month until paid in full.[27]

---

[26] Smith v. Zimbalist, 2 Cal. App. 2d 324, 38 P2d 170 (1934).

[27] Id. at 324, 38 P2d at 171. There was also a bill of sale that recited the particulars.

The problem was that neither the Guarnerius nor the Stradivarius was genuine and together they were not worth more than $300. Zimbalist refused to pay the balance due and Smith sued on the contract, but Zimbalist was able to defend successfully against the collection suit by asserting the defense of mistake and by arguing that the seller impliedly warranted authenticity, although there was no evidence of any misrepresentation. Smith fully believed at the time of sale that the violins were authentic masterpieces. The court said:

> [I]t is the opinion of this court that . . . the strict rule of caveat emptor may not be applied to the facts of the instant case, but that such rule is subject to the exception thereto to the effect that on the purported sale of personal property the parties to the proposed contract are not bound where it appears that in essence each of them is honestly mistaken or in error with reference to the identity of the subject matter of such contract.[28]

In addition, the court ruled that under both common law and California statutory law, there was an implied warranty that the goods transferred conformed to the description in the bill of sale.[29] This sensibly places the burden of identity and authenticity more heavily on the party who is in a better position to be aware of title, authenticity, and so forth.

Zimbalist illustrates some of the problems with remedies. The court's decision amounted to a reformation of the contract from one for $8,000 to one for $2,000. Although the greater loss measured by the terms of the contract fell on the seller, the buyer was certainly not without loss because he had paid a dear price for two rather ordinary violins.[30] If the mistake were indeed mutual, the buyer either could have sued for rescission and restitution or sought a reformation of the price term to accord with the real value of the two violins. However, he simply asserted the mistake doctrine as a defense to further performance and thus put the court in a

---

[28] Id. at 324, 38 P2d at 174.

[29] Id.

[30] This may have explained some of the sympathy he seemed to receive at the bar.

position similar to that in *Sherwood*. If the court were to enforce the agreement (i.e., make him pay the $6,000 balance), it would require the performance of a deal that it knew to be unfair through no fault or oversight of the buyer. (Indeed, the court's brief discussion of the implied warranty in the bill of sale may have been calculated to cast whatever blame may have existed on the seller.) By defending against further performance but not requesting affirmative relief, Zimbalist avoided the problem that faced Mrs. Wood: the undoing of a transaction that had seemed fair to both parties at the time of performance. This made Zimbalist's position seem especially fair, because he did not demand strict liability but willingly shared in the risk of loss from an honest mistake.[31]

The warranty discussion in *Zimbalist* brings up an issue that is important in a number of cases. Sometimes parties agree to a transaction about a subject matter that turns out not to exist or to be fundamentally different from what they both thought. For example, a buyer and a seller agree on the sale of a load of widgets, both believing the widgets to be in existence. They do not know that the warehouse in which the widgets were stored was destroyed by fire and that the widgets no longer exist. Thus, there may be no contract because there is no subject matter.[32] If the widgets do exist, however, and they are different in some fundamental way from the understanding of the parties, the seller may not be able to avoid performance by reason of mistake, even if both buyer and seller are mutually and honestly mistaken. The approach of some courts is to treat the problem as one of the seller's negligence or violation of warranty. In real estate transactions this is common because there is a doctrine of implied warranty of clear title and transferability on

---

[31] What we do not know is how long Smith had had the two violins and what he had originally paid for them. It may be that $2,000 actually gave him a profit over his own investment. That should not make any difference as a matter of law, but judges and juries are human, and it is shortsighted to think that such facts are altogether irrelevant. Why else would the California court have noted the advanced age of Mr. Smith? Surely it had little to do with the merits of the case, since it did not appear that his age had in any way impaired his ability to negotiate or to transact business.

[32] If the loss occurs in transit after contracting, the UCC provides rules to determine the risk of loss. See UCC §§2-319–2-322, 2-613. The common-law rule in such a case is that loss falls where there is title. Of course, both buyer and seller normally insure their respective risks.

the part of the seller whenever there is a contract for the sale of realty.[33]

An Australian case, *McRae v. Commonwealth Disposals Commission,*[34] is often cited to support the notion that some warranty exists on the part of a seller or someone in a position akin to a seller. The Disposals Commission published a request for bids to salvage an oil tanker on Jourmand Reef. The tanker was a casualty of World War II and was said to contain a considerable amount of oil. The plaintiff, who was the successful bidder, found that there was no ship where the Commission's directions led, although an old oil barge was abandoned some distance in another direction.[35] The bidder sued for damages. The lower court found that there was never any contract because there had never been a meeting of the minds on a subject matter that existed,[36] but found damages for the plaintiff on the count of deceit. In comparison, the High Court found that there was a contract that included a warranty that an oil tanker indeed existed at the location specified by the Commission. Despite the good-faith mistake of the personnel in the Commission's office, a failure of agreement had not occurred; rather, there was a breach of a warranty within the agreement.

The result in *McRae* further illustrates the difficulty in proving that there was in fact a mistake, or at least a mutual mistake, that justifies a court's intervention to void or to reform an agreement.[37] In *McRae,* the plaintiff did not want to avoid the agreement, and while he freely admitted that the barge was not what he had in mind

---

[33] See generally 7 *Williston on Contracts* § 923 (3d ed. 1968) (hereinafter cited as Williston).

[34] McRae v. Commonwealth Disposals Comm'n, 84 CLR 377 (Austl. 1951).

[35] There was no Jourmand Reef, although there was a Jomard Island and a Jomard Entrance. The tanker was said to be on the reef about 100 miles north of Samarai. Jomard Island was 170 miles southeast of Samarai. The Commission, in response to a request, gave the latitude and longitude of the location it had in mind. About eleven miles from that location was not a tanker but a wrecked barge.

[36] The lower court relied on Couturier v. Hastie (1852) 8 Ex. 40 [HLC 155 ER 1250]; (1853) 9 Ex. 102 [156 ER 43]; (1856) 5 673 [10 ER 1065], but the High Court disputed its reading of that case.

[37] These problems of proof are essentially factual and almost invariably are submitted to a jury. Printing Indus. Ass'n v. International Printing and Graphic Communications Union, Local No. 56, 584 F. Supp. 990 (ND Ohio 1984).

when he submitted his bid, he also objected strenuously to any claim of the defendant's good-faith error. The damage recovery in *McRae* was essentially a form of reliance recovery. Another approach might have been to treat the relationship not as one that gave rise to a contract with a subsequent breach of warranty, but simply as a relationship involving the reliance principle.[38]

[d] Mistake by One Party Only

As a general rule, no relief is available for a unilateral mistake. This is not a surprising doctrine in a system that includes doctrines of caveat emptor and vendor and a theory of strict liability for contracts.[39] The risk is put upon the person who could have avoided the problem if he had been more careful. Despite this general rule, however, the mistaken party can get relief in two kinds of unilateral mistake situations. The first arises in the course of performance [40] (e.g., a bidder submits a bid containing an arithmetic error that is too good to be true [41]). The second occurs where the nonmistaken party is guilty of blameworthy conduct, such as fraud or misrepresentation. Nevertheless, although there have been some incursions into the general rule that unilateral mistakes do not support a claim for relief, the rule retains most of its vitality.

There is nothing difficult about the concept of granting relief for a unilateral mistake that results from the other party's overreaching or misrepresentation. Contracts are agreements freely and fairly reached through arm's-length bargaining, a basic and fundamental concept. Deceit destroys the trust that is the necessary basis for contract and thereby destroys the contract itself.

---

[38] See generally Chapter 3.

[39] The objective theory of contracts that focuses on what the parties said rather than what they meant is illustrative of this approach. In the words of Judge Learned Hand, "A contract has, strictly speaking, nothing to do with the personal, or individual, intent of the parties. A contract is an obligation attached by the mere force of law to certain acts of the parties, usually words, which ordinarily accompany and represent a known intent." Hotchkiss v. National City Bank of NY, 200 Fed. 287, 293 (SDNY 1911), aff'd, 201 Fed. 664 (2d Cir. 1912), 231 US 50 (1913).

[40] See infra ¶ 12.02[4].

[41] See, e.g., Calamari & Perillo § 9-27, at 307.

Although a party who seeks to avoid performance may not have to prove all the elements of fraud as if he were suing in tort, he must substantially show that the other party did breach a duty implicit to the contract. As one court suggested in a well-known case that involved a settlement agreement with two former employees, an employee may owe a duty to his employer not to steal but he may not have the additional duty to confess to his theft as a condition to a settlement agreement.[42]

[4] Performance Mistakes

A party who seeks to avoid performance usually has little difficulty in reforming scriveners' errors unless the other party has relied on the errors in good faith to his detriment. Simple cases rarely make it to court, however. The usual problems in a case that involves a performance mistake lie in straightening out disputes about the materiality of the mistake, determining whether there is a loss and, if so, how it should be apportioned, and deciding whether there has been good-faith reliance by the nonmistaken party. What one person calls a mistake may seem to be nothing more than a breach of the contract to another.

Performance mistake cases often involve bids for construction contracts. A simple mistake in judgment (e.g., a bidder's wrong estimate) is no excuse; it is merely a normal risk of business. A clerical error must exist, such as a mistake in summing the bids of subcontractors. A rather loose doctrine that may be called the "too good to be true" rule runs through these cases.[43] The person, agency, or firm that invites bids usually makes a preliminary estimate of the project cost before receiving bids. Multiple bids usually fall within a fairly predictable range, and if one is well outside it, the recipient may be on notice that something is wrong with the bid. The recipient may not have the right to rely on an unusually

---

[42] See Bell v. Lever Bros., LR 1932 AC 161 (1931).

[43] See, e.g., Restatement (Second) of Contracts § 153 (1981); Chernick v. United States, 372 F2d 492 (Ct. Cl. 1967); Gardner v. Meiling, 280 Ore. 665, 572 P2d 1012 (1977); Geremia v. Boyarski, 107 Conn. 387, 140 A 749 (1928). Compare Steinmeyer v. Schoeppel, 226 Ill. 9, 80 NE 564 (1907) with Bromagin v. City of Bloomington, 234 Ill. 114, 84 NE 700 (1908).

low bid and thereby hold the bidder to it, although the order of magnitude of error may have to be fairly high in some jurisdictions.[44] In addition, the timing of the discovery of the mistake may be important. If the bidder corrects the error before the bid is accepted or otherwise relied upon, he may be in much better condition to argue for reformation or rescission than if he waits until after acceptance, especially if a statute exists that makes bids on public projects irrevocable after acceptance.[45]

The too good to be true rule applies in other contexts as well. The McDonald's Corporation entered into a long-term lease on a property in South Carolina. Because of a delay in closing the mortgage loan agreement for the construction of the McDonald's restaurant, the rent was two months in arrears before the first payment was made on the lease. For this reason, the first check was for twice the monthly rental. Through a bookkeeping error, McDonald's continued to pay double each month — it just kept repeating the first payment. The evidence showed that the recipient clearly understood this to be in error, but did not inform McDonald's of the mistake. McDonald's accountants discovered the problem during a routine audit three years later. McDonald's requested a refund of the overpayments, but the lessor refused and said that he had credited each overpayment to the last month of the term, the next-to-last month, and so on. He also argued that it was a unilateral mistake on McDonald's part and that the company should not expect any relief. In an action for restitution, McDonald's recovered all the overpayments plus interest from the date of demand. The court concluded that the lessor knew the terms of the negotiated agreement as well as anyone. He was on notice from the first overpayment that McDonald's was in error, and because he was on notice, he could not take advantage of the mistake by ignoring it. Furthermore, requiring a refund would not

---

[44] See, e.g., Triple A Contractors, Inc. v. Rural Water Dist. No. 4, Neosho County, 226 Kan. 626, 603 P2d 184 (1979) (bid of $812,000 was $169,000 lower than next lowest bid and was $486,000 below the defendant's estimate before receiving bids).

[45] See, e.g., Balaban-Gordon Co. v. Brighton Sewer Dist., 41 AD2d 246, 342 NYS2d 435 (1973) (bidder allowed to withdraw erroneous bid after submission but before acceptance even though statute made bids irrevocable upon submission).

work any hardship or impose any risk of loss; it would merely give both parties exactly what each had bargained for.[46]

Mistake in performance is sometimes an issue in a land sales contract, and the question often arises whether the contract was for a tract or for a number of acres at a price per acre. The seller is subject to the usual rule that he warrants title and ability to transfer, but there may be a mistake about the size of the parcel or its precise boundaries. With the ready availability of surveyors, title examiners, and title insurance companies, there really is little excuse for a fundamental error in the understanding or identity of a tract of real estate that is the subject of a contract, but these problems do occasionally arise. Although these cases are sometimes considered in the context of mistake, they are more often than not merely a matter of contract interpretation.

[5] UCC Provisions for Performance Mistakes

The basic substantive provision of the UCC that deals with mistakes in performance is found in Section 2-508.[47] This section provides that a seller may reject a nonconforming tender and that he also can cure if: (1) the time for performance has not expired; (2) he notifies the buyer of his intention to cure; and (3) he does in fact cure within the original contract time.[48] The cure provision applies even where the seller has taken back the nonconforming goods and

---

[46] McDonald's Corp. v. Moore, 237 F. Supp. 874 (DSC 1965); see also Gulf Oil Corp. v. Lone Star Producing Co., 322 F2d 28 (5th Cir. 1963); Gettinger v. Celebreeze, 218 F. Supp. 161 (SDNY 1963); First Nat'l City Bank v. McManus, 29 NC App. 65, 223 SE2d 554 (1976); Tarrant v. Monson, 96 Nev. 844, 619 P2d 1210 (1980); Pilot Life Ins. Co. v. Cudd, 208 SC 6, 36 SE2d 860 (1945); Thompson & Sebert, *Remedies: Damages, Equity and Restitution* 10-1 (1983) (hereinafter cited as Thompson & Sebert).

[47] Section 2-508 reads:

"(1) Where any tender or delivery by the seller is rejected because nonconforming and the time for performance has not yet expired, the seller may seasonably notify the buyer of his intention to cure and may then within the contract time make a conforming delivery.

"(2) Where the buyer rejects a nonconforming tender which the seller had reasonable grounds to believe would be acceptable with or without money allowance the seller may if he seasonably notifies the buyer have a further reasonable time to substitute a conforming tender."

[48] UCC § 2-508(1).

has refunded the purchase price or the down payment.[49] Section 2-508(1) avoids a breach or a failure of the contract when it is still possible for the parties to be made whole through self-help. Both the buyer and seller may have some transaction costs, but the buyer's costs should be minimized by the requirement that the cure occur within the original contract time.

Section 2-508(2) deals with the problem of poor communication or mutual misunderstanding. If the seller delivers goods that he believes, in good faith, conform to the contract that in fact do not conform, and that are rightfully rejected by the buyer, the seller has a reasonable amount of time (even beyond the contract time) to substitute conforming goods. To take advantage of this cure provision, the seller must give the buyer reasonable notice of his intention to cure in accordance with Section 2-508(2). This subsection is intended to protect a seller from a buyer's "surprise" rejection. The seller must prove, however, that he had "reasonable grounds to believe" that the goods were conforming.[50] The Official Commentary to Section 2-508 describes its standards of reasonability:

> Such reasonable grounds can lie in prior course of dealing, course of performance or usage of trade as well as in the particular circumstances surrounding the making of the contract. The seller is charged with commercial knowledge of any factors in a particular sales situation which require him to comply strictly with his obligations under the contract as, for example, strict conformity of documents in an overseas shipment or the sale of precision parts or chemicals for use in manufacture.[51]

Section 2-509 describes the shifts in risk of loss when no breach occurs. This section anticipates several possibilities and identifies the locus of the loss in different situations. The drafters of the UCC had in mind the use of a contract approach to shifts in

---

[49] See UCC § 2-508, Official Comment 1.

[50] See UCC § 2-508, Official Comment 2.

[51] Id.

loss rather than a purely property approach; that is, the guide for allocating loss is the contract itself and the anticipated allocation of risk of loss contained in the agreement rather than a determination of who held legal title to the goods at the moment of loss.[52] Section 2-509 only applies, however, when there has been no breach. If the seller's tender or delivery is nonconforming for any reason, Section 2-510 outlines the allocation of risk of loss upon a breach.[53] In general, Section 2-510 places the burden of loss on the party who is in breach, even if he has a reasonable time to cure before triggering the provisions on damages and other remedies. For instance, if a seller delivered nonconforming goods but announced his intention to cure under the provisions of Section 2-508, the risk of loss would remain on him until the contract requirements were fully cured and satisfied.[54]

[6] Releases of Claims for Personal Injury

Claims for personal injury are routinely settled by exchanging a sum of money for a release of any further claims by the injured party with respect to the incident that caused the injury. A release is no different from any other contract; there are at least two parties and there is a bargained-for exchange. Courts tend to be somewhat lenient, however, toward victims of bodily injuries who seek to set aside releases on the grounds of mistake. A person who accepts a settlement sum and signs a release must overcome the presumption of the doctrine of repose and must also show that he is acting in good faith. Nevertheless, courts seem willing to take judicial notice that the extent of an injury may not always be apparent and that both parties may be seriously in error about the magni-

---

[52] UCC § 2-509(4).

[53] UCC § 2-509(4); see also UCC § 2-509, Official Comment 1.

[54] Other UCC provisions of possible importance in deciding how to treat a mistake case include: Section 2-513 (giving the buyer a right of inspection before performance); Section 2-606 (defining the acts that constitute acceptance by the buyer); Section 2-607 (describing the effects of acceptance on buyer's rights); and Section 2-608 (describing how acceptance may be revoked under certain circumstances).

tude of the victim's problem and the costs associated with it.[55] As a result, a layman who is the victim of an automobile accident may not be held to quite as strict a standard in the analysis of his release to an insurance company as would a businessman engaged in common commercial transactions. The layman who is represented by competent lawyers, doctors, and other professionals, however, may not be able to draw as much sympathy from a court as one who relies almost exclusively on the advice of the insurer's claims agent.[56]

The standard rule is that mutual mistake justifies setting aside a release just as it justifies nonperformance of any kind of contract.[57] The same rule applies where one party is mistaken and the other is guilty of fraud, overreaching, concealment, or similar behavior.[58] What constitutes mutual mistake is essentially a matter of

---

[55] Judge Frank of the Second Circuit Court of Appeals used a case involving the validity of a release as an opportunity to discuss at length the problems of a purely objectivist approach to contract law and the interpretation of the words in a contract. Recognizing that the same words often convey quite different meanings to people in different circumstances and that courts should be aware of the peculiar nature of the parties and the context of their transaction (reflecting the influence of Legal Realism), Judge Frank said:

> "In short, the *'security of business transactions' does not require a uniform answer to the question when and to what extent the nonnegligent use of words should give rise to rights in one who has reasonably relied on them. That the answer should be favorable to the relier when the words are used in certain kinds of contracts does not mean that it should also be when they are used in a release of a claim for personal injury; and there may still be further reasons for an unfavorable answer when the claim is by an employee against his employer.*"

Ricketts v. Pennsylvania RR, 153 F2d 757, 766, 767 (2d Cir. 1946) (Frank, J., concurring) (emphasis in the original).

[56] Of course, if a professionally represented person has a problem, he may be able to seek satisfaction from his professional representatives.

[57] See, e.g., Robertson v. Douglas SS Co., 510 F2d 829 (5th Cir. 1975) (release based on a misdiagnosis); but there truly must be a mutual mistake. Castro v. Chicago, RI&PR Co., 83 Ill. 2d 358, 47 Ill. Dec. 360, 415 NE2d 365 (1980); cert. denied, 452 US 941 (1981); Young v. Robertshaw Controls Co., 430 F. Supp. 1265 (ED Pa. 1977). For a general discussion of releases, see Annot., 71 ALR2d 82 (1960).

[58] Benton v. Smith, 389 SW2d 392 (Mo. Ct. App. 1965) (unilateral mistake by itself is not enough; there must be some fraud or overreaching); Kennedy v. Bateman, 217 Ga. 458, 123 SE2d 656 (1961).

fact and is generally a question for a jury,[59] although there must be convincing evidence of mistake to send the question to a jury.[60] For instance, if a person has no history of heart disease and signs a release for a nominal sum based upon fairly minor physical injuries but later suffers a heart attack that is proven to be the result of the shock that accompanied the accident, the release may be set aside because neither party considered the latent problem of a weak heart.[61] It is as if there was no consensus ad idem because the parties never took into account a material fact, the existence of a weak heart. The risks thus were misallocated as a result of ignorance of an important fact.

Even if the parties know of a problem, a release may be set aside if they are in error about the seriousness of the problem. In *Kienas v. Patterson,*[62] a 1980 decision of the Montana Supreme Court, both parties knew at the time of the settlement that the plaintiff suffered from cerebral palsy. Neither party appreciated, however, that the superimposition of the physical trauma from an accident on the plaintiff's cerebral palsy condition would have a seriously disabling effect. Because neither party truly understood the full extent of the injury and all its ramifications, the court set aside the release on grounds of mutual mistake.

There is a distinction between mistakes about the course of healing and mistakes about the nature of the underlying physical problem. If there is no question about the identity of the injury or its seriousness, it is unlikely that a release will be set aside, even if it turns out that the time of convalescence is longer than anticipated.[63] Similarly, if a victim is not straightforward with his physician about his symptoms and either conceals or fails to disclose all of them, he may not be able to complain later that his problems are worse than anticipated and, therefore, that he should be excused

---

[59] Gust v. Consolidated Rail Corp., 116 Mich. App. 90, 321 NW2d 852 (1982).

[60] Schmidt v. Smith, 299 Minn. 103, 216 NW2d 669 (1974).

[61] Newborn v. Hood, 86 Ill. App. 3d 784, 42 Ill. Dec. 96, 408 NE2d 474 (1980).

[62] Kienas v. Patterson, 624 P2d 1 (Mont. 1980).

[63] Edwards v. Western and A RR, 552 F2d 137 (5th Cir. 1977); Loose v. Consolidated Rail Corp., 534 F. Supp. 260 (ED Pa. 1982), aff'd without op., 692 F2d 749 (3d Cir. 1982).

from the release.[64] On the other hand, an insurer's or tortfeasor's undue haste to have a release signed may be introduced as evidence in support of a claim of mutual mistake in an action seeking to avoid the release.[65]

[7] Remedial Issues: Reformation, Rescission, and Restitution

If a court determines that a mistake exists that excuses the performing party from further performance, it then has three options. First, it can do nothing more and simply leave the parties as they are but with no further obligations to one another under the contract. Second, it can reform the agreement to take into account the consequences of the mistake. Third, it can seek to undo the transaction and to return the parties to their status quo ante. This last alternative is known as the remedy of rescission and restitution. A court's ultimate course of action depends on the parties' own desires, their relative degree of culpability (if any), the seriousness of the mistake, the court's own ability to straighten out the problem, and, perhaps most important, the degree to which the parties and third persons have changed their positions in their reliance on the validity of the original agreement.

The remedy of reformation has its origins in equity and is most often used to correct clerical errors.[66] Often the parties are not in dispute, but must call upon a court for assistance because the correction of the problem requires its intervention (e.g., when a deed has been recorded with an incorrect legal description).[67] To clarify the record, the parties usually prefer to have an order of court directing the clerk to withdraw the incorrect deed and substitute a correct one or to have an order recorded that clarifies the chain of title for the purchaser and all subsequent purchasers.

The use of reformation in other kinds of situations is some-

---

[64] Davis v. Flatiron Materials Co., 182 Colo. 65, 511 P2d 28 (1973).

[65] Florkiewicz v. Gonzalez, 38 Ill. App. 3d 115, 347 NE2d 401 (1976); Hall v. Strom Constr. Co., 368 Mich. 243, 118 NW2d 281 (1962).

[66] See, e.g., Food Handlers Local No. 425 v. Valmac Indus., Inc., 528 F2d 217 (8th Cir. 1975) (court reformed union agreement to replace check-off provision that transcriber mistakenly omitted).

[67] See, e.g., Hartman v. Tillett, 86 Ohio App. 20, 89 NE2d 613 (1948).

what unusual. The plaintiff normally must prove by clear and convincing evidence that there was an agreement, that there was a subsequent agreement to reduce that original agreement to writing, and that there is a variance between the writing and the real agreement.[68] Obviously, a plaintiff who tries to meet these requirements will run into the parol evidence rule and will have to justify the admission of extrinsic evidence to vary the terms of the written contract.[69] Usually, this requires a demonstration of fraud, concealment, or other culpable behavior.

Neither reformation nor rescission and restitution may be available if one party to the contract has changed his position in reliance on the contract and the court cannot now undo the change in position without creating an injustice. For instance, if a buyer has sold to a third person who is a bona fide purchaser for value, a court generally will not reform or rescind the original agreement.[70] The reliance must have been reasonable, in good faith, and have caused a legal detriment. If a mistaken payment is received and

---

[68] See generally Calamari & Perillo § 9-31, at 312, 313, citing e.g., Pepsi-Cola Bottling Co. v. Peerson, 471 P2d 924 (Okla. 1970); Hardy v. Hendrickson, 27 Utah 2d 251, 495 P2d 28 (1972); Palmer, "The Effect of Misunderstanding on Contract Formation and Reformation Under the Restatement of Contracts, Second," 65 Mich. L. Rev. 33 (1966); and see Printing Indus. Ass'n v. International Printing and Graphic Communications Union, Local No. 56, 584 F. Supp. 990, 995 (ND Ohio 1984); Spitzer Hardware & Supply Co. v. Denver, 11 Ohio App. 2d 6, 227 NE2d 660 (1967).

[69] The parol evidence rule prohibits the introduction of oral or other extrinsic evidence at variance with the terms of a written agreement. There are a few exceptions — ambiguity in the language of the agreement, a trade usage that is not apparent to the court or to laymen, and fraud, duress, concealment, or similar culpable conduct on the part of the person who seeks to enforce the agreement strictly according to its terms.

[70] Holton State Bank v. Greater Milwaukee Food Merchants Ass'n, 9 Wis. 2d 95, 100 NW2d 322 (1960); Calamari & Perillo 316. The same rule applies with respect to completed gifts. Id., citing Restatement of Contracts § 506 (1932); *Clark on Equity*, §§ 258, 259 (1954); and see Restatement (Second) of Contracts § 155 (1981), which provides:

> "Where a writing that evidences or embodies an agreement in whole or in part fails to express the agreement because of a mistake of both parties as to the contents or effect of the writing, the court may at the request of a party reform the writing to express the agreement, *except to the extent that rights of third parties such as good faith purchasers for value will be unfairly affected.*"

(Emphasis added.)

subsequently used to pay a debt to a third party, it qualifies as a change in position, but not one that is detrimental because it can be rectified with no damage to the recipient's balance sheet as it stood when the mistaken payment was made.[71] The whole point is quite simple: Courts seek to avoid correcting one error by causing another separate injustice and perhaps making matters worse than they were in the first place. If there has been no change in position and the rights of third parties are not affected adversely, the most common remedy for mistake is rescission and restitution. It is consistent with the underlying rationale that if the parties to an agreement have been in error about some fundamental provision of the deal, then there really is no contract and the best course is to put them back where they started.[72]

[8] Mistake of Law vs. Mistake of Fact

At least since 1802 and the King's Bench decision in *Bilbie v. Lumley*,[73] courts and commentators have drawn a distinction between cases involving mistakes of facts and mistakes of law. Relief may be available in the former but not in the latter type of cases, or so the doctrine goes. The rule seems to be closely connected with the criminal-law rule that ignorance of the law is no excuse for malfeasance. Twentieth-century American commentators have been virtually unanimous in their criticism of the distinction between fact and law in mistake cases.[74] Professors Calamari and Perillo have even argued that the exceptions to the fact/law distinc-

---

[71] Ohio Co. v. Rosemeier, 32 Ohio App. 2d 116, 288 NE2d 326 (1972). For example, Green has a debt of $100. Brown mistakenly overpays Green $100, which Green then uses to discharge his debt. Green is no worse off than he was originally if he has to return $100 to Brown, even if he has to borrow the money to do so. Of course, Green may incur some transaction costs and he may wind up paying a higher interest rate on the second debt (he might pay a lower rate, also), but Green has the advantage of the use of Brown's money.

[72] Even if there is no contract, it may be that the best course in many cases is to consider the reliance interests of the parties and try to sort out the problem in that fashion.

[73] Bilbie v. Lumley, 2 East 469, 102 ER 448 (KB 1802).

[74] See, e.g., Dobbs, *Remedies* § 11.8 (1973) (hereinafter cited as Dobbs); 3 Palmer, *The Law of Restitution* §§ 14.27, 16.4 (1978); Thompson & Sebert 10-8, 10-9; Restatement (Second) of Contracts § 151 comment b (1981).

tion have swallowed up the rule and that there no longer is any real difference in judicial treatment of the two situations.[75] The critics of the distinction seem to be correct. There should be little conceptual difference between a misunderstanding between the parties about a material fact or a material provision of the law when it comes to trying to fashion a remedy for the error. The complexity of the law is now so great, especially in regulated industries, that it may be expecting too much to act as if every contracting party has perfect knowledge of applicable law.

Despite the criticisms of the distinction between fact and law, it does linger in the courts. It seems to arise most often in tax overpayment cases where a taxpayer seeks a refund of an overpayment made mistakenly or in the belief that a levy was valid, which subsequently turned out to be unconstitutional or illegal.[76] A taxpayer may prevail if the tax payment is made "under protest,"[77] but the unwary taxpayer who makes a mistake is usually out of luck.[78] In a different kind of case, a trucking firm was unable to recover overpayments to a union pension fund because they were made under a mistaken understanding of the firm's *legal* obligations pursuant to a collective bargaining agreement.[79]

There may not be many cases in which the fact/law distinction is important or determinative, but they appear from time to time, and lawyers should be aware of the lingering vitality of the distinction.

---

[75] Calamari & Perillo § 9-28, at 308, 309.

[76] Paramount Film Distrib. Corp. v. State, 30 NY2d 415, 285 NE2d 695, 334 NYS2d 388 (1972).

[77] See generally Dobbs § 11.8, at 764–766, citing, e.g., Farmingdale Realty Co. v. Borough of Farmingdale, 104 NJ Super. 314, 250 A2d 29, rev'd, 55 NJ 103, 259 A2d 708 (1969); Mercury Mach. Importing Co. v. City of NY, 3 NY2d 418, 144 NE2d 400, 165 NYS2d 517 (1957).

[78] He may be out of luck if he relies on the mistake doctrine as a basis for seeking a refund. Many state and local governments, however, have administrative procedures for rectifying overpayment problems, so the taxpayer may be able to receive a refund or a credit against other taxes.

[79] AAA Trucking Corp. v. Teamsters Pension Trust Fund of Philadelphia, 480 F. Supp. 579 (ED Pa. 1979), relying on Sellers & Co. v. Clarke-Harrison, Inc., 354 Pa. 109, 46 A2d 497 (1946).

¶ 12.03 IMPOSSIBILITY

[1] Differences Between Impossibility and Frustration of Purpose

The defense of impossibility or frustration of purpose is more common than the defense of mistake, although the facts of a case may fit equally well within either doctrine. There is a great difference between impossibility and frustration, which can be important in deciding what is an appropriate remedy. If an event occurs that makes performance objectively impossible, a court cannot very well require performance. The problem is to determine what to do with the parties after the problem has arisen, and that is essentially a question of risk allocation. Frustration of purpose is another matter altogether. It is not unusual for one party to decide that he has made a bad deal. From his perspective, the agreement has been frustrated because it no longer serves its intended purpose to provide a profit or a useful service. Although courts do not relieve parties from their obligation to perform just because they have made a bad deal, there are instances in which relief is available because performance is essentially useless or because the situation contemplated by both sides has changed fundamentally since the time of negotiation.

Despite their differences, frustration and impossibility are often considered together. The modern doctrine of frustration of purpose has its origins in impossibility cases, and marginal cases overlap greatly. Whether performance is impossible may be a matter in dispute, and it is often much simpler to think in terms of a frustration of purpose than in terms of impossibility. The disposition of a case may depend, however, on whether it is treated as an impossibility problem or one of a frustrated purpose. Professor Corbin described the fundamental conceptual problems:

> [W]hen a promisor is sued for nonperformance, he may set up, among various kinds of defenses, the three following that are very different in character: (1) he may assert that supervening events have made his own performance impossible; (2) he may assert that performance of the agreed equivalent has become impossible; (3) he may assert that the purpose for which he made the contract has been frustrated. These are alike in being asserted as a justifying reason for the defendant's not performing his promise; but the first is that he him-

> self can not perform, and the second is that the plaintiff can not. The second of these defenses is often called "failure of consideration"; but failure of consideration may be caused in many ways not involving impossibility. The third of these defenses is frequently not an assertion of impossibility of performance of either party's promise; it is an assertion that it has become impossible for him to attain the end and aim for which he had assented to the bargain.[80]

In considering the cases that involve the assertion of an impossibility or frustration defense, it is important to bear these differences in mind. They can have a profound effect on offers of proof and the remedies that courts are likely to consider.

[2] Origins of the Impossibility Doctrine

The discussion of impossibility usually begins with the seventeenth-century decision in the case of *Paradine v. Jane*.[81] The plaintiff sued for rent in arrears on a lease of lands. The defendant answered by saying that because Prince Rupert's army occupied the leasehold during the civil wars that culminated in the Puritan Revolution, he had not been able to use the lands.[82] Although he argued that the purpose of the lease agreement had become impossible because of Prince Rupert's invasion, the court rejected the plea, and Jane was required to pay rents even though his use of the property was frustrated. Jane might have been successful if he had pled Paradine's violation of a covenant of quiet enjoyment (if the facts supported the assertion of such a covenant), but the risk that Jane's use of the property might not turn out well was one of the risks he assumed. Paradine had completed his performance (as-

---

[80] *Corbin on Contracts* § 1320, at 1089–1090 (one volume ed. 1952).

[81] Paradine v. Jane, Aleyn 26, 82 Eng. Rep. 897 (KB 1647).

[82] The court described Prince Rupert as "an alien born, enemy to the King and kingdom, [who] had invaded the realm with an hostile army of men." In fact, Rupert was the grandson of James I of England. He was the son of Frederick the Winter King and Elizabeth of Bohemia, and he came to England in 1641 to assist Charles I in the civil wars. He returned to the continent after suffering a defeat at Marston Moor in 1644, but returned after the Restoration and served as an admiral for Charles II. He was also active in colonial ventures in the Hudson Bay area, and older maps describe the area of northern Canada held by the Hudson Bay Company as Prince Rupert's Land after Rupert, who served as its first governor.

suming the absence of a covenant of quiet enjoyment) when he transferred the leasehold interest to Jane, and it was not "impossible" in any objective sense for the defendant to pay the rent.

Although no one seemed to pay much attention to the decision in *Paradine v. Jane* for 150 years,[83] it established several principles that continue to govern the decisions of cases today. First, impossibility is not a defense at all unless performance is objectively impossible. The defendant asserted the defense of impossibility to a claim for rents, but did not show that it was impossible to pay the money. The frustration of the purpose of the agreement by a supervening event did not excuse performance. The corollary notion that it is never objectively impossible to pay money subsequently developed. This concept may be difficult to explain to someone who is impecunious, and it may be of small comfort to a plaintiff who is seeking to collect a judgment from an insolvent debtor, but the courts have consistently agreed that it is never objectively impossible to pay money in the way that it is impossible, for example, to deliver goods that have been destroyed by fire.[84] *Paradine* also stands as an example of the theory of strict liability in contracts. The key to enforcement is whether the defendant made a promise supported by consideration, not whether it is now just in any general sense to hold him to the letter of that promise.[85]

---

[83] See, e.g., Kessler & Gilmore 758 n.6.

[84] See, e.g., Levy Plumbing Co. v. Standard Sanitary Mfg. Co., 68 SW2d 273 (Tex. Civ. App. 1933). In support of this doctrine is the fact that money is fungible and cannot be identified to a contract. However, the bankruptcy law may intervene in some cases to make it legally impossible to pay money. But see City of Montpelier v. National Sur. Co., 97 Vt. 111, 122 A 484 (1923) (appointment of a receiver did not excuse performance). Farnsworth thinks that it is better to discuss these issues in terms of the assumption of risk. The ability to pay is usually within the control of a paying party, and, therefore, is a risk assumed by him. Farnsworth, *Contracts* § 9.6, at 688, 689 (1982) (hereinafter cited as Farnsworth), citing, e.g., Restatement (Second) of Contracts § 261 comment e (1981).

[85] Kessler & Gilmore provide an interesting bit of history about the nature of the common law. Kessler and Gilmore 757 n.2. The opinion in *Paradine* was apparently written by Rolle, who also wrote a treatise entitled *Abridgment des plusiers Cases et Resolutions del Commun Ley* (1668), in which he described the following case: "Si home covenant de edifier un maison devant tiel jour, et puis le plague est la devant le jour, et continue la tanque apres le jour, ceo excusera luy del breach del covenant pur non fesans de ceo devant le jour, car la ley ne voilt luy compell a venture son vie pur ceo, mes il doit ceo faire apres. . . ." Almost 200

Some courts and commentators fall into the trap of citing *Paradine* for the proposition that there is no discharge for physical impossibility unless it is made a condition of the agreement.[86] This notion is erroneous because *Paradine* was not really an impossibility case, but one that involved a frustration of purpose. The language is broad enough to support a general theory that physical impossibility is an assumed risk, but there is no factual predicate for such a reading of *Paradine*. The better approach, and the one generally followed today, is that impossibility is an assumed risk of the contract "only where the event causing impossibility was so probable as to be foreseen at the time of contracting."[87] In that case, it is not unreasonable to conclude that failing to include a contractual provision to deal with the possible future allocation of risk indicates an assumption of the risk. It is certainly true, nevertheless, that the popularity of force majeure clauses is related to the strict liability and assumption of risk understandings of *Paradine* and subsequent cases.

[3] Modern Examples of Impossibility

[a] Death

If the performing party dies before or during performance, his estate generally is excused from further performance, unless the

---

years later, Lord Campbell translated Rolle's statement as follows: "If a man covenant to build a house before such a day, and afterwards the plague is there before the day, and continues there till after the day, this shall excuse him from the breach of the covenant for not doing thereof before the day; for the law will not compel him to venture his life for it, but *he may do it after*." Hall v. Wright, El.Bl.&El. 746, 120 Eng. Rep. 688 (QB 1858) (emphasis added). The interesting point is that the better translation of the underlined phrase is probably "he *must* or *ought to* do it after." This would have been consistent with the strict liability approach of Rolle in *Paradine;* after one plague has passed, performance is not objectively impossible. By using the word "may," Campbell was able to use Rolle as an authority for a more expansive treatment of the impossibility doctrine that led to the development of the modern theory of frustration of purpose. Of course, a late twentieth-century translation of seventeenth-century legal French may be no better than a mid-nineteenth century translation, but there is the possibility that a loose translation suited Campbell's purposes better than one that was more technically accurate.

[86] See, e.g., L. Simpson, *Contracts* § 174, at 359 (2d ed. 1965) (hereinafter cited as Simpson), which does just that.

[87] John Soley & Sons v. Jones, 208 Mass. 561, 95 NE 94 (1911), cited in Simpson 359.

performance is nothing more than the payment of money. During medieval times, English courts generally refused to enforce a decedent's contracts against the executor for two main reasons. One was the maxim developed in trespass and early contractlike actions that actio personalis moritur cum persona (the acts of a person die along with him). Second, and more important, wager of law was the principal defense to a promissory action, and no executor could be absolutely sure of the truth of what he might be asserting in behalf of his decedent. For a believer, the consequence of false swearing was an eternity in hell. Courts were hesitant to make executors choose between fiduciary duty or eternal damnation.[88] As time passed and wager of law disappeared as the principal defense, courts became more willing to hold a decedent's estate to the contracts made during his lifetime,[89] but this did not apply to personal service agreements that depended upon the decedent's services. Even common-law judges agreed that they could not raise the dead, and the death of a principal was a normal risk to assume in a personal service contract. There may be a question about whether the decedent was the one actually expected to do the work, as when a partner in a law firm dies. (Was the work to be done by the deceased partner or by the firm? That is a question of growing importance as the size of law firms increases.) Subject to this caveat, the deceased can rest in peace, and so may the executor.[90]

[b] Destruction of the Subject Matter of the Contract

Generally, if the subject matter of a contract is destroyed by a supervening event, the performing party is relieved of his obligation to perform. The destructive event, however, must occur be-

---

[88] See generally AWB Simpson, *A History of the Common Law of Assumpsit* at 558–573 (1975).

[89] Id., citing Pinchon's Case, (1612) 9 Co. Rep. 860 and Morgan v. Slade, Yelv. 20.

[90] The usual result is to leave the parties where they are. This may result in a misallocation of risk, but the parties can usually handle such risks in advance by agreement or insurance. Key person life insurance is a common feature of small businesses and partnerships. See also Restatement of Contracts § 459 (1932).

tween the time of contracting and the time of performance,[91] and it must truly render performance impossible. For example, a contract to sell 100 bushels of beans does not become impossible to perform because the beans are destroyed; the seller can substitute another 100 bushels of beans. However, if the contract is for all the beans from a particular farm and the bean crop is destroyed by weather, pests, or other disaster, the impossibility defense holds because the contract was not merely for beans but for beans from a specific location.[92]

If the place for performance is destroyed (e.g., a theater burns down before a production is to open[93]) or the means for delivery are destroyed (e.g., the ship carrying the goods sinks), further performance is usually excused on both sides.[94] There is no excuse

---

[91] If the destructive event has already occurred at the time of negotiation, but both parties are ignorant of it, there may be no contract at all. Such a case fits better under the rubric of mistake. There was never a consensus ad idem because the subject of the contract did not exist. See supra ¶ 12.02[3][c].

[92] See, e.g., Michigan Bean Co. v. Senn, 93 Mich. App. 440, 287 NW2d 257 (1979); Ralston Purina Co. v. Rooker, 346 So. 2d 901 (Miss. 1977). Both cases involved the application of Section 2-615 on commercial impracticability. For further discussion of the UCC and commercial impracticability, see infra ¶ 12.04[2][c]. There may be an implied term in the contract that the crop will be from a specific location. This might be important, for instance, in connection with a contract for the supply of grapes to a winery. There may be thousands of tons of a grape variety on the market, but grapes vary greatly in their suitability for wine from area to area and farm to farm. The use of the crop is also important. It will make a difference if the buyer is making a small quantity of a high-quality vintage instead of making a varietal blend for mass marketing. For a similar case, see Squillante v. California Lands, Inc., 5 Cal. App. 2d 89, 42 P2d 81 (1935). Destruction of goods identified to the contract in a case falling under the UCC is governed by Section 2-613.

[93] Taylor v. Caldwell, 3 Best & S 826, 122 Eng. Rep. 310 (QB 1863). This case is very important in the development of the doctrine of frustration. See infra ¶ 12.04[1].

[94] But cf. Bende & Sons, Inc. v. Crown Recreation, Inc., 548 F. Supp. 1018 (EDNY 1982) (destruction of goods in a train derailment no excuse because the loss of goods was a foreseeable event; however, these goods were not identified to the contract). It is no excuse, moreover, that the normal route of delivery is closed if there is an alternative. In the cases that followed the closures of the Suez Canal in 1956 and 1967, impossibility was a generally unsuccessful defense. There was an alternate route, albeit a more expensive one, around Africa from Europe to the East. See, e.g., American Trading and Prod. Corp. v. Shell Int'l Marine, Ltd., 453 F2d 939 (2d Cir. 1972); Ocean Tramp Tankers Corp. v. V/O Sovfracht (The Eugenia) [1964] 1 All ER 161 (CA 1963); Schlegel, "Of Nuts, and Ships, and Sealing Wax, Suez, and Frustrating Things — The Doctrine of Impossibility of Performance," 23 Rutgers L. Rev. 419 (1969).

if one party has relied on a third person as a source of supply and the third party is unable to perform because of destruction or other disaster, unless the principal contract contemplates performance by the third person and the nonperforming party recognizes that his contracting partner will rely on the third person.[95]

[c] Illegality

The passage of a law or the promulgation of a regulation that renders performance illegal is almost invariably a sufficient excuse for nonperformance. Although a few older cases seemed to draw a distinction between domestic and foreign law, that no longer makes any difference.[96] Judicial orders, legislative acts, administrative regulations, and executive orders are all equally important in determining the validity of an excuse for nonperformance because of legal impossibility.

Foreseeability is an important issue in connection with legal impossibility, just as it is in other areas. If the performing party assumes the risk of performance knowing that there is a possibility that the contemplated performance may become illegal, he may not be able to claim the protection of the impossibility defense if the government does make performance illegal. In a well-known case, the lessee of commercial space in Beverly Hills that was intended for use as a car dealership was unable to avoid the obligations of his lease when World War II broke out and the federal government stopped the manufacture and sale of new private automobiles. He entered into the lease on August 4, 1941 for a five-year term beginning in September 1941. The California Supreme Court reasoned that American involvement in the war, either as a combatant or as a strong supporter of the Allies, was foreseeable and that this would likely cause dislocations in significant industries.[97]

[d] Strikes and Labor Actions

Most labor contracts include a standard clause to excuse performance or to allocate risk in the event of a strike or other work

---

[95] See, e.g., SCA Int'l, Inc. v. Garfield & Rosen, Inc., 337 F. Supp. 246 (D. Mass. 1971); Canadian Indus. Alcohol Co. v. Dunbar Molasses Co., 258 NY 194, 179 NE 383 (1932).

[96] See UCC § 2-615; Calamari & Perillo § 13-4, at 487.

[97] Lloyd v. Murphy, 25 Cal. 2d 48, 153 P2d 47 (1944).

stoppage. Without such a clause, there is some authority for the proposition that a strike by the performing party's employees is no excuse for nonperformance. The employer has some degree of control over the employees and their working conditions and, theoretically, can avert a strike.[98] On the other hand, the employer need not give in to unreasonable demands, and he may not be at risk for wildcat strikes or other unforeseen events.[99] In this as in other areas, foreseeability plays an important role in determining the proper allocation of risk.[100]

[e] Technical Impossibility

The impossibility defense is sometimes invoked as an excuse for the nonperformance of a building contract or a similar undertaking. Technical impossibility cases align more closely with frustration cases because they rarely involve problems of objective impossibility. The difficulty usually is that the project is economically inefficient. The first Restatement generally rejected the impossibility defense in such cases: "Impossibility of performing a promise that is not due to the nature of the performance, but wholly to the inability of the individual promisor, neither prevents the formation of a contract nor discharges a duty created by a contract." [101]

Many cases have followed the approach outlined in the first Restatement.[102] Classic examples include *Carnegie Steel Co. v. United States*[103] and *School Trustees of Trenton v. Bennett*.[104] In *Carnegie,* unforeseen difficulties in the new art of manufacturing armor plate did not excuse the contractor from performance. The contractor in *Bennett* had a terrible time making a school building

---

[98] See, e.g., 6 Williston § 1951A.

[99] See, e.g., Calamari & Perillo § 13-5, at 488.

[100] This can be a chancy business. In the words of Professor Corbin, "Where neither custom nor agreement determines the allocation of a risk, the court must exercise its equity powers and pray for the wisdom of Solomon." Corbin 1110.

[101] Restatement of Contracts § 455 (1932).

[102] See, e.g., Brasher v. City of Alexandria, 215 La. 887, 41 So. 2d 819 (1949); NJ Magnam Co. v. Fuller, 222 Mass. 530, 111 NE 399 (1916).

[103] Carnegie Steel Co. v. United States, 240 US 156 (1916).

[104] School Trustees of Trenton v. Bennett, 27 NJL 513 (1859).

stand up. Weather and other problems kept causing the building to fall down, but despite the contractor's claim that these were problems beyond his control, he was not excused from his contractual obligations. Other contractors have fared better, but from an application of the doctrine of frustration, not from the acceptance of an impossibility defense.[105] The risk is usually on the performing party,[106] unless the other party has provided detailed plans and specifications upon which the performing party is expected to rely.[107] A defendant cannot rely on the defense of frustration or impossibility if the problem is the result of the defendant's own actions or failures.[108] Similarly, a performing party has a duty to make a reasonable effort to avoid the asserted impossibility.[109]

¶ 12.04 FRUSTRATION OF PURPOSE

[1] Origins in English Common Law

The doctrine of frustration developed during the nineteenth century as a means to deal with cases that did not meet the strict common-law standards for the assertion of the defense of impossibility.[110] The absolute requirements of the common law precluded the use of the impossibility defense in cases that involved a frustration of purpose as long as it was physically possible to perform.

Beginning with the case of *Taylor v. Caldwell,*[111] decided in 1863, the English courts began to excuse performance in some

---

[105] See Mineral Park Land Co. v. Howard, 172 Cal. 289, 156 P 458 (1916); National Presto Indus., Inc. v. United States, 338 F2d 99 (Ct. Cl. 1964), cert. denied, 380 US 962 (1965).

[106] JA Maurer, Inc. v. United States, 485 F2d 588 (Ct. Cl. 1973).

[107] Coto-Matic, Inc. v. The Home Indem. Co., 354 F2d 720 (10th Cir. 1966); Helene Curtis Indus., Inc. v. United States, 312 F2d 774 (Ct. Cl. 1963).

[108] Martin v. Star Publishing Co., 50 Del. 181, 126 A2d 238 (1956).

[109] Chemetron Corp. v. McLouth Steel Corp., 381 F. Supp. 245, 257 (ND Ill. 1974), aff'd, 522 F2d 469 (7th Cir. 1975); Pennsylvania State Shopping Plazas, Inc. v. Olive, 202 Va. 862, 120 SE2d 372 (1961).

[110] See, e.g., Williams v. Floyd, 82 Eng. Rep. 95 (KB 1629), cited and discussed in 3 *Hawkland UCC Series* § 2-615:01, at 177 (1983) (hereinafter cited as Hawkland).

[111] Taylor v. Caldwell, 3 B&S 826, 122 Eng. Rep. 309 (QB 1863).

cases that did not present problems of absolute impossibility. In May 1861, the parties in *Taylor* entered into an agreement to rent a concert hall for several days in June. Between the time of the contract and the time of the performance, the hall burned down. The court excused performance on both sides. The opinion relied on the doctrine of impossibility, but the court made an important addition to the elements of the defense by stating that there was an implied condition in the agreement that the hall would be standing at the time of the performance. When it was destroyed by fire, through no fault of either party to the contract, the condition failed and the contract was no longer binding.[112]

Taylor provided the backdrop for the next step in the origins of the frustration defense, played out in cases that followed Edward VII's coronation in 1902. In anticipation of two days of celebratory processions, many people who owned or leased flats and offices along the parade route agreed to let them to people who wanted a good view and a comfortable setting for a party, and the lessees generally paid well for the privilege. Unfortunately, the King became ill and the processions were cancelled. In the famous case of *Krell v. Henry,*[113] the court of appeals ruled that the cancellation excused further performance because it was an implied condition (using the language of the *Taylor* decision) that the coronation procession take place. The only reason to rent rooms for two days at a high price along the parade route was to watch the parade, and when there was no parade, the contract served no purpose. This was a long step from the doctrine of *Paradine* and from the common-law standards of impossibility: It was certainly not impossible for the lessees to take possession of the premises for the designated days nor was it impossible for them to pay rent.

Krell did not answer all the remedial questions. The landlord sued for the unpaid balance of the agreed-upon price. At one point the defendant counterclaimed for the restitution of his down payment, but he later dropped that claim. All the court decided was that the defendant did not have to pay the balance — there was an excuse of future performance but no attempt to change the status

---

[112] For a discussion of the theory of conditions, see Chapter 5.

[113] Krell v. Henry, LR 2 KB 740 (Ct. App. 1903).

quo as it existed when the suit was filed. In *Chandler v. Webster,*[114] a case with virtually identical facts decided in the following year, the court's decision expressly left the parties in the position they occupied at the time of the frustrating event. In *Chandler* the lessee made a substantial down payment, and he sued for restitution. In a reversal of the roles in *Krell,* the defendant counterclaimed for the balance due. There were both left as they were, although they were excused from further performance.[115] In the midst of World War II, however, the English courts changed their minds and allowed restitution of down payments in similar cases.[116]

[2] Early American Approaches to Frustration and Implied Conditions

American courts were much more reluctant than their English counterparts to adopt the doctrine of frustration and, specifically, the notion of implied conditions. The uncertainty of American law was apparent in the first Restatement, which included sixteen separate sections on the subject of impossibility. The first Restatement made much of the distinction between objective and subjective impossibility: The former excused performance but the latter did not.[117] Objective impossibility related to the nature of the performance (e.g., a law rendered the performance criminal), whereas subjective performance related to the individual promisor's ability to perform (e.g., he had become insolvent). The distinction was far from clear, however. Death, illness, and physical incapacity, all of which affect the *promisor,* were included among the acceptable excuses and thus presumably were in the category of objective impossibility.[118] Section 461, which spoke in terms of the absence of facts "necessary for the performance of the promise," seemed

---

[114] Chandler v. Webster [1904] LR 1 KB 493.

[115] The moral was obvious: Buyers and lessees should make small downpayments; sellers and lessors should demand large ones.

[116] Fibrosa Spolka Akeyjna v. Fairbairn Lawson Combe Barbour, Ltd., HL [1943] AC32. The result in *Fibrosa* was codified in Law Reform (Frustrated Contracts) Act, 1943, 6 & 7 Geo. 6 c. 40.

[117] Restatement of Contracts §§ 455, 456, 457 (1932).

[118] Id. §§ 459, 460.

remarkably close to an implied condition approach, and Section 454 introduced the concept of "impracticability because of extreme and unreasonable difficulty, expense, injury, or loss" as a reason for excusing performance.

Until fairly recently, California was the only jurisdiction that clearly followed the lead of the English courts in developing a separate doctrine of frustration. *Mineral Park Land Co. v. Howard,*[119] a 1916 decision of the California Supreme Court, was the leading case. The defendant agreed to take all the gravel needed for the construction of a bridge from the plaintiff's land at a price of $.05 per cubic yard. It was estimated that about 100,000 yards would be needed. After excavating 50,000 yards, the defendant hit water, and the cost of removing the water and drying the gravel was so prohibitive that he went to another source. The owner of the property sued for breach of contract, but the court held that the extraordinary increase in cost frustrated the purpose of the contract and that the defendant was discharged from performance. Although the case might have been treated as one of mutual mistake (neither party knew of the water, which was a latent difficulty), the court chose to treat the problem as one of frustration, not of mistake. Subsequent California cases limited the *Mineral Park* holding to situations involving a fundamental change in the contemplated mode of operation.[120] Increased cost was not enough to justify a discharge; there had to be something more, such as the need for a change in the mode of extraction, as in *Mineral Park.*

In a 1921 decision, the United States Supreme Court also seemed to adopt the implied condition concept:

> [W]here parties enter into a contract on the assumption that some particular thing essential to its performance will continue to exist and be available for the purpose and neither agrees to be responsible for its continued existence and availability, the contract must be regarded as subject to an implied condition that, if before the time for performance and without

---

[119] Mineral Park Land Co. v. Howard, 172 Cal. 289, 156 P 458 (1916).

[120] See, e.g., City of Vernon v. City of Los Angeles, 45 Cal. 2d 710, 290 P2d 841 (1955); Transbay Constr. Co. v. City and County of San Francisco, 35 F. Supp. 433 (ND Cal. 1940).

the default of either party the particular thing ceases to exist or be available for the purpose, the contract shall be dissolved and the parties excused from performing it.[121]

Outside of California, perhaps the most interesting American decision came from the Court of Claims in *National Presto Industries, Inc. v. United States*.[122] During the Korean War, National Presto entered into a fixed price contract with the U.S. government to produce artillery shells for the Army. The contract required the shells to be produced by a new method designed to reduce waste. Unfortunately, the new method turned out to be technologically difficult. National Presto had cost overruns of $700,000, and it was not feasible to continue production using the new method. Although the contract was for a fixed price, National Presto sued to recover its cost overruns. The court mixed elements of mutual mistake and frustration theories and essentially decided that the agreement was as much a joint venture research and development project as it was a contract for the production of artillery shells. Neither side was familiar with the new technique, and although the method failed to work efficiently, that knowledge was worth something. The court's reasoning led to a reformation of the contract with an equal allocation of the risk of loss between the parties.

In comparison, in the case of *United States v. Wegematic Corp.*,[123] technical problems did not provide a sufficient basis for excusing performance. The defendant was trying to provide the government with state-of-the-art computer equipment in a rapidly changing market, and technological problems should have been foreseeable to both parties. However, the defendant made a number of promises and respresentations about its ability to perform. The court treated these as if they were warranties of performance and concluded that the defendant had assumed the risk of technological problems.

---

[121] Texas Co. v. Hogarth, 256 US 619, 620 (1921).

[122] National Presto Indus., Inc. v. United States, 338 F2d 99 (Ct. Cl. 1964), cert. denied, 380 US 962 (1965).

[123] United States v. Wegematic Corp., 360 F2d 674 (2d Cir. 1966).

In general, however, the American law of frustration remained largely undeveloped, partially due to the custom of including force majeure and other exculpatory clauses in business contracts. Many problems thus became matters of contract interpretation, and courts did not have to consider whether to develop new or different rules.[124]

[3] UCC Codification of Doctrine of Commercial Impracticability

[a] Section 2-615: Commercial Impracticability as Excuse for Performance

The relative paucity of American law and the sometimes restrictive approaches of courts to the assertion of impossibility defenses or the full implementation of force majeure clauses led to the drafting of UCC Section 2-615. This section embodies the concept of commercial impracticability as an excuse for performance. Although the concept of commercial impracticability antedated the adoption of the UCC, its inclusion in the UCC has significantly affected the development of the general doctrine of frustration.

Professor Llewellyn, the principal draftsman of the UCC, apparently intended Section 2-615 to provide a general theory of excuse from liability in a wide range of circumstances that covered not only impossibility but also the concept of frustration and the English notion of implied conditions.[125] The critical language is found in Section 2-615(a), which excuses performance by a seller if

---

[124] See generally 3 Hawkland § 2-615:01, at 180, 181.

[125] In the words of one commentator:

> "The private notes of Professor Llewellyn reveal that he had two things in mind in drafting this section. First, he wanted to free force majeure clauses from restrictive constructions that had deprived them of their commercial utility in some pre-Code states. Second, he wanted to provide a general doctrine of excuse to replace the concepts of frustration and implied conditions and to operate in appropriate circumstances even where no exemption clause appears in the contract."

Id. at 181.

> performance as agreed has been made impracticable by the occurrence of a contingency the nonoccurrence of which was a basic assumption on which the contract was made or by compliance in good faith with any applicable foreign or domestic governmental regulation or order whether or not it later proves to be invalid.[126]

This language accomplishes a great deal by introducing the concept of impracticability. The word itself implies a lesser standard than frustration and certainly less than impossibility. It expressly introduces a concept of subjectivity, because practicability almost invariably is a factor of the parties' specific circumstances and expectations. The language about contingencies that are a part of the basic assumption of the agreement derives directly from the English decisions in cases such as *Taylor v. Caldwell* and *Krell v. Henry,* with their emphasis on implied conditions. Section 2-615(a) also bows to the doctrine of impossibility by referring to governmental regulations, but even this is tempered by a concept of good faith because an invalid governmental order may excuse performance if it is followed in good faith. The drafters of the second Restatement used similar language in their modern definition of mutual mistake,[127] and their provision on frustration clearly shows the influence of Section 2-615:

---

[126] Section 2-615 reads:

"Except so far as a seller may have assumed a greater obligation and subject to the preceding section on substituted performance:

(a) Delay in delivery or nondelivery in whole or in part by a seller who complies with paragraphs (b) and (c) is not a breach of his duty under a contract for sale if performance as agreed has been made impracticable by the occurrence of a contingency the nonoccurrence of which was a basic assumption on which the contract was made or by compliance in good faith with any applicable foreign or domestic governmental regulation or order whether or not it later proves to be invalid.

(b) Where the causes mentioned in paragraph (a) affect only a part of the seller's capacity to perform, he must allocate production and deliveries among his customers but may at his option include regular customers not then under contract as well as his own requirements for further manufacture. He may so allocate in any manner which is fair and reasonable.

(c) The seller must notify the buyer seasonably that there will be delay or nondelivery and, when allocation is required under paragraph (b), of the estimated quota thus made available for the buyer."

[127] Restatement (Second) of Contracts § 294 (1981).

> Where, after a contract is made, a party's principal purpose is substantially frustrated without his fault by the occurrence of an event the nonoccurrence of which was a basic assumption on which the contract was made, his remaining duties to render performance are discharged, unless the language or other circumstances indicate the contrary.[128]

The close connection between the language of the second Restatement and the UCC indicates the influence of the UCC on the modern common law of contracts. Indeed, it is often impossible to distinguish the reasoning in a common-law case from the reasoning in a case governed by the UCC. This is especially true in cases that involve attempts to be excused from performance because of a sharp increase in costs.[129]

Before Section 2-615 comes into play, it must be shown that performance is commercially impracticable, that this impracticability is the result of the occurrence or nonoccurrence of a contingency, and that this contingency was a basic assumption of the agreement. Thus, there are three operative elements of proof, and Section 2-615 cannot be used to excuse performance unless all three elements are present.[130] The burden of proof for all three elements is on the party who is claiming excuse for nonperformance.[131]

[b] Proof of Commercial Impracticability

Although the Official Commentary speaks of commercial impracticability as a commonly understood term,[132] it is hardly self-

---

[128] Id. § 265 (1981).

[129] See infra ¶ 12.04[3].

[130] Iowa Elec. Light & Power Co. v. Atlas Corp., 467 F. Supp. 129 (ND Iowa 1978).

[131] Luria Bros. v. Pielet Bros. Scrap Iron, 600 F2d 103 (7th Cir. 1979); Ocean Air Tradeways, Inc. v. Arkay Realty Corp., 480 F2d 1112 (9th Cir. 1973); Bende & Sons, Inc. v. Crown Recreation, Inc., 548 F. Supp. 1018 (EDNY 1982), aff'd without op., 722 F2d 727 (2d Cir. 1983).

[132] UCC § 2-615, Official Comment 3. What is clear is that commercial impracticability is less than impossibility. RC Craig, Ltd. v. Ships of the Sea, Inc., 401 F Supp. 1051 (SD Ga. 1975).

defining. The determination of impracticability depends greatly on the peculiar facts that surround a transaction and the normal trade expectations of the industry. What often happens is that proof becomes circular. If it is shown that a contingency that is a basic assumption of an agreement has occurred or failed to occur, that demonstration often affects the determination of impracticability. The results in Section 2-615 cases may be difficult to predict, but that is largely a function of the section's purpose, which is to provide a mechanism for a court to mete out justice.[133] It provides a law court with the opportunity to act much like an equity court and to fashion a remedy that is sensitive to the relative positions of the parties without regard to any hard-and-fast rules of law.[134]

[c] Increased Costs as Basis of Commercial Impracticability

The most common issue that arises in Section 2-615 cases and common-law impracticability cases is whether an unexpected price or cost increase excuses performance. The Official Commentary to Section 2-615 rejects increased cost or a sudden rise or collapse of the market as a reason to invoke the section, but with a number of exceptions. If costs go up because of an unforeseen contingency that alters the nature of performance (e.g., the discovery of water in the gravel pit in the *Mineral Park* case[135]) or if there is a severe shortage caused by a natural disaster, war, or civil disturbance, the impracticability doctrine may apply.[136]

Despite the rejection of increased costs as a general basis for the assertion of commercial impracticability, defenses based on changes in costs continue to appear in the cases. One of the few cases in which the defendant has been successful was *Aluminum Co. of America (Alcoa) v. Essex Group, Inc.*,[137] decided in 1980.

---

[133] 3 Hawkland § 2-615:08, at 200–203.

[134] See generally Hurst, "Freedom of Contract in an Unstable Economy: Judicial Reallocation of Contractual Risks Under UCC Section 2-615," 54 NCL Rev. 545 (1976); Schwartz, "Sales Law and Inflations," 50 So. Cal. L. Rev. 1 (1976).

[135] See supra ¶ 12.04[2].

[136] UCC § 2-615, Official Comment 4.

[137] Aluminum Co. of Am. (Alcoa) v. Essex Group, Inc., 29 UCC Rep. 1 (WD Pa. 1980).

Alcoa agreed to process alumina for Essex to use in fabricating aluminum products. Both parties recognized that Alcoa's costs were likely to rise during the term of the agreement and took that into account in developing a pricing formula. Alan Greenspan, the noted economist, drafted the formula, which had two major parts. The first established a variable based on Alcoa's labor costs, and the second took into account Alcoa's nonlabor costs. These were computed by reference to the wholesale price index (WPI), which historically fluctuated in close harmony with Alcoa's actual nonlabor costs. After Alcoa began to perform, electricity costs skyrocketed to levels well beyond the increase in the WPI. Electricity is a major cost in the processing of alumina and Alcoa projected that it would lose $75 million over the life of the contract because the pricing formula failed to take into account the tremendous rise in electricity costs that resulted from the overall energy crisis. The court found for Alcoa, even though the parties specifically negotiated a formula that allocated the risks of cost increases, because the size of the increase was so large that it was beyond the reasonable contemplation of the parties. The reasoning of the court was based on the theory of mutual mistake. Both parties erroneously assumed at the time of contracting that the WPI would accurately reflect Alcoa's nonlabor costs over time. The court's analysis, however, borrowed heavily from discussions of frustration and commercial impracticability.

Other courts have not been as sympathetic to the assertion of commercial impracticability as a defense to performance because costs have increased, especially where the contract has included a risk allocation provision. As one court said in a case that arose from the closing of the Suez Canal in 1967, "a willingness (of the promisor) to assume abnormal risks . . . should legitimately cause us to judge the impracticability of performance . . . in stricter terms than we would were the contingency unforeseen."[138] For instance, a dairy was unable to avoid a fixed price contract for the supply of milk to a school system despite an unexpectedly large rise in milk prices because milk price fluctuations were foreseeable and the whole purpose of the fixed price contract was to avoid those fluctuations. The risk of a rise in the market was on the

[138] Transatlantic Fin. Corp. v. United States, 363 F2d 312, 319 (DC Cir. 1969).

supplier and the risk of a drop was on the buyer.[139] In *Eastern Airlines, Inc. v. Gulf Oil Corp.*,[140] Gulf was held to a supply contract for jet fuel even though the combination of the 1973 Arab oil embargo and the price stabilization program of the federal government wiped out Gulf's profit margin. The court said that the parties specifically contemplated cost increases because the contract contained an escalator clause, which amounted to an allocation of risk of a foreseeable occurrence. It did not matter that the precise cause of the problem had not been anticipated.

Another federal district court specifically rejected the reasoning of the *Alcoa* court. *Wabash, Inc. v. Avnet, Inc.*[141] involved a contract for the sale of the assets of IPM, an Avnet subsidiary, to Wabash pursuant to a consent decree entered into with the Federal Trade Commission. Wabash was to pay for the assets over time in accordance with a formula based on changes in the gross national product (GNP). Some time later, the GNP rose while IPM's fortunes declined and Wabash asked for a reformation of the agreement so that it would not have to pay a disproportionately high price for IPM's assets. The court considered the discussion of the formula in *Alcoa* and rejected that analysis because the GNP was a reliable indicator at the time it was chosen based on the historical performance of IPM and because the choice of a variable indicator always carries a degree of risk.[142]

---

[139] Maple Farms, Inc. v. City School Dist. 76 Misc. 2d 1080, 352 NYS2d 784 (1974).

[140] Eastern Airlines, Inc. v. Gulf Oil Corp., 415 F. Supp. 429 (SD Fla. 1975).

[141] Wabash, Inc. v. Avnet, Inc., 516 F. Supp. 995 (ND Ill. 1981).

[142] Other cases denying relief for large cost increases include: Roth Steel Prod. v. Sharon Steel Corp., 705 F2d 138 (6th Cir. 1983); Bernina Distribs., Inc. v. Bernina Sewing Mach. Co., 646 F2d 434 (10th Cir. 1981); Gulf Oil Corp. v. FPC, 563 F2d 588 (3d Cir. 1977), cert. denied, 434 US 1062 (1978); Printing Indus. Ass'n v. International Printing and Graphic Communications Union, Local No. 56, 584 F. Supp. 990 (ND Ohio 1984) (dictum — decision was to deny cross-motions for summary judgment because of fact issues); Louisiana Power & Light Co. v. Allegheny Ludlum Indus., Inc., 517 F. Supp. 1319 (ED La. 1981); Iowa Elec. Light and Power Co. v. Atlas Corp., 467 F. Supp. 129 (ND Iowa 1978); Eastern Airlines, Inc. v. Gulf Oil Corp., 415 F. Supp. 429 (SD Fla. 1975); see also Note, "UCC Section 2-615: Sharp Inflationary Increases in Cost as an Excuse From Performance of Contract," 50 Notre Dame Law. 297 (1974). In the words of one commentator, "Harshness alone cannot excuse performance . . . because it expresses a *result*, whereas this section [Section 2-615] centers its attention on the

One of the most extensive discussions of the commercial impracticability doctrine in the context of large cost increases is contained in a federal district court's opinion in a case that involved an agreement by Westinghouse to supply uranium and to process spent fuel for an electric utility.[143] In 1964, Congress made the private ownership of uranium legal, and this opened the door for the development of the nuclear power industry. Most utility companies depended on fossil fuels to generate power and they had no expertise in the use of nuclear equipment. Westinghouse was one of the major competitors for the sale of nuclear reactors and related equipment to the electric utility industry. To encourage Florida Light & Power to build a nuclear facility and to use Westinghouse equipment, Westinghouse committed to supply uranium for a substantial number of years and to dispose of the spent fuel.[144] These negotiations all took place in the mid-1960s when the industry was in its infancy, and, from all indications, Westinghouse considered the agreement to supply fuel and to dispose of the spent fuel to be a minor concession to close a deal in a highly competitive market. Unfortunately for Westinghouse, the cost of uranium increased dramatically over the next decade, and, due to a host of technological and environmental problems as well as new government regulations, the cost of dealing with the spent fuel became extremely onerous. Westinghouse reneged on its commitment and offered as defenses the doctrine of commercial impracticability under Section 2-615 and the doctrine of mutual mistake. The court, however, rejected the Westinghouse defenses and reasoned that Westinghouse had assumed the risk of cost increases, a risk that Florida Power & Light refused to assume during the negotiations. Furthermore, the contract was essentially for the sale of equipment,

---

causes of the result through the concept of contingency." 3 Hawkland § 2-615:08, at 201. Because price and cost changes are natural and foreseeable, the parties can avoid the harsh consequences of dramatic changes by negotiating appropriate exculpatory clauses. Only in more unusual cases will Section 2-615 provide an escape from a foreseeable problem.

[143] In re Westinghouse Elec. Corp. Uranium Contracts Litigation, 517 F. Supp. 440 (ED Va. 1981).

[144] The contract price for the uranium was determined from a formula based on the amount of electricity generated by Florida Light & Power. It had nothing to do with variables in the market for uranium.

not for the sale and processing of fuel. The uranium clause was an incidental part of the whole.[145]

[d] Other Excusing Contingencies in Commercial Impracticability Cases

Difficulties in obtaining necessary supplies of raw materials or in producing an agreed-upon crop sometimes provide a sufficient basis for an excuse under Section 2-615. In general, the approach is not too different from the common-law cases. For example, if there is a contract to deliver produce from a particular farm, the supplier may be excused if the weather destroys his crop,[146] but if the supplier merely has agreed to deliver produce, weather problems are no excuse.[147] It is so easy to avoid this kind of problem by careful drafting that it is difficult to understand why such cases continue to appear.[148] Other supply cases have similar results. If the contract contemplates a third-party supplier to the performing party and the supplier fails to perform, that may be an excuse. But if there is no agreement about a particular supplier, there is no excuse because the performing party has assumed the risk of finding an adequate source of supply.[149]

---

[145] If one examines the whole problem carefully, the court's result seems unduly harsh. Westinghouse and Florida Light & Power were both novices in the energy industry and they made a poor prediction of future events. Few businessmen in 1965 could have predicted the Arab oil embargo of 1973, the inflation of the next decade, or the international cartel that fixed uranium prices for a critical period in the early 1970s. There is enough flexibility in the doctrine of impracticability to have allowed the court to reform the agreement even if it did not want to excuse Westinghouse from all liability. Westinghouse was able to renegotiate or settle some of its other contracts with uranium clauses in them.

[146] Michigan Bean Co. v. Senn, 93 Mich. App. 440, 287 NW2d 257 (1979).

[147] Ralston Purina Co. v. Rooker, 346 So. 2d 901 (Miss. 1977) (unprecedented rains and floods causing crop failures did not excuse performance). But cf. Campbell v. Hostetter Farms, Inc., 251 Pa. Super. 232, 380 A2d 463 (1977) (unseasonably wet weather causing a crop shortage was an excuse); Mitchell Canneries, Inc. v. United States, 77 F. Supp. 498 (Ct. Cl. 1948) (total crop failure excused performance).

[148] For example, the supplier can specify in the contract the farm or farms or general geographic area from which the produce will come and include a crop failure or weather clause.

[149] See, e.g., SCA Int'l, Inc. v. Garfiedl & Rosen, Inc., 337 F. Supp. 246 (D. Mass. 1971).

The two key issues in most commercial impracticability cases are foreseeability and harshness. If a problem were foreseeable in the normal course of trade, most courts treat it as an assumed risk.[150] Protection should come from careful drafting of the agreement rather than reliance on the public law of sales. A good example is the decision in *Northern Corp. v. Chugach Electric Association.*[151] The defendant agreed to build a dam for the plaintiff. The contract specified that the rock and other materials for the dam were to be transported over a frozen lake, but it turned out that the ice was too thin. The defendant could have gone around the lake, but only at great cost in time and money. As a result, the defendant did not complete the job. The plaintiff argued against the defendant's assertion of an excuse for impracticability, relying on the Suez Canal cases in which carriers unsuccessfully sought to be relieved of their obligations of carriage because the Suez Canal was closed because of war. The court held for the defendant because the contract specified the route of carriage as an integral part of the transaction. In the Suez Canal cases, on the other hand, the route was not as important as the delivery of the goods, even by more circuitous and slower navigation.

[e] Applicability of Section 2-615 to Buyers

One of the questions about Section 2-615 is whether it applies on both sides of the transaction. The section speaks in terms of sellers and mentions buyers only where the seller is admonished to provide the buyer with seasonable notice of delay or nondelivery by reason of an event covered by Section 2-615.[152] The UCC generally treats buyers and sellers equally, and there is no good reason for Section 2-615 to be an exception. The doctrine of frustration that developed at common law did not distinguish between buyers

---

[150] See, e.g., Heat Exhangers, Inc. v. Map Constr. Corp., 34 Md. App. 679, 368 A2d 1088 (1977) (difficulty in obtaining parts was foreseeable). The second circuit has defined foreseeability as a "real possibility that [the event] would affect performance." United States v. Wegematic Corp., 360 F2d 674 (2d Cir. 1966).

[151] Northern Corp. v. Chugach Elec. Ass'n, 518 P2d 76 (Alaska), vacated on other grounds, 523 P2d 1243 (1974) and later appealed, 562 P2d 1023 (1977).

[152] UCC § 2-615(c).

and sellers, although a buyer would rarely be able to invoke the defense of impossibility because his performance usually consists simply of paying money. Official Comment 9 to Section 2-615 does discuss excuses for a buyer in an output or requirements contract as if buyers were covered by the section.[153] The two major treatises on the UCC agree that Section 2-615 should apply to buyers even if it does not do so by its own terms. One just bluntly says that it does.[154] The other says that buyers should be covered because that is consistent with the overall intent of the statute.[155]

[f] Relationship of Section 2-615 to Other UCC Sections

Section 2-615 is no different from other parts of the UCC in that its general approach is to interpret the various sections in pari materia, or as parts of a whole. In particular, there is a close relationship among Sections 2-614, 2-615, and 2-616. The applicability of Section 2-615 is expressly subject to the application of Section 2-614, which deals with substituted performance.

Under Section 2-614, if the agreed method of carriage becomes "commercially impracticable" but a "commercially reasonable substitute" is available, the seller must use the substitute and the buyer must accept tender.[156] Similarly, if the agreed method or manner of payment fails by reason of a domestic or foreign governmental regulation and a "commercially . . . substantial equiva-

---

[153] The comment says that the buyer in such a contract generally is covered by the section on output and requirements contracts (Section 2-306), but then goes on at some length to discuss what amounts to an expected contingency (an implied condition). That discussion would be redundant if there were no reason for Section 2-615 to apply to buyers.

[154] 4 *Anderson on the Uniform Commercial Code* § 2-615:4, at 270 (3d ed. 1983) (hereinafter cited as Anderson), citing Nora Springs Coop. Co. v. Brandon, 247 NW2d 744 (Iowa 1976).

[155] 3 Hawkland § 2-615:05, at 192, citing In re Brooks Shoe Mfg. Co., 21 Bankr. 604, 34 UCC Rep. 539 (ED Pa. 1982) (buyer not excused but court assumed that buyer could invoke protection of Section 2-615).

[156] Section 2-614(1) reads:

> "Where without fault of either party the agreed berthing, loading, or unloading facilities fail or an agreed type of carrier becomes unavailable or the agreed manner of delivery otherwise becomes commercially impracticable but a commercially reasonable substitute is available, such substitute performance must be tendered and accepted."

lent'' is available, the buyer must provide that equivalent and the seller must accept it.[157] The purpose of Section 2-614 is to avoid the destruction of the contract by a failure that is readily curable without loss to either side. The Official Commentary discusses the distinction in terms of whether the problem is an ''incidental matter'' or one that ''goes to the very heart of the agreement.''[158]

Section 2-616 focuses on the rights and duties of the buyer when he receives notice from the seller of a delay or an apportionment of performance by reason of one of the contingencies covered by Section 2-615. When an installment contract is at issue, if the delay or apportionment ''substantially impairs the value of the whole contract,'' the buyer generally may either terminate and discharge incompleted performance or modify by agreeing to take an apportionment in substitution.[159] The burden is on the buyer to go forward. If he receives notice from the seller pursuant to Section 2-615 and does not respond within thirty days, he will be held to have accepted the notice terms.[160]

Section 2-615 also contemplates that the seller may agree to a greater obligation than the one imposed by law, and the section only operates to the extent that the seller has not accepted a greater obligation. Official Comment 8 states in part:

> The provisions of this section are made subject to assumption of greater liability by agreement and such agreement is to be

---

[157] Section 2-614(2) reads:

''If the agreed means or manner of payment fails because of domestic or foreign governmental regulation, the seller may withhold or stop delivery unless the buyer provides a means or manner of payment which is commercially a substantial equivalent. If delivery has already been taken, payment by the means or in the manner provided by the regulation discharges the buyer's obligation unless the regulation is discriminatory, oppressive or predatory.''

[158] UCC § 2-614, Official Comment 1. It may also be helpful to examine Section 2-613, which deals with excuse by reason of the destruction of goods identified to the contract.

[159] UCC §§ 2-616(1)(a), 2-616(1)(b). For a discussion of installment contracts, see UCC § 2-612.

[160] UCC § 2-614(2). It is difficult if not impossible to avoid the effect of Section 2-616. Section 2-616(3) reads: ''The provisions of this section may not be negated by agreement except in so far as the seller has assumed a greater obligation under the preceding section.''

found not only in the expressed terms of the contract but in the circumstances surrounding the contracting, in trade usage and the like. Thus the exemptions of this section do not apply when the contingency in question is sufficiently foreshadowed at the time of contracting to be included among the business risks which are fairly to be regarded as part of the dickered terms, either consciously or as a matter of reasonable, commercial interpretation from the circumstances.

[g] Allocation of Goods Among Customers

When a shortage in supply excuses the performing party from full compliance with the contract, he must notify all his customers and allocate his deliveries among them in a manner that is "fair and reasonable."[161] In determining allocations, a seller may take into account that one purchaser bought goods before another. He also may prorate on the basis of the relative sizes of orders or may take into account the different manufacturing demands of various customers.[162] A seller may not discriminate among similarly situated customers and may not prefer a subsidiary over an outside purchaser.[163]

The problem that gives rise to an excuse under Section 2-615 may not last forever. When the difficulty is removed, the relationship between the parties depends on what has happened in the interim. If the contract has been rescinded, either by the parties themselves or as a result of judicial action, it is not revived.[164] When there has been an allocation among customers, but the contract has continued in existence, there is no good reason for it not to come back into full force when the disability is lifted. It may be that there should not be any retroactive effect, especially if a substantial amount of time has passed and parties have changed their positions, but there is no reason for the allocation to amount to a permanent reformation as to future performance.

---

[161] UCC § 2-615(b).

[162] See UCC § 2-615, Official Comment 11.

[163] Chemetron Corp. v. McLouth Steel Corp., 381 F. Supp. 245 (ND Ill. 1974), aff'd, 522 F2d 469 (7th Cir. 1975).

[164] Goddard v. Ishikawajima-Harima Heavy Indus. Co., 29 AD2d 754, 287 NYS2d 901, aff'd, 24 NY2d 842, 248 NE2d 600, 300 NYS2d 851 (1968) discussed in 4 Anderson § 2-615:25, at 282.

Despite the limitations that are imposed on the applicability of Section 2-615 and the often-repeated comment that it is to be strictly construed and applied,[165] it does codify the general law of frustration and makes it a central part of the American law of contracts. Article 2 of the UCC only applies to chattel sales, but its influence is great on common law. There is a natural tendency to treat contract cases similarly, and if the UCC provides a way to handle a certain kind of case it is not surprising that courts might follow this lead in other situations that are not expressly covered by the UCC.

¶ 12.05 WAIVER AND ACCORD

[1] Definitions

Terms such as "novation," "substituted agreement," "modification," "waiver," "accord," "executory accord," and "accord and satisfaction" can be confusing. There are technical distinctions among the terms that can have significant consequences, but each shares the underlying premise that one or both parties have agreed by words or actions to a change in the original agreement. This may be as fundamental as a change in the identity of one of the parties, or it may be as relatively inconsequential as a failure to complain about a payment that is a few days late. Because the terms are used so often, it is helpful to understand their distinctions.

[a] Substituted Agreement

Any mutually agreed-upon change in the original agreement is technically a substituted agreement. In fact, novation and modification are both subsets of the set of substituted agreements. Most courts, however, use the term "substituted agreement" to refer to a fundamental change in the subject matter of a transaction. For example, a buyer agrees to purchase condominium *A* from a developer for $100,000. However *A* is not available, and for the same consideration the buyer agrees to accept condominium *B* from the developer, all other terms remaining the same. The second agree-

---

[165] See supra ¶ 12.04[3][a].

ment is thus a substitute for the first.[166] A substituted agreement arises when the performing party accepts a promise to do something different from the originally agreed performance. Actual performance is not necessary to the creation of the new agreement and the extinguishing of the old.[167] If the nonperforming party accepts a performance that is different without complaint, that also extinguishes the original obligation if it is clear that the performing party has offered the different performance in substitution for the original.[168]

[b] Novation

Although sometimes used interchangeably with the idea of substituted agreement, novation more commonly refers to a change in the identity of the contracting parties. For example, White and Black reach an agreement, and subsequently White agrees to accept performance by Gray in lieu of Black's performance. In effect, a new agreement is created between White and Gray that takes the place of the original agreement between White and Black.[169]

[c] Modification

A modified agreement may be a substituted agreement or even a novation, although modification usually refers to a change in the original agreement that is less fundamental than a change in the identity of one of the parties or in the subject matter of the transaction. For example, the parties may agree to a different place for all or part of the performance, a different quantity of goods, a different price, or any number of other changes in the terms and condi-

---

[166] This simple example illustrates some of the complications that can arise. The substitution of *B* for *A* might be called a modification of the original agreement or even a substituted performance that amounts to an accord and satisfaction.

[167] Restatement (Second) of Contracts § 279 (1981).

[168] Id. § 278.

[169] Id. § 280. The second Restatement does not use the terms "novation" and "substituted agreement" interchangeably, although some courts do. Farnsworth § 4.24, at 284 n.4.

tions of performance. As a general rule, the parties are free to modify the agreement just as they are free to enter into a contract, and the rules of contract formation apply (i.e., there must be consideration, which may inhere in the mutual exchange of promises; the statute of frauds must be satisfied; and the modification must not be unconscionable). Even if the original agreement prohibits modification, the parties can modify the agreement by striking the antimodification clause and making whatever other changes they think are appropriate.

[d] Accord

An accord is an agreement to accept a substituted or different performance (e.g., a creditor agrees to take payment in kind rather than in money).[170] It is essentially the same as a substituted agreement in that the nonperforming party accepts a promise to provide a different performance. However, an important technical difference between the two is not always made clear in the cases. With a substituted agreement, the latter agreement governs and the original no longer exists. An accord that is still executory, however, may be withdrawn or further modified unless the nonperforming party has relied on the accord to his detriment. The nonperforming party may not sue on the original promise as long as an accord exists and the time for the performance pursuant to the accord has not yet arrived.[171] If the performing party does not perform at all or does not live up to the performance either of the original agreement or the accord, the nonperforming party can sue on either the accord or the original agreement.[172] Performance that comports with

---

[170] At one time the common law would not recognize an agreement to take a lesser sum in satisfaction of a debt, although a debtor could satisfy the obligation if the creditor agreed to a different consideration (e.g., a chattel or a service in kind in lieu of a money payment). See, e.g., Foakes v. Beer, 9 App. Cas. 605 (1884). That rule has little remaining vitality for the commonsense reason that creditors are often much happier to take partial payment and to discharge a debtor who is a poor risk than to be left with a valid but worthless obligation.

[171] There was once a doctrine that an executory accord was not a defense to a suit on the underlying obligation, but that has been discredited. Farnsworth 285 n.8, citing Gold, "Executory Accords," 21 BUL Rev. 465 (1941); Shepherd, "The Executory Accord," 26 Ill. L. Rev. 22 (1931).

[172] Restatement (Second) of Contracts § 281 (1981).

the accord is known as a satisfaction, and the performing party may plead accord and satisfaction to discharge his obligations under the original agreement and under the accord. To prove an accord and satisfaction, the defendant generally must meet the standards of proof that apply in pleading and proving an ordinary contract. This usually presents a case for a jury.[173]

[e] Waiver

A waiver involves no change in the underlying agreement, although that may be its practical effect. The doctrine of waiver relates to the actions of parties during the course of performance rather than during negotiations. It usually involves an excuse for performance that is at odds with the agreement because the nonperforming party has not demanded adherence to the original terms but has accepted nonconforming performance. Distinguishing waiver from modification, one commentator wrote:

> Waiver is the surrender of a right to object, or protect, or claim damages, by the person having the right to do so. Modification is the changing of the terms of the agreement which may diminish or increase the duty of either party as distinguished from the mere surrender of a right by one person against another.[174]

For example, a loan agreement with a bank may require that monthly installments be paid on the first business day of each month. Banks typically accept without question payments made by mail that arrive within a few days of the first day of the month. A bank that followed that customary practice would be estopped from suddenly demanding late charges — or even from claiming a default — for payments mailed on the first that arrive on the third day of the month.[175] Although this amounts to a de facto modifica-

---

[173] See, e.g., Clonts v. Scholle, 172 Ga. App. 721, 324 SE2d 496 (1984); Pennsylvania Threshermen & Farmers Mut. Ins. Co. v. Hill, 113 Ga. App. 283, 148 SE2d 83 (1966).

[174] 3 Anderson § 2-209:7, at 319.

[175] For an analogous situation involving an insurance company, see Horace Mann Life Ins. Co. v. Lunsford, 172 Ga. App. 866, 324 SE2d 808 (1984) (insur-

tion, the original agreement is still in force and, upon fair notice, the waiving party may be able to demand strict adherence to its terms in the future unless there has been detrimental reliance and a change in position by the other party.[176] In this latter situation, the doctrine of reliance coupled with the doctrine of waiver may result in a de facto modification that is as enforceable as any other modification that is freely and mutually reached by the parties.[177] As a general safeguard, courts tend to employ the doctrine of waiver with respect to fairly minor aspects of performance and not with matters central to the transaction. Waiver is a common issue in construction litigation because many variables are involved in performance (e.g., weather, bureaucratic delays in issuing permits, problems with transportation, difficulties with subcontractors) that are not anticipated in the original agreement. Rather than go through the formality of a modification or a change order, many parties simply accept performance at variance with the contract.

[2] Waiver and the UCC

Two provisions of the UCC are especially pertinent to a consideration of waiver and similar defenses. The first is Section 1-107, one of the general provisions that applies to transactions throughout the UCC, not just to sales transactions covered by Article 2. It reads: "Any claim or right arising out of an alleged breach can be discharged in whole or in part without consideration by a written waiver or renunciation signed and delivered by the aggrieved party."

---

ance company accepted late premium payments and was estopped to invoke forfeiture clause). In equity, the doctrine of unconscionability was used to prevent the enforcement of mortgage defaults when a late payment was tendered. See, e.g., Domus Realty Corp. v. 3440 Realty Co., 179 Misc. 749, 40 NYS2d 69 (Sup. Ct.), aff'd, 266 AD 725, 41 NYS2d 940 (1943).

[176] Restatement (Second) of Contracts § 84(2) (1981); UCC § 2-209(5); Hunt v. Smyth, 25 Cal. App. 3d 807, 101 Cal. Rptr. 4 (1972); Margolin v. Franklin, 132 Ill. App. 2d 527, 270 NE2d 140 (1971).

[177] The waiver of a condition after the time for the condition has expired is an election and is usually binding. See Farnsworth § 8.5, at 564, citing Restatement (Second) of Contracts § 84 (1981) and Wm. W. Bierce, Ltd. v. Hutchins, 205 US 340 (1907).

This provision eliminates the requirement of a separate consideration to support what amounts to a form of modification of the original agreement. According to the Official Commentary, it is to be read together with the general obligation of good faith contained in Section 1-203 and, for sales cases, in conjunction with Section 2-209, which deals with the modification of signed writings. The Official Commentary also states that an oral waiver or renunciation that is supported by consideration is enforceable as long as it comports with the statute of frauds. The fact that there are few cases interpreting or applying Section 1-107 is not surprising, since it is so straightforward and commonsensical. The requirement either of a writing or of consideration for an oral waiver ensures that the aggrieved party makes the waiver or renunciation seriously.[178]

The second significant UCC provision that directly relates to waiver is Section 2-209, which deals generally with the requirements for modification.[179] Section 2-209(1) eliminates the common-law requirement of separate consideration for a modification. Section 2-209(2) allows the parties to require in the principal agreement that any modification must be in writing and signed by both parties to be effective. Section 2-209(3) makes clear that if the principal contract is covered by the statute of frauds, any modification must also satisfy the statute. The provisions most important to

---

[178] One case held that a check is not a writing within the meaning of Section 1-107. Kane v. American Nat'l Bank & Trust Co., 21 Ill. App. 3d 1046, 316 NE2d 177 (1974).

[179] Section 2-209 reads:

"(1) An agreement modifying a contract within this Article needs no consideration to be binding.
(2) A signed agreement which excludes modification or rescission except by a signed writing cannot be otherwise modified or rescinded, but except as between merchants such a requirement on a form supplied by the merchant must be separately signed by the other party.
(3) The requirements of the statute of frauds section of this Article (Section 2-201) must be satisfied if the contract as modified is within its provisions.
(4) Although an attempt at modification or rescission does not satisfy the requirements of subsection (2) or (3) it can operate as a waiver.
(5) A party who has made a waiver affecting an executory portion of the contract may retract the waiver by reasonable notification received by the other party that strict performance will be required of any term waived, unless the retraction would be unjust in view of a material change of position in reliance on the waiver."

the notion of waiver are found in Sections 2-209(4) and 2-209(5). The first of these states that an attempt at a modification or rescission that fails may still operate as a waiver. The second provides that a waiver of an executory portion of a contract may be withdrawn before performance by reasonable notice unless to do so would be unjust because of the other party's detrimental reliance.[180]

The Official Commentary states that Section 2-209's general purpose is to facilitate modifications and to relieve parties from the technical requirements of the common law.[181] The drafters were especially clear about their intent with respect to the waiver clause. They said: "Subsection (4) is intended, despite the provisions of subsections (2) and (3), to prevent contractual provisions excluding modification except by a signed writing from limiting in other respects the legal effect of the parties' actual later conduct."[182]

There is no set rule about what constitutes a waiver within the meaning of Section 2-209.[183] Waiver is usually determined from the conduct of the parties[184] and is a fact issue for a jury.[185] Examples abound, however, that provide some guides. A buyer agreed to a payment in advance clause, but the seller delivered equipment without demanding payment. This was a waiver of the payment clause and the buyer was not in default for late payment.[186] A seller's acquiescence in repeated delays in performance and an election not to terminate when delivery was delayed was a waiver

---

[180] See, e.g., Hart v. Sims, 702 F2d 574 (5th Cir. 1983).

[181] Section 2-209, Official Comment 1 says: "This section seeks to protect and make effective all necessary and desirable modifications of sales contracts without regard to the technicalities which at present hamper such adjustments."

[182] UCC § 2-209, Official Comment 4.

[183] For a general discussion, see, e.g., Chemetron Corp. v. McLouth Steel Corp., 522 F2d 469 (7th Cir. 1975); Double-E Sportswear Corp. v. Girard Trust Bank, 488 F2d 292 (3d Cir. 1973).

[184] See, e.g., Federal Express Corp. v. Pan American World Airways, Inc., 623 F2d 1297 (8th Cir. 1980).

[185] See generally Anderson § 2-209:11, at 321.

[186] Westmont Tractor Co. v. Viking Exploration, Inc., 543 F. Supp. 1314 (D. Mont. 1982).

of breach of the delivery terms despite a time-is-of-the-essence clause.[187] Performance pursuant to an oral modification may be a waiver of the right to rely upon the statute of frauds even if it applied to a modification of the original agreement.[188] If one party breaches but the other continues to perform, it may be held that the nonbreaching party has waived the breach.[189] Practically anything can be waived. Courts have even held that parties have waived antiwaiver clauses.[190]

The moral of these cases is that the contract is not determined simply by the written agreement, no matter how carefully it may have been negotiated. The course of dealing between the parties is at least as important in determining their obligations to one another.

¶ 12.06 UNCONSCIONABILITY

[1] Origins of the Doctrine in Equity Courts

Discussions of unconscionability sometimes seem to treat the concept as if it were an idea of the consumer-conscious late twentieth century. In fact, there is nothing new about unconscionability. It has been a part of Anglo-American jurisprudence of contracts for at least three centuries. The modern definition of unconscionability comes directly from a 1750 English case, in which the court defined an unconscionable agreement as one that "no man in his senses and not under delusion could make on the one hand, and no honest

---

[187] United States ex rel. Shankle-Clairday, Inc. v. Crow, 414 F. Supp. 160 (MD Tenn. 1976).

[188] See, e.g., Farmers Elevator Co. of Reserve v. Anderson, 170 Mont. 175, 552 P2d 63 (1976); Nora Springs Coop. v. Brandon, 247 NW2d 744 (Iowa 1976).

[189] Dangerfield v. Markel, 252 NW2d 184 (ND 1977). This can become somewhat tricky. If the breach does not justify nonperformance (e.g., a landlord's breach of the duty to repair by not fixing a leaky faucet generally does not justify nonpayment of rent), the nonbreaching party does not want to waive any right to claim damages for breach by continuing to perform. Therefore, it is important to be explicit and to state that there is no waiver intended, that all one intends is to continue to perform one's own obligations and not to relinquish any rights under the agreement.

[190] Kropp v. Ziebarth, 601 F2d 1348 (8th Cir. 1979); CIT Corp. v. Jounet, 419 Pa. 435, 214 A2d 620 (1965); Gold Kist, Inc. v. Pillow, 582 SW2d 77 (Tenn. Ct. App. 1979).

and fair man would accept on the other; which are unequitable and unconscientious bargains; and of such even the Common Law has taken notice."[191] The doctrine of unconscionability was enough established as part of the mechanism of contract law that in 1795 the lawyers for one party in a Pennsylvania action sounding, in part, in contract argued the following:

> Inadequacy of price, known to the other party, is a ground to set aside a contract. So is imposition, as selling a horse for a barley corn for the first nail in his shoes, and so in a duplicate ratio for every other. A contract to be carried into effect, must be fair, reasonable, and free from circumvention.[192]

Unconscionability was not often used in the law courts, but was most often invoked as a defense to an action for specific performance in equity. This use was consistent with the general concern of the equity courts to do justice between the parties and to refrain from enforcing agreements that were unduly harsh or oppressive or that had been imposed on one party by another through sharp dealing or some other reprehensible action. Law courts reached somewhat similar results through traditional legal defenses such as failure of consideration, fraud, or incompetence.[193] One commentator searched the published American cases during the first 150 years of the Republic and found only six law cases that relied explicitly on the unconscionability doctrine,[194] although scores of cases in equity employed the doctrine.

---

[191] Earl of Chesterfield v. Janssen, 28 ER 82 (1750).

[192] Armstrong v. M'Ghee, Addison 261 (Westmoreland County Ct., Pa. 1795) reprinted in Kessler & Gilmore 109.

[193] Some have argued that this resulted in bad law because legal doctrines were stretched and twisted to achieve results consistent with the doctrine of unconscionability. It would have been preferable, the argument goes, for law courts to have attacked the problem directly with the unconscionability doctrine than to have twisted others out of shape. See, e.g., 2 Hawkland § 2-302:01, at 157, 158; Zapatha v. Dairy Mart, Inc., 381 Mass. 284, 408 NE2d 1370 (1980); Urdang v. Muse, 114 NJ Super. 372, 276 A2d 397 (1971). Professor Epstein, although critical of some applications of the unconscionability doctrine, has argued that it is a useful addition to the law because it allows law courts to police agreements against fraud, duress, incompetence, and similar problems without demanding their strict proof. Epstein, "Unconscionability: A Critical Reappraisal," 18 J. L. & Econ. 293, 302 (1975) (hereinafter cited as Epstein).

[194] Deutch, *Unfair Contracts* 44 (1977).

With the merger of law and equity in most jurisdictions, the historical distinction between law and equity courts in their use of the unconscionability doctrine may seem academic and, to a large extent, it is. Nevertheless, there is some lingering importance to the distinction. Remedies are still classified by their origins in law or equity, and there is a tendency to treat defenses the same way. It may be unconscionable to require a defendant to perform an agreement that he does not want to perform, but it may not be unconscionable to make him pay damages to the plaintiff for his refusal to perform. In addition, two of the premerger law cases employing the unconscionability doctrine introduced concepts that continue to be important in determining the scope of the defense. Both were Supreme Court cases and both date from the late nineteenth century, when freedom of contract was an especially strong concept. This adds some weight to their precedential value.

The earlier of these cases, *Scott v. United States,*[195] involved an exclusive agreement with Scott. He was to provide all necessary transportation for the U.S. government and its agencies through a particular area. The Army transported some troops through the covered area without compensating Scott, and he sought compensation through an action in the Court of Claims. The court ruled in favor of the United States by construing the contract narrowly to its terms as one strictly for round-trip transportation between Little Rock and Fort Smith, Arkansas, not one covering all movement through Little Rock and Fort Smith and the areas in between. In affirming the Court of Claims, the Supreme Court said in dictum: "If a contract be unreasonable and unconscionable, but not void for fraud, a court of law will give to the party who sues for its breach damages, not according to its letter, but only such as he is equitably entitled to."[196]

Although *Scott* does not include any serious or lengthy discussion of unconscionability, it is noteworthy for several reasons. First, the parties did not suffer from any disabilities. It was a negotiated commercial transaction between competent parties who presumably knew what they were doing. Second, the Supreme Court recognized the doctrine of unconscionability at law as sepa-

---

[195] Scott v. United States, 79 US 443 (1870).

[196] Id. at 445.

rate and distinct from doctrines of fraud or duress. Third, the Court made clear that unconscionability does not necessarily void an agreement. A court may not enforce the unconscionable provision or it may modify it to one that is conscionable, but the entire contract does not fail.[197] This is particularly important in terms of remedies, because a court is free to reform an agreement that has an unconscionable provision into one that the court finds acceptable and then enforce the latter.

Nineteen years later in *Hume v. United States,*[198] the Supreme Court examined a contract by which Hume had agreed to provide shucks to the U.S. government for a price of $0.60 per pound. The government refused to pay the full amount owed under the contract because the current market value for shucks was only $0.0175 per pound. Hume lost his suit for the balance due and was able only to recover the market value of the shucks. The Court found the contract price to be unconscionable and quoted with approval from the Court of Claims opinion:

> That an agreement to pay $1,200 a ton for shucks, actually worth not more than $35 a ton, is a grossly unconscionable bargain, defined in Bouvier's Law Dictionary to be "a contract which no man in his senses, not under delusion, would make on the one hand, and which no fair and honest man would accept on the other," nobody can doubt. Such a contract, whether founded on fraud, accident, mistake, folly or ignorance, is void at Common Law. It is not necessary to invoke the aid of a court of equity to reform it. Courts of law will always refuse to enforce such a bargain, as against the public policy of honesty, fair dealing, and good morals.[199]

In *Hume* the unconscionability defense was invoked in favor of the United States, hardly an incompetent or defenseless contract negotiator, as against a commercial trader in a common commercial context and in the absence of proof of fraud or mistake.

---

[197] This was consistent with English practice from at least the eighteenth century. See, e.g., Day v. Newman, 2 Cox Ch. 77, 30 Eng. Rep. 36 (Ch. 1788) and other cases discussed in Leff, "Unconscionability and the Code — The Emperor's New Clause," 115 U. Pa. L. Rev. 485, 531 (1967) (hereinafter cited as Leff).

[198] Hume v. United States, 132 US 406 (1889).

[199] Id. at 410.

Furthermore, it was used as a justification for the reformation of the price term to the current market price. To be sure, the contract price was more than thirty times the market price, but the contract was explicit and the remedy sought was simply money damages in the form of the unpaid balance. Whether a high price justifies reformation pursuant to the unconscionability doctrine continues to be debated; however, a high price alone rarely suffices as a reason to avoid performance. Indeed, all the modern cases in which there has been an adjustment because of the unfairness of the price term have been consumer cases, not transactions involving commercial parties.[200] The general presumption today is that the unconscionability doctrine does not apply in commercial contexts, although that presumption may be overcome.[201] A century ago, however, the Supreme Court seemed to have little difficulty applying the doctrine in a straightforward commercial setting because of a disproportionate price term.[202]

Aside from the few law cases in which the doctrine of unconscionability played a role before the merger of law and equity and prior to the UCC, the doctrine was invoked in scores of cases in equity. Most of the equity cases involved sharp dealing or overreaching by a commercial party or by one in a strong and knowledgeable bargaining position, against a consumer or a person in a weaker, more vulnerable position. Many involved standard form contracts offered by merchants with no real opportunity for negotiation. Many others involved real estate disputes, especially problems connected with mortgage foreclosures. In general, these cases focused on problems that occurred in the process of negotiation more than on the substance of the contract.

---

[200] See, e.g., Farnsworth § 4.28, at 312, 313; Quinn & Zaretsky, *Quinn's Uniform Commercial Code Commentary and Law Digest* 52–76 (1984 Cum. Supp. No.2) (hereinafter cited as Quinn & Zaretsky).

[201] See, e.g., Consolidated Data Terminals v. Applied Digital Data Sys., Inc., 708 F2d 385 (9th Cir. 1983); Earman Oil Co. v. Burroughs Corp., 625 F2d 1291 (5th Cir. 1980).

[202] The Court may have been influenced by public policy concerns. In both *Scott* and *Hume,* the Court was faced with claims on the federal treasury that were fairly extreme, considering the services or products being provided to the government. The Court may have been influenced by the desire to protect the public fisc as much as anything else.

Perhaps the most famous of all the pre-UCC unconscionability cases was *Campbell Soup Co. v. Wentz,*[203] a case sounding in equity that has strongly influenced subsequent developments in law, in equity, and under the UCC. Wentz was a farmer who agreed to supply his entire crop of carrots from a fifteen-acre tract to Campbell. The parties signed a standard form agreement drawn up by Campbell for use with its various farmer/suppliers. The contract provided for prices of $23 to $30 per ton, depending on the time of delivery. From all indications, the prices were fair at the time the contract was signed. The carrot market shot upward and by the time the Wentzes harvested their 100 tons of carrots from the fifteen acres, the market price was $90 per ton. Instead of delivering the carrots to Campbell, the Wentzes arranged to sell their carrots to a neighbor who would sell them to Campbell at the market price. Campbell sued to enjoin the Wentzes from selling their carrots to anyone else and to require specific performance.[204] In refusing to enforce the agreement, the Court of Appeals for the Third Circuit focused on a variety of provisions in the agreement that it considered to be unfairly one-sided. The court said:

> We think it is too hard a bargain and too one-sided an agreement to entitle the plaintiff to relief in a court of conscience. . . . We are not suggesting that the contract is illegal. Nor are we suggesting any excuse for the grower in this case who has deliberately broken an agreement entered into with Campbell. We do think, however, that a party who has offered and succeeded in getting an agreement as tough as this one is, should not come to a chancellor and ask the court's help in the enforcement of its terms. That equity does not enforce unconscionable bargains is too well established to require elaborate citation.[205]

What is particularly interesting about *Campbell Soup* is that Campbell was not really seeking enforcement of one of the more

---

[203] Campbell Soup Co. v. Wentz, 172 F2d 80 (3d Cir. 1948).

[204] The trial court avoided any theoretical difficulties by reasoning that carrots are fungible and that Campbell failed to show that they were unique chattels, thus justifying the intervention of equity.

[205] Campbell Soup Co. v. Wentz, 172 F2d 80, 83 (3d Cir. 1948).

onerous contract provisions. Rather, the court completely refused to give the aid of equity to Campbell because of what amounted to "unclean hands." According to the third circuit, the agreement was so one-sided that an equity court simply should have nothing to do with it. The opinion did leave open the possibility of a suit at law for money damages from the breach. Whether the difference between the contract price and the market price at the time of delivery would have supported an unconscionability defense to a claim for money damages is problematic.

[2] Section 2-302 and Contemporary Applications of the Doctrine

The most important development in the consideration of the unconscionability doctrine was the inclusion of Section 2-302 in the UCC. This section has far-reaching influence throughout contract law, not just in cases governed by Article 2. Section 2-302 has been the cause of a tremendous amount of academic commentary, which is almost equally divided between those who support the section and those who find that in its application it is contrary to the general principles of contract law and counterproductive.[206] Whatever the criticisms of the section, it is clear from its language and from the accompanying Official Commentary that it was intended to provide judges with a justification for refusing enforcement of contracts that were tainted by unfairness even if the unfairness did not amount to a traditional common-law defense. Section 2-302 reads in its entirety:

> "(1) If the court as a matter of law finds the contract or any clause of the contract to have been unconscionable at the time it was made the court may refuse to enforce the contract, or it may enforce the remainder of the contract without the unconscionable clause, or it may so limit the application of any unconscionable clause as to avoid any unconscionable result.
> "(2) When it is claimed or appears to the court that the con-

---

[206] Among the most important commentaries are: Ellinghaus, "In Defense of Unconscionability," 78 Yale LJ 757 (1969); Epstein; Kornhauser, "Unconscionability in Standard Forms," 64 Calif. L. Rev. 1151 (1976) (hereinafter cited as Kornhauser); Leff; Murray, Unconscionability: Unconscionability, 31 U. Pitt. L. Rev. 1 (1969) (hereinafter cited as Murray); Spanogle, "Analyzing Unconscionability Problems," 117 U. Pa. L. Rev. 931 (1969) (hereinafter cited as Spanogle).

tract or any clause thereof may be unconscionable the parties shall be afforded a reasonable opportunity to present evidence as to its commercial setting, purpose and effect to aid the court in making the determination."[207]

The question of unconscionability is expressly one of law for the court and not for the jury. It has been held that this does not violate the Seventh Amendment right to a jury trial because the doctrine of unconscionability has its origins in equity courts, where cases were tried to the court and not to the jury.[208] Section 2-302 also allows courts a wide range of discretion in deciding what to do when unconscionability is found. A court may let a party avoid the entire agreement, just a portion of it, or may even reform the agreement. This provides courts with much more discretion than is available when a defendant successfully invokes a doctrine such as fraud that renders the agreement void ab initio.[209]

The most significant omission from Section 2-302 is a definition of unconscionability. The Official Commentary does not help; it circuitously defines unconscionability in terms of itself.[210] This means that the determination of unconscionability depends almost entirely on a court's interpretation of the facts peculiar to each case and the context in which they arose.[211] The section makes no

---

[207] Official Comment 1 says in part: "This section is intended to make it possible for the courts to police explicitly against the contracts or clauses which they find to be unconscionable."

[208] County Asphalt v. Lewis Welding & Eng'g Co., 444 F2d 372 (2d Cir. 1971). This conveniently overlooks the use of the unconscionability doctrine in some cases tried at law. See also Mieske v. Bartell Drug Co., 92 Wash. 2d 40, 593 P2d 1308 (1979).

[209] For a discussion of how to enforce the remainder of a contract after declaring a portion of it to be unconscionable, see, e.g., Ashland Oil Co. v. Donahue, 223 SE2d 433 (W. Va. 1976), and see Vasquez v. Glassboro Serv. Ass'n, 83 NJ 86, 415 A2d 1156 (1980) (court implied a condition allowing a "reasonable time" to develop an alternative to performance that was unconscionable).

[210] "The basic test is whether, in the light of the general commercial background and the commercial needs of the particular trade or case, the clauses involved are so one-sided as to be unconscionable at the time of the making of the contract." UCC § 2-302, Official Comment 1. In other words, whatever is unconscionable is unconscionable.

[211] See, e.g., Fredonia Broadcasting Corp. v. RCA Corp., 481 F2d 781 (5th Cir. 1973); later appealed, 569 F2d 251 (5th Cir.), reh'g denied, 572 F2d 320 (5th Cir. 1978), cert. denied, 439 US 859 (1979); Office Supply Co. v. Basic/Four Corp., 538 F. Supp. 776 (ED Wis. 1982).

distinction between cases that involve merchants and those that involve consumers. Presumably, the identity and experience of the parties is one of the factors that a court should take into account.[212] The question of unconscionability is to be determined as of the time of contracting, not as of the time of performance.[213] The willingness of courts to apply Section 2-302 and its principles to all contract cases, not just to those covered by Article 2, has been significant.[214] The second Restatement contains a section on unconscionability that is essentially the same as Section 2-302; it is meant to restate the general law of contracts, not just the law of sales.[215]

[3] Procedural and Substantive Unconscionability

The late Professor Arthur Leff was largely responsible for the common distinction between procedural and substantive unconscionability.[216] Whether the distinction serves any useful purpose is

---

[212] See, e.g., Stanley A. Klopp, Inc. v. John Deere Co., 510 F. Supp. 807 (ED Pa. 1981), aff'd without opinion, 676 F2d 688 (3d Cir. 1982).

[213] See, e.g., Marcovich Land Corp. v. JJ Newberry Co., 413 NE2d 935 (Ind. Ct. App. 1980). A court may refuse to enforce a contract if there has been a fundamental change in circumstances since the time of contracting and cite the unconscionability doctrine. Camerlo v. Howard Johnson Co., 710 F2d 987 (3d Cir. 1983). In truth, that is more a matter of frustration of purpose or impossibility, but any court sitting in equity may refuse to enforce a fundamentally unfair agreement on general equitable principles. A determination of unconscionability, however, may affect the complainant's ability to recover money damages.

[214] See, e.g., BGW Assocs., Inc. v. Valley Broadcasting Co., 532 F. Supp. 1112 (SDNY 1981) (service contract); In re Marriage of Foster, 115 Ill. App. 3d 969, 71 Ill. Dec. 761, 451 NE2d 915 (1983) (divorce settlement); Jefferson Loan Co. v. Livesay, 175 NJ Super. 470, 419 A2d 1164 (1980) (consumer loan agreement); Weissman v. Blue Cross of W. NY, Inc., 116 Misc. 2d 1063, 457 NYS2d 392 (1982) (health insurance contract); Laudisio v. Amoco Oil Co., 108 Misc. 2d 245, 437 NYS2d 502 (1981) (lease of service station and related equipment); Hamm v. Taylor, 180 Conn. 491, 429 A2d 946 (1980) (mortgage and note). Contra In re Clinic Masters, Inc. v. District Court of County of El Paso, 192 Colo. 120, 556 P2d 473 (1976); First NJ Bank v. FLM Business Machs., Inc., 130 NJ Super. 151, 325 A2d 843 (1974).

[215] Restatement (Second) of Contracts § 208 (1981); see also Uniform Land Transactions Act § 1-311.

[216] Leff 488.

another question,[217] but it is often made nonetheless. Substantive unconscionability involves questions about the fundamental fairness of the agreement or clauses within the agreement: Regardless of the identity of the parties, is this a clause or a contract that should be enforced by a court? Procedural unconscionability involves questions about the manner in which the agreement was reached: Did one party adequately explain the content of the agreement to the other? Was the explanation in a language readily understood by the other party? Were there sharp practices or overreaching? Did one party take advantage of the other's lack of experience or naivete? The agreement might not be unfair in any abstract sense, but the process by which it was reached might have been tainted by the actions of one of the parties. Usually, elements of both procedural and substantive unconscionability exist when a court finds a contract or a clause to be unconscionable:

> Procedural unconscionability is broadly conceived to encompass not only the employment of sharp practices and the use of fine print and convoluted language, but a lack of understanding and an inequality of bargaining power. Most cases involve a combination of the two types of unconscionability and it is generally agreed that if more of one is present, then less of the other is required. It is unclear whether substantive unconscionability alone is enough, that is, whether a contract that is plainly oppressive in its terms can be legitimized by fairness in bargaining.[218]

---

[217] See, e.g., 2 Anderson § 2-302:43, at 446:

> The point is frequently made that unconscionability has both procedural and substantive aspects. The point is interesting but without significance. No court has ever made its decision turn on the classification of unconscionability as being procedural or as being substantive. To the contrary, the courts have always regarded the totality of all circumstances. The mandated hearing as to the character of the contract in its commercial setting necessarily requires the court to see the total forest without regard to whether a particular tree is procedural or substantive.

[218] Farnsworth § section 4.28, at 314, 315, citing as support for the suggestion that elements of both must be present Wade v. Austin, 524 SW2d 79 (Tex. Civ. App. 1975).

The second Restatement seems to contemplate that unconscionability may be found either for reasons of substance or procedure, and both need not be present.[219]

Three well-known cases illustrate the dichotomy between procedural and substantive unconscionability and the confusion that sometimes occurs in trying to determine whether unconscionability is a result of a problem in the bargaining process or in the underlying agreement. All three cases involve fairly typical consumer transactions.

American Home Improvement Co. v. MacIver[220] was a 1964 New Hampshire case. Mr. and Mrs. MacIver were visited in their home in the spring of 1963 by a salesman for American Home Improvement Company who induced them to enter into a contract for new windows, a door, and flintcoat siding. They agreed to pay for the goods and services in installments and signed, among other documents, an application for financing that included a blank note and power of attorney for the financing company. A few days later, Mr. and Mrs. MacIver thought better of the deal and ordered work to cease. By that time their financing was approved, a small amount of work was completed, and the company paid the salesman an $800 commission. (The total contract price was only $1,759.) The company sued for breach, but was unsuccessful.

The defendants moved to dismiss on the basis of a New Hampshire statute that required the disclosure of finance charges to a buyer before the execution of a financing agreement.[221] Admittedly, there was no disclosure and the financing charges over the five-year term of the agreement amounted to more than $800, or more than 45 percent of the principal. The defendants' statutory argument was a sufficient basis for a finding in their favor, but the New Hampshire Supreme Court went on to state that the contract

---

[219] Restatement (Second) of Contracts § 208 comment c says, "Theoretically, it is possible for a contract to be oppressive when taken as a whole, even though there is no weakness in the bargaining process and no single term which is itself unconscionable."

[220] American Home Improvement Co. v. MacIver, 105 NH435, 201 A2d 886 (1964).

[221] NH Rev. Stat. Ann. § 399-B, 1961 NH Laws 245:7.

was unenforceable in any event because it was unconscionable within the meaning of Section 2-302. The court seemed to be swayed by evidence that showed that the goods and services the defendants would have received had a current market value of $959, for which they agreed to pay a total of $2,568, including an $800 sales commission and $809.60 in finance charges.[222]

Technically, the discussion of unconscionability in *MacIver* is dictum, but because it indicated the court's view of the doctrine, the case has been cited frequently in subsequent opinions in other jurisdictions. The opinion of the New Hampshire Supreme Court focused on the price term. The MacIvers agreed to pay more for sales commissions and interest than for goods and services. This seems at first to make the case one of substantive unconscionability — the price was too high. But the case also involved procedural flaws. There was no disclosure of the finance costs, nor apparently of the sales commission. The defendants were induced to sign an application with a blank note and a blank power of attorney. The sale occurred within the defendants' home, and there is a tendency to examine home sales carefully because of the unsavory reputation (whether deserved or not[223] of door-to-door solicitations, especially for home improvements.[224] The MacIvers were ordinary consumers and their contract was not a transaction between merchants. It was prepared in a standard form by the seller, and the only negotiated terms were for the number of items and services.[225]

---

[222] American Home Improvement Co. v. MacIver, 105 NH 435, 201 A2d 886 (1964).

[223] Should the Fuller Brush or Avon salesperson be burdened with the bad reputation of less reputable door-to-door salespeople?

[224] To deal with this problem, a number of states have laws allowing rescission within a few days of signing an agreement with a door-to-door salesperson. This cooling-off period allows reason to prevail after a customer succumbs to an effective hard sell in his own living room.

[225] For further discussion of the case, see, e.g., Spanogle 964; Comment, 20 Maine L. Rev. 159 (1968). Unconscionability can be a useful concept in situations involving standard form agreements when there has, in reality, never been knowing consent to many of the provisions. See, e.g., Epstein 302 n.28; Murray 16–18; Slawson, "Mass Contracts: Lawful Fraud in California," 48 So. Cal. L. Rev. 1, 11–14 (1974).

In *Frostifresh Corp. v. Reynoso,*[226] the court was concerned with the disparity between the contract price and the market price for a deep freezer. After adding up finance charges, sales commissions, and other expenses, the buyers agreed to a price that was several times higher than the retail price for a similar freezer at most large department stores in New York, where the buyers lived.[227] This contract also was tainted by procedural irregularities. The consumer's language was Spanish, and the agreement was in English. The evidence tended to show that the contract had not been clearly explained in all its particulars to the buyer in a language that he could understand. The buyer was an unsophisticated consumer; the seller was an experienced merchant. The agreement was in a standard form. The procedural problems combined with the high price term satisfied the court that there was unconscionability.

Perhaps the most famous of this trio of unconscionability cases is *Williams v. Walker-Thomas Furniture Co.,*[228] a 1965 decision of the Court of Appeals for the District of Columbia. Mrs. Williams was an unemployed mother of seven children who lived on welfare payments of $218 per month. She purchased a stereo set from Walker-Thomas for $514, and signed an installment payment agreement. The key provision in the agreement was the security clause. Walker-Thomas retained title to the stereo, conditioned upon full payment of the price, and also took a security interest in items Mrs. Williams previously purchased from the store and in all items she subsequently would purchase. Apparently, she had been a customer of the store in the past and, by all indications, had been a good credit risk, despite her extremely modest income.[229] The net effect of the security clause was that if Mrs. Williams were to default on her payments for the stereo, Walker-Thomas could repossess the stereo plus all other items purchased by Mrs. Williams

---

[226] Frostifresh Corp. v. Reynoso, 52 Misc. 2d 26, 274 NYS2d 757, rev'd on other grounds, 54 Misc. 2d 119, 282 NYS2d 964 (1966).

[227] It was unlikely that these particular buyers would have qualified, however, for a department store charge account.

[228] Williams v. Walker-Thomas Furniture Co., 350 F2d 445 (DC Cir. 1965).

[229] She had made purchases of about $1,800 over a five-year period before buying the stereo, and at the time she bought the stereo her account balance was $164. She had not previously been in default. Id. at 447 n.1.

before and since the stereo purchase. Unfortunately, she defaulted and the store sought to enforce its security clause. Mrs. Williams asserted the unconscionability doctrine in her defense. The trial court rejected the defense, but the court of appeals remanded the case for fact findings on the issue of unconscionability and for further consideration of the doctrine in the common law of the District of Columbia.[230]

The court of appeals was certainly concerned with the substance of the security clause in the installment purchase plan, but in remanding the case the court was also careful to emphasize the importance of context and the details of the bargaining process. Much was made of the seller's knowledge of the buyer's precarious financial position, the misallocation of risk, the likelihood that the buyer did not really understand the details of the contract, the relative sophistication of the parties in commercial matters, and the use of a standard form agreement.

In all three of these cases the courts expressed concern about the fundamental fairness of important substantive provisions — the price terms in *MacIver* and *Reynoso* and the security clause in *Williams*. Moreover, in every case there were significant questions about the fairness of the bargaining process itself, and every one involved a standard form agreement that basically was not negotiable. It is possible to separate the substantive and procedural concerns of the courts, but a combination of factors rather than one specific incident caused the courts to be concerned about the enforcement of these contracts. This suggests that it may rarely be necessary to draw the distinction between procedural and substan-

---

[230] Because Congress adopted the UCC for the District of Columbia after Mrs. Williams made the purchase, Section 2-302 did not directly apply. The court of appeals intimated, however, that Section 2-302 might just be a restatement of the common law and not a new departure.

> "The enactment of this section, which occurred subsequent to the contracts here in suit, does not mean that the common law of the District of Columbia was otherwise at the time of enactment, nor does it preclude the court from adopting a similar rule in the exercise of its powers to develop the common law of the District of Columbia."

Id. at 448, 449. For an argument that Section 2-302 is a new statement of the doctrine of unconscionability and not simply an outgrowth of equity, see *Murray on Contracts* § 78 (1974).

tive unconscionability. Rather, the focus should be on the overall transaction and the facts peculiar to it, not on whether an aspect of the transaction should be categorized as either a substantive or procedural irregularity.[231]

These cases also illustrate the wide range of remedies available when a court employs the unconscionability doctrine. In *MacIver,* the buyers avoided the entire transaction. This left the seller with the loss of the sales commission and the amount expended in beginning the work at the MacIvers' home. The buyer in *Reynoso* was excused from further performance, but did not receive any refund. In effect, the court reformed the price term. Although this resulted in a price substantially below that in the contract, it was also substantially more than the ordinary retail price of a similar freezer. In *Williams,* the decision was simply to remand the case for further findings of fact. Even though unconscionability is a question of law for a court, it cannot be divorced from the facts surrounding the transaction and, indeed, is essentially a fact-based doctrine.

[4] Unconscionability in Commercial Contexts

There is a presumption of conscionability in contracts between merchants or other parties in a straightforward commercial setting.[232] Of the scores of cases employing the unconscionability doctrine, the majority have involved individual consumers. Nevertheless, the doctrine has found application in commercial settings despite the reasonable presumption that most merchants are (or should be) sophisticated enough to protect their own interests in negotiating transactions. Standard defenses, such as fraud or misrepresentation in the formation of an agreement or impossibility or

[231] For general criticism of the dichotomy between procedural and substantive unconscionability, see Eisenberg, "The Bargain Principle and Its Limits," 95 Harv. L. Rev. 741 (1982); Gordley, "Equality in Exchange," 69 Calif. L. Rev. 1587 (1981); Hillman, "Debunking Some Myths About Unconscionability: A New Framework for U.C.C. Section 2-302," 67 Cornell L. Rev. 1 (1981).

[232] Consolidated Data Terminals v. Applied Digital Data Sys., Inc., 708 F2d 385 (9th Cir. 1983); Earman Oil Co. v. Burroughs Corp., 625 F2d 1291 (5th Cir. 1980).

frustration in performance, usually suffice in protecting the interests of commercial contracting parties. By its very nature, the unconscionability defense seems more attuned to the protection of weaker, less knowledgeable parties who become involved in an oppressive deal than to the protection of businessmen who have made a bad contract. There are naive and foolish people in the business world, however, and courts sometimes come to their rescue.

In *Leasing Service Corp. v. Broetje,*[233] an experienced farmer entered a commercial lease for drilling equipment. Although he had the opportunity to do so, the lessee chose not to consult his lawyer nor to read the form lease agreement that was incorporated by reference into the transfer documents for the drilling rig. Not surprisingly, the form lease was drafted in favor of the lessor and included clauses establishing the choice of law, providing for acceleration on default in an installment payment, attorneys' fees, and so forth. In a suit for breach based on the farmer's default, the lessee asserted the unconscionability defense because of the one-sided nature of the lease agreement, which was sufficient to defeat the plaintiff's motion for summary judgment.[234] There was a substantial difference in the sizes of the lessor's and the lessee's businesses as well as differences in the relative experience of the parties in matters of equipment leasing, although the farmer was not an unaware businessman. According to the court, differences in size and expertise were not enough to raise an issue of unconscionability, but the issue became valid when these factors were coupled with the absence of professional advice.[235] The court seemed to ignore the traditional rule that a party to a contract has a duty to read it and that he cannot escape liability simply by saying

[233] Leasing Serv. Corp. v. Broetje, 545 F. Supp. 362 (SDNY 1982).

[234] Interestingly, this again illustrates the fact-based nature of the unconscionability doctrine. Even though it is a question of law, and presumably subject to disposition on a motion for summary judgment, the legal question cannot be answered without a detailed examination of the facts. In general, there must be a hearing on the issue of unconscionability. 2 Anderson § 2-302:94, at 475.

[235] Of course, this raises the question of why the lessor should have to bear the risk of the lessee's foolish decision not to consult his lawyer and not to demand a copy of the lease agreement before signing.

that he had not read the contract when it was available to be read.[236]

The New Hampshire Supreme Court refused to enforce a commercial agreement on grounds of unconscionability in *Pittsfield Weaving Co. v. Grove Textiles, Inc.*[237] The buyer was a small weaving company. The seller, a larger enterprise located in Pennsylvania, sold materials subject to a standard form contract that required obvious defects to be reported within fifteen days of the invoice and latent defects within sixty days. The buyer's problem was that some latent defects only showed up during processing, which often did not occur until more than sixty days after the invoice date. The court concluded that this clause, together with one on the choice of law, was oppressive and that because of an inequality of bargaining power, the buyer had had no realistic opportunity to negotiate the terms of the seller's standard form agreement.[238]

California courts have gone further than most in applying the unconscionability defense in commercial settings. In *Graham v. Scissor-Tail, Inc.*,[239] the California Supreme Court explicitly stated that bargaining inequalities between commercial entities could justify the use of the unconscionability defense. Graham was a promoter. The defendant was a company representing the interests of the musician Leon Russell, who was also a member of the American Federation of Musicians (AFM). Any promoter who wanted to present Russell had to sign an agreement with several clauses drafted and inserted by the AFM, including an arbitration provision that was heavily weighted in favor of the union member.

---

[236] See Calamari & Perillo § 9-42, at 328, 329. Professors Calamari and Perillo do admit, however, that courts may apply a different standard when faced with a contract of adhesion. Id. § 9-44, at 336–343.

[237] Pittsfield Weaving Co. v. Grove Textiles, Inc., 121 NH 344, 430 A2d 638 (1981).

[238] Take-it-or-leave-it contracts tend to fare badly when the unconscionability defense is asserted. See, e.g., Sunbeam Farms, Inc. v. Trocke, 110 Misc. 2d 501, 442 NYS2d 842 (1981); Neal v. State Farm Ins. Co., 188 Cal. App. 2d 690, 10 Cal. Rptr. 781 (1961).

[239] Graham v. Scissor-Tail, Inc., 28 Cal. 3d 807, 613 P2d 165, 171 Cal. Rptr. 604 (1981).

There was a dispute that went to arbitration, but the court refused to confirm the arbitration award because it was imposed on a take-it-or-leave-it basis and because the court did not think that it met the standards of integrity appropriate for a fair arbitration.[240]

A year later, California courts addressed the unconscionability question in another commercial context in *A&M Produce Co. v. FMC Corp.*[241] An experienced farmer purchased a tomato sorting machine. Although the buyer had been engaged in sophisticated farming activities for some time, he was new to the tomato-growing business. He relied on the seller's representative's oral representations about the quality and features of the machine and chose it over competitive models because of its lower price. The contract contained a disclaimer of warranty clause that complied with the requirements of Section 2-316 with respect to warranty disclaimers. The machine did not work as expected, and in the ensuing litigation the seller relied on the disclaimer clause. The court refused to enforce the disclaimer because it was too broadly drawn and was unconscionable.[242] There was both procedural unconscionability (the salesman said the machine would do things that it would not do) and substantive unconscionability (the disclaimer clause was too broad), and both were necessary to the result.[243]

---

[240] Again, this case involves a mixture of procedural and substantive issues. The clause was itself unfair in that it favored Russell, and the process was tainted because no negotiation was allowed. Criticizing the decision, see Rakoff, "Contracts of Adhesion: An Essay in Reconstruction," 96 Harv. L. Rev. 1174 (1983); Note, "Unconscionability of Presumptively Biased Arbitration Clauses Within Adhesion Contracts," 70 Calif. L. Rev. 1014 (1982).

[241] A&M Produce Co. v. FMC Corp., 135 Cal. App. 3d 473, 186 Cal. Rptr. 114 (1982).

[242] In the court's view, the effect of the disclaimer was to say that the machine was not warranted to do anything. Id. at 491, 186 Cal. Rptr. at 125. In Collins v. Uniroyal, Inc., 64 NJ 260, 315 A2d 16 (1974), the court struck a warranty limitation on consequential damages for much the same reason, although in a consumer case. For a criticism of the notion that a warranty disclaimer that complies with Section 2-316 still can be unconscionable, see Epstein 309, 310.

[243] The court also said that unconscionability was part of the common law of California and antedated the adoption of the UCC. In 1979, California also enacted a law applicable to all contracts that was identical to Section 2-302. Cal. Civil Code § 1670.5 (1979).

FMC Corp. is quite remarkable for four reasons. First, the UCC clearly contemplates the use of disclaimer clauses and specifies what they should include and how they should be presented in order to be enforceable.[244] It is ironic that a clause drafted in accordance with the dictates of the UCC would still be found to be unfairly broad under another UCC section. Some courts and commentators have argued that warranty disclaimers drafted in accordance with Section 2-316 are immune from the unconscionability defense,[245] However, there is support for the contrary view if there is evidence of procedural unconscionability in obtaining agreement to the exclusion clause.[246] Second, by considering evidence of the salesman's oral representations, the court showed its willingness to ignore the parol evidence rule and the concept of integration. Third, there was evidence that the buyer had received a competitive bid that was about twice that of the seller's. The court did not seem to think that the disparity in the two prices was sufficient to put the buyer on notice that the machine may not be all that it was said to be.[247] Finally, even though the buyer had years of experience in farming and in purchasing farm equipment, the court seemed moved most by the fact that he was new to growing tomatoes.[248]

Despite these and other similar cases, more often than not the unconscionability defense is unavailing in a commercial setting.

---

[244] The main point of Section 2-316 is to provide the buyer with notice so that he will be aware of the risk allocation before he enters into the agreement and may be able to consider alternatives.

[245] See Tacoma Boatbldg. Co. v. Delta Fishing Co., 28 UCC Rep. 26 (WD Wash. 1980); Avery v. Aladdin Prod. Div., 128 Ga. App. 266, 196 SE2d 357 (1973); Ford Motor Co. v. Moulton, 511 SW2d 690 (Tenn.), cert. denied, 419 US 870 (1974); Marshall v. Murray Oldsmobile Co., 207 Va. 972, 154 SE2d 140 (1967); Weintraub, "Disclaimer of Warranties and Limitation of Damages for Breach of Warranty Under the UCC," 53 Tex. L. Rev. 60 (1974).

[246] See Farnsworth § 4.28, at 319, citing FMC Fin. Corp. v. Murphree, 623 F2d 413 (5th Cir. 1980); Schroeder v. Fageol Motors, 86 Wash. 2d 256, 544 P2d 20 (1975); Ford Motor Co. v. Tritt, 244 Ark. 883, 430 SW2d 778 (1968); Note, 63 Va. L. Rev. 791 (1977).

[247] This ignores the too-good-to-be-true notion.

[248] For a general discussion of this case, see Comment, "Unconscionability and the Enforcement of Standardized Contracts in Commercial Transactions," 16 Pac. LJ 247 (1984).

The general idea is that merchants and businessmen know what they are doing and are capable of protecting their own interests. Courts are more reluctant to come to their aid than to assist an individual consumer who is the victim of sharp dealing.[249]

[5] Unconscionability in Specific Situations

The doctrine of unconscionability is so closely tied to the facts of each contract and to the context of its negotiation that it is difficult to develop any clear tests. Some guidance and a basis for prediction may be obtained, however, from examining a few of the situations in which unconscionability has or has not been found.

[a] Contract Price Terms

A perennial issue is whether a price term may be so out of line with the value of the performance or the goods that it is unconscionable on its face. The price term usually is negotiable; even in a take-it-or-leave-it situation the buyer rarely is faced with the necessity of making the purchase. Many consumer cases in which the unconscionability defense appears involve items that may be useful or desirable (e.g., deep freezers, aluminum siding, stereos) but are not necessary. The buyer always has the option not to buy. In commercial settings, prices or terms of payments are almost invariably flexible. Cases in which the only question is the relative equality of the consideration exchanged are extremely rare. When there is a dispute about the fairness of a price term, another issue about the fairness of the bargaining process or an aspect of the contract is almost inevitable. It can safely be said that there are hardly any cases in which the pure question of the conscionability of a price has been put squarely to a court.[250] Nevertheless, there are opin-

---

[249] See, e.g., FMC Fin. Corp. v. Murphree, 632 F2d 413 (5th Cir. 1980); Gelderman & Co. v. Lane Processing, 527 F2d 571 (8th Cir. 1975); Potomac Elec. Power Co. v. Westinghouse Elec. Corp., 385 F. Supp. 572 (DDC 1974); Gaynor v. Laverdure, 362 Mass. 828, 291 NE2d 617 (1973); Equitable Lumber Corp. v. IPA Land Dev. Corp., 38 NY2d 516, 344 NE2d 391 (1976); K&C v. Westinghouse Elec. Corp., 437 Pa. 303, 263 A2d 390 (1970).

[250] One of the closest was *Hume v. United States,* discussed supra at ¶ 12.06[1].

ions that indicate the price term may be crucial to the court's decision on unconscionability, and it may indeed be evidence of unconscionability.[251]

The decision in *Vom Lehn v. Astor Art Galleries, Ltd.*[252] is a case in point. The buyers paid $67,000 for twenty oriental jade carvings, but later decided that they had been taken. At trial their expert witness testified that the carvings were worth $14,750, although he agreed that this was a matter of opinion and that there were no hard-and-fast rules of valuation. The court agreed with the buyers and struck down the price term as unconscionable, although the court also seemed to be swayed by evidence that the seller knew that the buyers were unfamiliar with the art objects they purchased.[253]

Curiously, freezers and refrigerators have been the subjects of an inordinate number of unconscionability cases. In *Toker v. Paul,*[254] the court struck a price of $1,092.66 ($799 plus tax, insurance, and service charges) for a freezer that retailed for $300. The same court reached the same result in a case involving a refrigerator sold for two-and-one-half times the normal retail price.[255] In neither case was the buyer allowed to get the appliance free; the contract was reformed to amounts already paid. In each instance

---

[251] See, e.g., FN Roberts Pest Control Co. v. McDonald, 132 Ga. App. 257, 208 SE2d 13 (1974) (exorbitant price term in home improvement contract with 87-year-old woman was evidence of fraud or deceit). But cf. Morris v. Capitol Furniture and Appliance Co., 280 A2d 775 (DC 1971). See generally Kornhauser 1159.

[252] Vom Lehn v. Astor Art Galleries, Ltd., 86 Misc. 2d 1, 380 NYS2d 532 (1976).

[253] As two commentators said:

> "It is revealing to note that the court did not feel the slightest need to cite precedent or authority to justify its willingness to dump a sales contract on the basis of its excessive price. That went without saying. There is such precedent, but the court saw no need to rake over those coals, and that is the point. And that says a great deal about just how 'sacrosanct' the price term really is."

Quinn & Zaretsky 5-76.

[254] Tiker v. Paul, 103 NJ Super. 500, 247 A2d 701 (1968), aff'd on other grounds, 108 NJ Super. 129, 260 A2d 244 (1970).

[255] Toker v. Westerman, 113 NJ Super. 452, 274 A2d 78 (1970).

the amounts paid exceeded the usual retail price of the appliance.[256]

[b] Inflation and Changes in Currency Values

Courts have consistently rejected unconscionability defenses that were premised on inflation or dramatic shifts in currency values. This is not surprising, in view of the requirement that unconscionability be determined as of the time of contracting, not as of the time of performance. The risk of inflation is an ordinary and expected business risk and most courts assume that the parties take it into account during negotiations. To the extent that there is some dramatic and unexpected change in conditions, the frustration, impossibility, or commercial impracticability defenses may apply,[257] but not unconscionability.

The claim of unconscionability has most often been made in the context of long-term supply agreements with a pass-through or escalator clause in the price term. For instance, in *Kerr-McGee Corp. v. Northern Utilities, Inc.*,[258] the buyer complained about an escalator clause in a long-term contract for the supply of natural gas, which was keyed to price increases by other suppliers. The court was unsympathetic because the parties were equal in their bargaining strengths, the contract had been the subject of extensive negotiations, and as a balance to the price escalator, the buyer had the security of a long-term supply. Another court reached the same conclusion for essentially the same reasons in a case involving a pass-through clause in a long-term gas supply agreement.[259] Infla-

---

[256] For a similar result see Jones v. Star Credit Corp., 59 Misc. 2d 189, 298 NYS2d 264 (1969). Excessive price was a factor but not the only one in Milford Fin. Corp. v. Lucas, 8 UCC Rep. 801 (Mass. App. Ct. 1970).

[257] See supra ¶¶ 12.03, 12.04.

[258] Kerr-McGee Corp. v. Northern Utilities, Inc., 673 F2d 323 (10th Cir. 1982).

[259] Compania de Gas de Neuvo Laredo v. Entex, Inc., 686 F2d 322 (5th Cir. 1982). In Bernina Distribs., Inc. v. Bernina Sewing Mach. Co., 646 F2d 434 (10th Cir. 1981), the court refused to find a clause unconscionable simply because it tied payments to the relationship between the dollar and the Swiss franc and the dollar had dropped dramatically against the franc. The contract was fair at the time it was negotiated.

tion cases almost invariably involve risk shifting, and risk shifting is a normal incident of contracting. Without other instances of procedural or substantive unconscionability, inflation alone cannot support a finding of unconscionability.[260]

[c] Warranty Disclaimers and Exclusions of Remedies

A warranty disclaimer clause is not in and of itself grounds for a finding of unconscionability,[261] although it may contribute to such a finding. The same approach applies whether a clause excludes warranties or limits remedies.[262] Nevertheless, there have been several cases in which contracts with warranty exclusions or limitation of remedies clauses have been found to be unconscionable.[263] One court even ordered a seller to repair despite a sale that was "as is."[264] The one clear rule applies to blanket exclusions of personal injury recoveries in consumer transactions; because those clauses are against public policy, they are per se unconscionable.[265]

[d] Seller's Use of the Doctrine

The unconscionability defense usually is asserted by purchasers who seek to avoid payment for what they consider to be overpriced or inadequate services. (Of course, the doctrine is also

---

[260] Bowlin's, Inc. v. Ramsey Oil Co., 99 NM 660, 662 P2d 661, cert. denied, 99 NM 644, 662 P2d 645 (1983).

[261] See, e.g., JD Pavlak v. William Davis Co., 40 Ill. App. 3d 1, 351 NE2d 243 (1976).

[262] For a general discussion of limitation of remedies issues, see Chapter 10.

[263] In addition to the cases discussed supra at ¶ 12.06[4], see also Industralease Automated & Scientific Equip. Corp. v. RME Enters., Inc., 58 AD2d 482, 396 NYS2d 427 (1977); Johnson v. Mobil Oil Corp., 415 F. Supp. 264 (ED Mich. 1976).

[264] LaVere v. RM Burrit Motors, Inc., 112 Misc. 2d 225, 446 NYS2d 851 (1981). Normally a sale "as is" excludes any and all warranties, but this was a sale to a consumer of an automobile, a complex and potentially dangerous chattel, and the court was willing to hold the seller to a higher standard of duty to the customer than usual.

[265] See Farnsworth § 4.28, at 316. This doctrine dates at least to the famous case of Henningsen v. Bloomfield Motors, Inc., 32 NJ 358, 161 A2d 69 (1960).

used in connection with other contract provisions that have little to do with price.) There is apparently only one reported case, however, in which a seller employed the doctrine to avoid a low price term. In that case, the buyer presented himself as knowledgeable in the timber market and negotiated a purchase of timber for about $20,000. The seller, relying on the buyer's expertise, agreed to the price but then sought to avoid the deal when he discovered that the market value of the timber was closer to $50,000. The evidence showed that the buyer, contrary to his representations, was not much of an expert and that the difference in value was as much a surprise to him as it was to the seller. There were no indications of fraud or misrepresentation. The court held for the seller on the basis of Section 2-302, both because of the disparity between the price term and the true value of the timber and because of the seller's reasonable reliance on the buyer's mistaken estimate.[266] In such a circumstance there is certainly no reason to limit the application of the unconscionability doctrine to buyers, and the language of Section 2-302 does not do so. In fact, the case might have been handled as one of mutual mistake or as one involving a failure of consideration. There would have been some difficulties in using those approaches, however. Courts are more reluctant to undo transactions for a mistake about value when there is no mistake about the subject matter of the transaction.[267] There was also a fairly substantial consideration; the problem was in the relative values being exchanged, not in the absence of a consideration. Unconscionability provided the court with a convenient justification for refusing to enforce a flawed deal without the necessity of making the facts fit within the contraints of a traditional legal defense.

[e] Arbitration and Basis for Damages

Unconscionability is a proper subject for arbitration,[268] although an arbitration clause may itself be the focus of an uncon-

---

[266] Davis v. Kolb, 263 Ark. 158, 563 SW2d 438 (1978).

[267] See ¶ 12.02[3].

[268] In re Farker Co. v. RA Hanson DISC, Ltd., 583 F2d 68 (2d Cir. 1979).

scionability defense.[269] The doctrine cannot be used as the basis for a suit for damages.[270] It is a defense, not a justification for affirmative relief, although an argument to the contrary has been made by some commentators.[271] A defendant may sometimes be caught by his own actions in other contexts. In at least one case, a litigant was unsuccessful in asserting the unconscionability defense because he had himself used language for his own protection that was similar to the language he sought to avoid.[272]

[6] General Guide to Doctrine's Applicability

The main criticism of unconscionability is that it is an open-ended doctrine without clearly defined boundaries. It is difficult to predict with certainty how and when a court may apply the doctrine or what the results of an application might be — avoidance of the contract, reformation, partial rescission, or denial of specific performance without denial of a right to sue for damages. If abused, the doctrine can serve as an excuse for "courts to act as roving commissions to set aside those agreements whose substantive terms they find objectionable."[273] But if it is not abused, the doctrine can be a useful adjunct to more traditional defenses. It is flexible enough to allow a court to police agreements that are tainted by oppression or sharp dealing without necessarily destroying them. Fraud, for instance, is fairly difficult to prove because intent must be demonstrated, but when it is proven successfully, the remedy is severe: The agreement is destroyed. The requirements for proof of unconscionability are less rigorous and the remedies are much more flexible. The court simply deals with the

---

[269] See, e.g., Graham v. Scissor-Tail, Inc., 28 Cal. 3d 807, 623 P2d 165, 171 Cal. Rptr. 604 (1981).

[270] See, e.g., Pearson v. National Budgeting Sys., Inc., 31 AD2d 792, 297 NYS2d 59 (1969).

[271] King, "The Tort of Unconscionability: A New Tort for New Times," 23 St. Louis ULJ 97 (1979); Note, 29 Baylor L. Rev. 309 (1977).

[272] PQ Franz Chem. Corp. v. Philadelphia Quartz Co., 594 F2d 146 (5th Cir. 1979). The case involved two commercial entities of relatively equal knowledge and bargaining power. The clause that the defendant complained of was virtually identical to a clause in the defendant's own sales contracts.

[273] Epstein 293, 294.

portion of the agreement that presents a problem. Sometimes the result may be the destruction of the agreement, but more often than not it may be preserved with a few adjustments. This means that the parties may share the risk, as opposed to rescission, which casts the risk entirely on one party or the other.[274]

Despite the uncertain contours of the unconscionability doctrine some general guides determine when it may apply. There is some protection against uncertainty in that unconscionability is a question of law for the court and is not subject to emotional appeals to the jury.[275] Consumers are usually more successful in asserting the defense than are merchants or other businessmen,[276] but the doctrine may apply in business contexts.[277] One of the critical issues is the relative bargaining power and knowledge of the parties.[278] Courts tend to assume that consumers are in weaker bargaining positions than merchant sellers. The opposite presumption

---

[274] Despite his criticism of the unconscionability doctrine as it is sometimes understood and applied, Professor Epstein agrees that it is a useful adjunct to traditional common-law defenses. Id. at 302.

[275] See, e.g., County Asphalt v. Lewis Welding & Eng'g Co., 444 F2d 372 (2d Cir. 1971). It should also be considered together with the general obligation of good faith. See, e.g., UCC § 1-203. Good faith has been a somewhat amorphous concept at common law. See generally Gilmore, "The Commercial Doctrine of Good Faith Purchase," 63 Yale. LJ 1057 (1954); Kessler & Fine, "Culpa in Contrahendo, Bargaining in Good Faith, and Freedom of Contract; A Comparative Study." 77 Harv. L. Rev. 401 (1964); Newman, "The Renaissance of Good Faith in Contracting in Anglo-American Law," 54 Cornell L. Rev. 553 (1969); Summers, "'Good Faith' in General Contract Law and the Sales Provisions of the Uniform Commercial Code," 54 Va. L. Rev. 195 (1968).

[276] See, e.g., Stanley A. Klopp, Inc. v. John Deere Co., 510 F. Supp. 807 (ED Pa. 1981), aff'd without opinion, 676 F2d 688 (3d Cir. 1982).

[277] There is little doubt, however, that businessmen fail to prove unconscionability at least as often, if not more so, than they succeed in doing so. See, e.g., Spring Hope Rockwool, Inc. v. Industrial Clean Air, Inc., 504 F. Supp. 1385 (EDNC 1981); Melso v. Texaco, Inc., 532 F. Supp. 1280 (ED Pa. 1982); Phillips Mach. Co. v. LeBlond, Inc., 494 F. Supp. 318 (ND Okla. 1980); JD Pavlak v. William Davis Co., 40 Ill. App. 3d 1, 351 NE2d 243 (1976); Fedders, Inc. v. Monsanto Co., 33 UCC Rep. 541 (D. Minn. 1981); All-States Leasing Co. v. Tophat Lounge, Inc., 649 P2d 1250 (Mont. 1982); Smith v. Price's Creameries, 650 P2d 285 (N. Mex. 1982).

[278] See, e.g., Pittsfield Weaving Co. v. Grove Textiles, Inc., 121 NH 344, 430 A2d 638.

applies in commercial contexts,[279] but it is a rebuttable presumption because a businessman who is expert in one area may be as much of a novice as a consumer in another area.[280] Courts tend to examine standard form agreements much more closely than negotiated contracts,[281] especially if the form agreement is presented on a take-it-or-leave-it basis.[282] Substantive unfairness may be evidence of a problem with the agreement, but it is unlikely to support an unconscionability defense unless there is also some evidence of overreaching in the bargaining process.[283] Courts seem concerned to avoid unfair surprise because it upsets the expected risk allocation negotiated between the parties.[284] In the end, the unconscionability doctrine merges legal and equitable principles in the substantive analysis of contractual relationships. It is consistent with the formal merger of the two systems into one set of courts, and it works best when courts employ it with awareness of its essentially equitable origins. On the other hand, criticizing it as an equity principle grafted onto a legal system is inconsistent with the history of the doctrine because of its limited, but not insignificant, use at common law.

---

[279] See, e.g., Consolidated Data Terminals v. Applied Digital Data Sys., Inc., 708 F2d 385 (9th Cir. 1983).

[280] See, e.g., A&M Produce Co. v. FMC Corp., 135 Cal. App. 3d 473, 186 Cal. Rptr. 114 (1982).

[281] See, e.g., In re Hamby, 19 Bankr. 776, 33 UCC Rep. 1811 (ND Ala. 1982); Restatement (Second) of Contracts § 211 (1981).

[282] See, e.g., Sunbeam Farms, Inc. v. Trocke, 110 Misc. 2d 501, 442 NYS2d 842 (1981).

[283] See, e.g., Hahn v. Ford Motor Co., 434 NE2d 943 (Ind. Ct. App. 1982); Wade v. Austin, 524 SW2d 79 (Tex. Civ. App. 1975). But cf. Restatement (Second) of Contracts § 208 comment c (1981).

[284] For a discussion of risk allocation, see 2 Hawkland § 2-302:03, at 161 and Davenport, "Unconscionability and the Uniform Commercial Code," 22 U. Miami L. Rev. 121 (1967).

Table of UCC Sections

[References are to paragraphs (¶) and notes (n.).]

[*References are to paragraphs (¶) and notes (n.).*]

[*References are to paragraphs (¶) and notes (n.).*]

[*References are to paragraphs (¶) and notes (n.).*]

[*References are to paragraphs (¶) and notes (n.).*]

Table of Cases

[References are to paragraphs (¶) and notes (n.).]

[*References are to paragraphs (¶) and notes (n.).*]

[*References are to paragraphs (¶) and notes (n.).*]

[*References are to paragraphs (¶) and notes (n.).*]

B

[*References are to paragraphs (¶) and notes (n.).*]

[*References are to paragraphs (¶) and notes (n.).*]

[*References are to paragraphs (¶) and notes (n.).*]

[*References are to paragraphs (¶) and notes (n.).*]

C

[*References are to paragraphs (¶) and notes (n.).*]

[*References are to paragraphs (¶) and notes (n.).*]

[*References are to paragraphs (¶) and notes (n.).*]

[*References are to paragraphs (¶) and notes (n.).*]

[*References are to paragraphs (¶) and notes (n.).*]

D

[*References are to paragraphs (¶) and notes (n.).*]

[*References are to paragraphs (¶) and notes (n.).*]

[*References are to paragraphs (¶) and notes (n.).*]

[*References are to paragraphs (¶) and notes (n.).*]

[*References are to paragraphs (¶) and notes (n.).*]

G

[*References are to paragraphs (¶) and notes (n.).*]

[*References are to paragraphs (¶) and notes (n.).*]

[*References are to paragraphs (¶) and notes (n.).*]

H

[*References are to paragraphs (¶) and notes (n.).*]

[*References are to paragraphs (¶) and notes (n.).*]

[*References are to paragraphs (¶) and notes (n.).*]

I

[*References are to paragraphs (¶) and notes (n.).*]

[*References are to paragraphs (¶) and notes (n.).*]

K

[References are to paragraphs (¶) and notes (n.).]

[*References are to paragraphs (¶) and notes (n.).*]

[*References are to paragraphs (¶) and notes (n.).*]

[*References are to paragraphs (¶) and notes (n.).*]

[*References are to paragraphs (¶) and notes (n.).*]

[*References are to paragraphs (¶) and notes (n.).*]

[*References are to paragraphs (¶) and notes (n.).*]

[*References are to paragraphs (¶) and notes (n.).*]

[*References are to paragraphs (¶) and notes (n.).*]

O

[*References are to paragraphs (¶) and notes (n.).*]

P

[*References are to paragraphs (¶) and notes (n.).*]

[*References are to paragraphs (¶) and notes (n.).*]

[*References are to paragraphs (¶) and notes (n.).*]

Q

R

[*References are to paragraphs (¶) and notes (n.).*]

[*References are to paragraphs (¶) and notes (n.).*]

S

[*References are to paragraphs (¶) and notes (n.).*]

[*References are to paragraphs (¶) and notes (n.).*]

[*References are to paragraphs (¶) and notes (n.).*]

[*References are to paragraphs (¶) and notes (n.).*]

T

[*References are to paragraphs (¶) and notes (n.).*]

[*References are to paragraphs (¶) and notes (n.).*]

U

[*References are to paragraphs (¶) and notes (n.).*]

[*References are to paragraphs (¶) and notes (n.).*]

W

[*References are to paragraphs (¶) and notes (n.).*]

[*References are to paragraphs (¶) and notes (n.).*]

[*References are to paragraphs (¶) and notes (n.).*]

Y

Z

Index

[References are to paragraphs (¶).]

A

B

[*References are to paragraphs (¶).*]

C

[*References are to paragraphs (¶).*]

D

[*References are to paragraphs (¶).*]

E

F

[*References are to paragraphs (¶).*]

[*References are to paragraphs (¶).*]

L

M

N

[*References are to paragraphs (¶).*]

[*References are to paragraphs (¶).*]

R

S

[*References are to paragraphs (¶).*]

T

U

[*References are to paragraphs* (¶).]

V

W